LANGUAGE TEACHING ANALYSIS

INDIANA UNIVERSITY STUDIES
in the
HISTORY AND THEORY OF LINGUISTICS

Language Teaching Analysis

WILLIAM FRANCIS MACKEY

B.A., M.A., A.M., D.LITT.

*Professor of Language Didactics in the
Department of Linguistics of Laval University.
Sometime Senior Lecturer in the Division
of Language Teaching of the University of London*

INDIANA UNIVERSITY PRESS
Bloomington and London

Preface

Problems before being solved must first be analysed. The more complex the problem, the more is its solution dependent on a sound analysis.

Language teaching includes some of the most complex problems in the field of education. This book is an attempt, not to solve them, but to analyse them for those who are concerned with their solution. It is addressed to language teachers, teachers-in-training, school inspectors, local education authorities, and researchers. It therefore has the following uses:

1. To provide students with an analytic introduction to the entire field.

2. To present language teachers with an analytic view of language teaching, to suggest ways of examining and comparing the tools they use, their grammars, dictionaries and textbooks, and to encourage them to check their teaching techniques.

3. To assist school inspectors in their analysis of the language teaching which they supervise.

4. To help the language teaching committees of local education authorities to analyse and select textbooks and materials.

5. To serve as a framework for discussions on language teaching, and to delimit problems for research.

The book is designed as an integrated whole; but it is presented in such a way that each of its three main parts may be read independently.

Although examples are chosen mainly from the most usually taught foreign languages—English, French, German, Spanish, Russian, and Italian—the principles they illustrate apply to the teaching of any foreign language. Since the book is written in English, most of the examples are from that language; for it has been assumed that anyone able to read the book will also be able to understand the examples.

In the body of the text, a small, raised number refers to a work listed under that number in the bibliography. Where there is a colon as well, the number following the colon is the page number in the book cited.

The bibliography is meant as a systematic guide to works in the various divisions of the field delimited by the chapter headings. It is not intended as a complete bibliography on language teaching. The aim has been to include most of the general works in the field and some of the more important ones in different branches of linguistics not usually incorporated in

v

language teaching bibliographies. Those interested in bibliographies of special topics for term papers, reading lists, etc., should first consult the topical outline which precedes the actual list of works. This gives the contents, divisions and subdivisions of the bibliography and the numbers of the books included under each head. For more detailed studies and for reports of experiments, the reader is referred to the special bibliographies listed. No specific language-teaching courses were included in the bibliography, and those referred to in the text are anonymously labelled by means of letters, since the purpose of the book is not to favour one course over another, but to explain and illustrate a theory and technique of objective study in the hope that this may perhaps help encourage language teachers to consider language teaching as a matter not of allegiance but of analysis.

This book has been a long time in the making. During the past twenty years I have attempted in vain to read all of the vast literature in the field. Although I found most of it rather unrewarding as regards the analysis of language teaching, I did profit a great deal from the experience. I also benefited greatly from discussions with language teachers and teacher-trainers in many different parts of the world. Let me here thank all of them for what they may directly or indirectly have contributed.

I am particularly grateful, however, to those who have read the manuscript of my work. I wish first of all to express my sincere gratitude to Henri Frei, to Samuel Roller, and to Felix Kahn for having patiently read the entire manuscript in a number of versions and for having supplied valuable criticism and detailed suggestions for improving the work.

I owe a separate debt of thanks to each of those specialists who were, good enough to read individual chapters—to A. V. P. Elliott, J. C. Catford, M. A. K. Halliday, G. Herdan, W. E. Lambert, E. Ingram, J. Darbelnet, and G. L. Bursill-Hall. And finally to Ilonka Schmidt for having given her time and skill to the checking of the proofs, at all stages, I offer my sincere thanks. I must assume full responsibility, however, for errors of any sort which may have crept into the text.

Geneva, July 1961   W. F. M.

Contents

FOR MÓKI

Introduction

This study is a first approximation to a theory and technique of language teaching analysis. It is intended as a step in the evaluation of language teaching methods, in the investigation of the claims and counter-claims of conflicting schools, and in the delimitation of some of the century-old controversies in language teaching.

That such controversies have not yet been resolved is one of the causes of the periodical swing of language teaching opinion from one extreme to the other, a vacillation deplored long ago by scholars like Sweet [1274:31] and Palmer, [1245:19] since it makes language teaching a matter of fad and fashion, a matter of opinion rather than of fact.

Attempts since the end of the nineteenth century to resolve these conflicts by means of experimentation have as yet resolved none of them. [1318-20] For when analysed, most of these experiments prove to have little significance. This is not only because they applied to particular situations with extremely limited data subjectively interpreted, but also because so many variables were left uncontrolled, tests unstandardized and quite inadequate, experiments never verified by duplication, and above all, because the problems investigated had never been properly defined.

After going over the vast literature of the period, we cannot help but agree with the conclusions of Agard and Dunkel, in the survey connected with their investigation of language learning, that most of the opinions had been based on unverified results of personal experience resting on home-made and mostly invalid tests, reporting that students have done "someone's idea of well on someone's idea of an adequate test" as Dunkel has put it. [951:168] The results obtained in such tests may have been due to the causes suggested, or to a number of other variables on which no evidence is given. In other words, we are forced to the conclusion that the great majority of these past experiments were invalid as experiments.

Yet, even if these studies had been quite valid as experiments, they could not have constituted an adequate evaluation of the conflicting methods used in teaching languages. The very idea that such conflicts can be solved by experimentation is highly questionable. Yet this idea is immensely popular; as one educational official recently explained to the author, "It's very simple to find out which is the better method. Simply test the results." This fallacy of evaluating methods by the results of their teaching is as common as that of evaluating the teaching by the method used. A method is one thing; the teaching of it, quite another. Good teaching is no guarantee of good learning; for it is what the learner does that makes him learn. Poor learning can nullify the best teaching, just as poor teaching can devalue the best method. Analysing one in terms of the other is bound to lead to error.

Here we are chiefly concerned with the factors involved in language teaꞌ .ing, and only with language learning to the extent that it is a factor in theories of language teaching and language analysis. Good teaching must take the learning process into account since its very purpose is to promote good learning; but the one can and does exist without the other. They must therefore first be analysed separately, for each contains its own complex of factors.

In the analysis of language teaching, it is essential to maintain a distinction between the method and the teaching of it, without forgetting the obvious relationship between them—since one of the purposes of a language teaching method is to direct the teaching of the language.

A second distinction has to be made between the language and the method, between the description of the language as presented in grammars and dictionaries and the way this material is used in a particular language teaching method. Again it is important not to forget the relationship between both. All language teaching methods must be based on some knowledge of and about the language to be taught. The more that is known about the language, the more complete the method may become. But there are different ways of finding out about a language and of describing what it is made of; many of the differences rest on different ideas of what a language is.

We therefore have three distinct but related fields of inquiry: I Language, II Method, and III Teaching.

I LANGUAGE

Language teaching is influenced by ideas on the nature of language in general, by ideas on the particular language being taught, and by ideas on how the language is learned. A theory of language teaching analysis must therefore begin with a study of how ideas on language may differ (language theory), on different ways of finding out what a particular language is made of (language description), how it differs from the native language (language differences), and on differences in ideas of how a language is learned (language learning).

Differences in language theory affect language teaching in two ways. They may affect the analysis of the language on which a method is based, for example, by producing different types of grammar; and they may affect the classroom techniques of language teaching, for example, by stressing either meaning or form.

Differences in language description directly affect what is taught by producing analyses of pronunciation, grammar, and vocabulary which may vary both in type and extent. Differences in the type of description influence what is taught by considering parts of the language as being the same or different; for example, a method based on one description may teach as the same, sentence structures which would constitute several separate teaching points in a method based on a different description. Differences in the extent of the description affect both the completeness and the accuracy of what is taught; for example, a method based on a description whose phonetics includes little on intonation is likely to be incomplete in its presentation of intonation patterns.

Differences in ideas on language learning affect both the method and the teaching of it. A method or teaching technique based on the idea that we learn a second language as a child learns his native language will differ from one based on the idea that we fail to learn a second language because of interference from our native language. The latter view also promotes a type of language description aimed at bringing out the differences between the first language and the second. Because they affect both description and method, ideas on language learning are best studied after language description and before method; for this reason they are treated in the first part, immediately before the section on method.

II METHOD

A method determines what and how much is taught (selection), the order in which it is taught (gradation), how the meaning and form are conveyed (presentation) and what is done to make the use of the language unconscious (repetition). Since both presentation and repetition may also be the concern of the teacher, the analysis must first determine how much is done by the method and how much by the teacher.

III TEACHING

The actual teaching of a language may differ in the analysis of what is to be taught, in the planning of the lessons, in the teaching techniques used, in the type and amount of teaching done through mechanical means, and finally, in the testing of what has been learned.

The analysis of language teaching must therefore be concerned with three distinct but related fields of analysis: I. Language Analysis, II. Method Analysis, III. Teaching Analysis.

PART I

LANGUAGE
ANALYSIS

CHAPTER 1

Language Theory

OUTLINE

0. INTRODUCTION

1. THE VALIDITY OF CONCEPTS

   1.1 Language and the Concept of Man
   1.1.1 The Mechanist View
   1.1.2 The Mentalist View
   1.2 Language and the Concept of Knowledge
   1.2.1 The Inductive Approach
   1.2.2 The Deductive Approach

2. THE NATURE OF LANGUAGE

   2.1 Language as Substance
   2.1.1 Content-Substance
   2.1.2 Expression-Substance
   2.2 Language as Form
   2.2.1 Content-Form
   2.2.2 Expression-Form
   2.2.3 Content and Expression-Form
   2.3 Language as Form and Substance
   2.3.1 Content
   2.3.2 Expression
   2.3.3 Content and Expression

3. ASPECTS OF LANGUAGE

   3.1 Language as a State
   3.1.1 Dependent
   3.1.2 Independent
   3.2 Language as an Activity
   3.2.1 Of the Mind
   3.2.2 Of the Brain
   3.3 Language as Change
   3.3.1 In Time
   3.3.2 In Space

Outline

4. TERMINOLOGY

4.1 Different Languages
4.2 Different Terms
4.3 Different Meanings

5. CONCLUSION

0. INTRODUCTION

What is the relevance of language theory to the analysis of language teaching? Language-teaching methods and the teaching of them depend ultimately on what the teacher or method maker thinks a language is. If a method is based on the assumption that a language is a collection of words —and there are many such methods—it will differ considerably from one based on the assumption that a language is a system; language considered as traditional grammar will be taught differently from language as current usage. The basis may be an unconscious assumption influenced by popular and traditional notions about language, or it may be a conscious assumption forming part of one or more theories of language. As language-teaching method becomes more and more scientific, however, it rests to a greater and greater extent on conscious and explicit theoretical assumptions about language. Whether conscious or unconscious, such theories decide the ultimate outcome of language-teaching methods and the descriptions on which they are based. Where can such theories be found?

Many fields of knowledge have been concerned with language and some have elaborated theories to explain its workings. Since different fields of knowledge are concerned with different things, or study the same thing in different ways, it is not surprising that there is a large number of different answers to the simple question: What is language? To the philosopher, language may be an instrument of thought; to the sociologist, a form of behaviour; to the psychologist, a cloudy window through which he glimpses the workings of the mind; to the logician, it may be a calculus; to the engineer, a series of physical events; to the statistician, a selection by choice and chance; to the linguist, a system of arbitrary signs.

Modern theories of language, unlike those of ancient and medieval times, are more concerned with how language works than with why it exists. They therefore tend to base their principles on the observation of language and languages. The theory will therefore depend on what is observed and how it is observed. In each field of knowledge concerned with language, there are different and often contrary ways of observing linguistic facts.

In the field of philosophy, some writers regard language as an external expression of universal thought; others would reduce all differences in philosophy to differences in the use of language. In the field of psychology, theories of language tend to differ according to both the school of psychology and the branch of psychology practised—social, educational, or child psychology. For some psychologists, language is a type of symbolism with many functions; for others, it is a man-made instrument of communication. Linguists, whose special field is the study of language, maintain an

3

even greater divergence of theories. To the linguist, language may be form and not matter; or it may be a system of arbitrary vocal symbols; or it may be a system of systems, a system of hierarchies, or even a hierarchy of systems. To some, it may be material; to others it may be mental. To some it may include only vocal symbols; to others, it may also include written symbols.

If there are differences within each field, there are also points of similarity between theories in different fields—the agreement, for example, of certain linguists, psychologists and philosophers on the non-material nature of language.

To locate these points of difference and similarity, it is necessary to compare the theories according to their main characteristics. What are the main characteristics of a theory? A theory assumes the validity of certain basic concepts, states the nature of that part of the field of knowledge which it selects as its legitimate concern, and treats it from a certain point of view through the use of certain terms. These four characteristics, therefore, are the main lines on which we can place theories in order to compare them: (1) the validity of concepts, (2) the nature of language, (3) aspects of language, and (4) terminology. These are the four ways in which one theory may differ from another. By examining each of them, we can get some idea of the differences between language theories and the possible influence of these theories on language-teaching methods.

1. THE VALIDITY OF CONCEPTS

What sort of understanding does a theory of language convey? To what branch of knowledge does the study of language belong? What are its central problems? How should knowledge about them be acquired—by experience or reasoning? Should a language theory be based on a distinction between the physical and the mental? These are some of the questions which all theories of language must face. They must also face the possibility of being identified with one or other of the conflicting schools of philosophy. Indeed it is in the contemporary theories of language that the great conflicts of method in twentieth-century philosophy are most clearly reflected.

Some of the best-known philosophers of the twentieth century have based their philosophy on an analysis of language. The work of Russell with the language of mathematics and his view of mathematical knowledge as merely verbal knowledge led eventually to the notion that much of philosophy could be reduced to problems of language.[267] Wittgenstein devoted most of his philosophy to an analysis of everyday language and to a study of the function of words.[279] Others, like Cassirer, began to consider language as an independent mental form—scientific thinking as another, religious thinking as still another mental form.[235] Being thus independent, language could not be understood through the concepts and methods of other sciences. Urban used the very existence of language as a proof that metaphysics and ethics could be meaningful;[219] while Carnap rejected these as meaningless since they were not open to logical analysis, which he based on the analysis—or rather, reconstruction—of syntax. For Carnap the only proper task of philosophy was logical analysis. Philosophy became logic; logic became syntax.[225]

The basing of philosophy on language analysis is one thing; the basing of language analysis on philosophy is quite another. The preoccupations of the philosopher are not those of the linguist. Each makes a different use of the tools of language and logic. Although both may make use of formal logic, as do Carnap in philosophy and Hjelmslev in linguistics, they use it for different purposes: Carnap uses it to build up a language; Hjelmslev, to break it down. The philosopher is interested in the direct or indirect proof of linguistic statements. Not so the linguist; indeed, many of the statements the linguist is likely to analyse will be logically irrelevant, since they have to do with feelings and images. The linguist is interested in the form and meaning of all possible statements in a language—questions, commands, value judgments—which form the bulk of everyday discourse and have to be analysed as meaningful.

Some linguists claim independence of any philosophical assumption by adopting the pragmatic attitude that only facts verified by the senses are valid and that theories can only be summaries of such facts.[269] But this in itself is a philosophical assumption which shapes the theory.

It is such philosophical assumptions of linguistics, rather than the linguistic assumptions of philosophy, that are relevant to the conceptual foundations of language theory. And these may differ in two fundamental respects—(1) on the concept of man, and (2) on the concept of knowledge.

1.1 LANGUAGE AND THE CONCEPT OF MAN

Since language is a human activity, different ideas on what human activity involves produce different notions on what a language is. Human activity may be regarded (1) as wholly physical (the mechanist view), or (2) as largely mental (the mentalist view).

1.1.1. The Mechanist View

This view of man considers the mind as an extension of the body, different only in that the activity of the mind is more difficult to observe. The difference between the mental and the physical, between the animate and the inanimate, is in their complexity. They are essentially the same; the difference is only in degree. All human activity, including language, is a chain of material cause-effect sequences; if one knew the entire history of a person's nervous system one would know what he would say in any given circumstances.

This chain of sequences may be studied from evidence supplied by physical experiments, mostly of the stimulus-response type such as those performed on animals. For the linguistic responses of human beings are in essence considered to be the same as the physical responses of animals to their surroundings. But since so much of the stimulus and so many of the causes, the meanings expressed in speech, happen to be in the mind and therefore unseen, they are understandably neglected in the mechanist theories in favour of the physical manifestations of language in its spoken and written forms. These are the facts of language and are treated as the facts of a natural science.

Language descriptions and language-teaching methods based on such theories tend therefore to present the language mainly as a system of forms rather than as a collection of meanings. One outstanding example of a theory based on this mechanist view of man is that of Bloomfield and his school.[128,131]

1.1.2 The Mentalist View

In opposition to the mechanist view, the mentalist view maintains the traditional distinction between mental and physical. Acts of language are mainly mental acts and, although they may very well be correlated with the physical acts of speech, they are acts of a different type. The difference is not only one of degree; it is essentially a difference of kind. Linguistic activity cannot therefore be classed as physical activity.

Nor can human language be studied as animal behaviour. There is a fundamental difference. The animal can be conditioned to respond in a certain way; man, in addition to this, knows the right way to go on, on the basis of what he has been taught. Analogy, an instance of this capacity, is what makes language possible. Much of human behaviour is voluntary behaviour; it is essentially different from the conditioned behaviour of animals. Language, being a human and social phenomenon, cannot therefore be regarded simply as a physical or an animal act. It must be regarded from the point of view of the ideas and feelings peculiar to man.

Language descriptions and language-teaching methods based on a mentalist view are likely to give a great deal of importance to meanings, the mental part of language, and not exclusively to the physical forms. The best-known example of a language theory worked out from a mentalist point of view is that of Saussure and his school.[113,120]

1.2 LANGUAGE AND THE CONCEPT OF KNOWLEDGE

The validity of a language theory also depends on the type of knowledge it represents—knowledge obtained through the senses, or knowledge acquired through scientific intuition.

A theory may require (1) that languages be described through the observation and classification of facts (the inductive approach), or (2) through the intuition and construction of a model from which all possible facts may be deduced (the deductive approach).

1.2.1 The Inductive Approach

According to this approach, the only valid statements about languages are those arrived at by observing linguistic facts, classifying them and making generalizations on what is observed and classified. It is an imitation of the approach used by the sciences of observation. The linguist is to collect specimens of acts of speech, observe them, and classify the differences. Although he can obviously do this for only a small sample of all acts of speech performed in any one language, he makes generalizations on what he has observed and applies these to the unobserved remainder on the assumption that his sample contains everything of significance.

Since he arrives at his knowledge of language through the observation of its uses, there is no theoretical necessity for him to have any prior working knowledge of the language he describes. It is essentially a matter of gathering samples of the language from a native speaker and then "cracking the code" as it were, through techniques not unlike those of cryptography.

Such theories can therefore produce techniques and procedures of language analysis which are the same for all languages analysed (see Ch. 2 below). Any person trained in such procedures is able to make a grammar of any language of which he can get a sufficient number of samples. The approach is based on the belief that only the facts verified by the senses have any scientific validity.

Descriptions of language and language-teaching methods based on this approach are likely to give a great deal of importance to those features of language which lend themselves most readily to physical observation and classification, that is to the phonological features of language—the sounds and sound-patterns. Descriptive procedures such as those of Harris, for example, are based on this sort of approach.[431]

1.2.2. The Deductive Approach

If the inductive theorist of language imitates the sciences of observation, the deductive theorist follows the theoretical sciences. He perceives a pattern, constructs a theoretical model, and tests to see how much can be deduced from it.

The making of the right model is a matter of scientific intuition. It is done by making explicit the unconscious rules which every speaker of the language possesses; it is the codifying of one's intuitive notions of the structure of the language. One must therefore necessarily know the language before one can codify it in this way. A deductive linguist must first possess the language he wishes to describe.

In any language, the number and variety of utterances are infinite. And since it is impossible to describe all of them, the deductive linguist constructs theories to explain all possible utterances. The best deductive theory is that which gives the simplest explanation for all the known facts and is capable of predicting most of the others.

Descriptions of language and language-teaching methods based on this type of theory are likely to stress the largest patterns of the language—the type which can be arrived at most readily through intuition—the system of the parts of speech and syntactic relationships. An example of a deductive theory is that of Guillaume and the psychomechanic approach to language analysis.[162]

2. THE NATURE OF LANGUAGE

Devolving from the concepts of man and knowledge are the concepts of the nature of language. These may range from the conception of language as a sequence of sounds to the conception of language as everything that can be talked about, including the means used to talk about it. Language may be conceived as including not the sequences of sounds themselves but only our idea of them. It may include or exclude the meaning of the sound sequences. If it includes meaning, it may also include the thing meant—or it may exclude it. There is so much overlapping in what different concepts include that, in order to distinguish one from another, it is necessary to place each within a framework which includes all of them. The framework may be built on distinctions in the field as a whole, starting with the most general—the distinction between substance and form. This may be illustrated simply by a vertical line:

SUBSTANCE | FORM

In the areas of both form and substance, there is a further distinction between what is being talked about (the content) and the means used to talk about it (expression). This distinction may be indicated by a simple horizontal line, placed over the substance-form areas, since it is included in them:

CONTENT

EXPRESSION

The resulting framework may be shown thus:

AC=Substance
BD=Form
AB=Content
CD=Expression

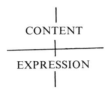

This gives us four distinct areas:

A: Everything that can be talked about (e.g. things like doors and gates, and our experience of them)=content-substance.
B: The formaliẓ tion of these into units of language or linguistic concepts (e.g. English *door*+*gate*=French *porte*)=content-form.
C: The physical media of language (e.g. sounds)=expression-substance.
D: The formalization of the media into units of expression (e.g. phonemes, letters of the alphabet)=expression-form.

Although this framework is sufficient to locate most theories, a refinement is necessary in order to make it completely functional. Area A includes not only things but also our experience of them, and Area C includes not only sounds but our experience of them.

Psychologically it is necessary to distinguish between things, etc. (phenomena), and our conception of them (experience). We can show this distinction by dividing the substance half of the framework with a vertical dotted line:

With such a framework placed over our field, we can plot some of the main concepts of the nature of language and see the location and extent of the area covered by each.

A language theory may be based on the assumption that language is by nature (1) substance, (2) form, or (3) both form and substance.

2.1 LANGUAGE AS SUBSTANCE

Language may be considered as made up of things that one can see and hear, feel and think. But there is a difference between (1) the substance of things we think about or talk about (Area A—Content), and (2) the substance of what we talk with—or write with—the sounds we utter and the marks we make on paper (Area C—Expression).

2.1.1 Content-Substance (A)

Modern theories of language no longer identify words with things; but even today, people act as if words and things were identical.

On the other hand, thoughts have long been identified with the words which represent them. The view that the content of words comes from universal mental concepts is responsible for the popular logical grammars which, since the early eighteenth century, have dominated the linguistic education of school-children.

Although twentieth-century linguists and psychologists have either completely overthrown or considerably modified this notion, it still remains the unstated assumption upon which many school grammars and language-teaching methods are based.

2.1.2 Expression-Substance (C)

Some theories of language deal exclusively with the material study of what can be seen or heard as language, that is, with the substance (e.g. sounds) used to express language.

Most of these are phonetic theories, which consider the language sounds either from a physical point of view (acoustic phonetics) as do such phoneticians as Fant, Zwirner, Ladefoged and Kaiser, or from the physiological point of view of how speech sounds are made (articulatory phonetics) as do Jones, Straka, Fouché, Viëtor, and many others. [484a–509,797,793]

Some phoneticians insist that the sound substance of expression is the very foundation of language. They have produced some detailed descriptions of it which have been the basis for a number of language-teaching methods.

2.2 LANGUAGE AS FORM

The best-known linguistic theories of the first half of the twentieth century consider language not as a substance but as a form. Language is not the same as the thoughts and things about which we speak; nor is it the sounds and tongue movements we use to speak about them.

It may, however, be (1) a labelling or classification of these thoughts and things (content-form), (2) an abstract grouping or image of the sounds and forms of the language (expression-form), or (3) the formalization of both— of what we talk about and how we talk about it (content and expression).

2.2.1 Content-Form (B)

Language has been considered exclusively as the formalization of thought. It is considered not as thought itself, but as a separate symbolic form. This is the view of Cassirer, who considers language as an independent mental form, separate from other symbolic forms like mysticism and scientific thought.[235]

Since such theories do not account for the sounds and forms of the language, and show no connection with either substance or expression, they have not been used as a basis for language-teaching methods.

2.2.2 Expression-Form (D)

Theories which consider language as the formalization of our means of expression, however, have been applied both to methods of language description and to language teaching. The best known of these theories is that of Bloomfield.

Bloomfield begins by excluding both mind and matter from linguistics on the ground that the linguist is not competent to deal with problems of psychology or physiology. Meaning cannot be analysed through linguistics.[128:162] The argument is that the totality of meaningful discourse must be "truth"—meaningful and truth being used in their pragmatic sense. And in dealing with the nature of language, the question of the nature of truth is irrelevant. For this reason, this school of language theory classifies speech by form and not by meaning.[127:24] And some of its adherents, in

11

order to keep the purity and exactness of their science, have handed over meaning to the anthropologists, phonetics to the physicists, and language learning to the psychologists. But since these "linguistic appendages" are central to none of these disciplines, they have not been incorporated into the main stream of either anthropology, physics, or psychology—disciplines which still look to linguistics to supply the answers to questions concerned with language.

Another theory which limits itself to expression-form is Carnap's logical syntax of language. This has been less applicable to language teaching than Bloomfield's theory, however; for while Bloomfield includes only the spoken form of a natural language, Carnap includes the written form of any language, but especially that of the artificial languages made up by logicians for the purposes of their study.

2.2.3 Content and Expression (BD)

Some of the better-known theories of language as form do not limit themselves to expression or to content, but include both. These theories insist on the formal relationship of expressions of language with what they mean.

Most such theories trace their origin to the teachings of Saussure. Saussure's theory first distinguishes language as a code or system (*langue*) from the use made of it in speaking (*parole*). For Saussure, the object of linguistics is the study of the code (*langue*) which is essentially form (Area BD) and not substance.[113:169] The thought substance and the sound substance do not concern linguistics. Language (*langue*) comprises neither ideas nor sounds, but simply conceptual and phonic differences. [113:166] The substance of both the content and the expression (Area AC) of a language is purely arbitrary; so are the connections between the real world, or our idea of it, and the signs used to talk about it.

A sign for Saussure is a fusion of a linguistic concept—the signified in Area B—with an acoustic image of the sound—the signifier in Area D. This may be illustrated thus:

The signified is made of distinctive characteristics isolated by the language from the events of the real world. The signifier includes acoustic images of the sounds of the language. Neither includes the physical qualities which such events or speech sounds may possess in themselves. What is relevant is the fact that one sign is not confused with any other.[113:164] The important feature of a sign is simply in being what the others are not.[113:162] It is the differences that count. In fact, language is made up entirely of differences.[113:166] The only positive fact is their combination; it is the only sort of fact that there is in language.[113:166] Any value which a sign may have lies in its opposition to or contrast with other signs.[113:168]

Although this is a more comprehensive theory than Bloomfield's, there are many points of similarity. Both Bloomfield and Saussure consider language as a form rather than a substance; they both make formal difference the main characteristic of language.[113:157] For Bloomfield, all that is necessary is that each phoneme be unmistakably different from all others.[128:128]

Saussure maintains that the patterning of the substance of language (Area AC) must be arbitrary.[113:100] So does Bloomfield.[128:93]

The main difference between these two important theories is in the place given to linguistic content. Bloomfield places it outside the realm of linguistics, claiming that meaning can only be described by the sciences whose object is the content in question. For the Saussurians, it is impossible to analyse the expression side as language without implicitly considering its content.[637:136] Linguistic content is inseparable from linguistic expression; linguistics is the study of their interrelationship.

Among the better-known theories which claim to stem from Saussure is the theory of Glossematics. The object of Glossematics is the study of linguistic form; other sciences study the substance. The theory therefore follows Saussure in considering language as form and not substance—as a totality which does not consist of things but of relationships.[154:22; 113:166] It is obvious to the Glossematicist that the description of language must begin by stating relations between relevant units, and that the description cannot include information about the substance of these units. The actual sounds (expression-substance: Area C) and the things they stand for (content-substance: Area A) are therefore irrelevant to the language system and may be completely altered without changing the language. But unlike the Bloomfield theory, Glossematics includes the study of form in both areas (expression and content) and stresses their constant relationship.

2.3 LANGUAGE AS FORM AND SUBSTANCE

While considering language as form, a number of important theories insist that language, by its nature, is also substance. It may be only (1) the substance of language content—the thoughts and things we talk about, or (2) the substance of language expression—the sounds we use to talk about them, or it may be (3) both the substance of content and expression.

2.3.1 As Content (AB)

Theories concerned with content are interested in how the content of reality (the things and experiences in Area A) become formalized as the content of language (the linguistic meanings and patterns of Area B). How are the things and ideas about which people talk attached to the units of meaning (content-form) through which the listener understands the speaker? In other words, where do our patterns of meaning originate?

Some theories seek the origin of these patterns in the real world; others find them in the language itself. For some, they are determined by experience; for others, by the particular language used.

At one time or other, philosophers, linguists and psychologists have seen in mind and matter the origins of patterns of meaning believed to exist in all languages. For them, the patterns in Area A shape all or some of the patterns of Area B. They shape all of them if nature is ultimately responsible for language. This is the view of Russell and Gardiner. Although nature and society may be ignored in discussions of language, they ultimately determine all language content.[217:234] Patterns of language depend ultimately on relations between non-verbal facts derived from nature. Countless acts of speech reflect this relation and result in the shadowy patterns we call meaning.[226:44]

On the other hand, the patterns of nature may be only partly responsible for the patterns of language. This is the view of Britton and Morris. Britton sees two types of patterns in language, the psychological type, which belongs to the human mind, and the linguistic type which belongs to the particular language.[218] Of the different types of linguistic meaning recognized by Morris, only identification, that is, the location in time and space, depends on the patterns found in nature.[211] This might suggest, however, that the space and time patterns of nature as shown by the physical sciences should be found in all languages.

In opposition to the above is the view that the content of language in Area B is entirely independent of our mental or physical experiences of reality in Area A. Indeed, the content of language, far from being shaped by thought, is itself the shaper of our mental categories. It is the language content that shapes the mental content. This hypothesis was advanced by Sapir and developed by Whorf.

Sapir saw language as a self-contained, creative symbolic organization which not only refers to experience largely acquired without its help, but actually defines experience for us by reason of its formal completeness and because of our unconscious projection of its implicit expectations into the field of experience.[206]

Elaborating this view into a theory, Whorf submitted that the structure or grammar of a language is not merely a reproducing instrument for voicing ideas, but rather is itself the shaper of ideas, the programme and guide for our mental activity, for the analysis of impressions, for the synthesis of our mental stock-in-trade.[200]

Theories of this type imply that a language is capable of expressing certain things and incapable of expressing others; and translators have not hesitated to supply examples. Language-teaching methods based on such theories tend to regard language instruction as the teaching of a new mode of thought.

2.3.2 As Expression (CD)

Language may be regarded as simply a means of expression, composed of both the substance of expression (Area C) and its formalization (Area D). It is the relationship between the hundreds of sounds we make when speaking and those selected and grouped by the language as being relevant (phonemes as reflected, for example, in the letters of the alphabet).

Among those who consider language thus are the phonologists of the Prague School, who, following the theories of Trubetzkoy, study the relationship between what they call the speech act (*Sprechakt*) of Area C and the speech structure (*Sprachgebilde*) of Area D.[173] According to Trubetzkoy, we can discover the structure of speech by first finding the distinctive or relevant units of Area D (phonemes, etc.), by determining exactly what in the speech act (Area C) keeps one unit separate from the others (phonetic contrasts), and by charting the relation between these. Contrasts such as the voice-vibration in the sound /z/ opposed to the lack of it in /s/, or between /s/ as a continuous sound and /t/ as a non-continuous sound, are all to be found in the actual substance of expression, the physical sounds of speech (Area C). The elements of speech structure, however, consist of the way such contrasts are arranged (Area D). This arrangement, which varies from language to language, determines the phonological structure of each language. (See also Chapter 2: 2.1.2.)

2.3.3 As Content and Expression

Theories which include both content and expression do so to different extents. It may be content and expression (i) only as regards substance (ABC), (ii) only as regards form (BCD), or (iii) as regards both substance and form (ABCD).

(i) *Substance (ABC)*

Language may be regarded as an activity in which the thing or idea referred to (A) gets its linguistic meaning by an act of reference (B) to a physical symbol (C). Language is thus a continual movement between Areas A and C (the areas of substance) via Area B. It is a movement between the thing or idea referred to (the referent in A) and whatever is used to refer to it (the symbol in C). This is done through an act of reference in Area B which is peculiar to the language in question. This may be illustrated thus:

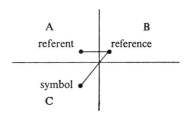

The type of movement between A (things and ideas), B (references) and C (symbols) varies from language to language. Teaching a language consists in establishing the relationships between A and B, and B and C.

In the language-teaching methods which this theory has produced, a great deal of care is devoted to establishing the right sort of connections (A-B) – (B-C) between the symbols of the language and what they stand for. Ogden and Richards' theory of reference is the original and most widely-known theory of this type.[233]

(ii) *Form (BCD)*

Language may be regarded as the expression of content form. All the sounds, words and inflections of a language exist only for the purpose of expressing this. Content form is regarded neither as substance nor as the ready-made representation of substance, but rather as a system of abstract outlines of mental operations whose use enables us to represent certain fractions of our experience. Language is primarily a system of representation (B) which makes use of a system of expression (D); both are form, not substance. But in order that the form be perceived, a language must make use of some physical means, some substance like sounds or letters (C). The act of speech as expression consists of a continual movement between B and C via Area D, between what is signified (content-form) and the signs used to signify it—the formal signs (expression-form) and the material used to express them (expression-substance). This may be illustrated thus:

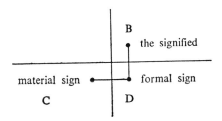

Such is the psychomechanic theory of Guillaume. Any language-teaching method based on it would presumably start from the most inclusive patterns of content form, the main outlines of representation, graduating through varying shades of abstraction from the most inclusive to the least. (See 3.2.1.)

(iii) *Substance and Form (ABCD)*

Of the theories which consider language as both the content and expression of form and substance (ABCD), the best known are those of Firth and Pike.

For Firth, language, being an essentially human activity, must not exclude the mind, thoughts and ideas of those who use it, nor the situations in which it is used (Area A).[134] A language groups and abstracts elements of these situations which have constant relationship with its vocabulary and grammar; this is the "context," a term which followers of Firth prefer to "content" (Area B). It includes all internal (formal) and external (contextual) relations. There is the relation of one utterance to another, and the relation of utterances to the situations in which they are made. The formal expression of this context of situation is the vocabulary and grammar of the language working through its spoken or written forms, its phonology or graphology (Area D). These in turn are a formalization of the phonic or graphic substance used by the language (Area C). If we plot this relationship on our framework, it appears as shown on the next page.

Students of Firth have elaborated this theory and made it more complete and rigorous. Halliday takes pains to point out that although the foundations of language are in the context of situation, the theory does not include an analysis of situations as such; it has nothing to do with the study of physical phenomena.[145] It is concerned with this area only to the extent that the forms of the language are related to situations. It is this relationship which is the context, and this context is expressed through the grammar and vocabulary of a language by means of its phonology or graphology, through the actual sounds or script it happens to use.

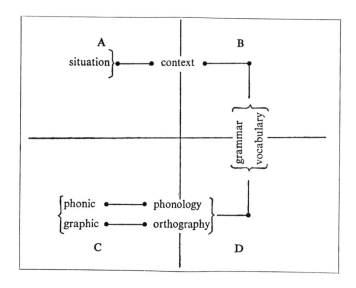

The grammar, no matter what the language, is necessarily made of certain units, certain structures, certain systems of relationship, and certain grammatical classes. These exist in all languages; but their type and number depend on the particular language. For example, in English the units include the morpheme, the word, the phrase, the clause, and the sentence. These can be arranged in order of increasing size, and each can be defined in terms of the other. Structures are the frameworks into which these units fit. Morphemes fit into word structures, words into a limited number of phrase structures, etc. In a phrase structure of the type ON THE TABLE, each position (like that of the article *the*) can be filled by a limited number of words (*this, that, his, a,* etc.) which operate as a system. Systems operate in a way that imposes limitations on the structure. For example, *the* can be replaced by *these* only if we make *table* plural. Systems group words and word-endings into classes, such as prepositions, conjunctions, etc. The number of items in any one grammatical class is limited, and these items form a closed series.

In the vocabulary of the language, however, the series is not closed. A language is always acquiring new words. The items in any word-class in the vocabulary must form an open series. Words may be arranged in two types of classes. They may be arranged according to their range of possible combinations with other words, and according to the range of situations in which they are used.

Although it operates likewise in all four areas, the theory of Pike is quite different from the above. Pike considers language in relation to a unified theory of the structure of human behaviour. Before elaborating his general theory, Pike developed special theories for determining the elements in the area of expression (CD)—the "phonetic" elements of C and the "phonemic" elements of D. Phonetic elements include all non-relevant variants found in language usage; phonemic elements are limited to the relevant ones. Extending this distinction to the areas of content (AB), and indeed to the entire field of human behaviour, in which language is included, Pike divides all activity into non-relevant *etic* elements in the area of substance (AC) and to the formalized and relevant *emic* elements in the area of form (BC).[192] (See 4.1 and Ch. 2.)

We can now compare these different types of theories of the nature of language, by placing them together within the same framework.

CONTENT

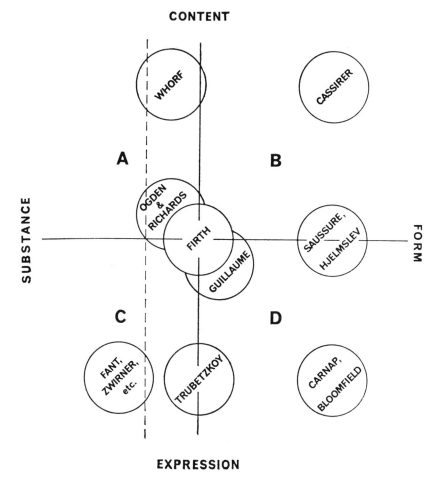

EXPRESSION

3. ASPECTS OF LANGUAGE

Within each of the above areas, a theory may consider language from three different points of view. It may be interested in (1) how the language sounds or looks (language as a state), (2) how it works (language as an activity), or (3) how it develops (language as change).

3.1 LANGUAGE AS A STATE

If it is interested in how the language sounds or looks, the theory will include something on language considered as a fixed state—either (1) as a state dependent on what people think and do, or (2) as one which is independent of this.

3.1.1 **Dependent**

Dependently, language may be considered as human thought or as human behaviour.

(i) *As Thought*

Language may be regarded as being composed of elements of thought. This is the traditional view. In the early twentieth century, Brunot developed this view into a theory treating of the relation between language and thought.[813] He first divided language into five categories of thought—beings, facts, circumstances, modalities and relationships—and then attempted to show how each of these is expressed by the French language. He made no distinction, however, between structure and vocabulary.

An example of an extensive analysis of a particular language based on mental categories is the French grammar of Damourette and Pichon, which considers language as a system of thought.[809] This voluminous work atomizes the language into a number of mental categories and sub-categories. Many traditional school grammars and language-teaching methods are based on this view of language as a set of mental categories.

(ii) *As Behaviour*

Language may also be regarded as being composed of units of behaviour. Not only the anthropologists and sociologists, but also certain linguists, consider language thus. Pike places language in the context of human behaviour in general, in which all social acts, including language, are divided into units of significance (*emic units*), each containing a number of non-significant variants (*etic units*).[192] (See 2.3.3.iii.)

Another linguist who regarded language as behaviour was Zipf, who made the state of language dependent upon the principle of least effort.

According to this principle, the forms of the language used in human behaviour become a compromise between the desire of the speaker to get his ideas and feelings across with the minimum of effort and the desire of the hearer to understand them, also with a minimum of effort.[208]

3.1.2 Independent

Language may be viewed as an independent state, either (i) as structure, or (ii) as a system of communication.

(i) *As Structure*

The idea of language as structure goes back to the teachings of Saussure and his disciples, who regard language as a structure of values between which systematic relations can be observed.

Saussure's basic notion is developed in a number of structural theories. Among these is Glossematics. Glossematic theory considers a language as a system of internal relations, as a self-subsistent whole which consists of nothing but relations or functions—"a web of functions", as it were. Using the methods of formal logic, it aims at describing the internal structure of a language completely, as simply as possible, and without contradiction. The language is therefore considered as an interplay of purely formal relations.

Other linguistic theories which consider language as structure are those of Bloomfield and Chomsky. Bloomfield considers the structure as a line or sequence of the smallest units of the language, that is, as a sequence of its phonemes. Chomsky, on the other hand, starts by considering linguistic structure itself as a theory which generates all and only grammatical sentences.[561] Considering language as a mechanism for generating sentences, his theory uses a chain of transformations to link the most general structures of language, the sentence patterns, to the sequences of phonemes uttered as sound patterns. The theory attempts to explain how the limited number of structural elements in a language can produce an unlimited number of sentences. (See Ch. 2: 1.3.2.)

The view of languages as structures is also the basis of typology—the study of language types. Typology disregards the traditional family classifications of languages as descended from a common parent (Germanic, Slavonic, Romance languages), since languages of entirely different origin may belong to the same structural type (*isomorphism*). Languages may also belong to the same type at one level of structure but differ at other levels. One of the aims of typology is to discover features common to all languages. All languages, for example, seem to have stop consonants like /p, t, k/; some, however, may have no fricative or continuant consonants. There are some languages lacking syllables with initial vowels, but none lacking initial consonants.[633:21] Any knowledge of features common to all or most languages has an obvious application to language teaching.

(ii) *As Communication*

Although communication is not language, language can be communication. It can also be much more—and much less.

Language considered from a communications point of view is the transmission of messages; it is the choice of a sequence of symbols from a reservoir of code. Indeed we use language as if we had to choose words one after another. Once a word or sound has been chosen, the choice of the one following is governed by the laws of probability. Thus, if the word is *the*, the probability of the next word in the sentence being an article or a verb is very small indeed. It is in this way that information theory regards language.[368] "Information" here is a technical term, different in meaning from its usual colloquial sense.

The language studied in the science of communication is the language of averages. It requires long statistical analyses of languages and specific methods for studying the results. These have been compiled and elaborated in such useful general studies of quantitative linguistics as those of Herdan and Guiraud.[371a-77]

Statistical analyses are of interest to the study of language teaching in so far as they give information on items which are most often used in a language (see Ch. 5). They are also of interest to those who base their structural analysis of a language on samples of texts. Since we cannot observe all of the spoken or written sentences used in any one language but only a relatively small sample, our analysis is to that extent necessarily statistical.

Linguistics, however, is not mathematics. Some linguists have tried to base the structure of language on statistics. The structure of a language is essentially non-statistical.[561] There is no demonstrable connection between the grammatical significance of a form and its relative frequency of occurrence.[243] Understanding the structure of a language is one thing; formulating statistics on the occurrence of its units is another. Statistics does not explain linguistic structure.

3.2 LANGUAGE AS ACTIVITY

In contradistinction to the view of language as a state made of elements of thought or behaviour, or of units of structure or communication, is the view of language as an activity. It is concerned with the way language operates or is operated by man. From this point of view, language may be considered as (1) an activity of the mind, or (2) an activity of the brain.

3.2.1 Of the Mind

As an activity of the mind, language may be regarded either (i) as mental movement, or (ii) as stimulus-response.

(i) *As Mental Movement*

The study of language as mental movement is called psychomechanics. Its basic postulate is that the mental operations involved in the use of language necessarily take a certain amount of time, infinitesimal though this may be. The task of psychomechanics is to identify these mental operations and to refer them to mental time in an effort to demonstrate the mental process involved in acts of language. The study starts by delimiting the degrees of abstraction through which our minds seize and represent the world of experience. Such an approach is fundamentally different from the traditional analysis of language as a group of static, logical categories.

Psychomechanics attempts to explain how language, the institutional system, becomes usage in the individual acts of speaking and writing. Usage is considered essentially as a process of mental expression by means of acts of abstraction capable of producing such different types of linguistic categories as the parts of speech, inflectional forms, and vocabulary.

(ii) *As Stimulus-Response*

Psychologists, and certain linguists as well, have long considered language as a verbal response to external stimulus. Language is regarded as an immediate animal-like reaction to what is perceived.[605] It is as if language were a long series of conditioned reflexes. A number of linguists and language teachers have regarded language in this way and have composed language-teaching methods from this point of view. Such methods present and drill unanalysed units of language as complete utterances, always given in association with the appropriate situation.

The contextual stimulus-response view differs from this in that it teaches the language as a constant variation in the stimulus to fit a corresponding variation in the language response, thus leading the learner to abstract the patterns of language by seeing the relation between each element of the situation and the corresponding element of the response.

This view of language teaching evolved from the contextual theory of Ogden and Richards.[233] According to this theory, the stimulus of experience comes to us in repeated contexts. These may be physical events which reach our minds through our senses; or they may be events in the mind itself—memories, associations of ideas. Whatever they be, these contexts are continually associated with certain elements (e.g. words) in the language which then become symbols of elements in the context. These symbols, from the speaker's standpoint, are always subordinate to what they stand for; from the hearer's standpoint, they are equal. The hearer first perceives the sound as sound. He then recognizes sounds as distinctive units; he does so because similar sound sensations in the past were always associated with signs. He then recognizes simple referents (e.g. names of things), and finally complex ones. The complexity of the referent, however, is not necessarily reflected in the complexity of the symbol; a single word can stand for a complex idea. But it is not the single word which determines the reference; it is its interconnection with the other words in the sentence.

Language may be considered as only partly a matter of stimulus-response. It is partly concrete activity; partly abstract activity. The concrete perceives and reacts to situations in an animal-like way, through verbal responses to immediately perceived cues and associations, in an automatic type of speech behaviour. The abstract conceptualizes and categorizes. Everyday speech is a combination of both. This is the view of Goldstein and Buyssens. Goldstein regards abstract and concrete behaviour as only two extreme poles, with fine gradations between them; similarly he makes no clear-cut distinction between conscious and unconscious verbal responses.[326,328]

3.2.2 Of the Brain

If some students of language regard language as an operation of the mind, others prefer to consider it as an operation of the brain. They study this operation of the human brain as a physical activity. In order to understand the nature of this activity, two approaches have been developed: (i) The first consists in an analysis of speech reactions during local interferences with the brain (the approach through neurology). (ii) The second is the construction of models and devices which function as analogues of the human brain (the approach through technology).

(i) *Neurology*

Since all stimuli leave a trace on the brain and a language sign is an association between two stimuli, the acoustic image and the concept, this sign may theoretically be found in the brain. The localization of speech areas in the brain goes back to 1861, when Broca pointed out the relationship between language and the cortex of man's brain. In recent years, neuro-surgeons have been able to locate the different areas in the cortex which control hearing and speech, memory and thought, and to formulate theories as to their function and interrelation. Penfield, working in this field for more than a quarter of a century, made verbal tests on hundreds of patients during brain operations. This enabled him to construct a theory based on speech areas and to assume that the organization and co-ordination of the speech mechanisms are carried out by nerve-cell connections, all within the same half of the brain, the dominant one.[321]

Most of those who study the linguistic activity of the human brain no longer believe that it is a matter of mental images. It is rather a matter of nerve impulses travelling along networks. These seem to correspond to the statistical properties of language. Recent neurological theories have led to speculation by theorists of language in a number of different directions. A science of "speculative neurology" has even arisen. Nerve-cells, which are all-or-nothing firing devices, operate in a two-unit system, building networks in which every linguistic form has its position. Some linguists believe that the nerve-cells are arranged in loops, around which signals circulate and may be remembered by firing one another in succession around the loop and back to the first cell, where the cycle is started anew on its next round.[620:166]

Similarities have also been found between certain brain disorders and certain fundamentals of language. Jakobson has compared the basic types of loss of memory with the basic characteristics of language. One type affects the ability to put words together in the right way; the other type affects the ability to substitute one unit for another.[166:60]

Students of linguistic psychology have asked whether the dividing of speech into units like phonemes and words is done in the mind of the speaker, or only in the mind of the linguist. To find out, they have set up experiments which aim to obtain from speakers and listeners certain responses which correspond to the theories and observations of the linguists. But this sort of experiment is more difficult than it seems, for each speaker and listener brings to the language his own special responses which are due to his peculiar nervous system and his own unique combination of memories and experiences in the use of the language; it would often seem that he interprets what he hears according to his own liking.[370:427]

(ii) *Technology*

The second approach to the linguistic operations of the human brain is through the construction of models of it, theoretical models and working models.

Theoretical models have been built for the purpose of studying the language as an activity of the brain. One of these is the chromatoscope, a sort of mechanical generator of linguistic hypotheses, in which both words and concepts are regarded as "molecules of experience", particles of "meaning" being the atoms out of which these molecules are built. The atoms of meaning are considered as active "packets of information" capable of activating other atoms. Theoretical models such as these only suggest possible approaches to the study of the linguistic activities of the human brain.[386:114]

As for the working models, it is the so-called "electronic brain" that is expected to lead to an understanding of how language operates in the brain of man.[383] These devices, although greater in working capacity and efficiency than the human brain, are extremely limited in the variety of their activities. Their greatest achievement has been in the field of mathematical computation.[385]

Efforts to design a machine for the translation of languages have resulted in a good deal of speculation on the linguistic activities of the brain.[384] It has seemed likely that the construction of an efficient mechanical translator will contribute to the design of an electronic analogue of the brain. The construction of such an analogue is one of the greatest ambitions of modern science and technology.

Some mathematicians, however, have denied any close analogy between such digital computers and the construction or activity of the human brain. They point out the historical and contingent character of both mathematics and the natural languages. Moreover, it is reasonable to expect that any adequate theory of brain functioning should have statistical characteristics which display plurality, probabilism, variability, redundancy, and tolerance of small errors. No machine having a unitary mechanism, a fixity of properties, an economy of connections, a certainty of output and an intolerance of small errors can successfully simulate the brain.[382] Batteries of machines of various types, however, have been suggested as capable of doing so. If and when such an analogue with the proper characteristics is developed, its contributions to linguistic psychology could be profitably correlated with the findings of the neuro-surgeons. If in turn these could be correlated with the analytical and inferential work of linguists, our knowledge of the two extremes of the act of human communication—two minds communicating through language—may yet reach the exactness of our knowledge of the sound-waves which occur between them.

3.3 LANGUAGE AS CHANGE

While some scholars consider language as state or activity, others regard it as something which is continually changing (1) in time, or (2) in space.

3.3.1 **In Time**

A theory may cover variations in language over a period of time, either (i) in the individual, or (ii) in the society in which the language has been used.

(i) *In the Individual*

Analysis of change in the speech of the individual is generally confined to the study of the linguistic development of children. This is a field in which important theories have been developed, in the first half of the twentieth century, as a result of studies based on more and more refined techniques of analysis. Since these theories are so very important in the study of language learning, they will be treated under that head (Ch. 4).

(ii) *In Society*

Analysis of variations of language in time—called historical linguistics—has been practised with great rigour for more than a century. Such linguists as Meyer-Lübke, Sweet, Schuchardt, Meillet, Jespersen, Nyrop, Wyld, Whitney, and Paul—to name only a few—have tried to explain the facts they found by theories ranging from phonetic law to selective variation.[95]

Today language is generally regarded as an ever-changing code. The changes are not considered as inventions designed by individuals to suit particular purposes; they are systems which arise from the interrelation of the many needs of thousands or millions of people. The mutually modifying practices of hundreds of non-relevant elements in the speech of many individuals eventually bring about changes in the relevant elements which form the code of the language. We are continually altering, continually building, the system of our language. It is as if the human mind were dissatisfied with the language it inherits and tries to correct and improve it. Usage seems to display a constant need to be brief, expressive, precise and consistent.

Frei describes an advanced state of the French language in which so-called mistakes appear as attempts to simplify the system.[228] It is through these mistakes that the language develops. Analogy, which reduces empty forms of no further value, is perfectly normal in the development of language. For example, frequently heard substandard forms like *we was* and *you was* reveal a tendency to regularize the only remaining English verb with an irregular past tense by bringing the plural form into line with the singular, and the second singular with the form of the first and third persons.

There is always room for change, for the vast majority of possible linguistic items and patterns are never used. Of all the possible sounds and forms, only a small fraction is selected by a given language. These are continually varied, combined and re-combined. Any language selects certain features or procedures (like word-endings or word-order), using them more or less consistently and varying the elements in as many combinations as needed.[620:169] This is how Whatmough's theory of selective variation explains the evolution of language in time. It is through selection and variation that languages evolve. Historical changes continually vary established patterns but only in certain ways. The variation is selective. As patterns are eliminated new ones are chosen to replace them. Each distinctive system evolves in a set pattern, whatever the phonetic or morphological process may have been which first set the pattern.[640:348]

Because of this continual change, language-teaching texts and the descriptions on which they may be based are rarely up-to-date. This is especially true when their authors hesitate to include the most recent forms of the language. In making a language-teaching text, their problem is to decide on a norm which is neither too old nor too new.

3.3.2 **In Space**

Variations in space have also given rise to various theories of language. Linguists have studied the variations in space of a single language in the present or of a group of languages traceable to a common ancestor. The first of these disciplines is known as area linguistics, the second as comparative linguistics.

(i) *Area Linguistics*

Area linguistics has produced theories to explain changes in a language from one part to another of the area in which it is spoken.

Some words are used in all parts of the country in which the language is spoken; others are limited to certain regions. Of the latter, some are limited to one region only, while others cover a number of different regions. The vocabulary of each region differs in both extent and extension.

The differences found from region to region are not limited to vocabulary; they also include pronunciation and grammar. Since many of these differences can be explained neither by the laws of phonetic change nor by the creation of new forms by analogy, some scholars, like Gilliéron, operated on the theory that each word must be treated as if it had a history of its own.[792]

In any area in which a language is spoken, however, we can find different forms of the same word, each representing a different phase of development; some of these are identical with words and forms found in areas in which a different but related language is spoken. In these areas too a word may have a number of different forms shading off into those of still another language area. So that there is no clear-cut distinction between adjacent languages like Spanish, Portuguese, Provençal, and Italian, or between German, Dutch, Flemish, Frisian, Plattdeutsch and certain dialects of English. For this reason, the delimitation of languages is arbitrary and, according to some area linguists, purely political.

Theories of area linguistics like that of Bartoli have tried to establish principles for arranging these shades of difference and for determining the form from which these arrangements should start.[212] According to Bartoli the older forms are found in areas which are either isolated (islands and mountains), extensive, marginal (language boundaries), first settled, or areas in which the language is disappearing.

In order to record the difference in words and the shades of differences in forms and pronunciation, samples of language usage have been gathered from all parts of the area in which the "same" language is spoken. These are plotted on maps of the area (often one map per word), and the result is a linguistic atlas. There are linguistic atlases for France,[792] Germany,[824] parts of the United States,[667] Switzerland, Italy, and other countries. In still other countries, notably in Scotland, England, Ireland, Spain, Canada and areas where Romance, Slavonic and Germanic languages are spoken, scholars have been building extensive dialect archives of usage in the various parts of their respective areas.

The relevance of area linguistics to language teaching lies in the possibility of deciding what forms to teach on the basis of proven usage. It helps the teacher and method maker distinguish between the regional and the national. It also enables them to make use of the regional peculiarities which the native language may have in common with the foreign language.

(ii) *Comparative Linguistics*

Along with historical linguistics, comparative linguistics profited greatly from the nineteenth-century studies of evolution and from the demanding techniques required to prove the origin and relationship of biological species. Proven relationships were formulated into scientific laws, like Grimm's Law and Verner's Law, some of them admitting of no exception. Genetic theories of the origin and spread of related languages were developed and refined from the comparative studies of Bopp, Schleicher, Brugmann, Delbrück, Diez, Miklosich, and others.[95] Schleicher's *Stammbaumtheorie*, or pedigree theory, has long given way to Schmidt's *Wellentheorie*, which disclaims the abrupt fusion into language families in favour of a gradual, wave-like spread from the centre.[405] But in order to explain the nature of the dialects on the edge of the area covered by a family of language, this *Wellentheorie* had later to be modified by Meillet's peripheral theory. Although the theories themselves have little application to the teaching of modern foreign languages, language teachers have made use of comparative linguistics to create formulas for the recognition of words which were common in the parent language. (See Ch. 2: 2.2.1.)

4. TERMINOLOGY

The most obvious way in which one language theory differs from another is in the words it uses or invents to talk about language. The differences may be due to the use of (1) different languages, (2) different terms, and (3) different meanings.

4.1 DIFFERENT LANGUAGES

Linguistic theories are not all written in the same language. The different languages in which they are written do not all have the same number of words for linguistic concepts, and even in cases where they do, the counterparts do not cover the same area of meaning. English, for example, has only the words *language* and *speech* to do the work of the French *langue*, *langage*, and *parole*. The English word *language* is not always equal to French *langue*; nor is French *langue* equivalent to the German word *Sprache*,[152:87] no more than *parole* is equal to *Sprechen*. French has *signification* and *sens* to cover the meaning of English *meaning*, *sense* and *signification*. Yet neither set of terms covers the meaning of German *Bedeutung* and *Sinn*.

This state of affairs has led some linguists to speculate on whether existing linguistic theories would have been different had they originally been formulated in a different language. In translating theories from one language to another, it has become the practice to preserve the key words in the original language in which the theory was first expressed.

4.2 DIFFERENT TERMS

A second difference is in the terms themselves. Some theorists invent new words for the categories which their particular theory distinguishes; they do so as one way of overcoming the possible confusion and inexactness in the use of everyday words. For the study of speech sounds, for example, they have invented such terms as *phone*, *phoneme* and *allophone* to distinguish between a segment of speech sound, a relevant speech sound, and its variants; and by analogy, *morph*, *morpheme* and *allomorph* were invented for the study of words. New terms such as these have filled a number of linguistic glossaries. (See Bibliography 2.3.3.)

The different terms used in different theories, however, do not always correspond to new concepts. Linguists have not hesitated to invent new terms for well-known concepts. Thus the study of relevant sounds might be called *phonemics, phonematics,* or *phonology,* depending on the school of linguistics in which the term is used. The new terms are created on the grounds that they do not stand for exactly the same concepts as those of the other linguists. Of course, they are unlikely to, since the theories are not the same.

Different schools of linguistics and language theory have turned out entire vocabularies of technical terms. Within each school, however, there are terms which are the property of a single writer; for example, Morris's glossary contains over a hundred terms, nearly all of which are of his own invention.[211:345]

Most attempts to date at compiling a general dictionary of linguistic terms have given unsatisfactory results. It is not surprising that the Permanent International Committee of Linguists (PICL) have considered it wiser to ask each school to prepare its own glossary, covering a limited span of time. (See Bibliography 2.3.3.)

4.3 DIFFERENT MEANINGS

The greatest confusion, however, is that created by giving different personal meanings to words in common use. Take for example the words *sign* and *symbol,* key words in many language theories. The word *sign* may mean simply an event which produces a response (Britton), or it may be more than a stimulus in that it controls behaviour toward a goal and means the same thing to speaker and hearer (Morris), or it may mean an abstract unit consisting of content and its expression (Hjelmslev), or it may be a class of events which produces the same reaction as another class of events (Russell), or any material thing having prearranged mental equivalents transferable at will (Gardiner), or a concept bound to an acoustic image (Saussure), or a universal entity (Maritain), or something which has meaning in the immediate environment to which it points (Langer).

Writers in the same tradition may use the same terms; but this is no guarantee that they carry the same sense. Both Saussure and Guillaume, for example, distinguish between *signifiant* (the signifier), *signifié* (the signified), and *signe* (the sign); but the latter uses *signifiant* with Saussure's meaning of *signe,* and *signe* with part of Saussure's meaning of *signifiant.*

The word *symbol* is another example. For some, linguistic symbols are units of communication; for others they are units of thought. For Saussure, symbols can even be natural phenomena; for Lasswell they are interpretations of communication and are opposed to signs, which are physical carriers of symbols from speaker to listener. According to Ogden, symbols are signs used by man for purposes of communication; they are signs of acts of reference. To Langer, a symbol is something which refers to a conventional concept and has meaning only in the mind; to Morris, a symbol is a sign produced by an interpreter and acting as a substitute for some other sign (an interpreter is defined as "an organism for which something is a sign"); to Maritain a symbol is a sensible thing signifying an object by reason of some presupposed relation of analogy; to Naumburg it is an expression, cultural or active, which contains an element of disguise or metaphorical allusion, etc., etc.

The words *symbol* and *sign* are by no means the only instances of the confusion of terms in linguistic theory. An equal number of different definitions could be given for almost any of the key words. Ries, for example, has been able to compile a hundred and forty definitions of the term *sentence*.[455]

This confusion in terminology has been largely responsible for the isolation of one discipline from another in matters of language theory and for the limitation of most linguists to their own theory—sometimes supplemented by a misinterpretation of a few others.

For this reason, the study of linguistic terminology is important; for linguistic terms often conceal significant differences and similarities in what has been said and thought about language, its nature and aspects.

5. CONCLUSION

The situation in language theory is not entirely unlike that prevailing in other fields of knowledge. As early as 1907, James remarked that so many rival formulations are proposed in all branches of science that no single theory is absolutely a transcript of reality.[269] Moreover, as sciences develop, it becomes evident that most of their laws are only approximations.

The great contrast in twentieth-century linguistic theory is between those who try to relate everything together and those who do one thing at a time. This is less a matter of doctrine than of method.

The consistent application of any one of these theories, however, has far-reaching practical consequences, not only for the theory of language teaching, but also for the linguistic descriptions on which the actual texts are based. If the language is regarded as a state, different theories produce different sorts of descriptions in the form of grammars and dictionaries which determine *what* is taught; if the language is considered as an activity, the theories produce different ideas on language learning which determine *how* the material is taught. It is therefore to the description of language as a state and to the study of language as an activity that the remaining chapters in this section are devoted.

Language Description

OUTLINE

0. INTRODUCTION

All language-teaching methods are necessarily based on some sort of analysis, for the very process of making a method involves the breaking down of the language into the elements which are to be taught. Language-teaching analysis depends ultimately on the recognition of these elements. The more we know about what a particular language contains, the more we can analyse the teaching of it.

Since the descriptive analysis of a language is the basis for the analysis of language teaching, it is important to determine (1) exactly how one description of a language may differ from another, and (2) what each type of description contains.

1. HOW LANGUAGE DESCRIPTIONS DIFFER

The descriptive analysis of language is of great antiquity. Although the ancient grammars were independent of any universal technique of linguistic description, the extension of Greek and Roman culture throughout the Western world resulted in the application of these classical grammars to the analysis and teaching of other, often unrelated, languages. This is the origin of the traditional grammars which still form the basis of language-teaching methods.

Modern methods of language description differ from the traditional ones; they also differ considerably from one another. This is because they are based on different theories of language or on different techniques of analysis used within the same theoretical framework. These are responsible for the four fundamental differences in the description of a language: (1) in the linguistic levels described, (2) in the units used to describe them, (3) in the direction or order in which these units and levels are treated, and (4) in the material on which the description is based.

1.1 LEVELS

Knowledge of such levels of description as the vocabulary, grammar and pronunciation of a language are obviously important both for its teaching and for the analysis of how it is taught. A method based on a detailed description of the pronunciation of a language will differ from one based mainly on its grammar.

For the description of a language may be only a grammar, or it may be mainly a treatment of its pronunciation, or of its vocabulary. It may include any of these three levels or all of them. Or it may include more than three, dividing grammar into morphology and syntax, and pronunciation into phonetics and phonology. Descriptions of a language may therefore differ (1) in the number of levels described, and (2) in the contents of each level.

1.1.1 **Number of Levels**

The number of levels into which a language description is divided has varied anywhere from the two of Harris (phonology and morphology) to the fourteen of Brøndal. It has been the tradition to recognize three— phonetics, vocabulary, and grammar. Many modern descriptions maintain these three levels; others reduce them to two or increase the number through subdivision or additions. By subdividing the traditional levels and adding new ones a procedure of language analysis may indeed produce more detailed descriptions than it otherwise would. The legitimate scope of interest permitted by a language theory also determines the number of levels in which a description will be made.

1.1.2 **Content of Levels**

The number of levels, however, is no indication of what a description in- cludes. The six levels of Firth contain just as much as the fourteen of Brøndal. Although Pike, Chomsky and Ullmann have each three levels, the contents of these are quite different; morphology, for example, which is a separate level in the first case, is combined with phonology in the second, and with semantics in the third. Some linguists restrict their analysis to one area of language, that of linguistic form, analysed exclusively from the point of view of expression and treated in detail by division into such levels as phonematics, phonotactics, morphomatics, morphotactics, inflection and construction.

The relationship between the number of levels can best be illustrated by a comparative table giving the contents of some of the more recent types of description. As the following table shows, by using Brøndal's com- pilation as a basis, and with slight changes in order, we can get some idea of the differences in both the number and the content of levels of language analysis as delimited by a few contemporary linguists. Since the types of an- alysis are not comparable, however, the horizontal correspondence between levels cannot of course be complete; for what to one linguist is one level may to another have to be distributed throughout several levels. A few of the levels are sometimes considered as inter-levels. Some students of language analysis have used the concept of language level as something that must include other levels; others, like Firth, have preferred to regard the levels as being interlinked, as Allen does when he conceives the levels of phonology and grammar as being linked by the phonic material of language.[450a]

LEVELS OF

<table>
<tr><th>BRØNDAL</th><th colspan="2">FIRTH</th><th colspan="2">HALLIDAY</th><th>PIKE</th></tr>
<tr><td>sound symbolism</td><td rowspan="15">↑ Context of Situation ↓</td><td rowspan="2">phonetics</td><td rowspan="2" colspan="2">SUBSTANCE phonic and graphic</td><td rowspan="2"></td></tr>
<tr><td>sounds and sound systems</td></tr>
<tr><td>syllabation and stress</td><td rowspan="3">phonology</td><td rowspan="3">phonology</td><td rowspan="11">↑ FORM ↓</td><td rowspan="3">phonology</td></tr>
<tr><td>phonetic function</td></tr>
<tr><td>phonetic syntax</td></tr>
<tr><td>shape of words</td><td>lexicology</td><td rowspan="7">lexis and grammar</td><td rowspan="4">morphology</td></tr>
<tr><td>word-formation</td><td rowspan="2">collocation</td></tr>
<tr><td>inflections</td></tr>
<tr><td>agreement</td><td rowspan="4">grammar</td></tr>
<tr><td>parts of speech</td><td rowspan="3">grammar</td></tr>
<tr><td>word-order</td></tr>
<tr><td>sentence and sentence elements</td></tr>
<tr><td>style</td><td rowspan="3"></td><td>context</td><td rowspan="3"></td></tr>
<tr><td>semantics</td><td rowspan="2" colspan="2">SITUATION extra-linguistic</td></tr>
<tr><td></td></tr>
</table>

LANGUAGE ANALYSIS

CHOMSKY	ULLMANN	HARRIS
morpho-phonemics	phonology	phonology
	lexicology	morphology
trans-formations		
phrase-structure		
	syntax	

This table is designed to give some idea of the extent to which levels of language analysis may differ. It shows only a few of the many ways in which linguists have cut up language for purposes of analysis. Vertical correspondences can only be approximate, since what one linguist includes in such concepts as phonology, morphology, grammar and lexicology is not always exactly the same as what another linguist may understand when using the identical term.

1.2 UNITS

Whatever enters into any of the above levels can only be analysed or described through some sort of unit. For the description of vocabulary, a unit like the word is needed; for pronunciation, a unit like the speech sound; for syntax, a sentence unit.

The linguistic units of a language, however, are neither clear nor self-evident.[114:149] This is because language is a continual flow of sound in which one unit merges into another. Whatever units do exist, they are not perceived as units, any more than one perceives the individual frames of a motion picture when one goes to the cinema. That is why descriptions of the same language differ in the number and type of units used.

Some descriptions use a large number of units; some, only a few. Some have traditional terms for them, terms like *sound, word, phrase, sentence*; others need special ones like *phone, phoneme, morph, morpheme, moneme, tagmeme*, and *seme*. But even these special terms, invented to avoid the confusion caused in the many meanings of the popular terms, are themselves used with a number of different meanings. Two descriptions of the phonemes of the same language are not necessarily identical. This is true for most linguistic concepts (see Ch. 1:4).

Differences in units and what they mean are determined not only by the linguist's choice of levels, but ultimately by his ideas on the nature of language (see Ch. 1: 2). Because of these, he may admit units (1) only of expression, (2) only of content, (3) of content and expression.

1.2.1 Units of Expression

Language may be described as a system of units of expression. These may be considered as physical units of sound or movements of the speech organs. Or they may be groups of these, formalized into the basic and relevant elements of the language, as when an alphabet represents all the relevant sounds of a language, but *only* the relevant ones, that is, its phonemes.

Basic units like phonemes may be used to describe all the other units of the language—syllables, affixes, words and word-groups.

1.2.2 Units of Content

In opposition to this are the units based on content, on meaning or reference. They may themselves be units of meaning or content, as for example, the concept of plural in English considered as the same whether it be expressed as *-es* in *foxes* or *-en* in *oxen*; or the classification of all questions as interrogative sentences, no matter what their forms of expression may be.

Or the content may be used to identify the units of expression, as when a native speaker of an unknown language is asked whether two similar-sounding words mean the same thing.

1.2.3 **Expression and Content**

Those who consider language as a form of expression and of content seek their basic units in the relation between these two areas, but without reference to their physical substance. A language is considered as forming its units out of two formless masses—experience and sounds. From each of these, it extracts what is relevant for the content and its expression; and by relating the one to the other, it creates linguistic signs. These are the basic units of a language. Each is composed of a concept (the content) and a sound image (its form of expression).

1.3 DIRECTION

The levels recognized and the levels included may be described in different order. In other words, descriptions may proceed in different directions. The direction may be of no theoretical importance. One may start with a description of the words, or of the sounds, or of the sentence types, and state any relation observed between one level and any other level. This is the practice of Firth, Halliday and their collaborators.[133-45]

On the other hand, the theory or technique may require that the description of levels and units follow one and only one direction. This may be (1) upward—from sound to sentence, (2) downward—from sentence to sound, (3) across—from word to word-position to pronunciation.

1.3.1 **Upward**

Following this direction, one starts by establishing the relevant sounds of the language (phonemes); one then proceeds to study how they combine into words, how the words combine into larger units, what the rules are for combining forms and words together, and so on, until the main sentence-types have been determined.

Levels are analysed separately and in the ascending order of complexity, starting with the phonology and ending with the syntax. There is often a strong injunction against anticipating the next higher level, against using material from a higher level to explain items in a lower level. The phonological description of the language must not only precede the morphological description, it must also be entirely independent of it. Among those who follow this direction are Hill, Trager and Smith, in their descriptions of English. [425,444,747]

1.3.2 **Downward**

Methods of description using this direction start with the largest units and work down to the smallest. The description may begin with a series of texts in the language. These are first broken down into sentences and sentence-types. With the sentence-types as a framework, word-classes (roughly equivalent to nouns, verbs, adjectives and adverbs) and groups of function words (articles, prepositions, etc.) are established. This is the technique used by Fries in his description of English structure.[745]

This sentence-to-sound direction is all-important for the transformation theory of analysis. Proceeding in this direction, Chomsky establishes the basic sentence-types and then moves gradually, through a series of transformations, down to the sequences of sounds.[561] Take, for example, the sentence-type Noun+Verb, or rather Noun-Phrase (NP)+Verb-Phrase (VP). This can become a sequence of sounds through a series of transformations which follow definite rules. For instance:

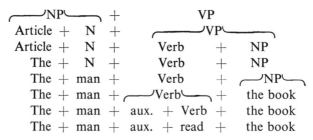

And a few morphological transformations of the verbal elements convert the sequence into the sentence:

The man has been reading the book.

Further morpho-phonological transformations produce the sequence of phonemes:

/ðə mæn həz bin riːdiŋ ðə buk/

It is in this way that an inventory of sentence-patterns is able to produce an endless text.

If transformation theory produces a text from an inventory, Glossematic theory produces an inventory from a text. Application of Glossematics results in such descriptions as Togeby's grammar of French.[810] In this grammar, the French language is first considered as if it were an endless text, to be analysed by dividing it into units and putting these into classes. The text is first divided into two planes—content and expression. Each of these is broken down into parts and described separately. The content is analysed into units according to the ways they combine and the systems they form (e.g. tense, number, case). The expression plane is also analysed into units according to the ways they combine (e.g. according to which sounds occur together) and according to the systems they form (e.g. the vowel system of the language). The larger units are then classified and sub-classified to give a list or inventory of the elements of the language and an outline of the systems which unite them. This appears as a series of tables. The phonological tables of French, for example, show 27 phonemes in all.

The main process of linguistic analysis is therefore the division and classification of the text (language) as a whole and of its expression and content separately. We can picture the analysis thus:

Language	*Division*	*Classification*
Expression-Content	Syntagmatic	Systematic
Content Plane	Syntactic	Morphological
Expression Plane ↓	Prosodic ↓	Phonological

1.3.3 Across

Distinct from this, is the technique of description which relates each unit of language to all other units at all other levels—phonological, morphological, grammatical. A word is described in terms of its pronunciation, its endings and its place in the different types of sentence. This is the technique advocated by Pike and his school.[192] The theoretical reason for advocating this technique of analysis is the view of language as a system of three hierarchies—lexicon, phonology and grammar. They are hierarchies because, within each, there is a number of levels, each more inclusive than the other; phonemes are included in syllables, syllables in stress-groups, stress-groups in pause-groups; morphemes are included in morpheme-clusters, morpheme-clusters in words, words in phrases; similarly with grammatical units like tagmemes (gramemes) and utteremes. We may picture the analysis thus:

Lexicon	*Phonology*	*Grammar*
morpheme	phoneme	tagmeme
cluster	syllable	(grameme)
word	stress-group	syntagmeme
phrase	pause-group	(uttereme)

The difference between this and the Glossematic technique is that it analyses language both as a system of hierarchies and as a hierarchy of systems.

1.4 MATERIAL

Descriptions of language may differ in the material on which they are based. A description of General American English will differ from one of Southern British. An analysis based on the spoken language is not likely to be the same as one based only on written materials. Materials of language description may vary in four respects: (1) in dialect, (2) in register, (3) in style, and (4) in media.

1.4.1 **Dialect**

The area from which the material comes makes a difference in the description which results. The American varieties of spoken English, Spanish, Portuguese and French differ from the European. A description of the pronunciation of Canadian English will not be the same as that of Australian English. In England the speech of the North differs from that of the South. And in the United States, the Southern accents differ from those of General American. The dialects included in the description may vary according to (i) the size of the area covered, and (ii) the size of the sample used.

(i) *Size of Area*

The analysis of a language may cover one or a number of the areas in which it is spoken. It may attempt to cover all areas or limit itself to one. In a single area it may include the speech of a large number of persons, as does either the French Grammar of Damourette and Pichon,[809] which includes some 850, or Fries' description of English based on the speech of 380 persons.[745] Or it may limit itself to the speech of an individual. The reason for this latter type of coverage is that it is likely to yield more complete, more accurate and more consistent results, since the language of each individual is regarded as a self-contained system. The technique has been clearly elaborated by Frei.[430] It has been applied in Kahn's description of French and Alemanic tenses.[807]

(ii) *Size of Sample*

Descriptions also vary in the amount of material on which they are based. For Frei, 2,000 sentences were sufficient; for Fries, fifty hours of telephone conversation were necessary. The size of the sample may vary from the relatively small amounts of English analysed by Hill, Trager and Smith to the masses of material used by Jespersen and Poutsma. The samples may also vary in the range of time covered. Frei covers a few weeks or months; Hill, a few years; Jespersen, a few centuries.

There are descriptions, however, which are based on no samples at all, but rather on the judgment of the author. This is sometimes a sample of what he himself would say, a sample of his own speech; but in most cases it is simply based on his rationalizations about the language—not so much on what he says, as on what he thinks others should say. This sort of thing soon ceases to be a description of what the language is, and becomes a prescription of what it should be.

Prescription is not to be confused with legitimate attempts to do away with the use of samples altogether, to eliminate from linguistic analysis the quantitative approach whereby samples of the language are divided into units and categories to be classified according to their relationships. What is proposed is a qualitative approach based on a theory of how a particular language works. This approach has been compared to that part of chemical theory concerned with the discovery of structurally possible compounds. It is a theory which can generate all physically possible chemical compounds. In the same way, a grammar should be able to generate all grammatically possible utterances. This is the approach to linguistic analysis, advanced by Chomsky, to replace the gathering and breaking-down of samples of language.[561]

1.4.2 Register

Register is a term employed by some linguists to indicate the uses to which a language is put—occupational, emotive, informative. A description based on samples of one register may be quite different from one based on samples of another. Hundreds of pages of scientific writing might be analysed without revealing a single instance of the first person pronoun; one page of a private letter might reveal several. A description of the occupational vocabulary of farmers will differ from that of fishermen or factory workers.

Language-teaching methods do not all use the same register. The language may be needed for commercial, scientific or military purposes. There are, for example, the well-known courses in Business English, German for science students, and the like.

1.4.3 Style

The style of the material analysed is likely to be reflected in the description of it, especially in languages where social distinctions are heavily marked. A description of the highly literate speech of a secondary school teacher and that of the language used by an illiterate, unskilled labourer would hardly be the same.

1.4.4 **Media**

Whether the material was collected through the medium of speech or the medium of the written language also makes a difference. A description of French based on its written form would put the French adjectives *fier* and *premier* into the same *-ier* category; but if the description were based on speech they would appear in two different categories, for although they are written alike they are pronounced differently. Many of the older descriptions like those of English by Jespersen, Poutsma and Kruisinga, are based on the written language. Some of the more recent ones, like those of Fries, Trager and Smith, are based exclusively on speech.

If techniques of description can differ in materials, direction, units, and levels of analysis, so can any part of the actual description, its phonetics, grammar, vocabulary, or meaning.

2. WHAT LANGUAGE DESCRIPTIONS CONTAIN

A language description may contain any or all of the following: (1) phonetics, (2) grammar, (3) vocabulary, (4) meaning. Each of these has its own particular problems of content and method.

2.1 PHONETICS

If we include phonology (the study of the relevant sounds) under this head, we find that descriptions may differ in the following respects: (1) in the range of accents described, (2) in the analysis of relevant sounds, and how they work together (units of phonology), and (3) in the symbols used to describe them.

2.1.1 **Range of Accents**

While the written form of the language is likely to be quite uniform throughout the area in which it is used, the spoken form is likely to differ with each region. That is why many manuals of phonetics have been limited to one accent or to a small number of related ones.

For English, there are a number of accents which have been acceptable in their respective regions. These include the speech of the educated speakers of South England, North England, Scotland, Ireland, Australia, New Zealand, South Africa, Canada, New England, the Atlantic Seaboard, and the American West, South and Mid-West, all of which have marked differences. In addition to this there are all the other regional standards in the English-speaking world and a number of formerly "dependent" accents like Anglo-Indian and Educated West African which are now regional accents in their own right.

Of all accents of English, the one which has been most fully described is English Received Pronunciation, known as RP. This, however, is not a regional accent but a social one. It is spoken throughout England by certain educated families, and kept alive in such private institutions as the Public Schools.[674] It is only one of several types of so-called "Educated English" spoken in England and reflecting the type, not the degree, of education. It is definitely a minority accent.

In contradistinction to this is a majority accent like General American, which is the next most fully described accent of English. Its importance lies not in its exclusiveness but in its inclusiveness. It is the native accent of more than a hundred and thirty million people and is spoken over wide areas of the United States and in parts of Canada. (For samples of dialect descriptions see Bibliography 659a–75, 788a–92, and 823–5.)

Faced with a number of acceptable accents, which is the language teacher to choose? There are two possibilities: (a) either he selects one pronunciation and sticks to it, or (b) he bases his teaching on an accent averaged from the major varieties. If a single pronunciation is chosen, it may be either a prestige accent or a majority accent. A prestige accent may be a social problem; a majority accent, a political one. Some politically centralized nations have propagated strong prejudices against anything regional. An average pronunciation, on the other hand, is based on a study of regional variations. The range of these variations must then be known. The vowel of *not*, for example, may be usually heard as [ɒ] in Southern England, [ɔ] in Scotland, [ɑ] in Canada, [à] in New England, and [a] in the American Mid-West. The two extremes are from [ɒ] to [a] therefore. (See Table of Vowel Varieties.)

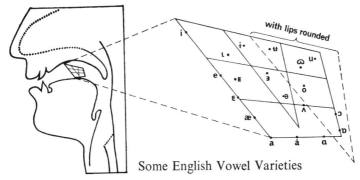

Some English Vowel Varieties

The above table of vowel varieties of English shows the usual tongue positions for the vowels of different accents accepted in the English-speaking world. It represents only the mouth, one of the cavities, along with the throat, responsible for these sounds. If the shape of the throat cavity changes, however, so may the tongue positions.

On these vowel varieties the following ranges have been suggested for English, as a nine-vowel system.[747] See also page 57.

Approximate Sound Ranges of English Vowel Phonemes

	Phoneme	*Sound Range*	*Example*	*Dialect Range*
HIGH	/i/ =	[ɩ] ... [ɨ]	*sit*	RP to American Southern
	/ɨ/ =	[ɨ] ... [ə]	*just*	General Amer. to Amer. South.
	/u/ =	[ɷ] ... [ə]	*put*	RP to Irish
MID	/e/ =	[e] ... [ɛ]	*then*	RP to General American
	/ə/ =	[ə] ... [ʌ]	*come*	General American to RP
	/o/ =	[o] ... [ɷ]	*road*	Irish to North English
LOW	/æ/ =	[a] ... [ɛ]	*that*	North English to Amer. South.
	/a/ =	[a] ... [ʋ]	*not*	Amer. Mid-West to Scottish
	/ɔ/ =	[ɔ] ... [o]	*bought*	North English to Scottish

In each dialect, however, there are a number of varieties, and the description of any one of them may vary from phonetician to phonetician, not only because of a more sensitive or better-trained ear, but also because each may classify differently the sounds he hears and relate them differently to his own dialect. Descriptions of the same variety of American pronunciation, for example, have recognized as few as six vowels[126:30] to as many as sixteen.[691:24] Vowels are only one example of how phonetic descriptions of the same dialect may differ.

What is the reason for such differences in descriptions which are allegedly equally scientific? Is it the language or the linguist that is responsible? Linguists have different ways of hearing and classifying sounds, and the sounds they hear differ from individual to individual. Not only do speakers of the same dialect have perceptible individual differences, even the pronunciation of the same person will vary according to sex, age, and state of physical and mental tension. It will also vary with his rate of speaking. For example, the word *extraordinary* may be pronounced by the same person in two different ways within the space of a few minutes as /ekstrəo:dinəri/ with six syllables and /stro:dnri/ with three. Some speech analysts go so far as to say that it is highly unlikely that one ever makes exactly the same group of speech movements twice in a lifetime; and if one does, it is to be attributed to chance rather than to law.[311:218] It is necessary, therefore, to make abstractions from the physical sounds and to determine what is relevant. This is the function of phonology.

2.1.2 **Units of Phonology**

Phonology is the study of the system behind the speech sounds. Its fundamental problem is to extract from the substance of pronunciation the relevant units of speech. These are the units of (i) articulation, (ii) catenation, (iii) rhythm, and (iv) intonation.

(i) *Units of Articulation*

Although the varieties of articulation are almost unlimited, the number of relevant units of articulation (phonemes) in any one language is restricted to less than 100. Not all sounds in use form part of the language. A person may speak with a nasal accent without having any nasal vowel phonemes. No matter how he speaks Standard French, however, he needs nasal vowels (phonemes) to make himself understood; otherwise such words as *lin-laid* /lɛ̃/ - /lɛ/ and *grincer-graisser* might sound the same. The phonemes are the units which keep one word from sounding like another.

Linguists have different views on what phonemes are and how to find them. The fundamental differences, however, are simply instances of varying views on the nature of language and the validity of linguistic concepts (see Chapter 1: 1 and 2). Are phonemes mental or physical units, or are they both? Are they absolute or relative? Are they actual occurrences of sound or only classes or families of sounds? Do they exist as units in the mind, or are they paths followed by it through "a forest of contrasts?" These are but a few of the different concepts of the phoneme. A summary of the different theories on the phoneme may be found in Twaddell[522] and Jones.[512]

But speech is not only a string of isolated phonemes; it is a flow of sound based on a system through which phonemes are connected (catenated), grouped, and modified in certain combinations.

(ii) *Units of Catenation*

Catenation includes the features which chain sounds together. It is concerned with (a) the grouping of phonemes into syllables (syllabification), and the grouping of syllables through (b) junction, (c) assimilation, (d) elision, and (e) word-linking.

(a) Syllabification: Languages differ in the way they divide the stream of speech into syllables. They also differ in the structure or make-up of their syllables. Each language makes use of only a limited number of possible combinations of its phonemes, and it resists the rest. In English, for example, there are no initial consonant groups of four consonants, and of the 11,000 possible combinations of three consonants, the language tolerates only 40; and of two-consonant combinations, only 137 out of a possible 576. Languages differ not only in the phonemes which they can combine together but also in those which can occur in certain positions. Some phonemes, like /h/ can be used only at the beginning of a syllable; others, like /ŋ/ and /ʒ/ only at the end and in the middle, but never at the beginning. It is possible, therefore, to reduce the phonetic structure of the syllable in a given language to a formula which any speaker of the language —even when uttering non-sense syllables or invented words—is forced to follow. Whorf has given such a formula for the single-syllable word in English.[200:223]

(b) Junction: This is the feature which links and separates syllables. It prevents the identical pronunciation of such similar sentences as *Send them aid* and *Send the maid*, *It's an aim* and *It's a name*. The way this is done varies from language to language.

There are conflicting views on exactly what junction (or juncture) includes, on whether it is simply a matter of different lengths of pause between syllables, or whether features of assimilation, linking, vowel length and tone are also involved. Some linguists have attempted to describe the juncture system of English by means of four "juncture pho-nemes."[747]

(c) Assimilation: When sounds occur together in a language they under-go certain changes which are regular and peculiar to that language. For example, *don't you know* in English is often heard as /dountʃ ə nou/ where the /t/ of *don't* combines with the /j/ of *you* to yield /tʃ/. Similarly, *open the door* is often heard as /oupmðədoə/, where /n/ takes on the lip position of the preceding /p/. Some of these changes are so regular that they may be said to form part of the grammar or morphology of the language; yet because they are also part of the phonology, they are called morpho-phonological. For example, the adding of *-s* in the plural comes out in speech as an /-s/ or a /-z/ or an /-əz/, depending on how it assimilates to the preceding sound; we say *cats* /kats/, but *dogs* /dogz/ and *matches* /matʃəz/.

(d) Elision: Related to this is the leaving out of a sound when too many come together. Just as the system of assimilation varies from language to language so does the system of elision. In English, for example, we can, and do, drop the /t/ when uttering words like *postpone, directly, next station.*

(e) Linking: Languages also differ in the way they divide and link words. German does it with glottal stops. English and French, through linking sounds, English making use mostly of the glides /ʷ/ and /ʲ/ when two vowels come together. For example:

You /ʷ/ always want to /ʷ/ eat.
She /ⁱ/ always takes my /ⁱ/ arm.

(iii) *Units of Rhythm*

Each language has its rhythm. This strikes the ear as a sequence of changes in loudness and length. Each unit of rhythm is made of a number of syllables; the unit of rhythm has been called the foot.[473] The length and loudness of each syllable is affected by the number of syllables in the foot and by their relative importance. The vowel of *good*, for example, is longer than the same sound in *goodness*, longer in *that's good* than in *that's good enough for me*. The first vowel of French *pâte* is longer than the same sound in *pâteux*, which in turn is longer than in *pâtissier* and *pâtisserie*.

Rhythm also influences the loudness of syllables. Note, for example, the decrease in loudness in the syllable *-bout* in the following series of sentences: *He was walking about. What's he talking about? It's about a mile.* Variations in length and loudness are usually called stress; but there is little agreement on what should be included under this term. Some linguists recognize four levels of stress in English, /ˊ/ primary, /ˆ/ secondary, /ˋ/ tertiary, and /˘/ weak, as for example, in *ĕlĕvàtŏr-ôpĕràtŏr*. They may do so on the basis of phonetics,[703] or for reasons of phonological analysis.[747]

(iv) *Units of Intonation*

We hear the intonation of a language as a continual raising and lowering of the voice. This change is due not only to what we say, but to the way we say it. We all know that there are many ways of saying the same thing to convey different meanings. We can say *yes* to mean "Yes, of course" or "what?" or "maybe" or even "no". It is said that Stanislavsky, when he was director of the Moscow Art Theatre, required his pupils to speak the word *tonight* in some fifty different ways while an audience of assessors wrote down their impressions of what sense was conveyed each time.[363: 84] Kingdon listed some sixty intonation-stress variants of the four-syllable sentence *I can't find one.*[712: xvi] And even then he was far from listing all the possibilities. If we add to all these meaningful variants the differences in intonation from region to region and from person to person, including variations due to sex, age and temperament, we have an almost endless number of possibilities.

To describe the intonation of a language therefore it is necessary to establish units of intonation. These may be considered as fixed tones or as moving tones. If the units are fixed tones, they can correspond to neither real tones nor even to a range of tones, for each human voice may be different in level ǀ ǀ ǀ and also in range ǀ ǀ ǀ. Such units can only correspond to relative differences in the speech of each individual. This is perhaps what linguists like Pike, Hill and Trager mean when they give four tone phonemes to English.

If the units are considered as moving tones, however, they need not represent fixed levels, but simply the direction of movement. What is important here is whether the voice goes up or down. English intonation has been analysed into five moving tones, such as the rising tone, the falling, the falling-rising, etc. These have been subdivided into high and low varieties.[712]

Instead of regarding these tones as superimposed on the sounds of the language, the unit of intonation may be considered as a tone-group, which is composed of one or more feet (the rhythm unit), which in turn includes one or more syllables (length unit) made up of one or more phonemes (the articulation unit).[721]

2.1.3 Phonetic Notation

One of the most confusing things for a beginner in the use of phonetics is the difference in the symbols used to represent sounds, especially when he is forced to switch from one type of phonetic notation to another.

Not all types of phonetic notation are equally good. Some have been constructed with much more care and thought than others. A good notation cannot be elaborated by arbitrary afterthought. Devising a good notation is a technical and difficult piece of scientific invention.

What are some of the principles of an efficient notation? There are at least eight. First, *analytical adequacy*; the notation must be able to represent the results of the analysis. Secondly, *clarity*; the relation between parts must be self-evident, for example, the relation between syllable, tone and stress. Third, *legibility*; it should be easily read and not have to be deciphered. Fourth, *produceability*; it should be easy to write, type, or print. Fifth, *concision*; there should be economy in the use of configurations. Sixth, *visual suggestion*; the forms should suggest what they stand for. Seventh, *range*; while expressing the analytical minimum, the notation should also be capable of recording the perceptible maximum, for example, the regional variations needed for the description dialects. And finally, *synthesis*; although each level may be noted separately in analysis it should be capable of appearing again in a synthesis which constitutes a reflection of the utterance as a whole; for example, it should be possible to read the whole utterance at once, not one level at a time, starting with the phonemes, then adding the stress, then the intonation, then the features of catenation.

Let us now examine some of the current phonetic notations from these points of view. Since the units of articulation and catenation, which are segments, differ from those of rhythm and intonation, which are pattern modifications, we examine each pair separately.

(i) *For Articulation and Catenation*

Despite the standardizing efforts of the International Phonetic Association since the end of the nineteenth century, there is still a considerable difference in the use of phonetic symbols for the articulated sounds of speech. The main difference may be outlined in the following table.

If we examine the table, the first thing we note is that the columns on the right have more double symbols than those on the left. For example, for the sound of the vowel in *seat*, most of the left-hand columns have a single symbol /i/ or /iː/; the others have a double symbol, some including /i/ and another symbol, /j/ or /y/, to render the diphthongal quality of this English vowel as /ij/ or /iy/.

Those using /ij/ or /iy/ for *seat*, also use the first symbol of this combination, /i/, for the vowel in *sit*. Those using /iː/ for the vowel of *seat*, use the same symbol /i/, without the length mark /ː/, for the vowel of *sit*. The reason for these differences in notation is not so much that the phoneticians hear different sounds, as that they interpret what they hear in different ways. In fact, if we examine closely the difference between the vowel of *seat* and that of *sit*, we notice that there is more than a single difference. To begin with, there is a difference in kind; in going from one to the other we notice a difference in the lip position, in the mouth opening, in the position of the tongue, and in the tenseness of the muscles. On the principle of one-symbol-per-sound, therefore, we can show the difference in kind by writing simply /sit/ and /sɪt/. But if we listen further we notice that a difference in kind is not the only difference; there is also a difference in degree, in the length of the vowel—*seat* being longer than *sit*. For some phoneticians, this is the important difference, and they show it by writing /siːt/ and /sit/, or by indicating the length by doubling the symbol thus: /siit/ and /sit/, imagining length as the pronunciation of the same sound twice in succession. Now if we listen carefully to this long sound /ii/, we notice that the first part is not exactly the same as the second, for while closing our mouth to end the vowel, we produce one that is more closed. This is even more evident when a word ends in the vowel, as the word *three* in the sentence *I didn't want three!* The very long sound at the end of the exclamation is generally a movement from an open /ɪ/ of *sit* to the closed /i/ of *seat*, or even to the semi-vowel /j/ as in *yes*. In other words, it is a diphthong, and this is the most important feature of the

	Jones	Scott	Ward, Palmer	Pike	Fries	Kenyon	Thomas	MacCarthy	Trager and Smith	Hill	Bloomfield	Bloch and Trager	Sledd
seat	iː	iː	i	i	i	i	i	ii	iy	iy	ij	ij	iː
sit/silk	i	i	ɪ	ɩ	ɪ	ɪ	ɪ	i	i	i/ɨ	i	i	ɪ/ɨ
say	ei	ei	eɪ	e	e	e	e	ei	ey	ey	ej	ej	eː
set	ɛ	e	ɛ	ɛ	ɛ	ɛ	ɛ	e	e	e	e	e	ɛ
sat	a	a	æ	æ	æ	æ	æ	a	æ	æ	ɛ	a	æ/æː
salve	–	–	–	–	–	a	–	–	æh	–	–	–	–
suit/food	uː	uː	u	u	u	u	u	uu	uw	uw	uw	uw	uː
soot/put	u	u	ʊ	ʊ	ʊ	ʊ	ʊ	u	u	u	u	u	ʊ
so	ou	ou	oʊ	o	o	o	o	ou	ow	ow	ow	ow	o/oː
sought/saw	ɔː	ɔː	ɔ	ɔ	ɔ	ɔ	ɔ	oo	ɔh	ɔh	ɔ	oh	ɔː
sot/not	ɔ	ɔ	ɒ	–	–	ɒ	ɒ	o	ɔ	ɔ	ɑ	o	ɑ/ɔ
psalm/calm	ɑː	ɑː	ɑ	a	a	ɑ	ɑ	aa	ah	ah	a·	ah	ɑː
sun	ʌ	ʌ	ʌ	ə	ə	ʌ	ʌ	ʌ	ə	ə	o	ə	ə/ɑ
the	ə	ə	ə	ə	ə	ə	ə	ə	ə	ə	ə/o	ə	ə/ɨ
sir (RP)	əː	əː	ɜ	–	–	ɜ	ɜ	əə	əh	–	–	əh	əː
sir (Gen. Amer.)	–	–	–	r	ər	ɝ	ɝ	–	ər	ər	ər	ər	əːr
lesser (Gen. Amer.)	–	–	–	r	ər	ɚ	ɚ	–	ər	ər	r	r	ər
sigh	ɑi	ai	aɪ	aⁱ	aɪ	aɪ	aɪ	ai	ay	ay	aj	aj	ɑi/ai
sow/now	ɑu	au	aʊ	aᵘ	aʊ	aʊ	aʊ	au	aw	aw	aw	aw	ɑu/au
soy/boy	ɔi	oi	ɔɪ	oⁱ	ɔɪ	ɔɪ	ɔɪ	oi	ɔy	oy	ɔj	oj	ɔi/oi
ship	ʃ	ʃ	ʃ	š	š	ʃ	ʃ	ʃ	š	š	š	š	š
measure	ʒ	ʒ	ʒ	ž	ž	ʒ	ʒ	ʒ	ž	ž	ž	ž	ž
church	tʃ	tʃ	tʃ	č	č	tʃ	tʃ	tʃ	č	č	č	tš/č	č
judge	dʒ	dʒ	dʒ	ǰ	ǰ	dʒ	dʒ	dʒ	ǰ	j	ǰ	dž/ǰ	ǰ
thin	θ	θ	θ	θ	θ	θ	θ	θ	θ	θ	θ	θ	θ
then	ð	ð	ð	ð	ð	ð	ð	ð	ð	ð	ð	ð	ð
young	j	j	j	j	y	j	j	j	y	y	j	j	y
which	hw	ʍ	hw	hw	hw	hw			hw				
huge	hj	hj		hy	hj	ç			hy				

Comparison of the Most Usual Styles of English Phonetic Notation sound as far as some phoneticians are concerned; so they write it as /siyt/ or /sijt/. Therefore the different notations interpret the difference between the two vowels as either a difference in kind (/sɪt/ and /sit/), a difference in length (/sit/ and /siːt/), or a difference in diphthongization (/sit/ and /sijt/). If we again look down the respective columns we find that the same differences of interpretation apply to the vowel of *suit*—/sut/, /suːt/, or /suwt/; and in other columns to the vowel of *say*—/se/, /seː/, /sei/, /sej/, /sey/. Similar differences may be seen in the notation of the vowels of *so, psalm,* and *sought.*

Another difference is the treatment of the vowel of *sun,* as compared with the vowel of *the* in phrases like *the man.* Both these vowels occur in the word *above,* which some linguists would transcribe as /əbʌv/ and others as /əbəv/. The main difference behind these two transcriptions is not one of pronunciation but rather a difference in the basic principles of phonetic notation. One principle is that a notation should note only significant differences and that two sounds, although they may be heard as different, may be written with the same symbol, provided they have the same function. For example, there is need for only one /l/ symbol in English, although the actual sound of the beginning /l-/ in a word can be heard as different from that of the final /-l/; the difference between the first and last sounds of the word *lull* is quite noticeable, but need not be written, since it always corresponds to its position at the beginning or the end of the word. No word in English can become another word simply by changing one of these /l/ sounds to the other, since there is only one distinctive and relevant /l/ in English—one /l/ phoneme. If we thus have only one symbol for each significant sound we get an alphabet that contains only what is absolutely essential in recording or writing down the language— not one symbol too many. For one symbol too many would be useless; one symbol too few would be confusing, since two different words might be written in the same way, e.g. if /i/ and /e/ had only one symbol, *pin* and *pen* would be written as the same word. This absolute minimum list of symbols is a notation of all and only the phonemes of a language; it is a phonematic (or phonemic) alphabet of the language. Applying the phoneme principle to our example of the two vowels in *above,* we find that although they may sound different, they can never be confused since the first occurs only in unstressed or weakly stressed syllables and the second only in stressed or strongly stressed syllables, so that the one symbol is sufficient for both cases, since there is only one /ə/ phoneme. Phonemes may be indicated by placing the symbol between / / slanted lines.

In contradistinction to this rigid phoneme principle of notation is the more elastic phonetic principle, which makes the notation supple enough to indicate anything which a phonetician or a teacher of pronunciation may wish to indicate. It ranges from a broad transcription, which shows only the phonemes, to a very narrow form, which may indicate all the features which the ear of the phonetician can perceive. If, for example, the teaching situation requires that the difference between the initial and final /l/ should be kept before the eyes of the learner, it is simply a matter of making the phonetic transcription somewhat narrower, writing /l/ for the initial sound and [ł] for the final sound, thus: [lʌł]. Most partisans of this principle of transcription see enough difference between the two vowels of *above*, for example, to justify the use of two different symbols, and to write [əbʌv]. To indicate speech sounds which may or may not be phonemes, or are components of phonemes, it is customary to use [ ], square brackets.

A third cause of differences in phonetic notation is the purpose for which the notation is intended. The purpose may be the description of a certain dialect or regional standard with sufficient accuracy for practical teaching,[693,676] or it may be the creation of a framework into which all dialects may fit.[747] This framework is built by plotting the vowels against the semi-vowels (glides), giving a certain number of possible stressed vowel groups (vowel nuclei). Each syllable nucleus in the language may be any one of nine simple vowels or any combination of a simple vowel (V) with one of the three glides /j/, /w/, or /h/, giving a possible total of 36 vowel nuclei, which may be tabulated as shown in the table opposite, with examples from a variety of dialects.

Of course, no one speaker makes use of all these thirty-six nuclei. Some will make use of a larger number than others. Lists which take care of the needs of a single speaker include no more than about twenty-one. The point of arranging the possible sounds in nuclei is that speakers with the same number of vowel nuclei do not all make use of the same ones. And even when they do, they may not use them in the same words. Thus the vowel sound of the word *house* might be /həws/ in Canada, /haws/ in the South of England, and /hæws/ or /hews/ in South-eastern United States.

Another thing that must be kept in mind is that the key words may not correspond to comparable sounds in the other words of the various dialects. For example, both Jones and Bloomfield may say /put/ for *put*; but that does not necessarily mean that if one of them says /sut/ for *soot*, the other does likewise. This is a matter not of notation but of distribution of sounds throughout the vocabulary; and it varies from dialect to dialect, and indeed from individual to individual.

As for symbols of catenation, apart from linking marks and small letters written above or below the line, the only special symbols are those of junction. These are: $+$, $/$, $//$, $\#$, each longer or more open than the following.[747]

ENGLISH VOWEL NUCLEI

	Pure Vowel (V)	V+j	V+w	V+h
/i/	sit	see	new	near
/ɨ/	sugar	see	moon	fur
/u/	put	buoy	do	boor
/e/	set	say	house	fair
/ə/	pump	bird	go	fur
/o/	obey	boy	go	paw
/æ/	pan	pass	house	bar
/a/	pawn	buy	house	psalm
/ɔ/	got	wash	law	paw

Finally, not all symbols are accepted without controversy. Note, for example, the many objections to the use of /h/ as a glide or semivowel,[538,535] and the objections to the use of the length mark /:/ to show the only distinction between two vowels which also differ in quality.[480]

(ii) *For Rhythm and Intonation*

In examining current notations, we are first struck by the lack of uniformity in symbols used for rhythm and intonation in comparison with those used for isolated speech sounds. This should not be surprising, however, since the units are not so obvious and much less attention has been given to the standardization of symbols for them.

In the absence of a standard notation, many a linguist, after having analysed the rhythm and intonation of a language, has tended to devise a personal notation which best fits his analysis. This is unfortunate because it is sometimes copied by other linguists and influences their results. If there is one thing that a linguistic notation should not do, it is to prejudice linguistic analysis. We also find cases of linguists inventing a notation and then proceeding to name the entities they believe to have discovered after the notation which they have invented.

We may classify the notations of rhythm and intonation into three categories—(a) numerical, (b) linear, and (c) accentual. (See tables below.)

NUMERICAL TYPES

N–1: **The Scale Type**

```
9.................9
7.................7
5.................5        6-1    1 3   4   9   1
3.................3
1.................1        Why, I never had one.
```

N–2: **The Level Type**

Type *A:*

```
_____1              "Every "man must "go.
_____2
_____3              °2–3    °2–3    –    °2–4
_____4
```

Type *B:*

```
_____4                2        3        1
_____3                 \        /
_____2              That was kind of you.
_____1
```

N–3: **The Frequency Type**

	All right, then.		
Speaker A:	270	210	235
Speaker B:	275	215	240
Speaker C:	300	205	225

LINEAR TYPES

L–1: **The Dot Type**

Type *A:*

But   how d'you manage?

Type *B:*

Hello, I thought I recognized your voice.

L–2: The Dash Type

Type *A:*

Type *B:*

L–3: The Dot-and-Dash Type

Type *A:*

Type *B:*

L–4: The Line Type

Type *A:*

Type *B:*

L–5: Musical Notation

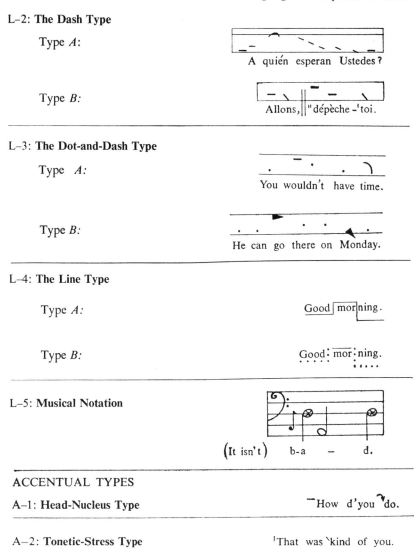

ACCENTUAL TYPES

A–1: Head-Nucleus Type

A–2: Tonetic-Stress Type

(a) Numerical types

Numerical notations are those which use numbers to indicate changes in tone. There are three types, the scale type, the level type and the frequency type.

The *scale type* is based on an average total range of nine semitones. The

59

tone is marked over each syllable. The rhythm may be marked in the text. This type has been used by Coleman and his followers.[503:1]

The *level type* assumes a certain number of significant levels, and numbers each of them. Most adherents to this school of notation admit four levels for English; but some recognize only three, while others claim five and see the possibility of even more. Some, like Pike,[716] Fries and Lado,[680] read their levels from top to bottom; whereas others, like Trager and Smith,[747], Sledd[727] and Hill,[425] read them from bottom to top; so that Level 4 of one group corresponds to Level 1 of the other. One group writes the tone notation below the line of the text, whereas the other group indicates intonation above the text. The four or three stress levels recognized are indicated by accent marks over the syllables of the text. This notation shows a clear correspondence between syllable, stress and pitch. Any number of pitch levels may be added as the analysis reveals them to be significant. But the notation does not distinguish between moving tones and fixed ones, and there is no visual suggestion of what the forms stand for. An association must be made between a number and a pitch level if the intonation contours are to be read off at sight. This is difficult enough to develop into a habit. Once the habit is formed, however, it becomes most inconvenient to switch from texts written by the down-up group to those of the up-down faction.

A third numerical notation is the *frequency type* in which number of vibrations in cycles per second is indicated for each speaker under each syllable of the text. Stress is indicated separately in decibels (measure of relative loudness). The advantage of this type of notation is its accuracy. But it is difficult, if not impossible, to read aloud. Its use is highly restricted to laboratory notation for acoustic and psycho-acoustic research. This type of notation has been used by Jassem, Zwirner, and others.[715]

(b) Linear Types

The linear category of notation invites the user to visualize the material as a sequence of dots, dashes, curves, or notes, or as a continuous or broken line. There are five types: the dot, the dash, the dot-and-dash, the line, and musical notation.

The *dot-type* marks intonation by a sequence of dots within two or three lines, representing the normal voice range. Stress is indicated by the size and blackness of the dots. Sometimes tails are added to dots to indicate changes in the direction of pitch variation. This type has been used by Jones, MacCarthy, and others.[676]

The *dash-type* regards the material as a sequence of dashes. Stress is noted by the thickness of the dash, and voice change within a single syllable by the direction of the dash. This type has been used by Tomás Navarro, Coustenoble, and others.[801]

In the *dot-and-dash type*, the dot represents a weakly stressed syllable and the dash indicates a more strongly stressed syllable. Voice-change within a single syllable is indicated by curving the dash. Instead of straight dashes and curves, one type uses a wedge which points in the direction of the voice movement. This is visually more representative than the dash, because it pictures the strongest part of the stress at the beginning of the syllable. Kingdon,[712] Armstrong and Ward[717] have used the dot-and-dash type in their work.

These three linear types all require staves above or below the line of text. The *line-type*, however, can be woven directly into the text, the height of the voice being indicated by how close the line comes above or below the text. The line may be solid or broken. If it is solid, the stress has to be indicated separately. If it is broken, the solid part may be used to indicate the stress. The line-type has been used by Jones, Pike,[716] Prator,[685] Fries, and Lado.[680]

The use of *musical notation* constitutes a fifth linear type. Since all speech has tone and rhythm in common with music, a notation which has proved adequate for music has been used to note the rhythm and tones of speech. This may be quite helpful for those who can read music, but it cannot be written with anything like the speed required for a good notation.

When we examine these five types of linear notation, we find that they are on the whole clearer and more easily visualized than numerical notations, and may be analytically just as adequate. But they lack concision and produceability. They are difficult to write and type, are costly to print, and cannot be written along with the text at verbatim speed.

(c) Accentual types

Finally, there are the accentual types. These include all those types of notation which indicate rhythm and intonation by use of diacritic marks of any sort, whether they be arrows, dots, or grave, acute or circumflex accents, written with the body of the text.

There are two main types of accentual notation: the head-nucleus type and the tonetic-stress type.

The *head-nucleus type* divides the tone pattern into head, nucleus and tail. The head is marked by a dash above, below, or across the line of text; the nucleus, that is, the changing tone which takes the main stress, is marked by arrows of different sizes and directions. The tail is unmarked. This type has been used by Palmer, who distinguishes three heads and five nuclei for English,[718] and by the Polish phonetician Jassem, who has a notation of eight heads and twelve nuclei.[715]

The *tonetic-stress type* makes a primary distinction between static tones and moving or kinetic tones. The static tones are indicated by a vertical accent in front of the stressed syllable whereas the kinetic tones are shown by grave, acute and circumflex accents, written below or above the line, depending on the degree of stress. This type has been used by Kingdon,[712] Halliday,[721] Allen,[714] Lee,[711] and Schubiger.[713]

While retaining all the clarity, legibility and much of the visual suggestion of the other types, accentual types can synthesize both stress and intonation into a single system of notation. Compare, for example, A-2 with N-2(b); both contain the same amount of information. The easiest type of notation to produce is also the accentual type; it can be written on any typewriter with a single grave-acute accent key, is easy and cheap to print, and takes little space. Moreover, it can be written with the text at verbatim speed and is therefore excellent for phonetic transcription. Since the linear types are by far the most visual, however, they seem to be pedagogically preferable as an introduction.

(For samples of phonetic descriptions, see Bibliography 675a–724, 793–802, and 826–35.)

2.2 GRAMMAR

Grammars differ (1) in their types of purpose and scope, (2) in the categories they use, and (3) in the terms and notation which they employ.

2.2.1 Types of Grammar

The purpose of grammars may be historical, comparative or descriptive.

The purpose of a historical grammar is to trace the development of the structure of a language back to its origins. A grammar like Wright's, for example, traces the development of the sounds and forms of English from about the thirteenth century to the present day.[763] Related to this is comparative grammar, which traces the movement by which the most primitive form of a language group develops into a number of different languages. For instance, the grammar of Prokosch shows how Primitive Germanic branched out into such different languages as Gothic, Old Saxon, Old High German, Old Norse, and Old English.[753] If the native language is genetically related to the second, comparative grammar may offer formulas for the identification of related words. For example, since English and German were once the same language, a German *z*- often corresponds to an English *t*-, as it does in *Zinn/tin*, *Zunge/tongue*, or a *pf*- to a *p*-, as in *Pfeffer/pepper*, and *Pflaume/plum*. But these can only be hints.

Neither historical nor comparative grammars are likely foundations for a modern language method, concerned as they are with forms no longer in use. It is on the contemporary descriptive grammars that such methods are likely to be based.

Not all descriptive grammars, however, are relevant to modern language teaching. A grammar may well be a description of an older form of the language, one like Campbell's, for example.[729] Yet this does not mean that grammars of Modern English which refer to the origins of the modern forms of the language are not useful in the preparation of materials for teaching purposes. Jespersen's is of this type; it has a wealth of information about Modern English forms and at the same time gives the historical background of these forms.[748] Nor does it mean that all grammars based exclusively on the contemporary forms of the language are useful in the teaching of the language as a foreign language, for many are intended for native speakers, who already know the language. Such grammars are often concerned mainly with definitions, classifications and correct usage.[755] Some are concerned with training the student in techniques of analysing his own language.[736]

The sort of descriptive grammar which is the most relevant to modern language teaching is that whose purpose is to describe the contemporary forms of the language.[765] Some of the most complete ones have been written by grammarians for whom the language described is a foreign one; they are such grammars as those of Poutsma,[762] Jespersen,[748] Kruisinga[761] and Zandvoort.[750] These grammars are not chiefly concerned with definitions, analytical techniques or correct usage; they are mainly reservoirs of information about the language.

Like any description of a language, a descriptive grammar may be based on the usage of any region or regions, in which the language is used. Although most descriptive grammars have been based on written documents, a few, such as Palmer's, and that of the *français fondamental*, have been based on the spoken forms of the language.[754] And the tendency is more and more in this direction. Descriptive grammars may also vary as to the type and amount of material on which they are based. Some grammars make use only of literary documents—novels, plays, etc. Others, like Fries', are based exclusively on contemporary letters.[752] The amount of material may vary from a few hundred sentences to many thousands. (See also 1.4 above.)

2.2.2 Grammatical Categories

One of the most significant ways in which one grammar may differ from another is in the categories into which it puts the different forms of a

	GREEK				ROMAN	MEDIAEVAL	RENAISSANCE	18TH–20TH CENTURIES
	Plato	*Aristotle*	*Stoics*	*Thrax*	*Priscian & Donatus*	*Modistae*	*Lyly & Jonson*	*Lowth, Murray, et al.*
	noun	noun	noun	noun*	noun*	noun*	noun*	noun
								adjective
			article†	pronoun	pronoun	pronoun	pronoun‡	pronoun
				article				article §
				participle	participle	participle	participle	participle §
	verb*	verb	verb	verb	verb	verb	verb	verb
		indeclinables		adverb	adverb	adverb	adverb	adverb
				preposition	preposition	preposition	preposition	preposition
			conjunction	conjunction	conjunction	conjunction	conjunction	conjunction
					interjection	interjection	interjection	interjection §

* includes adjective. † includes pronoun. ‡ includes article. § sometimes omitted.

Evolution of Traditional Parts of Speech

language. Of these, by far the most important are the word-classes, or parts of speech, as they have been traditionally called.

All grammars do not agree on the parts of speech, what they are and how many there are. In English, the number has ranged from two to fourteen. Up to the early part of the twentieth century, most grammarians accepted the traditional parts of speech handed down from antiquity. But even in antiquity there was not always universal agreement, as the facing table shows.

The table, however, does not show all the attempts at analysis of all the grammarians of antiquity—Varro, Apollonios Dyskolos, Quintilian, Donatus, even Caesar and Lucretius. It gives only a representative sample of grammarians. It gives no indication of the differences which early Greek philosophers inferred between logical and grammatical categories. Nor does it show all the contributions to a growing tradition on the parts of speech, such as the fact that in the first century A.D., Palaemon added the interjection to the list. A tradition, however, was established fairly early. It was maintained during the Middle Ages by the Modistae, named after their method of speculative grammar, *de modis significandi*.[89] The tradition was taken up by the Renaissance scholars and has continued to persist.

We can see from the table that the evolution of the idea of parts of speech seems to have taken place independently of the language. Differences in the number of parts of speech recognized were due not so much to the language observed as to differences in principles of analysis.

It is true, however, that the parts of speech of Greek did provide a useful framework for the description of Latin. But they fitted English less well; and it took a few centuries before this was fully realized. The delay was due largely to the prestige of Latin, but also to the fact that the parts of speech were maintained by definition rather than by analysis.

English grammarians of the twentieth century made an attempt to break with this tradition when they realized that their parts of speech were those of another language. They tried to re-establish the word-classes of English on the analysis of the contemporary forms of the language. But those who attempted the analysis got different results; and this was again due, not to differences in the language, but to differences of analysis. Some of the analyses were logical; some, empirical. Some were based on form; some, on meaning; others, on both. The following table gives some idea of the results. It compares the traditional parts of speech with those arrived at in twentieth-century descriptions of English. (See following table.)

Again the table is only representative of the main types. It does not include the names of all contemporary grammarians of the language, notable exceptions being Poutsma, Kruisinga, Curme and Zandvoort.[724a–66]

TRADITIONAL	SWEET		SLEDD		
	Declinable	Unde-clinable	Morpho-logical	Syntactic	
				Minor	Ma;
article				determiner	
pronoun	noun†		pronoun	reflexive	nomi.
noun			noun		
adjective	o adjective		adjective		adjecti
verb	verb		verb	auxiliary verbals	
adverb		adverb	adverb	adverbs of degree	
				interrogative adverbs	
preposition		preposition		preposition	
conjunction		conjunction		conjunction	advert
interjection		interjection			

* *includes adjectives*   † *includes pronouns*

English Parts of Sp

ESPERSEN		ROBERTS		FRIES		HILL
ks	Parts of Speech	Form Classes	Structure Words	Form Classes	Function Word Groups	
	Pronouns ‡		deter-miners		A	
ries			pronouns	1		pronouns
	nouns *	noun				nouns
aries		adjective		3		adjectives
	verbs	verb	auxiliary verbs	2	B / G	verbs
	particles	adverb	inten-sifiers	4	C / D / H / I	adverbs
			question words			
			preposi-tions		F	preposi-tions
			conjunc-tions		E	conjunc-tions
			sentence-connectors			
			subordin-ates		J	
			etc.		K / L / M / N / O	

‡ *includes articles*   o *includes participles*

Twentieth Century

Although the name and number of parts of speech may coincide, they do not necessarily include the same thing, and are not necessarily arrived at in the same way. For some of the parts of speech are forms of expression; others are categories of content (see Ch. 1). Although both Sweet and Roberts admit the noun as a separate part of speech, they define it differently; for Roberts, it is simply a form-class of words which can take certain endings and fill certain positions in the sentence.

Similar tables of the other categories of grammar would reveal the differences in the number and variety of tenses, inflectional groups, sentence patterns, etc. All these differences affect language-teaching methods. In the teaching of sentence patterns, for instance, one method puts the sentences: *His house is there* and *The house is there* under two separate patterns on the grounds that *his* and *the* belong to separate parts of speech; another method considers the sentences as examples of the same pattern since *his* and *the* can occupy the same position before the noun and therefore belong to the same group of structure words.

Other languages like French[810] and German[837] have modern grammars which also differ radically from the traditional grammatical categories into which the forms of the language have been classified. (For samples of current descriptive grammars, see Bibliography 724a–66, 803–13 and 836–843.)

2.2.3 Grammatical Terminology and Notation

Most evident, of course, are the differences in terminology. Two grammarians, for instance, using almost identical categories, may scarcely have a term in common. Some adapt the traditional terms and add a few of their own. Others do away completely with the traditional terminology. Fries, for example, insists on doing away with all traditional terms like "noun" and "verb" on the grounds that they are associated with false definitions.[745]

Some attempts, however, have been made to standardize grammatical terms. In 1913 the report of the American Joint Committee on Grammatical Nomenclature was adopted by both the Modern Language Association of America and the National Education Association of the United States. Because of the revolution in English grammar which took place between 1940 and 1960, introducing many new terms and techniques, this report on grammatical terms is now very much out of date. Contemporary grammatical terms may be found in the glossaries of the different schools of linguistics.[650-56]

Even more diverse than differences in terms are the differences in syntactic notation, since these include not only different definitions, different categories and different symbols, but also different principles of syntactic analysis. To illustrate some of the differences, let us take a sentence from Jespersen[565] and reduce it to the notation of Fries;[745] then let us take one from Fries and write it in Jespersen's notation. Jespersen: S (subject), V (verb), O (object), P (predicate); 1 (primaries), 2 (secondaries), 3 (tertiaries); Fries: 1, 2, 3, 4 (form-classes); D (any determiner). (See preceding table.)

	He	eats	very	little.
Jespersen:	S	V	0 (2	(3)1)
Fries:	1	2	3	1

	The	board	appoints	a	teacher	the	secretary.
Fries:		D	1	2	D 1^b	D	1^b
Jespersen:			S	V	O^r		(S$_2$P)

2.3 VOCABULARY

Of the systems which make up a language that of vocabulary is the least stable. It is continuously changing, bringing in new words from other languages, losing words, adapting others to changing conditions. It is voluminous; no man possesses it all, and no dictionary has ever recorded all the words in any language.

The description of vocabulary includes (1) lexicography, the inventory of the words, and (2) lexicology, the study of the relations between them.

2.3.1 **Lexicography**

In the cataloguing tradition of language analysis, the most prolific descriptions have been the dictionaries—perhaps because their problems are less complicated than those of grammar and phonetics. Dictionaries, which are compilations of the vocabulary of a language, with explanations of the meanings by paraphrase definition, are the sort of description on which language learners have traditionally most depended.

How do dictionaries differ? They differ mainly (i) in their aims and range, (ii) in the type of definitions, and (iii) in their use of notation.

(i) *Aims and Range*

Before a dictionary is started there is generally established a definite purpose which answers the questions: Whom is it for? and What is it supposed to do?

The aim of the bilingual dictionary is to give people learning another language equivalents or translations of words; the aim of the one-language dictionaries is not entirely the opposite, since some of them have been designed mainly for foreign learners.[774] Some dictionaries have a historical aim. In a historical dictionary, which gives the history of the vocabulary, dates and old spellings are of course of great importance.[784] The encyclo-paedic type of dictionary gives not only the meanings of words, but also condensed information about persons, places and institutions. There are also the numerous technical and specialized dictionaries, dictionaries of place names, dictionaries of slang, etc.

The purpose of the dictionary will of course determine the range of material which it includes. A dictionary intended for home and office is likely to have more contemporary technical terms and fewer archaic words than one intended for secondary school students, who may have to read literary works written three or four hundred years ago.

Dictionaries differ most in how they decide what goes in and what stays out. A word may be excluded because of its age, because of its social stand-ing (e.g. it may be considered slang), or because of its frequency of use. Some school and desk dictionaries include only the words in current use. This is often determined by a frequency count of the occurrence of words in contemporary writing (see Ch. 6). An example of this type is the Thorndike-Barnhardt series of dictionaries, based on Thorndike's Teachers' Word Book of the 30,000 most frequent words.[1396]

Differences between dictionaries may also depend on the extent to which they are based on previous dictionaries. Many dictionaries are adaptations of previous works; note, for example, the many adaptations of Webster's Dictionary. On the other hand, some are based on original material.[769, 784] Few lexicographers, however, do not make some use of previously-published dictionaries.

The date of publication of a dictionary is no sure indication of whether or not it is up-to-date. Two dictionaries, first published in the same year, may differ widely in their use of new material. No dictionary, however, contains all the latest words and meanings, since new ones are continually appearing, even while the new dictionary is in the press. Realizing this, some publishers maintain a permanent staff to keep the dictionary up-to-date; others publish a house organ, with information about new words.

Dictionaries also vary considerably in the type and amount of informa-tion which they give on each word. This ranges from the one-spelling-one-definition item of the pocket dictionary to the several spellings, dates, definitions, dated quotations, classified meanings, etymology, and indica-tions of pronunciation found in the larger dictionaries.[784] Some diction-aries supply material on the grammar of the words[781]—the sentence patterns into which they can fit,[774] prepositions which accompany them, and other sorts of information useful to the foreign learner.

(ii) *Definitions*

The most significant differences, however, are in the types of definition and the number of meanings included. Theoretically the words used in the definition should be simpler than the word being defined. But this is not always the case; some come close to Johnson's definition of the simple word *network* as "anything reticulated or decussated, at equal distances, with interstices between the intersections." There are some words, however, which are so simple, that they are difficult to define in simpler terms. For example, in one dictionary the word *cat* is defined as "a carnivorous animal which has been long domesticated as a household pet, and for catching mice."

Eventually the problem of what constitutes a simple definition had to be faced. In the 1930s, attempts were made to establish a simple vocabulary in which all the words of the English language could be defined. The problem was studied by Michael West, who established a minimum defining vocabulary of 1,490 words.[782] With these, he defined some 18,000 words and 6,000 idioms, and published them in dictionary form.[767a] This was especially intended for students of English as a second language who presumably already understood the words in the defining vocabulary. Another defining vocabulary was a by-product of the elaboration of Basic English (see Ch. 6). Although not intended exclusively as a defining vocabulary, Basic English was developed by the technique of definition and re-definition developed by Ogden and Richards as a logical outgrowth of the principles laid down in their *Meaning of Meaning*.[233] The result was a list of 850 words, plus 50 international words. These were eventually used to define the 20,000 English words of Basic English Dictionary.[780]

(iii) *Notation*

Despite a great effort on the part of such organizations as the International Phonetic Association to standardize phonetic notation, there are still a number of minor and major differences in the use of notation in dictionaries. The major differences are between those using the Alphabet of the International Phonetic Association (the IPA) and an important group, including Webster's dictionaries, which persists in the use of a notation based on re-spelling according to the conventions of orthography, supplemented by diacritic marks over letters of the conventional alphabet.

The problems of making dictionaries are far from being solved. There remain such questions as the classification of homonyms under one heading or under two. As linguistic theory and research advance, however, we may expect changes and improvements in our dictionaries. That dictionaries can be improved is beyond discussion; that they lag behind linguistic theory and research is also evident.[633:96] (For samples of dictionaries in current use, see Bibliography, 766a–88, 814–22, and 844–9.)

2.3.2 Lexicology

Lexicology is the study of the relationships in the vocabulary of a language. These may be formal or semantic. Formally, a word is related to all the other words of which it is part. In this way, *man* is related to *manly*, *mannish*, *manlike*, *unmanly*, *mankind*, etc. Semantically, it is related to all other words of which its meaning is part; but the relationships differ according to the role of the word within the series. For example, *man* is related in a different way to *fellow*, *sir*, *chap*, *mister*, than it is to *father*, *uncle*, *nephew*, *son*. In this way, each word in the language is associated with the others in a sort of network of relationships.

Each word is the centre of a sort of constellation in which all items inter-animate one another. The important thing for language teaching is that this constellation, or network, differs from language to language. For example, the English word *line* does not have the same network of relations (semantic constellation) as the French word *ligne*. For the network of the French word *ligne* does not touch the semantic areas of conformity (*fall in line*), correspondence (*drop me a line*), limit (*draw the line*) or policy (*the party line*); whereas the English *line* does not include eminence (*hors ligne*), commencement (*aller à la ligne*) or importance (*en première ligne*).

A second important feature of these networks of semantic relations is that they change their shape from generation to generation. If we were to use the words *awful* and *artificial* in describing a work of art, it would be a sign that we did not admire it. But when King James II told Sir Christopher Wren that the architect's new St. Paul's Cathedral was awful and artificial it was received as a great compliment. For in the time of James II, *awful* was not associated with the idea of *bad* and *horrible* but with that of *amazing* and *inspiring*, and *artificial* did not go with *false* and *unnatural* but rather with *perfect* and *skilful*. A striking example of the fact that the network of associations changes with time is seen in the fact that each generation has its own slang.[788]

Studies in lexicology may appear in essay form under conceptual headings or alphabetically. Roget's study has been arranged under both conceptual and alphabetical headings. [766a]

2.4 MEANING

Although there are no manuals of meanings as there are grammars and dictionaries, meaning is one of the most important aspects of language, and the most difficult to describe. It is necessary: (1) to see what meaning involves; (2) to analyse the attempts to describe it.

2.4.1 What Meaning Involves

The notion of meaning, like that of sound, is not limited to language. Smoke means fire; clouds mean rain. Meanings are relationships between certain impressions made on the mind. The relation may be between an event in nature (clouds) and another event (rain), a relation studied by the physical sciences. It may be a relation between a graphic image (painting) and a conception, a relation cultivated by the arts. Or it may be a relation between a series of sounds (words) and a concept, in which case we have language. With language, there is the big difference that the two end-points are purely arbitrary, not necessary relations like smoke and fire. Each type of meaning pervades every level of human activity. Language is used to represent all of them—everything that takes place outside the individual and everything that goes on inside him.

In what takes place outside the individual, language is supposed to have a meaning or symbol for everything we sense, the phenomena of Area A (see Ch. 1). This can only be a fiction. It is impossible that everything should have a distinct name. If it did, we should require a much more powerful memory than most of us can exercise. We are forced to reduce the names of things and events of our experience to a number we can manage. We do this by neglecting much of what we experience and by grouping the rest into a number of abstractions. Meanings are abstractions from our experience.

The sort of abstractions varies with the language, since each language groups the things and events of experience in a different way. The classical example is the grouping of colours. Some languages divide the colour spectrum into two colours, others into three, four, five, or as many as twelve. Yet languages with the same number of colours do not have the same grouping. English *brown* includes part of French *jaune* (yellow), *gris* (grey), *bistre* and *marron*.[870] English green and blue are equivalent to a single colour in Welsh. Colours are not the only example. Such differences apply to all experience, even to such obvious things as the parts of our body. Most Slavonic languages group the hand and the arm together (*ruka* in Serbian) and similarly, the leg and the foot into one (*noga*). Differences are most common in the abstractions made from nature. Whereas English has only one word for snow, Eskimo has three.

If languages vary in the way they group the phenomena of nature, they differ even more in the way they represent it. Any grouping or abstraction may be represented by any device which the language may possess—sounds, words, grammar, etc. What appears as grammar in one language is vocabulary in another. The idea of an incomplete event is expressed by grammar in English; by a fixed word-group in French. The idea of the present continuous (*I'm dressing*) can be rendered by the words *en train de* in French (*Je suis en train de m'habiller*). Meaning pervades all levels of language.

In addition to the use of different devices of language there is the use of different combinations of them to represent the same situation. The response to a *thank you* in some varieties of English may be *not at all* or *you're welcome*; in German it is the same as *please* (*bitte*).

So much for what goes on outside the individual; the most complicating factor is what goes on inside him. The same devices are used to represent his ideas, feelings, imaginings, etc., the experience of Area A (see Ch. 1). These are so numerous and diverse that no language can convey all of them. There is no line of demarcation between them, and there are so many shades and gradations that it is impossible to have a name for each. So they have to be grouped by the language into concepts. This grouping is not only arbitrary, but it varies from language to language, and often from individual to individual. Any label representing one of these concepts cannot stand for exactly the same thing for even two individuals, since no two people have exactly the same experiences. Words like *good, truth beauty* mean different things to different persons. Much of education, law and politics is an effort to make such labels mean the same thing to everybody.

Another factor is that two or more of such labels may in fact mean the same thing, like the words *fire* and *conflagration*, or *six* and a *half-dozen*. There may be more of them in one language than in another. Conversely, a number of different groupings may use the same label, as when *nut* is used to indicate both a food and a piece of ironware. Yet these may be indicated not by the same but by different labels in another language, such as French, where *noix* is used for the one, and *écrou* for the other.

What labels go together is another matter. And this too varies from one language to the next. In English, soap is associated with cake (*a cake of soap*); in French it is associated with bread (*un pain de savon*).

Any one of these aspects may be what is described as "meaning."

2.4.2 Attempts to Describe Meaning

If meaning cannot be seen, how can it be described? It cannot, according to some linguists, notably of the Bloomfield school—at least, not as language. For words like *wolf, fox,* and *dog* do not, in themselves, tell us anything about the differences between these animals. And a zoologist's description of them cannot be verified by a science of language.[128]

Attempts, however, have been made to describe meanings (i) as the response of individuals, (ii) as expression, (iii) as content, and (iv) as content and expression.

(i) *Meaning as Response*

Meaning, like value, must be referred to someone; to describe the meaning of a sign, we observe habits it produces in people.[227] To describe the meaning of a word is to give an account of how it is used within a context of situation.[234, 223] Or meaning may be described as certain dispositions to respond to a stimulus by means of words, actions or things.[297] Or it may be the mediating element in the response, conditioned by the individual's past experience, a sort of pattern of value judgments.

Meaning has also been considered as a series of events, determined by their previous history, and described as different types of content words which identify, designate, prescribe, etc., in such contexts as legal, poetic, scientific and religious language.[211:291] Or meaning may be regarded simply as the regularly recurring "sames" in a stimulus-response situation.[441]

(ii) *Meaning as Expression*

Although the workings of the mind cannot be observed, their results as expressed in linguistic forms can be. Without taking mental or social situations into account, meaning has been described by showing which forms occur with which, that is, by the correlation of forms.

Another type of mechanical analysis of meaning is based on the probability that the forms will occur in a given text. If a form is sure to come up, the fact that it does, conveys nothing. But if it is uncertain to occur, it always carries some meaning whenever it does in fact occur.[224, 368]

(iii) *Meaning as Content*

Meaning has been described as a chain of verbal abstractions made from the content of reality. We start abstracting at the moment of perception when we observe only certain characteristics of the thing we see. Then we verbalize it (That's a cow); we generalize this (Cows give milk), leaving out more and more particular characteristics as we do. Then we continue climbing up the ladder of abstraction when we call the animal a bovine, quadruped, organism, etc. This is the view of General Semantics. [359]

But any element of language, as Saussure pointed out, has no meaning

75

by itself. It acquires meaning only through opposition to other elements in the same field. For example, a word like *language* (F. *langage*) has a different meaning in a language containing three related words (*langue, parole, discours*) than it has in one containing two (*speech, discourse*). Meaning is not a list of isolated abstractions; it can only be a system of such abstractions. Words and other elements of a language unite into conceptual areas of meaning forming a system of concepts covering all the needs of a community of speakers. If this system is pieced together, it shows the community's image of the world. This is meaning described as a semantic field.[590]

The semantic field reflects the social patterns of the community. It is made of basic key-words, which command an army of others.[588] The semantic area may be regarded as a network of hundreds of associations, each word of which is capable of being the centre of a web of associations radiating in all directions. A word like *man* might have as many as fifty such associations—chap, fellow, guy, gentleman, etc. The network is different for different languages, and for this reason has to be mastered by anyone learning a new language. (See also 2.3.2).

The concept of the semantic field may be important for language teaching. In our native language we know the part that each element occupies in the field. In a foreign language, we have to learn, not only the central meaning of each word, but also the part of the semantic field which it covers in relation to all other words of similar meaning.

(iv) *Meaning as Content and Expression*

Finally, meaning has been described as a relationship between content and expression. It may be an imputed and conventional relationship between a referent of content (e.g. an object) and a symbol of expression (e.g. a word), mediated by an act of reference (thought). This is imagined by Ogden and Richards in the form of a triangle.[233:11] (See Ch. 1.)

Meaning operates when the sign is a member of a certain context in the mind. When only part of the context recurs, it produces the same effect as if the entire context had occurred. This is the basis of the contextual theory of reference. Even though mind may here be regarded as an activity of the nervous system, it is not studied as such.

Had Saussure elaborated the science of signs, the semiology which he foresaw, he would have agreed with this as far as it goes.[113:33] Yet, from what he says in his course in general linguistics, he would have added the relationship between the word and our image of it. The entire relationship might be presented as in the following diagram.

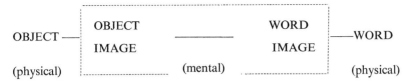

The relation between the object and its image depends, as Firth has pointed out, on the context in which it occurs. The language abstracts what is relevant from the context and distributes it throughout its system of expression, which includes sounds, words, word-patterns, word-endings, etc. Each of these handles its own share of the meaning. In Firth's technique of description, meaning is described as a complex of contextual relations.[143]

This complex of relations is what characterizes language as a whole. In a language, everything can be related to everything else. For the most distinctive feature of a language is that it is a system of systems.

2.5 THE SYSTEM OF SYSTEMS

If we add together the elements in all these systems—phonetics, grammar, vocabulary, meaning—we still do not get a complete picture of a language. For a language is not a group of these systems; it is a system of them—a system of systems. Many points in each of these systems are related to points in the other three systems. For example, every time a plural or third singular is used in the grammatical system, it brings into play a relationship with the phonetic system to determine whether the ending will be uttered as an /-s/, a /-z/, or an /-əz/, as in *cats, dogs,* and *matches*. The study of such relationships is sometimes called morpho-phonology or morpho-phonemics. Words in the vocabulary are connected with points in the grammar. For example, *tell* and *say* may be regarded as equivalent in the vocabulary, but the choice of one rather than the other forces the speaker to connect with a different series of sentence-structures; for instance:

I told him to go.
I said that he should go.

In these two sentence-structures the verbs are not interchangeable:*I said him to go* and *I told that he should go* are impossible.

The idea of a language as a system of systems can be illustrated, in its barest outline, by a diagram such as the one on the next page.

This system of systems functions as a whole whenever a person finds himself in a situation which requires speech, when he makes conversation, gives orders, argues, or relates an anecdote. What he says through this

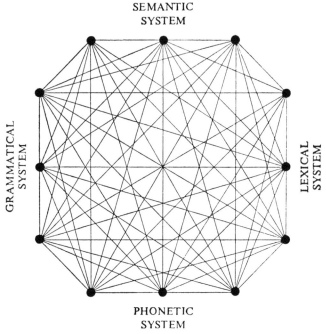

SEMANTIC
SYSTEM

GRAMMATICAL
SYSTEM

LEXICAL
SYSTEM

PHONETIC
SYSTEM

Language as an Interrelated System of Systems

system of systems, however, depends only partly on what he has to say. It also depends on what language he happens to be speaking.

It is well known that the formulas for greeting people, offering something, making requests, and giving thanks vary from language to language. Learners of a foreign language tend to assume that these should be the same in the second language as they are in the first. And they tend to make the same assumptions for the phonetics, grammar, and vocabulary of both languages. To discover what precisely these assumptions may be it is necessary to analyse the differences between the learner's language and the foreign one. How this may be done is the subject of the next chapter.

CHAPTER 3

Language Differences

OUTLINE

0. INTRODUCTION

Learning to speak a foreign language is the acquiring of an ability to express oneself in different sounds and different words through the use of a different grammar. Any sounds, words or items of grammar of the foreign language may or may not have counterparts in the native language. And these counterparts may have meanings, or content, which are similar to or considerably different from those of the other language.

Since such similarities and differences may be used as foundations for language-teaching methods, it is important to know what they are and how they may be analysed. They include those similarities and differences in pronunciation, grammar, vocabulary and usage between the first language and the second. An analysis of these results in differential descriptions of the two languages.

Differential description is of particular interest to language teaching because many of the difficulties in learning a second language are due to the fact that it differs from the first. So that if we subtract the characteristics of the first language from those of the second, what presumably remains is a list of the learner's difficulties.

If the description of a single language is a highly complex affair, the differential description of two languages is more than twice as complex. It involves not only the analysis of two languages, but a comparison of the differences in separate items and of the way they work together. It covers all levels of language and the relations between them—(1) Phonetics, (2) Grammar, (3) Lexicology, and (4) Stylistic usage.

1. DIFFERENTIAL PHONETICS

Comparing the phonetics and phonology of two languages involves not only the phonemes themselves but also their variants, the way they work together and the patterns superimposed upon them in complete utterances. It therefore involves differences in (1) articulation, (2) catenation, (3) rhythm, and (4) intonation.

1.1 DIFFERENCES IN ARTICULATION

In analysing differences in articulation we determine which phonemes of the second language do not exist in the first and which ones are simply pronounced differently. This is done for both (1) the vowels, and (2) the consonants.

1.1.1 **Vowel Phonemes**

Taking the vowels of English (RP) and Standard French as an example, we first make a table of the vowel articulations in each language. By putting these tables side by side, we can see at a glance which vowels are lacking in each language. This gives some idea of the differences in pronunciation. (See Ch. 2: 2.1.1 and notation table in 2.1.3.)

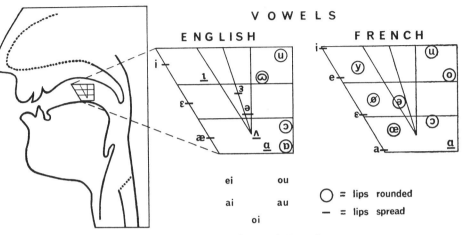

V O W E L S

The Vowels of English and French

When we examine the table, we find that French lacks the following English vowels and diphthongs: /ɜ/ *bird*, /ʌ/ *bud*, /æ/ *bad*, /ɪ/ *bid*, /ɒ/ *put*, /ou/ *boat*, /ei/ *bate*, /ai/ *bite*, /au/ *bough*, /oi/ *boy*; these are the ones which would have to be learnt by native French speakers learning English. On the other hand, English lacks the following French vowel phonemes: /o/ *tôt*, /e/ *thé*, /y/ *lune*, /ø/ *feu*, /œ/ *boeuf*; these are the ones which, along with the nasals, give English speakers difficulty when they learn French.

But the solution is not so simple as that. A comparison of the diagrams of lip and tongue positions of French and English shows that the differences are largely a matter of degree. Both English and French have the /ɛ/ sound, but in English it is located between the French /ɛ/ and /e/ sounds. And the English sound is further apart in tongue position from the French sound than are the two different phonemes, the French /ɔ/ and the English /ʌ/, which were listed as separate phonemes to be learned. The difference here, however, is mostly in lip position; so that if a French learner of English spreads his lips when he utters his sound /ɔ/ as in *comme*, he gets an acceptable equivalent of the English sound /ʌ/ as in *come*; or he gets an equally good approximation by retracting his tongue when uttering the /a/ of *batte* to sound like the English word *but*.

Secondly, although a sound may not exist as a phoneme in the mother tongue, certain words may nevertheless contain a close approximation to it. French, for example, does not have the English phonemes /ai/ as in *eye* or /ei/ as in *bay*, but it does have in many of its words certain combinations of sounds which come very close to the pronunciation of the English phonemes, words like *ail* /aj/ and *abeille* /ej/, which can be used as starting-points;[852] likewise with French *beurre* and Southern British *burr*. Any two languages are bound to contain a number of similar approximations.

1.1.2 Consonant Phonemes

In comparing the consonants of two languages, it is convenient, for ease of comparison, to arrange them into a single table:

CONSONANT DIFFERENCES: ENGLISH–FRENCH

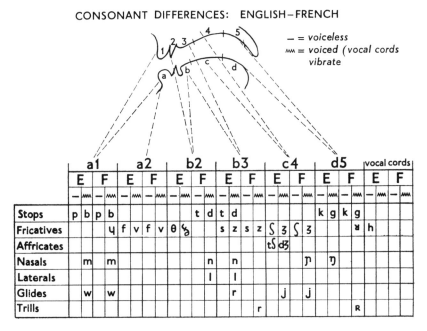

— = voiceless
ww = voiced (vocal cords vibrate)

Legend for each group: columns are E (English) and F (French); within each, the first symbol is voiceless (—) and the second is voiced (ww).

	a1 E	a1 F	a2 E	a2 F	b2 E	b2 F	b3 E	b3 F	c4 E	c4 F	d5 E	d5 F	vocal cords E	vocal cords F
Stops	p b	p b					t d	t d	k g	k g				
Fricatives			f v	ɥ f v	θ ð		s z	s z	ʃ ʒ	ʃ ʒ		ʁ	h	
Affricates									tʃ dʒ					
Nasals	m	m					n	n		ɲ	ŋ			
Laterals							l	l						
Glides	w	w					r		j	j				
Trills								r				R		

If we look at the table of consonants, we find the same sort of differences as we did in comparing the vowels of the two languages. We find, for example, that French does not have the phonemes /θ/ and /ð/ as in *thin* and *this*; and English lacks the French phoneme /ɥ/ as in *huit*.

But as we have seen in the case of the vowels, a simple comparison of phonemes does not reveal all the differences, and difficulties. For example, both English and French have an /r/ phoneme, but in English it is a glide and in French it is a fricative or a trill. And this difference is sufficient to make the sound one of the most difficult to master for the English or French learner studying the other's language. An added complication is that there are different varieties of /r/ in French; there is the fricative or breathed /ʁ/, the rolled guttural /ʀ/ (uvular trill) and the trilled alveolar (gum-ridge) /r/. A further example are the phonemes /n/, /l/, /t/, and /d/, which exist both in English and in French but are not pronounced in the same way, since in French the tongue is here more advanced than it is in English. But what the table does not reveal is the fact that there are words in English in which these sounds are pronounced with the tongue touching the teeth as it does in French, words like *tenth, health, wealth*, where the following dental /θ/ causes the advance of the tongue as far as the teeth.

A similar table of German and English sounds would show that English has no /ç/ phoneme as found in German words like *Chemie, ich, manches, Mädchen*. But that does not mean that English speakers never make the sound; for they often pronounce it in the first sound of words like *huge* and *hue*. The reason they have difficulty with the German sound is not because of the sound itself but because of its position in the word. In German it occurs before or after the vowel; in English, always before. For a similar reason it is difficult for English speakers to begin a word with the sound /ŋ/; for speakers of some African languages this is by no means difficult, for there are many words in these languages which begin with such a sound. In English, although the sound is very frequent at the end of words like *long, hang*, and *sing*, it never occurs at the beginning. Many mistakes in pronunciation are due, not to the fact that the sound or phoneme does not exist in the language being learned, but to the fact that it does not exist in the same positions. When a North German says that he likes the English pubs /pʌps/, it is not because he lacks a /b/ phoneme in his language, but because the final /-b/ in his language is always devoiced and becomes a /-p/, or something very close to it.

Comparative tables cannot reveal everything about the exact quality of each sound. For instance, they do not show the essential difference between English and French stop consonants. They do not reveal the fact, for example, that English initial voiceless stops are followed by a puff of air and that French stops are not, except in marginal and emphatic speech and in interjections like *hop* and *hep*. These differences in quality could be put into the table, however, by making it more complicated and by using a more detailed or narrower notation; but the tables would then not be limited to a comparative list of phonemes (the sounds which made a difference to the code of the language) but would include all speech sounds which made a difference to the ear.

Speech sounds themselves, however, do not give the whole picture.

What is equally important for the comprehension of the language is the way the sounds work together.

1.2 DIFFERENCES IN CATENATION

Catenation involves the answers to three main questions:

(1) What combinations of sounds does each language permit? (2) What changes occur in each language when different sounds come together? (3) How does each language separate or join together its words and phrases?

1.2.1 **Combinations Permitted**

Two languages may differ considerably in the combinations they permit; this may be a great source of difficulty in learning to pronounce a second language. For example, English, French, and Russian have the sounds /f/, /s/, /j/, but the English or French learner of Russian has difficulty in combining them into Russian words.

Not only the combinations themselves are different, but so are the positions in which they occur. There is, for example, a big difference in English in the number of combinations permitted before stressed vowels and the number allowed after them; there is also in Russian. But those permitted before the vowel in Russian are not the same as those permitted before the vowel in English; so that it is easy for an English speaker to end a word in /-ts/ as in the word *cats*, but harder for him to begin a word with /ts-/, as he will need to, if he happens to be learning Russian. For the same reason, Spanish learners of English will pronounce the word *steak* as /estek/ and *drugstore* as /drogestor/; for although Spanish has the combination /-st/ after a stressed vowel it does not have it before one, and never begins a word with /st-/.

In differential phonetics, therefore, a distinction must be made between combinations permitted before the stressed vowel and those allowed after it. As an example let us take those consonant combinations of English (RP) which occur before the stressed vowel or begin a word, tabulate them, and then superimpose on the table the consonant combinations of Spanish (Castilian) which can occur before the stressed vowel or begin a word. (See opposite table.)

When we look at the table, the first thing that strikes us is that English permits more consonant combinations than does Spanish, that those which are permitted in Spanish are limited to single consonant plus /l/ or /r/, and that of the English combinations not permitted in Spanish, most begin with an /s/, accounting for the Spanish pronunciation of words like *steak*, as we have seen above.

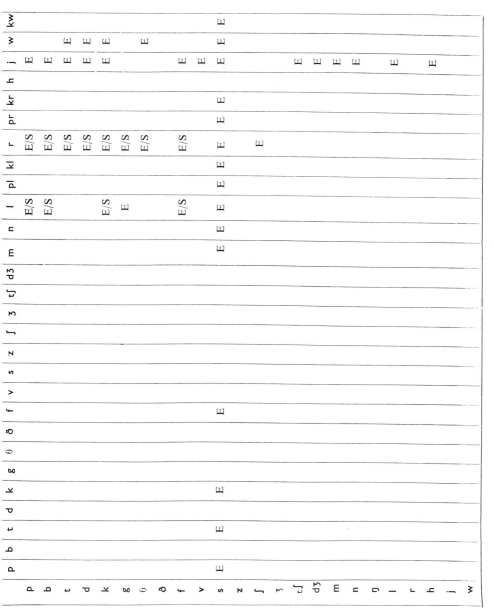

Initial Consonant Combinations in English (E) and Spanish (S)

1.2.2 Combinations Causing Sound Changes

Different languages react differently when two or more of their speech sounds come together.

When two sounds come together, one of them may change so as to become more similar to its neighbour (assimilation). It may do so in two ways: it may change its voicing, as when /n/+/s/ in the word *pens* is pronounced /penz/ (voice assimilation); or it may change its position in the mouth so as to have a place nearer to its neighbour, as when the /n/ of *tenth* touches the teeth because that is the place of the neighbouring /θ/ (place assimilation).

But which sound influences which? The influence may go in two directions: it may go forward, changing the sound that follows, as when *pens* is pronounced /penz/ (progressive assimilation); or it may go backward, changing the sound that precedes, as when alveolar /n/ becomes dental in *tenth* (regressive assimilation). With the same combination of sounds, one language may use one type, and another language, the other type. One language may assimilate in one direction; another language, in another. Although English and French make use of both forward and backward assimilation, English often goes forward in situations where French goes in the opposite direction; so that a French person learning English is likely to apply his backward-tending type of assimilation to the language he is learning and say /ðizbuk/ for *this book*, and /teigðis/ for *take this*. On the other hand, English learners of French, failing to apply this very type of assimilation tend to say /absolymã/ *absolument* for the usual /apsolymã/ and pronounce *médecin* with a voiced instead of a devoiced [d̥].[798]

When two or more sounds come together, languages differ in the tolerance with which they may let one of them drop (elision). A word like *clothes*, especially in such combinations as *clothes-closet* will generally be uttered without /ð/ as /klouzklɔzit/, and *waistcoat* without /t/ as /weiskout/. Elision in some languages may depend on whether or not the syllable is stressed. In English, for example, in unstressed syllables /h/ is often not pronounced; the sentence *He had his hat at the hotel* in normal speech, might be /i əd iz 'hat ət ði ot'el/. (See Ch. 2: 2.1.2, ii.)

1.2.3 Linking and Separating Words

Languages differ in the way they link together or separate words and phrases. The rules of liaison in French are well known to those who have studied the language in school, e.g. *les êtres* /lezɛtr/, but *les hêtres* /le ɛtr/. English has a different system of linking. It has three linking glides: /ʷ/, /ʲ/, and /ʳ/, *two* /ʷ/ *oranges*, *three* /ʲ/ *apples*, *more* /ʳ/ *apples*. French speakers of English, who do not use this system of glide-linking in their language, often seem to be adding an /h/: *two/h/oranges, three/h/apples*.

The differences in junction, or juncture, between languages are not always easy to analyse because so many different elements come under this rather abstract and very general notion—special linking sounds, as we have just seen, special separating sounds like the glottal stop in German, stress and intonation patterns, and even time, have all been suggested as elements. In test sentences like *Not all blackboards are black boards*, what separates the word *blackboards* from being identical to *black boards* may be the stress pattern, intonation pattern, co-articulation (pronouncing /k/ and /b/ together), pause, or any combination of these factors. And this combination may differ from one language to the next. (See also Ch. 2: 2.1.2, ii.)

1.3 DIFFERENCES IN RHYTHM

Of all differences in the pronunciation of two languages, rhythm is often the most noticeable. Faulty rhythm in English is perhaps responsible for more misunderstanding than any other feature.

What makes a differential description of rhythm complicated is that in some languages, like English, it is closely connected with a number of different factors. For example, as an English phrase increases in length, the number of syllables per beat of rhythm naturally increases, and this changes the stress of the words involved.

Examine the series:

> It's an 'old 'house.
> It's a 'nice old 'house.
> It's a 'very nice old 'house.
> It's a 'very, very nice old 'house.

Notice how the word-stress shifts from *old* to *nice* to *very*. In French, on the other hand, the stress is much more predictable. It is most often at the end of the word, phrase, or sentence—except when certain words are emphasized, as they frequently are in conversation.

1.4 DIFFERENCES IN INTONATION

Some pairs of languages have much greater differences in intonation than others. A Welshman is most easily recognized by his intonation—that is, when he uses the intonation patterns of his own language in English sentences.

When making a differential description of intonation patterns, it is necessary to show, not only which patterns exist in each language, but also when and for what they are used. The first task is difficult enough and it is hampered by lack of standard principles of analysis and of a standard notation. (See Ch. 2: 2.1.3, ii.)

The second task of giving a content or meaning to each intonation pattern is much more difficult, for a sentence structure may be used with a number of different intonation patterns. And intonation patterns may add special subtleties to the contexts in which they are used.[721]

2. DIFFERENTIAL GRAMMAR

By superimposing the grammatical patterns of one language upon those of another we can determine some of the main grammatical difficulties involved in learning the second language. We find for example that there is agreement in number and gender between noun and adjective in French, but not so in English, that the modifier comes before the noun in English, whereas it usually comes after it in French, *United Nations* giving *Nations Unies*, *some fresh air/de l'air frais*.

This gives us only the features which each grammar lacks or possesses in relation to the other. Differential grammar is not, as some practitioners of it would have us believe, simply a matter of superimposing an outline of the grammar of one language on that of another. What is required is a special type of description which accounts for all types of differences and equivalences.

To begin with, we must distinguish between what may be said and what must be said. When a French learner speaks English he is forced into making certain distinctions that he has always ignored in the grammar of his own language. The grammar of English forces him to decide on whether he is referring to a state or an action, whether the action is incomplete and continuous or simply habitual. In his own language, he does not, for example, have to make the distinction between a person who plays the piano regularly as a hobby or profession and one who happens to be playing on the piano at any given moment; the utterance *Il joue du piano* covers all such situations. In English, however, the distinction is compulsory, and the French learner must get into the habit of making it, for in one case he will have to say *He plays the piano*, and in the other, *He is playing the piano*. It is not that he is unable to make this distinction in his own language for he can distinguish *Il joue du piano* from *Il est en train de jouer du piano*; it is that he is not forced to make the distinction.

Secondly, in what must be said, we must distinguish unique forms from alternate ones. The grammar of our native language may provide a number of different ways of saying the same thing. Only one of these may be possible in the second language. Conversely, a single form in the native language may be equivalent to a number of different forms in the second language. For example, the adverb *well* in *He spoke well of you* may be equivalent to an adverb in French (*Il a très bien parlé de vous*) or it may be equivalent to a noun (*Il a dit du bien de vous*).

Although the examples we shall use are of the obligatory type, a complete differential grammar would also show what choices exist in each of the four grammatical categories—(1) the systems of the grammar, (2) the structures of the grammar, (3) the grammatical classes, and (4) the grammatical units.

2.1 DIFFERENCES IN SYSTEM

Not all languages have the same grammatical systems. Some languages have no cases, for example. A French learner of German has to get used to the whole idea of case inflection in nouns—nominative, genitive, dative and accusative—in addition to the use of the right case in the right place.

Languages with the same systems, however, do not use them in the same way. An English learner of French knows that both English and French have a passive voice; but he must learn to avoid equating one with the other, for an English passive may be equivalent to the French "pronominal voice". (E. *It's not done* / F. *Ça ne se fait pas.*)

Not only do different languages have different inflectional categories, but the same category may function differently in one language from the way it does in the other, so that the function of number, case, person and tense is different in each language.

Of the differences with the systems of the verb, let us take as an example the use of tense in English and French. The fact that English and French have many tenses in common does not mean that these are equivalent. Both English and French have a simple present tense, but the English present may often be equivalent to the French perfect, future, or future perfect:

I *hear* he's coming. =E. PRESENT / F. PERFECT =*J'ai appris* qu'il viendra.
I hope he *comes*. =E. PRESENT / F. FUTURE =J'espère qu'il *viendra*.
After we *finish*. =E. PRESENT / F. FUTURE =Après que nous
PERFECT *aurons fini.*

Both English and French have simple past tenses, but the English simple past is often the equivalent of the French imperfect, subjunctive, or present perfect:

He said he *knew*. =E. PAST / F. IMPERFECT =Il a dit qu'il le *savait*.
It's time he *shut up*. =E. PAST / F. SUBJUNCTIVE =Il est temps qu'il se *taise*.
I *saw* him yesterday. =E. PAST / F. PRES. PERF. =Je l'*ai vu* hier.

Conversely, if we were to take the French tenses as a starting-point, we would find a similar lack of equivalence with those of English. For example:

F. PRESENT   E. PERFECT
Nous le *connaissons* depuis des   We*'ve known* him for years.
    années.

2.2 DIFFERENCES IN STRUCTURE

Languages differ in the way they put words and phrases together. They differ in the order and interdependence of their items. A description of the structural differences between two languages will show such things as differences in word-order. For example, although adverbs are used in both French and English they do not always occupy the same relative position in the sentence.

F. Il répond *toujours* en français. / E. He *always* answers in French.
F. J'aime *beaucoup* le thé.   / E. I like tea *very much.*

A differential description will also show the differences in the type of interdependence of words in the sentence. In French, the tag-question is completely independent; in English, it depends on the main verb and must agree with it. A French learner of English must get used to making this agreement.

In the following example, note how the French *n'est-ce pas* always remains the same, being independent from the main clause with which it is used. On the other hand, the English equivalent is a dependent group which always has to agree with the main clause.

Il est prêt, n'*est*-ce pas?	He's ready, *isn't* he?
Il était prêt, n'*est*-ce pas?	He was ready, *wasn't* he?
Il sera prêt, n'*est*-ce pas?	He will be ready, *won't* he?
Il semble prêt, n'*est*-ce pas?	He seems ready, *doesn't* he?
Il semblait prêt, n-*est*-ce pas?	He seemed ready, *didn't* he?
Il n'est pas prêt, n'*est*-ce pas?	He isn't ready, *is* he?
Il n'était pas prêt, n'*est*-ce pas?	He wasn't ready, *was* he?
Il ne sera pas prêt, n'*est*-ce pas?	He won't be ready, *will* he?
Il ne semble pas prêt, n'*est*-ce pas?	He doesn't seem ready, *does* he?
Il ne semblait pas prêt, n'*est*-ce pas?	He didn't seem ready, *did* he?

2.3 DIFFERENT CLASSES

Although most languages have such word-classes or parts of speech as nouns, verbs and adjectives, the number of classes is not necessarily the same for all languages.

In languages with the same number of word-classes, each class does not necessarily do the same work as its counterpart in other languages. And in actual use, a word (e.g. a verb) may be equivalent in one language to a word belonging to an entirely different part of speech, in another language. This sort of equivalence is called transposition. [851:50]

A French verb, for example, may be equivalent to an English adverb, or adjective, or noun:

Il ne *tardera* pas à rentrer.   F. VERB / E. ADVERB   He'll *soon* be back.
Dès qu'on *essaie* d'être
    arbitraire.   F. VERB / E. NOUN   Any *attempt* to be arbitrary.

A French noun may be equivalent to an English adjective:

Au *début* du 19ᵉ siècle.   F. NOUN / E. ADJECTIVE   In the *early* 19th century.

And some French nouns are equivalent to English phrasal verbs:

Attention!   F. NOUN / E. PHRASAL VERB   *Look out!*

2.4 DIFFERENT UNITS

Words, phrases, sentences, etc., are the units of grammar. Not all languages have the same sort or the same number. Those that exist in both languages do not always correspond. A word in the first language may be equivalent to a phrase in the second, as when the English word *agenda* is equated to the French *ordre du jour*, or when the German word *druckfertig* has to be rendered into English as *ready for printing*.

Some of the difference may form a pattern, as may be seen by comparing English phrasal verbs with their French and German equivalents. Examine, for example, the following:

F. VERB	E. PHRASAL VERB		G. PREPOSITION	
Entrez.	Come in.	Go in.	Herein.	Hinein.
Sortez.	Come out.	Go out.	Heraus.	Hinaus.
Montez.	Come up.	Go up.	Herauf.	Hinauf.
Descendez.	Come down.	Go down.	Herunter.	Hinunter.

Many French verbs are equivalent to an English verb followed by some sort of modifier, giving such combinations as phrasal verbs. The structure of phrasal verbs enables English to make distinctions like the one between *come in* and *go in* which the French single verbs like *entrer* do not reveal.

The most important word units in a language are its structure words— its articles, prepositions, etc. Although these are limited in number, they are found in almost every utterance. Structure words of the first language, however, are not always equivalent to those of the second. For example, although the English structure word *some* is equivalent to the French partitive *du* in a few of its uses, it must very often be equated with other French structure words such as:

en	Give me *some*	Donnez m'*en*
un	*Some* fool has . . .	*Un* imbécile a . . .
quelque	For *some* time	Pendant *quelque* temps
environ	*Some* forty persons	*Environ* une quarantaine
certains	*Some* say that . . .	*Certains* disent que . . .

Structure words, however, are limited in number, forming part, as they do, of a closed system. (See Ch. 1.) If the word is not a structure word, it is part of an unlimited series requiring a different technique of differential description. This is the function of lexicology.

3. DIFFERENTIAL LEXICOLOGY

By far the most numerous items which distinguish one language from another are the items of vocabulary. Some of these may have the same form in both languages, but differ in content; or they may have different forms and the same content. The vocabulary of both languages may be compared from these two points of view: (1) equivalence in their forms of expression (expression equivalence), and (2) equivalence in meaning, or content (content equivalence).

3.1 EXPRESSION EQUIVALENCE

Words with similar expression forms in both languages may be described as to (1) what they stand for (their reference), and (2) the combinations, or collocations, into which they enter.

3.1.1 **Reference of Cognates**

If a word has the same form in both languages, it may (i) have the same referent, (ii) have different referents, or (iii) have some referents in common.

(i) A few words, like *jeep* in French and English, which look and sound alike in both languages may also refer to the same thing.

(ii) There may be a number of words which look and sound alike in both languages but which refer to different things. The word *car* in French has not the same referent as it has in English.

(iii) Many of the words which look and sound alike have some referents which are the same and some which are different. The word *administration* which looks alike in English and French sometimes refers to the same thing. It sometimes, however, refers to something different. In business texts, for example, *administration* in French is equivalent to *management* in English. When the reference is not external but internal, a reference to feelings or thoughts, the analysis of common and different referents is necessarily more complex, as the following example will indicate.

ENGLISH	FRENCH
Suggestions for improvement.	/ *Suggestions* en vue d'une amélioration.
It conveys a *suggestion* of regret.	/ Cela suscite une *nuance* de regret.
A *suggestion* of an accent.	/ Une *pointe* d'accent.

3.1.2 Collocation of Cognates

Cognates vary greatly in the combinations which each language allows them to enter. The German word *Winter* may seem like a close cognate of English *winter*, but in German, winter cannot be "around the corner" it can only be "at the door" (*vor der Tür*). Even identical geographical place names may have collocations which are quite different. The word *Rome* may refer to the same city in English and French; but to find the French equivalent of the collocation *When in Rome do as the Romans do*, one would have to consider howling with the wolves, *Il faut hurler avec les loups*.

Are such cognates of expression easier to learn than entirely different words? It depends on what we mean by learning a word. In the first place, we must distinguish the understanding of a word from its use. And in the understanding of the word we must further distinguish the spoken from the written form. In the understanding of speech, words spelt the same may be similar in a way which is not of much help. Words like *nation* which have the same spelling in English and in French sound quite differently when spoken: English /neiʃn/ and French /nasjɔ̃/. Nevertheless, it would be an exaggeration to jump to the conclusion that "there are no cognates of the ear."[888:204] German *Haus* and English *house* represent the same sequence of phonemes (homophones). As for those words with identical spellings in both languages (homographs) it may be a real help in reading a foreign text to recognize a familiar word; but it may lead the learner to assume that it is exactly the same word simply because, in a particular sentence, it happens to have the same form and meaning as in the native language.

Yet in the actual use of the language, homophones and homographs can be more of a peril than a help.[878] In order to use them safely, one has to go to all the trouble of learning the cases in which they are cognates and the cases in which they are not; and when they are similar, to what extent they are similar. For example, English *hound* and German *Hund* are similar in form and meaning. But in order to use the English word correctly, the German learner has to forget about the word *hound* and learn the word *dog*, the usual equivalent of German *Hund*.

There are many such confusing similarities between genetically related languages like English and German, languages that once have been identical and still are classed in the same family. But each language develops in its own way and undergoes different influences, so that what was once the same has become different in pronunciation, spelling or meaning.

There is also a great number of confusing similarities between languages which have been in close contact, languages like English and French. Although thousands of English words have been imported from the French language, few are now identical with their French counterparts. The reason is that only part of the meaning may have been imported in the first place, or the meaning may have changed and developed in a different direction from the original. Moreover the imported word has to be fitted into a different phonetic, grammatical and semantic structure. [866, 855, 871]

A third case is where the cognate has been imported from a common language. Words like *sugar—sucre—Zucker, coffee—café—Kaffee, tea—thé—Tee*, imported ultimately from the Near and Far East, may differ in spelling and pronunciation but have a number of formal and semantic elements in common.

3.2 CONTENT EQUIVALENCE

If two words are different in expression-form in both languages, they may likewise be analysed according to what they refer to and how they combine with other words, that is, according to (1) the reference of the counterparts in the other language, and (2) the collocations into which these counterparts enter.

3.2.1 Reference of Counterparts

If the two words are different in their form of expression, they may be identical in reference. The English word *cod* and the French word *morue* refer to the same fish. This one-to-one equivalence is popularly supposed to exist between all the words of both languages. And this is what many learners expect to be taught when they study a foreign language or when they look up words in a bilingual dictionary.

What is usually the case, however, is that the content equivalence is only partial, that a word in one language has a number of counterparts in the other. The English word *head*, for example, has a number of counterparts in French, since it covers an area of content which is only partly equivalent to that covered by the French *tête*, as a glance at the following list will reveal:

	tête	(of a person)
	chevet	(of a bed)
	face	(of a coin)
	pomme	(of a cane)
head =	bout	(of a match)
	haut bout	(of a table)
	directeur	(of an organization)
	mousse	(on beer)
	rubrique	(title)

Similarly, the French language makes a distinction between rivers which flow into the sea (*fleuve*) and those which do not (*rivière*); for English they are all rivers. It is this unexpected and seemingly unreasonable difference in grouping of referents that is responsible for so many of the errors in second language learning. When a German learner of English says "Close the door, please; there's a train." he has no reason to believe that the concepts of train and draught should not have a single label in English as they do in German, where the word *Zug* covers both.

3.2.2 Collocation of Counterparts

Even when the counterparts are equivalent, however, the equivalence rarely extends to the complete range of collocations into which each word may enter. The English verb *laugh* may be the counterpart of the French *rire* and the German *lachen*; but when we laugh up our sleeve in English we laugh in our beard in French (*dans sa barbe*), and in our fist in German (*ins Fäustchen*).

Differences in range of collocations have not been determined for any two languages. There have been studies of deceptive cognates,[878] useful treatments of certain areas of content in two languages,[870] and a large number of isolated instances unearthed in the compilation of some of the more complete bilingual dictionaries.

4. DIFFERENTIAL STYLISTICS

All the above differences in vocabulary, grammar and pronunciation do not add up to a complete differential analysis. This is because all levels of language work together as a whole (see Ch. 2). In the final analysis, what must be known is how each language, working as a system of systems, differs in the production of complete utterances in any given situation. One language may require a long utterance, and in the same situation, another language may require not more than a word or simply a gesture. It is a matter of style.

No differential analysis of two languages can be complete unless it includes (1) such differences in the contents of the responses to conventional situations. And since responses may themselves be made through different levels in each language, vocabulary, grammar, or pronunciation, the description must also include (2) the differences in the levels of expression.

4.1 DIFFERENT CONTENT OF RESPONSES

It is not sufficient to know that words and phrases in two languages may differ in content. These words and phrases appear in different sequences which may relate differently to the same situation. In all sorts of everyday situations involving such things as requests and courtesy, giving and getting, what is normally said in one language does not correspond in either form or content to what may be said, in the same circumstances, in another. For example, if a German speaker offers a stranger his seat, he will probably begin and end the act with what might be interpreted as *please* (*bitte*). Not so in English, where he may begin with a slight gesture or remark and end with a *Not at all* or *That's quite all right*. The German speaker of English, transferring his native stylistic pattern for such situations, will put his English words into the wrong situations, as the following little dialogue will illustrate:

SITUATION	GERMAN	ENGLISH	LEARNER
X. (offering his seat)	Bitte.	(gesture)	Please.
Y. (sitting down)	Danke.	Thanks.	Thanks.
X. (answering thanks)	Bitte.	Not at all.	Please.

Spanish is also quite different from English in the content of responses which it requires in conventional situations. Whereas a *This way, please* might be sufficient in English, Spanish may require of the same situation something like *Please do me the favour of coming this way*.

SPANISH	ENGLISH
Hagan ustedes el favor de pasar por aquí.	This way, please.

The stylistics of courtesy vary a great deal from language to language.

4.2 DIFFERENT LEVELS OF EXPRESSION

Equivalents lie often in entirely different levels of language. It may be a matter of vocabulary in one language and of grammar in another, of grammar in one language and of phonetics in another.

An item in English grammar may be equivalent to an item in the French vocabulary. For example, English: *I'm packing*/French: *Je suis en train de faire mes bagages.*

English word-order may be rendered at times by French intonation:

Are you a doctor?   Vous êtes médecin?

A change in English stress can be equivalent to a change in French vocabulary.

That's 'my business.   C'est mon *affaire.*
That's my 'business.   C'est mon *métier.*

And a change in English vocabulary often corresponds to a change in French tense.

He *heard* you were coming   Il *a su* que vous viendriez.
He *knew* you were coming.   Il *savait* que vous viendriez.

He *attempted* to escape   Il *a voulu* s'échapper.
He *wanted* to escape.   Il *voulait* s'échapper.

He *was able* to do it.   Il *a pu* le faire.
He *could* do it.   Il *pouvait* le faire.

Because each language is absolutely free to represent what it likes with its structure words, inflections, and parts of speech, in any level or combination whatever, the differential analysis of two languages can be a highly complex affair. Such an analysis, however, is necessary if we are to get a picture of the internal problems of foreign-language learning. As for the external problems of language learning, they will be the subject of the following chapter.

CHAPTER 4

Language Learning

OUTLINE

0. INTRODUCTION

This complex system of systems that has so long defied analysis by superior minds in so many fields of knowledge is mastered by an ordinary child before he starts school. And this involves duplicating the system of systems into a number of skills, each of which is a system of habits.

From the thousands of different speech sounds that strike the ear, each varying in quality, pitch, length, and loudness, the child learns to recognize a few significant dozen. He learns their possible combinations and the way these combinations may in turn vary in pitch, length and loudness. He learns not only the word and sentence forms of the language, but also the way these words and forms cut up, classify and label everything he sees, hears, smells and touches. He learns not only to recognize and comprehend all these features; he learns also how to use them.

Of the many possible sounds, the child succeeds in limiting himself to the significant ones and their possible combinations and modifications. He becomes skilled in making the complex relationships between the system of sounds, the system of words, the grammatical system, and in relating all these three to the system of meaning. He knows not only what is significant but what counts as significant and what does not.

In addition to the imitation of someone else, the speaker uses expressions which he could not have imitated. This implies the making of utterances never heard before, the capacity to go on doing the same sort of thing, the ability to extend indefinitely the use of the patterns in this complex system of systems and to use them to say whatever he may want to say.

How is such a thing possible? And if it is possible for one language, why not for two, three or more languages? What precisely is involved in learning a language? Is it different from learning anything else? Does it involve thinking or intelligence? And how is it possible to remember it all? All such questions closely affect language-teaching methods and techniques. But the answers to them are many and conflicting; they concern: (1) the learning of the first language, (2) the learning of the second language, and (3) the learning process itself and its relation to thinking and remembering.

1. LEARNING THE FIRST LANGUAGE

Learning to talk has been called the most difficult skill which we ever acquire as human beings. Although we manage to do so in the first few years of our lives, it takes us more than fifteen years before our language reaches what might be called our adult level. And indeed we continue increasing our knowledge of our language as long as we live, if only by learning new words for new things.

Our language is first of all an instrument through which we find out about our surroundings; it is a means of getting what we want, not a goal to be achieved. But we cannot start learning a language until we are physically ready for it. Although there may be differences between individuals, and although specialists in child speech do not agree on the details, most writers on the subject mention the same general stages of development. We shall consider these from two points of view, topic and time.

1.1 TOPICAL DEVELOPMENT

To understand the development of child speech it is necessary to take each of its components as separate topics. We therefore examine separately the development of the child's (1) phonetics, (2) vocabulary, (3) meanings, (4) grammar, (5) abstractions, (6) verbal behaviour, (7) comprehension and expression.

1.1.1 **The Child's Phonetics**

The main stages of a child's phonetic development are: (i) crying, (ii) babbling, (iii) lallation, and (iv) talking.

For the first few months, the noises the child makes are mostly oral or vowel-like sounds. For this period, the vowel-consonant ratio is about 5 to 1, as against the adult's which is about one to one, or 1 : 1.5, depending on the language.[367:143]

By the eighth or tenth month, a great variety of sounds have appeared, and the infant amuses himself by playing with them. He has now entered the babbling stage. His playing with sounds seems as aimless as any other form of infant play; but its function is to give needed exercise to his vocal organs, to those muscles and reflexes which he will need for speaking.

While this is going on, the child starts to acquire another ability without which he would never learn the language, the ability to imitate. It begins with babbling or jargon. The infant utters a sound which strikes his ears, and this stimulates him to repeat it again and again, until he becomes as it were, "trapped in the cycle of his own voice"; he does this with sounds, later with words and still later with sentences. This lallation, or echoing, performs the function of fixing the bond between the action of the speech organs and the acoustic results. If a sound from someone else enters the circuit, the child will also repeat it, reproducing the clearest part of the utterance.

As his imitation of others becomes better and better, his intelligibility also increases—an average of between 65 per cent to 99 per cent from the ages of two to three and a half. His phonological system, which begins as a limited one, becomes more and more like that of an adult. But it seems that the child has to re-learn, through imitation, sounds which he produced by muscular accident, during the babbling period; and he must learn when to use them. As he thus progresses, and as his imitative ability develops, he produces these sounds with greater and greater accuracy, since they no longer depend exclusively on the development of his organs of hearing and articulation.

1.1.2 The Child's Vocabulary

As a general rule, a child's first word appears in his first year. It may sometimes be heard as early as the eighth month. But many parents often find the first word earlier because, of all the combinations of sounds the child makes in his babbling period, some are bound to sound like real words, especially repeated syllables like [mama], [dada], [papa]. It is often difficult to say, however, when these syllables take on meaning.

From this point until the second year, the rate of increase in vocabulary is slow. Most of the words are nouns, which may also function as verbs or as whole sentences.

After the second year, however, the increase is extremely rapid, and the curve continues rising until the seventh or eighth year, when the rate of intake slows down again. By the third year, parts of speech other than the noun are being used, as the child grasps the structure of the language. But the majority of the words, until the age of five, are limited to the immediate surroundings. After the age of six, there is another rapid expansion, as the child listens and talks more and more, using words to learn words. And at the age of eight or nine, when he becomes skilled in reading, there is an even greater rate of increase in vocabulary. For since he has already mastered the essentials of the phonetic and grammatical structure of the language, he is able to concentrate on words.

1.1.3 The Development of Meaning

If crying is the first stage in the learning of sounds, it conceals three separate stages in the acquisition of meaning.

The first stage is muscular response to discomfort due to some physical stimulus. The resulting cry often brings about an improvement in the infant's environment. It is through such cries that the infant enables the parents to make his life more comfortable; this reinforces the cries and makes them regular.

In the second stage, the infant cries *in order* to bring about a change in his environment. With the aid of gestures, he helps his hearers to get at the meaning of his cries. The infant has now reached the stage where he controls his environment by the utterance of sounds.

In the third stage, the infant uses cries as a means of expression. When his needs have been satisfied, he can express his feelings of comfort; he can also express fear, loneliness and anger. As these cries become more and more differentiated, each is reinforced by the parents' interpretation of them, that is, by the meaning which they give them.

When this differentiation develops into a greater and greater variety of sounds, which result in the syllables of the babbling stage, the parents continue to try to give meaning to the sounds which their child makes. They may hear the child repeat a syllable like [da] again and again with all varieties of dental to palatal sounds: interpreting it as *dada*, the mother will repeat it, while taking every opportunity of pointing to the father as she does so. And eventually the child, by now used to imitating himself, will imitate others, repeating their words while pointing to things.

This pointing-and-naming stage soon develops into the naming-and-getting stage. At this stage, instead of using cries to get what he wants, he begins to use words for that purpose. He soon realizes that he usually gets better results by doing so. These words have meaning for him, therefore, in so far as they produce the results he wants to produce. Later on, he gets even better results with combinations of words and sentences.

The child always learns his meanings through contexts of situations. The more the context comprises, the greater the probability of his guessing the right meaning. Although sounds are learned by imitation, meanings are acquired by association and developed through reinforcement.

The child learns one meaning at a time. The first meaning may not always be the most usual. It may even be a rare, figurative or idiosyncratic meaning, But it is the meanings which best fit his needs that survive.

Having often more meanings than words, however, more things to say than means of saying them, the child extends by analogy those meanings of words which he already knows. For example, he might extend the meaning of *dada* to include all men. It is only in such cases as these, where the analogy is incorrect, that we notice what the child's mind is doing.

By now the child is continually making use of analogy, continually trying to apply a rule, as it were, always trying to find the regularly recurring elements of the language. And here again his analogy may not always be right, for he will regularize all plurals to produce utterances like *tooths* and *foots* and invent regular past participles like *bringed* and *teached*. Here he enters the realm of grammar, where he must learn to make further distinctions.

1.1.4 **The Development of Grammar**

It is through analogy that the child learns the grammar of the language. But he does not usually acquire a mastery of all its forms until after he has entered school.

A child's first sentences are single words with a variety of meanings, mostly imperative. Later he makes use of word groups, with these same sentence meanings, but only as if they were long words. After the age when he begins to count, the child can remember the order of sequences, and this gives him a basis for his mastery of sentence structure. As he masters sentence structure, the emotionally intoned word-sentence of his earlier period becomes less and less frequent. Plurals, word-endings and different parts of speech begin to appear. After the age of four, simple sentences become more and more complex. But we may have to wait until after the age of ten before we can expect the child to understand grammar as grammar.

1.1.5 **Abstraction**

It is generally after the age of ten that the unilingual child begins to make a distinction between a word and its context. Yet the development of the power of abstraction begins at a much earlier age, as early as the age of four, according to Stern.[938]

Both Stern and Piaget have demonstrated that concepts of volume, quantity, weight, time and dimension, being abstractions, are not self-evident to the child. They have to be learned. It is not self-evident to the child that a part must necessarily be a part of a whole, that a brother must be a brother to someone. Nor does the child always realize that speech and thought may be distinct. Ideas come from the mouth.[931:256] Thought is contained in the voice, and the wind comes from the trees. As the child develops mentally, he first distinguishes speech from thought and only later sees the relationship between them.

1.1.6 **Verbal Behaviour and Environment**

Contact with parents and playmates forces the child to make distinctions and to form abstractions. From the age of three or four, the child gets more and more of his language from his playmates. If his parents should have a foreign accent, the child will rarely adopt it. As Jespersen has pointed out, the main factors in the development of the language of children are the children they play with.[632]

A child learns his language in a social environment and for social purposes. But once he has acquired the language, his whole inner life is changed. He is now independent of people around him, no longer relies on them, and can make his own judgments and decisions.[935] And as he thus develops, he relies less and less on imitation and more and more on analysis. The more he uses the language, the more he becomes a prisoner of its structure and the structure of the society in which it is used.

1.1.7 Comprehension and Speech

Parents are often surprised to hear their child utter a word which they believe he has never heard. The fact is that a child may repeat a word only after a fairly long interval of time. The interval between his first hearing a word and his first use of it may be as long as several months.

What happens during the interval? The child first makes a record of the meaning of the concept and of the sound of the word. He then establishes a link between them. To do so, he has to make a generalization from a number of particular instances. But little is known about the process. For although researchers have often noted what a child says, no one seems to have recorded what a child hears. The exact relationship between both cannot yet therefore be established. But we do know that the growth of understanding does have a different chronology from that of utterance.

1.2 CHRONOLOGICAL DEVELOPMENT

The chronological development of child speech may be seen on the next page in an outline based on the findings of Grégoire,[935] Piaget,[937] Stern,[939] Leopold,[945] Kaper,[920] Gesell,[934] and others.

Child language starts with a cry, which becomes more and more differentiated as time goes on, until it develops into a sentence. The first distinction is between different emotions, cries of pain and pleasure. Then after a few months, the child tries out different sounds, exercising his speech organs (babbling). He then imitates his own sounds (lallation), and later those of others. When the parents hear certain sound combinations they take them for words, and by acting as if they had meaning for the infant, they help establish associations between these sound combinations and certain persons or objects. These single words eventually take care of whole situations, functioning as sentences, especially as imperatives. As the infant increases his vocabulary, he begins to differentiate in the situation between elements like actor and action, and to combine these into two-word phrases like the noun-verb combination.

The number of words in these phrases increases and, as it does so, the child perceives distinctions in word-order, syntax and inflections. At this stage the child is qualitatively able to speak. He has most of the basic

CHRONOLOGY OF CHILD LANGUAGE

	Understanding	*Utterance*
3 months	Recognizes human voice. No memory. Bound to present. Little co-ordination between grasping and mouthing.	Social smile. Spontaneous, disorganized sounds. Babbling.
6 months	Recognizes friendly and unfriendly tones.	Many vowel sounds. Lallation.
9 months	Reacts to gesture. Preference for certain words.	All varieties of sound and sound combinations.
12 months	Responds to simple commands.	Verbal play. Jargon stage. First few words as conditioned responses.
18 months	Points to simple things on command. Follows simple directions.	About a dozen words or more. Verbal behaviour accompanied by gesture. Beginning of language as communication. Jargon begins to disappear. Beginning of two-word phrases. Vocabulary begins sharp rise.
2 years	Understands commands referring to present situation. May understand several hundred words.	Jargon dropped. Language as communication. Great individual variation in pronunciation. Vocabulary in the hundreds. Simple phrases. Pronouns. Verbalizes wants.
3 years	Understands questions referring to past.	Large increase in vocabulary. Gets structure right. Plurals, tenses, parts of speech, sentence patterns. Narrates past experience. Language as a substitute for action.
4 years	Great range of understanding. Still confuses periods of time.	Speech skills perfected. No baby talk. Rambling torrent of speech. Age of loquacity.
5 years	Understands past events of childhood. May understand over two thousand words.	Briefer and more critical responses. Begins counting and printing. More complex sentences. Large vocabulary.
6–8 years	Complete understanding of everyday utterances. Begins reading, thus increasing passive vocabulary.	Complete speech habits of the language. Only need is reinforcing them through practice. Holds on to patterns learned.

elements of the language, but he has to increase their number and refine his distinctions in grammar and meaning. Note that, in the process, the child proceeds from sounds to distinctive sounds, to words, to phrases, to sentences.

The various elements of language seem to develop at different rates, as can be noticed by anyone who has heard a child speaking fluently without using all the sounds of the language, using /w/ for both /r/ and /w/, for example.[947]

We can now sum up by enumerating the main procedures involved in learning the first language. They are: (i) trial-and-error, (ii) rote memory, (iii) imitation, (iv) association, and (v) analogy.

Can these procedures also apply to the learning of a second language? We must first see what the learning of a second language involves.

2. LEARNING SECOND LANGUAGES

The learning of one language in childhood is an inevitable process; the learning of a second language is a special accomplishment. Every year millions of people start learning a second language, but very few succeed in mastering it. Why is this so?

The first and most obvious reason is that the learner of a second language has had experience with another language. The type and amount of experience varies from person to person. A person who has been using only one language since early childhood has habits of thought which are closely tied to his habits of language. The language he uses is now part of his experience with the world of actions and things. When he was a child, an increase in this experience was always connected with an increase in language learning.

Now he is faced with the problem of dealing with these same surroundings and this same experience in an entirely different way, not only with different sounds and words and sentences, but with different groupings of things, persons and actions, and different arrangements of time, space and matter, all of which may conflict with the structure of his native language. It is this native language structure—so much a part of his thought—which is his first obstacle to learning a new language. For he will always tend to put the raw material of his experience into the groups fashioned for him by his first language. What he now needs is a second grouping of his surroundings and experience. And this second grouping cannot be made in the same way and under the same conditions as the first.

The older the second-language learner is, the more he wants to know the what and the why of anything he is doing. So he tends to form consciously the habits which, in his native language, he had formed unconsciously. And if he knows something of the grammar of his native language he will try to find in the second language grammar features which are equivalent to those of his first language.

By the time he has reached the period of adolescence, the beginner in a second language has so overlearned his first language that it is hard for him to get used to saying the same things in a different way. In his native language, he knows what to expect. Even though he should hear only a random half of what is said, his built-in statistical feeling for the language helps him to make out the whole of it. This is not true for the language he is learning.

The learning of the first language follows the same pattern for everyone; the learning of a second language can take on a variety of patterns. Dozens of factors are involved, each highly variable, and each related to other factors. It is doubtful whether the present state of our knowledge can make possible a complete analysis of all these factors, for we are even not sure what precisely the understanding and speaking of a language involves. [951:27] Nevertheless, there are all sorts of notions, opinions and beliefs on what influences language learning. And these affect the teaching of languages, through syllabus, texts, policy, and teaching techniques. What are the main influences which determine the type and degree of second-language learning? They are of three types: (1) linguistic, (2) social, and (3) psychological.

2.1 LINGUISTIC

Process and progress in second-language learning depend on (1) how the second language differs from the first, and (2) on how much the first language interferes with the second.

2.1.1 **Differences**

The problem of learning a second language which is highly similar to the first is not the same as learning a language which is entirely dissimilar. The problems of the Frisian who is learning Dutch are not the same as those of the Chinese who is learning English.

Similarities between languages may be of different sorts and different origins. The two languages may be similar because they belong to the same family, as is the case for Spanish and Italian. Or they may be similar because one is a modified or creolized form of the other, as is the case for French and Haitian. Or one language may have had a great influence on the other through past contact, as is the case for the influence of French on the English vocabulary. Or both may have contributed elements to a mixed language which serves as a lingua franca.[975] The similarities and differences may be in phonology, grammar, vocabulary, stylistics or graphics.

In the realm of phonology, the difficulty of a second language depends both on the sounds themselves and on their ability to combine. For example, a Japanese learning English has more phonology to learn than a German learning English.

Differences in grammar make it more difficult for an Englishman to learn Russian than for a Bulgarian, whose language belongs to the same family. Similarities, however, are not limited to related languages; similar grammatical features may exist in entirely unrelated languages such as Hungarian and German, both of which have separable prefixes.

In the field of vocabulary, the importation of large numbers of words into a language can make learning it easier for those from whose language the words originally came. A Frenchman reading English can recognize a good percentage of familiar words like *page, nation, religion,* since the language he is reading has been importing French words since the Middle Ages.

Because of similarities in units of meaning and style, it is often easier to understand a language belonging to the same civilization than it is to make out one embedded in a strange culture.

One of the first differences which strike the eye, however, is the way the language is written. For an alphabet-based Englishman, Chinese looks more difficult than Russian, which is at least alphabetical; Russian, more difficult than Polish, which uses the same alphabet as English does.

Each of these types of differences may interfere in a different way with the learning of a second language.

2.1.2 Interference

The type of interference depends on whether the learner is speaking the language or simply trying to understand what he hears or what he reads.

If he is learning to speak the language, the deeply ingrained patterns of his first language will interfere with those of the language he is learning. When a situation presents itself, the stronger associations of his first language will unconsciously respond; this is the cause of much of the difficulty in learning to speak a second language.

On the other hand, if he is learning simply to understand the language, the greater the similarity between the first language and the second, the easier the latter will be to understand. In using the language, however, it is the similarity that may cause interference by the misuse of such things as deceptive cognates, like *local* and *location* in French and English. For there is a big difference between learning an item and learning how to use it. It is of course true that if a learner does not have an item in his first language he is likely to have trouble with it when learning the second language, especially if the item is a phonetic one. He will first tend to make the new language conform to the patterns of his first language. But how he will do so is hard to predict.

Interference may take the form of replacement of one item by another. Or it may be only a partial influence. For it is not a single feature, but a complex of features, that strikes the learner when he copes with a new language. It is never one sound that strikes the learner's ear, but a complex of sounds. A /b/, for instance strikes the learner's ear, not as a simple sound, but as an acoustic complex, resulting from an articulatory complex which includes lip closure, stoppage of the air and vibration of the vocal cords to produce voice. And the amount of voice varies from language to language, as can be illustrated by the approximate relative differences in the voicing (. . . .) of a /b/ in German, English, French and Russian:

——— . . . . . . ———	German
——— . . . . ——–	English
— . . . . —	French
– . . . . –	Russian

Anyone studying the interference in the pronunciation of a learner studying a second language cannot afford to ignore such phonetic facts, as some linguists have done, limiting themselves to a comparison of only the relevant sounds, the phonemes, of both languages (see Ch. 3). A purely phonological analysis of German, for example, would reveal the fact that German words do not end in voiced stops like /b/, /d/ and /g/ but in voiceless stops like /p/, /t/, and /k/. Reasoning from this, one would predict that when a German learner imitated a word like *herb* or, better still, its French equivalent *herbe*, he would come out with the pronunciation [herp]. But he might just as well imitate it as [herm], as the author's experiments have in fact indicated. This is because his /m/ phoneme in certain positions has almost as much voice as the foreign /b/ which strikes his ears.

A simple sound like /b/ may also differ from language to language in the amount of air stopped by the closing of the lips. Some languages close them more tightly than others. Take for example the difference between the English and Spanish /b/ in the pronunciation of such words as *Cuba*. The Spanish /b/ is so open that it sounds almost like a /v/ to an English ear.

There are also such differences as the action of the tongue and throat when the lips are closed. Some native French speakers will accompany their /b/ or /p/ with a catch in the throat or glottal stop whenever they stress such words as *bébé* and *père*. There is a further difference between languages in what happens when the lips are opened. In some languages, like English and German, there will be a puff of air or aspiration, of which there are different degrees in different languages. To a French ear this may sound almost as if the speaker is adding an /h/.

All this multiplicity of sound features strikes the ear of the learner. Some he may notice; others he may not. He will more readily notice those that are found in his first language; but these too are complexes of sound. And since he has the choice of a number of combinations, it is very difficult in practice to predict accurately what he hears or what he will consequently say.

The problem is considerably more complex in the realms of grammar and meaning, since there are more elements that may vary.

Not all errors in the second language, however, are due to the structure of the first. Many are due to incomplete learning. The learner may have "covered" the foreign pattern only in so far as he responds to the stimulus "different" from that of his own language. But he cannot remember how it is different. So rather than halt the flow of speech he simply makes a wild guess, making sure not to say something similar to his native language.

A third cause of errors in learning a second language is the extension by analogy of patterns one has already learned in that language. When a foreign speaker of English says: "I would like to get married and have a couple of childs," he may simply be extending by analogy the regular endings of English plurals which he has heard in the same grouping of words, *couple of kids: couple of childs*. He is not necessarily transferring the pattern of his mother tongue into the second language.

A fourth cause is confusion. When a German learner of English says *What that is?* he is not imitating the sentence pattern of his native language, since it happens to be the same, *Was ist das?* He is simply being confused, perhaps because he is trying to absorb too much at a time. An incorrect pattern hit upon this way may become just as habitual as one imported from his first language, as was the case of the old German shopkeeper who, for the rest of her life, always greeted American soldiers with a "How do you do you do."

Certain linguists have tried to reduce the prediction of error in second language learning to an exact science on the analogy of the way the physical sciences, studying the laws of nature, can predict such things as eclipses and chemical reactions. But in the field of linguistic usage one is in a different realm from that of the physical sciences. One cannot predict a person's use of language in the same way as an astronomer predicts an eclipse. If mistakes are made in language learning one may indeed discover their causes; but one cannot say with certainty which mistakes will be made and when they will be made. Moreover, the first language itself is not the only influence on second language learning. There are also important and complex social and psychological influences.

2.2 SOCIAL

Since language is essentially a social phenomenon, the social influences on its acquisition are numerous and interrelated in complex ways. It is the play of these influences on the growing mind that results in the learning of the first language; social influences are also responsible for the learning and maintenance of second languages. These may be analysed as (1) a number of language contacts operated by (2) a number of different factors.

2.2.1 **Contacts**

The groups of persons with whom we continually use a language have some effect on the manner and skill with which we use it; so do the situations in which we are placed. These groups or contacts may be enumerated as follows: (i) those with whom we live (the home group); (ii) those near whom we live (the community); (iii) those with whom we work (the occupational group); (iv) those with whom we learn (the school group); (v) those of the same national background (the ethnic group); (vi) those with whom we pray (the church group); (vii) those with whom we play (the play group); (viii) such non-personal and passive contacts as radio, television and the cinema; and (ix) such contacts with the written language as provided by our reading matter.

(i) *Home*

Learning a second language at home is an older practice than learning one at school. Long before modern foreign languages were introduced into the schools, it was usual for families who could afford it to have a foreign person in the home as governess to the children. French governesses were common in well-to-do families in England and Russia during the eighteenth and nineteenth centuries.

Despite the fact that the schools now claim to do the job for them, some families still initiate their children into a second language by engaging foreign maids and nurses. Others send their children to live or work in a foreign family for the purpose of acquiring the language. There are even agencies which arrange a temporary exchange of children between families speaking different languages; and there are many sorts of private arrangements through the intermediary of friends and newspapers.

Some families who speak a language other than that of the community insist on keeping it as the home language. Whether or not this becomes the predominant language of the children depends on the influence of other factors as well. In families where one of the parents knows another language, that language may be used as one of the home languages. Studies of the effects of such a practice have been made by Ronjat,[984] Pavlovitch,[983] and Leopold[981] to test the theory that two languages can be acquired for the same effort as one. Each experiment used Grammont's formula: *une personne, une langue*, whereby the child always spoke the same language to the same person, one language to the mother and another language to the father.[946] None of the studies found any permanent interference of one language with the other. But the predominant language of the child was eventually the language of the community.

(ii) *Community*

The community is perhaps the most important context for the learning and maintenance of a language. A child is surrounded by the language of the community into which he is born, and this soon takes the place of the home as the most important influence on his speech. Children talk like other children.

A learner of a second language, however, may have no contact with a community in which the language is spoken, and this may be one of the reasons for his failure to learn or maintain his second language. A corrective to this has been the periods of foreign residence which language learners have long found profitable. They have been so profitable, in fact, that some countries now require a period of foreign residence as part of the qualifications of their language teachers.

(iii) *Occupation*

Although the majority of people generally use in their work the same language as that of the community, there are many whose occupation involves the use of a second language.

Aside from those who work for foreign firms, there is an ever-increasing number of people who deal with foreign customers in various parts of the world.

In occupations like medical work, hotel work, salesmanship and others that serve the public, a person's clients may determine the language which he generally uses at work.

In technical occupations, it is often the subject-matter which determines the language. An increasing number of technicians trained through a second language prefer that language when speaking about their speciality.

(iv) *School*

The first contact that most people have with a second language, however, is in school; and for the majority, this is often the only contact they ever get. Many have to wait until secondary school before they begin the second language.

It makes a big difference, however, if some or all of the instruction in the school is given in the learner's second language. Some parents go to a lot of trouble and expense to send their children to such schools in foreign countries, ethnic communities or bilingual areas.

In certain schools, for purely linguistic reasons, a second language has been known to be used as a medium of instruction for one or two subjects. This is the practice in certain bilingual schools. It is important, however, to determine which subject-matter is taught in the second language, since it will have an influence on the vocabulary of the learner. If it should be history, literature, and religion, the influence will be different from that where it happens to be biology, geography and arithmetic.[994]

Schooling may also be a matter of private tuition. Many people believe that they learn more from a private tutor because they have a longer period of direct contact with the language, and because of this they are quite willing to engage one for themselves or for their children.

(v) *The Ethnic Group*

Ethnic groups tend to maintain the use of second languages through meetings, public lectures and social functions. In a community with no other possible contact with the language, regular attendance at such social and cultural functions may maintain and even improve a person's skill in a second language.

(vi) *Church*

Church groups are often connected with the ethnic groups. But a person may associate with one and ignore the other. It is not unusual for a foreign family to ignore their ethnic group and yet bring the children to their church and Sunday school, where the sermon and instructions are given in a language which is not that of the community.

(vii) *Play Group*

The language of the group of persons with whom one plays, is not limited to the school. It is true that a group of foreign students in a unilingual school may always play together. But adults in a foreign environment tend to do likewise.

In the field of sports and recreation, certain clubs may have a majority of members who speak a language which is not that of the area. Persons who join such clubs may hear nothing but their second language.

(viii) *Radio, Television, Cinema*

These powerful media of mass communication can give millions of people their only contact with a second language. People have been known to succeed in learning a second language and develop an acceptable accent in it, simply through the radio, although their opportunity for speaking the language was limited. Television is an even greater and more powerful medium of contact, since the objects and gestures the viewer sees are often a clue to the meaning of what he hears. The cinema has the same advantages. Regular attendance at foreign films may succeed in maintaining a person's comprehension of the second language.

(ix) *Reading Matter*

Although this involves neither listening to the language nor speaking it, reading is an important means of maintaining contact with a second language. This is because it may give all the features of the spoken language except the sounds.

Moreover, it is often the most available form of contact with the language, since it is something that one can always have at hand. People with no other means of contact with a language they once knew, have often kept themselves from forgetting it completely by frequent and abundant reading of books, newspapers, or magazines.

2.2.2 Factors

Each of these types of contact may vary according to the following factors: (i) time, (ii) population, (iii) use, (iv) skills, (v) standard, (vi) attitude, (vii) pressure.

(i) *Time*

The amount of time spent in learning a second language is one of the most important factors in mastering and maintaining it. Persons who start a second language in the first years of primary school and use it continually are obviously further ahead than those who start only in secondary school.

The time element is often confused with other factors, however. Some language-teaching methods have been judged as excellent when the time element, not the method, was the most important factor involved. After World War II, the so-called "army-method" was said to be better than methods employed in schools. But some army courses lasted nine full months during which the learners did nothing but study the language.

Time is one of the main reasons why the first language is so thoroughly mastered. In learning the first language a lot of time is first spent in listening, and once the language begins to be used, almost all the schooling is done in it. It is practised for the rest of the speaker's life. But when a language is considered as just another school subject, the amount of time given to it is extremely limited; F. Marty estimates an average of 250 hours a year for the second language as taught in school as against some 5,000 hours a year for the learning of the first language at home.[1704]

It is difficult to say the number of hours needed to learn a second language. It depends not only on the proficiency aimed at, but also on a great number of personal and social variables. Nevertheless Gouin was bold enough to claim that it takes 900 hours.[1277:294] This figure could hardly be accurate for everyone and for every language.

(ii) *Population*

Occasions for speaking a second language largely depend on the number of persons with whom one comes in contact. If the community is a large metropolis there will be more occasions of contact than if it is an isolated hamlet. If two persons in a factory speak a second language there will obviously be less opportunity than if there are several hundred factory workers who speak the language.

(iii) *Use*

Another important factor in the mastery or maintenance of a second language is what the language happens to be used for. If it is used as a medium of instruction it will not have the same effect as if it is used as a medium of entertainment. Part of the success in learning the first language is due to the fact that it is used for almost everything. For a child "everything" is not very much; but he has great success in operating in his limited area, although he may take a lot of time to master the language.

Part of the failure in learning a second language is that it is used too soon for too much. If an adult learner were to remain within a range of ideas and vocabulary as narrow as that of the child, and if nothing more were demanded of him, his performance might be quite surprising.[951:71]

(iv) *Skills*

Whether a person makes use of all the language skills or only one of them, will also have some effect on his mastery of a second language. His occupation might involve him in all the language skills or only in one of them.

The skill with which a person starts might decide his eventual mastery of the language. If he begins with reading and becomes skilled in it, he may have a different pronunciation from that which he would have had if he had started with the spoken language.

There is a common element, however, in all skills, and that is the language itself. And knowledge of this is presumably transferable from one skill to the other (see Ch. 8). Goldstein found that those who read rapidly also understand the spoken language more rapidly than do those who read slowly.[952]

(v) *Standard*

The social, regional and cultural level at which the language is spoken is another factor. A person's most important or most frequent contact may be with speakers of a regional or social dialect of the language. Or it may be with persons having an imperfect knowledge of it.

The sort of hearer also affects the language of the person speaking. Persons who continually speak to foreigners have been known to develop a special sort of accent based, not on the speech of the foreigners, but on their own word-for-word effort to make themselves understood—much of it unnecessary.

(vi) *Attitude*

A speaker may have different sorts of attitudes to his various contacts, attitudes toward the persons he meets, toward certain situations, and even toward the language itself, and to language-learning in general. And his hearers may have certain attitudes toward him as a foreign speaker.

His attitude may be informal at home, formal at school, solemn in church, and colloquial at play. With some persons he will be intimate, with others respectful. He may avoid using his second language in certain situations because he is ashamed of his accent. In other situations, he may prefer the second language because he is ashamed of his first, since it may be a small dialect, or the language of an unpopular country or community. It has been said that some speakers of minority languages even harbour an attitude of disrespect toward their first language and an admiration for their second. Certain speakers of majority languages, like German, may even consider languages like Italian more "beautiful" than their own.

(vii) *Pressure*

In any of the areas of contact with others, a variety of social pressures may influence an individual's use of his second language. These pressures may be (a) economic, (b) administrative, (c) cultural, (d) political, (e) military, (f) historical, or (g) religious.

(a) Economic: People may have to learn a second language in order to find a job or to improve their economic standing. For speakers of a minority language in an ethnic community, the knowledge of the majority language may be an economic necessity. Foreign parents may even insist on making the majority language the language of the home, in an effort to prevent their children from becoming economically under-privileged. This of course, depends on what the language is. For the contrary may also be true; if the foreign language has a high economic value this may be a sufficient reason for retaining it.

(b) Administrative: In some countries, administrators and civil servants are required to master a second language. A few governments even give an annual bonus for each language the civil servant succeeds in mastering or in maintaining.

(c) Cultural: The cultural riches available through some languages make a knowledge of them almost essential for any educated man. Greek, Latin, and French have long been learned for purely cultural reasons.

A language may be so cultured, however, that it may be quite inaccessible to some speakers. In Sanskrit drama, for example, women and slaves speak a Prakrit.

(d) Political: Political pressure can make the learning of certain languages compulsory. This may be due to the fact that two countries are close together or on friendly terms. There is a tendency to learn the language of friendly countries or of rich and powerful neighbours. Or a language may be politically imposed on a nation by a power having dominance over it. This is the case with certain colonial languages. After many years of such dominance the imported language may become the most important one, serve as the language of the country, and develop its own regional standard. Contrariwise, a political regime may be so nationalistic as to discourage citizens from acquiring a native-like knowledge of the foreign language for fear of losing their loyalty.

(e) Military: People serving in a foreign army must learn something of the language which the army uses. The fact that two countries make a military treaty may result in large-scale language teaching, such as the teaching of English to parts of the Chinese Navy during World War II to permit them to take instruction in the manning of American ships. The large-scale teaching of English to the Indian Army during the same period is another example. Military occupation may also result in second-language learning, either by the populace, by the military, or by both.

(f) Historical: Past relationships between two countries may determine which languages will be learned. The historical role of Britain in India has made English an important second language in that country.[401]

(g) Religious: The expansion of great religions has resulted in the widespread learning of second languages—Arabic with Islam, Greek and Latin with Christianity. And today persons in different parts of the world entering religious orders may have to learn either Latin, Greek, Coptic, Sanskrit, Arabic, or Old Church Slavonic, depending on the religion, rite, or sect of the order.

As with all the other factors, each of these pressures may operate in any area of contact. We can best show this interrelationship through the following table. If units of measurement could be established for the factors of time, population, use, skill, standard, attitude and pressures, a social profile of language learning could be drawn for both individuals and groups.

Factors \ Contacts	HOME	COMMUNITY	OCCUPATION	SCHOOL	ETHNIC GROUP	CHURCH	PLAY GROUP	RADIO & TV	READING
TIME									
POPULATION									
USE									
SKILLS									
STANDARD									
ATTITUDE									
PRESSURES :									
Economic									
Administrative									
Cultural									
Political									
Military									
Historical									
Religious									

Social Variables in Language Learning

2.3 PSYCHOLOGICAL

The ability to learn a second language varies from person to person. There are persons who immigrate in their youth and yet never succeed in mastering the language of their new country, while others succeed in learning a second language after a few periods of foreign residence.

Some of the reasons for their differences are (1) age, (2) motives, (3) native skill, (4) intelligence and personality, (5) auditory memory span, (6) intention, or readiness to learn, (7) emotion, and (8) drive.

2.3.1 **Age**

It is popularly assumed that the younger a person starts a second language, the better.

Studies of cases where both languages were learned at the same time give some indications of what happens. In the most notable of these, the studies of Ronjat,[984] Pavlovitch,[983] and Leopold,[981] one language was used exclusively by one parent and another by the other parent (see 2.2.1, i).

Although Leopold noticed an effort on the part of the child during the first two years to weld two phonetic systems together, there was no lasting ill effect on the first language. Ronjat reports the use of two languages from the beginning; his child eventually used them just as well as children who learn only one language.

Leopold's study, however, shows that much was forgotten in the second language. Indeed, at an early age it is easy for a child to forget his first language completely and acquire another. This was demonstrated by Tits in his experiment with a six-year-old Spanish girl who, transferred to a completely French environment, ceased completely to use Spanish after only 93 days; and in less than a year she had a knowledge of French equal to that of the neighbouring children.[982]

To explain such cases, Penfield has put forth a theory based on his research into the physiology of the human brain. Before the age of nine, the child's brain seems particularly well suited for language learning. But this capacity decreases with the years, as the speech areas become "progressively stiff". Experienced teachers and some psychologists, however. have claimed that there is no decline up to the age of twenty-one.[977]

As proof of his theory, Penfield points to the difference between adults and children who have had serious brain injuries of the speech centres. The child's brain adapts itself and he nearly always learns to speak again; but many adults never do. There are numerous examples of children under four completely transferring their speech mechanism from the left to the right half of the brain. Penfield also suggests that those who learn more than one language in early childhood find the learning of later additional languages easier.[1008:242]

In the field of language learning, childhood has been called the age of form; adulthood the age of content. Children learn the structure of a language, although they may not have much to talk about. The adult has a lot to talk about and finds that the structure of the language gets in his way when he tries to use the vocabulary of all the things he wants to say.

The reasons advanced for starting the study of a second language as early as possible are the following: (i) greater facility in imitation, (ii) flexibility of the speech centres, (iii) less interference from previous experience, (iv) lack of self-consciousness. Most of those who advocate starting early put the stress on the phonetic aspect of the language; they also assume that once started, the training will continue indefinitely.

Most school systems find it convenient, however, to start the second language in the secondary school, for reasons such as the shortage of time and the lack of trained language teachers. The argument against starting as late as in the secondary school is that the child's mind has now entered the stage of abstraction. He therefore tends to regard the second language in terms of his first, begins to translate and by doing so develops a new brain process on which he begins to rely. Although his capacity to acquire new material is greater, his native vocabulary has expanded so much that he cannot hope to say all he wants to say in the second language.

To solve the administrative problem it has been suggested that most of the elementary education, including that in the kindergarten, be conducted by teachers whose mother tongue is the children's second language.[1008:255] Some advocates of starting the second language early would be satisfied if it were started at the age of eight—provided, of course, that it were continued throughout the school years.

In the introduction of a second language, practice in schools throughout the world varies from starting at the age of five to the age of fourteen. In some countries, national and social ideas prompt the early introduction of a second language. In countries where the native language has no recorded literature, a second language is introduced early enough in the primary school to permit the second language to be used as a medium of instruction. In most European countries, however, a second language has been introduced only after the age of ten.

Although there seems to be a great deal of evidence on the question of the ideal age for second-language learning, there is no agreement among educators, psychologists and neurologists on any universally valid optimum starting age. (See also 3.3.2, i.)

2.3.2 **Motives**

The reason a person wants to learn a second language and how much he wants to learn it, how well and in what manner, may determine the amount of effort he is willing to put into it. Psychologists have claimed that practice without willingness gives poor results.

For the first language, the motives are most compelling. The language gives the child control of his surroundings and makes him a member of the community. But once these vital purposes have been achieved, the reasons for learning to communicate in another language are generally less urgent. Whereas the first language is simply an unconscious means to an end, the second may first have to be learned as an end in itself. So that, for the second language, the immediate objectives may be scholastic rather than social.

If he is old enough, the second-language learner is conscious of both the end and the means. So the closer the relation between the two, the better the learning is likely to be, especially if the learner sees that he is getting what he wants. Methods and teaching techniques sometimes include material to stress this relationship by suggesting motives and reproducing situations in which the learner is likely to need the language.

2.3.3 **Native Skill**

Not all persons learn their first language at the same rate and with the same degree of success. Individuals vary in the skill with which they acquire the different elements of language. Some may have a rich vocabulary and a poor enunciation; others have a good enunciation but little grammatical versatility.

The question here is: Are such differences carried over to the learning of a second language? There have been famous writers who were masters of their first language but very poor at learning a second. But that may simply mean that they had little ability to pronounce the foreign sounds. It is possible to be good at one linguistic skill and poor at another. This is demonstrated by the fact that some of the best translators have been unable to speak the language out of which they were translating.

2.3.4 **Intelligence and Personality**

While the first language is part of the development of the learner's intelligence and personality, the second language is generally learned when the mind is more mature and in no great need of an extra mental tool. Moreover, the mental needs of the child are seldom much greater than the growing language can handle.

The adult, on the other hand, is able to talk about a great range of things in his first language before he is able to talk about them in a second language. And the more intelligent he is, the greater his range.

Does intelligence make for better language learning? Some studies seem to indicate that if intelligence is a factor, it is not the most important one. The simple imitation which the learning of everyday formulas seems to involve may indeed have little to do with intelligence, as Angiolillo's experiments with imbeciles seem to indicate.[968] More is involved in speaking, however, than simple imitation.

When it comes to the comprehension of a language, intelligence seems to play a greater role, especially in reading, where a person's reasoning ability and general knowledge are a great help in enabling him to guess meanings from the context.

2.3.5 Memory Span

Memory, especially the auditory memory for sounds immediately after hearing them, is considered a factor in language-learning ability.[1068] An analogy is seen in the learning of sound codes like those used in telegraphy. It has been shown that the difference in span of auditory comprehension distinguishes the beginner in telegraphy from the expert. Whereas the beginner can handle only one word at a time, the expert can deal with ten, keeping them all in his memory before interpreting them. As the language learner progresses he also keeps more and more words in his memory before deciding on the meaning of an utterance. There is conflicting evidence, however, on the role of rote memory in language learning.

2.3.6 Readiness

A person who wishes to do something gets ready to do it by awakening certain responses and mental associations.[951:57] This is what gives direction to his learning; and it is an important factor in comprehension. Witness the initial lack of understanding when we are addressed by a friend in a language we know, but do not expect from him.

2.3.7 Emotion

Added to the above factors is the effect of emotions and emotional associations on second-language learning. For a variety of reasons, some persons connect certain emotional associations with certain languages; they like certain languages more than others. They may also associate a language with past experience, gained directly or through books, or with feelings for the people who speak the language.

2.3.8 **Drive**

Individuals vary in their determination to finish a job of work and the energy they expend in the process. This applies to all sorts of formal learning in addition to certain types of language learning.

Many of the psychological factors involved in second-language learning apply equally well to formal learning or to learning in general. Psychologists have studied these factors, and educators have applied them to the entire curriculum, including the teaching of second languages. It is therefore important for the analysis of language teaching to take into account these theories of learning, thinking and remembering which are so often uncritically applied to foreign-language instruction.

3. LEARNING, THINKING AND REMEMBERING

Language learning, being largely a psychological problem, benefits, along with other psychological problems, from our knowledge of the process of learning, thinking and remembering. How many kinds of learning does language learning involve? What sorts of understanding affect language learning? Does the understanding of content facilitate the learning of expression? What sort of motivation most affects the learning of a language? What sort of learning theory best applies? If trial-and-error is an important element in language learning should a trial-and-error psychology be applied to language teaching? What does thinking in a second language involve? Do we need language in order to think? What does remembering involve? And how is a language forgotten? These are some of the psychological questions related to the study of language learning. First there is the basic question of what is involved when one learns.

3.1 LEARNING

What is learning? When we ask this simple question we get results as diverse as those produced by our equally simple question on the definition of language. We find that there are many answers which take the form of a number of different and often conflicting theories. We have already seen how language theories differ. Let us now see some of the differences between the theories of learning.

3.1.1. **Theories of Learning**

Like theories of language, theories of learning differ in their fundamental doctrinal approach toward the field, in their concentration on one part of the field to the neglect of others, and in their interpretation of the things and events observed.

Theories of learning may be divided into two main categories: cognitive theories and associative theories. Cognitive theories are concerned with knowledge; associative theories with responses. Whereas cognitive theories claim that we learn by insight, interpretation and by solving our problems, associative theories maintain that we learn by trial and error. A cognitive theory sees learning within a central mental organization; an associative theory considers it as a chain of responses.

Within each category there are theories which differ greatly in many respects. For example, theories differ in the number and types of learning which they recognize. Some recognize only one type, others argue for two types, and some can see as many as seven different types of learning. Differences may be traced to various interpretations of the facts, to terminology, and to degrees of refinement in analysis.

Theories also differ in the number and types of learning which they recognize. Some recognize only one type, others argue for two types, and some can see as many as seven different types of learning. Differences may be traced to various interpretations of the facts, to terminology, and to degrees of refinement in analysis.

The different theories, however, are not all mutually exclusive; there is a certain measure of agreement among them on the factors which affect the learning process, factors which determine *what* a learner is actually learning, in which *direction* he is headed, *how fast* he is going, and *how long* it will take him to get there. These factors are: (i) motivation, (ii) capacity, (iii) repetition, and (iv) understanding.

(i) *Motivation*

Motivation determines how much a person will learn and when he will learn it. This depends on what he wants to know and how badly he wants to know it. It depends on how he thinks he can learn it, and on what he believes to be to his advantage. It depends on the needs, interests and sense of values of an individual. It is the justification in language-teaching methods and techniques of the efforts expended to make the learner want to learn the second language.

Most theories agree that the more and better the motivation, the better the learning; that an incentive of reward is to be preferred to one of punishment; that hope of success is a better motivation than fear of failure. Since success is an element of motivation, material arranged in small and easy steps may be preferred to material taught in long and difficult leaps, especially in the learning of a skill. (See Ch. 7.)

(ii) *Capacity*

Capacity has to do with how much a person is able to learn in comparison with other individuals. It depends on his native ability, his previous training, and also on his age.

The theoretical possibilities of developing the learning capacity of an individual are indeed great. Neurologists claim that the individual normally exploits only a very small fraction of his brain capacity. Only a small number of the 10,000 million-or-so nerve cells in our central nervous system is ever put to use.[1009:28] Our capacity to use these develops throughout childhood; older children learn more easily than younger ones. There has been a slight but steady decline noticed after the age of thirty; but this largely depends on the subject matter being learned.

(iii) *Repetition*

Nearly all theories of learning give some importance to repetition. Repetition permits the reinforcement of patterns and their conversion into habits or skills. Once these patterns are established, they resist interference from any conflicting patterns which may present themselves to the mind, as in the learning of a second language.

Repetition, or practice, is essential in learning any sort of skill, like language, music, painting, and certain sports. Active repetition is considered better than passive repetition, so that a person who tries to speak a language may learn it better than one who simply tries to understand it. Spaced repetition is generally considered better than concentrated repetition, especially if the material is to be retained for any length of time. Repetition is one of the most important elements in remembering what is learned. (See Ch. 9 and 3.3.2, vi, below.)

(iv) *Understanding*

Many theories, especially the cognitive ones, consider understanding as an important learning factor. Learners learn some things better if they understand what is involved and if they know exactly what they are doing. For other types of learning, understanding what is involved may not be important. For example, we can pronounce all the sounds of a language without knowing all the tongue positions; but it would be difficult to learn the words of a language if we did not understand what they meant.

Our understanding and interpretation of anything is dependent on our perception of it. And our perception of it depends on what we expect, what is familiar and what makes sense to us. Anything unfamiliar, unexpected or senseless is difficult to perceive and to learn. We see it as something else and distort it in our minds.

Things that have meaning, therefore, are more readily mastered than things that do not; and the better the learner understands the meaning, the better he will learn the material.

3.1.2 Learning Theory and Language Learning

In the present state of our knowledge, many theories of learning must still be concerned with the simpler acts, rather than with the complex activity of language learning. In order to limit the complexity of the problem, empirical theories have been based on controlled observation of animal learning. In many tests of human learning, any item is considered learned after it can be recalled or recognized. This is hardly sufficient as a test for the learning of such a skill as language. Theories that are tested for verbal learning base the test on isolated words and nonsense syllables; language learning is not a matter of learning isolated words but the mastery and use of a number of complex systems (see Ch. 2).

Much of comprehension is a matter of interpretation and expectancy. Our expectancy is most often confirmed in a system with which we are familiar. The more experience we have with a language, for example, the more we know what to expect from it. And because of this we need to hear less in order to understand. For instance, we can understand a very bad gramophone record of a language we know well, better than we can make out an equally bad record of a language we are still learning. It seems that the more we hear of a language, the less we need to hear in order to understand it.

A word must fit into our idea of the phonetic structure of a language if we are to grasp it. Note how many foreign names we hear for the first time and fail to grasp, especially if these names do not fit into the patterns of a language we know.

Familiarity with words and their forms is not the only factor to be taken into account in the study of comprehension. There is also our familiarity with what the words are supposed to convey, our knowledge of the content or subject-matter. Facial expressions also play some role in comprehension. Cotton's experiments, for example, have suggested that distorted speech, made unintelligible to the listener, is understood when the listener can see the speaker.[1089]

We obviously do not learn to say everything we may want to say. We are only able to learn general patterns for representing concepts which we can apply when we need them. The question is, however, whether we apply them before or when we speak. Some writers on the subject assure us that we must conceive most of an utterance before uttering it.[311:111] But here surely a distinction must be made between content and form.

It seems that content is conscious and prior to expression, but that the actual expression of the content is automatic. In other words, a speaker has to be conscious of what he is going to say, but not of how he says it. But since both are so closely linked, how is this possible?

One theory which attempts to explain speech is the neurological theory of speech mechanism and language learning.[1008] According to this theory, a person's ability to speak is due to the growth and use of specialized speech mechanism in the dominant half of the brain. Comprehension precedes expression and is made possible by the presence of concept units and sound units in the brain. When both are interconnected a person is able to understand—so are most animals. Man, however, tries to imitate what he hears, and his ability to do so is the basis of speech.

Speaking depends on the operation of two mechanisms: a mechanism of articulation and a mechanism of ideas, concepts, or forms of representation. Man is born with an articulation mechanism which he learns to control. This mechanism contains in each side of the brain (in the cortex) two areas of control for the voice and additional areas for controlling other speech organs like the tongue and lips. But man does not inherit his mechanism of ideas. At birth it is a completely blank area located in the dominant half of the brain. It is soon filled, however, with units which, after the first ten years of life, can hardly be erased.[1008:250] Language learning is the formation of nerve patterns in these areas. The patterns are created by streams of electrical impulses which alter the nerve cells, their links and branches. Four types of patterns are possible: sound patterns for listening, verbal patterns for speaking, visual patterns for reading, and manual patterns for writing.

Writing, which is also controlled by the dominant half of the brain, is usually done by the hand on the opposite side. It is at first voluntary, later becomes an automatic skill without losing its capacity to be controlled. A written word follows a nerve pattern formed by a stream of electrical impulses flowing from the idea mechanism to the muscles of the hand. What we write or say, however, and our decision to do so, depends on an initial impulse from our central brain system which links all nerve mechanisms of the brain and makes them available for use in thought and speech.

Proof of this theory has been suggested by the different effects of motor and sensory injuries to the brain. Motor injuries involve speaking but not understanding; sensory injuries involve understanding but not speaking, although most cases are mixed. This suggests that the areas of expression are separated spatially from the areas of comprehension. When certain areas of the brain are removed, the speaker can still use the language as he did before; when other areas are removed, he cannot. The effect depends on the area. When certain parts are removed, the speaker can no longer find his words, although he may know what he wants to say. He may think of something; but the connection between what he thinks and the corresponding symbol no longer exists. This theory, however, does not explain whether the concept units—what persons want to say—can be acquired without language; nor does it show the exact relationship between language and thinking. Moreover, concepts and language units are not verified in the same way as the presence of nerve cells and electric impulses.

3.2 THINKING

It is important to consider some of the ideas on the relationship between thinking and language because these often have an effect upon methods and policies of second-language teaching. When a directive on teaching technique exhorts teachers to make the learners think in the second language or when a method is designed to do so, what exactly is meant? Is it possible to speak a language without thinking in it? What is the relationship between thinking and speaking? Is one dependent on the other? These questions have been considered, not only by different schools of psychology, but also by certain linguists, philosophers and mathematicians.

For some, speaking and thinking are independent; for others the dependence of thought on speech is a fundamental principle. "No thought without speech; no speech without thought," says Révész.[1056] Peirce claimed that when we think, we talk or argue with ourselves. Moreover, since thinking involves seeing one's actions as they appear to others, it cannot be done without language.[1054]

A number of experimental studies have tried to discover the relationship between language and thought. It has been demonstrated, for example, that deaf-mutes use their finger muscles when they dream.

On the other hand, there are a number of scholars who hold that thinking and speech are not identical, that they are two separate functions of the mind, since there exists such a thing as non-verbalized thought.[1055] Not all concepts are necessarily verbal.[1026:113] Some mathematicians have claimed that neither formulas nor words are necessary to mathematical thinking. Einstein once stated that neither written nor spoken symbols played any part in his thought.[1052] Thinking connected with creative activity is said to take place without speech.[326:91] It has even been suggested that language may be harmful to the solution of mental problems.[1053]

It is well known that the laws of logic are not the laws of thought. Grammatical gender is different from logical gender; grammatical number is not logical number. According to Saussure, the structure of language cannot be explained by the structure of thought, since language structure is a closed system and cannot be added to, whereas thought can. Linguistic signs obey the rules of the language, not the rules of thought. Their value is dependent, not on thought, but on their own internal interrelations. According to Frei, language is a manifestation of thought; the act of speaking, a manifestation of language.

Thinking creates language and precedes speech. The impulse to speak comes always from thinking, and our thinking is fixed and aided by our language.[328] Language can therefore be considered as the chief manifestation of thought, and speech one of its possible results.[326:104] Gesture, music and painting are other manifestations of thought.

Speech is not reason; it is only an indication of reason. It helps reasoning by delimiting an idea and holding it before us, and by presenting us with a set of symbols. Speech and thought, as Piaget has pointed out, are supported by each other in perpetual interaction.[326:60] Yet both depend on intelligence, which is independent of speech and comes before it. Both have the same source in our symbolic function, of which speech is only part. But speech has also a social function, for without it all our actions would remain individual and independent of others. In the mental development of the child, the relation of thought to language is affected by the degree to which thought loses its relation to images and becomes attached to words. The mere fact of telling our thoughts to others, or to ourselves, is of great importance for the structure of our thought and for its functioning.[937:43] Although all thinking, especially the concrete thinking of animals and children, may not be connected with linguistic symbols, much of the thinking of literate adults undoubtedly is.

The exact relation between thought and speech, however, still remains an unsolved problem, and much about it remains to be discovered. This being so, of more immediate importance to language teaching is not the question of whether we think in words but the problem of how to remember them.

3.3 REMEMBERING

One of the most important processes in language learning is the remembering of what is learned.

Psychologically, memory is not a reservoir of past events. It is rather an adjustment between past impressions and present demands. It is not a faculty but a process, or rather, a group of mutually related processes. From the point of view of behaviour, memory is the reproduction of previously encountered responses to a given stimulus.

Apart from abnormal causes like injuries and diseases of the brain, forgetting may be due to the fact that the material had been repressed by the mind as too difficult, that new patterns have replaced or interfered with it, that the patterns have been too long without use, or that the material was badly patterned in the first place. A study of the causes of forgetting gives a clue to some of the factors involved in remembering.

Some of the factors of remembering are: who does the remembering, (i) his age, (ii) his intentions, and (iii) his experience; what is to be remembered, (iv) the material and its context, (v) how it is learned, (vi) the amount of practice or repetition, and (vii) the amount of time elapsed.

(i) *Age*

People often use the argument of age as an excuse for not learning a language. They say that they are too old to remember. An equally valid excuse might be that a person is too young.

It is popularly supposed that the younger the person, the better he can remember. But this is by no means the case. In fact, it has been demonstrated that memory for both rote and meaningful materials increases with age.[1066] As a general rule, a person's capacity to remember increases steadily during the first two decades of his life, levels off in the third and starts declining in the fourth. The rate of decline depends on the type of material remembered and the past experience of the individual.

Psychologists have attempted to measure remembering capacity of different ages by determining the number of digits a person can remember.[367:210] The results might be indicated as follows:

No. of Digits		Age
1		
		2
2	—————————————	
3	—————————————	3
4	—————————————	
		4
		5
		6
5	—————————————	7
		8
		9
6	—————————————	10
7		
8	—————————————	16–20

This gives an idea only of the rate of development of the capacity of immediate memory. But the figures are more striking than they seem,

131

since the difference in difficulty increases proportionately with the number of digits to be remembered.

There is much more to remembering, however, than the immediate memory for digits. A great deal remains to be discovered on the precise relationship between memory and age, especially in the field of language.

(ii) *Intention*

Remembering depends to a great extent on the intention to remember. How often have people dialled the same telephone number again and again, looking up the number each time! These same people, if they had really intended to remember the number, could have done so after having looked at it for less than a minute. It is undoubtedly similar in the case of language learning; if a learner does not intend to remember, he probably will not.

(iii) *Experience*

It is well known that the more experience one has in a particular field, the more one can remember in it. It has also been noticed that the more experience a person gains in a second language, the easier it is for him to learn and remember more of it. This may be due to the fact that the more experience we have with anything, the more meaning it has for us.

(iv) *Material and Context*

If the material has meaning for the learner, he remembers it more readily than if it has not. The effort to make sense out of something greatly influences a person's ability to remember it. And what makes sense is determined by a person's cultural background and past experience.[1064]

Related to the effort after meaning and the familiarity with the material is the fact that the learner should know what to expect. In language the familiar word-sequences and word-connections play a role in remembering. A person familiar with a language has developed an unconscious feeling for its statistical structure, a feeling for what can go with and come after what.

(v) *Learning the Material*

The more thoroughly anything is learned, the longer it will be remembered. Good teaching, which promotes good learning, may therefore make remembering easier. It is often true that pupils of good teachers need less time to remember material which has been well presented in class. (See Ch. 8 and Ch. 14.)

(vi) *Repetition*

This has long been considered the most important factor in remembering especially where a skill such as music or language is concerned.

There is always a definite relation between the amount remembered and the amount of practice devoted to it. It is therefore profitable to continue practising something even after it is considered as known; that is, until after it can be immediately recalled. Any repetition beyond this point is called over-learning, and it is most important in the acquisition of a second language. Yet a point is eventually reached where the amount of time and effort spent on a learning point does not justify the additional gain.[1062:42] It may even reach a point of satiation, especially in the perception of meaning.[963a] This may be due to the fact that the significance of constantly recurring stimuli is eventually ignored, since its high expectancy reduced the amount of new information conveyed—as is the case when a person gets used to working in noisy surroundings. This may not be true, however, for the formal elements of expression, which are analogous to the mastery of physical skills.

Active repetition is generally considered as having greater effect than passive repetition. Given an equal amount of time, a person who speaks a language every day will remember it better than one who only hears it daily; one who writes it, better than one who only reads. (See Ch. 7 and 3.1.3, iii, above.)

(vii) *The Time Factor*

We are well aware that with the passage of time, we tend to forget anything which we do not continually recall. Yet the precise relationship between time and memory is not very well known. Experiments with certain types of material indicate that we forget on the average about three-quarters of the material after a week and about four-fifths after a month. If this applies to language learning, it is no wonder that learners who devote only an hour or so a week to it, do not succeed in remembering very much.

Because the time elapsed is such an important factor in remembering, regular and frequent practice, even for short periods, is necessary. Several short periods are considered more effective than one long one. But the periods must not be so short that there is no time to get involved in the subject. And the interval between the periods must not be so long that the material is forgotten or is allowed to lose its interest. (See Ch. 7 and Ch. 15.)

The importance of such factors as these for the remembering of material has led some psychologists to formulate certain "rules" of memory. Here is a list adapted from those suggested by Hunter.[1062:60]

1. Find suitable incentives. 2. Combine them with activities already interesting. 3. Present together things to be remembered together. 4. Whole method for short things; part method for long ones. 5. Gain accurate first impressions; avoid errors. 6. Early recitation; but not so early as to encourage guessing. 7. Make material meaningful and as rhythmic as possible. 8. Have short memory drills; stop when tired. Distribute effort. 9. Frequent revision at first, and at progressively longer intervals. 10. Integrate what has been learned into further activities and larger contexts.

Therefore incentive, interest, accuracy, significance, practice, revision, and integration, in relation to the learner's capacity, understanding and motivation, and the use of rote memory, association, analogy, and trial-and-error activities of language learning by children, are the psychological principles on which language-teaching methods and techniques can be based. We shall first see how these may apply to the analysis of methods.

PART II

METHOD
ANALYSIS

The Meaning of Method

OUTLINE

0. INTRODUCTION

The second field of analysis in language teaching is method. It is partly determined by the different principles of language analysis, and itself determines to a large extent the teaching techniques.

The method used has often been said to be the cause of success or failure in language learning; for it is ultimately the method that determines the what and the how of language instruction. But it is also the "method" that enables commercial language schools to give their customers "complete command of another language . . . in just a few short months". For the method is all-important.

At the other extreme is the view that methods are of little importance wherever there is a will to learn; the quality of the learner is what counts.

Thirdly, there is the view that the teacher is the only important element; methods are only as good as their teachers. They are simply instruments in the hands of the teachers.

Yet teachers are continually being invited to give up these instruments, to discontinue the books and teaching methods they have been using and to adopt newer methods and textbooks. They are also expected to re-examine their methods from time to time in the light of new theories and new research. But invitations to alter old methods or try out new ones generally meet with resistance; for there is much doctrinaire controversy and misunderstanding in the field of modern-language method.

This has been true for a long time. In 1929, after analysing the most extensive survey of language teaching ever made, Fife concluded: "New ideas seem to germinate and take root with exasperating slowness. An outworn methodology and threadbare dogmas continue to hold the centre of the stage, with no support except constant iteration, and the same old songs are sung in tones of special propaganda and *a priori* conviction that long ago ceased to thrill the audience."[1197:48] When new methods do take hold, however, it is at the expense of both the good and the bad in the older methods, indifferently overthrown. For example, methods have swung from wholesale learning by heart to the highly logical techniques of linguistic analysis[1207:180]—and back again to learning by heart.

While sciences have advanced by approximations in which each new stage results from an improvement, not a rejection, of what has gone before, language-teaching methods have followed the pendulum of fashion from one extreme to the other. So that, after centuries of language teaching, no systematic reference to this body of knowledge exists. The quality of some of the work is so poor as to discredit the entire field of language method, putting the charlatans and the scholars in the same boat. As a result, much of the field of language method has become a matter of opinion rather than of fact. It is not surprising that feelings run high in these matters, and that the very word "method" means so little and so much. The reason for this is not hard to find. It lies in the state and organization of our knowledge of language and language learning. It lies in wilful ignorance of what has been done and said and thought in the past. It lies in the vested interests which methods become. And it lies in the meaning of method.[1286]

Any meaning of method must first distinguish between what a teacher teaches and what a book teaches. It must not confuse the text used with the teacher using it, or the method with the teaching of it. Method analysis is one thing, therefore; teaching analysis, quite another. Method analysis determines how much teaching is done by the book; teaching analysis shows how much is done by the teacher.

The purpose of method analysis is to show how one method differs from another, what is new in new methods, and what is old in old ones. It is limited to the analysis of materials through which learners can study the language. These include textbooks, workbooks, courses on tapes, discs, and films, package courses, and the programming of teaching machines. Since these are all fixed or textual materials, an analysis of them can be much more accurate than the measurement of the results they achieve when used. And such an analysis logically precedes a study of the results. Before elaborating a theory of method analysis, however, it is necessary to determine what exactly a method involves: (1) its relation to language analysis, (2) the development of methods likely to be analysed, (3) types of methods in use, and (4) what methods are made of and the ways in which one method may differ from another.

1. LANGUAGE ANALYSIS AND METHOD ANALYSIS

Differences in methods may be the result of (1) different theories of language, (2) different types of language description, and (3) different ideas on language learning.

1.1 METHOD AND LANGUAGE THEORY

Different theories of language are responsible for differences in method when they are limited to certain areas or neglect others. Methods based on theories which limit their study to linguistic form will differ from those which concentrate on linguistic content, or on the relationship between language and reality. (See Ch. 1.)

1.2 METHOD AND LANGUAGE DESCRIPTION

Differences in language description produce differences in the social or regional dialect studied, differences in the styles and registers taught, and differences in the linguistic categories recognized. The categories established in a description of a language will be those taught by the method using that description. A certain method, for example, has assumed that the sentences *Where do you get on the bus every morning?* and *Do you live far from school?* belong to the same pattern and consequently come under the same teaching point; while another method considers them as two separate teaching points. Such a distinction depends on the sort of grammar or descriptive technique which the method maker has used. Of course, the grammar in the mind of the method maker may be nothing more than his *ad hoc* description of what he thinks the language to be. But it is nevertheless still subject to analysis. (See Ch. 2.)

Some methods stress the differences between learning the first language and learning the second. These may be based on either a differential analysis of both languages or on studies of difficulties peculiar to certain types of language learners. (See Ch. 3.)

1.3 METHOD AND LANGUAGE LEARNING

A large number of methods are based on ideas of how languages are learned. Some methods, for example, are supposed to reproduce the conditions under which the first language was acquired; such methods stress imitation, rote memory, association and analogy. On the other hand, there are those built on the belief that such a thing is impossible, that there can be no such thing as a natural method since a method is a system which is necessarily artificial.[1277: 85] They may yet nevertheless try to approximate to the conditions under which the first language was acquired. (See Ch. 4.)

There are methods with neither theoretical background nor indication of any analysis of the language. They may be simply collections of some of the lessons of experienced teachers. Nevertheless such methods are inevitably based on certain assumptions.

These different and often conflicting principles of language theory, language description and language learning have been, consciously or unconsciously, assumed and applied to a greater and greater extent as the study of language teaching has developed. It is important therefore to examine this development, if only in brief outline.

2. DEVELOPMENT OF LANGUAGE TEACHING

2.1 ANTIQUITY AND THE MIDDLE AGES

Before the beginning of the Roman empire the Romans studied Greek as a second language. They did so by engaging Greek tutors and also by having Greek-speaking slaves and servants in the household. As the empire expanded, however, other peoples began to learn Latin until that language became the international language of the Western World, the language of church and state, and for a long time the sole language of learning, the only medium of instruction in the schools. And it remained so in some European countries until modern times.

The first concern with language-teaching method in Europe, therefore, had to do with the teaching of Latin. During the Middle Ages Latin was the language of teaching. Methods were mostly limited to Latin grammars designed to enable clerics to speak, read and write in their second language, the language in which nearly all academic learning was done.

2.2 THE RENAISSANCE

It is significant, perhaps, that the first complaints about bad methods of teaching Latin appear after the invention of printing. One of the first uses to which the printing press was put was the reproduction of Greek and Latin classics. These were distributed and taught throughout Europe. But the language in which Latin classics were written was several centuries older than and consequently quite different from the Latin spoken in academic Europe at the time. Yet the language of these classics came to be regarded as the original and correct form of Latin, the form on which Latin grammars and methods of teaching the language should be based. Latin grammars based on the classics gradually became longer and more complicated, until the study of them, instead of being a preparation for the reading of the classics, became an end in itself. Decrees that this sort of Latin was to take the place of the form of the language spoken at the time were largely responsible for converting Latin into a dead language, and it gradually ceded its place to the national languages of Europe.

But before this happened, there were a number of attempts to improve the teaching of Latin by doing away with the learning of grammar for grammar's sake. In 1532 a brief grammar (67 pages) by Di Marinis, was published "to make Latinists and not grammarians out of the students". Luther and his contemporary, Melanchthon, were also opposed to too much formal grammar and to the teaching of rules.

In one of his essays Montaigne makes the point that he learned Latin without rules because his father made everyone in the household, including a German tutor engaged for the purpose, speak to him only in Latin —in the case of the children, even before they started learning their mother tongue. But once Montaigne entered the Collège de Guyenne, where he presumably started learning only the rules of the grammar, he quickly began to forget the Latin he knew so fluently.

About this time, Ratichius also complained about the contemporary methods of language teaching which stressed grammar at the expense of reading. But it remained for his successor, the famous Czech educator, Jan Comenius, to devise new methods of language teaching based on new principles. Instead of rules, Comenius used imitation, repetition and plenty of practice in both reading and speaking. The grammar was acquired indirectly by induction. In 1631 Comenius published his *Ianua linguarum reserata* (The Gate of Languages Unlocked), which included a limited vocabulary of a few thousand words, each used in a sentence which gave some indication of the meaning. In the following year, appeared the *Didactica magna*. This was a more ambitious work, which went beyond language and laid the foundations for modern pedagogy. But language teaching remained the main interest of Comenius. His *Linguarum methodus novissima* contains one of the first attempts to teach grammar inductively, and one of his later works, the *Orbis pictus* (1658) was the first to teach language through pictures.

2.3 THE SEVENTEENTH AND EIGHTEENTH CENTURIES

Although much of the work of Comenius was forgotten soon after his death and remained so for more than two centuries, some of his ideas were from time to time revived by persons interested in language teaching. Some of the ideas of both Comenius and Montaigne were shared by John Locke and published in his *Some Thoughts Concerning Education* (1693).

For Locke, "languages were not made by Rules of Art, but by Accident, and the Common Use of the People. And he that will speak them well, has no other Rule but that; nor any thing to trust to, but his Memory, and the Habit of speaking after the Fashion learned from those, that are allowed to speak properly, which in other Words is only to speak by rote . . ."[1103:138]

The ideas of Comenius were also followed by Basedow who later, in 1763, also came under the influence of the nature-education ideas of Rousseau. But he was violently opposed by educators of the time, who believed that he endangered the secure position of the classics in education.

Up to the last quarter of the eighteenth century the usual practice in schools was to translate from the second language into the first. This practice was largely reversed through the influence of Meidinger who, in 1783, published his *Praktische französische Grammatik* which advocated translation into the second language through the application of rules of grammar.

By the end of the century, the teaching of Latin grammar had become an end in itself. Latin had ceased to become the medium of instruction and the teaching and application of its rules had become formalized into a sort of intellectual exercise. It was not surprising that the few modern languages which had been introduced into some of the schools of the time were taught with the same methods as Latin and justified by the same arguments of mental discipline.

2.4 THE NINETEENTH CENTURY

At the beginning of the nineteenth century there was a reaction. Following the lead of James Hamilton (1764–1829), Jacotot and Toussaint-Langenscheidt encouraged a return to inductive grammar through the study of texts in the second language. But the texts they used, being literary or biblical works, proved too difficult for beginners. To overcome this difficulty, Seidenstücker in 1811 succeeded in writing a text based on simple sentences containing most of the grammatical features of the language. This innovation of his was taken up by Ahn and later by Ollendorf. But the one to erect Seidenstücker's disconnected grammar-teaching sentences into a principle was Karl Plötz (1819–81) who dominated language teaching in Europe until long after his death. His method was divided into two parts: (1) rules and paradigms, and (2) sentences for translation into and out of the second language. Throughout the nineteenth century, language teaching in schools followed Plötz's techniques. It was a matter of using the first language to acquire the second, this included rote learning of grammar rules, learning to put grammatical labels on words, and learning to apply the rule by translating sentences.

During this time, especially in the later half of the century, there began a number of individual reactions which finally developed into a movement. One of the pioneers of the movement was Claude Marcel whose 1867 treatise on the study of language advocated the abolition of translation and grammar rules and the teaching of language first through comprehension of texts, through abundant listening, then through the reading of simple and familiar material, followed later by speaking and writing. In 1874 Sauveur advocated similar principles, adding grammar and translation only when the learners were able to understand the language.[1281] By 1866 Heness had started a private school for teaching languages by a "natural method" which was intended as an extreme reaction against the grammar-translation methods of Plötz, Ahn and Ollendorf.

About 1880 a new element was added to language teaching—physical activity. It was in that year that Gouin first published his *Art d'enseigner et d'étudier les langues*. Although first ignored in France, this book, in translation, had a great influence in England, Germany, and the United States, and its ideas were used as a source for the elaboration of the Direct Method.[1277] Gouin, a friend of Humboldt, applied principles of the growing science of modern psychology to the learning of languages, the principles of the association of ideas, visualization, learning through the senses, centres of interest, play and activity in familiar everyday situations. Each sentence in his course was linked with other sentences into a "selection" and each selection associated with another selection in a "series" and each series combined with others into a general series. Each sentence was to be acted out while it was being uttered. The language was first introduced through the ear, and then reinforced through the eye and hand by reading and writing. All the vocabulary, about 8,000 words, was related to activity. For Gouin, the sentence was the basic unit of speech, and each sentence was to be associated with another to form a chain. These chains of sentences dealt with everyday acts and activities based on the interests of the learners, not on those of the teacher.

About this time, another new element was added to language teaching—descriptive phonetics. Although this had been studied since the middle of the century by Brücke, Ellis, Bell, Sweet, Sievers, Klinghardt, Passy and others, having also been applied by Sayce to modern-language teaching, it was Viëtor who incorporated it into a language-teaching method. In a much-discussed pamphlet, first published anonymously in 1882, Viëtor analysed and violently criticized the grammar-translation methods of the Plötz school; but he also proposed a new approach to language teaching.[1270] Using the spoken language as a starting-point, he and his supporters elaborated a method whereby words were to be used in sentences and not in isolation, since the sentence was considered the basic unit of speech. Sentences were not to be disconnected; they were to be used in contexts along with other sentences all of which dealt with subjects of interest to the learners. New material was to be taught through gestures and pictures and through the use of words already known. Reading was to be introduced later, and only through graded reading-material leading to a knowledge of the foreign country and its culture. Any knowledge of grammar was to be acquired inductively through the study of texts.

These ideas started a long and voluminous controversy.[1320] Yet they found some immediate support in Germany, Scandinavia, and at the turn of the century, in France, England and later in the United States. The great debate on this method, called the Phonetic Method or Reform Method, ended in something of a compromise; combining with some of the principles of Gouin, it gave rise to the Direct Method movement.

The sort of teaching engendered by the Direct Method movement was at first quite disorganized. The teacher took the place of the book, had no technique of teaching through actions, and on the whole, did whatever he pleased. Sometimes a native speaker of the language would be used as a sort of model or, as he might be called a half-century later, an informant. What happened is that the principles of Viëtor and Gouin were over-simplified in practice. They were confused with the "natural method", in which the language was to be learned the same way as the child learns his mother tongue. If the learner understood only a fraction of what he heard, it made little difference; the principle of "natural selection" would eventually give him what he needed. If he made nothing but mistakes when he spoke, he would at least gain a familiarity with the language and eventually identify and correct his own mistakes. Language-teaching method had thus swung from the strict application of principles of logic to the single-minded practice of principles of psychology.

The Direct Method did not lack critics. These were quick to point out that the theory of natural selection by the child did not apply to a second language, that too many difficulties at once caused only confusion, error, waste of time, and inaccuracy. They also noted that the method required a teacher with a fluent command of the second language and with plenty of vitality and resourcefulness to teach it.

The need for system was at length admitted by the exponents of these techniques. The primary role of the spoken language and the need to train the ear to hear it led to an effort to standardize pronunciation. The result was to incorporate into the method systematic drills on vowel and consonant sounds from the very beginning, often with the aid of phonetic notation. When the sounds were mastered, whole sentences were taught along with their meaning, which was conveyed through objects. These sentences were later incorporated into dialogues and anecdotes.

2.5 THE TWENTIETH CENTURY

It was only at the turn of the century that the Direct Method textbooks began to follow a definite pattern. Maintaining the principle that no use whatsoever be made of the learner's language, the typical text started with the spoken language, and only after some time went on to reading, and later to writing.

Work on the spoken language started with the study of sounds through the aid of phonetic notation. These sounds were used in sentences whose meaning was taught through pictures and definitions, aided by the gestures and ingenuity of the teacher. The structure of the language was assimilated through inference and abstraction. Material for reading was written in a contemporary style and often dealt with the life and culture of the foreign country.

There was also some effort to systematize the teaching of the structure and meaning of the language. The material was now roughly graded so that one class led to the next. The need for training teachers in special teaching-techniques was also admitted; special holiday-courses were started for this purpose. The movement was also strengthened by the international congress of modern language teachers in Vienna in 1898, which accepted the principle of giving some time in each elementary lesson to some aspect of the Direct Method, such as the use of dialogues or dramatization. And at the Leipzig congress of 1900 a motion was passed to apply the new principles in advanced classes. These principles included almost exclusive use of the second language in the class, the use of texts in modern prose, material on the foreign culture, inductive grammar, modern literary texts and written work in the form of reproduction exercises.

It was in 1901 that the term "direct method" seems to have been established when it was described in a circular of the French Ministry of Public Instruction. By 1902, through a decree of Leygues who was then the Minister, the *méthode directe* had become the only officially approved method for the teaching of foreign languages in France. The same year, the Direct Method also became official in Germany, along with Viëtor's phonetics. Before the turn of the century, the method had already been introduced into England by Walter Ripman, without however becoming the official method.

The imposition of the Direct Method as an official method created many difficulties in the countries which adopted it. In the first place, there were few teachers trained to use the method. Most of them had neither the fluency, the techniques, nor the energy which the method required. As far as techniques were concerned, a great need was felt for the interchange of information among teachers using the method. Language teachers began visiting centres where the method was successful, and they published descriptions of the techniques which they had observed. For example, after seeing the direct method in action at the Lycée de Bordeaux in 1909, Pitschel published his findings and comments on the effective use of diagrams, wall pictures, advertisements and songs.[1263]

As the principles of the Direct Method spread there was more and more compromise with them in order to meet the growing demands for measurable standards of accuracy. Vocabulary exercises and systematic grammar drills were added. At a more advanced level, translation was included. And at all levels certain standards of correctness were required.

In practice, each country made its own compromise with the Direct Method. In Germany, after being propagated by Walter, Wendt, Hartmann, Klinghardt, Kuhn and Hausknecht, the method was adapted to more traditional language-teaching and combined into what was eventually called the "eclectic method". The combination included the phonetics, intuition, induction and modern texts of the Direct Method, combined with a systematic study of grammar along more traditional lines. In France a similar compromise resulted in the *méthode active*, which kept most of the features so ardently proclaimed by Passy, Carré, Pinloche, Schweitzer, and Simonnot. In Switzerland, as early as 1887, Alge had accented the intuition element of the method by adding the use of wall pictures and other similar devices. His writings on teaching techniques (e.g. *Leitfaden für den ersten Unterricht im Französischen*) were the forerunner of a rich literature on Direct Method techniques. In Belgium the method had been supported by Melon and, indirectly, by the government when in 1895 it decreed that the spoken language be made the basis of all elementary language-instruction and be taught through natural and intuitive teaching-techniques. But here too the method ended in a compromise.

In England, owing largely to the efforts of such exponents as Sweet, Ripman, and Findlay, the method was used with enthusiasm and success by its supporters, and it remained in vogue between 1899 and 1924. As it spread to the average school, however, its use began to decline because it demanded highly competent teachers, willing to spend a great deal of time and energy on each lesson, for results which were not always worth the effort. Teachers gradually drifted back to some forms of the grammar-translation approach.

In the United States, little was heard of the Direct Method before the publication of a short description of it in the *Report of the Committee of Twelve*.[1271] This committee was a group of a dozen prominent American teachers of languages, appointed in 1892 by the Modern Language Association of America to advise the National Educational Association on curriculum and methods in language teaching. Its influential report stated that "the ability to converse should not be regarded as a thing of primary importance for its own sake but as an auxiliary to the higher ends of linguistic scholarship and literary culture."[1271:20] Moreover, under conditions prevailing at the time in America, it was possible to learn only to read a second language and not to speak it.

Under the chairmanship of Thomas, the Committee outlined what has been called the Grammar-translation Method. It included teaching of grammar, translation of simple prose, and practice in hearing and pronouncing foreign words. For the Committee, the main purpose of foreign-language teaching was to enable the learner to translate at sight in order eventually to be able to read the language. Great importance was given to the proper use of the learner's first language. The need for better textbooks for grammar-translation work was soon satisfied by the publication between 1900 and 1914 of such influential texts as those of Fraser and Squair for French, Thomas for German, Ramsey for Spanish and Grandgent for Italian. The ultimate objective was always to train the learner to read the language. For example, the purpose of Grandgent's Italian grammar was to prepare students to read Dante in the original. The aims of the method did not include teaching the learner to converse in the language.

Conversational skill in the foreign language, which the curriculum and methods of the schools had failed to give, was offered by a growing group of language merchants, the best known of whom was Maximilian Berlitz, who had started a language school in Providence in 1878. The demand for the spoken language was so great that the Berlitz family was able to increase the number of its schools to almost two hundred in various countries of the world. Some of these schools were prepared to teach 60 different languages. The method used was similar to the Direct Method, for under no circumstances was anything but the foreign language to be used in the teaching of it. All instruction was oral from the very beginning. The material was based on the phrases and vocabulary of everyday conversation.

Because of the demand for the spoken language, some American and Canadian teachers tried out the techniques of the new "reform" methods which had been imported from Europe. But many became disillusioned with them for they felt that what the grammatical method neglected, namely, practical and correct use of the spoken language, the reform methods had pushed to extremes. In making mastery of the spoken language the chief objective, the nature and function of secondary schools was overlooked, because such an objective under the normal conditions of mass instruction was only attainable in a modest degree. The reform methods not only required a teacher who possessed a perfect mastery of the foreign language, but they made such claims on his nervous and physical energy as to entail premature exhaustion. The abilities and ambitions of average pupils, not to mention those of the weaker ones, do not justify the demands made by the oral use of the language.[1221:19]

A vast project was therefore planned to solve the methods problem by means of experiments. Between 1920 and 1935 there was an active period of experimentation in America. Aims were appraised. There was much planning, and even some agreement, based on a number of factual studies. The net result was the largest and most systematic study of its kind ever undertaken. Called the Modern Foreign Language Study, it began in the United States in 1923 and ended in Toronto in 1927 at a joint meeting with the Canadian Committee. The results were reported in seventeen volumes devoted to different aspects of language teaching—enrolment, achievement, testing, reading, vocabulary control, and bibliography.

The findings of the study were summarized by Coleman in a volume which started much discussion. Some refused to accept the conclusions, which, according to Coleman were the following: Since most pupils waste their time in trying to achieve the impossible, especially in two-year courses, it is better to try for something attainable, a limited reading knowledge of the second language. Use of word counts, syntax and idiom lists, and replacements texts, better methods, and definite standards of achievement were advocated. These were the conclusions which governed language teaching in America between the two World Wars.

The effect of the study was to spread the Reading Method, with texts based on a controlled and limited vocabulary. Only a comprehension of the text was required; what was stressed in practice was rapid, silent reading, and plenty of it. But since silent reading was a private affair and not a group activity, teachers, for want of something to do, began to spend classroom time talking in the learner's language, about the foreign language and the people who use it.

These were the conditions which prevailed until the time the United States entered World War II and found itself incapable of supplying the language needs of its huge army and navy, which was then taking up positions in all quarters of the globe. To train fluent speakers of a considerable number of languages for its far-flung operations, the American Army, with the help of the Universities, set up its own schools under the Army Specialized Training Programme, popularly known as the ASTP.

In some of these schools, language learning was a full-time job, and the results after a few months seemed so impressive that it was believed that the "Army Method" contained the secret of successful language teaching. Actually no such method existed. All that the Army had asked for was results, including a fluent speaking knowledge of the language; a variety of methods and techniques were used to achieve these results. Advice had been sought from a number of specialists, especially from linguists and anthropologists who had learned some of the more exotic languages in their field work. Among them was Franz Boas, who suggested that the bulk of the time be spent on accurate imitation of the natural conversation of native speakers of the language. He was supported by Sapir and also by Bloomfield, who had already pointed out that pseudo-grammatical doctrine and puzzle-solving translation had been largely responsible for the failure of the schools to give even a small percentage of the population a working knowledge of a second language. What was needed was abundant contact with the spoken language. In order to give the maximum contact with the spoken language there was to be a minimum of reading and writing and only the essentials of grammar. Small classes were to meet frequently for imitation and drill with a native speaker (called an informant) operating under the direction of a linguist.

The results achieved by some of the wartime language schools were apparently so satisfactory that, after the war, military language schools using the same patterns of instruction were organized in the United States and other countries on a permanent basis. But a few modifications were made. Instead of an informant there was only the teacher, who had to be a native speaker of the language. Reading and writing were added in larger doses. Systematic grammar was used to summarize what had been learned. The emphasis was on memory-work, aided by pictures, charts, tapes and discs, and film-strips. The length of the course varied with the language; some full-time courses lasted forty-six weeks.

Another effect of the impressive results of war-time language centres was a post-war attempt by schools and colleges to duplicate them. But this proved practically impossible in most cases, since full time could not be devoted to language learning. Moreover, the motives were not so urgent; and the classes were far too big. Although a few private schools did attempt full-time programmes, the great majority of secondary schools could devote only five hours a week, and in addition, had to deal with classes of over thirty. The best that could be done was to double or triple the number of class hours per week into the so called "intensive course", to increase the number of contact hours with the language by the use of recordings on magnetic tape or discs to be imitated in groups or in the individual recording-booths of the increasingly popular language-laboratory. (See Ch. 15.) These laboratories were first introduced in the universities, where intensive courses totalled fifteen hours a week of classes plus an additional fifteen hours of practice in the laboratory.

Some adaptations of ASTP techniques also produced impressive results. When the extra time was not available, however, the "Army Method" did not succeed in producing anything like a fluent command of the spoken language. [951:293] The fact was that there was nothing really new in the ASTP techniques used in the military language schools. All of its main features had already been mentioned half a century earlier in the Report of the Committee of Twelve, which rejected them as inapplicable at the time; and all of them had been used in Europe during the latter part of the nineteenth century and the beginning of the twentieth. Since these methods and techniques, like those of the Direct Method, required the services of highly competent language-teaching specialists, language teachers reverted to the use of grammar and translation, to the Reading Method, and to other methods which had been developed in the past.

If we now glance back at the development of language-teaching method, we see that it first swings from the active oral use of Latin in Ancient and Medieval times to the learning by rule of the Renaissance grammars, back to oral activity with Comenius, back to grammar rules with Plötz, and back again to the primacy of speech in the Direct Method. During this development, the demand had also switched from the classics to the modern languages. Because of the expansion of trade and commerce during the period following the Industrial Revolution, training in Latin and Greek came to be considered as insufficient for the future businessman and industrialist. The demand was now for modern foreign languages; but the argument that had to be used to get them into the schools was that they could be reduced to the same sort of academic subjects as the classical languages. It is perhaps because they have had to compete with Latin and Greek that modern languages have so long been taught as if they were dead languages. But as the teaching of modern languages became the rule rather than the exception, there was a reaction against techniques and objectives which had been adapted from the teaching of the classical languages. By the middle of the twentieth century, however, modern languages were still being taught by such techniques; they were also being taught by a great variety of other types of "methods", most of which had originated in the nineteenth or early twentieth centuries.

3. TYPES OF METHODS

Most of the methods developed over the past few centuries are still in use in one form or another in various parts of the world. The most common types in use are (1) the Direct Method, (2) the Natural Method, (3) the Psychological Method, (4) the Phonetic Method, (5) the Reading Method, (6) the Grammar Method, (7) the Translation Method, (8) the Grammar-Translation Method, (9) the Eclectic Method, (10) the Unit Method, (11) the Language-Control Method, (12) the Mimicry-Memorization Method, (13) the Practice-Theory Method, (14) the Cognate Method, (15) the Dual-Language Method.

3.1 THE DIRECT METHOD

This is one of the most widely known methods and the one that has caused the most controversy. Its main characteristics are: 1. The use of everyday vocabulary and structure. 2. Grammar taught by situation. 3. Use of many new items in the same lesson to make the language sound natural and to encourage normal conversation. 4. Oral teaching of grammar and vocabulary. 5. Concrete meanings through object lessons; abstract ones through the association of ideas. 6. Grammar illustrated through visual presentation. 7. Extensive listening and imitation until forms become automatic. 8. Most of the work done in class; more class hours needed for the method. 9. The first few weeks devoted to pronunciation. 10. All reading matter first presented orally.

3.2 THE NATURAL METHOD

This is similar to the Direct Method in so far as it starts its courses with questions on objects and pictures. New words are explained by means of known words. Meaning is taught by inference. There is no use of the first language, no translation, no talk about the second language. Grammar is used to correct mistakes; the dictionary, to help in remembering partly forgotten words. The order of presentation is: listening, speaking, reading, writing, grammar.

3.3 THE PSYCHOLOGICAL METHOD

This is also related to the Direct Method. It is based on mental visualization and the association of ideas. Some of its chief characteristics are the following: Objects, diagrams, pictures, and charts are used to help to create a mental image and to connect it with the word. Vocabulary is arranged into groups of short idiomatic sentences connected with the subject. One such group forms a lesson. Lessons are collected into chapters; several chapters form a series. Teaching is at first exclusively oral; later it is based partly on the book. The vernacular is rarely used, but is sometimes permitted. Composition is introduced after the first few lessons. Grammar begins early; reading, late.

3.4 THE PHONETIC METHOD

This is also known as the Reform or Oral Method; it has had close links with the Direct Method movement. It starts with ear training, then goes on to pronunciation in the order: sounds to words to phrases to sentences. These are later combined into dialogues and stories. Phonetic notation, not spelling, is used in the texts. Grammar is inductive, and composition consists in the reproduction of things heard and read.

3.5 THE READING METHOD

This method was devised for schools whose only objective was a reading knowledge of the language. The text is divided into short sections, each preceded by a list of words to be taught through context, translation or pictures. After a certain vocabulary level is reached, supplementary readers in the form of stories or simplified novels are introduced, in order to enable the learner to consolidate his vocabulary.

3.6 THE GRAMMAR METHOD

In this method, rules of grammar are learned, along with groups of words. The words are then put together according to the rule, thereby giving practice in the application of the rule. Knowledge of the rule, however, is more important than its applications. There is no oral work or teaching of pronunciation. One of the advantages claimed for this method is that it can be classed as mental discipline. It is easy to apply and does not require a teacher who is a fluent speaker of the language. It is also simple to test and easy to control.

3.7 THE TRANSLATION METHOD

This consists of practice in translating texts of increasing difficulty, first from the second language into the first, and later from the first language into the second.

A variant of this is the Interlinear Translation Method. Here both an interlinear word-for-word translation and an idiomatic one are given. The story is divided into sections of lesson length, each with a series of questions and answers to accompany it, followed by a number of exercises in two-way translation.

Like the Grammar Method, the Translation Method can be taught to classes of any size, by teachers with an imperfect knowledge of the language and no special teaching-techniques. It is easy and cheap to teach and administer, and the number of class periods may be as few or as many as administratively feasible.

3.8 THE GRAMMAR-TRANSLATION METHOD

This is simply a combination of the activities of grammar and translation. The main features of the method are as follows: The grammar is an outline of formal grammar. The vocabulary depends on the texts selected. The teaching begins with rules, isolated vocabulary items, paradigms and translation. Easy classics are then translated. Vocabulary is divided into lists of words to be memorized; but there is little relationship between the vocabulary of successive lessons. Pronunciation either is not taught, or is limited to a few introductory notes. Grammar rules are memorized as units, which often include illustrative sentences.

3.9 THE ECLECTIC METHOD

This has been called the *méthode active* in France. It is essentially a compromise between the Direct Method, with its many demands on the teacher coupled with its alleged inaccuracy for the learner, and the more formal methods based on grammar rules and translation. The language skills are introduced in the following order: speaking, writing, understanding and reading. Activities include oral practice, reading aloud, and questions and answers. There is a certain amount of translation, with some deductive grammar, and some audio-visual aids.

3.10 THE UNIT METHOD

This is an application to language teaching of the five steps of the Herbartian system of teaching, viz., student preparation, presentation of material, guidance through induction, generalization, application. It can be applied at all levels. At the elementary level, for example, a unit would develop thus: 1. A unit of interest is chosen by vote by the class. 2. A committee of learners prepares a dialogue in the native language. 3. The teacher translates it, trying to stress one grammatical point. 4. From a duplicated sheet, the learner studies the content vocabulary of the situation, e.g. *travel, ticket, train*, etc. 5. A list is made of the grammatical constructions. 6. The vocabulary is learned by association. 7. Phrases and sentences, especially the ones with new grammatical points, are repeated and memorized. 8. The teacher sees whether the student has discovered the rule inductively. 9. The whole scene is acted out. 10. Finally a list of words is studied for free composition, translation, filling-in exercises or reading.

3.11 THE LANGUAGE-CONTROL METHOD

The main thing in this method is the limitation and gradation of vocabulary and structure. This limitation may be based on studies of word frequency or on the usefulness of the items taught. The meanings may be taught through controlled actions and pictures, through objects and visual material. It can be similar to the Direct Method, but it must be patterned and controlled. Both oral and written drills are included.

3.12 THE MIMICRY-MEMORIZATION METHOD

This is also sometimes called the Informant-drill Method. In it the teaching is divided into demonstration and drill, generally in the proportion of one of the former to two of the latter. The demonstration lessons teach grammar, pronunciation and vocabulary through a teacher and a native informant. In the drill lessons, the native informant, or drill-master, reads a few sentences, and the class, after listening a few times, mimics him again and again, until the sentence is partly memorized. Grammar is taught inductively or through model sentences. Beyond the elementary level there are lectures, dramatizations and discussions. A variation of this, without drill-master but with added recordings of dialogues and drills, is sometimes called the "Audio-lingual Method".

3.13 THE PRACTICE-THEORY METHOD

This is to some extent the reverse of the preceding method. Here theory follows practice, generally in the proportion of seven units of practice to three of theory. Model sentences are memorized, through constant repetition, by imitating informants and recordings. The model sentences are then analysed phonetically and structurally to permit their expansion into new sentences of the same type.

3.14 THE COGNATE METHOD

In this method the learner starts by learning a basic vocabulary made up of words which are similar in form and meaning to those of his own language. These are then immediately used for oral and written expression.

3.15 THE DUAL-LANGUAGE METHOD

Similar to the Cognate Method, this is based on the similarities and differences between the first and the second language. These are not limited to vocabulary but include the sounds, forms and syntax of both languages. The material is arranged according to the length and complexity of its formal elements. The first language is used to explain differences in phonetics, grammar and vocabulary. Each point of difference is used as the basis of systematic drills.

In addition to these methods, there are less widespread variants such as the Situation Method, the Simplification Method, the Conversational Method, the Film Method, the Laboratory Method, the Basic Method, not to mention the hundreds of methods named after their authors.

4. WHAT METHODS ARE MADE OF

In all these names of methods, the Direct Method, the Grammar-translation Method, the Phonetic Method, what does the term "method" mean? Does it refer only to what is taught, how it is taught, and when it is taught? It should be quite evident from the foregoing history and description of language-teaching methods that the meaning of "method" depends on the method. "Method" means different things to different people. For some, it means a set of teaching procedures; for others, the avoidance of teaching procedures. For some, it is the primacy of a language skill; for others, it is the type and amount of vocabulary and structure.

Different meanings of "method" can be inferred from the regulations on language-teaching method issued by departments, boards, and ministries of education. Some have decreed that the "Direct Method" shall be used to teach foreign languages. The name "Direct Method", however, says only *how* the language is to be presented. It simply says that the meaning is taught by making a direct connection in the mind of the learner between what he sees and what he says, and later between what he thinks and what he says. In other words no use is made of the learner's own language. It says nothing about *what* is to be taught or *when* it is to be taught. In fact, there is nothing in the Direct Method which makes it essentially different from the Phonetic Method, the Natural Method, the Situation Method, the Unit Method, the Language-Control Method, or the Dual-language Method. Although these are different from the Grammar-translation Method, the latter can also include many of their features, such as dual-language description, situations, and grouping into units, and still remain the same "method". All of these, in turn, can be included in the Language-Control Method, provided, of course, they control their language.

Lack of understanding on exactly what method means can lead to unfortunate results. The author was once asked by a certain government to design an experiment to determine whether the Basic Method or the Direct Method would be better for a certain area. Had the government realized that the Basic Method could also be taught as a Direct Method, they would have predicted the futility of such an experiment. They would have seen that the one is a list of words; the other, a set of teaching procedures. And neither a list of words, nor a set of teaching procedures, can of itself constitute a method.

Such terms as "the Direct Method", "the Simplification Method", "the Situation Method", "the Natural Method", "the Film Method", "the Conversational Method", "the Oral Method", "the Linguistic Method", can only be vague and inadequate because they limit themselves to a single aspect of a complex subject, inferring that that aspect alone is all that matters. Consequently as language-teaching methods, they often fail to consider what methods are made of and how one method differs from another.

One method can differ from another only in what a method, as a method, must include. The first question that needs answering therefore is: What must a method include? Surely it includes what all teaching includes, whether it be the teaching of arithmetic or astronomy, of music or mathematics.

All teaching, whether good or bad, must include some sort of *selection,* some sort of *gradation,* some sort of *presentation,* and some sort of *repetition.* Selection, because it is impossible to teach the whole of a field of knowledge; we are forced to select the part of it we wish to teach. Gradation, because it is impossible to teach all of what we have selected at once; we are forced to put something before or after something else. Presentation, because it is impossible to teach without communicating or trying to communicate something to somebody. Repetition, because it is impossible to learn a skill from a single instance; all skill depends on practice.

All language-teaching methods, by their nature, are necessarily made up of a certain selection, gradation, presentation and repetition of the material. It is therefore through these four inherent characteristics that one may discover how one method differs from another. Let us first consider differences in selection.

CHAPTER 6

Selection

OUTLINE

0. INTRODUCTION

1. PURPOSE, LEVEL AND DURATION
    1.1 Purpose
    1.2 Level
    1.3 Duration

2. CHOICE OF TYPE
    2.1 Dialect
    2.2 Register
    2.3 Style
    2.4 Media

3. CHOICE OF AMOUNT
    3.1 External Factors
        3.1.1 Purpose, Level and Duration
        3.1.2 Type
    3.2 Internal Factors
        3.2.1 Number
        3.2.2 Composability
        3.2.3 Information
        3.2.4 Probability
        3.2.5 Combinability
        3.2.6 Structurization

4. CHOICE OF CRITERIA
    4.1 Frequency
        4.1.1 What is Counted?
        4.1.2 How Much is Counted?
        4.1.3 What is Counted as What?
        4.1.4 Sorts of Frequency Lists
        4.1.5 Limitations of Frequency Counts
    4.2 Range
    4.3 Availability

0. INTRODUCTION

Selection is an inherent characteristic of all methods. Since it is impossible to teach the whole of a language, all methods must in some way or other, whether intentionally or not, select the part of it they intend to teach.

No method can teach the whole of a language. No native speaker knows all of it. Even the greatest writers never master the whole of the vocabulary of the language in which they write. The average native speaker knows an even smaller fraction of his native vocabulary. And he may have only a vague idea of a great many words he continually sees. The average worker, for example, according to the Princeton Opinion Research Corporation, understands only 12 per cent of the content words in the house organ of his company; he has only an uncertain idea of the meaning of words like *revenue* and *excise tax*. One can hardly expect a method for foreigners to include more of the language than the average native speaker possesses. And yet that is what many a method attempts to do.

The great amount of material taught by some methods includes much that is never used and soon forgotten. A learner often memorizes as many as 12,000 words in order to be able to understand a particular 1,000. This is because there is no relationship between the wide selection made and the limited purposes of the learner. It is partly through its relationships with the purposes, level and duration of a course that we can evaluate a selection of items, of words, structures and forms of a particular language.

If the course is short, the more important it will be to limit the course to the essentials, and the more difficult it will be to determine exactly what these essentials are. The selection is limited by the type of dialect, register, style and medium taught. A person may have a most extensive vocabulary in the literary language and still not have enough to order a meal. The well-known French writer, André Gide, for example, who had such a wide knowledge of the English literary vocabulary, as shown by his excellent translations of Shakespeare and Conrad, was quite unable, according to his friend Julian Green, to ask a London bus driver where to get off.

Another important factor is the amount of language involved. The problems of selecting a vocabulary of 300 words are quite different from those for a 4,000-word vocabulary. Determining the vocabulary size for a given purpose is itself a complex problem. Foreign-language methods used in many European countries teach 500 to 1,500 words a year over a period of six years. Of these a maximum of only one-third is remembered, according to the Vocabulary Committee of the Sixth Conference of the International Federation of Modern Language Teachers. But the amount selected and the efficiency of the selection is dependent above all on the very possibilities of limitation contained within the language itself.

Some languages can be limited in certain ways much more than others.

Since all methods must select, we must determine to what extent they can do so; we must find out how selectable a language is. Since many methods use selections of the language already made—word lists and syntax lists, for example—we must also determine how such selections differ. Finally, what is taught is also affected by the choice of principles or criteria on which selections are based. These must be compared and evaluated.

In analysing the selection which a method has made we must therefore find out the why and the how of the selection: (1) the purpose, level and duration, which affect (2) the type, and (3) the amount selected, all of which are influenced by (4) the way the selection is made, and determine (5) the items selected from the phonetics, grammar, vocabulary and semantics of the language.

1. PURPOSE, LEVEL AND DURATION

In order to evaluate or compare selections of a language, we must first know the purpose for which the selection was made, its level and duration.

1.1 PURPOSE

The questions to ask about the purposes of a selection are: why was the selection made, and for whom? Was it made for purposes of teaching, of examinations, of travel? Is it intended as a basis or foundation for second-language learning, or as a self-contained language for purposes of international communication?

The committee of the Interim Report on Vocabulary Selection recognized nine possible purposes for the selection of words: (1) The island vocabulary (closed); (2) the foundation vocabulary (open); (3) the standard examination vocabulary; (4) the purification of style and usage; (5) the practical vocabulary; (6) the cultural vocabulary; (7) the vocabulary for the simplification of texts; (8) the lingua franca vocabulary, and (9) the vocabulary of travel.[1401:18] The list, however, is far from complete, for there are a number of other special purposes. For example, during World War II, the U.S. Navy training manuals were reduced to a vocabulary of 250 general words plus 150 nautical terms in a special course of lectures, demonstrations and instructional films used to prepare foreign trainees.

Secondly, for whom was the selection made—for children, adults, adolescents?—for Indians, Africans, or Europeans?—for students, soldiers or tourists? The committee of the *français fondamental* recognized three types of people for whom a selection could be made: (1) Students in school; (2) Foreign peoples and immigrants, and (3) Tourists and travellers.[1453] But here again a number of special groups must be considered.

The greatest word-count selection ever made was for stenographers;[1491] one of the earliest was intended for the blind.[1424]

1.2 LEVEL

The amount of the language mastered and the skill which the learners may already have acquired in using it will obviously affect the selection. A course for absolute beginners will probably not contain the same type and amount of material as a course for advanced learners.

Level also has an effect on the relative importance of purposes for which the selection may have been made. The lower the level, the less the selection is affected by the purpose of the course. This is because there are certain fundamental elements in every language that anyone speaking it must know, no matter who he is or where he lives.

1.3 DURATION

The length of time covered by the course or syllabus affects both what and how much is taught. A selection intended for a two-week emergency course for newcomers will differ in kind and amount from one intended for a three-year course for immigrants. The material in a two-year school course at two hours a week cannot be the same as that in a six-year course at five hours a week.

It is the purpose of the course, its level and duration which determine the choice of the dialect, register, style and media which will be taught.

2. CHOICE OF TYPE

Selection of the language type to be taught includes a choice of (1) dialect, (2) register, (3) style, and (4) media.

2.1 DIALECT

The teaching of a language with a number of dialects poses the problem of selecting one of them. The pronunciation of General American differs from that of Southern British (see Ch. 2). There are differences in British and American usage and vocabulary. A method for teaching German may have to select either a Southern or a Northern variety of the language. In Spanish there is the choice between standard Castilian and a number of American varieties.

The choice depends not only on the variety most useful to the learner, however, but also on the type and amount of descriptive material available, on the type and completeness of grammars, dictionaries and phonetic manuals (see Ch. 2). A method may, for example, intend to teach Canadian

English to French Canadians but may be forced to make a choice between American or British varieties of the language because of the lack of adequate descriptions of Canadian English.

2.2 REGISTER

Methods may be written at different registers—military, scientific, commercial, etc. There are language courses for business, for science students and for soldiers. The importance of certain words, idioms and constructions is not identical in all registers of the language (see Chap. 2).

2.3 STYLE

A method may choose to teach the literary or colloquial style, standard usage or popular usage; the importance of items in the language may vary greatly from one to the other. The relative importance of words like *so* and *and*, for example, is not the same in popular usage as it is in standard usage (see 4.1.1 below).

2.4 MEDIA

Methods may choose between the spoken or the written language, since they may limit themselves to the teaching of reading, writing or speaking.

The degree of difference between the spoken and written forms varies from language to language. The difference in vocabulary between spoken and written English is about 15 per cent, according to Schonell.[1393] In other languages, like Arabic, for example, it may be considerably greater (see 4.1.1). Selection may be limited to what is common to speech and writing.

In each of these types of language, courses vary in the amount they select and in the way in which they select it.

3. CHOICE OF AMOUNT

If a language is a system of systems in which everything is interdependent, how is it possible to limit its amount? The limitation of a language is made possible by the fact that some parts of it are less systematic than others.

Items in a language differ in how closely they are linked into a system and how easy it is to dispense with them. Some items are therefore more selectable than others. Selectability depends ultimately on what one can eliminate and still have a language, and on the degree to which one can do without it in a given circumstance.

The selectability of any item is inversely proportional to its restrictability, that is, to the capacity of the language to do without it. If the item is a phoneme, its restrictability is low because a language cannot easily be deprived of one of its phonemes without modifying its system, no more than it can eliminate one of the letters of the alphabet. One cannot speak English without the phoneme /m/, for example. On the other hand, one can spend an entire lifetime speaking and writing the language without using a word like *viatic*. In fact, one may have to wait a long time before finding a situation in which such a word could be used. It is reported, for example, that a certain Judge Arthur Thomsen of Omaha, pondering a traffic damage suit, told the jury, "A careful driver ought reasonably to anticipate some vehicles making viatic use of the road," and then added, "I have been waiting two years to get a case where I could use the word '*viatic*'." It is easy for the language to do without such words as *viatic*, and the advantages of selecting them for teaching are therefore very low; in fact, their restrictability is so great that a method—like the judge—may have to do without them.

There are items, therefore, which one must necessarily exclude and items which one must necessarily include. Between these two extremes of what we have to use and what we cannot use lie the problems of selection. The two extremes are the end-points of a scale of restrictability the degrees of which correspond to the number of items a language can do without. The main outline of the scale is indicated in the figure on the following page.

Examining the scale, we find that the most restrictable items, the easiest to do without, are some of the meanings of the language, especially those "phonetic" meanings conveyed by the many variations in stress and intonation. They are also the most numerous; for there are more meanings in the language than there are different words to express them. Of the millions of meanings in the total vocabulary of a language only a small percentage can ever be taught. On the other hand, the lowest in restrictability are the letters and the phonemes, the choice of which is easy, since they all have to be included; it is difficult to restrict their number and still have a language.

Within each category of items there is also a scale of restrictability which fits into the general scale. Verbs have not the same degree of restrictability as nouns. And within the category of the verb, there are different degrees represented by the number of contexts to which each can apply. For instance, both *put* and *swim* are important verbs; but *put* is much less restrictable because it supports a larger number of contexts than *swim*; you can put more things in more places than you can swim.

The degree of restrictability is governed by two sets of factors, (1) external, and (2) internal.

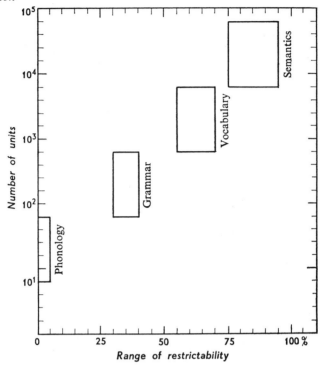

Within any level—phonology, grammar, vocabulary or semantics—the total number of units varies from language to language. This variation is indicated in powers of ten along the upright axis to the left. Along the horizontal axis, the corresponding estimates of restrictability are shown as percentage ranges based on average frequencies regrouped from the figures available. [1381–1514]

3.1 EXTERNAL FACTORS

The external factors are related to (1) purpose, level and duration, and (2) type of selection (see 1 and 2 above).

3.1.1 Purpose, Level and Duration

External factors affecting restrictability depend on the purpose, level and duration of the course. A course with limited objectives is more restrictable in its elements than is one with wide or multiple purposes. The higher the level of language learning, the higher the degree of restrictability and the greater the number of selectable alternatives. The lower the level, the lower the degree of restrictability, and the smaller the number of selectable alternatives. In other words, the closer we are to the beginning, the more our language is limited to that part of it which we cannot do without. For example, no course at the beginning level can leave out the articles; all courses at that level must necessarily include a fairly high percentage of structure words. A course at an advanced level, however, can teach an almost entirely different vocabulary from that of another course at the same level. The higher the level of language, the greater the amount of option in restricting its components.

The longer the course, the greater the possible range of selection; the shorter the course, the narrower the range. For example, a number of different short courses of two weeks' duration at the same level will all have to include a high proportion of the same words; whereas a number of six-year courses can be quite different in their concrete and abstract vocabulary.

3.1.2 Type

The greater the difference in type, the greater the range of selection; the smaller the difference, the lower the restrictability.

As the capacity to restrict a language increases, so does dependence on type, register, style and medium in the choice of items. For example, as restrictability increases, the meanings of a language depend more and more on situation and context of registers, so that technical and professional language includes a number of ordinary words with special meanings. These meanings are easy to do without, their restrictability is high because they are closely dependent on type.

Governing these external factors are six internal factors.

3.2 INTERNAL FACTORS

These internal factors are (1) number, (2) composability, (3) information, (4) probability, (5) combinability, and (6) structurization. The first three of these increase restrictability; the second three limit it. Restriction therefore increases with number, composability and information; it decreases with probability, combinability and structurization. It is directly proportional to the former and inversely proportional to the latter.

3.2.1 Number

Number includes the relationship between the size of a class of items and the frequency of the items it contains.

Restrictability is directly proportional to class-size; and inversely proportional to frequency. The more items there are in a category, the easier it is to eliminate one of them; for example, there are more words to eliminate than there are phonemes.

Selection

(i) *Class Size*

The following figures show the relative number of items in each class of the English and French vocabularies.

English Word-classes at the Thousand-word **Level**

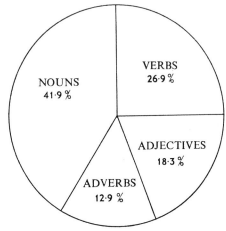

Relative size of word-classes in an English vocabulary of a thousand words. Figures based on Fries. [745:105] *Percentages corrected to exclude structure words.*

French Word-classes at the Thousand-word **Level**

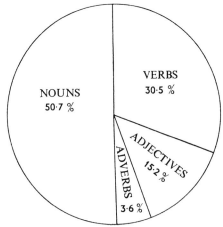

Relative sizes of word-classes in a French vocabulary of a thousand words. Figures based on Guiraud. [374:36] *Percentages corrected to exclude structure words.*

It is obvious from the figures for French and English that nouns form the most restrictable class of words.

The smallest class, as the following figure shows, is more frequent than most larger classes. In English, less than 200 structure words occur more often than all verbs, adverbs and adjectives combined, and almost as often as nouns.

Relation between Class-size and Frequency

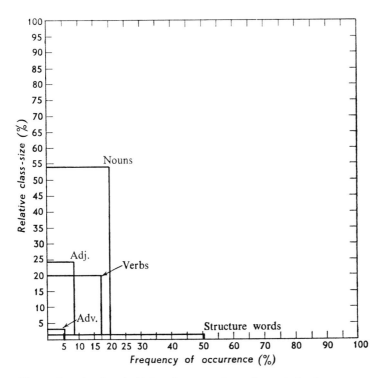

The smallest class has the highest frequency. It consists entirely of structure words, which make up less than 1% of the total vocabulary but almost half of our talk. Percentages are based on figures supplied by Guiraud.[374:36]

(ii) *Frequency*

Language statistics reveal a very high frequency of use for a very small number of items. Here is an example of this relationship, compiled from various word-counts of written English.

Number of different words	*Make up what Percentage of any text*	
4,500	99%	Thorndike
3,000	97.5%	Bongers
3,000	95%	Palmer
1,000	90%	Ayers
732	75%	Dewey
50	50%	Ayers
9	25%	Dewey

Results for the spoken language are even more striking:[139][93:73]

Different Words	*Percentage*
1,000	94%
100	72%

The small classes of words are used more often in speech than they are in writing. According to Miller fifty words make up 60 per cent of our talk and 40 per cent of our writing.[367:89]

The proportions are about the same in other languages. Only ten different French words on Henmon's list account for 25 per cent of the total uses.[1467] They are words belonging to small classes, like articles, determiners, prepositions (*à, de, dans, sur*), conjunctions (*et, ou, que*) and structural adverbs (*ne, pas, y*). These all form part of the structure of the language, of course; in other languages like Hungarian their equivalents might be counted as part of the morphology, or inflectional system.

At the other end of the scale it takes a large number of words to get an extra percentage point. Michéa has shown that although 3,000 words account for 95 per cent of language usage, and derivatives from these for an extra 2 per cent, it would take an extra 6,000 words to increase this by another 1 per cent.[1346] For the extra one per cent, Whatmough estimates an additional 9,000 words. But this extra one per cent cannot be entirely disregarded, since in a reading text it represents one word in a hundred, something like three to five words a page. Moreover, it has been shown that about half of the words in any text occur only once. The great word-count of Kaeding[1491] totalled 11,000,000 running words, giving 258,000 different word forms. Yet fully half this number occurred only once in the eleven million.

Number is related to the external factors of level, duration, and type. The lower the level, the higher the percentage of structure words. (See graphs on the relation of class-size to level.)

Relation of Class-size to Level

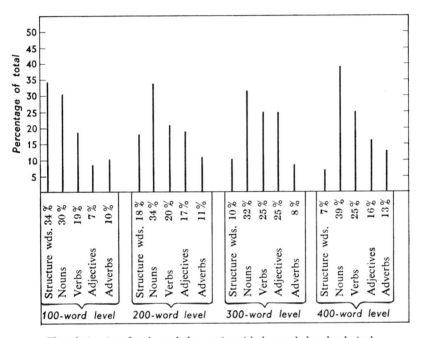

The relative size of each word-class varies with the vocabulary level. At the lowest level, structure words are the most numerous, although in the language as a whole they form the smallest class. Even at the 200-word level they are outnumbered by nouns, which become relatively more and more numerous as the level of vocabulary increases.

As the vocabulary increases with the length of the course it becomes less and less general. In practice, however, the relation between size of vocabulary and duration of course has varied from 500 in three years to the 10,000 in ten days, advertised in a certain new method for the teaching of Spanish.[1117:59] Most people reading such advertisements do not realize that they use less than that number of words in their own language. Many general vocabularies are larger than native speaking vocabularies, which total 4,539 for English-speaking adults as recorded by Schonell,[1393] and

Selection

7,500 for French according to the researchers of the *français fondamental* project.[1453]

Language teachers themselves are not in agreement on how many words constitute a general vocabulary. The Sixth Conference of the International Federation of Modern Language Teachers suggested objectives between 1,500 and 3,000 words for a six-year course. But surely the total must vary according to the number of hours per week. (See graph on the relation between duration and percentage of total units.)

As the number of selectable items increases, so does their dependence on type, on dialect, register, style and media. The dependence on media is

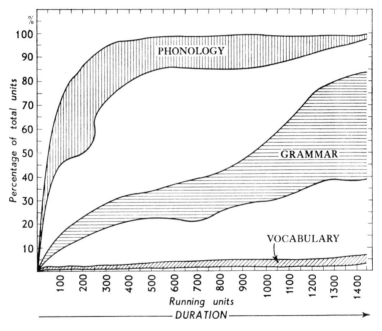

Restrictability decreases with duration, but it does so at a different rate for each level of language. At the level of phonology, the number of phonemes left to restrict may be limited to one or two after less than a thousand have been uttered in context. This is indicated as a percentage of the total by the scale along the upright axis. The horizontal axis refers to the appropriate unit of the level in question—sounds, forms, or words, as the case may be. The graphs represent ranges found in a count of running words, grammar forms and phonemes of a hundred English texts. The ranges between maximum and minimum lie within the shaded areas.

best seen in the relative sizes of active and passive vocabularies.[1376] Although the average person speaking on the telephone makes use of a vocabulary of only some 2,240 words (Berry), he will nevertheless understand many more when he sees them in print. College students are said to be able to understand between 60,000 and 100,000 words.[1384] For it takes fewer words to express our ideas than it does to understand those of others.

The restrictability of an item is inversely proportional to the stability of its frequency. For the more generally necessary an item is, the less its frequency varies from situation to situation or from text to text. And the more restrictable it is, the more its frequency will vary from situation to situation.

3.2.2 Composability

Restriction is directly proportional to composability, that is, to the possibility of making up larger units from smaller ones, sentences from clauses, clauses from phrases, phrases from words, words from morphemes, and morphemes from phonemes. As the units decrease in size, so does our capacity for composing our own items and our ability to restrict them. We make up our sentences more readily than we make up our own words. We can express this concept more clearly in the form of a diagram designed to

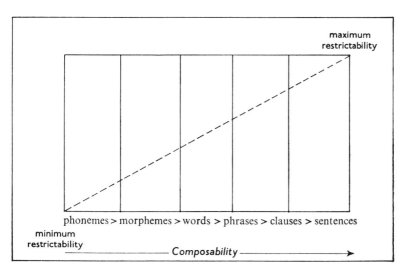

Relationship between Restrictability and Composability

show the relation between our capacity to compose our own items and our ability to restrict their use.

Our capacity to make up our own items increases with the level and duration of the course. At a very advanced level it is possible to compose not only a great number of new sentences, but also a number of new words. This is also true for differences in type; as the language becomes more and more specialized, the composition of new words and extensions of meaning become more and more necessary.

3.2.3 **Information**

Information is used here in its technical sense, which is related to the degree of freedom with which we choose the different elements of the language as we speak. For example, if we say, "I put it in the ———", what we choose next must be a noun; but it can be one of a great number of nouns. Whereas if we say, "It is a part ———", there is only one word which is most likely to follow, the word *of*. Information theorists calculate that in English our choice is restricted to about 50 per cent in this way.[363,368] And that 50 per cent carries no information because it can be predicted. The information is carried in the other free, unpredictable half of the language.

The more information carried by an item, the greater its restrictability. In other words, the less one can predict the occurrence of an item, the easier it is to do without it. Restrictability is therefore proportional to our freedom of choice in the use of the language. The freer we are to choose an item, the more restrictable it is.

An increase in level, duration, and variety of types is also an increase in the relative amount of information carried, and hence in the degree of restrictability.

These three factors—number, composability, and degree of information —increase the possibility of restricting the language. Three other factors— probability, combinability, and structurization—limit the possibility of restriction.

3.2.4 **Probability**

The greater the probability, the less the possibility of restricting the language. The more likely an item is to occur, the more difficult it is to do without it.

An increase in the level, duration, or number of types means a decrease in the probability of each new item, and hence a corresponding increase in its restrictability.

3.2.5 Combinability

This is the capacity of an item to combine with other items. Restrictability is inversely proportional to this capacity. The more an item can combine, the less easy it is to eliminate. This is true for the language as a whole, for all its levels and the categories which they contain. Phonemes can combine more than syllables, syllables more than words, and different sorts of words combine more than others. Structure words combine with more other words than do adjectives, adjectives more than nouns.

Combinability is one of the most fundamental characteristics of any item in a language. For it is the capacity of an item to combine with other items that largely determines its frequency and its probability of occurrence. Words that occur everywhere again and again are those which combine most readily with other words. Most of the structure words have a high degree of combinability. Words like *a* and *the*, *can* and *do*, *in* and *on*, can combine with thousands of others.

Combinability, however, is not limited to structure words. Certain verbs, adverbs, adjectives and nouns are more combinable than others. Verbs like *put*, *take*, *give* and *get* can combine with a great number of different nouns, and also with a relatively large number of adverbs and prepositions. A limited number of adjectives like *big* can combine with a large number of nouns. Among the nouns themselves a limited number of abstract nouns like *part* can apply to a great number of concrete nouns. And a number of concrete nouns whose meanings are easily extended combine with a large number of other nouns. For example, a word like *head* (of a person, a bed, a table, a cane, etc.) has a greater combinability than a word like *clock*. Within each class, therefore, there are different degrees of combinability, noun with noun, adjective with adjective, etc.

Combinability is limited by an increase in level, duration and differences in type. As the level increases the percentage of combinability of each new item decreases. The lower the level, the greater the potential of each item to combine with others, either at the same level or at a higher one. The longer the course, the lower the average percentage of combinability of each item it contains. And as the language grows more and more specialized, the degree of combinability of each new item decreases.

3.2.6 Structurization

This is the degree to which an item is structured or takes part in a structure. It is not limited to structure words. Some verbs, for example, are more structured than others. The verb *get* may be the opposite of *give*, but it is not its structural equivalent, since *get* but not *give* can be used with other verbs to express grammatical aspect, as in *get married, get going*, etc.

The more an item or class of items is structured, the less possibility there is of restricting it, or of choosing whether or not to use it. The highly structured elements of a language—its phonemes, sound-clusters, syllables, and structure words—will be found at that end of the scale where the restrictability is low, for the more an item is linked to a closed system the more difficult it is to do without it. On the other hand, items like concrete nouns and adjectives are found at that end of the scale where the restrictability is high, for the less an item is structured, the easier it is to do without it.

As the level, duration and number of types increase, the degree of structurization of each new item decreases. Conversely, the lower the level, the shorter the course, or the more general the type, the greater the degree of structurization of what is included. The more elementary the course, the higher the percentage of structure, for the simple reason that most of the items required to build sentences are structural ones.

These external and internal factors of purpose, level, duration, type, number, composability, information, probability, combinability and structurization, and their interrelations answer the question: How much of what? The specific items selected, however, depend upon the choice of criteria, or the principles which determined how the selection was made.

4. CHOICE OF CRITERIA

When we learn our first language, we automatically make our own selection. We learn words as we need them; and the more we need them, the more we use them. This so-called principle of "natural selection" has been applied to the teaching of second languages. Although it is possible for a teacher to attempt to apply to the second language the same principles used to learn the first, it is not possible for a method to do so, in so far as it must present its material in some form to the learner, in textbooks, films, recordings, etc.

Secondly, there are methods where selection is based purely on the random choice or whim of the author, often under the influence of the situation with which he happens to be concerned. Although such methods are not based on principles of selection, they can nevertheless be judged by them.

Apart from the principle of "natural selection" and no principle at all, there are a number of criteria on which selections have been based and through which they can be evaluated. These are: (1) frequency, (2) range, (3) availability, (4) coverage, and (5) learnability.

4.1 FREQUENCY

Selection by frequency is made by taking samples of the sort of material the learners are likely to read or hear, counting the items that occur the most often, and arranging them according to their frequency of occurrence.

Since the items occurring the most frequently are those which the learner is most likely to meet, they are the ones which are selected for teaching. Moreover, since frequent items are more readily recognized than infrequent ones, fluency in a language depends on the frequency of what is taught.

Frequency counts appear as lists of the most usual words in a language, often in their order of frequency. Not all frequency counts give the same results, however. Differences in results depend on what is counted, how it is counted, and how much is counted.

4.1.1. What is Counted?

Items do not occur everywhere with equal frequency. The number of times an item is used will vary with dialect, register, style, medium, and time.

(i) *Dialect*

The frequency of words varies from region to region. A word like *tonic*, for example, in many regions of the English-speaking world, would be no more frequent than other medicaments like *aspirin* and *vitamins*. But in the English of Boston and parts of New England, its frequency is likely to be closer to that of *tea, coffee, milk* and *beer*, since it is the usual word for non-alcoholic drinks made with soda-water. In Schonell's list of the oral vocabulary of Australian adults the word *bloke* appears as a very usual word;[1393] in other areas where *chap*, *guy* and *fellow* are the usual words, *bloke* appears as a much rarer word.

(ii) *Register*

Frequency is also affected by what the language is used for. Words like *invoice*, *cheque* and *sale* occur more often in commercial texts than they do in medical material. The first person pronoun makes up almost one and a half per cent of the words in personal letters, whereas in scientific texts it may have a frequency of zero (see 1.1.2).

To make the study more generally representative of a number of registers, some frequency counts are made from a number of sources. Hoz used private letters, newspapers, books and official documents.[1498] Josselson used newspapers, non-fiction, and the prose and dialogue of fiction.[1510]

Selection

(iii) *Style*

Differences in style influence the frequency of items at all levels of language. If the data is gathered from colloquial texts the relative frequency of words will not be the same as it would if only literary texts were included. The word *so* will be found to occur six times as often in popular usage as it does in standard usage; and *and* twice as often.[620:146] The interrogative verbal phrase is much more frequent in a radio dialogue than it is in a radio description of a horse-race.

(iv) *Medium*

Items occur in the spoken language with a frequency different from that in the written language. In written English, especially in literature, the past tense is more often used than it is in spoken English. In the spoken language the use of the first person pronoun is as high as five per cent of the total usage (in telephone conversations), but in written English it varies from 1·2 per cent to zero (in technical publications).[367:92] On the telephone our favourite word is *I* whereas in writing it is *the*.

In the past, most word-counts were based on written sources; this was justified on the grounds that the results were to be used in the making of methods for reading and writing. Thorndike's word-count was intended for native-language reading texts,[1410] Horn's for writing,[1417] and Kaeding's for stenographers.[1491] But the lists established by these counts were later used as a basis for selecting words for second-language teaching, including the teaching of the spoken language. There was some disagreement, however, on whether frequency counts based on written material gave results suitable for work on the spoken language.

The improvement of recording equipment facilitated large-scale counts of the spoken language. French,[1449] Berry[367:166] and Fries[745] used telephone conversations, the *Recuento de vocabulario español* made use of radio material,[1497] and the *français fondamental* project in France[1453] and Schonell in Australia[1393] sent out teams of researchers equipped with magnetic recorders to record the speech of people in their everyday occupations.

(v) *Time*

Frequency varies in time. The words of one generation have not the same frequency as those of the next. This is not only because a language is continually evolving, but also because fashions, opinions, and living conditions are continually varying and constantly affecting the frequency of the words which represent them. The frequency of *satellite* was quite low until man started making his own. The popularity of *jet aircraft* (*avions à réaction*) set the frequency of *réaction* rising in France. Industrial firms through advertising and publicity are continually trying to increase the frequency of the words after which they name their products; they have succeeded in establishing *kodak* and *hoover* as household words; but *exercycle*, *skijamas*, and hundreds of similar inventions may not last a generation.

All frequency lists are marked by the date of the materials on which they are based. Vander Beke's reflects the vocabulary of the many nineteenth-century French novels which he included, giving a much higher frequency to *carrosse* than to *automobile* or *avion*, and making *comtesse* and *duchesse* appear as everyday words.

So as not to appear dated, some frequency counts select materials from a number of different periods. Josselson's Russian word-count, for example, distributes the material over three periods: 1830–1900, 1900–1918 and 1918–1950.[1510]

4.1.2 How Much is Counted?

It is not only what is counted that makes a difference in the results, but also how much is counted. Statistically, the greater the number of items counted, the greater the reliability of the count. Kaeding's count was based on a study of eleven million running words, the *Recuento* on seven million, and Thorndike's count on four and a half million.

In frequency counts based on mixed sources, the amount of material from each will affect the results obtained. Some counts assume that all sources are equally valuable. Hoz takes 100,000 words from each of his four sources.

Range of sources is also indicative. Although Thorndike averaged 50,000 words from each of 200 sources, the differences between the sources are not as great as they might be, since most of the sources could be classed as literary.

4.1.3 What is Counted as What?

An important question affecting the results of frequency counts is: What was counted as a unit? In counting meanings, for example, the results of two studies of the same text may be quite different, since there is no agreement on how many meanings each item has and exactly what these meanings are. Similarly, there can be no agreement on the frequency of sentence patterns until we identify the different types. For it is no use starting to count something until we know what exactly we are counting.

The importance of this was evident from the very beginning of the vocabulary counts. Some word statisticians classified words by form; others by meaning or function. For some, like Kaeding, forms like *Bruder* and *Brüder* or *go* and *went* would be counted as an occurrence of two different words since they differed in form; for others, these were counted as two occurrences of the same word, since they had a common meaning. Or the distinction may be between system and discourse. In the system of the language, each of the above pairs is one word, but in the relation between words in discourse they are two. Contrariwise, a word like *du* in French is a single word in discourse but two words—*de la* (*de l'eau*)=*du* (*du vin*)—in the system.[467]

4.1.4 Sorts of Frequency Lists

In order to make use of lists based on different sorts of linguistic analysis and different amounts, dates, and types of materials counted, various lists have been grouped together, correlated, corrected and combined into new lists, some of them to be used for purposes quite different from those for which the original counts were made.

(i) *Grouped Frequencies*

Items in frequency counts can be re-analysed after they are counted and re-grouped to form a different list. For example, if a word-list based on a count of the different word forms includes *men, men's, man, manly,* and *mankind* as separate words with separate headings, these can all be re-grouped under a single heading and their frequencies added. This establishes a difference between vocabulary and inflection, and increases the relative frequency of words having a large number of derivatives. This is the sort of list first established for English by the committee of the Interim Report on Vocabulary Selection,[1401] for French by West, Bond and Limper,[1459] and for German by Morgan.[1485]

(ii) *Combined Frequencies*

Since the number of words counted increases the validity of the frequencies, some word-statisticians have added the frequencies from other lists to those they determined themselves. This is equivalent to increasing both the size and range, and hence, statistical validity, of their word list. Vander Beke[1465] added his frequencies to those of Henmon,[1467] whose list originated from a count of 400,000 words made to check and correct the validity of a list of 5,000 words which he had established subjectively. To these combined Vander Beke-Henmon frequencies, Verlée added his own.[1456] In this way, frequencies have become more and more reliable.

(iii) *Correlated Frequencies*

The relative importance of words in different lists can be correlated, in order to select words which are agreed as important. For example, the fact that a number of lists agree on the relative frequency of a certain word makes that word all the more important. Dottrens' list[1462] is a correlation of those of Dubois, Prescott and Haygood,[1461] which in turn is based on 2,000 words from Vander Beke.

(iv) *Corrected Frequencies*

Frequencies may be corrected for certain reasons or for special purposes. For example, Schlyter[1457] and Tharp[1458] made lists based on corrected versions of Vander Beke. Although they accepted more or less the majority of the first 2,000 words, the further they advanced into the lower frequencies, the more they relied on their judgment.

If a list is not entirely satisfactory for some reason or other, it can be corrected for special purposes, for a certain dialect or register, for example. More regional words can be added or more words of a certain register—technical, commercial or literary. For example, although words like *sword* and *treasure* may not appear in a list of everyday English vocabulary, they may have to be added if the list is to be used as a basis for reading material for adolescents, since such words are found in the sort of adventure stories which they read.

4.1.5 **Limitations of Frequency Counts**

The frequency of an item is not equally important for all purposes. It is more useful for comprehension, for example, than it is for expression. Although a passive vocabulary can be based on frequency, an active vocabulary must take other sources into account. For while it is possible to predict what a person will have to read, it is impossible to know everything he may want to say.

Frequency does not reveal the relative importance of concepts. It is not concerned with the code of the language (*langue*), but rather with its manifestation, its use (*parole*). Frequency is simply a statistical reflection of the usefulness of words in the materials analysed. The more materials are analysed, the more the new items added depend on the nature of the materials themselves.

Counts made for one purpose may be quite unsuitable for others. For example, if one were selecting vocabulary for a classroom text in the order of importance given by Thorndike's frequencies, one would have to teach about 4,000 words before introducing the words *chalk, blackboard, shelf* and *drawer*.

Moreover, certain items in the language have frequencies which are not at all stable, being high in some texts and situations and low in others. Such items are the great majority of concrete nouns and adjectives the statistics for which are inconsistent and therefore unreliable.

Frequency lists also disrupt word classes. If a method were based on the list of Vander Beke or on Schlyter's adaptation of it, it would have to teach the French word for the first day of the week (*dimanche*) in the first thousand words, the fifth day (*jeudi*) in the second thousand, the seventh and fourth days (*samedi, mercredi*) in the third thousand, and the second and third days (*lundi, mardi*) in the fourth thousand. Whereas if one were to use the uncorrected frequencies of the *français fondamental*, the words *dimanche, lundi* and *samedi* would appear in the first thousand, *mardi* and *jeudi* in the second. In any case, the days of the week would not appear together, because of the difference in frequency in the materials analysed.

The frequency of an item is greatly influenced by the material on which the counting was done. A verb like *sift* will be highly frequent in cookery books, but rare in most other works.

Because of these limitations of frequency counts, other principles have been used instead of or in addition to them. These are: range, availability, coverage, and learnability.

4.2 RANGE

The number of samples or texts in which an item is found is its range. A word that is found everywhere is more important than one that can be found in one particular text or situation only, even though its frequency there may be very high.

The greater the range of an item, the more important its frequency. The frequency of an item used in many contexts and situations is more important than that of an item used in only one. The items of widest range are generally the structure words, certain types of adverbs, adjectives, verbs and abstract nouns.

Vander Beke, for whom range eventually took precedence over frequency, noticed that of the 19,253 different words in the material he analysed, 13,186 (i.e. 68·5 per cent) occurred in less than half the texts. They were therefore eliminated because their range was not great enough. This left only 6,068 for the final list.

As might have been predicted, the words remaining showed an abnormally high ratio of verbs to concrete nouns (see 3.2.1, above). For it is the concrete noun that varies most from situation to situation and has consequently the narrowest range. And because of this, the frequency of concrete nouns varies a great deal from text to text. This characteristic of concrete nouns suggests that their main importance lies not in their frequency or range, but in their availability for use in a given situation.

4.3 AVAILABILITY

In a critical study of word-frequencies, Michéa noticed that the instability in the frequencies of certain words was not corrected by increasing the number of words counted.[1339] Their importance, therefore, could not depend on their frequency. Their usualness must depend on another factor; this other factor was found in the fact that they happened to be the most appropriate and necessary words for certain situations. Even though *blackboard* may not be a very frequent word elsewhere, it is a necessary word in the classroom. Any classroom vocabulary would have to include it.

Such words constitute the thematic vocabulary available for certain situations. The frequency of such words is quite unstable if based on texts or samples of speech; but it is quite stable if based on the situations themselves or on opinions about these situations.

The degree of availability of a word corresponds to the readiness with which it is remembered and used in a certain situation. To test his theory, Michéa divided vocabulary into sixteen main themes or general situations. He then asked a large number of people to list the twenty most useful words in each situation. The results showed a great degree of stability; they were used as a basis for correcting the frequencies in the oral records of the *français fondamental* project.[1453]

Even in available vocabulary, however, there are differences due to the peculiarities of certain areas or individuals. In country areas, for example, *bottes* predominated over *chaussures* 100 to 21, whereas in city areas *chaussures* predominated over *bottes* 100 to 50. For 181 boys listing *cravate* as an important article of clothing there were only 73 girls who thought likewise; but for 101 girls listing *corset*, there were only 62 boys.[1453:172]

The most noticeable result, however, is the great difference between this available vocabulary and vocabularies based on frequency. For example, there is only one item in common between the ten most frequent and the ten most available French verbs; this is the verb *aller*, which functions as both a structural and a content verb. The two sets of verbs are well worth comparing in the manner shown on the next page. Note that the frequent verbs are more abstract and more structural.

Most Frequent	*Most Available*
être	manger
avoir	boire
faire	dormir
dire	écrire
aller	lire
voir	marcher
savoir	aller
pouvoir	parler
falloir	travailler
vouloir	prendre

4.4 COVERAGE

The coverage or covering capacity of an item is the number of things one can say with it. It can be measured by the number of other items which it can displace. For example, there are at least nine ways of saying "How long have you been here?" in French; but *"Depuis quand êtes-vous ici?"* will cover all of them. And since the learner does not have to decide among a number of possible ways of saying the same thing, he is able to express himself more readily.[1704:62]

If there are two or more possible forms, the one which covers the greatest number of uses is preferable. For example, in French *quand* covers more than *lorsque*, *plus* more than *davantage*, and *à peu près* more than *environ*, since each is composed of elements which themselves can say a great deal. Similarly in English, *bag* can displace *suitcase, valise, handbag* and *sack*.

How is it possible for words to displace other words? They can do so by four means: (1) inclusion, (2) extension, (3) combination, and (4) definition.

4.4.1 Inclusion

A word which already includes the meaning of other words can be used instead of them. In English, for example, *seat* includes *chair, bench, stool* and *place* (reserve a seat, go to your seats). It can therefore be used instead of these words. The word *chair* on the other hand cannot be used instead of *seat, bench* or *stool*.

4.4.2 Extension

Words whose meanings are easily extended metaphorically can be used to eliminate others. For example, *tributary* of a river can be covered by *branch* or *arm*. Words such as these are the ones with the most meanings and are therefore those most worth selecting.

4.4.3 **Combination**

Certain simple words can displace others by combining either together or with simple word-endings. For example, the combination *news+paper+man* makes *journalist* unnecessary. *Handbook* can eliminate *manual*; *parting* can be used for *separation*. Between two similar words at the same frequency Verlée selected the more efficient, that is, the one which can produce the most compounds and derivatives.[1456]

4.4.4 **Definition**

Certain words can be replaced by simple definition. For example, *breakfast* can be defined as the *morning meal*, a *pony* as a *small horse*, and even a word like *pancreas* can be a part of our inside which changes our sugar into energy. Such words as *part* and *small* are useful because they can define and therefore help displace others. This is because these words represent characteristics and activities common to a great number of things; they can therefore be used to talk about these things. The mechanic can talk about the *parts* of an automobile; the mathematician about the *parts* of an equation. The physician can refer to the *parts* of the body, and the physicist, the *parts* of the atom. Chemists make different *parts* of a formula stand for different *parts* of a compound. The coal miner is interested in the *parts* of the mine which he has been working. Yet all these persons may talk to one another about the *parts* of the town in which they live and about the *parts* of their own house. It is words of such wide coverage as these that West included in his definition vocabulary, a selection of 1,490 words designed to enable a learner to read any text with the help of a unilingual dictionary using only this vocabulary to define all the other words.[1402]

The problem of coverage, therefore, is to decide on what needs to be said and to find out one acceptable way of saying it. It is essentially a problem in word economy.[1336] Some selections are built exclusively on these principles of coverage. Rigid application of them through a logical analysis of a language can result in a small self-contained or island language, the best known example of which is Basic English.[1400]

Basic English is a self-contained language of 850 English words used with a few inflections and sentence patterns and designed to express any idea. The logical basis of the system, reminiscent of the universal languages of Leibniz (*Caractéristique universelle*) and Condillac (*La langue des calculs*), was an outgrowth of work on the *Meaning of Meaning*, the work in which Ogden and Richards elaborated a theory of definition applicable to the simplification of language. By defining words with words and these with other words, they arrived at an irreducible core capable of defining all the other words in the language.

The language was first reduced to 7,500 words and, by redefinition, cut down to 1,500, which were further reduced to the eventual 850 by a technique of "panoptic" definition. This involved an effort to eliminate each word on the grounds that it was some sort of modification of other words, a modification in time, number, size, etc. For example, *puppy* was a temporal modification of *dog* (young dog), *army* a numerical modification of *soldier*. Similarly, a *crowd* was a *great number*, a *gale* a *strong wind*. This left 600 names of things which could combine to displace a great number of words such as *locomotive* (steam engine).

Verbs were reduced by a similar analysis. The verb *enter* was reduced to *go into*; *descend*, to *go down*, etc., until there remained a number of verbs like *go, give* and *take* which could be reduced no further. These turned out to be very few in number, only 18 in all, namely: 12 simple bodily or manual acts (*give, get, come, go, put, take, say, see, send, keep, let, make*), 4 variable auxiliaries (*do, have, be, seem*), and 2 invariable auxiliaries (*will, may*). Since verbs were eliminated on principle they were classified under operators, which also included prepositions and other structure words. Prepositions were reduced to 22, all except *of* and *for* referring to position or direction in space.

A great number of adjectives and adverbs were eliminated along with the nouns and verbs derived from them. Many of these, like *duty, honour, avarice*, and *thrift* were considered as fictions, that is, words which seemed to represent things, but actually referred to ideas, feelings, conditions, and emotional overtones. These could be made neutral by separating what is being talked about from what is being felt about it. So that both *avarice* (bad) and *thrift* (good) could be reduced to a *love of money*. This also eliminated such adjectives as *thrifty* and *avaricious*. What was left of the adjectives and adverbs of the language was 100 quality words plus 50 of their opposites which, along with the 600 nouns and 100 operators, gave the basic vocabulary of 850 words. These were to be put together in sentences, according to a few basic principles of grammar, namely: (1) Plurals with -*s*; (2) Derivatives in -*er*, -*ing*, -*ed*, from 300 nouns; (3) Adverbs in -*ly* from the quality words; (4) Degree with *more* and *most*; (5) Questions by inversion + *do*; (6) Operators and pronouns fully conjugated; (7) Numerals, measurement, calendar, currency and international terms as in full English.

The resulting limited language was subjected to a great deal of scrutiny and analysis by scholars engaged in vocabulary limitation by other or more varied principles.[1405] The system was criticized[1330] and compared with other limited vocabularies.[1399] For it had become the centre of a whole generation of controversy on vocabulary control, indulged in not only by specialists in the subject but also by persons with no knowledge of it. An anthology of the literature (pro and con) has been compiled by Johnsen.[1395]

Basic English, which was founded essentially on the principle of coverage, was a conscious reaction against the over-application of the principle of frequency in selection; it was not devised in ignorance of the principle. For at the time, Ogden had at hand the works of Horn, Thorndike and Dewey; but he believed that what a word will do for us is not the same as the number of times it is used. For him, it was not the frequency of a word which makes it useful; it was its usefulness which makes it frequent.

4.5 LEARNABILITY

Some selections are based on a preference for items easily learned. What makes an item selectable on these grounds? Any one or any combination of five factors are involved. These are: (1) similarity, (2) clarity, (3) brevity, (4) regularity, and (5) learning load.

4.5.1 Similarity

Some items are selected because of their resemblance with those of the native language and because cognates, like English *mother* = German *Mutter*, are easy to remember. On this principle, a class of French learners of English might start English with words like *table, page, nation, moustache, souvenir*; whereas a class of German learners might begin with *man, house, mouse, warm, ox, hound*.

Words and structures selected on this principle, however, are rarely the exact equivalents of those in the native language, and they are not always the most useful (see Ch. 3). For example, the similarity in form and meaning between English *brown* and French *brun* hides the fact that *brun*, being less generic, does not cover the meanings: brown bread (*pain bis*), brown paper (*papier gris*), brown shoes (*souliers jaunes*), brown sugar (*cassonade*), and brown shading (*en bistre*).[870]

It has also been suggested that some items in language are universal, and can be found in all languages. In 1952 the Committee on linguistics and psychology of the American Social Science Research Council started an investigation of this possibility. Their tentative conclusion is that there seem to be large areas in which most languages operate psychologically if not structurally in the same way.

4.5.2 **Clarity**

Some items are included in a selection because their meaning is easy to make clear. Words like *radiator*, which are the names of things which can be pointed to, are considered easier to teach and to learn than words like *insurance*, which require a complex definition or translation. But opinions vary on what exactly constitutes easy teaching and easy learning.

4.5.3 **Brevity**

Items are sometimes included in a selection because they are short and easy to recognize or to pronounce. Long words and constructions are considered difficult to learn. On these grounds a word like *foe* would be included in preference to the more usual word *enemy*, regardless of frequency.

4.5.4 **Regularity**

Items which follow the regular pattern of the language are sometimes selected to the exclusion of those which do not. Some methods, for example, include only the regular verbs in their beginning course.

4.5.5 **Learning Load**

An item may be added to a selection because the extra effort required to master it is so small in comparison to the potential value of the word. For example, for learners who already know the words *hand* and *bag*, the addition of the compound *handbag* does not add very much to the learning load. And although the item is already covered by *bag*, the learner does get an extra word with very little extra effort.

4.6 CONFLICTING CRITERIA

These five principles of selection—frequency, range, availability, coverage, and learnability—are not mutually exclusive. They are not all necessarily in conflict. Many words, for example, have a high frequency, a wide range, are readily available in a number of situations, cover a great deal of meaning, and are easy to learn.

Other items, however, may be justified by one principle but not by another, so that one of the following conflicts may have to be resolved:
1. Frequency *vs.* Availability: e.g., *pouvoir* vs. *manger*, *pouvoir* leading in frequency, *manger* in availability.
2. Frequency *vs.* Range: Words like *cheque* may be frequent in business letters, but not elsewhere.

3. Frequency *vs.* Coverage: The word *number* covers *many* and *few* (great number, small number), but *many* and *few* are more frequent. *Thank you* is frequent, but it can be covered by *It's very good of you.*

4. Frequency *vs.* Learnability: Many items are easy to learn but not very frequent, e.g., French *corsage* and German *Kindergarten.*

5. Range *vs.* Availability: The range of *pot* may be limited to kitchen vocabulary; it is, however, one of the most available words within that vocabulary.

6. Range *vs.* Coverage: Although range and coverage are often complementary, there are still a number of possible sorts of conflict. For example, a word like *want* has greater range than *to have a desire for*, but the latter has greater coverage.

7. Range *vs.* Learnability: An item may be found in a great many contexts and still be difficult to learn. For example, the morphology of the Russian numbers.

8. Availability *vs.* Coverage: The word *chair* is one of the most available to express the vocabulary of furniture, but it can be covered by *seat.*

9. Availability *vs.* Learnability: Although *hound* is easy for a German to learn, since it reminds him of *Hund*, the word *dog* is much more available.

10. Coverage *vs.* Learnability: For a French learner of English *valise* is more familiar to him than *bag*, but the latter has the greater coverage.

How are such conflicts to be resolved so as to permit an evaluation of items selected for teaching? Here is one possible technique:

1. First subtract that part of the list in which there is no conflict. Some lists will have a much higher percentage than others.

2. List conflicting possibilities under the principles which justify their inclusion. For example:

Frequency	Range	Coverage	Availability	Learnability
many	many	seat	dog	hound
		number		

3. Relate the table to the purpose of the selection to level and to type. For example, does the course stress comprehension or expression? If it stresses comprehension, frequency and range within the sort of material used will take precedence. If the course is mainly for expression, coverage and availability take precedence. If it is both comprehension and expression the order is: (i) Frequency, (ii) Coverage, (iii) Range, (iv) Availability, (v) Learnability.

4. The remaining (unjustified) items are totalled and their percentage of the total list calculated. The lowest percentage represents the best selection.

5. CHOICE OF ITEMS

All or any of the foregoing criteria may be used to determine and evaluate the specific items selected in the language from its (1) phonetics, (2) grammar, (3) vocabulary, and (4) meanings.

5.1 PHONETIC SELECTION

Some sounds are easier to pronounce than others. These are generally the ones most easy to produce and clearest to distinguish. This is the case for consonants like the alveolars /t/ and /d/ which account for more than 50 per cent of our consonant usage.[367:86] But, as the above tables indicate, the possibility of restricting the sounds of a language is extremely limited. Most languages have fewer than fifty significant sounds, and most of these are needed in the basic vocabulary. English has only 40; only nine of them are used half of the time. The most frequent /ɪ/ is used a hundred times more often than the least frequent /ʒ/ (0·05 per cent) according to Miller (quoting Denver).[367:86] Indeed, this is one of the few sounds that can be restricted in English by the avoidance, for example, of words like *rouge, measure* and *leisure*. But the number is so limited that any further restriction would greatly reduce the efficiency of vocabulary selection based on principles other than frequency.

The restrictability of the phonemes of a language is further limited by the fact that about half the phonemes of the first language are bound to occur in some form or other in the second. Trubetzkoy has suggested that the following phonemes occur in some form or other in most languages: /a, e, i, o, u/, /p, t, k/, /m, n, j/, /w, s/. If this is true, nearly all people learning a second language can be expected to produce some version of these phonemes. It is the way they are pronounced, however, that will cause difficulty.

If phonemes are not restrictable for use, they may nevertheless be selected for drilling. Some methods select one or two for each lesson and include exercises for drilling them. When analysing such methods it is necessary to notice whether these drills are based on useful words or on the vocabulary already taught. For example, is the English interdental fricative /θ/ practised through words which the learner is likely to have to utter, words like *thick* and *thin*, or through words like *thrall* and *thwart*, words which he will only run across in his reading, if at all?

Sound-clusters have greater possibilities of limitation than the sounds they contain. For example, it would be possible to limit words containing the English /st/ cluster, if there were any real need for it. (See 2 : 2.1.2.)

Syllables can also be restricted, since a quarter of what we say is limited to 12 different syllables; half of our speech makes use of only 70 syllables. But 1,370 more syllables would be required to add another 43 per cent.[1450] The selection of syllables is of less use in languages like English and German, where half of all speech is in monosyllables.[224]

What is more significant is the frequency of syllabic structure. In English the simplest structure V (vowel) accounts for only 9 per cent of occurrences, whereas CVC takes up 33·5 per cent. CV 21·8 per cent, VC 20 per cent, CVCC 7 per cent. and CCVC 2 per cent.[367:88]

It is in the area of catenation, rhythm and intonation that phonetic selections have the greatest range. This is not because there are more units, but because of our great degree of freedom to combine such features, and because of the great number of alternatives. For example, in the teaching of French pronunciation it is possible to select only those types of liaison which are compulsory, to eliminate emphatic stress from sentences and to limit the selection of intonation patterns to those devoid of special emotional overtones.

If the structures of a language form a framework which can support all the words of the language, the corresponding rhythm and intonation patterns may be considered as forming a framework for all the sounds and sound-clusters. The basic framework of rhythm and intonation patterns may be selected not only on the basis of frequency, range, availability, coverage and learnability, but also on the basis of suitability in the selected structures.

5.2 GRAMMATICAL SELECTION

The grammar of a language is made up of (1) structures, (2) inflections, and (3) structure words.

5.2.1 Structures

Structures include (i) sentence structures, (ii) clause structures, phrase structures, and collocations.

(i) *Sentence Structures*

Since there is still uncertainty and disagreement on how sentences should be analysed and classified (see 2 : 2.2), much less research has been done in the selection of sentence patterns than in the field of vocabulary. Inventories, however, have been made by Palmer,[758] Thorndike,[1441]

Jespersen,[565] Fries,[745] and Hornby,[1440] for English, and by the team of the *français fondamental* for French.

Although the possibilities of grammatical selection are not so great as those for vocabulary selection (see tables, above), selection of structures is important if only because it eliminates rival patterns and avoids duplication. This may be done on the basis of frequency. For example, the *français fondamental*[1453:222] has made use of such structure frequencies as these in the selection of its question patterns:

Où = *où, quand, comment, pourquoi, combien.*

Où va ton père?	11	Où est-ce qu'il va?	30
Où ton père va-t-il?	4	Où c'est qu'il va?	12
Où ton père va?	32	Où qu'il va?	5
Où va-t-il?	123	Il va oú?	45
Où il va?	45	Total occurrences:	307

Another basis on which sentence structures have been selected is the number of words and phrases which can fit into them. For example, the *it is here* structure can include more changes in words and phrases than the *here it is* structure.

To illustrate the problems of method analysis by means of comparison, eight courses starting at the beginning level have been chosen at random and simply labelled as Methods A, B, C, D, E, F, G, and H.

Suppose we are examining or comparing two methods for beginners (Method A and Method B), how would we go about comparing the sentence structures which each has selected?

We will probably not find them in the index. We may find them at the head of each lesson either in the textbook itself or in the teaching manual, under such headings as: *syntax patterns, model sentences,* and *sentence patterns.* Failing this, we shall have to look for them within the body of the lessons themselves. When we do find them, we may note for example, that Method A has only such fundamental structures as: *It is here; I got it for you; Joseph is coming; He was a stranger.* But in Method B, we find such structures as: *Yonder comes Joseph; A stranger he was, at that; You have made yourself to me a father; The boy studied with a perseverance of which he was not thought to be capable.*[1364]

The choice of the latter can be explained neither on the basis of any of the above criteria, nor by their capacity to absorb vocabulary.

(ii) *Clauses, Phrases and Collocations*

Sentence structures may be broken down into clause structures and these in turn into phrase structures and collocations—groups of words which usually occur together.

Here is an example of a sentence with two clause structures: *It is here, if you want it*. Some types of clause structures are included in Thorndike's inventory.[1441]

Certain words in a clause may be replaced by a group of words, that is, by a phrase. For example, the word *here* in the above example may be replaced by the following groups of words:

It is   here

in this box
on this box
on that box.
on that table.

In the group *in this box* all the words have been changed to *on that table*, but the phrase structure remains the same. Another type of replacement is where the word-classes change, but syntactic relations remain. For example:

It is here.
Fido is here.
The dog is here.

Collocations are phrases made of words which usually occur together, groups like *for the time being*. A tentative selection of these has been made by Palmer.[1443]

We have seen that we can change all the words in a phrase or sentence and still have the same structure. In certain expressions this is not possible. For example, if we change the *do* to *did* in *how do you do*, we get much more than a change from present to past; we get a change from a fixed formula to a free structure. Fixed formulas are a necessary part of the language, but they have to be selected and taught at the right level. For example, formulas like *thank you, yes please*, and *good-bye* are not on the same level as *I beg your pardon, much obliged*, and *well, I never*.

Clause structures, phrase structures, collocations and formulas may be selected according to any of the above criteria; or they may be chosen according to the number of selected sentence structures into which they can fit. On either of these characteristics we have little information. Here again research is retarded by disagreement or uncertainty on what exactly constitutes a collocation and what the differences are between collocations, phrases and formulas.

Selection

5.2.2 Inflections

Words may vary their meaning and function by changing their form or by combining with certain structural words; for example, *dog – dogs, man – men, ask – asked, go – went, has taken – was taken*. These formal changes include the various grammatical devices for indicating number, person, tense, mood, voice, and comparison.

Inflections may be selected on the basis of frequency, range, availability and complexity of form. Frequency studies of French tenses for example, show that two tenses cover 90 per cent of all indicative tenses used, and that the remaining seven tenses cover only about 10 per cent. The relative frequencies of these tenses have been given as follows:[807:116]

Present	66·89%
Perfect	22·98%
Imperfect	4·81%
Future	3·32%
Near Future	1·27%
Pluperfect	·41%
Future Perfect	·14%
Recent Past	·14%
Near future with past reference	·05%

The percentages, of course, may vary slightly according to the material analysed and the method of analysis.[808:152]

Because of low frequency of occurrence, certain inflections may be excluded entirely. It has been suggested, for example, that the simple past, the imperfect and pluperfect subjunctive be eliminated from elementary French courses along with irregular plurals and the feminine of rarer words.[1704:63]

Some courses, however, completely disregard the relative frequency of inflectional forms and teach all of them together so that the paradigm may be complete in the learner's mind. Courses in elementary Spanish, for example, teach the preterite perfect, despite the fact that it will occur only once in about 10,000 verb forms used; it is given the same time and importance as the present indicative which occurs 3,764 times more often.[620:208]

But the frequency and availability of a form is not related to its degree of difficulty;[808:153] nor is its similarity with forms in the learner's language. Both English and French, for example, have the present perfect tense, *I've finished / j'ai fini*, but this is precisely the tense which gives French learners the most difficulty. The point is not whether the form exists in both languages, but whether it has exactly the same semantic function.

194

In examining a method, we may find the inflections listed in a grammatical index or summary, or more usually, at the beginning of each lesson. In examining a text for beginners, it is necessary to check carefully not only the inflections which are formally taught, but also those which happen to be used. Are the tenses, for example, limited to the present continuous and the simple past, present and future, as they are in Method A, or do they go on to such forms as the pluperfect, and the future perfect continuous, *I had gone, I shall have been going*, as in Method B?

5.2.3 Structure Words

If these are not listed separately in either the learner's book or the teacher's guide we shall have to look for them in the general vocabulary. They will not be difficult to find, for they are generally very few in number (less than 200) and include the prepositions, the conjunctions, the pronouns, the auxiliaries, the determinatives, the negative particles, the interrogative adverbs, and the adverbs of degree.

Examining our sample methods, therefore, we find that Method A includes only such common structure words as *a, the, it, he, in, on, to, is, does*. Method B teaches less useful and less frequent words like *lest, hence, yonder, hitherto*. Of course, a certain number of structure words will be found in any course in which we find sentences, for the simple reason that it is impossible to speak or write a language without them. They are the words which are capable of putting thousands of other words into operation, although they are themselves very few in number.

These words in their proper places make up the framework or skeleton upon which the rest of the language rests. For this reason, their selection does not depend upon physical environment or on the age of the learner. They are the words which have to be mastered by anyone who learns a language. They are, in fact, the most useful words in the language; it is no wonder they are also the most frequent.

5.3 VOCABULARY SELECTION

It is in the field of vocabulary that there has been the greatest amount of work in language limitation. This is not only because words are the most numerous units to choose from, but also because they are most easy to identify, partly because of our fixed conventions in writing them.

There therefore exists a long tradition of vocabulary selection which goes back to about 900 A.D. when the Talmudists of the time organized the first word counts.[367:88] A history of vocabulary selection may be found in Bongers[1330] and in Fries.[1399]

Selection

What makes comparisons between different word-lists difficult is the difference in linguistic analysis on which they were based. Some have considered any two forms as two different words; *mouse* and *mice*, for example, are counted as two words by some and as a single word by others (see 4.1.3) above. Secondly, there is the difference in meaning necessary to make the same form a different word. Is the *claim* staked by a prospector and the *claim* made by his lawyer the same word or two different words? Thirdly, are the structural words to be counted as vocabulary or as structure? If they are counted separately, how about words like *have* and *get*, which can be classed as both structural and content words? Fourthly, if words are listed under separate parts of speech, how about those words like *round* which can function as any part of speech?

In judging or comparing selections of vocabulary it is necessary to consider each word in relation to the total number selected. For example, if the word *colt* appears in a beginner's course of 300 words, it will require more justification than if it were to appear as one item in a list of 2,000 words. One of our methods, for instance, includes the following in its first 400 words: *wheelbarrow, pew, hydrant, buffet,* and *ciborium*. These would be very difficult to justify at that level.

In examining a vocabulary selection, it is necessary to analyse not only the words which have been included, but also those which have been excluded, and the relationship between these and the selected vocabulary. For example, in the first 400 words of this same method, we find *colt, brace, spout, mould, spirit-level,* but not *road, clock, minute, night, river, fruit* or *baby*. And in the first 800 words we find *peep, pliers, diligent, chisel, peddler,* but not *cotton, fall, sort,* or *dark*. And after four years on this method the learner would have been taught *muskrat, churn, brood, crib,* but not *ticket, land, noise, office*. He would have the verb *skim,* but not *shut* or *laugh,* the adjective *shabby,* but not *cheap*. After five years, he would not yet have encountered *company, middle, knot, common, simple, sharp, flat, button, page, skin, drawer*; but instead he would have learned *waddle, germinate, knead, extract,* and *decay*.

We must also keep in mind that the usualness of a concept is not the same thing as the usualness of a word. Some concepts are expressed by a number of word forms. Does the method we are examining give all of these forms or only the most usual one? For example, the learner using the above method is taught *abdomen* in his third year and *stomach* by the end of his fifth.

The relative difficulty of the words selected can only be studied in different categories; verbs are usually more difficult than nouns, abstract nouns more difficult than concrete nouns. We must therefore examine separately the selection of the different sorts of nouns, verbs and modifiers, since there is a fundamental difference in their learning and teaching difficulties. Some methods have separate lists for each in the vocabulary index.

5.3.1 Concrete Nouns

Does the beginner's book include such concrete nouns as *table, hand, head, house, sun, water*, names of concrete things of our everyday experience, things which we all have in common and which we cannot do without? Or does the book include such replaceable and dispensable nouns as *helmet, cauldron, casement, hinge, pebble, chancel*?

5.3.2 Abstract Nouns

The difficulty with abstract words is not only that they cannot be taught by pointing to an object, but that they may have to be taught in combination with certain other words. For example, the word *part* must be taught with the word *of*, so that the learner can use it in its most usual context, *a part* OF *something*. Similarly, we have to teach *an answer* TO *a question, an attack* ON *or* AGAINST *someone, arrival* AT *a place*.

Some of these abstract words, however, may be of great use to the beginner, since they include the general names of the essential aspects of everyday experience. A word like *part*, for example, may be used when speaking of a great number of things—the parts of the body, of the house, of the city, of the country, of a machine, of an equation (see 4.4 above). One can do the same sort of thing with words like *sort, thing, number, idea, colour, form, size, middle*; but not with words like *venture, prophecy, sloth, sojourn, fortitude, soliloquy*.

5.3.3 Modifiers

Do we find, in the beginning course, such basic modifiers as *long, short, black, white, thick, thin, cold, warm*? Or does the textbook include words like *lengthy, frigid, bashful, illusive, nimble, thorough*, modifiers which any principle of selection could hardly justify at that level?

Is there at the beginning a sufficient proportion of defining words, like *square, wide, smooth, hollow, straight, hard, sharp*, which fill the gaps in the concrete vocabulary and enable the teacher to give meanings in the second language (see 4.4)? Or are the majority of modifiers words like *frank, stout, clumsy, sincere, elegant*, which are merely descriptive?

5.3.4 Verbs

The most difficult words to master in a language are generally the verbs.

Selection

They have to be learned along with the changes in form and auxiliaries required for person, number, tense, and voice. Many of them have irregular forms, which have to be learned for each verb. Moreover, verbs have much the same difficulty that we find in abstract nouns and adjectives. One cannot teach them simply by pointing to something. And one has to learn which prepositions or adverbs go with them. The learner has to learn *to listen* TO *someone, to go* TO *a place, to take something* FROM *some place*, and to *look* AT *or* FOR *something*.

Moreover, a distinction has to be made between features of agreement and phrasal verbs which are separate units in themselves. In the method we are examining, therefore, are phrasal verbs like *come in, go up, get over, put up with*, selected as such?

Some of these combinations are not the sum of their parts. *To give up*, for example, does not equal the meaning of *to give* plus the meaning of *up*; and *to fall out with* has nothing to do with *falling, out*, or *with*. Some phrasal verbs made up only of known elements are fully as difficult as additional words.

Because of these difficulties and many others, some methods select as few as a dozen verbs for beginners, verbs like *go, come, give, get, put, take*. Others go so far as to include verbs like *guess, pretend, hide* and *remind*, but not so far as to teach *waddle, vacillate*, and *ruminate*, as does the above method.

5.4 SEMANTIC SELECTION

Although meanings are those elements of language which are the most numerous and hence the most restrictable, less work has been done on their selection than on the selection of words. This is because there is no line of demarcation where one meaning begins and another ends. Whereas the form can tell us that *estuary* is one word and *mouth* is another, there is nothing in the form of the word *mouth* when it means *estuary* to tell us that it does so. Only the other words (*mouth of a river*) used with it can do that. But if these alone determine differences in meaning, the number of different meanings for a single word would be very large indeed for the meaning of the word *give* in *giving a pen* would be different from that in *giving a pencil*; the meaning of *on* in *on the table* would be different from *on* in *on the floor*. Most people would agree that there is no change in meaning in either of these cases. But if one considers the *on* in *on the ceiling* as against *on* in *on the wall*, is there a difference in meaning? Is there in *words on the blackboard, keys on a chain, a ring on your finger*? If we do not know where one meaning begins and another ends, how is it possible to select between them, or to count them, as some researchers have done?

Lorge got around this difficulty simply by accepting the meanings numbered as different in the *Oxford English Dictionary*.[1438] But these were based only on the material read by the dictionary-makers which, although voluminous, was mostly written before 1900 and hence was far from reflecting the actual semantic possibilities of present-day vocabulary. Moreover, the semantic divisions imposed by the editors, ingenious as they were, were largely subjective and in each case represented only one of a number of possible divisions into different meanings. West, for example, who incorporated Lorge's semantic count into the *General Service List*, found it necessary to reclassify the meanings into larger units.[1394]

The closer we get to the beginner's level, the more acute does the problem of semantic selection become. The reason for this is the fact that the more usual a linguistic sign, the greater the number of its meanings. If a method maker decides to introduce a common everyday verb like *take* into his course, he is immediately confronted with the problem of deciding which of its many meanings he will include. Even if he limits himself only to the definitions of the *Oxford English Dictionary* he will have to select from a total of 317 different meanings.

Meaning, however, is not limited to vocabulary; the structural elements of a language also convey differences in meaning and a difference in word meaning in one language is often rendered by a difference in the structure of another (see Ch. 3).

Finally, phonetic differences, especially changes in stress and intonation, can also convey differences in meaning, as can be seen when a difference in the relative stress in one language has to be rendered by a difference in vocabulary in another (see Ch. 3).

The different meanings which methods teach will rarely be found in the index of words or structures taught. Some vague reference to the selection of meanings may be found in the preface. Meanings therefore may have to be culled from the contexts in which they are introduced. In any case, in examining the lexical meanings, structural meanings and the phonetic meanings, it is always wiser to see the contexts in which these meanings are used rather than to rely on some general statement in the preface.

5.4.1 Lexical Meanings

Each of the words selected, as we have seen, may have a number of meanings. The word *make*, for example, has 97 different dictionary meanings. Some of these meanings may be quite useful for beginners; others may be unsuitable even for advanced learners. For example, the meaning of the word *make* in *to make a dress* is quite useful, teachable, and frequent; but the meanings of the same word in *to make for the door* and *to make out somebody's writing* might only be confusing for a beginner.

Many words which are the names of things in our everyday experience can be gradually extended in meaning; and this adds to their usefulness. The word *head*, for example, may mean a part of the body, the head of a pin or of a match, the head of a firm, or the head of a bed. Similarly, with *hand* and *face*; we have hands and faces, and so have clocks.

Some of these extensions of meanings are so usual and obvious that they are well worth teaching to beginners. Other extensions are not at all obvious; some are so far from current usage that, even at the intermediate level, an entirely new word might be better. For example, at a certain level the verb *to happen* may be better than the extension *to come to pass*.

Certain meanings are so idiomatic that they are fully as difficult as new words; for example, *to come to heel, to boot* (in the sense of *as well*), *to be a lemon, to stand fast* (after *to run fast*).

In examining a method, therefore, it is important not only to find out which meanings of each word have been selected, but also how closely these selected meanings are connected. Are words which have the same or almost the same meaning taking the place of more useful words? In the method we were just examining for vocabulary selection, for example, we find such redundant pairs in the elementary oral text as *among* and *amongst, cross* and *crucifix, autumn* and *fall*. And in the farm vocabulary of one of the early lessons we find both *goose* and *gosling* but neither *plough* nor *pump*.

5.4.2 Structural Meanings

Such general notions as the distinction between the person spoken to and the person spoken about (2nd and 3rd persons), the number of things referred to (singular and plural), the relationship between things and actions, and the time of actions are generally conveyed by the structure of the language. A number of these notions may be expressed by a single form; and a number of different forms may be used for the same notion. For example, the idea of the future in English may be expressed in the following different ways: *I'll go to London, I'm to go to London, I'm going to London, I'm going to go to London,* and *I go to London.* Some methods may select only one of these to convey future meaning; others may use all of them. Some methods may not even teach future meaning in their beginner's course, but may limit themselves to the simple or progressive present and/or the simple past. Others may include such distinctions between aspects of action as we find in the perfect tense. Still others may include special meanings of tenses such as *I would go* (meaning *I often went*).

Although methods differ in the phonetic, grammatical, lexical and semantic items which they select, all these added together do not make a language; for a language is not composed of separate items, but of a number of interconnected systems (see Ch. 2). A number of methods may have the same selection of items; but each may organize them quite differently. It is to this important characteristic of methods that we devote the next chapter.

CHAPTER 7

Gradation

OUTLINE

0. INTRODUCTION

After we have discovered *what* is taught we can ask *in what order is it taught*? Everything selected obviously cannot be taught at once; something must come before or after something else. Two methods may have the same selection of structure, vocabulary and meaning, and yet differ widely in the order in which they teach it. In other words, they may have the same selection, but a different gradation.

Although both *gradation* and *grading* are terms used to refer to the ordering of the language for teaching purposes, we use the former term because it avoids confusion with the grading of language tests and examination papers and with *grading* as a grammatical term.[206:122] Also because *gradation* suggests not only the act of ordering the language but the end product as well. Gradation answers the questions: What goes with what? What comes before what?

Does it matter what goes with what and what comes before what? If a language is a system and not a list of words or a collection of clichés, it matters a great deal. It means that we cannot start anywhere or with anything; for in a system one thing fits into another, one thing goes with another, and one thing depends upon another.

The importance of this in language teaching was long ago recognized. We shall therefore take a rapid glance at (1) the principles of gradation which have appeared from time to time in the history of language teaching, before outlining (2) a technique for the analysis of gradation.

0.1 HISTORY AND PRINCIPLES

Principles of gradation in language teaching had been established in Europe at least by the end of the Renaissance. In 1531 Vives, in his *De disciplini*, outlined principles of graded instruction whereby one lesson automatically introduced the next. Comenius, however, was one of the first to establish systematic principles of gradation.[1094] His main principle was that knowledge must necessarily come in successive steps, and that proficiency could be obtained only by degrees. Any language could be divided into degrees in such a way as to encourage good teaching. For Comenius, good teaching was that which enabled someone to learn rapidly, agreeably and thoroughly. In order to achieve this end in language teaching, it was necessary that the method be specially graded, for "the method of languages is more difficult than the method of knowing and working".[1094:158]

Comenius claimed that systematic gradation reduced the difficulties of language learning by distributing the extensive material of a language into steps arranged in specially prepared texts in which everything progressed, not by leaps and bounds, but gradually. To begin with, the foundations should be properly established, by devoting to them the best models and the best teaching. The beginning should be slow and accurate, rightly understood, and immediately tested. Unless the first layer is firm, nothing should be built on it; for the whole structure will be developed from the foundations. All parts should be bound together so that one flows out of the other, and later units include earlier ones.[1094:117] Whatever precedes forms a step to what follows, and the last step should be traceable to the first by a clear chain of connection. When the learner realizes that everything is in regular steps he has a desire to go ahead.

Uniformity makes for rapidity. In order to encourage uniformity, related things should be taught together; opposites should also be taught together because when placed side by side they become clear, and one helps in teaching the other. Parallelism also makes for greater clarity. No opportunity to draw parallels should therefore be missed. Larger units should be taught before smaller ones and the material should be arranged so that the few come before the many, the brief before the long, the simple before the complex, the general before the particular, the near before the remote, the analogous before the anomalous, and the regular before the irregular.[1094]

One of the purposes of such careful gradation was to avoid the confusion caused by a casual or perfunctory arrangement in which a confused mass of words retards, repulses or perplexes the mind.[1094:143] It seems, however, that after the death of Comenius these principles of gradation in language teaching were either ignored or forgotten.

In the nineteenth century they begin gradually to reappear. In 1885, Heness, writing on the language-teaching principles of his *Leitfaden*, says that his method "consists simply in questions spontaneously but naturally and logically connected and built up one on the other, each suggesting the next."[1280]

Later, Gouin, applying principles of association psychology to language teaching, insisted on teaching together what was normally associated together.[1277] Gouin grouped the vocabulary of a language under five headings: home, man in society, life in nature, science, and occupations. Each of these was subdivided.

Home:	dress, water, fire, etc.
Society:	school, church, games, etc.
Nature:	hunter, shepherd, fields, etc.
Science:	plants, animals, birds, etc.
Occupations:	carpenter, shoemaker, tailor, etc., etc.

Gradation

In the early twentieth century Bréal was proclaiming the principle of starting language teaching with whole sentences, of starting with sentence structures instead of with word-lists and grammar rules.[1260] The order in which new items are introduced was given a great deal of importance by both Jespersen and Sweet.[1274:178] And Palmer included "gradation" as a major division of his work on the scientific study and teaching of languages.[1245:119]

In 1922, Briod outlined principles for the gradation of words, meaning and grammar. According to him, each item that is added should reinforce what has gone before, not erase it by giving contradictory impressions. Each new item should confirm what has been taught and prepare for what will follow.[1235:24] One meaning should be mastered before others are taught; and these meanings should be closely related to the known ones.[1235:48]

By the 1930s some of the American language-teaching specialists connected with the Modern Language Survey were urging the teacher to replace the "jigsaw-puzzle" by the "snowball" conception of language learning. But no definite principles were given as to how this should be done.

It was only in the 1940s that principles of gradation began to be rigidly and systematically applied to beginners' courses in limited vocabularies. Richards conceived language-teaching method as an arrangement of graded sentence-situation units forming an "organic" sequence in which each step supports and is supported by the others.[202:92, 96] A sentence-situation unit was defined as one in which the elements of the sentence are made clear by the situation in which it is used. The structure of the sentence is taught by varying its elements along with the corresponding elements in the situation.[1517] In this way the most confusing forms of a language could be made clear if they were presented in the right place in the sequence.[1397:82] The essential vocabulary was organized into graded sentence sequences, each building outward from the preceding ones.[1516]

This notion of breaking a repertoire of language behaviour into a progressive series, moving from simple to complex stages, bore little resemblance to traditional theories of learning, since it did not include rote memorizing as an essential element.[1704:174]

Most principles of gradation have been justified on purely psychological grounds. One of the justifications of the principle that each new item should confirm what has been taught and should prepare for what is to come, is the prevention of what the psychologists call *retroactive inhibition*, whereby new material is confused with old material in such a way that neither can be remembered. In a good gradation, new material would strengthen the known material by the process of *facilitation*.

Psychologists have also discovered that a greater number of items can be learned in a fixed amount of time if these fit into established and interconnected patterns.[367:212] We learn systematic and regular series more easily than irregular ones. The irregular ones lead to error by analogy. The more such errors appear in the learning process, the more likely they are to appear later in the use of the language. Responses associated with one stimulus will also be associated with all similar ones; the greater the similarity, the stronger the association. Therefore, the smaller the difference from one step to the next, the better the learning.[1523]

0.2 ANALYSIS

Regardless of the principles on which they may be based, all methods include (1) some sort of grouping of their material, and (2) an arrangement of it into some sort of sequence. It is by comparing the grouping and sequences of material that we can see how one gradation differs from another.

The material, being a language, is both system and structure. It is made of a system of sounds, words, phrases and meanings which can be taught either separately or together. Each of these sounds, words, phrases and meanings can be fitted into structures, which in turn can be arranged in different sorts of sequences. The questions arising out of the grouping and sequence of system and structure may be illustrated as follows:

	Grouping	*Sequence*
System	What goes with what?	Which items follow which?
Structure	What fits into what?	Which structures follow which?

Let us see first how the grouping may vary from one method to another and how it can be compared and evaluated.

1. GROUPING

The grouping in some methods may be better organized than it is in others. To illustrate this, we shall from time to time compare the grouping in a number of methods which are actually in use. (See Ch. 6: 5.2.1.*i*.)

Grouping concerns (1) the systems of a language, and (2) its structures.

1.1 GROUPING IN THE SYSTEM

To analyse the grouping of the system of a language is to answer the question: What goes with what? What sounds, words, phrases and meanings are taught together?

What are the phonetic, grammatical, lexical and semantic groupings of the method?

1.1.1 Phonetic Grouping

This includes the grouping together of phonetic units with each other and with other elements of the language.

The occurrence of units of articulation and catenation will depend on the words used at any particular point in the course. But the grouping of units of rhythm and intonation may be independent of both words and phrases, since many of their different patterns may fit into the same structures.

A graded system of phonetic units can be made the phonetic counterpart of a graded system of grammatical units. If the method starts with a few highly useful sentence structures which it will repeat again and again with varying elements, then the most usual rhythm and intonation patterns of these structures may be well worth teaching at the same time.

1.1.2 Grammatical Grouping

Methods differ in the way they group grammatical items with themselves and with items of other systems.

Some structural words, for example, are best grouped with others. *What* goes with *this* and *that* (*What's that?*); *where*, with prepositions (*Where is he? In his office*). Certain inflections may best be grouped with certain nouns, adjectives or adverbs. The simple present (present habitual) tense may be grouped with words like *usually, often, frequently*, and *every*. (*They go to the country every week-end.*)

If we examine our sample methods (labelled A, B, C, etc.) we find that one method (Method A) has a better grammatical grouping than another (Method B), since the only tense taught, the present, is grouped with the structure words which go with it. Method B, on the other hand, groups the present tense with superlatives, possessives, and regular and irregular plurals; and it fails to group the plural with the corresponding singular forms, or the superlative with either the comparative or the uninflected adjective.

1.1.3 Lexical Grouping

Words may be grouped together (i) by association, or (ii) by collocation.

(i) *Association*

The association of words is justified on both linguistic and psychological grounds. The more links there are between words, the more we can say with them; ten words from the same context give more possibilities than one word from ten different contexts.

Psychologically, the association of words helps us to remember them. But the associations are not the same for all persons and for all languages. The majority of persons of one language may have one predominant set of word associations. For example, in English, more than half the speakers of the language associate the word *chair* with *table, seat, furniture,* or *sit.*[367:177]

There are several different types of association. They are: contrast (man – woman), similarity (blossom – flower), subordination (animal – dog), co-ordination (dog – cat), superordination (spinach – vegetable), part-whole (day – week), derivation (deep – depth), completion (black – board) predication (dog – bark), egocentrism (success – I must), and assonance (pack – tack). Methods differ in the types of association used and the extent to which they use them. If we examine Method C, for example, we find that the whole goes with its parts (*house – roof, door, windows*); the general with the particular (*fruit - apples, oranges*); the object with its attribute (*sun – heat*), or its complement (*teacher – learners, school*). Some words are linked by a common denominator (*hat and coat, soap and water*); some reflect the interlinking of things and events (*journey – train – taxi – bags – tickets*). Method C groups its words by association to a much greater extent than does Method D, which begins with the sequence: *aeroplane, ants, apple, arm, ass, axe.*

On the other hand, in Method B, which uses word association as one of its main principles, we can find such gaps as *day* without *night*; *thoughtful* without *thought*; *peck measure* and *tape measure* without *size*; *rake* and *hoe* without *plant*; *raft* without *boat* or *ship*; and *bugle* without *sound*.

(ii) *Collocation*

Certain words necessarily go with others, some depend on others and cannot be easily used without them. For example, *long* and *short* go with words for things that can be long or short—pencils, string, blades, hair, rope, and grass. And it is with these words that Methods A and C group these adjectives. Method D, on the other hand, teaches *blue* and *brown*, without including words for objects which have different colours.

Certain words in a language may be collated with a certain structure word. This sort of grouping makes the course more systematic. For example, the word *of* goes with certain nouns like *box* (of matches), *glass* (of water), *head* (of a pin), *page* (of a book), or any *part* (of anything).

1.1.4 **Semantic Grouping**

Some words have a large number of meanings. Any one of them can be grouped with the meanings of another word. Some of these meanings go together better than others. For example, the temporal meaning of *on* goes better with ordinal numbers and days of the week than does the temporal meaning of *at* or *in*. The temporal meanings of *on* and *in* also go together with such words as *when* and *now*. (When? On Monday, in January.) Method A teaches them together. (When? On the 21st, on Friday, in June.)

On the other hand, a number of different words may have meanings so similar that it is uneconomical to group them together. Method B introduces *river*, *stream* and *brook* together at the beginning level, where *river* could easily have included the meaning of the two other words.

1.2 GROUPING IN THE STRUCTURE

If a language is a system of systems where everything is interrelated, a method approximates to the language to the extent that its selected items fit one into the other. The better they fit, the better the system, and the more there is that can be done with it. How well they fit depends on the extent to which (1) the sounds fit into the words, (2) the words fit into the phrases, (3) the phrases fit into the clauses and sentences, and (4) the sentences fit into the contexts.

1.2.1 **Sounds into Words**

Do the phonetic elements of the course fit into the lexical and grammatical items taught? Are the new phonemes found in the new vocabulary? Does each intonation pattern fit into the phrases and sentences at the level in which it is introduced?

Method F lists the words in each lesson under their stressed vowel. But it leaves out the vowel /ə/, which is the most frequent in English and which is the most important in unstressed syllables. Method A recommends stress drills from the first lesson. Yet the phonetic drills of these two courses are based on the vocabulary taught. Method D, on the other hand, has an entirely different vocabulary for phonetics, obliging the learner to spend his time repeating a number of words he will not be using.

1.2.2 **Words into Phrases**

Not all words fit into the same phrases, clauses and sentences. The word *make*, for example, does not enter the same structure as *ask*. You can say *I asked him to do it* but not *I made him to do it*. And both *I asked him to do it* and *I made him do it* are structures which are of no use to a person wanting to use the verb *prevent*; what he needs is the structure pattern *I prevented him from doing it*.

Some phrase structures can absorb more words than others. For example, the French structure *d'une voix* (etc.) *basse* (etc.) can include more adjectives than the structure *à voix* (*basse, haute*), which in turn absorbs more than *à haute voix*.

In examining this part of the grouping therefore, we should find out not only the degree to which the words fit into phrases, but also the extent to which phrase structures can absorb the selected vocabulary. In Methods A and C most words fit into the phrase structures being taught. For example, *in the box* (*bag – drawer – bottle*); *in the box – on the box*; *on the board – off the board*. All the words in the first few lessons of A and C fit into all of the phrase structures used:

in the box	in the box
bag	on
drawer	over
bottle	under

Concrete nouns like *hat, pencil* and *book*, combined with *table, floor* and *shelf*, help make clear a structure word like *on*, and the phrase structure into which it fits. Because any of the first three can be *on* any of the second three, the choice and grouping of the words can bring out the usefulness of the structure. This is not the case in Method D, which includes less useful concrete nouns, the grouping of which is merely alphabetical: Lesson 1 uses words beginning with the letter *a* (*ant, apple, arm*); Lesson 2, words starting with a *b* (*bag. basket, bat*); Lesson 3, with *c* (*cat, coat, cot*), and so on.

1.2.3 Phrases into Clauses and Sentence Structures

Phrases fit into certain clause and sentence structures. For example:

He	put	it	there.
His mother	will put	a sandwich	in his school bag.
Jimmy Smith	is putting	his exercise-book	on the teacher's table.

If we look at the first five structures of Method C we find that all the phrase structures fit into all the clause-sentence structures; for example, *He put it on the table* (*on the wall – over the door – in the box*). In Method D, less than half of them fit together.

1.2.4 **Sentences into Contexts**

Finally, do the sentences fit into the contexts? In Method A, all sentences are linked together through a series of interrelated situations. But in Method B, more than half the number of sentences have no relationship with any context or situation to which the lesson might be referring.

The sentences in some methods are simply a series of numbered and unconnected items illustrating a grammar rule; for example, a certain English method popular in the early 1940s starts out, in its first lesson (devoted to the substantive), with the sentence *He gave a large sum to his cousin*, followed by *Here is Baby calling Nurse*.

There are methods in which sentences are not only disconnected but unrelated to any real context in which they could possibly be used. In such methods we find sentences like: *The garden of my father is larger than the pen-knife of my uncle*, and *The big dog wants but the little dog does not*.

Some methods group their material exclusively around a series of topics in such a way that words and sentences used in the contexts of one topic are useless in dealing with later topics. This makes it difficult to incorporate the material of one lesson into another; it discourages the natural repetition of material from lesson to lesson.

2. SEQUENCE

Since any item taught must necessarily come before or after some other item, all methods have sequences in which their material has been arranged. There are (1) the sequences of individual items within each system—phonetics, vocabulary, grammar, and meaning—and (2) the sequences of combinations of these items into the various structures.

2.1 SEQUENCE IN THE SYSTEM

The larger the number of items, the greater the number of possible sequences; the more open the system, the greater the possibilities of arrangement. Phonetic items, being relatively small in number, have the least number of possible sequences, (2) grammar has more, (3) vocabulary still more, and (4) meaning most of all.

2.1.1 **Phonetic Sequences**

The range of phonetic sequences depends on the type and number of phonetic items and on the extent to which they are dependent upon other sequences in the grammar and vocabulary of the language.

Phonemes have the least possibilities, not only because their number is relatively small but also because they are dependent upon the order in which words and inflections are introduced.

By making the sequences of words and inflections depend on the sequence in which the sounds are introduced, it is sometimes possible, at the very beginning, to bring in the sounds of the language one after another, postponing the difficult ones until the learner is ready for them. But some phonemes are easier to postpone than others. In English, for example, the /ʒ/ phoneme can be postponed the longest since it occurs in very few words of high frequency. But it is most difficult to postpone phonemes like /ɩ/ and /ə/, not only because they are so very frequent but also because they occur in the most basic structure words and inflections like *is, it, a,* and *the.*

In practice, however, most methods do not permit phonetic considerations to interfere with the order in which words and inflections are introduced. They simply teach the pronunciation of the language separately, using sequences based on principles which vary from one method to the next. Some courses simply ignore sounds which are similar to those of the learner's native language and treat the others in the order of frequency or relative difficulty—vowels first, then consonants, then rhythm and intonation. Others may start with rhythm patterns, including phonemes in the order of their frequency of use.

Methods also differ in the relationship between the sentences and words used in the phonetics and those used in the grammar. In some methods they are entirely different; in others, they are identical, sentence-stress patterns being taught through sentences from the text, phonemes through the vocabulary already covered. Some courses will wait until enough words containing the same phoneme have been taught before attempting to treat it systematically. Method C, for example, waits for seven lessons before it treats the phoneme /ʌ/; from these seven lessons it brings together words like *under, come, does, us, brother, mother, oven, button, son, sun, Sunday, Monday, money, brush, thumb,* and *number.*

Some words, especially the structure words, have a number of different pronunciations, depending on the rhythm of the phrase into which they fit. For example, *can go* can be /kan gou/, /kən gou/, /kn gou/, or /kŋ gou/. Some methods insist on the stronger form first, on the grounds that it is acoustically clearer; they start with the pronunciation /kan/ before /kn/, /ði/ (*the*) before /ðə/ and /ei/ (*a*) before /ə/. Others do the contrary, introducing the weak forms first since they are the most usual when normal conversational rhythms are used.

The order in which allophones or non-relevant variants are taught may also differ from course to course. Some will begin with only the significant distinctions; any sort of /t, d, n, l/, for example, will be acceptable if it does not get mixed up with other sounds. Others will insist from the very beginning on the right sound with its allophones; the /t, d, n, l/ must be alveolar (gum-ridge) sounds in English and dental sounds in French. There are some courses, however, which go still further and include at the beginning cases of assimilation where the English alveolar /t, d, n, l/ changes to dental before interdentals /θ/, as in *eighth*, *width*, *tenth*, and *health*.

Intonation patterns pose quite a different problem, because of the many variants that can be superimposed on a single phrase. There are several ways of saying *I don't know*, and these can be taught in any possible order. Some methods start with the intonation having the least number of semantic overtones. In French, for example, a pattern without emphasis may come before any of the emphatic ones. But if frequency of occurrence is used as a principle, an emphatic form may well be the first taught, because it is often the most usual.

2.1.2 Grammatical Sequences

The grammar of a language offers a greater number of alternative sequences than does the phonetics.[1523] There are the sequences of (i) the structure words, (ii) the inflectional forms, and (iii) the different types of word-order.

(i) *Structure Words*

Although they are among the hardest to teach, the structure words must be introduced as soon as sentences are used, because it is impossible to make sentences without them. For although they are very few in number, they constitute about one-third of the words used in most sentences. The first to be taught are those which fit into the simplest structures.

As examples of different sequences of structure words, let us examine the first lessons of two of the methods which we have before us, and list the first twenty structure-words in the order of their appearance:

> *Method A:* this, is, I, that, you, he, she, a, to, from, it, on, off, in, there, and, they, are, there, the.
>
> *Method B:* what, do, you, in, this, I, a, and, the, are, on, but, still, in, they, which, how, where, has, to.

Method A begins with those general reference words to persons and things that can be pointed to (*this – that*); later it brings in their space analogues (*here – there*); and some time later in the course, their time analogues (*now – then*). It combines these with the most useful form of the most frequent verb (*is*) to form a simple structure. On the basis of the opposites (*this – that*; *I – you*; *he – she*), it teaches the directional opposites (*to – from*). Immediately after having established a few pointing words it brings in the indefinite article in *This is a . . . .* But, to avoid confusion, it does not bring in the definite article *the* until six lessons later. Method B, regardless of possible confusion, introduces both articles together. The structure word *still* is taught in the first lesson, long before the more obvious adverbs *now, then, before, after*, which *still* supposes; for *I am still here* infers *I am here now* and *I have been here for some time*. Although formally simple, *still* is semantically complex.

The place which a structure word has in the sequence may affect other sequences of word-order or inflection. The early introduction of *y* in an elementary French course involves the teaching of new types of word-order, *Il est ici, Il n'est pas ici; Il n'y est pas*. Method B begins the course with the question words *what* and *do*, which involve complex changes in the basic word-order.

The sequence of structure words may also involve social considerations. In French, *tu* may fit into a situation involving two children; but *vous*, the politer form and the more generally useful, may be the one to teach, since a foreigner speaking the language to adults has generally to wait a long time before he can ever allow himself to address one of them as *tu*.

(ii) *Inflectional Forms*

Both the structure words and the content words may appear in different inflectional forms. Let us examine the gradation of the first dozen of these as they appear in Methods A and B.

Method A: this, is, my, your, his, her, him, here, gives (*pres. tense*), these, those, are.

Method B: see (*pres. tense*), boys (*plural*), getting, dressed, teeth, his, saw, whose, has, youngest, day's, gladly.

Method A starts with the most productive form of the most frequent verb *is*, brings in the third person before the second, the singular before the plural. Method B brings in the plural before the singular, the superlative (*youngest*) before the uninflected form (*young*) and the adverbial *-ly* (*gladly*) before its adjective base (*glad*).

Principles on which inflectional sequences are based may conflict with those on which vocabulary sequences are built. For example, it might be better to postpone irregular forms like the plurals *feet* and *men*, or irregular verb forms like *went* as the past of *go*; but it may be necessary to include their basic uninflected form because of its immediate usefulness. It may be possible to postpone difficult agreements without postponing the words themselves, like the agreement in French, for example, of the past participle of *avoir*.

Gradation

(iii) *Word-Order*

Sentences, clauses, phrases, collocations and formulas may have different types of word-order. Methods differ greatly in the sequence in which these types of word-order appear.

In order to get an idea of some of the possible differences of word-orders, let us look at the first few lessons of Methods C and D.

(a) Sentences and Clauses

Let us compare the first five types in each method. Here they are, in the sentences and in the order in which they appear in the text:

Method C	*Method D*
(1) I am here.	Point to the picture of an aero-
(2) This is a man.	plane.
(3) He will take his hat off the table.	This is a book, is it not? Yes,
(4) Now it is in the man's hand.	it is.
(5) It is in the man's hand now.	Colour this square blue.
	This is not a book, is it?

In Method C the word-order is limited to the general pattern of Subject + Verb + Complement. The aim is to establish this pattern before another one is introduced. The Method D list, on the other hand, contains different and more complex patterns: imperatives (Verb + Complement), positive and negative statements with positive and negative question-tags (Subject + Verb + Complement + Verb + Subject + Negative and Subject + Verb + Negative + Complement + Verb + Subject), and the short reply form. The reason for introducing these forms, it seems, is to give the teacher the structures he needs to keep the class doing things and answering questions. Method C avoids this on the grounds perhaps that it is not necessary to ask questions in order to make learners speak, nor to give commands in order to make them act.

In Method D, the sentences, being mostly imperatives, questions and negatives, assume that the learner understands the language already; for sentences which ask for physical or verbal responses must assume that the person to whom the order or question is addressed understands what is said.

(b) Phrases

Here are the first five types in Methods C and D, in the order of their appearance:

Method C	*Method D*
(1) a man	to the picture of an aeroplane
(2) this man	to the map of Africa
(3) my hand	of a boy bending
(4) in my hand	to the black square
(5) my right hand	this square

We note that Method C starts with a simple combination (*a man*) and goes on gradually to more complex ones (*my right hand*); whereas Method D starts with the complex (*to the picture of an aeroplane*) and goes on to the simple (*this square*). Method C brings in only the modifier + noun combination; Method D also uses it (*black square*), but only after the less usual noun + modifier pattern (*boy bending*).

(c) Formulas and Collocations

Both Methods C and D avoid formulas and collocations at the beginning; others, like Method E, start with simple greetings like *Hello* and *Good morning*, limiting them to those with regular structures.

Method A introduces formulas in the following order: (1) Hello – Goodbye; (2) Please – Thanks; (3) Good morning – Good afternoon; (4) How are you – Fine, thanks; (5) How do you do – See you later. Formulas with the same word-order as found in the phrases and sentences are considered preferable to those with a different word-order.

Method F begins with less useful expressions like *of course* and *on the other hand*. Some methods using a small vocabulary give beginners such confusing collocations as *all along, not at all, have to do with*.

2.1.3 Lexical Sequences

The problems of sequence are not the same for all classes of words.[1523] It is therefore necessary to make an initial distinction between sequences of (i) concrete nouns, (ii) abstract nouns, (iii) verbs, and (iv) modifiers.

(i) *Concrete Nouns*

The order in which concrete nouns are introduced may be due to their use in making the grammatical sequences clear. It may also depend on the sequence of contexts, which in turn depend on external factors like dialect, register, and style. A military course, for example, may well teach *rifle* before *pencil*, and *belt* before *blackboard*. But a general course like Method D can hardly be justified in introducing, as it does, *dumb-bell* and *Indian club* before *comb* and *brush*, *silo* before *hospital* and *post-office*, and *aisle* before *way*.

Gradation

(ii) *Abstract Nouns*

The main question here is this: Are the higher abstractions based on the lower ones, and are these in turn based on the concrete words which define them? In Method C, *apples* and *oranges*, after ten pages, become *fruit*, which combines with *milk*, *meat* and *bread*, twenty-four pages later, to become *food*. Method A has a similar treatment of abstract nouns; Method D avoids abstractions altogether, and B brings them in haphazardly from the first lesson.

Not all concrete nouns can precede abstract ones. Some low-level abstractions are of greater utility than a dozen concrete nouns. In Method B, for example, more could have been said earlier by introducing *liquid* before *sap* and *pus*.

(iii) *Verbs*

Because verbs have more forms than nouns, some methods begin with very few and bring these in gradually. Methods A and C start with verbs like *give* and *get*, *put* and *take*, actions through which a great number of objects can be manipulated. Method D also starts with verbs which manipulate objects, but with the less frequent ones like *point, find, colour,* and *draw*. Method B starts with some useful verbs, but it also includes many less useful and less frequent ones, with which it overloads its first lessons. For comparison, here are the content verbs in the first three lessons of Methods A and B:

Method A: give, get.
Method B: see, get, dress, brush, put, like, watch, come, play, belong, splash, begin, look over, ask for, give, raise.

Not only are the verbs more numerous in B but some of them are complicated to teach. Even highly useful verbs like *see*, which simply express sensation, are not so easy to demonstrate as verbs like *give* and *get*, which can be expressed in the moving of physical objects, and are more generally useful than verbs like *brush* and *splash*. Some verbs in B (*look over, ask for*) have the added difficulty of having to be learned along with the preposition with which they are used.

Method B introduces more specific verbs of narrow application, verbs such as *tug*, before more generally applicable equivalents like *pull*. It also brings in derived verbs before the more usual adjectives or nouns on which they are based, *to sharpen* before *sharp, to land* before *land*.

(iv) *Modifiers*

Since modifiers may have different degrees of abstractions, the above questions apply to them. Though a certain number of them are useful in a foundation course, quality words are not indispensable parts of the structure of English. It is possible to speak English without them; in fact, we do so half of the time. They need not therefore appear in the first few lessons, as they do in Methods D and B.

Method B not only teaches a large number of modifiers, it introduces the complex derivatives before the simple base forms, *loudly* (*loud* + *ly*), before *loud*, and *frequently* before *frequent*.

2.1.4 Semantic Sequences

Both the structures and the vocabulary of a language have meaning—(i) structural meanings, and (ii) lexical meanings.[1523]

(i) *Structural Meanings*

Structural meanings may be found in (a) structure words, (b) inflectional forms, and (c) types of word-order.

(a) Structure Words

Although they are often called meaningless or empty words, the structure words may each have a large number of meanings. Let us take for example the various meanings of the definite article. Which of its many meanings take us gradually and furthest into the others? Method A starts in this order: (1) the sun (absolute uniqueness), (2) the floor (uniqueness within context), (3) the book on your table (limitation of context), (4) this is a pencil; the pencil is in my hand (previous reference). These meanings are introduced gradually one at a time; later on, the course could also include: (5) to go to the cinema (any one), (6) the ant is a hard worker (all of them), (7) a bullet hit him in the leg (a definite part), (8) cheaper by the dozen (fixed unit of measure), and so on. Whereas Method A uses a sequence which goes gradually from the general to the particular, Method B brings in the above meanings haphazardly in the order (5), (4), (8), (7).

Most prepositions have a great number of meanings. These may be arranged in a highly teachable order. For example, Method A teaches the various senses of *on* in roughly the following order, starting with the physical meanings: (1) on the table, (2) on the wall, (3) on the blackboard, (4) on the ceiling, (5) put a ring on, (6) put gloves on, (7) on Friday, (8) on your knees. At a more advanced level it could go on to: (9) play on the guitar, (10) on the phone, (11) on the radio, (12) on the market, (13) tax on cigarettes, (14) on the committee, (15) on a trip, (16) on your mind, (17) and so on. The gap between these different senses can be bridged by intermediate meanings which make the lesson-to-lesson development of the meaning of *on* even more gradual. Methods B and D show no such gradual development; B starts with an extension of Meaning 6 and from there goes on to (7), (2) and (8).

(b) Inflectional Forms

Some of the grammatical forms of both nouns and verbs may have a number of meanings. For example, the addition of the final *'s* in the genitive case may mean any of the following: (1) the owner of a thing (*Tom's book*); (2) the doer of an action (*Tom's question*); (3) the receiver of an action (*Tom's education*); (4) a certain type (*a men's shop*); (5) a certain measure (*a day's work*). Method C begins with the first of these, which is the most frequent; Method B begins with the last.

The various meanings of verb forms must also appear in a certain sequence. Take some of the meanings of the simple present tense, for example:

(1) Habitual action:	He goes to town every Saturday.
(2) Future time:	He goes to town next Saturday.
(3) Past time ("Historic" present):	One morning he goes to town, goes up to the Mayor and says . . .

Method A limits its meaning to that of habitual action. One recently published course, however, introduces both the meanings of past time and habitual action in its third lesson.

(c) Word-Order

Some types of word-order have a number of structural meanings. For example, the Subject + Verb + Complement combination may mean that a person or thing:

(1) is identified –	This is Tom.
(2) is located or described –	Tom is here.
(3) does something to somebody –	Tom sent him.
(4) undergoes an action –	Tom was sent here.
(5) results in the action undergone –	Tom was sent a letter.

If the course starts with this pattern, which of its meanings does it teach first? Method A first identifies persons and things before it describes them; Method C locates them before it identifies them; and Method B puts them into action before either identifying or locating them.

Phrases have likewise a number of structural meanings. For example, the modifier + noun combination may mean that a person or thing (1) has a certain quality (*a small bag*), (2) is made of something (*a 'paper `bag*),

(3) is used for something (*a ˋpaper bag, a ˋpaper knife*), (4) is in the state of (*an open door*), (5) does something in a certain way (*a fast speaker*). Of these meanings, Method A starts with the first, whereas Method B begins with the fourth and goes on to the fifth.

(ii) *Lexical Meanings*

It is in the content words that differences in meaning are most easily seen. Many of them have physical meanings which can be extended metaphorically; *mouth*, for example, may refer to the mouth of a man, the mouth of a bottle, or the mouth of a river. The word *case* may mean a box (a case of beer), a circumstance (in that case), a legal action (he has no case), and a category of disease (a bad case of 'flu). The word *power* may mean physical strength (the power of his muscles), mechanical strength (this motor has a lot of power), general capacity (the power of a lens), legal right (power of arrest), political leadership (the party in power), influence (to be in someone's power).

Verbs have often more meanings than nouns. For example, here are some of the many meanings of the verb *run*: the boy ran up the hill; the road ran up the hill; he ran the car up the hill; he ran the rope through his hands; his car runs smoothly; these colours don't run; the contract runs for three years; the thought ran through his mind; he ran a knife into the man and then ran away; he ran away with his neighbour's wife; we're running short of envelopes; feelings run high in these matters; do not run the risk of failure; let's run over the details again; I ran across Bill this morning; the clock is running down; he ran up a big bill. These meanings may appear in various orders, be spaced differently throughout the course, and be fitted in different ways into the lessons which teach them.

In the first lesson of Method A, we find the first meaning of *head* as part of the body; ten lessons later it is extended to mean the head of a nail, a pin, and a match; after a further ten lessons it is linked, as the controlling part of the body, to the heads of a family, of a school, of the army and of the government. The purpose of this analogical sequence of meanings is to increase the range of the words taught while keeping the learning load light.

This can be applied to verbs as well as nouns. Let us take the verb *give* as an example. Starting with the most physical sense, it is easy to act out the meaning of giving a pencil to someone, and to go on gradually from there to giving a push to something, giving our name, giving a message, giving answers to questions, giving information, giving a party, giving someone work, giving our word, and so on. The main question is whether

221

the physical senses are taught first, and of these, the most obvious and expansible.

Let us compare the first meanings of a few of these content verbs in Methods C and B.

First meanings of:	*Method C*	*Method B*
GIVE	He will give his hat to the man	The teacher will gladly give it (some information) to her.
GET	I will get my hat.	They are getting dressed.
HAVE	A man has two eyes.	The boys are having a game.

The meanings which Method C starts with are among the most physical and expansible; those in Method B are not. If both methods continue like this, C is bound to have better semantic sequences than B.

A semantic sequence is not translatable from one language to another for the simple reason that two words are rarely equivalent in all their meanings. Compare, for example, the following sequence of meanings of French *mettre* and English *put*:

METTRE

French		*English*
1. le mettre sur la table	–	put it on the table
2. mettre le couvert	–	lay the table
3. se mettre au travail	–	to get to work
4. mettre du temps	–	take time
5. se mettre à table	–	be seated
6. se mettre à parler	–	start talking
7. le mettre à la porte	–	show him the door
8. être bien mis	–	be well dressed

PUT

English		*French*
1. put it on the table	–	le mettre sur la table
2. put him up	–	le loger
3. put up with him	–	le supporter
4. put it in	–	l'insérer
5. put it on	–	le poser
6. put it out	–	l'éteindre
7. put it down	–	le descendre
8. put it against	–	l'appuyer

Note that, although the first meaning may be the same in both languages, the other meanings are quite different. So that not only will the sequences be different, but also the grouping. What is grouped with clothes is

Meaning 8 in French, but Meaning 5 in English. A semantic gradation in one language cannot be transferred to another.

2.2 SEQUENCE OF STRUCTURES

Sequences of structures may differ in (1) where they go (direction), (2) how they grow (expansion), (3) how they change (variation), and (4) how long they take to get there (length).

2.2.1 Direction

In which direction is the sequence progressing? Is it continuous or is it interrupted by detours?

As an example, let us examine the directions in which the sequences of structures are arranged in Methods C and D.

In Method C, the first structure, *He is here* (*I am here*, etc.) incorporates the elements of the second structure, *This is a man*, thus:

	1. He is here
2. This is a man.	3. This man is here
4. This is his hat.	5. His hat is here
6. This is a table.	7. His hat is on the table

Once these elements have been established, they are used in building new structures, by adding one new element at a time – *He is **putting** his hat on the table*, etc. Method D, on the other hand, shows no such gradual build up, but abruptly goes from *Point to the letter 'a'* to *This is a book, is it not?*, the latter being a structure of an entirely different type containing entirely different elements.

A sequence may go from one structure to the next by the use of expansion and variation.

2.2.2 Expansion

A sentence structure with a minimum number of elements can be expanded by adding clauses, phrases and words to the positions into which they fit. A single position can be expanded thus:

It is there
    the shelf
    on the shelf
    the teacher's shelf
    the book on the teacher's shelf
    under the book on the teacher's shelf.

Gradation

Or positions can be added to form an expanding sequence, such as:

> It is.
> It is coming.
> It is coming here.
> It is coming here alone.
> It is coming here alone now.

Such expanding sequences are to be distinguished from conflicting sequences like: *She is here now – Now she is here*; *I got a book for her – I got her a book*. If we examine the list of the first five structures of Methods C and D (2.1.2, iii a), we notice that in C there is no conflict until we come to the last two structures. In Method D, however, conflicts in the sequence of structures are greater and more numerous. For example, *This is a book, is it not?* is followed by *This is not a book, is it?* Some methods, like Method A, separate any two structures which are thus in conflict; for example, the structure *I gave him something* may be confused, and often is, with the structure *I gave something to him* so as to produce such sentences as *I said him good-bye* and *I put him my coat*. For the same reason, Method A teaches question forms only after the most usual statement forms are sufficiently familiar, so that the word-order in *This is Tom* does not develop into *What this is?* For a learner may use a structure, not only by analogy with those of his mother-tongue, but also by analogy with part of a structure already taught.

This uncontrolled analogy, encouraged by the early introduction of complex and conflicting patterns, has been suggested as a cause of such structural errors as: *Point the picture. This square brown. I go every week to cinema. Will be tomorrow some English course?*

There is also the question of whether the sequence of structures follows the order of their expansibility. Are the more expansible structures taught first, and how gradually are they expanded? In the table in 2.2.1 we see how Method C gradually expands the *He is here* structure to *His hat is on the table*, expanding *He* to the semantically equivalent *This man*, and *here* to *on the table*. In this way, the structure is further expanded as the course advances. Method D starts with *Point to the picture of an aeroplane*, an already expanded structure which soon approaches its maximum expansion in the sentence, *Point to the picture of a boy catching a ball*.

How gradually structures are expanded depends on the extent to which the elements in each expansion are varied before another expansion is made.

224

2.2.3 **Variation**

The greater the variation of each element, the clearer the structure appears. Here, for example, are the variations which C makes in its first two structures, *I am here* and *This is a man.*

(1) I (*he, she, it, they, you, we*) am (*is, are*) here (*there*).
(2) This (*that, these*) is (*are*) a man (*a woman, a table, a hat, the fingers, my head, his hat*).

Note that all elements are varied. Now compare these variations with those in the first two structures of D:

(1) Point to the picture (*map, letter 'a'*) of an aeroplane (*Africa, North America, ants, an apple, an arm, Asia, an ass, an axe*).
(2) This is a book (*a box, the door, an aeroplane, an ant*), is it not?

2.2.4 **Length**

The number of variations and expansions determines the length of the series or text. A long series can be better graded than a shorter one only if the sequence expands continually in the same direction. If the direction of two sequences is the same, however, the longer one is better graded, since it generally indicates the use of a greater number of variations and hence a better exploitation of the possibilities of the gradation. (See Ch. 10: 2.1.)

Any of these sequences in which the elements or a combination of elements are introduced may be presented in written form or spoken form, for the teaching of reading, writing, listening or speaking. The order, or stages, in which these four skills appear is not, however, a matter of gradation; it has to do with the presentation of the material which has been selected and graded. This will be the subject of the following chapter.

CHAPTER 8

Presentation

OUTLINE

0. INTRODUCTION

1. EXPRESSION
   1.1 Staging
      1.1.1 Number of Stages
      1.1.2 Order of Stages
      1.1.3 Spacing
      1.1.4 Units
   1.2 Demonstration
      1.2.1 Spoken Forms
      1.2.2 Written Forms

2. CONTENT
   2.1 Differential Procedures
      2.1.1 Explanation
      2.1.2 Translation
   2.2 Ostensive Procedures
      2.2.1 Objects
      2.2.2 Actions
      2.2.3 Situations
   2.3 Pictorial Procedures
      2.3.1 Type
      2.3.2 Media
   2.4 Contextual Procedures
      2.4.1 Definition
      2.4.2 Enumeration
      2.4.3 Substitution
      2.4.4 Metaphor
      2.4.5 Opposition
      2.4.6 Multiple Context

0. INTRODUCTION

Having seen how the selection and gradation of a method may be analysed it is now possible to examine its presentation. Presentation means communicating something to somebody. It is an essential part of the method; the most carefully graded selection of a language is useless unless it gets into the minds of the learners.

Getting the language into the minds of the learners depends on the technique of presentation peculiar to the method; it also depends upon the teaching technique of the individual teacher. We shall here study the technique of presentation which can be examined in a particular method. Some methods have elaborate teaching-manuals; since these do not concern the learner directly but rather the teacher-text relation, they come in at a later stage of the analysis (see Ch. 11). We are here concerned with the analysis of the teaching text which is put into the hands of the learners and with its recorded or pictorial equivalents. What does the learner see when he opens his textbook? How much of the language does it teach him? How are the forms and meanings of the language taught? Does the quantity and quality of the teaching vary from one part of the text to the other? These are some of the questions which must be answered in making an analysis of presentation.

Some methods do all the presentation; others do none at all. Some present the meaning of the language; others present only its form. For example, there are textbooks made up exclusively of pictures; others made up exclusively of words. The former may give only the contents or meanings of the words spoken by the teacher; the latter, only the written forms, leaving the teacher to supply their content. Teaching a language involves the presentation of both (1) expression and (2) content.

1. EXPRESSION

This includes (1) the number, order, spacing and units in which the different forms of the language—spoken and written—are presented to the learner (staging), and (2) the techniques used by the method to teach them (demonstration).

1.1 STAGING

Staging involves (1) the number of forms of the language included in the method and the number of stages into which these are divided, (2) the order in which these are taught, (3) the spacing between them, and (4) the units into which their presentation is divided.

1.1.1 **Number of Stages**

How many forms of the language does the method present and which are they? Does the method include only the written forms, only the spoken forms, or both? Is it exclusively an "oral method" or a "reading method"? Some methods limit themselves to establishing a firm foundation in the spoken language, on the grounds that it is the more active form and that the learner is more "highly motivated" by it. Some do so because of the universality of speech; since most people speak, many people read, but relatively few write. In any single day, the average person spends more time speaking than he does writing. The number of persons whose professions involve daily writing is small; there have been whole civilizations which have remained illiterate throughout their entire history.

Other methods present only the written language because their learners will have little contact with the spoken form, or because the written form is the easiest to teach and to test in examinations. Many methods present both the written and spoken forms of the language, however, because they may both be equally necessary and because the learning of one may reinforce the learning of the other.

Learning both the spoken and written forms of a language necessitates the acquisition of a number of abilities, some of which are common to both forms, some of which are different. This may be represented as in the next table.

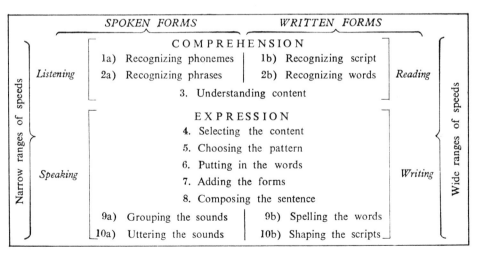

Primary Language Skills

Presentation

From the above table we can count six common abilities and eight different ones, fourteen in all, involved in the four primary skills of listening, speaking, reading, and writing.

In addition to these, there are four partial or secondary skills which involve much less. They are: imitation, copying, oral reading, and dictation. Their interrelationships would appear as in the figure below.

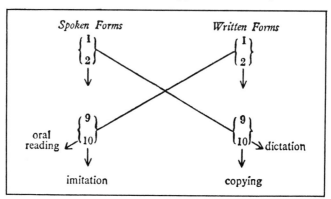

Secondary Language Skills

These four secondary skills and the fourteen different abilities in the primary skills may each be divided into a number of stages. For example, on the side of the written forms of the language, spelling (No. 9b) may be presented in at least three stages:

A. Presentation of letters which always correspond to the same phoneme, e.g. English /p/ as in *put*, or French /i/ as in *midi*.

B. Whole words of very high frequency presented as units, e.g. English *here, there,* or French *est, elle.*

C. Presentation of regular forms within a limited system, e.g. English *-ed* as in *asked* and *wanted,* or French *-ent* as in *ils marchent,* the *-ent,* of course, being purely graphic.

In this way a method may include as many as several dozen stages.

Methods may differ widely in the number of stages into which they divide the course. Method G, for example, divides an eight-year course into five stages, whereas Method H divides a two-year course into sixteen. (See 1.1.2 below.)

1.1.2 Order of Stages

Methods differ also in the order in which the spoken and written forms of the language and their various stages appear. One course may start with the written form; another with the spoken form. Whichever form is introduced first, an understanding of it must, in the nature of things, come before its use. The relationship is as follows (refer to the table in 1.1.1, above):

(i) In order to speak or to write a language, we must first be able to understand it.

(ii) In order to understand a language, we do not have to be able to speak it or write it.

(iii) Although speaking, writing, listening and reading may be separated, they have the following in common:

   (*a*) Understanding the content of words and sentences is needed for both reading and listening. The ability to understand the content of spoken forms could therefore be transferred to an understanding of the content of written forms, and vice versa.

   (*b*) Deciding what we want to express, selecting the content, choosing the right words and sentence patterns, and putting them together with the necessary grammatical forms into sentences which correctly express our meaning are activities needed for both speaking and writing (4–8). Speaking ability can therefore be transferred to writing ability once we know how to shape the script and spell the words. But can writing ability be transferred to speaking? In speaking, all the complex actions of expression (4–10a) have to be done simultaneously or within a limited range of speeds. In writing, it is possible to separate these complex actions and to do them at a wide range of speeds (4–10b).

(iv) The written forms may be just another way of expressing the spoken forms; but there may be certain differences. Some of these differences are sources of confusion and error, making it sometimes necessary to separate the spoken from the written language at certain points. In some languages, there is a difference between the way we write words and the way we say them (5a–b). In writing English, for example, we add a T to HERE and get THERE, both words having four letters in common; but if we pronounce these two words they have only one sound in common, the /ə/ in /hiə/ and /ðeə/. Often there is a fixed relationship between the sound and the letter, as there is for most of the English consonants; sometimes there is no fixed relationship at all, as is the case for most of the English vowels (10a–b). But the fact that a learner can write and pronounce all the letters of the alphabet does not mean that he can pronounce all the sounds of the language. For there may be more sounds than there are letters to write them. Spelling cannot be transferred to pronunciation. In some languages like English and French, if the learner pronounces words as they are spelt, his speech becomes incomprehensible. If he spells the words as they are pronounced, his written work will be full of mistakes. This difference between speaking and writing has been an argument for presenting them separately. If, however, we use a special phonetic alphabet with the same number of letters as there are significant sounds and with a fixed relationship between them, the written words may be regarded as pictures of the spoken words. Although a phonetic alphabet may be a help in learning the spoken forms, the learner may still have the problem of developing the ability to spell if he is ever going to write the language. Since in some languages there is no consistency between the letters and the sounds they represent, some methods separate the foundations of speech from the foundations of writing; for it is impossible to speak without making sounds and impossible to write without spelling words. If the learner starts writing before he knows the sounds of the language, he may form his own idea of pronunciation, basing it partly on the spelling, partly on the sounds of his own language.

This is the argument for starting to learn a language orally, even though the sole aim may be to read it. "Reading readiness" in the first language involves ability to understand speech. This so-called "oral approach" requires that the learner should hear much more than he speaks, speak only on the basis of what he has heard, read only what he has spoken, and write only what he has read.[888:50]

But all these skills, as we have seen, are made up of a number of different abilities, each of which may be divided into stages. By the order in which these stages are presented, it is possible to cover varying degrees of one skill before starting another. In the way this is done there may be a great difference between one method and another. For example, the order in which Methods G and H arrange the stages into which they divide their courses is shown on the facing page.

In each method, after the four fundamental skills have been started, they are used to help in teaching one another. Materials from the reader for example, are used as topics for speaking and writing.

Method G	*Method H*
(eight years)	(two years)

Method G (eight years)

1. Speaking:
   Situations in dialogue form.
   Speech patterns of the dialogues.
2. Reading:
   Reading first taught orally.
   Dialogues and original prose, first prepared as speech.
3. Writing:
   Dictation.
   Completion.
   Copying.
   Composition based on oral work.
4. All skills:
   Long responses.
   Discussion of reading.
   Unprepared home reading of plays and novels.
   Use of dictionary in the foreign language.
   Writing of précis and directed composition.
5. Discussion of reading:
   Modern and Classical Literature.
   Composition.
   Translation.

Method H (two years)

1. Recognizing sounds and sound-groups.
2. Understanding speech.
3. Pronunciation.
4. Speaking I: Look and say.
5. Recognizing letters and words.
6. Reading I: Look and say.
7. Speaking II: Situations.
8. Reading II: Silent reading of oral work.
9. Writing I:
   (a) Shaping the letters.
   (b) Copying.
10. Speaking III: Questions and Answers.
11. Writing II: Spelling.
12. Reading III: Silent reading of short anecdotes.
13. Speaking IV: Questions on the reading.
14. Writing III: Prepared dictation.
15. Speaking V:
   (a) Action chains.
   (b) Model dialogues.
   (c) Songs.
16. Writing IV: Look and write.

1.1.3 Spacing

Methods also differ in the amount of one form they use before introducing the other, that is, in the amount of spoken language used before the written forms are presented, or vice versa. In each of these there may also be a difference between the amount of comprehension which precedes expression in speech and writing. The amount may vary from a few sentences as in Method C to an entire text, as in Method D. Some courses are arranged so that the written form of a word or sentence is shown immediately after the spoken form is heard; other courses will want the learner to hear and speak the language for a couple of years before presenting it to him in print.

Method D causes the learner to listen to the language for the first few months while checking his comprehension through picture-pointing and responses to spoken commands. When he has covered simple questions and commands he starts learning the sounds of the language and the beginnings of the spoken language. Reading, considered more of a personal or at-home activity involving a different "passive" vocabulary, is introduced only in the second volume of the course.

Spacing may depend on age and ability. Some primary-school language courses may not include any reading or writing, since the child is not yet literate enough in his first language. In the secondary school, however, the learner is so letter-bound that a long delay between speech and reading may result in the learner's forming his own idea of how the language must look in writing and in his devising his own system of spelling, resulting in such transcriptions as *feeneesay* and *shantay* for the French *finissez*, *chanter*. For at the secondary-school stage, the learner may believe what he sees more than what he hears.

Ability is another factor; it has been suggested that the able learner is not affected by the gap between one skill and another. Some methods include independent and optional courses in speech, reading and writing. A course may start with one or two years of silent, rapid reading, in order to give the learner the feel of the language before introducing speech.

Courses which teach both forms close together may do so on the assumption that what is learned through all the senses is better understood and longer remembered. All avenues of approach are used in the same lesson, the ear and the eye reinforced by the motor reflexes of hand and mouth. The lesson may begin with listening and speaking and end with reading and writing. Reading may be used to help to sharpen attention to the sounds, an association being formed between sounds and letters, which is in turn reinforced through the written exercises. Some methods teach both forms close together in their beginner's course only, on the principle that for beginners nothing is unimportant enough to remain merely passive. The belief is that basic vocabulary and structure should be mastered orally, even though the ultimate aim is only a reading knowledge of the language.

1.1.4 Units

How are the units of presentation organized?

Textbooks may divide their material according to different principles; some organize it into centres of interest, some into steps, some into sequences, and some into teaching points. These may vary from large units built around a thematic picture, each of which may take from two to three weeks to cover, to small teaching points three or four of which may be covered in a single lesson.

Method B, for example, divides its entire elementary course into ten centres of interest, whereas Method D divides a comparable amount of material into a hundred and twenty teaching points.

1.2 DEMONSTRATION

How does the method present the forms which it includes?

At this point in the analysis, it is important not to confuse presentation with repetition. Presentation is here concerned with what the method does to show the learner (1) the spoken forms, and (2) the written forms of the language. What it may do to convert these forms into habits is another matter. (See Ch. 9.)

1.2.1 **Spoken Forms**

We are here concerned with what the method does to teach the learner to distinguish and produce the spoken forms of the language. Understanding the spoken forms involves the recognition of the different relevant sounds of the language. The hearer must be able to keep these in mind long enough to understand them as groups of words.

Does the method teach the learner to distinguish the phonemes of the language? If so, how does it go about it? Are the phonemes taught by means of tapes or records which accompany the method? What is included on these records or tapes? What is the quality of the recordings? The fact that they may be quite comprehensible to a native speaker is not a test of their suitability for teaching. With a familiar language we can reduce audibility and accuracy of production to a very great extent and still have material which is entirely understood; but this is not true for an unfamiliar language, where the hearer may be listening to every sound. A good recording can be clearer than classroom speech, since a sensitive microphone can pick up all the details of speech almost as if they were placed, as it were, under a magnifying glass.

But the learner must go beyond the phoneme in order to be able to understand a language. So long as he hears only the individual sounds, or even individual words and phrases, he will not understand the larger structures. For the relations among the components of a pattern must be known before its individual members can be understood. It has even been suggested that we really start putting meaning into a word in context before we hear it; the context permits us to predict the word and, on the basis of this prediction, we anticipate the meaning of the word-group. Our verbal habits and knowledge of the language influence our perception of it. That is why it is easier to understand a word correctly in context than it is in isolation. Does the method therefore present sounds, words, or sentences first?

Presentation

The recognition of sounds, words and sentences, as we have seen, comes before their use. Because of this, some oral courses begin with a period of gestation or auditory assimilation in which the learner does nothing but listen and identify different sounds and words. This period often includes a series of lessons on pronunciation, given in the learner's own language. It may also include the learning of phonetic symbols and the phonetic transcription of texts. After a series of lessons in which the learner is taught to produce the new sounds, he may be introduced to texts in phonetic notation. The first year textbooks of some courses are entirely in phonetic notation; conventional spelling is sometimes delayed until the second year.

In addition to lessons in pronunciation, or instead of them, there may be periods of systematic imitation. The model may be the pronunciation of the teacher and/or recorded materials. For this purpose, some methods, like Method A, include records as part of the course. In examining these records we should note such things as clarity and speed. Some records for beginners are much too fast; others manage to start with sentences spoken as slowly as possible without breaking the normal rhythm of the language.

In distinguishing the sounds of the spoken language, it is sufficient to be able to tell one phoneme from another; in speaking the language, however, this is not enough. For we cannot speak in phonemes; we have to utter the particular combinations of allophones which comprise them. Some methods completely ignore this; others give so much attention to details of pronunciation that no time is left for the other elements of speech.

Speech is not a succession of allophones or phonemes, or even of words composed while speaking; it is a stream of sound which simultaneously operates four interrelated systems—meaning, vocabulary, grammar and speech sounds.

In listening to a language we have only one form to deal with at a time; in speaking it, we must select from among a number of possible forms. There are many forms available for each concept. There are at least ten polite ways of asking someone to close the door; the learner may have heard all of them, but now that he has to use one of them, he must make up his mind which one he is going to use. How does the method enable him to do this? Some courses use questions on pictures, questions on texts, anecdotes to be retold, various devices for oral composition, and model dialogues.

1.2.2 Written Forms

The recognition of letters of the alphabet is no problem for learners whose script is the same as that of the language they are learning. The problem arises with non-alphabetic learners like Chinese, learning to read an alphabetic language like English, Russian, or Hebrew; or vice versa, with alphabetic learners learning to read a non-alphabetic script like Chinese or Japanese.

In addition to the transfer from an alphabetic to a non-alphabetic writing system or vice versa, there is the problem of transfer from one alphabet to another, as when English people learn to read Russian, Hebrew, or Greek.

Does the method take into account the possibility of a difference in script between the first language and the second? Does it include a section for learners with a different system of writing? How does it go about presenting to them the written forms of the language?

Recognizing the written forms of a language may be purely visual, with little connection between the sound of a word and its shape. In a language with an alphabetic script, however, each sound may be represented by a letter. This representation may be quite consistent, as in Spanish, Hungarian, and Serbian; or it may be inconsistent as in English and French. Where it is inconsistent, the recognition of individual words may be necessary in addition to or instead of the recognition of the letters which compose them.

There are a number of different ways to teach the beginnings of reading. Two of the best known are the phonic method and the whole or sentence method.

The phonic method goes from letter to word, establishing a link between speech-sound and letter. For languages with consistent and phonological systems of spelling this may be considered an advantage. But for languages with non-consistent one-to-one correspondence between letter and sound, the sentence method, going from sentence to word to letter, is sometimes used. It has been combined with a slow letter-intake, so that after the whole word is recognized, the recognition of its letters comes shortly after. New letters are very few in number; and the ones which look alike, *p* and *b*, for example, are spaced as far apart as possible.[202:94]

Both Methods A and D contain sections for the teaching of non-alphabetics; but they proceed in entirely different ways. Method A starts with the sentence and breaks it down into words and letters; Method D starts with the letter, builds letters into words and words into sentences. Method A uses a technique whereby the learner reads whole sentences and words and then goes on to recognize the individual letters. For example,

in the first stage he recognizes *this* only as ⌐▢ and *that* as ▢⌐

Later he sees that the ▢ of *this* and *that* are both made up of *t* and *h*, but that the letters (*i* and *a*) which follow are not the same. If he sees too many different letters at once, however, it will be hard for him to recognize all of them; just as if he goes to a party and meets 26 different people, he recognizes fewer the next day than if he had met only four or five. On this principle, one text starts by presenting sentences containing only seven different letters, viz., *m, h, n, s, t, i, a.* These letters form such sentences as *This is a man, That is a hat, It is his hat.* After a number of such sentences, one or two new letters are added; these are combined with known letters to form new words and new sentences. Letters which may be taken for each other are not presented close together; they are letters like *d* and *b, p* and *b.* The learner is allowed to become completely familiar with one before being shown its upside-down or mirror-image equivalent. The sentences and words are illustrated and presented in a special pre-primer text with accompanying film strips, both the primer and the film strips present the meaning of each picture.

Method D, on the other hand, starts with isolated letters, each of which is to be associated with a certain sound. It then gives small two- or three-letter words made of these sounds for the learner to read aloud—words like *cat, rat, mat.* The material is presented in an illustrated pre-primer accompanied by a series of flash-cards showing pictures of an object or animal over the word it represents.

For learners who do not yet know the alphabet, each method also includes a section on handwriting to accompany the reading course. Some courses bring in handwriting gradually, starting with a few simple strokes, then a few letters in simple words and sentences, gradually adding one new letter at a time.

Even for learners using the same script, training in the recognition of words is an essential part of learning to read and write a language. This is especially true where the spelling system of the new language differs from that of the mother tongue. If the spoken language is taught first, the learner will have to learn what the words he utters look like when written. If he understands the spoken before the written language, he may have to learn that some words that strike his ear as different may in fact be written alike: For example, /dʌz/, /touz/, and /ʃuːz/, which are heard with three different vowels, are written with the same pair of letters as *does, toes,* and *shoes; danger* and *anger* look alike but sound different, as do *low* and *how, word* and *lord, dull* and *bull, home* and *some, roll* and *doll, comb* and *bomb, golf* and *wolf, singer, finger* and *ginger,* and many others. Because of such difficulties the beginning course of some methods supplies flash-cards for every new word taught.

A method may present irregular spellings either through the ear or through the eye. The reason for a visual presentation is that once the learner has observed the word and remembers what he has seen, he is usually able to write it. The problem is to make the learner observe the shape of the words which the method presents.

2. CONTENT

One of the most debated questions in language-teaching method is how the meaning of words and phrases should be conveyed to the learner.

To begin with, there are a number of different views on the nature of meaning (see Ch. 2). Whereas some teachers may believe that each word has a central meaning which is an inseparable part of the word, most modern philosophers reject the view that there are entities called meanings existing separately from people and their utterances. For Wittgenstein, for example, the meaning of a word is simply its use. To understand a word is to be able to use it correctly according to customary social practice. What *counts* as the meaning *is* the meaning. We acquire meanings by seeing or looking for some common element in a situation.[282]

According to some linguists, words do not have meanings; they are only cues or hints to possible meanings. Most of them are ambiguous. In every particular case the thing meant has to be discovered in the situation or context by the listener's alert and active intelligence.[226:50]

A word can only have meaning by virtue of its opposition to other words; even in the presence of an object, a word has only a vague meaning if it does not, through its opposition, concentrate on a particular property of the object. Our reaction to a word is not to what it means but to what we think it means. A meaning can only be a meaning to someone, and this meaning depends on the person's attitude toward meaning. For certain persons, the word may be the thing (as in magical meaning), or it may represent a personal experience (subjective meaning), or it may refer to some thing or concept (logical meaning), or it may be a stimulus (behavioural meaning).

These different attitudes may be re-created in a second language. A person may be taught to respond unconsciously to foreign commands, to acquire concepts unknown to him in his native language, and to associate foreign words with things experienced in the second language. A method might use different devices to re-create all these attitudes, or it might limit itself to a single impersonal this-means-that approach.

In addition to the different attitudes toward meaning, the method must also cope with its different levels (lexical and structural), and with types at each level. Each type may pose a different problem. The problem of verbs, for example, is different from that of nouns; that of concrete nouns, different from that of abstract nouns; that of nouns at one level of abstraction, different from nouns at another level of abstraction.[1524]

To solve these problems, a method may use any or all of four possible procedures: (1) differential, (2) ostensive, (3) pictorial, and (4) contextual. Which of these does the method use? How and for what does it use them?

2.1 DIFFERENTIAL PROCEDURES

These are procedures based on differences in meaning between the first language and the second. They include the use of the native language to get meanings across.

Some methods teach all meaning through the native language; others make no use of it whatsoever. The reasons for using the native language to get meaning across is that it prevents any misunderstanding, saves time, and makes the gradation of the language free from physical demonstration. The main reason for avoiding it completely is that any use of it encourages the learner to think in it. The more he does this, the less will he think in the language he is learning and the more likely will he be to fuse its structure with that of his own language. Between these two extremes there are methods which use the native language to a greater or lesser extent.

Methods may make two different uses of the native language: (1) explanation, and (2) translation.

2.1.1 Explanation

If the native language is used for explanation, what does it explain?

In addition to explaining the meanings of words and their usage, the native language may also be used to explain such things as grammar rules, the production of sounds, differences in the structure of the two languages, and situations about which the language is to be used.

Some methods avoid native language explanations altogether on the grounds that such explanations can only be abstract and confusing to the learner and that they make him spend his time, not in learning the language but in learning about it.

2.1.2 Translation

If the method makes use of translation, how does it do so? Does it, like Method B, begin each lesson with a list of words opposite equivalents in the native language? Or does it limit itself to the translation of sentences in the body of the lesson? Does it translate into the native language, out of the native language, or in both directions?

Most methods which make use of translation assume that the learner will translate anyway in his mind, and that it is useless to try to prevent him from doing so. Other methods, while avoiding translation as much as possible, are forced to use it for certain words and structures which they would be unable to teach by any other means, or without a great waste of time. Some methods may add this caution: If translation leads to mistakes, avoid it; if it helps to avoid mistakes, use it. But the causes of mistakes are not always evident.

Methods which make no use of translation may give strong arguments for avoiding it. One of these is the fact that many words have no exact equivalent in the learner's own language, and vice versa. This is especially true, of course, for structure words like *the*, *still*, and *quite*. It is also true for other classes of words as well. In most Slavonic languages, the English *foot* and *leg* are the same term; and there is only one term for *hand* and *arm*. It is also true for structures, most of which do not have the same functions as their vernacular counterparts; the same situation may call for one structure in the mother tongue and for an entirely different structure in English. (See Ch. 3.)

Languages differ not only in specific terms for objects and actions; they differ even more in the kind of linguistic and social contexts in which these terms are used. Individual words and their meanings are embedded in a unique semantic field, or world-view, reflected by the language. They also form part of unique constructions and contexts occurring in that language. Translation, therefore, presupposes abstractions.

When we listen to familiar words in our language, we do not really listen to them as words. We put a certain set of meanings into the sounds immediately; so long as we do this we can grasp a wide range of equivalents. But in translation, what we do is first to identify the word and structure, put meaning into it, and then re-compose with different words and different structures. Translation is therefore regarded as a complex process whose complexities are often the cause of mental confusion in the minds of those not equipped to deal with them.

Some methods take into account the learner's attitude toward translation, especially the usual assumption that, for any word in one language, he will be able to find an equivalent in the other. Since the learner tends to make mental makeshift equivalents in his own language, the meaning of what is taught is made clear and simple and the rhythm of presentation such that there is no need, no time and no desire for mental translation. This is sometimes achieved through the skilful use of ostensive procedures.

2.2 OSTENSIVE PROCEDURES

The principle of learning meaning through the senses goes back to Aristotle's *Nihil est in intellectu, quod non prius fuerit in sensu,* whatever is in the mind must first have been in the senses. Educational theories have been repeating this principle ever since. It has been responsible for the application of the theory of direct association to the teaching of languages. The stronger the association between visual stimulus and vocal response, the shorter the time needed for learning. To what extent, therefore, does the method rely on direct association for the teaching of meaning, and how does it apply the principle?

Some proceed with plenty of activity and plenty of language, dispensed by a sort of hit-or-miss technique. They supply a great deal of talk and gesticulation in the hope that some link will be formed in the learner's mind between what is said and what is done. In this way, some do succeed in teaching the meaning of a number of concrete nouns; but they often fail to teach the meaning of all the rest of the language, the abstract words, verbs, structural words, forms and structures. In the use of ostensive procedures, the first thing is to make clear which words refer to which objects and actions. Neglect of this has caused the failure of many attempts to teach a foreign language without the use of translation.

The text, however, cannot itself make use of ostensive procedures; it can only instruct the teacher to do so. It cannot, therefore, be part of the teaching done by the text which is put into the hands of the learner, but only of the teaching notes or teaching manual.

Some methods are designed to have all meaning taught by the teacher through ostensive procedures. These procedures include the use of (1) objects, (2) actions, (3) situations.

2.2.1 Objects

Objects or models of them may be used to teach, not only vocabulary, but structure as well. Some methods use objects for the meaning of content words only; others use them to teach the meaning of abstract words, quality words, structures and structural words. The easier these objects can be seen and felt, the easier it is to get the meaning across.

(i) Names of things like pencils, pens, tables and books may be taught by a pointing-and-naming technique, the success of which lies in making clear what is being pointed at.

(ii) Quality words have meanings which may be effectively presented in contrast with their opposites by means of objects which best bring out their opposing qualities. For example, *long* is clearer when contrasted with *short,* and taught by means of contrasting pairs, such as long and short lines, pencils, sticks.

(iii) Certain abstract words like *food, metal, plant,* and *substance* may be taught by grouping together a number of objects, models, or samples of material belonging to the same class. For example, bits of lead, tin, or iron have been used to teach *metal.*

(iv) Structure words which indicate relationship—words like *on, in,* and *under*—may first be presented through objects which illustrate their particular type of relationship. The clarity of the first meaning taught depends on the objects used. A hat on the table, a bottle on a shelf, or a book on the floor may be a clearer introduction to the meaning of *on* than is a town on a map. For position in time, objects like clocks and calendars may be used to teach such structural meanings as *on Friday* and *at noon,* and the present, past and future tenses.

2.2.2 Actions

Objects alone are not sufficient to teach meaning. Much has to be taught through gestures, like pointing and touching, and actions, like giving and taking. These may be used, alone or with objects, to convey the meaning of demonstratives (*this, that*), directional prepositions (*to, from*), verbs of action (*go, come*), and nouns of action (*smile, fall*).

The connection between the actions and the meaning may be quite haphazard in some methods; in others it may be quite systematic. The type of gesture may be left to the teacher, or it may be rigidly defined by the method. The teaching manual of Method C, for example, gives a long description of each gesture to be used, and how it is to be timed with the spoken words. To convey structural meaning through actions, this method insists on the following: (i) that the action should be completely isolated from other actions, significant or non-significant; (ii) that the timing of the action should reflect the tense of the verb; (iii) that the gestures should be clear and conventional.

When examining the gestures which the method recommends we should find out whether each gesture can mean only one thing to the learner. Methods C and D, for example, both start the first lesson of their beginner's course with the same gesture: the teacher is supposed to face the class and point to himself. In one method, this gesture means one thing; in the other, it means something else. In the first case the gesture goes with the words "This is I"; in the second case, it goes with "I am standing up". In both methods, the next gesture is pointing. In the first method it is supposed to mean "That is you"; in the second, it is supposed to mean

"Stand up". The effectiveness of gestures is more easily examined in the teaching technique of the individual teacher than in the pages of a textbook.

2.2.3 Situations

Some methods teach structural meaning by varying the situation together with the sentence. In Method C, for example, the teacher is instructed: (i) to do what he is saying, "I am giving my pencil to Tom"; (ii) to point to a learner to do the same action and say what he is doing. Learner (giving pencil to his neighbour): "I am giving my pencil to Mary"; (iii) to repeat his first action with other objects while the learner says what he (the teacher) is doing, "You are giving your book to Tom"; (iv) to say what the other learners are doing, "Tom is getting my book from me. John is giving his pencil to Mary. Mary is getting his pencil from him"; (v) to get the learners to say what the other learners are doing, "Tom is getting your book from you. John is giving his pencil to Mary". Each element of the situation is thus varied with the corresponding element of the sentence.

In Method D, on the other hand, the teaching of structure through situations consists in the formation of conditioned reflexes through stereotyped responses. These take the following pattern: Teacher: "I am giving my book to Martin, am I not?" Class: "Yes, you are" (or "No, you aren't."). Teacher: "He is giving his book to John, is he not?" Class: "No, he is not giving his book to John. He is giving his pencil to Alice."

Situations may be dramatized quite early in the course. One method dramatizes material from its first lesson by making the learners introduce one another with the simple form, "Tom, this is Bob Smith. Bob, this is Tom Brown." Later, as structure and vocabulary permit, the course dramatizes more complex daily activities like shopping and posting a letter.

Although some methods instruct the teacher to present meaning through situations and actions, this is often impossible because of the type of arrangement or gradation of the material. The eventual question is: How "presentable" is the method? Is it possible to get the meaning across by the means which the method intends? If the method is graded along the lines of teachability and one step leads to the next, then the meaning of every sentence may be made clear to the learner through the use of objects, actions and situations. Well-graded methods which succeed in making clear the whole of the language do so through a technique which leaves nothing to chance; one which isolates one situation at a time, timing actions with words and words with actions so that each part of the sentence stands out. It is a technique in which clarity of meaning depends upon the timing and clarity of gestures.

But presenting meaning in a limited vocabulary through controlled gestures consumes a great amount of time, and limits the situations to what can be produced in the classroom. Some methods overcome these limitations through the right use of pictures.

2.3 PICTORIAL PROCEDURES

The use of pictures in language teaching is as ancient as the *Orbis pictus* of Comenius (1658), written in Hungary between 1653 and 1654. For Comenius, it was above all the picture which could be most easily impressed upon the mind, giving the most real and lasting of impressions. Like many others of Comenius' ideas, however, this one was long neglected.

It was only towards the end of the nineteenth century that pictures seem to have come back into language teaching. In 1885 Hölzel used coloured pictures to teach Austrian school children their native language. In Switzerland pictures were introduced into second-language teaching. In 1887 Alge published a series of wall-pictures of trades, seasons, country and city life; these were also reproduced in the text. From then on, pictures and pictorial procedures have been used more and more.

Pictorial procedures may differ in two essential respects: (1) in type, and (2) in media.

2.3.1 Type

There are three types of language-teaching pictures: (1) thematic; (ii) mnemonic, and (iii) semantic.

(i) *Thematic Pictures*

Thematic pictures are those used simply to illustrate a theme or a text. Their use in getting meanings across can only be incidental to their function as illustrations. They may give the learner a desire to read the text in order to understand the significance of the illustration, or they may furnish an occasion to comment on a theme. A picture may illustrate the text of a lesson in order to focus the attention of the learner on what the text says by helping him to imagine it. If pictures are simply illustrative, we may analyse them for their appropriateness, atmosphere, liveliness, technical perfection, and personal appeal.

Thematic pictures most often come in the form of crowded scenes, illustrating a single theme, like the family leaving on a holiday, the countryside, in winter, etc. Although they usually do not give the meaning of everything, it is likely that the meaning of a certain percentage of items, especially that of the concrete nouns, is conveyed through the picture.

(ii) *Mnemonic Pictures*

Mnemonic pictures are those designed to remind the learner of certain words or sentences. They may be pictures of situations, presented simultaneously with sentences about these situations, and used later to remind the learner of these sentences.

They may represent situations broken up into sequences and presented in a sort of comic-strip technique. Here, too, a certain amount of meaning is likely to be conveyed by any sequence of pictures used in this way.

(iii) *Semantic Pictures*

Semantic pictures are those whose sole function is to get a specific meaning across. If the pictures are all intentionally semantic, that is, if they are exclusively a means of teaching meaning, we may examine them for the amount of meaning they teach and for their efficiency in teaching it. In doing so, we apply the same principles of evaluation as we did for objects, actions and situations, considering the context, the function of the picture in the pictorial sequence, and the amount of linguistic, cultural and general knowledge it assumes in the learner.

Where a picture is used for the teaching of meaning, it is important to make sure that the picture is not ambiguous. For purposes of clarity, a drawing is often better than a photograph; a simple drawing, better than a complex one. To be clear, the picture must contain only what the words mean; there must be nothing in the picture that is not contained in the sentence. For example, one picture in a beginner's text has a man pointing to a hat hanging on a hook in the wall; but there also happens to be a portrait hanging on the same wall, and it is not clear whether the man is pointing to the portrait or to the hat. The portrait is therefore not only superfluous but confusing. If the meaning of a picture is to be purely semantic, all irrelevant detail must be removed; otherwise the picture is merely illustrative.

2.3.2 **Media**

Any of these types of pictures may appear: (i) in the text, (ii) in separate class pictures, and (iii) on films.

(i) *Text Pictures*

What types of pictures are used in the text? To what extent is each type used?

Some methods teach all meaning through pictures. Some use pictures to teach content words only; others teach all structural meaning through pictures. One method uses a number of pictures to teach the meaning of a single word; in the very first lesson of its beginner's text it has ten different pictures of heads of persons and animals all of which teach the word *head*. Another method has a picture for almost every sentence; it makes the structure of the picture parallel to the structure of the sentence.

(ii) *Class Pictures*

A series of separately printed pictures for classroom use may be supplied by the method in the form of (a) picture cards, and (b) wall-pictures.

(a) Picture Cards

Picture cards may be uncaptioned or captioned, in front or on the reverse side. They may depict only objects, or they may show actions as well. Method D supplies a picture card for each concrete noun in its vocabulary, including pictures of objects obtainable in the classroom, but no pictures of actions or situations.

(b) Wall-pictures

Wall-pictures, with details large enough for the entire class to see, may be used in place of things such as clouds, the sea, mountains, the sun, and the sky, which are impossible to bring into the classroom. Each of these wall-pictures may be reproduced in the text, as they are in Method B. Conventional wall-pictures, however, are usually of the thematic type, and may be too confusing in all their detail to be used as a means of teaching any one specific meaning; they may be excellent, nevertheless, for practice in oral composition, and question-and-answer drill. (See Ch. 9.)

(iii) *Films*

The entire course, or part of it, may be available on films of the thematic, mnemonic or semantic type. These may be supplied in the form of (a) fixed film-strips or slides, and/or (b) motion-picture films.

(a) Film-strips and Slides

Pictures may be supplied in the form of slides or film-strips, either to convey meaning, to teach reading, or as aids in oral and written composition. We are concerned here only with those which teach meaning. These should be examined for the same sort of clarity which applies to the teaching of meaning through pictures in the text. Such slides or film-strips may be in the form of photographs or drawings, with or without captions.

The advantages of slides and film-strips is that they direct the attention of the class to the screen and to the pictures and words on it. The superiority of film-strips over slides is that the order of the picture is fixed and follows the gradation of the method.

Film-strips and slides free the teacher from the reality of the situation, which he must completely control if he is going to make his meaning clear. They control the situation, leaving the teacher free to control the class. For this reason the entire course of Method A is duplicated on film-strips.

Film-strips can depict not only those situations which the teacher can present in class, but also many of those which he cannot; and they can present these situations more rapidly than the teacher can act them. Moreover, a situation on film-strip can be shown over and over again without tiring the teacher and without changing the quality of the presentation. Some film-strips are synchronized with recorded material either on tape or on discs.

In examining semantic film-strips and slides, we should find out whether each frame, or sequence of frames, makes the meaning clear, and contains only the meanings being taught, or those already known.

The disadvantages of film-strips and slides are that they are not real situations and that they are seldom flexible enough to vary the situation to meet the difficulties that are liable to arise at any moment in the mind of the learner. Only the teacher can give the learner the individual attention he needs. Yet in a large class where the learner gets little or no individual attention anyway, film-strips and slides may be the best available means of getting the meaning across.

(b) Motion-picture Films

Motion-picture films are not only visual aids; if specially designed, they may be the chief means of presenting both the meaning and the form of a language. They can do all that film-strips can—and more. They can teach more in a shorter time because of the high degree of attention which they compel, partly through isolation of context, partly through movement.

Gestures, looks, and movements of lips may help the viewer to interpret what is said. In looking at a motion-picture film, he is no longer aware of time, as he is when viewing film-strips. Whereas film-strips may convey the meaning of simple actions, they are poorly suited to conveying results, causes, reasons and feelings. Here the motion-picture is superior, for its visual portrayal of movement, synchronized with sound, closely simulates reality to such an extent that it is even able to communicate emotional experiences. It can come as close as possible to giving the illusion of living in a foreign country. The sound motion-picture has the possibility of a wider context of meaning than any other semantic procedure, for

248

it can convey all types of meaning with all their associated overtones.

As a technique of presentation, the sound film can reduce a situation to its essentials; it can prevent anything irrelevant from taking the learner's attention away from the teaching point. Whereas a teacher can indeed teach *hand* by pointing to his hand and saying, "This is my hand" the camera can make it even clearer by filling the entire screen with a picture of a hand. It can show any situation which can be demonstrated in class; it can also show the world outside the classroom, which semantically is just as important. It can show a plane crashing, a house going up in smoke; and it can do this with a vividness impossible in the classroom. This very vividness increases the meaning of the accompanying language. The sound film can also maintain much more continuous action than can a teacher; and it can do so with a wide variety of speaking voices.

There are different types of sound films—animated drawings, photographic films with actors and live dialogues, and photographic films with commentary only. The animated drawing gives the film-maker the greatest control of meaning and context because it can regulate all actions and free any object or part of an object from distracting background. Photography on the other hand produces a greater illusion of reality, and with the help of actors and live dialogue, it can be made to look very much like real life. But background, gesture and timing are more difficult to control.

Films which merely present a teacher in action are less effective than a good teacher. Language-teaching films have to be designed specially for teaching at a specific level; to be most effective, they must exploit those teaching advantages peculiar to the film. When examining elementary language-teaching films, we use the same criteria as for objects, actions and situations. The most relevant questions are the following: (1) Is the object action or situation sufficiently isolated? Does the camera show only what is spoken about, or does it also include other irrelevant things, persons, actions and situations? (2) Do all actions have meaning, or are some meaningless? (3) Do the gestures of the actors convey the meaning of their actions? (4) How close is the union between the structure of each sentence and the structure of the situation in the picture? (5) Is the dialogue natural, or is it forced into grammar-making sentences? (6) Is there a story interest? (7) Is the sound-track at least as clear as the unrecorded voice of the teacher? (8) Can everything in the film be understood?

2.4 CONTEXTUAL PROCEDURES

The extent to which pictures, objects, actions and situations are used in order to convey meaning depends on the language level at which the method is operating. The smaller the vocabulary of the learner, the more ostensive and/or pictorial the procedures. Once the learner has acquired a certain vocabulary, known words may be used to teach the meaning of new words and structures. This is done by putting the new words in verbal contexts which give them meaning.

Words are known by the company they keep. If we learn things in company with others, we expect to find them in similar company when we see them again. There are groupings of words common to all users of a language, and these become likely in certain contexts. One of the reasons for teaching in sentences or larger units is that connected discourse, by cutting down the range of expectancy, makes comprehension much easier and more accurate. Moreover, connected and meaningful discourse is much more resistant to interference from the native language. It is also far easier to learn than unfamiliar sequences, or no sequence at all; for the greater the associative value, the easier the learning. The more connections we note, the more we know what is connected. The more abstract the meaning, the more it relies on verbal contexts. These verbal contexts include: (1) definition, (2) enumeration, (3) substitution, (4) metaphor, (5) opposition, and (6) multiple context.

2.4.1 Definition

New words may be defined by words already known. For example: *Breakfast* is the meal we have in the morning. Some words are more useful for defining than are others. A method may intentionally teach a good number of such words early in the course so as to be able later to expand vocabulary by definition.

Teaching definitions are not dictionary definitions, and dictionary definitions are not scientific definitions; they are only illustrations or explanations of artificial divisions of meaning. This is necessarily so, for the many meanings of a word merge one into the other and blend into the meanings of other words. All boundaries must be made for special purposes. Teaching definitions can therefore be quite different from dictionary definitions. They can include simple comparison or synonym, e.g. This is something like that. This word can be used instead of that word.

2.4.2 Enumeration

A meaning may be taught by listing what it includes. For example: dogs, cats, cows, horses and pigs are *animals*; pens, pencils, books, tables, coats and hats are *things*; black, white and red are *colours*. It is neither necessary nor possible to give a complete enumeration; it would be impossible, for example, to explain the word *integer* by listing all of them.

2.4.3 **Substitution**

The meaning of some words may be taught by substituting them for other words or groups of words. For example, in the following sentences *it*, *there* and *which* are taught as substitutes:

The parcel was on the table.

It   was *there.*

He has the parcel. | *It* | was there.

He has the parcel | which | was there.

The important thing here is that the nature of the substitution be made clear to the learner.

The meaning of a word may be made clear by words which can take its place. The difference in French between *marcher, se promener* and *aller à pied* may be taught by the words which can be substituted for each. *Marcher* can be replaced by *courir, grimper* and other kinds of performances; *se promener* by *jouer, patiner* and other pastimes; *aller à pied* by *aller en voiture, aller en avion*, and other means of locomotion.

2.4.4 **Metaphor**

If two or more things have a common feature, the same word may be used for them; if one of these is already known, we may assume that the learner will see the analogy with the other. For example, if the learner already knows the names for the main parts of the body, it would not be too difficult for him to identify the *legs* of a table, the *foot* of a mountain, or the *mouth* of a river. He may also understand what part of an aeroplane we are referring to when we speak of the *nose* of the plane, the *tail*, the *body*, and the *wings*. Some methods teach structural meanings through a similar but more abstract use of metaphor. They may teach the main adverbs of time, for example, in opposing pairs, as metaphorical extensions of words for space and matter, already taught by context of situation, since:

	this and *that* are to MATTER.
what	*here* and *there* are to SPACE.
what	*now* and *then* are to TIME.

2.4.5 **Opposition**

If the learner knows the meaning of a word, he simply needs to be told that another word is its opposite in order to get an idea of the meaning of the new word. For example: *Peace* is the opposite of *war*. *Easy* is the opposite of *difficult*. There are many types and degrees of opposition; some are much more teachable than others.

2.4.6 **Multiple Context**

Context helps us to guess the meanings of the words. In fact, that is what we do when we learn our native language. A child learns many of his words by drawing tentative conclusions from a variety of contexts. Multiplication of contexts helps to make meaning clear.

Since the meanings of all the words in a sentence interact upon one another, the meaning of a new word may be inferred from its use in a number of different sentences. For instance, if we see the sentence: "Squirrels ..X.. from tree to tree", we may get the idea that X means some sort of movement like running, jumping, or hopping. Later when we see the sentence "The horse..X.. over the fence", we may feel sure that the movement must be some sort of jump or hop. Still later, with sentences like "How high did he ..X..? Four feet three", we are almost certain that the meaning is that of the word *jump*.

The reader may not know the meaning of the word *távolság*; but he will, after reading the following paragraph:

> It's a long távolság from my home to the office. The távolság between the earth and the sun is 93 million miles. What's the távols´g from here to the next town?

In such series of contexts the first sentences may give only a general idea of the meaning; the second makes it more specific; the third makes it even more precise, and so on—the new word becoming clearer and clearer, and acquiring more and more meaning as contexts are multiplied.

It is in this way, by using words in many different contexts, that graded and supplementary readers help to make the meaning of their vocabulary clearer, more specific, and more complete. The meaning is clearest when all the words except the new one are already known. The more general the meaning, the greater the number of contexts needed to cover it; the more particular the meaning, the fewer the contexts needed.

Familiarity with both the form of the language and the content of a text helps us to understand its meaning. Knowledge of the subject-matter helps us to understand the meaning of a text in a foreign language. Familiar passages from the Bible, for instance, may be easier to understand in a foreign language than a simpler text about something entirely unfamiliar.

Context used to teach meaning can also be cultural. As the level advances, the closer the link between language and culture becomes. If culture is the aim of the method, how efficiently is this achieved? Does the cultural content help language learning, or does it hinder it? In some methods, most of the space is devoted to telling the learner *about* the peoples who speak the language.

Finally, are the sentences used in likely contexts? Some methods are more interested in making sentences than in making sense. The following sentences, for example, have appeared in language-teaching methods: *I have not seen your father's pen, but I have read the book of your uncle's gardener. My doctor's great-grandfather will be singeing the cat's wings. The philosopher pulled the lower jaw of the hen. The merchant is swimming with the gardener's son, but the Dutchman has the fine gun.* And in a beginner's Spanish course: *El hijo de la blanca Albion se pone algo melancólico.*

Each of these fundamental semantic procedures—differential, ostensive, pictorial and contextual—may be used, not only to present meaning, but also to drill it. In the analysis of a method it is an important distinction to make. A method may, for example, use differential procedures to present its meanings but make no use of translation in its exercises. Another method may use the same procedures for both presentation and drill. Or it may use pictures both as a semantic procedure and as a technique of repetition. It is to this final characteristic of method, to repetition, that we now turn.

CHAPTER 9

Repetition

OUTLINE

0. INTRODUCTION

    0.1 Nature of Repetition

    0.2 Types of Repetition

        0.2.1 Rote

        0.2.2 Incremental

        0.2.3 Variational

        0.2.4 Operational

    0.3 Media of Repetition

        0.3.1 Contextual

        0.3.2 Formal

1. LISTENING

    1.1 Recognition

        1.1.1 Phonetic Identification

        1.1.2 Phonetic Transcription

    1.2 Auditory Comprehension

        1.2.1 Listening Exercises

        1.2.2 Look-and-Listen Exercises

        1.2.3 Read-and-Listen Exercises

2. SPEAKING

    2.1 Pronunciation

        2.1.1 Sound-Bracketing Drills

        2.1.2 Minimal-Pair Drills

        2.1.3 Oral Reading

        2.1.4 Listen-and-Repeat Drills

        2.1.5 Songs

    2.2 Oral Expression

        2.2.1 Model Dialogues

        2.2.2 Pattern Practice

        2.2.3 Oral Drill Tables

        2.2.4 Look-and-Say Exercises

        2.2.5 Oral Composition

Repetition

3. READING

3.1 Visual Recognition
    3.1.1 Letters or Graphemes
    3.1.2 Words and Word-Groups
3.2 Reading Comprehension
    3.2.1 Intensive Reading
    3.2.2 Extensive Reading

4. WRITING

4.1 Graphics
    4.1.1 Tracing
    4.1.2 Copying
    4.1.3 Transcription
4.2 Spelling
    4.2.1 Completion
    4.2.2 Transliteration
    4.2.3 Dictation
4.3 Composition
    4.3.1 Sentence Modification
    4.3.2 Sentence Composition
    4.3.3 Paragraph Writing

0. INTRODUCTION

The ultimate aim of a language-teaching course is to teach the learner to use the language accurately, fluently and independently. To achieve accuracy, errors or their repetition must be avoided; to achieve fluency, a great amount of practice is needed. Between controlled accuracy and fluency and the independent use of the language lie many types of repetition.

0.1 NATURE OF REPETITION

All human acts are interrelated and tend to become habitual. They become habits, not in isolation, but as part of other acts. This is especially true of language. Language is mainly a matter of interrelated habits; if it were not, it could not be used as it is. A habit is not established by one or two performances but by many. The more often we perform a given act in a given arrangement, the more likely we are to repeat the act in the same arrangement. Linguistically, the more often an incorrect form is used, the more ingrained it becomes, even though the user knows it to be undesirable.

The problem is to obtain the maximum amount of repetition with the minimum of mistakes. The correct form must therefore be uttered more often than the incorrect form; for the more often the incorrect form is uttered, the more it becomes a habit. To correct this habit, the right form would presumably have to be uttered at least as often as the incorrect form had been. Preventing mistakes is therefore better than correcting them. Mistakes may be prevented in the design of the method through careful selection, orderly gradation, and clear presentation, where the selection is small enough to control, and productive enough to use; the gradation, gradual enough to be absorbed and systematic enough to avoid confusion; the presentation clear enough to be understood and varied enough to be interesting. This makes for accuracy of repetition. Fluency and independence of use, however, are matters of frequency and variety of repetition. There are many varieties of repetition; some types are more suited to one language skill than to others.

0.2 TYPES OF REPETITION

The many varieties of repetition may be reduced to four fundamental types: (1) rote, (2) incremental, (3) variational, and (4) operational. A method may use any or all of these throughout the course; or it may make use of one type for a particular purpose.

Repetition

0.2.1 **Rote**

This is the most rudimentary type of repetition. It is one in which exactly the same forms are used again and again. In some methods this is the only type used. In others, it may be limited to the learning of such things as songs and model dialogues for the purpose of fixing in the mind certain patterns of structure and intonation, certain clichés and idioms which the learner may later draw upon in oral composition and conversation. It does not in itself assure the learning of the language, since it does not necessarily require an understanding of the meaning or structure of the sentences. People have been known to read the same passages and use the same telephone numbers hundreds of times without remembering them.

Rote repetition may be used in listen-and-repeat drills, model dialogues, songs, oral reading, copying and transcription.

0.2.2 **Incremental**

In this type of repetition each new utterance adds a new element to the structure. A new word or word-group may be added with each repetition, requiring the learner each time to repeat a longer and longer sentence. The model may be available on recordings, supplied by the method.

Teacher:	It's warm.
Class:	It's warm.
Teacher:	Here
Class:	It's warm here.
Teacher:	Today
Class:	It's warm here today.

This sort of repetition does not necessarily involve an understanding of the meaning of what is uttered. Incremental repetition is used in expansion and addition drills and in sentence-building exercises.

0.2.3 **Variational**

In this type of repetition, sequences are repeated while changing their elements—one, two or more at a time. The possible changes may be arranged in the form of chains or tables (see below). In oral drills, the element to be substituted may be presented as a call-word:

Text or Recording:	Now he's eating at the restaurant.
Call-word:	Yesterday?
Learner:	Yesterday he ate at the restaurant.

In written exercises, this may be represented as a blank to be filled:

Yesterday he . . . . (eat) at the restaurant.

The variation may be arranged so that each repetition requires an understanding of the meaning, or constitutes an effort in expression. An example of this is the matching table and the look-and-say sequence, where the learner varies each part of a sentence along with changes in the corresponding elements of a picture.

The variation type of repetition is used in exercises of completion, conversion, transformation, transposition, multiple choice, inclusion and re-statement (see 2.2 and 4.3).

0.2.4 Operational

This is repetition considered as performance, as the operation of one of the language skills—listening, speaking, reading or writing. Here all the abilities comprising a particular language skill have to be co-ordinated into a complex of habits. This co-ordinated use must be constant if the skill is to be kept up, since a habit once acquired must be put to use. Some methods are designed as if any item once known will remain for ever on the tip of the tongue. If a method exercises only the items being taught, those already taught will cease to be known. On the other hand, every time a method re-uses an item everything associated with that item is reinforced and made more habitual.

Since the full use of a skill has a wider field of association and context than the isolated repetition of any of its elements, operational repetition does not require the same sort of organization as do the other types. But since all the elements and abilities comprising the skill are used together, it supposes that these have already been acquired. Some methods give abundant practice in the operational use of a skill without first having built it up from the elements and abilities which comprise it. Certain so-called conversation courses, for example, completely ignore the complex abilities which comprise speech, or simply assume that they have already been acquired. (See Ch. 8: 1.1.1.)

The operational type of repetition may be used in question-and-answer exercises, look-and-say drills, reproduction exercises, description, exposition, narration, and translation.

To what extent therefore does the method being analysed make use of these four fundamental types of repetition, and for what purpose? Method A limits itself almost entirely to the variational type; Method B uses nothing but rote repetition.

0.3 MEDIA OF REPETITION

Any and all of the above four types of repetition may be used through different media. These may be of two sorts: (1) contextual, and (2) formal.

0.3.1 Contextual Media

Language may be practised in the contexts of action, of pictures, or of words.

For the context of action, the method can only give a plan of what is to be done in class—outlines of drills, for example, such as the do-and-say type. Only the teacher in the class can see that the actions are rightly performed and that they fit the words uttered. Such drill may include action chains, games and dramatization. (See Ch. 13.)

In pictorial contexts, however, pictures of actions and situations can be included in the text, on wall-pictures, on films and film-strips. These may include such speech exercises as the look-and-say type; or they may be the basis of exercises in reading and writing.

Language may also be practised through the medium of verbal context in the form of stories, songs, anecdotes and various types of verbal drills.

Which media does the method under investigation use? Method A uses pictures in the text, films and film-strips. Method B uses wall-pictures and anecdotes. And Methods C and D limit themselves mostly to the context of actions.

0.3.2 Formal Media

Any of the contextual media may be used with either form of the language, the spoken or the written. Drill in the spoken form of the language may be presented in recorded exercises on tape or on discs.

The written form may be presented either exclusively in the text, as exercises in reading and writing, or in separate readers and workbooks. In comparing our methods we find that Method A drills the two forms through both records and workbooks; Method B uses only records, Method C, only workbooks, and Method D only supplementary readers.

The materials supplied and the media of repetition depend ultimately on the skills which the method sets out to teach and the order in which it stages them. The whole purpose of repetition is the conversion of the language presented into these skills of listening, speaking, reading and writing. It is only within each of these skills that the different types and media of repetition can ultimately be analysed and evaluated.

The main question is: Through which contexts, verbal and pictorial, and in what ways, does the method repeat the material taught? We must answer this question for each of the primary skills—listening, speaking, reading and writing.

1. LISTENING

Perception of speech is not passive. The skill of listening to a foreign language and understanding what is said involves (1) the immediate and unconscious recognition of its significant elements, and (2) the comprehension of the meaning which the combination of these elements conveys. (See Ch. 8.)

How do the methods under analysis convert the abilities of recognition and comprehension into unconscious habits? Do they use in any of their exercises pictures and recordings in addition to the text, or instead of it?

1.1 RECOGNITION

What sort of recognition-drills does the method provide for the spoken language? In the past most methods included none at all, leaving the task entirely to the teacher. But with the availability of discs and tapes, methods began supplying such drills as part of the course. They appeared under such headings as ear-training exercises, distinction-drills, or some other name.

Recognition-drills may include (1) phonetic identification, and (2) phonetic transcription.

1.1.1 Phonetic Identification

Learners may be drilled in identifying contrasting sounds by a same-different type of exercise whereby the learner simply checks whether two sounds are the same or different. Or the exercise may ask him to indicate the sound he hears by writing down its number.

Skill in recognizing foreign phonemes may take a great deal of time. Morton reports that it took his most intelligent college students 28 to 56 hours of listening to distinguish only 14 of the significant sounds of Spanish with from 90 per cent to 96 per cent accuracy.[704:129]

In order to understand the spoken form of a language, however, it is not sufficient to recognize isolated sounds. How then does the method enable the learner to distinguish the significant elements in the normal flow of speech?

Methods make use of contrasting sentences with one different element in each. These can be presented in a number of different ways. The sentences can be uttered and numbered in sequence. The learner is required to identify, in the text, the sentence which he hears. Or three or four contrasting sentences may be included in the text so that the learner may check the one he thinks he hears on the record. A variation on this is to ask the learner to indicate the number of the picture which corresponds to the spoken sentence.

Some methods make the learners familiar with the sound-groups and word-groups of a language by training them to learn by ear some highly frequent sentences. They do so on the grounds that the more the learners learn by heart, the more easily will they be able to understand the foreign speech. Over-learning is said to be essential to comprehension.

1.1.2 Phonetic Transcription

To what extent does the method use phonetic notation, and what type does it use? Some methods may require the learner to take down recorded sounds and sentences in phonetic notation and to compare their transcription with that in the text or phonetic handbook. (See Chap. 2.)

Some methods arrange the sounds in minimal pairs, that is, into words or phrases with only one relevant difference in sound; pairs like *tin–thin, nut–not, I'm leaving here–I'm living here.* All relevant sounds are contrasted with one another, until all the phonemes of the language are indentified. Certain methods go no further than this, seeming to assume that to understand the spoken language it is sufficient to be able to recognize its phonemes.

It is not only the individual sound that gives the meaning of a word, but also the context in which it is used. The better a person understands a language, the more he is able to lag behind the speaker in order to get more context and to relate it all the better to the total situation. Repetition of words in context is also important for comprehension.

1.2 AUDITORY COMPREHENSION

Whereas methods may give abundant practice in the visual comprehension of the language through graded and supplementary readers (see below), few courses supply anything like a comparable amount of practice in auditory comprehension. The material supplied is often limited to the same vocabulary and situations used in the speech section of the course. The justification for this at the elementary level is that the speed of comprehension is inversely proportional to the size of the vocabulary. So that the smaller the vocabulary, the greater the comprehension. The more different words that have to be perceived, the longer it takes to perceive them. Of these, the frequent words are recognized more quickly than the others. Fluency in comprehension is therefore a function of size of vocabulary and of frequency of use.

But if the learner is to be trained to understand anything he hears, he will eventually have to have practice in listening to more than he is able to say. As Epictetus put it long ago, nature has given man one tongue and two ears that he may hear twice as much as he speaks.

Auditory comprehension involves the understanding of both the form and the meaning of utterances. It may be practised through (1) listening exercises, (2) look-and-listen exercises, and (3) read-and-listen exercises.

1.2.1 Listening Exercises

Practice in listening to the language may be supplied in the form of recorded materials on discs and tape. These may include samples of every-day conversation recorded in the country in which the language is spoken, giving a variety of voices and accents. They may also include extracts from plays and literary readings. Each exercise may also be accompanied by a series of written questions to enable the learner to test his comprehension. Exercises of this sort, of course, assume that the learner has already mastered the foundations of auditory comprehension in the language he is studying.

1.2.2 Look-and-Listen Exercises

The recorded text may be accompanied by a sequence of pictures which gives it its meaning. These may be either in the form of a picture-book, wall-picture, film-strips, or sound motion-picture films.

Method A includes a picture-book and film-strips to accompany the records: it also includes a series of sound motion-picture films with sequences of actions which explain the spoken sequence of sentences.

1.2.3 Read-and-Listen Exercises

The recorded material may be listened to while reading an accompanying text supplied by the method. This may be either in the language taught or in the learner's native language.

One method has the foreign-language text available on tape, with a translation of it printed in the text. Here the auditory comprehension drill consists in reading the translation while listening to the recorded text of the original.

2. SPEAKING

Speaking is the most complex of linguistic skills, since it involves thinking of what is to be said while saying what has been thought. In order to be able to do this, structures, it seems, must be chosen in the decreasing order of size.[623:93] Words must be put in at a rapid rate and with a spacing of about five to ten words ahead of the utterance.[367:192] In addition, patterns and words must be chosen to fit the right situation or attitude intended. All this supposes a certain reservoir of structure and vocabulary. And it requires a great deal of practice, since it includes (1) pronunciation, in which the entire phonetic system comes into play, and (2) expression, in which the grammatical, lexical and semantic systems are used simultaneously and in a regular rhythm.

2.1 PRONUNCIATION

Pronunciation-drills may include the same materials used to present sounds and the same exercises as those used for sound recognition. In examining pronunciation-drills, it is important to see how they fit into the vocabulary, structure and contexts likely to be used by the learner. Is the vocabulary in the phonetic drills the same as that used in other parts of the course? Or is it different? Does the beginner, for example, have to learn to use words like *rile* and *fie* just in order to get practice in the /ai/ diphthong? Does he have to repeat such sentences as *The good bull put his sooty foot into the brook* to exercise the English open /ɒ/ ? Does he have to achieve perfection in the French /y/ by learning to say *Le curé a su ce qu'il a lu sur les murs de la cure,* or equally improbable things?

Is the phonetic drill related to what is being done in the morphology and syntax of the language? Is the drill in the French plurals in -*s*, for example, related to exercises in its pronunciation, in liaison groups such as *les enfants, leurs affaires*?

Pronunciation-drills may be given in the form of recordings, and/or in the text. They may include (1) sound-bracketing drills, (2) minimal-pair drills, (3) oral reading, (4) listen-and-repeat drills, and (5) songs.

2.1.1 Sound-Bracketing Drills

These give practice in making unaccustomed sounds by going from one phoneme boundary to another. For example, the difference between the French /i/ and /y/ can be practised by a shift of the lip position from maximum spread to maximum rounding: /i/ – /y/, /i/ – /y/, /i/ – /y/, etc. These drills, either in phonetic notation or orthography, may also include mouth-position reminder diagrams like:

/i/   /y/

2.1.2 **Minimal-Pair Drills**

Some methods are based on a phonological theory that regards the phoneme as a minimal unit of sound difference, as the smallest change in sound which can cause a change in meaning. To drill the pronunciation of the phonemes of a language, therefore, is to give practice in making these minimal differences. These may be presented in English pairs like *sit – seat*, or French ones like *si – su*. Or they may be given as sentences which make sense only when the minimal oppositions are respected, as when the French proverb *Poisson sans boisson est poison* is used to drill the contrast between voiced and voiceless stops /p – b/ and fricatives /s – z/ with which speakers of certain German, Chinese, and other dialects have so much difficulty. (See also 1.1.2 above.)

2.1.3 **Oral Reading**

Reading aloud has been used to such an extent in primary schools that some language teachers make extensive use of it for the second language, without knowing exactly why. A method making use of oral reading as a pronunciation-drill may include passages for this purpose. These may be either in orthography or phonetic notation. In certain languages like English and French, oral reading of texts in conventional orthography at the beginning level may, if read as written, lead to habits of spelling pronunciation like /listɛn/ instead of /lɪsn/ for *listen* and different versions of such unphonetically written words as *through, tough, women, nation*. For this reason some methods present texts for oral reading in phonetic notation only. This requires the learner to study a special alphabet. If he is very young, however, and is still having difficulty with the alphabet of his first language, this may confuse him. If, on the other hand, he has had so much experience with the written language as to have to see a word in writing before being able to pronounce it, phonetic notation may become a necessity.

2.1.4 **Listen-and-Repeat Drills**

These consist of individual sounds and/or sentences, spaced with pauses for imitation by the learner. They may be made available on tape or disc, and may be used to drill phonemes, stress, intonation patterns and features of catenation.

The recorded part of the course may be arranged in such a way that the learner is made to repeat the parts of the sentence before repeating the sentence as a whole. For an example, see overleaf.

Repetition

> *Recording:* Where
> *Learner:*   Where
> *Recording:* can I get
> *Learner:*   can I get
> *Recording:* Where can I get
> *Learner:*   Where can I get
> *Recording:* some toothpaste
> *Learner:*   some toothpaste
> *Recording:* Where can I get some toothpaste?
> *Learner:*   Where can I get some toothpaste?

The length of the unit to be imitated may vary from method to method. Some courses divide their material into units of no more than five syllables, so that the learner nearly always hears and repeats bits of the sentence before repeating the sentence as a whole.

2.1.5 Songs

These may be included in the text and/or on recordings. Although songs are a fruitful device for the repetition of sounds and sound-groups, it is necessary to check whether their text conforms to the level and utility of the language taught. Does the rhythm of the music correspond to the natural rhythm of the sentence? Or is the stress placed on a normally unstressed syllable? Are the structures used all current and frequent? Or is the song an occasion for drilling obsolete structures? The structures of such lines as *We three kings of Orient are*, and *I'm going to Alabama my true love for to see*, repeated often enough, may later lead a learner to say *We three students of English are*, and *I'm going to town my young brother for to see.*

2.2 ORAL EXPRESSION

It is a long way from pronunciation exercises to the ability to converse fluently in a language. Oral expression involves not only all the features of auditory comprehension, with the use of the right sounds in the right patterns of rhythm and intonation, but also the choice of words and inflections and their arrangement in the right order to convey the right meaning.

A method may give practice in oral expression through verbal and/or pictorial exercises, with or without recordings. These exercises may include (1) model dialogues, (2) pattern-practice, (3) oral drill tables, (4) look-and-say exercises, and (5) oral composition.

2.2.1 **Model Dialogues**

Dialogues are the commonest sort of oral expression. They can include the high frequency small-talk which is the stuff of everyday conversation. They can be placed within a wide context which gives all the overtones of meaning and allusion, lending significance to the slightest change in intonation. Since all elements in a dialogue are interrelated, they are more significant than isolated sentences. Dialogues can be adapted and dramatized; they can also be used as a basis for other exercises, like pattern-practice drills, giving each drill sentence a contextual referent.

Dialogues, however, do not always exercise the independent use of the language. Yet they suppose the use of nearly all the complex abilities of speech; for this reason some methods do not use them until these have been mastered.

In examining dialogues, we first note their length and the range of their content. Does the content include references to subject, person, place, time, age, and tone—features necessary to make the dialogue seem real and believable? Are the dialogues original, or are they extracted from plays and novels? What is the average length of the dialogues? If they are going to be memorized, they cannot be too long. About six sentences with an average of six words each has been suggested as a possible optimum.[888:180]

How is the dialogue presented? In one method the recordings give dialogues, without pauses, for the learners to study and imitate. In another the dialogue is first presented as a unit for the learner to hear. It is then repeated, with pauses for the learner to imitate. And finally it is divided in such a way that the learner hears only one of the speakers and supplies the responses for the other.

At a more advanced level, the recording gives an account of a situation in which the learner is invited to place himself. It then gives only one half of the dialogue of the situation, letting the learner invent the other half. For example:

Recording: Somebody phones to ask you why you didn't turn up at the last meeting. You reply: (1) that you didn't know there was a meeting; (2) that you didn't get the announcement; (3) that you're sorry to have missed it; and (4) that you'll make sure to come to the next meeting.

Recording: I was wondering why you didn't come to our last meeting.

Learner: I didn't know there was a meeting.

Recording: Didn't you get our letter?

Learner: No, I didn't, etc., etc.

Dialogue drills may be supported by picture sequences on film-strips or sound motion-picture films designed to supply a visual context.

2.2.2 **Pattern-Practice**

Most of the various types of pattern-practice drills force the learner to make a grammatical or semantic choice in response to a question or call-word. Pattern-practice makes grammatical explanations superfluous and encourages learning by analogy. Since it always involves the making of some sort of change in a sentence along a certain pattern, the drill must make clear the type of change which it requires the learner to make and the way he is supposed to make it. The drills may consist of isolated and unrelated sentences or may include material from a story or dialogue (2.1.1).

The method may supply any of the following types of pattern-practice drills in the text and/or on recordings (R). Recordings have a pause after the call-word to permit the learner (L) to supply the correct response. In self-correcting drills, the pause is followed by the correct response, permitting the learner to compare immediately what he has said with what he should have said.

The various types of pattern-practice drills include: (i) addition, (ii) inclusion, (iii) replacement, (iv) integration, (v) conversion, (vi) completion, (vii) transformation, (viii) transposition, (ix) rejoinder, (x) contraction, and (xi) restatement.

(i) *Addition*

This is a drill of the incremental type whereby the text or recording gives an additional form which the learner simply adds at the end or the beginning of the previous phrase. For example:

    R: He's working
    L: He's working
    R: Here
    L: He's working here
    R: This afternoon
    L: He's working here this afternoon
            *   *   *
    R: Elle pense
    L: Elle pense
    R: Toujours
    L: Elle pense toujours
    R: À son fils
    L: Elle pense toujours à son fils.

Or there may be a fixed phrase for the learner to add:

R: À la campagne
L: À la campagne
R: Je reste
L: Je reste à la campagne
R: Je veux rester
L: Je veux rester à la campagne.
R: Je veux toujours rester
L: Je veux toujours rester à la campagne.

(ii) *Inclusion*

In the inclusion type of drill, a sentence structure is given and followed by a number of isolated words for the learner to include in their proper place in the structure. It may be used to drill such things as the position of certain words, like the English adverbs, for example.

R: Jim is working at his car. Always.
L: Jim is always working at his car.
R: Jim is always working at his car. Usually.
L: Jim is usually working at his car.
R: Jim is usually working at his car.
    *   *   *

R: I know him. Hardly
L: I hardly know him.
    *   *   *

R: Je l'ai donné. Lui
L: Je le lui ai donné.

(iii) *Replacement*

The text or recording gives a sentence, with instructions to replace one of its elements. This may be always the same element, or it may be a chain replacement in which all elements are changed, one after another.

R: I put a clean shirt in your drawer. Handkerchief.
L: I put a clean handkerchief in your drawer.
R: I put a clean handkerchief in your drawer. Pullover
L: I put a clean pullover in your drawer.
R: I put a clean pullover in your drawer.
    * * *

R: He lost his pen. She
L: She lost his pen.
R: Found
L: She found his pen.
R: My
L: She found my pen.
R: Watch
L: She found my watch.
    *   *   *

Repetition

> R: Elle joue dans le jardin. Il
> L: Il joue dans le jardin.
> R: Travaille
> L: Il travaille dans le jardin.
> R: À la maison
> L: Il travaille à la maison.

(iv) *Integration*

Two phrases, clauses, or sentences are given for the learner to join together into a single structural unit, making the appropriate changes.

> R: I know the man. He owns the garage.
> L: I know the man who owns the garage.
> R: I know the man who owns the garage.
>   *   *   *
> R: J'ai rencontré cette demoiselle. Elle enseigne ici.
> L: J'ai rencontré cette demoiselle qui enseigne ici.

(v) *Conversion*

A number of forms are given, with instructions to change all of them to a given pattern.

> R: (Convert to the negative:)
>   He was there last week.
> L: He wasn't there last week.
> R: He wasn't there last week. I saw the director.
> L: I didn't see the director.
>   *   *   *
> R: (Dites au futur:)
>   Il va chez lui.
> L: Il ira chez lui.
> R: Je passe la journée en ville.
> L: Je passerai la journée en ville.

(vi) *Completion*

In this type of drill, the learner is required to give the complete sentence in response to an incomplete one.

> R: He has all of them and I . . .
> L: He has all of them and I have none.
> R: He has all of them and I have none. You take your share and I'll . . .
> L: You take your share and I'll take mine.
>   *   *   *
> R: Mieux vaut tard . . .
> L: Mieux vaut tard que jamais.

(vii) *Transformation*

A sentence is transformed in a certain way in response to a call-word.

    R: Today we came to school at nine. Tomorrow.
    L: Tomorrow we'll come to school at nine.
    R: Tomorrow we'll come to school at nine.
          *   *   *
    R: Il commence ses vacances demain. Nous
    L: Nous commençons nos vacances demain.

(viii) *Transposition*

Here the learner is required to transpose a sentence into a related one.

    R: (Ask for some.) I like ice-cream.
    L: Give me some ice-cream.
    R: Give me some ice-cream.
          *   *   *
    R: Dites que vous en avez besoin.
       Il y a du papier.
    L: J'ai besoin de papier.

(ix) *Rejoinder*

This type of drill may be used to practise fixed formulas of politeness, surprise, etc. Instructions are given the learner to use a formula appropriate to the situation or to the attitude intended.

    R: (Answer affirmatively and politely.)
       Did you enjoy the meal?
    L: Yes, indeed.
    R: Yes. indeed. May I borrow your pen?
    L: Of course.
          *   *   *
    R: (Vous êtes surpris.)
       Gaston se marie.
    L: Pas possible!

(x) *Contraction*

The text or recording gives the longer form, instructing the learner to contract it.

    R: I have the keys.
    L: I have them.

Repetition

> R: I have them. It's my pencil.
> L: It's mine.
>
>   *   *   *
>
> R: Je connais cette dame.
> L: Je la connais.

(xi) *Restatement*

The learner restates in a given form the content of a statement or question given by the text or recording.

> R: Ask me how old she is.
> L: How old is she?
> R: How old is she? Tell me that you're going to give your bicycle to your brother.
> L: I'm going to give my bicycle to my brother.
>
>   *   *   *
>
> R: Dites-lui que vous êtes d'accord.
> L: Je suis d'accord.

Pattern-practice drills may provide a considerable amount of repetition of the variation type; but the learner cannot be expected to know the limits or range of possible variations until he has had some experience with the language.

2.2.3 Oral Drill Tables

These are drill devices to enable learners to compose sentences along certain patterns. They include (i) substitution tables, and (ii) matching tables.

(i) *Substitution Tables*

A substitution table is a sentence-structure with a list of words under each of its elements.

There are two types of substitution tables, those that make sense all the way, and those that do not. In using the ones that make sense all the way, the learner has simply to read across from left to right, picking any one item from each of the succeeding columns in order to get a sensible sentence. In the other type the learner has actually to compose a sensible sentence from the elements given.

Any number of elements in the structure may be varied. Methods may supply tables of one, two or more variables.

(a) One Variable

He's putting his	pen pencil book key	on the table.

It is simple enough for the learner to memorize this table and to utter from memory all the possible variations. Yet he will be able to make only four. But by converting it into a table of two variables he will be able to make sixteen different sentences.

(b) Two Variables

He's putting his	pen pencil book key	on the table. in the basket. over the bag. under the desk.

4   x   4   = 16

Later the course may proceed to tables with three variables, which permit even more sentences.

(c) Three Variables

He's putting his	pen pencil book key	on in over under	the table. the basket. the bag. the desk.

4   x   4   x   4   = 64

Four variables are still not too difficult to memorize:

(d) Four Variables

He's putting	my your his her	pen pencil book key	on in over under	the table. the basket. the bag. the desk.

4   x   4   x   4   x   4   = 256

(e) Five or More Variables

A table of five or more variables, however, may be a little hard to control But it is most productive. With the following table of five variables the learner can make 1,024 different sentences.

He	puts is putting will put put	my your his her	pen pencil book key	on in over under	the box. the basket. the bag. the desk.

$$4 \quad \times \quad 4 \quad \times \quad 4 \quad \times \quad 4 \quad \times \quad 4 \quad = 1,024$$

With this pattern it is possible to go on to seven variables, which would yield as many as 16,384 different sentences. The value of substitution tables as habit formers is the great number of sentences which they permit the learner to make and the ease with which he can make them.

Substitution tables can be used in a variety of ways. As a preparation for using the table, it is necessary to start by making sure that the learner has the correct pronunciation, the stress, the intonation and the rhythm of the model. Then the model is given, with one variable, and the learner repeats. Next, instead of the whole sentence, only the variables are given, in the form of call-words, and the learner gives the complete sentence. For example:

> *Call-word:* Pencil.
> *Response:* He's putting his pencil on the table.
> *Call-word:* Book.
> *Response:* He's putting his book on the table, etc.

The learner may later memorize the table and compose as many sentences as he can with it.

When the negative and interrogative forms have been taught, the text may convert the table into them, and include the intonation and rhythm patterns which these forms require.

Substitution tables which make sense all the way give excellent practice in the forms and patterns of the language, but not necessarily in the expression of meaning. This disadvantage may be overcome by the inclusion of matching tables.

(ii) *Matching Tables*

In matching tables, columns of sentence elements are arranged in such a way that by selecting an element from one column and matching it with an element from another column, the learner gets a sentence which makes sense. To use the table, he must understand the meaning of what he says.

There are different types of matching drills. Some are suitable at the beginning stage; others can be used only at an advanced level. Here are examples of simple sentence matching drills which may be found at the elementary stage:

		shoes			heads
We put		hats	on our		fingers
		rings			feet

To produce sentences like, *We put shoes on our feet, We put hats on our heads, We put rings on our fingers,* from the above table, the learner must of course understand the meaning of what he is saying. Later in the elementary stage he may be offered something like this:

		knife			go fishing
I need a		hook	to		cut bread
		ticket			get on the bus

When teaching the use of clauses in complex sentences, a course may use matching drills to drive home the correct relationship between the clauses. For example, when it gets to the stage of the if-clause, it might include a drill like this:

		shelf			leather
		dress			paper
I'd make a		cake	if I had some		cloth
		belt			flour
		poster			wood

It can have the learner match not only clauses, but sentences as well. For example:

		A			farmer			patients
		B			fisherman			pupils
Mr.		C	is a		shopkeeper	He has lots of		cattle
		D			teacher			customers
		E			doctor			fish

Matching drills may also be based on reading texts. The text may give a list of questions and a list of answers about the story. The order in each list is mixed.

Questions	*Answers*
Who came to the house?	He gave her a box of chocolates.
Where did he put his coat?	She put it on the table.
What did he give to the woman?	Mr. X came to the house.
Where did she put the box?	He put it in the bedroom.

Repetition

Certain types of matching tables may be intended for use as fluency drills. In the following type the learner has to make as many good sentences as he can in a given time. Sentences may be positive or negative.

Bicycles		feathers
Houses	have	tails
Horses	have no	wheels
Chickens		faces
Clocks		roofs

2.2.4 Look-and-Say Exercises

Pictures may be used to promote speech. The method may include speech-drill pictures in the text, on picture-cards, wall-pictures, films or film-strips as part of the course. From a point of view of teaching method, such pictures, as we have seen, may be thematic, semantic or mnemonic. (See Ch. 8.)

Thematic pictures are generally found in the text, in the workbook, or as wall-pictures. They are often rather crowded scenes of the beach, the station, the farm, the factory, etc. Each includes a number of situations on which the vocabulary and structure can be drilled through series of questions and answers. In evaluating these pictures it is important to check whether the situations pictured can be discussed within the vocabulary and structure already presented. Method B is built entirely around a dozen such thematic wall-pictures, each reproduced in colour in the text. An analysis of the elements in each picture, however, reveals a number of objects and situations the words for which are not taught in the course.

The main characteristic of the semantic type of picture is that there is only one meaning possible within the sequence. Such pictures may appear in the text, on accompanying picture-cards, or on films and film-strips.

In the text, they sometimes appear as individual postage-stamp sized drawings, picturing objects, actions and situations. Method A is made up entirely of such pictures, each of which is meant to be entirely unambiguous within the sequence in which it appears. At the end of each section there is a series or sequence of pictures with questions for the learner to answer orally.

Not all postage-stamp type pictures, however, qualify as purely semantic. Method B contains quite a number of them but few are entirely unambiguous; most would have to be classified within the thematic or mnemonic categories. Others are limited to pictures of objects, persons or animals, which are easy enough to make clear, but which exercise only vocabulary. Method D has a few hundred of such small pictures which it uses in the oral introduction of the course. Each picture is numbered.

Some methods supply a set of picture-cards for use in the oral part of the lesson. These may be limited to single objects or actions. For situations to be unambiguous, however, the text may require a sequence of pictures. Method D supplies a picture-card for each concrete noun in its elementary course. Films and film-strips can be designed so that the sequence of pictures in them can make actions and situations entirely unambiguous. Method A supplies sets of both films and film-strips of this sort.

Mnemonic pictures are pictorial sequences which are designed to remind the learner of the text. One method is organized with a sequence of pictures going from top to bottom on every left-hand page of the book, with the corresponding text on the right-hand page. The learner studies the pictures while referring to the text, and then tries to repeat the text orally while looking at the pictures.

Some methods for the teaching of beginners are wholly based on an application of this technique to film-strips, synchronized with an oral text on magnetic tape. The learner listens to the recorded text while looking at the film-strip, then tries to repeat after the recording, while looking only at the picture on the screen. Later he tries repeating the text without the recording, in response only to the visual stimulus. Finally he is expected to recount the sequence with the support of neither recording nor pictures. A variant of this is the technique whereby the film-strip or motion-picture loop is designed to permit the learner to play the role of one of the characters. The first version of the film enables the learner to listen to the characters and imitate them; in the second version, one of the characters is left blank so that the learner can take his place.

2.2.5 Oral Composition

This involves the composition by the learner of sequences of sentences on material supplied by the course. It may include (i) question-and-answer exercises, (ii) reproduction exercises, and (iii) free composition.

(i) *Question-and-Answer Exercises*

These are often based on a reading passage or a series of pictures. They consist of a series of questions to be answered orally by the learner. In Method D, for example, there is a series of such questions for each section of the story in the supplementary readers which go with the course.

(ii) *Reproduction Exercises*

The text or recording gives a passage for the learner to study a few times. He is then required to reproduce it in his own words.

Repetition

(iii) *Free Conversation*

At a certain level, the course may supply outlines of topics on which the learner is asked to talk freely. Some conversation courses contain an entire volume of such outlines.

3. READING

Reading involves skill in (1) the visual recognition of words, and (2) the comprehension of their content.

3.1 VISUAL RECOGNITION

The skill of reading is based ultimately on the recognition of written symbols. For learners unfamiliar with the symbols of the script used, the method may include books of exercises in visual recognition, based either on the phonic or the whole-sentence principle. (See Ch. 8.)

3.1.1 Letters or Graphemes

The problem of recognizing the different elements of the script depends on the number of configurations which the script includes. Alphabetic scripts have fewer than syllabic or ideographic scripts. To read any European language requires the recognition of only a few dozen symbols; some Oriental languages require several hundreds.

Has the method under analysis any exercises in reading designed for learners with a different script? Method A, for example, has supplementary texts and workbooks to prepare non-alphabetics and illiterates for the use of the regular course.

When examining such texts and materials, it is important to determine how many letters or other elements are taught at a time and the order in which they are introduced and drilled, their spacing and the amount of drill on each. Some methods include exercises in reading within a limited alphabet so that the learner may have only a few new symbols to cope with at a time. (See Ch. 6 and Ch. 8.)

3.1.2 Words and Word-Groups

Words may be easier to recognize than the letters which are contained in them. They can, for example, be read at a distance at which individual letters are unrecognizable. And if the letters form a familiar sequence they are easier to read than when they do not.

Word and sentence recognition may be drilled through flash-cards, reading cards, films and film-strips, and passages for oral reading. Method D supplies cards with the word on one side and the picture on the other.

The student looks at the picture and gives the word. The card is turned over and he reads the same word out loud. Method D has also a set of reading cards of words and word-groups, graded in length and difficulty, for exposure by the teacher for shorter and shorter periods as the reading speed of the learner increases. Some of the cards are simple commands of actions to be performed by the learner; this enables the teacher to find out whether the learner has read and understood the sentence. Method A supplies a complete set of film-strips, each frame of which can be left exposed for any length of time by a timing device attached to the projector. Certain reading methods also supply motion-picture films which train the learner in the control of the eye-span and eye-movements necessary for efficient reading.

All these techniques are used for the promotion of rapid silent reading which, according to some methods, makes for fewer bad habits of both reading and pronunciation. On the other hand, if a method has devoted a long beginning period exclusively to oral work, reading aloud may be stressed in order to teach the learner the relationship between the pronunciation of words and their spelling.

3.2 READING COMPREHENSION

The main activity of reading is putting meaning into word-groups; this involves a certain amount of expectation, visual skipping, and intelligent guessing.

Most of the reading may be done in the text itself or in special readers. When examining these, we should find out whether they contain only the words which have already been taught. Some courses teach all the words orally first, so that the learner reads only what he understands. Others teach all new vocabulary and structure in the reading books through contexts and pictures.

Methods may give practice in the comprehension of the written language through (1) intensive reading materials, and (2) materials for extensive reading.

3.2.1 **Intensive Reading**

Courses may give drill in reading by accompanying the reading material with (i) textual aids, (ii) pictorial aids, and (iii) recorded aids.

(i) *Textual Aids*

These may take the form of explanation or comprehension exercises.

A reading text may be explained by another text either in the same language or in the native language of the learner. Explanations in the same language may be within a limited vocabulary, presumably one already mastered by the learner. A number of literary texts, for example, have appended explanations or re-statements in limited vocabularies.

An older form of textual explanation is the type which uses the native language either to comment on the text or to translate it. Some methods have been based entirely on this procedure. They appear as reading texts with interlinear translation or with the translated text facing the original on the opposite page.

A course may also add comprehension exercises to its reading passages. These may take the form of completion exercises, sentence scrambles, or questions about the text.

Completion exercises for reading are designed in such a way that the learner is unable to fill in the blanks unless he understands the text. They are quite different from the type of completion exercise used to drill the structure of the language (see 2.2.2).

Sentence scrambles are made of sentences from a summary of the reading passage. These are disconnected and arranged in random order. The learner puts them in the order which best gives the sense of the original text.

Questions on the text may be either of the multiple choice type, the true-or-false type, or the type which requires a full oral or written answer.

(ii) *Pictorial Aids*

Many methods make use of pictures in the reading sections of their texts. These may simply illustrate the passage as a whole or some interesting incidents in the story. Some texts include in their margins small pictures giving the meaning of new words as they appear in the text; but these are generally limited to a few concrete nouns. Other courses illustrate key sentences in the text by a series of pictures. Nearly every sentence in Method A, for example, has a corresponding picture to enable the learner to check his comprehension of the text.

A variant of this is the comic-strip technique whereby the drawing gives a key to the situation, and all dialogue is put into balloons emanating from the mouths of the speakers.

(iii) *Recorded Aids*

The recordings may be either in the language being studied or in the learner's native language. Recordings in the language being studied may include comments and questions on the reading passage or they may be simply recorded readings which the learner listens to while reading the text.

Recordings in the native language may also include comments on the reading text; or they may be simply a translation of the text into the native language to which the learner listens while reading the text in the foreign language.

3.2.2 Extensive Reading

As the learner develops a certain facility in silent reading, he may be given more and more material in a vocabulary which increases gradually. The method may start with short illustrated anecdotes and go on to short stories written in a vocabulary the learner understands. It may also include special supplementary texts written or re-written for the level he has reached. Extensive reading supposes that the learner reads the text without difficulty, and if possible with pleasure. What he needs is a wide choice of reading material which fits, not only his vocabulary, but also his interests. These interests will depend on his age, his sex, his surroundings, his past experience, his attitudes and his ambitions.

Reading books should therefore be checked for content, in order to make sure that they contain the sort of material which is likely to interest the learners who use them (see Ch. 11). Some reading courses begin with dull "grammatical" sentences, building up to equally dull stories. Others offer material written within the mental and linguistic level of the learner and include the sort of anecdotes, folk-tales, short stories and short plays which appeal to his attitudes and background; that is, the sort of material he would read for pleasure in his own language.

We should therefore examine the contents of the reading books for their appeal to the emotions of the learner. We should examine them for plot, characters, action, surprise, dialogue and humour. To take care of differences in individual and group interests, some courses supply a wide choice of supplementary readers at various vocabulary levels, ranging from about a 500-word level to beyond the 3,000-word level. These are continually being added to, and include collections of short stories, plays, abridged novels, short biographies, and a variety of factual and cultural reading. These offer the learner a wide choice of books, in words he understands, books he may read for his own pleasure.

Some extensive readers include a series of questions to enable the learner to test his comprehension of the text. These may be answered in writing or orally, and may be used as topics for conversation.

Supplementary readers may be of two types, (i) the progressive type, and (ii) the plateau type. The progressive readers gradually bring in new vocabulary; the plateau readers do not, since they are written throughout at a fixed level.

(i) *Progressive Readers*

New words used in the progressive readers are generally explained in footnotes. They may be used in the text a number of times, immediately after their introduction, so as to give the learner an opportunity of assimilating them. In this way the learner increases his reading vocabulary while reading.

(ii) *Plateau Readers*

The purpose of the plateau reader is to consolidate the vocabulary which the learner has already learned, either through speech or through print. It is written throughout at a fixed vocabulary level.

In some countries reading is the only skill taught. Such a policy is often based on the assumption that reading is the only foreign language skill which most learners are able to acquire at school and continue to use and employ after having left school, since they may have plenty of opportunity to read books, newspapers and periodicals, but little need for speaking the foreign language. They may need it later only for the reading of scientific or technical writings. Or the language may be available only in written form.

4. WRITING

Writing involves (1) the ability to shape the letters of the alphabet (Graphics), (2) knowledge of the right combinations of letters (Spelling), and (3) skill in expressing oneself through the written word (Composition).

To what extent do the methods being examined exercise these three interrelated skills?

4.1 GRAPHICS

Methods intended for persons whose native language uses the same alphabet have little need to include handwriting as part of the writing course. Methods likely to be used by non-alphabetics, however, or by persons with a different script, must begin the writing course with some sort of introduction to the new script.

Some of the same principles applied to the teaching of reading apply equally to the teaching of writing. It is not necessary to teach the whole alphabet at once; a few letters at a time, taught in the most teachable order, are sufficient. (See Ch. 8.)

A certain amount of preliminary muscular drill will be necessary, especially for young beginners who have to learn to control the small muscles of the hand and arm. There are a number of techniques for preparing the small muscles of the hand to shape the letters of the alphabet. They begin with the making of straight lines, circles and curves. Some start with big lines and gradually make them smaller and smaller until they approach the size of normal letters.

When it comes to exercising the new configurations, courses may do so through (1) tracing drills, (2) copying drills, and (3) transcription drills.

4.1.1 Tracing Drills

Some methods supply lined workbooks, filled with separate and linked letters and words. These are written in dotted lines over which the learner writes. In some books these are followed by blank lines for the learner to fill in, continuing the same outline that he has just traced.

4.1.2 Copying Drills

The writing course may include lines of model letters, words and sentences which the learners are to copy and imitate. For this purpose there may be a number of blank lines included in the workbook after each model.

4.1.3 Transcription Drills

Beyond the exact tracing and copying of letters further practice in writing may be given by the transcription of printed texts. Some methods often include mottoes or useful sentences for this purpose. Others include substitution and matching tables, which have to be transcribed and memorized for later use in the oral work (see 2.2.3 above).

4.2 SPELLING

Once the learner can shape the letters, he must learn which ones to use for each sound or word. Even though he has the same alphabet as that of the language he is learning, he will find that the use of the alphabet to represent certain sounds varies from language to language. For example, the combination of letters *ch* represents the sound /tʃ/ in English, /k/ in Italian and /ʃ/ in French.

If the learner does not form the habit of associating the right sound with the right letters, he must at least form the habit of associating the right words with the right combinations of letters. In languages like English, with little regularity in the relation between sound and letter, it might be preferable to practice the spelling of many words separately.

Repetition

One of the reasons why English spelling is not exact is that there are not enough letters to represent all the sounds. For instance, there are only five letters for the vowels, and these have to represent 21 spoken vowels and diphthongs. But this is a difficulty which could be overcome. The main difficulty is the haphazard and unsystematic way the letters are combined. The same combination of letters is used for entirely different sounds. The letter *a*, for example, represents entirely different sounds in each of the following words: *that, palm, fall, came, about, any*. And the same sound is represented by different combinations of letters; *receive, machine, believe, be, people, see* and *sea*, though spelled differently, are all pronounced with the sound /iː/.

The spelling drills of a course may include oral and written exercises in (1) completion, (2) transliteration, and (3) dictation.

4.2.1 Completion

The purpose of word-completion exercises is to train the learner in observing the shape of words which he may already have recognized as wholes in his reading. One or two letters are omitted, and the learner fills in the blanks to form a correctly spelled word. For example: *t_is, _hat, her_ fa_her, p_ncil, bal_*.

4.2.2 Transliteration

If the method is staged so that the spoken language is taught first, with the aid of phonetic transcription, its writing course may include texts in phonetic notation to be re-written in conventional orthography.

4.2.3 Dictation

Exercises in associating the spoken with the written word may be included in the text, or in the recorded part of the course in the form of material spoken at dictation speed. Using conventional orthography, the learners write what they hear, and check it against the text of the dictation which is reproduced in the textbook or workbook.

4.3 COMPOSITION

Written work may start with the vocabulary and structure which the learner has either learned to use orally or simply learned to read. Some courses include in the text or the workbooks a series of written exercises for each lesson. These exercises may be of various types. They range from filling in blanks to free composition and may be grouped into three main types: (1) sentence modification, (2) sentence composition, (3) paragraph writing.

4.3.1 Sentence Modification

There is a variety of exercises which consist in giving practice in the structure of the language by asking the learner to complete or modify one or more elements of a sentence in one way or another. The main types of sentence modification exercises are (i) multiple choice, (ii) conversion, (iii) word jumbles, (iv) matching, and (v) alteration.

(i) *Multiple Choice*

This sort of exercise includes the familiar supply-the-missing-word type, often used to give practice in grouped grammatical elements or to recapitulate what has been taught. For example, suppose the course has just presented the prepositions *over*, *under* and *between*, and the course practises them in contrast with other prepositions which it has already covered (*on, in, to, from*). It may supply an exercise giving a number of sentences, each of which can have only one of the above prepositions. The exercise might look something like this:

> Put the following prepositions in their right places: *over, under, in, to, between, from, on.*
>
> 1. He put three words........the blackboard.
> 2. The pages are........the covers of the book.
> 3. The clouds are........the city.
> 4. I am going........the post-office.
> 5. I put the book........the drawer.
> 6. My mouth is........my nose.
> 7. The station is far........my house.

Another type of multiple choice exercise involves giving for each sentence, two or more choices, only one of which is correct. For example:

>   sheep.
> 1. They went across the sea in a bow.
>   ship.
>
>   laugh
> 2. Don't see   at him.
>   love

When the course has covered a sufficient number of words which are opposites, it may include an exercise on opposition:

> 1. Hot is opposite to *cold.*
> 2. Big is opposite to ......
> 3. On is opposite to ......

Repetition

Another variation is the type of exercise whereby the learner fills in the blanks, using one of the words in parenthesis. For example:

Clocks have . . . . . . (hands, legs, ears).

Any of these may use pictures instead of, or in addition to, the words and sentences included in the exercises.

(ii) *Conversion*

One way of giving practice in a new form is to make the learner use it in place of a known one. For example, if the course has covered a number of statement structures and is now teaching the inverted question, it might include a drill made up of a number of statements for the learner to convert into fixed questions:

Text	*Learner*
He is here.	Is he here?
She was there.	Was she there?
He is going.	Is he going?
She is coming.	Is she coming?
He put it in his pocket.	Did he put it in his pocket?
She goes to school.	Does she go to school?

Or it may ask the learner to convert from statements into free questions:

That's a school.	What's that?
His book is in his pocket.	Where's his book?

The learner may be asked to change positive structures into negative structures:

I went to the library.	I didn't go to the library.
Did you go to the library?	Didn't you go to the library?

He may convert one tense into another:

Now	*Yesterday*
I'm going to the door.	I went to the door.
I'm putting a sentence on the board.	I put a sentence on the board.

Or he may change direct into indirect speech:

"Are you ready?" I asked her.	I asked her whether she was ready.
"Go home," I said to him.	I told him to go home.

(iii) *Word Jumbles*

This exercise is used mainly for drilling sentence structures. Words are mixed in a random order, and the learner is required to make a sentence out of them. For example:

TROUSERS CHILD PAIR WOMAN A IS OF FOR HER THE MAKING.

The text may include a drawing for each sentence, in this case, a drawing of a woman making something out of cloth.

For beginners who have not yet mastered the basic word-order of the language, however, word jumbles may sometimes be more of a hindrance than a help.

(iv) *Matching*

The text gives two lists of words or word-groups. By matching them, the learner composes sentences which make sense. For example:

I am	in my pocket.
My pencil is	on the blackboard.
The words are	a learner.

(v) *Alteration*

This exercise appears as a series of sentences with certain words under-lined. The learner re-writes the sentences using the opposites of the words underlined. The exercise may also require the learner to change all the nouns, or the tenses of all the verbs, or make similar changes in the text.

4.3.2 Sentence Composition

There is a difference between filling in blanks and composing original sentences. Practice in sentence composition may be offered through (i) caption writing, (ii) sentence translation, and (iii) composition tables.

(i) *Caption Writing*

The text or workbooks may include a series of pictures under each of which the learner writes an appropriate sentence describing the picture. Or there may be larger and more crowded pictures, about which the learner is required to write a number of interconnected sentences. These pictures may be reproduced in the text.

(ii) *Sentence Translation*

Many methods in the past have used this as the main type of written exercise. Each lesson contained a number of sentences to be translated into the second language. Since translation is more difficult than composition (see Ch. 8), it is important to note at what level this sort of exercise is introduced. And since context is most important in translation, one must examine the sentences from this point of view. If they are disconnected sentences, as many are in fact, are their referents clear enough, or are there a number of time-wasting ambiguities?

Some methods consciously exclude translation exercises on the grounds that, if the activity of translating is started before both languages have been mastered, it hitches these languages together and confuses the beginner in translation once and for all. They may regard translation as too difficult and too damaging to the learner to be part of his activities until he has reached a high level of proficiency in the second language.[888:107]

Some courses limit themselves to translating in one direction only, either into the second language, because that is what is being practised, or into the native language, because it is easier. We can give the native equivalent of a foreign word or text more easily than the foreign equivalent of a native word or text, because recognition is easier than recall.

(iii) *Composition Tables*

The course may require the learner to write out full sentences from substitution tables or to make substitution tables from sentences. The tables or sentences may be the same as those used in the oral part of the course. Some courses supply carefully planned substitution tables to enable the learner to write a series of sentences which form a natural sequence. This leads to the first type of controlled composition.

The purpose of composition in a second language is to drill the learner in the use of the language, not in the use of his imagination. Some methods supply all the ideas to the learner beforehand, so that he will not have to think them up in his own language.

4.3.3 **Paragraph Writing**

The number of written exercises done before composition is attempted may vary from course to course. Some courses spend a great amount of time on simple sentence-modification exercises before introducing any sort of composition. Even then the introduction is gradual, starting with the description of simple actions, and proceeding to the recounting of the learner's daily activities, simple anecdotes which he knows well, and in general, topics which require no effort of the imagination. Other courses, however, start exercises in formal composition after the first few lessons.

Composition exercises at the paragraph level and beyond may include: (i) précis and paraphrase writing, (ii) narration, (iii) description, (iv) exposition, (v) free composition, and (vi) translation.

(i) *Précis and Paraphrase*

The course may include selected passages for the learner to summarize in précis form or to paraphrase in his own words. Some advanced and intermediate courses devote an entire volume exclusively to this sort of exercise.

(ii) *Narration*

The text gives a sequence of pictures, and the learner writes the story which they tell. Exercises may require the learner to write in full sentences the actions which he performs during the day, from the time he gets up until the time he goes to bed.

(iii) *Description*

Some texts may supply a series of pictures, each rich in detail. On each the text may include a number of questions to lead the learner into writing a description of the picture.

(iv) *Exposition*

The learner is required to tell how he does an action with which he is likely to be familiar, how, for example, he sharpens a pencil or rides a bicycle. The text may include questions on the details of such actions.

(v) *Free Composition*

This is often regarded as the culminating point of that part of the course devoted to writing. Composition may be required only on topics with which the learner is absolutely familiar. A detailed outline of each composition may be given in the text. This may also include a number of questions on each topic, so that when the learner sits down to write he may not be at a loss for ideas.

(vi) *Paragraph Translation*

This is perhaps the most advanced type of written exercise that can be given in a second language, since it requires a good knowledge not only of the structure and vocabulary of the language, but also of its semantic fields with their many shades of reference, their various ways of expressing what in the native language may be the same thing, and their allusions and references to the foreign culture.

| EXERCISE | TEXT | | RECORDINGS | | | | PICTURES | | | | | | Films | | |
	Orthography	Phonetic Notation	Tape	Disc	Spaced	Unspaced	Book Untitled	Book Titled	Class Untitled	Class Titled	Filmstrips Untitled	Filmstrips Titled	Sound	Silent	Titled
LISTENING															
Sound-Identification															
Phonetic Transcription				A	A										
Look-and-Listen Drills				A	A							A	A		
Read-and-Listen Drills	A			A	A			AC							A
SPEAKING															
Sound-Bracketing															
Minimal-Pair Drills															
Oral Reading															
Listen-and-Repeat				A	A										
Songs					A										
Model Dialogues												A	A		
Pattern Practice — Addition															
Inclusion															
Replacement															
Integration															
Conversion															
Completion															
Transformation															
Transposition															
Rejoinder															
Contraction															
Restatement															

Oral Drill Tables								AC				
Look-and-Say Drills	C							C				
Questions and Answers												
READING Visual Recognition												A
Intensive Reading												
Extensive Reading	C							C				
Handwriting Drills												
Word Modification	A											
Transliteration												
WRITING Dictation	C											
Sentence Modification	A											
Sentence Composition	C											
Précis Writing	C											
Free Composition										A		
Translation												

The many types of exercises in a method may vary in so many ways, in media, context, oral and visual, that they are best shown in the form of a table, in which the various types of repetition and contexts are indicated for each of the four primary skills. We have filled in the table, by way of example, with those two of our sample methods (A and C) which differ most in the types of exercises used.

Repetition

Translation is really a skill in its own right. Persons may be able to write well in two languages without being able to translate very well from one into the other. In examining the type and amount of translation required we must note the level at which it is introduced and the preparation the course gives in the elements of this difficult skill.

In many countries, writing is the main language activity taught, since success is determined solely on the basis of written examinations. In many schools this becomes a case of the examination determining the method.

If methods may be analysed, as we have just seen, they may also be measured. The next chapter attempts to outline how this may be done.

The Measurement of Method

OUTLINE

0. INTRODUCTION

1. SELECTION
   1.1 Quantity
      1.1.1 How much of the Phonetics?
      1.1.2 How much of the Grammar?
      1.1.3 How much of the Vocabulary?
      1.1.4 How much of the Semantics?
   1.2 Proportion
   1.3 Utility
      1.3.1 Frequency
      1.3.2 Range
      1.3.3 Availability
      1.3.4 Coverage
      1.3.5 Learnability

2. GRADATION
   2.1 Productivity
      2.1.1 Types of Productivity
      2.1.2 Rates of Productivity
   2.2 Intake
      2.2.1 Types of Intake
      2.2.2 Rates of Intake

3. PRESENTATION
   3.1 Expression
   3.2 Content
      3.2.1 Differential
      3.2.2 Ostensive
      3.2.3 Pictorial
      3.2.4 Contextual

4. REPETITION

    4.1 Amount of Repetition
        4.1.1 Number
        4.1.2 Distribution
    4.2 Ratio of Repetition
        4.2.1 Skills
        4.2.2 Media
    4.3 Variety of Repetition
    4.4 Types of Repetition

5. THE METHOD PROFILE

    5.1 Design
    5.2 Uses

0. INTRODUCTION

We have devoted the foregoing chapters to an analysis of the characteristics which make one language-teaching method different from another. But in order to get any sort of detailed analysis for purposes of evaluation and comparison these characteristics must be quantified.

What are required are techniques for the measurement of the four inherent characteristics of method—selection, gradation, presentation and repetition. To what extent are these measurable? These characteristics are all measurable in so far as they are internal to the method; that is, they can be measured in the text, its supplements and substitutes on films and recordings. It is the teaching done by these that we measure here.

There are four types of measurement: nominal (number), ordinal (rank), interval (scale), and ratio (relation); all of them can be applied to the measurement of method.

If the purpose of measurement is comparison of methods, we must first make sure that the methods are comparable. It is useless, for example, to try to compare a one-year elementary course with a seven-year course. The two must first be equalized. The simplest way of doing this is to cut the longer course at a point where it is quantitatively equal to the shorter one. This can be done by counting the number of running words in each course and using them as a measure of length; these include the running words of the course as a whole—words in textbooks, workbooks, readers and recorded material.

Each characteristic is then measured, in the following order: (1) selection, (2) gradation, (3) presentation, (4) repetition, and (5) the factors of all these are reduced to percentages and united in a general picture or profile of the method as a whole.

1. THE MEASUREMENT OF SELECTION

The measurable factors of selection include: (1) the quantity or amount of the language selected, (2) the proportion in each class of items, and (3) the utility of the items chosen.

1.1 QUANTITY

How much of the language does the method teach? How much of (1) the phonetics, (2) the grammar, (3) the vocabulary, (4) the semantics?

1.1.1 **How much of the Phonetics?**

This is often the hardest to determine, since not all methods list the phonetic items which they teach. Methods A and B, for example, do not.

But an examination of the accompanying discs reveals the use of all the phonemes of the language, as might be expected, by the first tenth of each course.

Method G, on the other hand, devotes an entire volume to the phonetic features of the language. This teaches 39 phonemes, 112 clusters, 9 types of catenation, 16 rhythm patterns, and 11 intonation patterns.

1.1.2 How much of the Grammar?

How many structure words, inflectional forms, sentence structures, phrase structures, formulas and collocations?

Comparing Methods A and B we get the following:

	A	*B*
Structure Words	93	101
Inflectional Forms	14	28
Structures:		
Sentences	4	5
Clauses	6	8
Phrases	21	31
Formulas	5	26

1.1.3 How much of the Vocabulary?

After counting the total vocabulary, exclusive of structure words, we determine the totals for each part of speech, as taught in the text. It is important to specify this, since many words may be used in more than one part of speech—as nouns, verbs, adjectives and adverbs. The total vocabulary for Method A, for example, is 503 words; for Method B, 407 words. And here are the totals for the different parts of speech as taught in the texts:

	Method A	*Method B*
Nouns	365	210
Verbs	16	70
Adjectives	82	74
Adverbs	40	53
	503	407

Method A teaches 96 more words than does Method B. The totals can be expressed in percentages of the total number of words in a common list, 2,000 for the *General Service List*, for example, giving 25·1 per cent for A and 20·3 per cent for B.

1.1.4 How much of the Semantics?

How many meanings are taught? We distinguish between lexical meanings and structural meanings. Here is a comparison of the numbers taught in Methods A and B, with reference to those included in the *General Service List*.

	Method A	*Method B*
Lexical:		
Nouns	537	380
Verbs	97	121
Adjectives	102	114
Adverbs	66	79
Structural:		
Structure words	152	215
Inflections	30	43
Sentence Structure	16	23
Clause Structure	9	12
Phrase Structure	24	41
Formulas	7	34
Total	1040	1062

Method A, we note, makes up in the semantic extension of its verbs what it lacks in number. Since there is little agreement on the classification and counting of meanings, another list might show fewer meanings or many more. The important thing, however, is that the same list be used for both methods.

1.2 PROPORTION

How is the selection balanced? What proportion of the selection is devoted to each class or category? To answer this question we simply convert the above amounts to percentages of the total vocabulary. As an example, we give these for the vocabulary of Methods A and B.

	Method A	Method B
Nouns	72·6%	51·5%
Verbs	3·2%	17·2%
Adjectives	16·3%	18·2%
Adverbs	7·9%	13·1%

Note the great difference in A and B in the proportion of verbs taught.

These proportions, however, are not to be evaluated by comparison with those for the language as a whole because they must necessarily vary with the level reached (see Ch. 6: 3.2.1). And the proportion does vary from one part of the course to another, and varies differently according to the method.

1.3 UTILITY

How useful is the selection? How much wastage is there? What percentage of the material will rarely be used? These questions can be answered quantitatively with reference to the five criteria of selection (see Ch. 6: 4). These are: frequency, range, availability, coverage and learnability. Each of these can be measured to the extent that statistics are obtainable. The most easily obtained are those for word-frequency; for there are a number of studies in various languages which give such frequencies, either for the written language, the spoken language, or for both (see Bibliography 1393–1514).

1.3.1 Frequency

We can compare the frequency of two or more selections by adding the accepted frequencies of each word. These may be obtained, for English, from such lists as those of Thorndike, Schonell, and the *General Service List*; for French, from Vander Beke, the *français fondamental*, and others; lists are also available for German, Spanish, Italian, Russian and other languages (see Bibliography 1474–1514).

If the methods are mainly oral, the frequencies can be those of the spoken language, where they are obtainable; for reading methods, frequencies can be found in a wider choice of lists, based on the written language. If they are all-skill courses, frequencies can be combined, or obtained from lists which take both the written and the spoken language into account. In comparing the total frequencies of the vocabularies of Methods A (503 words, not including structure words) and B (407 words), for example, we can use those found in the *General Service List*. And we get for Method A, 698,072, for Method B, 503,223. If we wish to reduce these to percentages, the most convenient base seems to be the total number of running words or occurrences on which the list was made, in this case,

5 million. This would give 14 per cent for Method A and 10 per cent for Method B. These percentages will be needed in the final synthesis of the factors analysed. Meanwhile we might note that although the vocabulary of Method A was selected on a criterion of coverage, it comes out better as to frequency than the vocabulary of Method B.

1.3.2 Range

A similar procedure can be followed in comparing the range of items in each method. We may either add the ranges of all the words in each method as we did for frequency, or take each word and note its percentage of the total range of the list or highest range-frequency credit number (Thorndike), and then average all the percentages. This latter procedure is preferable since it gives results in a form which can be directly incorporated into the final synthesis. With it we get the following average vocabulary ranges: Method A, 57·3 per cent; Method B, 44·7 per cent.

In our final calculations we use only vocabulary range and frequency as examples because of the lack of available information, not only on the statistics of usage in grammar and phonetics, but also of the availability, coverage and learnability of vocabulary. Yet these factors may be of great importance in certain types of selection.

1.3.3 Availability

As for availability, a similar procedure can be adopted. The difficulty, however, is the lack of basic studies. For French, there are those made for the *français fondamental*, but few others.

1.3.4 Coverage

For coverage, statistics are also lacking. It should be possible, however, to determine the degree of coverage of a word by the number of combinations in which it is capable of entering. For example, the word *piece* enters into more than does the word *chalk*. What should be measured is the number of cases the word occurs as a secondary, not as a primary, element; *piece work* is a point for *piece*, not for *work*; *red chalk* is a point for *red* and not for *chalk*. All words could thus be arranged in the order of coverage. Of course, some words might be more combinable in some texts than in others. Here the principle of range could be applied to determine which had the widest coverage. Indices of coverage could also be made by establishing occurrences of words used in definition, simplification and compounding. Meanwhile, we can take for each method the percentage of its items appearing in a list based only on coverage.

1.3.5 **Learnability**

For learnability, statistics could also be computed to measure brevity, regularity, clarity and relative learning load (see Ch. 6: 4.5). One type of similarity is that which relates to the native language of the learner. Figures would have to be based on a detailed differential description of the two languages involved. As far as the two vocabularies are concerned, it should be quite possible to count the number of cognates in each text.

Although we have given examples only for the vocabulary, similar studies are possible for the phonology, grammar, and semantics taught in the texts.

2. THE MEASUREMENT OF GRADATION

Gradation includes grouping and sequence (see Ch. 7). Grouping is measured by productivity; sequence by intake.

2.1 PRODUCTIVITY

Productivity is the answer to the question: How much can you say with what you have? With certain groupings of grammar, vocabulary and meanings you can say more than with others. Two methods might teach identical vocabularies, yet one may be much more productive than the other, if it includes structures into which more of the vocabulary can fit.

It is not the number of structures, however, that makes the difference. One method may have twice as many as the other and yet be less productive.

Productivity is a function of combination (see tables in Ch. 6). The more combinations permitted by the grouping of the material, the higher the productivity. Productivity is the maximum number of combinations obtainable from a minimum number of elements. It is a measure of the number of elements in a system which fit into an immediately superior structure—sounds into forms into words into phrases into clauses into sentences.

The productivity of a gradation is the sum of the productivities of its constituent structures. The productivity of a structure is the number of possible combinations which it can produce from elements of its immediately inferior level—sentences from clauses from phrases from words from morphemes from phonemes.

2.1.1 **Types of Productivity**

There are three types of productivity: (i) combinatorial (CP), (ii) semantic (SP), and (iii) textual (TP).

(i) *Combinatorial Productivity*

This is the product of all possible combinations in a structure. Let us, for example, take a structure from Method A, the phrase-structure of the type Preposition + Determiner + Noun (e.g. *on the table*). What is its combinatorial productivity? How many phrases can be composed out of it? This depends on the number of words in the method which can fit into it. We have seen that Method A contains 365 nouns and 93 structure words, of which 10 are prepositions and 20 determiners. Therefore, the combinatorial productivity of this structure in Method A is 20 × 10 × 365 = 73,000. In Method B it is somewhat less, viz. 53,130 (23 × 11 × 210). Not all of these possible phrases, however, will make sense. If we assume that the number of non-sense combinations will have roughly the same proportion in each case, we need go no further in our calculation of the relative productivity of a particular structure in a particular method. And for the method as a whole, or for any part of it, we simply total and average the productivity for each structure. For example, for Methods A and B we get the following:

	Method A		Method B	
	Total	Average per structure	Total	Average per structure
Phrases	956,550	45,550	975,878	31,479
Clauses	18,010	3,000	12,118	1,505
Sentences	378	94	345	70

Average combinatorial productivity figures give only the possibilities. Since certain structures used only once can considerably raise the total average combinatorial productivity of the method, it is sometimes preferable to take a more representative measure such as the median.

To get a more accurate idea of the possibilities of a method, therefore, we can select the median productivity (MP)—that of the structure, in the order of increasing productivity, which has as many structures before as it has after, i.e., the one in the middle. An even more complete picture may be obtained by comparing this with the average productivity

$$AP = \left(\frac{CPG \text{ (combinatorial productivity)}}{S \quad \text{(number of structures)}} \right) \text{ to give the degree}$$

of variations from the average: $AP - MP = AD$. For certain purposes, it may be useful to calculate the deviation for each structure: $PS_1 - MP = D_1$.

The Measurement of Method

The utility of the structure whose productivity varies greatly from the median can be judged by its frequency of occurrence.

Productivity is cumulative. A structure can make use of all previously used elements which it is capable of absorbing, so that the second structure in the gradation (C_2) may use as many elements as is possible from the first (C_1). And the third (C_3) may absorb elements from both the second and the first. Conversely, at the level of C_3 (Level 3), C_1 will absorb the C_3 elements along with those of C_2. The productivity of a structure at any given point depends on the number of elements it can absorb *at that point*. The productivity of C_1 at Level 1 was 12; but at Level 3 it is 80, since it absorbs many of the same elements used in C_3. And at this level, C_2 will be 260 and C_3 will be 420. The sum of all these gives the combinatorial productivity of the gradation (CPG) up to that point. So that:

$$CPG_3 = CP_1 + CP_2 + CP_3 = 80 + 260 + 420 = 760.$$

Or more concisely,

$$CPG_3 = \Sigma C_1 \ldots _3 = 760.$$

The general formula for the calculation of the productivity of a gradation (G) is therefore $CPG = C_1 + C_2 \ldots C_k$, meaning that the productivity of a gradation up to any point is equal to the sum of the productivities of each of its constituent structures up to that point.

(ii) *Semantic Productivity*

Combinatorial productivity indicates the number of sentences which a gradation can produce. But this does not mean that all of them make sense semantically. To find out, we must consider the sentences as a combination of words, not as above, as a combination of clauses made up of phrases, which in turn are composed of words. The best way to find out how many sentences make sense is to put them in the form of a substitution table (see Ch. 8) and work it out from there (see Ch. 9: 2.2.3). For example:

This	is	my	key
That	was	your	bag
These	are	his	book
Those	were	her	pen

(+ S)

$$= 2 \times 2 \times 4 \times 4 \times 2 = 128$$

In other words, the semantic productivity (SP) of the structure (S_1) up to this point (4 nouns, 4 verb forms, 8 determiners and 1 inflectional form) is 128.

Suppose we made a similar table for S_2 and got 440 and S_3 yielded 764, the semantic productivity of the gradation (SPG) up to that point would be: $SPG_3 = S_1 + S_2 + S_3 = 1,332$. This does not mean, however, that the text makes use of as many as this. How many the text actually uses is quite another matter.

(iii) *Textual Productivity*

Some methods exploit their possibilities more than do others. And this is something that has to be calculated in our evaluation of a method. What is the difference between what it can say and what it does say? In other words, what is the difference between its semantic productivity (SP) and its textual productivity (TP)? The difference in productivity (PD) is simply one minus the other, $SP - TP = PD$. The PD (productivity differential) represents what the method could use but does not. It shows what the teacher is able to use over and above the method.

For example, the first sentence structure of Method C has an SP of 160 but uses only 36 of these; whereas the first sentence structure of Method A has an SP of only 64 but uses 52 of them. Method C has a greater potential semantic productivity; Method A has a greater textual productivity. The practical, classroom significance of this is that, although Method A does more actual teaching, Method C has greater potential in the hands of a teacher willing and able to exploit it (see Ch. 11).

Since the SP is relative, and requires a separate judgment for each of several thousands of possible sentences, it is simpler to calculate the PD as the difference between combinatorial and textual productivities. The possible margin of error is small, since so many things are considered sensible only if they become habitual and familiar, and senseless if strange and unpredictable. If we thus calculate the difference for Methods A and B, we find that Method A uses 56·8 per cent of its numerical potential whereas Method B uses only 24·4 per cent.

To get an idea of the extent to which individual structures are exploited by the method, we can calculate the PD for each structure and list the results in the order of magnitude.

2.1.2 **Rates of Productivity**

A method does not have the same degree of productivity in all parts of the course. There are variations from one part to the other in all types of productivity.

Some methods, like Method B, have a very low combinatorial productivity at the beginning of the course, but pick up toward the end. This means that not very much can be said with them until a great deal of material has been covered. Other methods, like Method C, have a very high combinatorial productivity from the very beginning, indicating that the learner can say a great deal very early in the course with the little he has.

But this shows only what *can* be said as the course advances, not what is actually used in the method. One method may not be able to use much at the beginning but it may use everything it can. Another method, like Method C, may be able to use a great deal but may in fact use very little, and this difference between the potential productivity and the actual productivity may vary from one part of the course to the other. The productivity gap is not necessarily uniform.

For purposes of comparison it is more expedient, as stated above, to calculate the difference directly between the combinatorial and textual productivity curves. The difference can be calculated for a number of points along each course—say, every 300 words—to give two curves, one for the combinatorial productivity, and the other for the textual productivity, the number of sentences which the course actually produces with its material. The gap between the two curves represents the relative number of potential sentences which remain unused. This might increase or decrease as the course advances. A study of the gap for each structure will help identify those structures which are not used enough to make them habitual, but whose potential is sufficiently high to enable one to make up the deficiency.

The calculation of productivity does not, as might be imagined, make the measurement of selection redundant. For the independent use of a language productivity is not a substitute for structures of wide range and high frequency. It simply means the number of different sentences a person can produce with given material, not the number of topics about which he can speak. In free conversation, a wide variety of structures are needed, including not only those with a high productivity, but also those with a low productivity but with a wide range or a high frequency. We cannot consider only productivity and eliminate selection from our calculations for the method as a whole. Should we wish to determine, therefore, the general usefulness of a course up to any given point we should need to take into account, not only the productivity, but also the range and frequency of all items included up to that point.

2.2 INTAKE

Intake is a measure of the gradualness of a sequence. It is the answer to the question: How much comes in at a time? How many unknown items are introduced in relation to the known items used? In other words, how many new types are there in relation to tokens or uses? The general formula is:

$$\text{Intake} = \frac{\text{Token}}{\text{Type}}$$

2.2.1 Types of Intake

This applies to the phonology, grammar, vocabulary and meanings of the language. The simplest to calculate is the vocabulary of the language, or word-intake. The special formula for this is:

$$\text{Word-intake} = \frac{\text{Running Words}}{\text{Different Words}}$$

Method A, for example, teaches a vocabulary of 596 different words. To teach these, it uses 16,750 words of text, that is, 16,750 word-tokens for the 596 different word-types. So that the word-intake ratio (WI) is

$$\text{WI} = \frac{16,750}{596} = 28$$

Therefore the text repeats every word taught about 28 times, on an average.

This gives the ratio for the vocabulary as a whole. But the structure words of the vocabulary may not have the same intake ratio as the verbs; the verbs will differ in intake from the nouns, etc. The ratio has to be calculated for each class of word. For example, the verb-intake (VI) of Method A is quite different from that of Method B:

$$\text{Verb-intake} = \frac{\text{Verbs used}}{\text{Verbs taught}} \quad \begin{array}{c} A \\ \hline \frac{2611}{16} = 163 \end{array} \quad \bigg| \quad \begin{array}{c} B \\ \hline \frac{1649}{70} = 23 \end{array}$$

Intake is conveniently reduced to percentages of the total number of tokens. Of all the items used in a text, what percentage is made up of different items? Here are the intake percentages for nouns, verbs, adjectives and adverbs in Methods A and B.

	Method A		*Method B*	
	Type/Token		*Type/Token*	
Nouns	365/3755	19·7%	210/2252	9·3%
Verbs	16/2501	·6%	70/1656	4·2%
Adjectives	82/1012	8·1%	74/502	14·7%
Adverbs	40/243	16·4%	53/149	35·5%

Grammatical intake includes the introduction of new structure words, inflectional forms and structures. It can be calculated with the above formula. Applying this formula to the sentence structures of Methods A and B, for example, we count all the sentences, and divide them by the number of different sentence structures, to get the sentence intake (SI) of both methods.

$$A \qquad\qquad\qquad B$$
$$SI = \frac{2551}{4} = 625 \qquad\qquad SI = \frac{1500}{5} = 300$$

Reducing the structural intake to percentages, as we did above for the lexical intake, we get:

	A		B	
	Type/Token		*Type/Token*	
Structure Words	93/9252	1·0%	101/3879	2·6%
Inflections	14/1398	1·0%	28/624	4·5%
Sentence Structures	4/2551	·1%	5/1500	·3%
Clause Structures	6/2611	·2%	8/1599	·5%
Phrase Structures	21/8356	·2%	31/6006	·5%
Formulas	5/14	35·7%	26/43	60·4%

2.2.2 Rates of Intake

The rate at which new items are introduced may vary from one part of the text to another. In order to get an idea of how gradual the intake is, averages are not really enough.

The intake rate may be calculated for every type of unit in the language. It is simply a matter of plotting the type against the token. For example, for vocabulary we use the running words as a base, and plot the new words against them in the order of their appearance. The rate of intake for Methods A and B is shown opposite.

The rate of intake for the structure of the language, however, may be quite different. Opposite, for example, are the rates of intake for the structure words of Methods A and B.

Similar curves may be calculated for the different units in the phonetic and semantic systems of the language.

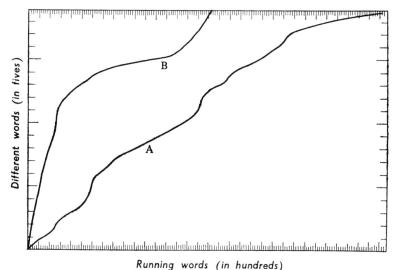

Vocabulary Intake Rates in Methods A and B

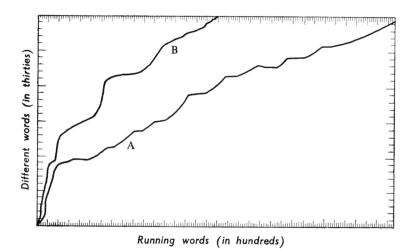

Intake Rates of Structure Words in Methods A and B

3. THE MEASUREMENT OF PRESENTATION

Presentation is a question of the staging of forms and the demonstration of content. It is concerned with what skills come before what and with the procedures used to get the meaning across. The presentation of both expression and content can be measured. In measuring these, it is important to make a distinction between how much may be taught and how much must be taught, between what the method actually does and what the teacher using the method may be advised to do.

3.1 EXPRESSION

The main problem in the presentation of expression is the stage at which the different skills are introduced. Quantitatively the question is: How much of one skill before how much of the other?

We are here interested only in what the method does. If it starts with a purely oral section presented through recorded materials, with or without accompanying pictures, it will not have the same textual staging as it would if a printed text accompanied this recorded material.

Method A, for example, has pictures, texts and recorded material. The learner, while looking at the pictures, listens to the recorded material and again listens to it while looking only at printed words. He then repeats after the record, and finally utters sentences while looking at the pictures only. This is done sequence by sequence. After a number of sequences have been covered the learner does written exercises on them. The order is therefore listening-reading-speaking-writing, or LRSW for short.

There are methods with an order identical to this, but with quite a different spacing; they might devote as much as a quarter of the course to listening before starting reading, and another quarter to reading before introducing speech.

The difference in spacing can be expressed in terms of percentages of the entire course, using as a base the total number of running words or their equivalent. An equivalent would be necessary only where oral material was neither recorded nor written, but elicited by pictures only. In this case, we count the minimum number of words necessary to give a caption to the picture. This is the case, for example, for Method B, which has a long oral introduction based on captionless pictures used to promote speech before the written word is shown. Method A, on the other hand, includes captions from the very beginning. Method B has not only a different spacing in its staging, but also a different order.

We can indicate both the spacing and order by the following table, which shows the order in which listening (L), speaking (S), reading (R), and writing (W) are introduced, and the amount of each used before the next skill is started. In Method A, for example, listening, speaking and reading are introduced in the first lesson, and writing shortly after. In

308

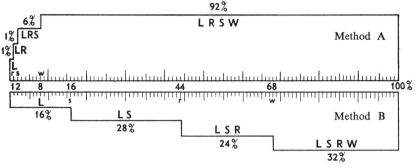

Presentation of Skills

Method B, the course is a quarter over before reading and writing are introduced.

3.2 CONTENT

The second element is the presentation of the content of the language. The main question is: How does the method get the meaning across? We have seen that there are four possible procedures—differential, ostensive, pictorial, and contextual. How much of each does the method use? How much of the native language, how much action, how many pictures, and how much verbal context?

3.2.1 **Differential**

The simplest way to measure the use of the native language in the text is to count the total number of running words in it, exclusive of drills and exercises, and calculate how many of these are in the first language and how many in the second. The results can be expressed as the percentage of total running words (exclusive of drills) in the second language.

For Methods A and B it is 100 per cent, since both make exclusive use of the second language. For Method E, however, it is 75·5 per cent—the 24·5 per cent being devoted to explanation in the native language (16·5 per cent) and to translation from and into the second language (8 per cent). This, of course, does not include the many translation exercises; these are not a matter of presentation, but of repetition (see 4.3 below).

3.2.2 **Ostensive**

This represents teaching not done by the method, but possibly by the teacher. It answers the question: How much of the presentation of meaning *must* the teacher do through objects, actions, and situations? It is not a question of how much he *can* do. For, in addition to any means used in the text, the teacher can use his own teaching devices and techniques (see Ch. 14). For Method A, it is nil, since it does all the teaching of its 1,040 semantic items through the text, by means of verbal contexts and pictures. In Method B, however, of the 1,062 semantic items taught, 351 or 33 per cent are taught through pictures or verbal context, leaving 711 or 67 per cent to be taught ostensively as the method requires.

3.2.3 **Pictorial**

Strictly speaking, only semantic pictures, those which get meanings across, would be counted here. But this may sometimes be difficult to determine. If we assume, therefore, that each picture in the course can convey at least one meaning, we may get a rough idea of the relative amount of pictorial presentation by counting each picture as a unit—but duplicates only once. If pictures in the text, for example, are reproduced as picture-cards, wall-pictures, or film-strips, these reproductions are here ignored for our present purposes (see 4 below). We then express the total as a proportion or percentage of our base, the number of words in the text, written and recorded, exclusive of drills. This gives us the word-to-picture ratio of the course.

Method A, for example, which teaches 596 words including 93 structure words, uses 1,252 pictures to do so. The word-to-picture ratio is therefore 1 : 2. Method B, on the other hand, has 427 pictures and teaches a vocabulary of 508 words, a word-to-picture ratio of 5 : 4.

A more precise calculation would be to take the total number of meanings taught, i.e. 1,040 for A and 1,062 for B (see 1.1.4), and determine what percentage of these are taught through pictures, i.e. 814 for A and 326 for B. For Method A, this comes to about 78·3 per cent; for Method B, it is 30·7 per cent.

3.2.4 **Contextual**

Here again, as in the case of meaning through pictures, we are faced with the problem of finding a simple criterion for measuring the amount of presentation done through contexts. One thing we do know is that the greater the number of contexts in which an item is used, the greater the likelihood of its meaning becoming clear. Using this as a criterion we can determine the average number of sentences in which each item is used. For Method A, each semantic item is used on an average in 16 different sentences; in Method B it is used in half that number. This includes all contexts—enumeration, definition, metaphor, substitution, opposition and multiple context.

If this is not precise enough, we can, as in the case of pictorial presentation, take the total number of meanings taught and calculate the percentage of these presented through contexts. If we do this for the same two methods we get 232 out of 1,040 for A (22·3 per cent) and 139 out of 1,062 for B (13·1 per cent).

4. THE MEASUREMENT OF REPETITION

In any course, we can measure (1) the amount, (2) the ratio, (3) the variety and (4) the types of repetition.

4.1 AMOUNT OF REPETITION

In measuring the amount of repetition we must take into account (1) the total number of repetitions per item, and (2) their distribution or rate of recurrence in the texts, its supplements and substitutes.

4.1.1 **Number**

Here the first thing is to find out how much repetition the course gives as a whole. The simplest way to do this is to start from the intake figures (see 2.2.1) using the total number of running words in the course, including those on films and recordings—but not those in the native language. We find that Method A has 16,750; and Method B totals 8,452.

These figures, however, are not comparable, since Method B teaches less than Method A. In order to compare the amount of repetition in the two methods we divide the number of items used by the number of items taught to get the average number of repetitions per item (see 2.2.1).

For the vocabulary of Method A it is $\dfrac{16,750}{596} = 28$,

or an average of about 28 repetitions per word.

For Method B it is $\dfrac{8,452}{508} = 16$.

In other words, the repetition of lexical items in Method A is so frequent that only about 3·5 per cent of the items are different; in Method B, it is 6 per cent.

4.1.2 **Distribution**

It is not only the number of times an item is repeated that counts; it is also how these repetitions are distributed throughout the course. An item repeated many times in the first lesson may be entirely forgotten if it is never repeated again. How well does the course keep up what it has taught?

Opposite each item in our list of words and structures taught, we indicate the teaching unit or running-word-level at which it recurs. This gives us not only the number of recurrences, but also their distribution. This distribution of recurrences can be plotted, for each item, against the number of running words, to give a detailed picture of the entire course.

In some courses, especially advanced reading courses, the relative frequency of each word is supposed to be "normal" or the same as in the usage of the language. This can be checked for any word by comparing its recurrence in the text with its expected frequency. This is obtained by multiplying the known frequency, taken from a list like the *General Service List*, by the length of the text, and dividing the product by the total number of running words on which the list is based, in this case, 5 million. For example, the word *make* occurs 9,600 times in the 5 million running words on which the *General Service List* is based. Its expected frequency in a reading text of 10,000 words would therefore be

$$\frac{9,600 \times 10,000}{5,000,000} = 19$$

If what is required, however, is simply an idea of the average distribution of items in the course as a whole, we may use a sampling technique. For example, we may divide the course into ten equal parts on the basis of units or running words. We then determine in how many of these a random sample of known or taught vocabulary and structure words recurs. For ten equal sections of Methods A and B, a random sampling of ten words already taught gives the following recurrences:

Vocabulary	A: 9, 10, 9, 8, 8, 7, 6, 6, 4, 3 = av. of 7, or 70%
	B: 7, 7, 6, 5, 4, 3, 3, 4, 1, 0 = av. of 4, or 40%
Structure Words	A: 10, 9, 9, 9, 10, 9, 9, 8, 9, 8 = av. of 9, or 90%
	B: 10, 9, 8, 7, 8, 6, 5, 6, 6, 5 = av. of 7, or 70%

4.2 RATIO OF REPETITION

This includes both the proportion of repetition allotted (1) to each skill, and (2) to each medium—textual, pictorial, or recording.

4.2.1 **Skills**

First we count the number of sentences or responses in exercises practising each of the four primary skills, listening, speaking, reading and writing. We then reduce the totals to percentages of the total number of sentences or responses in all exercises in the course. Calculating this for Methods A and B, for example, we get the following results:

	A		*B*	
	Responses		*Responses*	
Listening	812	24%	316	21%
Speaking	881	26%	225	15%
Reading	1,016	30%	884	59%
Writing	677	20%	76	5%

4.2.2 **Media**

How much of the repetition is given through the texts (including workbooks), through recordings (disc and tape), and through pictures (including films and film-strips)?

To calculate this, we take the total number of sentences or responses through all media and then the totals for each medium, reducing each to a percentage of the total for the course as a whole.

For Methods A and B, this is what we get:

	A		*B*	
Texts	1,392	41·1%	1,273	84·8%
Recordings	650	19·2%	76	5·1%
Pictures	1,344	39·7%	152	10·1%

4.3 VARIETY OF REPETITION

There is a difference between a method that always uses the same sort of drill and one that uses a variety of drills and exercises. How many different sorts of exercises does the method use? The simplest way is to count the number of different sorts used for each skill, and to express the results as percentages of all possible sorts. We may use a list such as the one in the table at the end of the preceding chapter. Here, for example, are the results for Methods A and B:

	A	*B*
Listening Drills	3 out of 5, or 60·0%	1 out of 5, or 20·0%
Speaking Drills	3 out of 23, or 13·1%	3 out of 23, or 13·1%
Reading Exercises	2 out of 7, or 28·6%	1 out of 7, or 14·2%
Writing Exercises	6 out of 19, or 31·6%	4 out of 19, or 21·1%

This may be sufficient for the comparison of two courses. It indicates the relative number of different exercises, but not the amount of repetition devoted to each sort of exercise. It is possible to get a detailed picture of the extent to which each sort of exercise is used by writing in the appropriate blank of the table at the end of the preceding chapter the *number* of responses called for in each sort of exercise.

4.4 TYPE OF REPETITION

Finally it is important to determine the type of repetition which predominates—rote, incremental, variational, or operational. This is not the same thing as the different sorts of exercises used, since it is possible to have a wide variety of exercises using only one sort of repetition (see Ch. 9).

The different sorts of exercises, however, as indicated in the table at the end of the preceding chapter may be used as a starting point. We can count the number of sentences or responses used in each sort of exercise and then add together those representing each type of repetition. We express the results as percentages of the total number of sentences or responses in all the exercises and drills in the course. For Methods A and B we have the following:

	A		*B*	
Rote	1,757	51·9%	1,128	75·2%
Incremental	119	3·5%	103	6·8%
Variational	1,290	38·1%	76	5·1%
Operational	220	6·5%	194	12·9%

5. THE METHOD PROFILE

5.1 DESIGN

The main factors comprising the four fundamental characteristics of method can now be brought together and expressed in percentages on a single decimal scale. Here, for example, is a synthesis of the measurements of these factors in Methods A and B:

	Method A		*Method B*		
	0- - - - - - - - - 100		0 - - - - - - - 100		**Code**
1. SELECTION					
1.1 Quantity	25·1%	- -'- - - - - - - - -	20·3%	- -'- - - - - - - - -	Q
1.2 Proportion:					
Nouns	72·6%	- - - - - - -'- - -	51·5%	- - - - -'- - - - -	N
Verbs	3·2%	'- - - - - - - - - -	17·2%	-'- - - - - - - - -	V
Adjectives	16·3%	-'- - - - - - - - -	18·2%	-'- - - - - - - - -	Adj
Adverbs	7·9%	'- - - - - - - - - -	13·1%	-'- - - - - - - - -	Adv
1.3 Utility:					
1.3.1 Frequency	14·0%	-'- - - - - - - - -	10·0%	-'- - - - - - - - -	F
1.3.2 Range	57·3%	- - - - -'- - - - -	44·7%	- - - -'- - - - - -	R
2. GRADATION					
2.1 Productivity	56·8%	- - - - -'- - - - -	24·4%	- -'- - - - - - - -	PD
1.2 Intake:					
Nouns	9·7%	-'- - - - - - - - -	9·3%	'- - - - - - - - - -	NI
Verbs	·6%	'- - - - - - - - - -	4·2%	'- - - - - - - - - -	VI
Adjectives	8·1%	'- - - - - - - - - -	14·7%	-'- - - - - - - - -	AjI
Adverbs	16·4%	-'- - - - - - - - -	35·5%	- -'- - - - - - - -	AvI
Structure Words	1·0%	'- - - - - - - - - -	2·6%	'- - - - - - - - - -	StI
Inflections	1·0%	'- - - - - - - - - -	4·5%	'-- - - - - - - - -	InI
Sentence Structures	·1%	'- - - - - - - - - -	·3%	'- - - - - - - - - -	SI
Clause Structures	·2%	'- - - - - - - - - -	·5%	'- - - - - - - - - -	CI
Phrase Structures	·2%	'- - - - - - - - - -	·5%	'- - - - - - - - - -	PhI
Formulas	35·7%	- - -'- - - - - - -	60·4%	- - - - - -'- - - -	FI
3. PRESENTATION					
3.1 Expression					
Points	0·0%	'- - - - - - - - - -	0·0%	'- - - - - - - - - -	L
at which	1·0%	'- - - - - - - - - -	16·0%	-'- - - - - - - - -	R/S
skills are	2·0%	'- - - - - - - - - -	44·0%	- - -'- - - - - - -	S/R
introduced	8·0%	'- - - - - - - - - -	68·0%	- - - - -'- - - - -	W

3.2 Content:

Differential	0·0%	- - - - - - - - - -	0·0%	- - - - - - - - - -	D
Ostensive	0·0%	- - - - - - - - - -	67·0%	- - - - - -'- - - -	O
Pictorial	78·3%	- - - - - - -'- - -	30·7%	- - -'- - - - - - -	P
Contextual	22·3%	- -'- - - - - - - -	13·1%	-'- - - - - - - - -	C

4. REPETITION
4.1 Amount
4.1.1 Number   3·5% '- - - - - - - - - - 6·0% '- - - - - - - - - - No
4.1.2 Distribution:

Vocabulary	70·0%	- - - - - - -'- - -	40·0%	- - - -'- - - - - -	Dv
Structure	90·0%	- - - - - - - - -'-	70·0%	- - - - - - -'- - -	Ds

4.2 Ratio
4.2.1 Skills:

Listening	24·0%	- -'- - - - - - - -	21·0%	- -'- - - - - - - -	Rl
Speaking	26·0%	- -'- - - - - - - -	15·0%	-'- - - - - - - - -	Rs
Reading	30·0%	- - -'- - - - - - -	59·0%	- - - - -'- - - - -	Rr
Writing	20·0%	- -'- - - - - - - -	5·0%	'- - - - - - - - - -	Rw

4.2.2 Media:

Texts	41·1%	- - - -'- - - - - -	84·8%	- - - - - - - -'- -	Mt
Recordings	19·2%	-'- - - - - - - - -	5·1%	'- - - - - - - - - -	Mr
Pictures	39·7%	- - -'- - - - - - -	10·1%	-'- - - - - - - - -	Mp

4.3 Variety:

Listening	60·0%	- - - - - -'- - - -	20·0%	- -'- - - - - - - -	Vl
Speaking	13·1%	-'- - - - - - - - -	13·1%	-'- - - - - - - - -	Vs
Reading	28·6%	- -'- - - - - - - -	14·2%	-'- - - - - - - - -	Vr
Writing	31·6%	- - -'- - - - - - -	21·1%	- -'- - - - - - - -	Vw

4.4 Type:

Rote	51·9%	- - - - -'- - - - -	75·2%	- - - - - - -'- - -	Ro
Incremental	3·5%	'- - - - - - - - - -	6·8%	'- - - - - - - - - -	In
Variational	38·1%	- - -'- - - - - - -	5·1%	'- - - - - - - - - -	Va
Operational	6·5%	'- - - - - - - - - -	12·9%	-'- - - - - - - - -	Op

All these are now arranged in a circle, around a circular percentage grid, so that the measurement of all the factors can be seen at a glance. For ease in reading, all plottings are connected by a continuous line to give the profile of the method as a whole. See, for example, the profiles of Methods A and B.

5.2 USES

Such profiles enable us to see all the characteristics of a method together. They give us a quantitative picture of a method and enable us to determine at a glance to what extent any factor in one method predominates over the same factor in another.

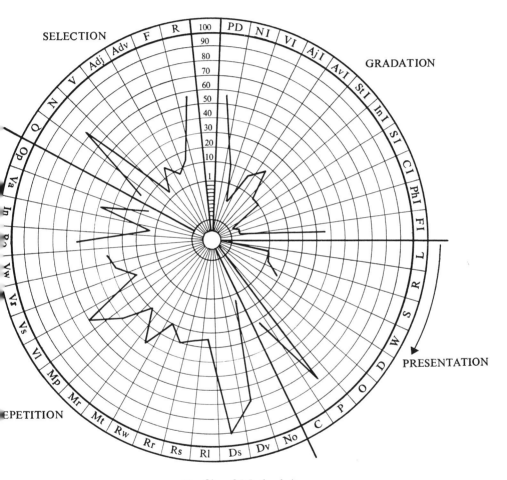

Profile of Method A

The profile can be used not only in comparing one method with another, but also in finding out in what measure a course is suited to a particular teaching situation; a method might be quite suitable for some situations,

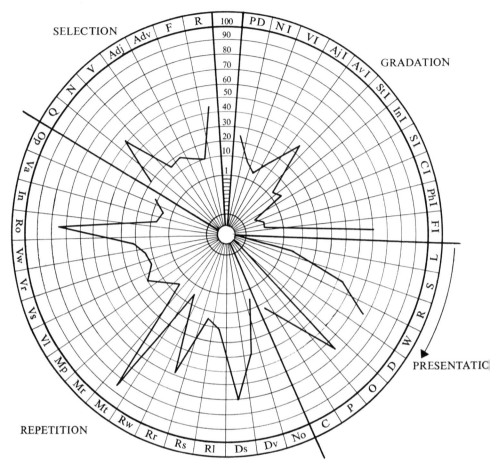

SELECTION

GRADATION

PRESENTATIC

REPETITION

Profile of Method B

but not for others. One method may be preferable for some types of teaching and teachers; other methods, for other types.

After having determined how methods differ in design, it remains to be seen how they differ in use; how they suit the syllabus, the learner and the teacher using them; what use is made of their materials; how these materials are converted into lesson plans; what techniques are used to teach the lessons; how far the teaching is mechanized; and how the material taught is tested. These are the problems with which teaching analysis, the final division of our inquiry, is concerned.

318

PART III

TEACHING ANALYSIS

CHAPTER I

The Suitability of Methods

OUTLINE

0. INTRODUCTION

1. SYLLABUS AND METHOD
    1.1 Analysis of the Syllabus
        1.1.1 Content of Syllabus
        1.1.2 Specification
        1.1.3 Justification
        1.1.4 Attainability
    1.2 Suitability of Method to Syllabus

2. LEARNER AND METHOD
    2.1 Age
        2.1.1 Content of Method
        2.1.2 Presentation and Practice
    2.2 Aptitudes
        2.2.1 Memory
        2.2.2 Imitative Ability
        2.2.3 Intelligence
        2.2.4 Personality
        2.2.5 Background
    2.3 Level
    2.4 Interests
        2.4.1 Listening and Speaking
        2.4.2 Reading and Writing
    2.5 Time
    2.6 Size of Group
    2.7 Culture Group

3. TEACHER AND METHOD

3.1 Suitability of Teachers
3.1.1 Language Skills
3.1.2 Professional Skills
3.1.3 Teaching Loads
3.2 Suitability of Methods
3.2.1 Adaptation
3.2.2 Preparation
3.2.3 Teaching Guidance

4. TEACHER AND LEARNER

0. INTRODUCTION

Starting with our method profiles we try to determine to what extent any method suits the syllabus, the learners and the teachers using it. The ideal would be to have profiles for the syllabus, the learner, and the teacher as a language teacher, to superimpose one profile on the other and to see how well they fit. To what extent is this possible? This depends on what we fit with what. The method may be related to (1) the syllabus, (2) the learner, and (3) the teacher.

1. SYLLABUS AND METHOD

Both the method and the teaching techniques which it requires can be judged only in the light of the objectives which they are supposed to meet. These are found in the syllabus.

Before judging the suitability of a method to a syllabus, we must first begin by analysing the syllabus itself. A syllabus may or may not be suitable to the situation in which it is to be used. We therefore (1) analyse the syllabus, and (2) see how the method suits it.

1.1 ANALYSIS OF THE SYLLABUS

When analysing a syllabus there are four main questions which have to be answered: (1) What does it include? (Content); (2) How specific is it? (Specification); (3) Why does it include what it does? (Justification); and (4) How attainable is it by the majority of learners for whom it is intended? (Attainability).

1.1.1 Content of Syllabus

What objectives does the syllabus include? The most usual are: understanding, speaking, reading, writing, grammar, translation, acquaintance with the history, civilization and literature of foreign peoples, better understanding of the native language, mental discipline, social adaptability, and use of foreign discoveries.

The list is typical of many a syllabus which makes no distinction between reasons for teaching a second language and the objective to be achieved. Such reasons as the understanding of foreign civilizations are listed together with reading ability under the general heading of "aims".

In examining the content of a syllabus the main question is this: What skills are required and how much of each?

1.1.2 Specification

How specific is the syllabus? The degree of specification may vary from a few vague cultural objectives to detailed instructions on reading, writing and speaking, including lists of words and structures for each skill.

A syllabus may be quite specific in content but vague in the degree of skill required. Such terms as "speaking ability" and "ability to understand a foreign speaker" are much too vague to permit quantification.

1.1.3 Justification

How does the syllabus justify its objectives? What reasons does it give for the requirements which it specifies?

A syllabus may require skills which are quite useless for the area in which it is used. It may, for example, for purely traditional reasons, require a knowledge of grammar rules which may be traced back to the formal study of Latin grammar during the Renaissance (see Ch. 5).

1.1.4 Attainability

How attainable are the objectives laid down by the syllabus? This will depend on the time available for foreign-language practice, on the abilities of the learners, and on the qualifications of the teachers.

Some objectives are quite unrealistic, requiring unqualified teachers to teach large classes of indifferent learners in two hours a week for a period of two years what may normally be attempted in other areas by highly skilled teachers with selected students in six hours a week over a period of seven or eight years.

Because of the limited time available, some objectives may be restricted to an elementary knowledge of only one of the primary skills. During the 1930s in the United States, reading knowledge became the sole objective because an extensive survey had revealed that 87 per cent of secondary-school students studied a foreign language for a maximum of two years.[1212:29]

1.2 SUITABILITY OF METHOD TO SYLLABUS

How does the method meet the objectives of the syllabus? Does it concentrate on the same skills as the syllabus prescribes? If the syllabus emphasizes a speaking knowledge of the language, a reading method may not be the most suitable. On the other hand, if the syllabus is limited to a reading objective, the reading section of an all-skill method may, under certain conditions, be the most appropriate method available.

The degree of suitability can be determined only to the extent that the syllabus is specific. In the present state of language teaching, the syllabus is generally not specific enough to permit any sort of measurement. It would be difficult, with most existing types of syllabus, to construct a profile such as the one designed for the quantitative analysis of methods.

2. LEARNER AND METHOD

The suitability of a method to a learner depends on (1) his age, (2) his aptitudes, (3) his second-language level, (4) his interests, (5) the time he can devote to language learning, (6) the size of the group with whom he practises the language, and (7) the culture group to which he belongs.

2.1 AGE

One cannot expect a child of fifteen to learn in exactly the same way as a child of five. A learner's age affects the suitability of a method in (1) content and (2) presentation and practice.

2.1.1 Content of Method

We must distinguish linguistic content from situation content. Age has the least effect on linguistic content the closer we come to the foundation level. For the most important words and structures of a language must be known by all ages. Differences in content vocabulary at a more advanced level, however, are greatly affected by age. At an advanced level, a method meant for business men would hardly be suitable for children of eight or nine.

Age also affects the form in which reading matter is presented. Young learners require a maximum amount of narration and a minimum of description.

Situation content depends largely on age for its appropriateness. A reading method for children would not be expected to contain the same situations as one for adults. Adults also demand something more sustained and coherent.

2.1.2 Presentation and Practice

The way the material is presented in the method may be more appropriate for one age group than for another. Children are more sensitive to anything that touches the senses; they react easily to physical stimulus.

In the presentation of the structure and meanings of the language children may need only the examples, whereas more mature learners may demand to know the rules. New associations are established more easily in children; adults have a body of associations not so easily disturbed.

The Suitability of Methods

2.2 APTITUDES

Learners differ in the number and degree of their language-learning aptitudes; a method may favour some of these more than it does others.

Aptitudes needed in second-language learning involve (1) memory, (2) imitative ability, (3) intelligence, (4) personality, and (5) background.

2.2.1 **Memory**

A method may favour any one of the three memory types—eye, ear, or motor. A reading method favours the eye type, the listening material of a course favours the ear type, and writing and speaking methods favour the motor type. These types represent of course only the predominant sense; only the blind and the deaf are all of one type, to the exclusion of the others.

Yet the predominant memory type of the learner may well affect the skill he will most easily acquire and also his preference for one sort of staging over another. It may also affect the relative proportion of recognition to productive vocabulary which he is likely to master. (See Ch. 4 and Ch. 8.) Learners with fugitive memories, however, may have difficulty with all the language skills.

2.2.2 **Imitative Ability**

Ability to discriminate foreign sounds and to imitate them with accuracy is one of the main aptitudes involved in learning to speak a second language. Methods with recorded sections favour this aptitude of imitation.

Tone-deaf learners will, of course, have difficulty with methods which rely heavily on imitation of the spoken word; so will lispers and stutterers.

2.2.3 **Intelligence**

A clever learner may get relatively more out of a method based on ostensive presentation than will a less intelligent one. From a point of view of language learning, intelligence may be semantic or structural.

The semantic aspects of intelligence include the ability to grasp meanings rapidly and intuitively. The structural aspects involve the ability to arrange, alter and co-ordinate forms simultaneously. This can be tested by requiring the learner to study a limited artificial language in a limited time.

The reading material supplied by the method is most obviously related to the intellectual level of the learners for whom it is intended. A class of seven-year-olds may have gone beyond the thousand-word level in the second language and yet be unable to understand a work of Plato, rewritten in a vocabulary even lower than this.

2.2.4 **Personality**

Some personality types learn languages more readily than others. The type who works hard but in periodic outbursts of activity, no matter how brilliant he is, may be less successful than the regular, routine type of learner of average intelligence.

2.2.5 **Background**

Persons with a multi-lingual background of spoken languages may find it easier to learn to speak a new language.

Learners may find a language easy or difficult to understand in so far as it approximates to the phonology, grammar or vocabulary of their native language. A good foundation in the native language may well be an advantage.

Background also affects the presentation of meaning. People from different cultures react differently to the same pictures and situations, since they may contain different cultural meanings for them. For them, the pictures may be connected with chains of associations different from those intended by the authors.

2.3 LEVEL

The suitability of a method to a learner depends on the level he has already reached in his study of the second language. Apart from the method not being intended for his scholastic level in years of study, it may not be suited to his real level of attainment.

What a learner may have been taught is no indication of what he knows. If he has covered the first book of a particular course, it does not mean that he is ready to start the second, even though he may have had high marks in the examination at the end of the first year. Language teaching cannot be built on what the learner knew; it can only be built on what he knows.

2.4 INTERESTS

To what extent does the content of the course meet the motives and interests of the learners?

If the learner does not want to learn the language, the best method will probably not succeed in teaching it to him. On the other hand, if he does not know what he wants the language for or what skills he wishes to acquire, he may still be sufficiently curious about the language itself or about the country in which it is spoken to develop an interest in the course.

The degree of interest may vary in different sections of the course, since the sort of material used in practising speech may not be the same as the sort used in reading and writing. We must examine separately the elements of interest (1) in the listening and speaking parts of the course, and (2) in the reading and writing sections.

2.4.1 Listening and Speaking

Are the situations used in the listening and speaking sections of the course those which the learner is likely to find believable? Are they situations which he can connect with something familiar and useful—the home, the family, occupations, travel? Are they associated with his purposes in learning the language?

2.4.2 Reading and Writing

Does the reading material suit the interests of the learner? Does it appeal to his emotional level? The more emotion the reading arouses, the deeper the impression on the learner and the longer will he remember and more quickly recall the stories and their language. There may be the appeal of suspense by the use of conflict, competition and incomplete situations such as are found in certain types of mystery stories. But different types of learners will have different sorts of reading interests. Adolescent boys, for example, are more likely than girls to be interested in stories of mystery and adventure. Other learners may prefer factual and informative reading matter. Does the course supply reading matter within the range of interests likely to be found in the group of learners for which it is intended? (See Ch. 9: 3.2.2.)

2.5 TIME

The time factor is of great importance in deciding whether a method is suitable for a particular group of learners. It is not the length of the course in running words that is the main factor, however; it is the amount of material taught. If the learner has only two hours a week of practice it is not necessarily preferable to replace a three-volume course covering a thousand-word vocabulary by a one-volume course covering the same material.

Learning a language takes practice, and practice takes time, at least as much time as learning any other skill, such as the ability to play a musical instrument. If little time can be devoted to language learning, the most suitable method may be the one with the minimum learning load and the maximum range of meaning and expression, in other words, the one with the greatest relative productivity (see Ch. 10).

Other factors to be considered here are the length, frequency, and distribution of periods into which the learning time is divided. If a method is used in an elementary school, daily periods of fifteen to twenty minutes, preferably in the morning, may be the most suitable. For the initial primary stages, more periods of short duration may be the most effective division of time; whereas the advanced stages may require fewer periods of longer duration.

In some cases, an intensive course of several hours a day may be better than an extensive course of a few hours a week over a longer period. Here learning plateaux and saturation points have to be taken into consideration.

2.6 SIZE OF GROUP

This is another important factor affecting the suitability of a method. A method suitable for a small class of fifteen learners or less may be unsuitable for classes of forty or fifty, and quite impossible for classes of more than a hundred. For the latter, methods with effective and abundant audio-visual materials may often be preferable.[1632] On the other hand, the teacher may devise techniques whereby a very large group is divided into teams of four or five learners, the best teams giving practice to the poorer ones. This, however, is not a matter of method but of teaching technique (see Ch. 14).

2.7 CULTURE GROUP

A method may not be equally suitable for all national and cultural backgrounds. The content may be so unfamiliar as to be incomprehensible. Or the text may not be the type which interests certain cultures. Some Oriental groups, for example, have a preference for the picturesque and the romantic.

3. TEACHER AND METHOD

A good method can be useless in the hands of a teacher who does not know how to use it; a good teacher can be ineffectual with a poor method. We must therefore examine (1) the suitability of the teacher to the method, and (2) the suitability of the method to the teacher.

3.1 SUITABILITY OF TEACHERS

The suitability of a language teacher is a matter of (1) his language skills, (2) his professional skills, and (3) his teaching load.

The Suitability of Methods

3.1.1 **Language Skills**

Does the teacher know enough of the language to use the method? If the method teaches the spoken language and does not include recordings, is the teacher's pronunciation alone good enough to serve as a model? If it is not, the phonetics part of a course and the availability of recordings may take precedence over other features of the method.

Of course, we should expect the teacher to know the language he is teaching. But this is not always the case, and it is not a simple either-or question. It is not sufficient that he should know the language well in order to teach it. If it were, the best language teachers would be native speakers with higher degrees in their own language and its literature. Such persons have sometimes turned out to be not the best teachers of their mother tongue as a foreign language. What is important is a mastery of the language at the level at which it is being taught. Some outstanding elementary language teachers can never compete with a native speaker in range of vocabulary, but they may have no need to do so. They may have a good pronunciation, a mastery of the structure of the language, speak it fluently and on top of this, be able to out-teach some of the best native speakers.

3.1.2 **Professional Skills**

Has the teacher the necessary teaching skills to use the method? Is he clear on language-teaching principles and procedures? Is he able to make the necessary adaptations of the texts? Does he know how to prepare drills and assignments?

If the method relies heavily on ostensive procedures, is the teacher skilled in using these? Is he willing to use them—or are they beneath his dignity?

Is the teacher's professional training orientated towards a different level from the one at which he is teaching? If he has few qualifications, this does not mean that he should be teaching at an elementary level. It has even been suggested that the contrary is the case, that none but the most experienced and most skilled teachers can properly handle young beginners, that teachers of beginners should know phonetics, have a keen ear, a good pronunciation, an intimate acquaintance with the foreign country and its people, and be able to teach what they know efficiently and with enthusiasm. Only mature and experienced teachers can do this.[1138:47]

Elementary language teaching, however, has often been considered as a period of "penal servitude" to be endured until the teacher has acquired sufficient seniority and reputation to be allowed to teach what he really wants—literature, grammar, textual criticism and the like.[951:6]

3.1.3 **Teaching Loads**

Has the teacher the time to use the method? Some methods require more preparation than others. The less preparation done by the method, the more will have to be done by the teacher, and the more time will he need to devote to the preparation of his lessons. But teachers with six or more hours a day of elementary language teaching may not have sufficient time to prepare each lesson.

The method may be an excellent one and the teachers employing it highly skilled in the teaching and use of the language; yet there may not be enough time to undertake the amount of lesson preparation which the method requires of the teacher. In such situations a less perfect method which does more teaching may be what is needed.

3.2 SUITABILITY OF METHODS

The suitability of a method to the skills and teaching load of the teacher depends on (1) the amount of adaptation it requires for use in the particular teaching situation, (2) the amount of preparation needed to use it, and (3) the amount of guidance or help which the method gives the teacher through the teaching manual or teaching notes.

3.2.1 **Adaptation**

What can the teacher do with the method? How much adaptation does it need for the situation in which he has to teach? How adaptable is the course?

A method intended for other purposes than the one for which it is being used may be well worth adapting because of its general teaching qualities. Some methods, however, are more easily adapted than others. Some characteristics are easy to alter, while others are quite complicated. It is easier, for example, to take a well-graded method and alter its presentation than it is to take a method with a good presentation and alter its gradation.

3.2.2 **Preparation**

How much preparation does the method require in order to be properly taught? A method relying heavily on the presentation of meaning through objects, actions and situations may demand more preparation than the teacher can handle. Many methods give only a fraction of the amount of practice needed for a mastery of the material presented. The authors of some methods simply assume that the teacher will have plenty of time to prepare the necessary drills and exercises. These persons seem either unwilling or unable to realize that the preparation of exercises for language learning is an undertaking of vast proportions. It is so time-consuming that some writers on the subject have suggested that if teaching is a full-time occupation, so is the preparation of exercises.[888:146]

Many teachers, however, have neither the time nor the competence to prepare the right sort of exercises. This is a job for the specialist. Therefore in some teaching situations, the number and variety of exercises supplied by a method may be the deciding factor in its adoption.

Related to this is the question of equipment. Some methods, excellent though they may be, may require film-projectors, tape recorders and other equipment. Are these available to the teacher who is expected to use the method? Lack of proper equipment may be a factor in the choice of one method rather than another; so may the willingness or ability of the teachers to make use of the equipment available.

3.2.3 Teaching Guidance

How does the method help the teacher to do the teaching? How much guidance does it give him? This may vary from a few paragraphs at the beginning of the text to an elaborate teaching manual. Quite common is the method with separate texts for the teacher and the learner. The teacher's text may contain everything found in the learner's book and, in addition, more or less elaborate teaching notes appended to each teaching unit. The quality and amount of these notes may be a deciding factor. A method with a good teacher's book or an elaborate teaching manual may enable semi-skilled language teachers, given the necessary time, to use the method adequately. Some such manuals give step-by-step teaching plans for each lesson. Others avoid this on the ground that they must not take the initiative away from the teacher. The plans, however, may have been included only by way of suggestions to the teacher and on the assumption that if he can make better ones he probably will. A teacher's time may be so limited that he will welcome anything which takes the burden of preparation off his shoulders. Some methods include a standard teacher-training course as a prerequisite to the use of the materials in class.

In evaluating teaching manuals or teaching notes, it is also important to examine the completeness, clarity and precision of the instructions given. Some teaching manuals are of little help because they lack precision. One method, for example, has a teacher's book which instructs the teacher to make the pupils associate a new word with its meaning, without giving any indication whatsoever how this can be done. Such vagueness of instruction makes the teaching manual superfluous for the skilled teacher, and unsuitable for the unskilled.

4. TEACHER AND LEARNER

Although it is not directly related to the suitability of methods, the problem of the relationship between teacher and learner is one which must eventually be analysed. Aside from the general compatibility of the teacher's personality with those of his students, there is the question of the teacher's ability to make good language learners out of the persons he is teaching. To begin with, it may be necessary to discover and remove certain psychological obstacles to language learning. The teacher may have to make an initial effort, for example, to improve the learner's attitude towards the language and the people who speak it. It may be necessary for him to inculcate in the learner the importance of correctness in oral or written expression. Or the teacher may have to remove a number of inhibitions which prevent the learner from making what appears to him as a series of funny sounds and grimaces. There is also the problem of doing away with the fear of being laughed at, either because of these strange sounds or because of mistakes in the language.

It is also most important that the teacher create in the classroom the sort of climate most conducive to the learning of a foreign language. In certain cases, this may be just as important for the success of a language class as is the suitability of the method.

We must distinguish, however, between the suitability of a method and its use. The fact that a method suits a teacher's qualifications does not guarantee that it will be used effectively. The use of a method can only be examined in the lessons which come from it. To get an idea of how effectively a method is used we have to analyse a series of lessons over a certain period of time. To facilitate the analysis, tape recordings and kinescopes may be made of each lesson. In fact, this may have to take the place of the method and its teaching materials for the learner-linguist working alone with an informant and in cases where neither the teacher nor the learners make use of a textbook or of any sort of materials prepared in advance. It is to the analysis of the lesson, therefore, that we must now turn.

What does the analysis of a lesson involve? It involves an examination of the three basic characteristics which all language lessons are necessarily made of: (1) the items of language included; (2) the plans or arrangements made for their teaching; (3) the techniques used to teach them. It is to these characteristics of lesson analysis that the next three chapters are devoted.

CHAPTER 12

Lesson Analysis I: The Language

OUTLINE

0. INTRODUCTION

1. ADAPTATION
   1.1 What is added?
   1.2 What is omitted?
   1.3 What is changed?

2. EXPLOITATION
   2.1 Formal Analysis
       2.1.1 Listing
       2.1.2 Tabulating
   2.2 Semantic Analysis
       2.2.1 Delimitation of Items
       2.2.2 Determining Semantic Relations
       2.2.3 Grouping into Teaching Points
       2.2.4 Ordering the Points

0. INTRODUCTION

A distinction has already been established between the amount of teaching done by the text and the amount done by the teacher. Two teachers may use the same text in entirely different ways, and each to a different extent, both in what the text teaches and the way it teaches it. We first consider what use the teacher makes of the text. To what extent is the language of the method (1) adapted, and (2) exploited?

1. ADAPTATION

The adaptation of a text may take three forms: (1) something may be added, (2) something may be omitted, and (3) something may be changed.

1.1 WHAT IS ADDED?

A teacher may add new items to the method either in his lesson plan or, *ad lib*, during the lesson. To find which these are, both the lesson and the lesson plan must therefore be examined (see below). How many items are added? What are they? Why are they added?

The most justifiable additions are concrete nouns in the form of highly frequent and available regional words; the least justifiable are likely to be structural items.

The number of items added is an important factor, since it alters the learning of all others. For example, if a teaching unit in the method has fifteen nouns and five structure words, and the teacher adds another ten nouns to these, he either decreases the relative amount of learning time per item or will have to increase the total learning time required. Which of these alternatives has the teacher chosen?

Are the items added incorporated into the method? Are they combined into sentences with other items taught? Are arrangements made for their recurrence in subsequent lessons, or are they used in one lesson and then forgotten? Does the addition of one item involve the teaching of others? For example, if a word like *look* is added, it may involve the addition of the preposition *at* or *for* and the groups *to look at* or *to look for* something. In making additions, has the teacher taken such things into account?

1.2 WHAT IS OMITTED?

Anything omitted reduces the learning load: but the extent to which it does so depends on what is omitted. As a general rule, the omission of structural items makes the greatest reduction in learning loads.

If the teacher omits an item from the method, however, he must make sure to omit it, not only in one lesson but in all subsequent lessons. Otherwise, the learner is up against unknown items which the method assumes he knows.

1.3 WHAT IS CHANGED?

Items may be grouped differently or arranged in different sequences. Some things may be taught earlier; some later. The problem facing the teacher who teaches an item earlier than does the text he is using is that of making sure that it is not forgotten by the time it comes up in the text. He has also the problem of seeing that it can be absorbed by the structures which have been or are being taught.

If, on the other hand, the teacher postpones an item taught in the text, he is faced with the task of continually eliminating it from the method until he reaches the point where he decides to introduce it.

2. EXPLOITATION

Some methods exploit their possibilities more than others. A method, chosen for its excellence, may nevertheless rely heavily on the teacher for its maximum effectiveness in use.

The potentialities of a method may be both formal and semantic. In order to exploit these, the teacher must know what they are. He can do so only through a formal and semantic analysis of the items in the text. If the method does not supply such an analysis, he will have to do his own.

2.1 FORMAL ANALYSIS

In order to get the most out of the method, it is important for the teacher to know which forms (phonological, grammatical, and lexical) are taught, and how much can be said with them. To find this out he needs (1) lists of items included, and (2) tables of their use in the structures taught.

2.1.1 Listing

If the method does not supply a list of items taught in the order in which they appear, the teacher will have to make his own. For before he can make any sort of analysis, he must know what is taught and when it is taught.

Using the text and the teaching manual as guides, the teacher can start by making separate but parallel lists for the phonology, grammar and vocabulary in the order in which the items appear. Each item represents a potential teaching point. Once completed, the lists tell him what the method teaches and the order in which it is taught.

The lists will not, however, show to what extent material which precedes can help to teach the material which follows. This can be done for the forms of the language by making cumulative tables of all the structures and the items which fit into them. Some teachers require the learners themselves to do this as the course proceeds.

2.1.2 Tabulating

In order to be able to exploit the method fully, the teacher must know what he has to teach with, and what can be said with what is taught. In other words, he must have some idea of the semantic productivity of the lesson he happens to be teaching (see Ch. 10: 2.1.1).

This will give the raw material necessary to introduce, present and drill each new teaching point effectively. To get an idea of the language he has to teach with, the teacher must put the known vocabulary into the new patterns (sentence, clause and phrase structures) and the new vocabulary into the known patterns. This gives him a series of tables from which he may extract the sense-making sentences he needs for the presentation and drill of the new teaching points.

(i) *Known Vocabulary into New Patterns*

Suppose that the new pattern to be taught is THE X IS ON THE Y. The teacher puts under X all the known words that take this place in the pattern, and under Y all the known words which can take the final position. The result is a table which might look something like this:

NEW PATTERN

	The	X	is on	the	Y	
KNOWN WORDS	The	book pen pencil watch key chalk brush	is on	the	table shelf floor seat book	KNOWN WORDS

Using this as a substitution table one can select a large number of sentences for the presentation and use of the new material. If *my, your, his, her* have been taught, one can get an even larger number of sentences by substituting them for the article *the* in the above pattern.

(ii) *New Words into Known Patterns*

Suppose that the new words to be taught are *door, window, roof, wall, ceiling, station, hospital, restaurant,* and *post-office.* A list is made of the patterns already taught (THIS IS X, I'M GOING TO THE X, etc.), and as many as possible of the new words are fitted in.

KNOWN PATTERN

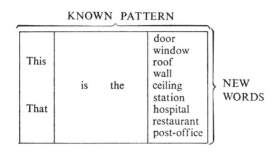

In some patterns, known words may be combined with new ones:

KNOWN PATTERN

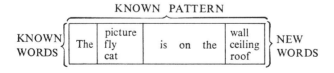

or, more elaborately:

KNOWN PATTERN

Known Words			New Words
The man woman taxi car	is	at the	door window station hospital restaurant post-office
Mrs. Smith Mr. Smith He She It			
The men women taxis cars	are		
Mr. and Mrs. Smith My bags We You They			

If the new teaching point is a structure word, both the known patterns and known words can be combined with it. For example, if the new teaching point is *in* there may be such a combination as this:

KNOWN PHRASE STRUCTURE

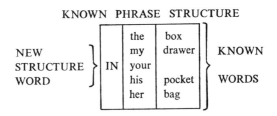

NEW STRUCTURE WORD } IN

the	box
my	drawer
your	
his	pocket
her	bag

KNOWN WORDS

And this:

KNOWN SENTENCE AND PHRASE STRUCTURE

KNOWN WORDS AND STRUCTURES					WORD → IN ← NEW		
I	am						
You / We / They	are	putting	the / my / your	knife / pen / book		the / my / your / his / her	box / drawer / bag / pocket
He / She / The woman / That man / Tom	is		his / her / their	pencil / watch / key			

With tables such as these in front of him, the teacher sees at a glance the possibilities of using the known to teach and drill the unknown.

2.2 SEMANTIC ANALYSIS

For the semantic exploitation of a method, a different analysis is necessary. If the teacher is to use the meaning of one item to teach, drill and reinforce the meaning of others, (1) he will have to know which items are semantically separate, that is, he will have to delimit the various meanings, (2) he will have to know the relation between the meaning of one item and that of another; this will permit him (3) to group the items into teaching points, and (4) to evaluate and arrange them in the order in which they are best taught. All, little or none of this may already have been done by the method; much of it may have to be done by the teacher.

2.2.1 Delimitation of Items

This operation may start from the list of forms taught (see above). Since the list gives only the forms taught, however, and not the meanings, it can be used only as a starting point.

It is important for the teacher to know all the meanings in which each form has been used. The list may, for example, include the structure word *on* in the fourth lesson; in order to exploit this fully, the teacher must know whether its spatial sense (on the table), its temporal sense (on June 23rd), or both, have been or are being taught.

2.2.2 Determining Semantic Relations

Once all the meanings of all items are listed, it is possible to find out which can be used to help teach and drill which. For example, if the temporal sense of *on* has been taught, it can be used for drill in the use of the days of the week (on Friday), or vice versa.

2.2.3 **Grouping into Teaching Points**

When the semantic relations of all items are known, they can then be divided into teaching points made of simple items or of groups of items which inter-teach one another. For example, the relation between *on* and *off* is one of opposition. If both words occur together at the same level, they may be grouped together into a single teaching point since the meaning of one helps to teach the meaning of the other by exclusion. There may be a number of such pairs, one of which excludes the other: *to–from, this–that, put–take, up–down.*

On the other hand, items of vocabulary may be grouped together because of some common semantic characteristic. For example, *table, chair, shelf,* and *floor* may be grouped into a single teaching point because they are all surfaces. The justification of this depends, of course, on the items with which they are going to be used. If the structure word *on* is being taught, *table, chair, shelf,* and *floor* may be the words which represent the only surfaces available for presenting and drilling this item, since any number of known objects can be placed on them.

2.2.4 **Ordering the Points**

Once the teaching points are established, the order in which they appear in the lesson will finally have to be determined. This may depend on their relative importance, or on the semantic or formal relations between them. For example, the structure word *on* is more important a point than *table, chair, shelf* and *floor*; that does not mean, however, that it has to appear as the first point in the lesson. If no words for surfaces have been included up to the stage where *on* is introduced, *table, chair, shelf* and *floor* may have to precede *on* for the simple reason that they are needed to teach it.

All this grouping and ordering of teaching points may have been done thoroughly or partially by the method; or it may have to be done by the teacher. It is the function of method analysis to determine how much of it is done by the method and how much remains to be done.

Once the teaching points have been determined and grouped, the teacher must then decide how he is going to teach them. His plan may be sketchy or elaborate, it may be made on paper or only in his mind, it may be entirely original or taken wholly or partly from the method; but it has to exist, since he has to decide what he is going to do before he does it. It is this decision, this teaching plan, that we now analyse.

Lesson Analysis II: The Plan

OUTLINE

0. INTRODUCTION

1. OBJECTIVES

    1.1 Level
    1.2 Type
    1.3 Skills
    1.4 Teaching Points

2. PROCEDURES

    2.1 Equipment
    2.2 Preparation of Learner
        2.2.1 Psychological
        2.2.2 Linguistic
    2.3 Presentation
        2.3.1 Forms
        2.3.2 Meanings
    2.4 Guidance
        2.4.1 Comprehension
        2.4.2 Production
    2.5 Habit Formation
        2.5.1 Expression Drills
        2.5.2 Content Drills
    2.6 Application: Expanding the Context
        2.6.1 Conversation
        2.6.2 Extensive Reading
    2.7 Checking-up and Summing-up

3. ORDER

    3.1 Order of Items
    3.2 Order of Skills
    3.3 Order of Procedures

4. PROPORTION

    4.1 Proportioning the Items
    4.2 Proportioning the Skills
    4.3 Proportioning the Procedures

Lesson Analysis II: The Plan

0. INTRODUCTION

Language-teaching efficiency may be examined by analysing a series of lesson plans over a period of time. Even a superficial analysis of the lesson plans can tell us the procedures of presentation, the predominance of skills, and the frequency of reviews. It can tell us how much teaching is done by the teacher and how much by the method, what the teacher has omitted or added to the text, and the extent to which he exploits his material.

The first thing in analysing a teaching plan is to ask who made it and for what purpose. Does it come entirely from the teacher or partly from the teaching manual, or from a series prepared by another teacher?

The nature of the lesson plan will depend on the sort of lesson, the length of the lesson and the level of teaching. There are three sorts of lessons: informative, affective, and practical. All of these may appear as language teaching, which can be informative when the lesson is about the language, its grammar or evolution, affective when it appreciates the literature, and practical when it teaches people to use the language. It is this last sort of lesson which concerns us here. It is a sort which necessarily involves a certain amount of learner participation; and the more participation involved, the more planning required.

Lesson plans may differ in (1) objectives, (2) procedures, (3) order, and (4) proportion.

1. OBJECTIVES

The objectives of a lesson plan may vary according to (1) the level of teaching, (2) the type of lesson being taught, (3) the language skills used and (4) the teaching points presented.

1.1 LEVEL

For what level is the plan intended? Is it suitable for this level? Quite often a lesson plan may be excellent for advanced learners but not at all appropriate for beginners.

1.2 TYPE

What type of lesson does the plan outline? This depends on whether the lesson is devoted to presenting new material, revising old material, or correcting bad habits. Remedial lessons, for example, although they may look very much like lessons for beginners, may cover a great deal more material.

1.3 SKILLS

If the lesson is not to be about the language, its literature, or culture, it will have to present one or more of the four primary language skills— listening, speaking, reading and writing. Which of these are included in the plan? Some plans may be limited to only one; there are plans for reading lessons or conversation lessons, for example. A lesson plan may be limited to one aspect of a single skill; it may be a plan for a lesson in pronunciation and may be further limited to the identification of the relevant sounds.

1.4 TEACHING POINTS

What items are taught and how are they grouped in the plan? What sort are they—phonetic, lexical, structural? How many are there? A lesson which teaches ten structure words in a half-hour period will be more difficult than one which teaches ten concrete nouns in the same time.

2. PROCEDURES

A lesson plan necessarily involves a number of teaching procedures. Each of these may include a variety of different activities. There are some fundamental ones, however, that one might expect to find in any complete lesson plan.

Language lesson plans include: (1) A list of equipment; (2) procedures for preparing the learner; (3) presentation of the teaching point, (4) guidance of the learner in his first attempts; (5) habit formation; (6) application of language items taught, and (7) a final checking-up and summing-up. Which of these procedures does the plan under analysis include?

2.1 EQUIPMENT

Does the plan include a list of equipment which the teacher will need, to present and drill the items in the teaching point? If he is using ostensive procedures of presenting meaning, is there an ordered list of all the objects or models he needs to get the meaning of the new point across?

Of course, the materials listed depend on both the teaching point and the type of drills included in the plan. Some drills may require flash-cards, word-strips, film-strips, or recordings.

The list of equipment may be placed at the head of the plan since it must be consulted before the lesson begins.

2.2 PREPARATION OF LEARNER

A learner who knows what he has to do and is well disposed to do it, gives a better performance than one who does not know what to expect. In language learning, the preparation of the learner has to be (1) psychological, and (2) linguistic.

2.2.1 Psychological Preparation

It is important to prepare the mind of the learner for the lesson and the teaching point it includes. It is first of all necessary to attract his attention to what is being taught. In some cases it is possible in a few sentences to fill his mind with examples of the importance, agreeableness and facility of what he is going to be taught. Is there anything at the start of the plan that is meant to attract the learner's attention either to the new point or to something which leads to it?

It may simply be an indication of some action, either by the teacher or by a learner, designed to attract attention. For example, if the teaching point includes *whose*, the teacher might begin by collecting some of the learners' belongings—pens, pencils, knives, books—with the intention later of returning them or asking the learners to return them in answer to the question: *Whose X (pen, etc.) is this?* Or if the first sentence in the sequence is *Where's my book?* the teacher might begin by putting his book on the floor or by asking one of the learners to do so.

2.2.2 Linguistic Preparation

In addition to training learners in language learning—in exploiting limited vocabularies, native speakers, documents—there is the more specific preparation for each new teaching point by showing its relation with the items already taught. If the known material is to be used to present and drill the new teaching point, the learner will have to be reminded of what this material is; and the teacher will have to make sure that it is still known. Is there anything in the plan, therefore, that takes this into account?

Once the teacher has the attention of the learners, he may start immediately building a bridge from what they have already been taught to the new point which he is going to teach them. For example, starting from the above introduction, where a learner put his book on the floor, there may be the following bridge leading to the presentation of *was*.

1. Having put book on floor, ask: Where's my book?
2. Class: It's on the floor.
3. Take book off the floor, put it on the table and ask the class: Where's my book?
4. Class: It's on the table.
5. Point to table and say slowly: Yes. It *is* on the table.
6. Point to floor and say slowly: It *was* on the floor.

In this case, the new teaching point, *was*, first appears in Number 6 above and is based on a knowledge of Numbers 1 to 5, which form a bridge to the new point. If this bridge does not exist in the minds of the learners, it is up to the teacher to build it; if it is not strong enough, it is up to him to strengthen it. For if the learners are still struggling with *is*, they will not easily master *was* or *will be*. If they do not know *It is on the table* they can hardly be expected to use this sentence as a means of learning *It was on the table*. The teacher may have to re-teach or review all the words (*on, where,* etc.) in the first five sentences before he can go on to the new point in the sixth. He may have to go over his old lesson plans for these points and have them ready in case he needs them.

But he will first have to analyse the meaning of the new point and see how it could be linked to or made to depend on something which has already been taught. Just as the above use of *was* depends on a knowledge of *is* (since the past assumes a knowledge of the present), so the plural assumes the singular; *part* depends on the names of things that have parts; *high* and *low, long* and *short,* on the names of things that can be high or low, long or short.

2.3 PRESENTATION

How are the forms and meanings of the new point to be presented?

2.3.1 **Forms**

Which forms are to be taught, the spoken form, the written form, or both? Are these presented in context or in isolation?

Any new form of a language, spoken or written, must have a model. What is this model to be? If the form is to be spoken, is the teacher to rely on his own pronunciation, or is he to use recordings? If, in addition to the spoken form, the written form is to be presented, is it to be shown before, after or at the same time? How is the written form to be first presented—with flash-cards, word-strips, film-strips, or on the blackboard? (See Ch. 8: 1.2.2.)

2.3.2 **Meanings**

What procedures are to be used to get the meanings across to the learner—the learner's own language, objects, actions, situations, pictures, or the words he already knows? How many of these procedures are used? (See Ch. 8: 2.)

If the new point is a new pattern, does the teacher present it by means of words already known? These words will be found in the analysis he has previously made for each of the teaching points. (See Ch. 12: 2.1.2.) If the new point is a word, he may present it by means of known patterns, the possibilities of which he can find in the tables which were the results of the same analysis. By means of what is known, he is thus able to make the meaning and form of the new point clear.

He may decide to present important points such as structural words in more than one way, and follow up with a number of useful examples, so as to give the learners the idea that they are learning something of importance.

In making his plan, the teacher lists what he and the learners are going to do and say during the presentation. Keeping the above example of *was*, here is one teacher's plan for presenting it:

Equipment: Books, pencils, watches and other objects the names for which are known to the learners.

DO	SAY
1. Put book on the floor, and ask:	Where's my book?
2. Encourage class to respond:	It's on the floor.
3. Take the book off the floor, put it on the table, and ask:	Where's my book?
4. Class:	It's on the table.
5. Point to table and say slowly:	Yes. It's on the table. It *is* on the table.
6. Point to floor and say slowly:	It *was* on the floor.
7. Put pencil on the table and ask:	Where's my pencil?
8. Class:	It's on the table.
9. Now take it off the table, and put it on a seat and ask:	Where's my pencil?
10. Class:	It's on the seat.
11. Point to the pencil on the seat and say:	It is on the seat.
12. Point to the table and say slowly:	It was on the table.
13. Put watch on the table and ask:	Where's my watch?
14. Class:	It's on the table.
15. Put watch in pocket and ask:	Where's my watch?
16. Class:	It's in your pocket.
17. Put hand over pocket and say slowly:	Yes. It is in my pocket.
18. Point to the table and say:	It was on the table, etc.

2.4 GUIDANCE

Before the learner can be drilled in the new teaching point, it may be necessary for him to know that he is capable of using it, so that he can start with a realization that he is able to achieve what he has been taught. If bad habits are to be avoided, the first efforts of the learner must be carefully guided, both for (1) comprehension of the teaching point and (2) its production. What is there in the plan that takes care of this?

Guidance may take the form of checking comprehension and guiding production.

2.4.1 Comprehension

Comprehension may be checked (i) by asking the learner to point to something, (ii) to do something, (iii) to answer a question, or (iv) to explain in his own language. Which of these procedures is used?

2.4.2 Production

If the lesson includes oral or written production of the new teaching point, does the plan make room for a try-out of the new point under the supervision of the teacher? Is enough time allowed for this?

After the learners have been taught the meaning and expression of the new teaching point, they try using it themselves at their own speed in order to get the feel of it. For example, continuing the above sequence for the presentation of *was*:

1. Point and say:	My watch was on the table.
2. Ask:	Where was my watch?
3. Answer question:	It was on the table.
4. Ask the class:	Where was it?
5. Let the class answer:	It was on the table.
6. Ask:	Where is it?
7. Class:	It's in your pocket.
8. Ask:	Where was my pencil?
9. Answer question:	It was on the table.
10. Ask class:	Where was it?
11. Class:	It was on the table.
12. Ask class:	Where is it?
13. Class:	It's on the seat.
14. Ask:	Where was my book?
15. Answer question:	It was on the floor.
16. Ask class:	Where was it?
17. Class:	It was on the floor.
18. Ask class:	Where is it?
19. Class:	It's on the table, etc.

Such sequences are designed to give the class confidence that they can use the new word or pattern correctly, though perhaps hesitatingly.

Lesson Analysis II: The Plan

2.5 HABIT FORMATION

Any language-teaching plan must take into account the fact that a language is a system of habits. What provision is there in the plan, therefore, for converting what is taught into a habit? Language habits include (1) expression, as in the case of pronunciation, and (2) content, as in the use of the right words in a given situation.

2.5.1 **Expression Drills**

Formal habits may be developed in the use of (i) the spoken forms, and (ii) the written forms.

(i) *Spoken Forms*

Although the class may now be able to give correct formal responses, they will not yet have mastered the teaching point. Drills are needed to make their pronunciation, rhythm, and intonation natural and fluent. Drills include articulation and catenation, rhythm and intonation, and pattern.
(a) Articulation and Catenation Drills:
These include the articulation and catenation features connected with the teaching point. To continue the above example, this part of the lesson might show and drill the use of the strong form in such sentences as *Where WAS it?* Or it may concentrate on the weak form in such sentences as *It was on the table.* So as not to take up too much time in the teaching point, the drills may be in chorus. Here the teacher might also drill any difficult sounds with which the learners may be having difficulty.

(b) Rhythm and Intonation Drills:

This type of drill gives practice in the rhythm and the intonation of the new teaching point and incorporates it into sentence structures already taught, preferably in those in which it most usually appears.

When the new teaching point happens to be a new sentence structure, this is the place where its particular rhythm and intonation patterns might be drilled. For example, the class may be required to repeat in chorus as the teacher makes the necessary variations in the wording, while using the same rhythm and intonation again and again.

Teacher	It was in the room.
Class:	It was in the room.
Teacher:	It was on the floor.
Class:	It was on the floor, etc.

350

So as to make sure not to make any rhythm or intonation changes from one sentence to the next, the teacher might indicate in his teaching notes a rhythm and intonation which is both natural and simple. If rhythm and intonation, however, is the subject of the course, the point of the drill might be to keep the same words and structures and to change the rhythm or intonation in response to changing situations signalled by the teacher.

If the teacher has recordings spaced for repetition, this might be the time to bring them into the plan. Group singing and oral reading might also come in at this point.

(c) Pattern Drills:

The purpose of this type of drill is to lead the learner to pronounce the new teaching point not only correctly but also independently. It is the same sort of chorus repetition as the above rhythm drill except that the teacher gives only the variation, and the class, the complete form. For example:

1.
Teacher:	It was on the floor.
Class:	It was on the floor.
Teacher:	Table.
Class:	It was on the table.
Teacher:	Seat.
Class:	It was on the seat, etc.

2.
Teacher:	It was in the box.
Class:	It was in the box.
Teacher:	Drawer.
Class:	It was in the drawer.
Teacher:	Water.
Class:	It was in the water, etc.

To prepare such pattern drills, the teacher simply refers to his analysis and draws up a list of known words which can fit into the pattern being drilled. (See Ch. 12: 2.1.)

(ii) *Written Forms*

These include drills in the reading and writing of letters, words and sentences.

(a) Letter Drills:

If some of the learners are not able to read the alphabet or if they have different alphabets, the teacher may have to give them a special course in recognizing letters and words.

After learning to read, the first thing that the learner must know in order to write is to be able to shape the letters. He may already have learned to do this in his own language; but if he has not, it must be taken into account in the plan.

(b) Word Drills:

In order to read and write, the learner must develop habits of recognizing words and of spelling them correctly. These skills may be practised through copying and spelling drills like word-alternation, word-completion, and word-building (see Ch. 9: 4.2.1).

Once the learner can shape letters, the teacher may give him some practice in both language and penmanship by making him copy sentences which he is able to read. The teacher may also make him copy substitution tables, especially those which he is attempting to memorize. Later the learner may be asked to copy material which he has already memorized; this is a sort of auto-dictation.

If the learner is a literate adult who has started by reading phonetic script, transcription from phonetic script into ordinary spelling may be used as an exercise in writing as well as in ear-training. If the teacher is going to use the blackboard, he may include in his plan an outline of what he is going to put on it.

(c) Sentence Drills:

Skill in writing and punctuating sentences may be developed through such exercises as dictation and transcription (see Ch. 8: 4.2.2). A teacher may prefer to use dictation sparingly, however, since it may sometimes do more harm than good. He may decide to use only material with which the learner is thoroughly familiar, material so well prepared beforehand that no mistakes are made. Dictations which are full of mistakes are of little value as drills.

2.5.2 Content Drills

Although the learners understand the new teaching point and can pronounce it fluently in a number of sentence patterns, they still have to learn to use it as an automatic response to the appropriate situations. At this point, therefore, the teacher may give the class a number of situation drills, drills which force the learner to use the new teaching point in response to certain situations, often in contrast with something already known, for example, *was* contrasted with *is*, the future with the present, the plural with the singular.

Situation drills force the learner to use the new point to convey meaning. Conveying meaning in a language may be done in (i) speech, or (ii) writing.

(i) *Speech*

A learner may be given practice in speaking the language through the use of actions, pictures, and speech. Which of these are included in the plan?

(a) Speech through Actions:
Practice in speech may be developed through look-and-say drills, do-and-say drills, and action games. These drills involve the creation of situations the response to which makes the learners use the words and patterns covered in the form drills while combining the new teaching point with what they have already been taught. The number and range of these combinations will be found in the analysis already made of the possibilities of the teaching point (Ch. 12: 2.1.2). To continue with the same illustration of the teaching of *was*, suppose that the analysis reveals that among other known patterns into which *was* can fit are the patterns WHERE WAS THE X? and IT WAS IN (on, at) THE X. The analysis will also show a number of words that can take the place of X, such words as *book, table, seat, pen, pencil, key, knife, watch*. This information would permit the teacher to devise the following situation drill for *was*:

1. Collect different objects the names of which have already been taught—a pen, a pencil, a book, a knife, a key, a watch, etc.
2. Put them in various places—in a drawer, in a bag, in a box, on the floor, on a table, on a seat, etc.
3. Ask the class where each is:
   Where's the key?   *Class:* It's in the bag.
   Where's the knife?   *Class:* It's in the drawer, etc.
4. Now collect all the objects and put them on the table. Ask the class where they are now, and where they were:
   Where's the key?   *Class:* It's on the table.
   Where was it?   *Class:* It was in the bag.
5. Ask the learners to do the asking.

Or suppose the teaching point is *what*. The above objects might be used in the same places; but instead of asking where they are and where they were, each learner takes his turn in asking the class what is on (or in) what: What's on the table? What's in the drawer? What's in the bag? (For further examples of speech drills through actions, see Appendix A.)

The large number of drills necessary to convert a teaching point into a habit may result in boredom and in failure to maintain the amount of attention needed for learning. If there is danger of this happening, the teacher may find it necessary to bring a few language games into the plan. The sort of games needed are those which raise the interest of the class while giving them practice in using the new teaching point in response to changing situations. To continue our above example of the teaching of *was*, here is a game which might follow after a number of ordinary situation drills:

Guessing Game for Drilling WAS

1. Have cards put in different parts of the room to represent the different parts of a town—station, post-office, etc.
2. Ask one of the learners to leave the room.
3. Go to one of the above places.
4. Return and call the learner back into the room.
5. Now ask the learner to try to guess where the teacher went. Other learners take their turns in asking the guessing learner: "Where was Mr. X?"
6. Guesses must be made in full sentences: "He was at the station. He was at the post-office, etc."
7. The learner whose question results in a correct guess has to replace the guessing learner, leave the room, and return to do the guessing.

As an additional example, here is a game for the drilling of *what*:

Guessing Game for Drilling WHAT

Ask a boy and a girl to stand in opposite corners of the room. Give each a complete collection of objects the names of which have already been taught. Put them in a box or a bag so that the class cannot see them. The boy and the girl take turns in putting a hand into the bag, taking a small object from the bag, concealing it in the hand, and in asking each learner to guess what it is. Each learner takes his turn in going through the following procedure:

1. Learner stands up and faces the boy in the corner.
2. The boy in the corner asks him: What's in my hand?
3. The class asks him: What's in his hand?
4. He guesses: It's a key.
5. If his guess is right he takes the object.
   If his guess is wrong he asks the boy
   in the corner: What's in your hand?
6. The boy in the corner shows the object
   to the class and says what it is: It's a book.
7. The learner must now face the girl in the opposite corner and go through the same procedure.
8. The girl in the corner asks him: What's in my hand?
9. The class asks him: What's in her hand?
10. He guesses: It's a ticket.

11. If he is right he keeps the object.
    If he is wrong he must ask: What's in your hand?
12. The girl in the corner shows the object
    and says what it is: It's a pencil, etc.

The learner with the greatest number of objects wins the game.

Some games may be presented as team games. These sometimes appeal to the competitive instincts of certain age-groups. Do language games such as these appear in the teaching plan? (For further examples of language games involving action, see Appendix B.)

Many situations, however, cannot be produced in the classroom; others cannot be changed rapidly enough to make them useful as drills. This is where the use of pictures and film strips may be incorporated into the plan. Some textbooks supply a series of numbered pictures, each showing a different situation.

(b) Speech through Pictures:

Pictures of objects, actions, and situations may be shown and the learners may be asked to describe them or answer questions on them.

Different drills may be used with picture-cards, blackboard drawings, wall-pictures, flannel-boards, picture books, films and film-strips. Some of these may be used in picture-games as well. (See Appendixes A and B and Ch. 9: 2.2.4.)

(c) Speech through Speech:

The stimulus used to make the learner speak may, of course, be the most usual one, speech itself. The learner may be given speaking practice through question-and-answer drills, conversion, completion, matching and substitution drills. (See Ch. 8: 2.2 and Appendix A.)

(ii) *Writing*

Does the plan include writing drills? If so, what sort? Practice in writing may be given through actions, pictures, and texts.

(a) Written Action Drills:

These include all drills whereby the learner observes actions and writes down what he sees. They may be of the do-and-write type, where the learner describes actions he has just performed, or of the look-and-write type, where he describes the actions of others (see Appendix A).

(b) Written Picture Drills:

These are similar to the speech-through-picture drills (see above), but instead of saying what he sees the learner writes it down (see Appendix A).

(c) Written Textual Drills:

Practice in writing may be provided through texts which have been either written on the blackboard, duplicated by the teacher, or supplied in the workbooks of the course. These include drills in sentence modification, sentence composition and paragraph writing (see Ch. 9: 4.3).

Written exercises on the teaching point might be given either as class work or as homework. These exercises may range from filling in blanks to writing compositions, depending on the level. One possible exercise for *was* at the blank-filling level is to contrast it with *is* and later with *were*, *are*, and *am*. For example:

IS, WAS *and* AM

1. He........here now.
2. She........here yesterday.
3. The table........in this room now.
4. I........at my table now.
5. It........there last night, etc.

2.6 APPLICATION: EXPANDING THE CONTEXT

In order that the new teaching point may become part of his usable language, it is important for the learner to get a feeling for the spoken and written contexts in which what he has learned is normally used. Its use will therefore have to be expanded beyond the limited contexts of the drills.

After the learners are able to use the new teaching point automatically in response to the right situations, the teacher may decide to give them practice in using it within the wider, more natural contexts of everyday conversation, reading and writing.

Does the plan make provision for expanding the context through (1) conversation, or (2) extensive reading?

2.6.1 Conversation

The new teaching point may be linked with contexts of everyday conversation. This may, for example, be done through the learning and dramatization of model dialogues. The model dialogue may first be studied in class as a series of phonetic and pattern drills (see above), perhaps with the aid of recordings. The memorizing process may then be completed at home. Next day the dialogue may be dramatized in class.

If dialogues are used, where do they come from? Does the teacher compose his own? Do they follow the interests and vocabulary of the class? Elementary dialogues are often more difficult to write than the more advanced ones; for as the vocabulary and structure increase, so does the productivity, and hence the possibilities for natural, everyday conversation.

2.6.2 Extensive Reading

It may be decided to expand the context further through reading. By thus being associated with a wide variety of contexts, the new point becomes all the more meaningful and all the easier to remember. This may be achieved through the use of reading material incorporating the new teaching point, and written within the learner's vocabulary.

The reading may be started in class and finished at home; or it may be done entirely at home. If the question forms have been taught, the learners, for homework, may be asked to prepare questions on the reading.

2.7 CHECKING-UP AND SUMMING-UP

Does the plan include a section devoted to a recapitulation of the items taught? Does the teacher leave time for checking the extent to which the lesson has been mastered by the class, and time for clearing up any difficulties which may have arisen?

Although this section may be short, it may be important, since both the summing-up of a point and the testing of it reinforce all the impressions with which it has been connected throughout the lesson.

Before going on to the next teaching point, therefore, the teacher may want to find out whether or not he has succeeded in teaching this one. From the oral responses already given he may have some idea of how well the class has mastered the new point. Yet it may be necessary for him to have a rapid, final check. Picking individual learners at random, he may present them orally with a number of questions or situations the response to which includes the new teaching point. For example:

Teacher:	Where was my watch, Tom?
Tom:	It was in your pocket.
Teacher:	Where was my book, Jane?
Jane:	It was on the floor, etc.

He may thus, in a short time, make some intelligent soundings to find out the percentage of the class with a sufficient knowledge of the new point.

From time to time, he may, of course, give more elaborate written tests which he can collect, correct, and study after the class. They may give him some idea of the sort of remedial teaching needed, and determine what his next lesson plan will be. He must not wait until improperly mastered teaching points become unchangeable habits.

3. ORDER

Teaching plans may differ considerably in the order in which their constituent parts are arranged. This applies to (1) the items presented, (2) the skills taught, and (3) the procedures used.

3.1 ORDER OF ITEMS

Two plans teaching the same items may present them in a different order. For example, if they include presentation of the structure words *on* and *off*, one plan may represent and drill *on* with *table-shelf-floor*, then present *off* and drill it similarly; whereas the other plan might have both *on* and *off* presented and drilled together, as opposites.

3.2 ORDER OF SKILLS

In what order are the skills arranged in the plan? Some teachers present reading and writing first because these may be considered the most accessible; others present listening and speaking first because they consider them the most active and often the most useful.

3.3 ORDER OF PROCEDURES

In what order are the procedures arranged? The most important differences in the order of procedures are in those concerned with content and expression in presentation and habit formation. Some plans may put expression before meaning (content); some, after.

Some present expression first and meaning later. There is an advantage, however, in starting the presentation with the meaning, and in starting the drills with expression forms. In this way the learner knows what he is saying during the form drills and knows how to say it during the semantic drills. This is because all drills involving meaning also involve the use of the expression forms of the language-phonemes, stress, etc.; but not vice-versa. So that, if a learner has learned to pronounce the new teaching point correctly, every sentence he utters in the semantic drills reinforces his good pronunciation; otherwise, it reinforces his errors in pronunciation, in which case more form drills may have to be devoted to erasing these errors.

4. PROPORTION

Finally, teaching plans differ in the way they apportion the lesson time for (1) the teaching of the items in the lesson, (2) the exercise of the skills, and (3) the use of the procedures.

4.1 PROPORTIONING THE ITEMS

What proportion of the lesson time is given to each of the items taught? Is it justified?

Some plans may devote no more time to the presentation of structure words than they do to concrete nouns; others may give much more time to the structural items, presenting each in a variety of different ways.

4.2 PROPORTIONING THE SKILLS

How much time is calculated for listening, speaking, reading and writing? The class-time which the learners may have to devote to some of these skills may depend on a number of external factors outside the control of the teacher. If home reading is out of the question, for example, reading in class may take up a greater proportion of the time than it otherwise would.

Time spent on each skill may also depend on the level reached. In some methods, the elementary course requires that more than three-quarters of the time be devoted to speech. This proportion, however, gradually decreases as the course advances. In other methods, reading and writing may be required as the main skills taught.

4.3 PROPORTIONING THE PROCEDURES

What proportion of time is allotted to such procedures as learner preparation, presentation, guidance, habit formation, application through context expansion, checking-up and summing-up? Some plans may allot most of the time to presentation; others, to drill. If many types of drills and games are used, what is the relative amount of time given to each? Some teachers may be so taken up with one type of drill that they ignore all the others.

The amount of time devoted to a procedure may, of course, depend on the age of the learners. Children need more variety than adults and have a shorter attention span. They may require a change of activity every five or ten minutes. In the 1920s, in "direct method" classes in France, there was a break of five minutes per quarter-hour to allow the children "to rest their ears" because of the concentration required when listening to a strange language.[1207:66]

Finally, is the plan usable? Is it easily followed? Is it confused, badly arranged, or too detailed? If the plan is too detailed, is there a simple, single-page summary for easy reference in class?

There may be a great difference, however, between a plan and its performance. We cannot therefore have a complete lesson analysis until we have observed the teacher in action, until we have analysed the teaching techniques used to convert the plan into a lesson. It is the analysis of teaching techniques, therefore, which will be our next concern.

CHAPTER 14

Lesson Analysis III: The Techniques

OUTLINE

0. INTRODUCTION

1. USE OF THE PLAN

2. EQUIPMENT AND LAYOUT
   2.1 Type of Room
   2.2 Equipment
       2.2.1 Furniture
       2.2.2 Teaching Equipment
   2.3 Layout
       2.3.1 Layout of Equipment
       2.3.2 Seating Arrangement

3. TECHNIQUES OF PRESENTATION
   3.1 Expression Techniques
       3.1.1 Spoken Models
       3.1.2 Written Models
   3.2 Content Techniques
       3.2.1 Differential
       3.2.2 Ostensive
       3.2.3 Pictorial
       3.2.4 Contextual

4. TECHNIQUES OF REPETITION
   4.1 Speech
       4.1.1 Amount
       4.1.2 Accuracy
       4.1.3 Types of Responses
       4.1.4 Contexts of Speech
       4.1.5 Variety of Speech Drills
       4.1.6 Techniques of Questioning
       4.1.7 Techniques of Correcting
   4.2 Reading
   4.3 Writing

Lesson Analysis III: The Techniques

0. INTRODUCTION

In the analysis of the teaching techniques, we are concerned only with the teacher's performance, with how he does his job, with the use of his material facilities, and with his teaching tactics. What are the questions we must ask, therefore, in analysing the actual performance?

The performance of a lesson includes: (1) the use of the lesson plan, (2) the equipment and layout, (3) techniques of presentation, and (4) techniques of repetition.

1. THE USE OF THE PLAN

The best teaching plan will have little effect if it is not properly used. In the first place, we must ask whether the teacher is qualified to use it? Are the activities called for within his linguistic and professional competence? If the plan requires him to use his own pronunciation as a model, is he capable of pronouncing the language properly?

Secondly, is the teacher sufficiently familiar with the plan? Does he know it well enough to be able to give his whole attention to the class instead of to his teaching notes? Does he have to hesitate every few minutes to find out what he is going to do next? If he does, he may not only lose valuable classroom time; he may also lose the attention of the class.

Thirdly, how closely does the teacher follow the plan? Are there any deviations or digressions? What is the reason for them?

2. EQUIPMENT AND LAYOUT

Physical surroundings are important for efficient language teaching, especially for techniques with a physical basis. The surroundings most relevant to language teaching techniques are: (1) the type of room, (2) the teaching equipment, and (3) the layout of the class.

2.1 TYPE OF ROOM

Are the size and shape of the room appropriate for the type of lesson to be taught? Is it too small, or too large, for the purposes of language teaching at the particular level? Does its shape permit a good distribution of the learners, or does it place them all, one behind the other, in a long corridor-type of room?

Does the room permit the accurate hearing and seeing necessary for language teaching? Can the foreign sounds be heard distinctly in all parts of the room? Can everything used be clearly seen? Is it also possible to darken the room for the use of films and film strips?

362

2.2 EQUIPMENT

What does the room contain in the way of (1) furniture, and (2) teaching equipment?

2.2.1 Furniture

Is the furniture suitable for the level at which the teaching is done? Is there a place for storing the teaching equipment needed? What sort of demonstration table is there? Are the seats of the right sort? Are they movable or fixed?

2.2.2 Teaching Equipment

Has the teacher all the teaching equipment he needs for the lesson? Has he the right properties—objects, models, pictures? Or does he have to use some readily available classroom object and pretend that it is something else?

Has he the projector and record-player he requires for the audio-visual part of his lesson? Are there suitable records, films or film-strips at his disposal?

2.3 LAYOUT

How efficiently are (1) the equipment and (2) furniture arranged from the point of view of the teacher and from the point of view of the learner?

2.3.1 Layout of Equipment

Is all the teaching equipment which will be required properly laid out before the lesson begins? Are the properties which are going to be used in the lesson close at hand and arranged in advance in the order in which they will be needed? Is all equipment ready to operate—projector and record-player loaded and checked, screen in the proper position? Or will class-time be wasted in threading and focusing the projector, or in rewinding upside-down tapes and inside-out film-strips?

2.3.2 Seating Arrangement

Are the seats arranged so that everyone can see the teacher, the blackboard and the screen? If ostensive techniques are used, can all the learners see what is on the demonstration table?

If the learners are to be asked what they are doing, can each learner see all the other learners? If some learners are to move about, does the seating arrangement permit each to leave his seat and return without disturbing the others?

Some forms of seating arrangement that fill these requirements are the U-shape, the semi-circle, and the hollow square. In some classrooms, however, such seating arrangements may be impossible because all seats are fixed in rows, one behind the other.

3. TECHNIQUES OF PRESENTATION

How does the teacher execute his plan for the presentation of (1) the forms, and (2) the meanings of the teaching points?

3.1 EXPRESSION TECHNIQUES

Are new forms presented in sentences or as isolated words? Are the sentences presented in context or in isolation?

Does the teacher give a model for each new form presented, (1) a spoken model, and (2) a written model?

3.1.1 Spoken Models

The main formal requirement of a spoken model is that it should be clear and audible. Standards of acoustic clarity and audibility sufficient for the native language, however, are not high enough for the foreign language, especially for the beginning level. It is believed that the learner must be able to hear the foreign language at least three to five times more distinctly than he hears the mother tongue in order to understand it.[888:72] For the learner may have to listen for each significant sound.

Are the significant sounds of the language, therefore, clearly distinguishable? Are they demonstrated as significant? Are the new words and forms spoken clearly, loudly, and slowly enough, and at the same time with a natural pronunciation?

Is the learner required simply to imitate the model (teacher or recording) or is he also taught through diagrams, minimal oppositions, phonetic bracketing or approximations to his native language? Are any phonetic laboratory techniques used to teach pronunciation—speech-stretching, spectrography, palatography? When there are facilities for filtering sound-frequencies, some frequencies which overlap with those of the mother-tongue may be filtered out, thus permitting the learner to hear sound distinctions which he would not otherwise perceive. Similar results may be had by reconstructing sounds from frequency ranges which do not overlap with those of the mother tongue. If these modifications and reconstructions are made from the learner's own voice, and simultaneously fed back into his earphones, he has the impression of hearing his faulty pronunciation as if it were correct.

Is a check made on the learner's auditory perception to make sure he is hearing correctly the sounds which he is expected to make?

3.1.2 **Written Models**

How is the written form of the teaching point first presented to the learner —on flash-cards, film-strips, word-strips, or on the blackboard? Are the letters large and legible enough?

Are learners presented with isolated words or complete sentences? Are sentences given in contexts?

3.2 CONTENT TECHNIQUES

How efficiently does the teacher use his plan to present the meaning of the new teaching points? Are the techniques used suited to the level of the class? Do they hold the interest of the learners? Is vividness of presentation and emotional appeal kept for the important points?

In how many different ways is the same meaning presented? Does the importance of the item justify all of them? How is each procedure used? How much is (1) differential, (2) ostensive, (3) pictorial, and (4) contextual?

3.2.1 **Differential**

Does the teacher make use of the learner's own language? How much of it does he use? For what purpose? Does he use it to give rules, or to ask for them? Does he translate from one language into the other?

3.2.2 **Ostensive**

How effectively is the meaning conveyed through (i) objects, (ii) actions, and (iii) situations?

(i) *Objects*

The meaning of the teaching points may depend on objects that can be seen, felt and manipulated. If the object is too big or inappropriate to bring into the classroom, is there a model of it? Whether object or model is used, is it clearly visible? Is it isolated from all the others when used for demonstration? Is it held in such a way that every learner sees it and understands that the teacher is referring to it? Do the learners handle the objects?

(ii) *Actions*

If meaning is taught through actions, the clarity of the meaning will depend on the skilful use of appropriate gestures, especially at the very beginning when further clarification by means of language already taught is not possible. Because each gesture in the demonstration may have meaning, each gesture will count. Each meaningful gesture will have to be clear and distinct, stylized, stereotyped, and conventionalized. Superfluous and meaningless gestures will have to be avoided.

Are actions carried out, therefore, in such a way that they convey only the meaning they are supposed to convey? Are gestures clear-cut, distinct and significant? Are the significant gestures made with deliberateness or with nonchalance? Do they give the impression that the teacher is performing something significant and is making an effort to get the meaning across to the learners? Is the attention of the learners during the demonstration on the gestures of the teacher, or on their books? Are the books open or closed?

How are the gestures timed? Timing of gestures is one of the most important aspects of ostensive techniques, especially at the beginning level. An understanding of the entire tense system may depend on it. If the teacher uses sentences from the beginning, each sentence will have at least one verb, corresponding to the action or state of the situation. The verb will appear in one of its recognized tenses, and the meaning of the tense will be the time relation between the words and the action. If, for example, the tense is the present continuous, the action of the teacher or learner will have to be controlled so that it takes place while the sentence is being spoken, that is, between the beginning of the sentence and the end of the sentence. If the timing is wrong, the present continuous verb may be given the meaning of past or future action. If the verb is future, the action cannot begin until the sentence is completed. If the verb is past, the sentence must begin only after the action is completed.

Another sort of timing is teaching rhythm. Each action-sentence unit may have a rhythm of its own; so might each sequence of these units. In order to achieve this, the sentences cannot be interpunctuated with awkward pauses in which the teacher thinks out what he is going to do next—and in which the learner's mind wanders off to thinking in his native language. In order to be able to go smoothly from one situation to the next it is necessary for the teacher to be well prepared and well practised in teaching techniques.

A third sort of timing is the gearing of the rate of presentation to the class's average rate of mental intake, its capacity for analogic creation (usually higher among children) and its capacity for abstraction (usually higher among adults). When the number of errors to be corrected is very high, either the rate of presentation is too fast or the plan has been badly graded.

(iii) *Situations*

Does the teacher make use of situations to convey meaning? In what way? Many fundamental structural meanings can be presented by means of real or realistic situations. These may be either classroom situations, isolated for the purpose, or selected everyday situations re-enacted in the classroom with the appropriate properties. Classroom situations like giving and getting books and pencils, going to the board or to the door, opening and closing the window, may be acted out and used to demonstrate structures.

Everyday situations such as shopping and posting letters may also be acted out in class with the suitable properties. Are the situations used the sort which particularly interest the type of learner being taught? Have they some connection with his environment? Is the number of elements in both the situation and the linguistic structure the same? Are there situations which require linguistic responses beyond the language level taught?

3.2.3 **Pictorial**

If pictures are used to get meaning across, what sort are they—picture-cards, wall-pictures, flannel-board cuttings, films, film-strips, blackboard drawings? Are they made by the teacher or supplied by the course? Are they clear and unambiguous? Do they convey only the meaning they are intended to convey? (See Ch. 8 : 2.3.)

3.2.4 **Contextual**

If the teacher uses words to teach the meaning of the new items, does he use only those which the learner already knows? Through what sort of verbal context does he teach—definition, enumeration, metaphor, substitution, opposition, multiple context? (See Ch. 8 : 2.4.)

4. TECHNIQUES OF REPETITION

How does the teacher execute that part of the plan devoted to making the language a habit? How efficiently does he drill the skills of (1) speech, (2) reading, and (3) writing?

4.1 SPEECH

We can examine the efficiency of speech-drill techniques from the points of view of (1) amount of learner's speaking time, (2) accuracy of his speech,

(3) types of response, (4) contexts of speech, (5) variety of speech drills. (6) techniques of questioning, and (7) techniques of correcting.

4.1.1 **Amount**

The more practice the learner gets in speaking, the sooner will he become fluent in the language.

For what proportion of the class time do the learners do the talking? Some methods recommend at least 30 per cent in the first year and 40 per cent in the second. Do all the learners participate, or do only some of them?

4.1.2 **Accuracy**

The number of sentences spoken by the learner is not the only indication of the efficiency of speech drills. If these sentences always contain the same mistakes, these mistakes become language habits.

How accurate are the first attempts of the learner? What percentage of errors is made in the oral exercises?

How much incorrect speech does the learner hear? To cut down on the amount of incorrect speech some teachers always call on one of the best learners first and on the poorest ones last. Does the teacher display incorrect forms, or does he try to keep them out of sight and out of mind?

What is the standard of accuracy and fluency required from the learners before they proceed?

4.1.3 **Types of Responses**

What is the proportion of chorus to individual responses? Does the teacher repeat with the class in chorus work, or does he keep his attention on the performance of the learners?

What is the length of unit used in chorus repetition? Is it short enough? Some methods recommend a maximum of eight syllables. What is the length of the pause between the model and the imitation? The greater the pause, the less the accuracy. Is a regular tempo maintained in the chorus drills? What proportion of the responses are rote, incremental, variational and operational? (See Ch. 9 : 0.2.)

4.1.4 **Contexts of Speech**

In what sort of contexts are the speech drills performed—actions, pictures, texts? What proportion of each? Do the learners do actions while speaking about them? Do they talk about the actions of other learners? Do the learners repeat the actions of the teacher? Is their timing controlled?

4.1.5 **Variety of Speech Drills**

How many types of drills are used to practise the teaching point? What are they? (See Ch. 8 and Appendix A.)

What use is made of speech games? Are they brought in at an appropriate moment in the lesson—when they are needed to maintain interest in additional repetition? Are the games used to drill the teaching point or merely to amuse the learners? Is it first made clear to the learner what is expected of him in the game or drill? (See Appendix B.)

4.1.6 **Techniques of Questioning**

How efficient is the questioning? Are the questions clear and to the point? Are the questions so worded as to avoid unprofitable yes-or-no answers? Are the efforts of the learner given to answering the question or to finding out what it means? Are the learners asked to speak on things for which they have no words?

Does the teacher require the use of foreign manners in the responses? Does he create a foreign atmosphere in the class by such devices as giving foreign names to the learners?

4.1.7 **Techniques of Correcting**

This is one of the most important of classroom techniques. The teacher may first try to diagnose the cause of the error. The error may be due to a transfer from the native language, an analogy with something correctly learned in the foreign language, a wild guess, vagueness in remembering the right form, or general lack of accuracy and language skill.

The teacher may try to avoid errors by eliminating the causes. Or he may drive them out by driving in the correct form through plenty of practice of the right sort. Another precaution the teacher may take is to make sure that the learner knows whether or not his first tries are acceptable; for if they are not, and he is not made aware of it, the wrong response is very likely to be learned instead of the right one.

In the correction of errors, there are three possibilities for the learner: He may hear his error and correct it, he may hear it and not correct it, and he may neither hear it nor correct it. Does the teacher make sure he hears it and tries to correct it?

What is the delay between the response and its correction? The longer the delay, the harder it is to make the correction. The shorter the time lapse between the learner's attempt and his realization of his degree of success, the better. But the delay must not be so short that it interrupts the learner in mid-sentence. Nor must the correction of an individual interrupt the flow of the lesson or distract the others.

Does the teacher concentrate on correcting one learner to the point of making the others lose interest? Does he concentrate on individuals or on the group? Does he correct one thing at a time? Does he ask other learners to do the correcting?

If there are too many corrections to be made, what is the cause? Is it the level of the course, or the quality of the teaching?

4.2 READING

How much reading is done in class? Is it oral or silent? Does the teacher use flash-cards? For what purpose?

Are reading-comprehension drills used? Which sorts? (See Ch. 8 : 3.1.) Are there questions on the reading? Is reading used as a basis for speaking? Is any use made of comprehension games? (See Appendix B.)

What techniques are used for teaching rapid silent reading? Rapid silent reading needs special training. One technique is to ask the learner to read the first paragraph as fast as he can in order to get the general idea, and later to re-read it for the details. He then writes down what he remembers. He repeats this procedure for each paragraph, and ends by making a summary of the whole text.

How much extensive reading is done? Do the learners read different books or the same one? Is there a committee of those who have read the same book? Has the class an adequate supply of graded supplementary readers?

Are book reports required? What sort? One type of book report used in modern-language teaching requires comments on the author, the type of book, the theme, setting, a synopsis of the plot, something about the author's purposes and intentions, a few highlights, something about the characters, some comparisons with other books, and the learner's personal reactions.

4.3 WRITING

Which writing drills are used (see Ch. 8 : 4 and Appendix A)? How much time is devoted to re-writing, imitation and re-telling a story? Is writing based on speech, on reading matter, on neither, or on both? How is composition taught? Is it first done orally? Is any use made of pictures?

How is the written work corrected? Is the learner given the correct form, or does he have to find it himself and re-write the entire sentence correctly?

After we have examined all the techniques used in the lesson and the efficiency with which they were used, we can calculate the amount of time lost. What proportion of time was wasted? On what was it spent, on comments not connected with language teaching, on problems of discipline, on questions of learners wanting to know *about* the language, its grammar or evolution?

Finally, does the teacher take time at the end of the lesson to evaluate it in the light of the plan, and vice versa? Does he make notes for improving the plan and the lesson?

The answers to all these questions, added to our study of lesson plans and teaching points, will permit us to analyse a series of lessons in the teaching of language courses. The effective planning and teaching of some courses, however, may require more time and energy than the teacher is able to offer. And the results of his efforts may be diluted by the large number of his learners and the small number of hours they spend in the language class.

A remedy for these difficulties has been to impose upon language teaching a certain degree of automation. In some countries, language teaching with the aid of machines has become widespread. Our next problem, therefore, is to determine how such automated language teaching may be analysed and evaluated.

CHAPTER 15

Automated Language Teaching

OUTLINE

0. INTRODUCTION

1. ACCOMMODATION AND EQUIPMENT
   1.1 Accommodation
       1.1.1 Quarters
       1.1.2 Arrangement
   1.2 Equipment
       1.2.1 Types
       1.2.2 Suitability

2. FUNCTIONING
   2.1 Range of Uses
       2.1.1 Input
       2.1.2 Output
   2.2 Recording
   2.3 Control
       2.3.1 Central Control
       2.3.2 Individual Control
       2.3.3 Optional Control

3. OPERATION
   3.1 Staff
   3.2 Scheduling
   3.3 Laboratory Routine
       3.3.1 Orientation
       3.3.2 Attendance
       3.3.3 Monitoring
   3.4 Administration

4. TEACHING PROCEDURES

- 4.1 Teaching Media
    - 4.1.1 Auditory Media
    - 4.1.2 Visual Media
- 4.2 Teaching Plans
- 4.3 Teaching Units
    - 4.3.1 Design
    - 4.3.2 Repetition
    - 4.3.3 Length and Speed

5. RELATION TO TEXT AND TEACHER

0. INTRODUCTION

Under the heading of automation we analyse the use of machines in the teaching of languages. Since the invention of the gramophone, the film-projector and the tape recorder, machines have been doing many of the operations involved in language teaching. Any analysis of language teaching must take this into account; it must determine the extent to which such machines are used, what they are used for, and how much of the teaching is done through them.

The use of machines in language teaching may vary from the playing of gramophone records in class to the teaching of all language skills in a language laboratory. It includes language teaching through radio and television, and the use of audio-visual aids in class.

When analysing *what* is taught through machines, however, it is necessary to make the same sort of analysis of the selection, gradation, presentation and repetition of the material as we have for methods and teaching techniques (Chs. 5–14). But there are certain characteristics peculiar to the use of machines that must be analysed separately.

First, what language learning facilities can machines supply? Machines used in language teaching can supply the following: 1. Listening—to develop the ability to understand the language spoken at normal speed. 2. Imitation—to develop the sounds, stress, rhythm and intonation of a native pronunciation. 3. Repetition—to develop the ability to speak the language at a normal rate of speed, to master the complex of skills involved in speaking a language. 4. Observation of Context—learning language as a co-ordinated system of behaviour. 5. Semantic Drill—to give practice in putting words in the right contexts, thus leading to independent use of the language. 6. Pronunciation Drill—to give practice in forming the right sounds and sound patterns. 7. Practice in reading and writing. 8. Testing—to test auditory comprehension, pronunciation, speech, reading and writing. In short all language skills and essential language-teaching procedures—presentation, repetition, testing, re-teaching and contextual expansion—may be subject to automation.[1707]

Secondly, what is the difference between teaching by machines and the teaching of a teacher? 1. The learner has no control over the teacher, but he can have control over the machine. 2. The learner cannot ask questions of the machine, but he can question the teacher. 3. The machine cannot interfere with the gradation and content of the course. 4. The machine takes care of the great amount of oral repetitive drill necessary for the mastery of a language. This saves valuable class time and relieves the teacher of much of the routine of repetition. 5. Some learners need more repetition than others. The machine gives the slow learner as much repetition as he requires without retarding the others. In fact, each learner may advance at his own rate. Slow learners may need to listen much more often than gifted learners before being able to repeat. The machine allows the slow learner to take the time needed. 6. The machine permits up to 100 per cent individual participation by giving each learner, as it were, his own room with his private electronic tutor. 7. With machines it is possible for a teacher at a control panel to correct and coach individually any learner without wasting the time of twenty or thirty others. 8. The machine permits the class to be divided and subdivided into any number of levels, without increasing the number of teachers. It thus multiplies the efficacy of each teacher. 9. The machine permits learners to start the language course at different times. A learner may thus start the course in the middle of term and begin at the beginning, instead of trying to follow, as he would in a classroom, a course which is already beyond him. 10. It is possible for the machine to standardize instruction at the best level of teaching proficiency. All learners go through the same course, hear the same voices and do the same drills. 11. The machine may encourage self-evaluation. It does this by making the learner continually compare his performance with that of a standard model. He hears himself objectively and can always have some idea of how far he has to go to achieve native-like ability in the spoken language. 12. Machines can be so connected as to permit a class to be grouped in pairs for simultaneous conversational drill. 13. With the machine the learner may devote as much time as he wishes to practice. Batteries of recording machines may operate very much like a library; in such cases, an ambitious learner may work as long as he likes. 14. With the use of machines a record of each learner's progress in speaking the language can be automatically preserved. Tests of pronunciation, auditory comprehension and speech can be made and preserved for comparison at a later date. 15. The machine cannot, however, adapt its teaching techniques to the moods and psychological peculiarities of the individual.

The degree of automation in language teaching depends on the extent to which this potential of the machine is actually put to use. But it is not the machine that determines the quality of the automation; it is what we put into it. The most highly automated programme of language teaching is no better than the material it contains. It is the material put into the machine that is analysed as method and teaching technique. Since all the machines usable in language teaching can be brought together and operated at full potential in the language laboratory, it is within this flexible concept that the automation of language teaching is best analysed. The concept of the language teaching laboratory varies from that of a classroom with machines, to that of machines without a classroom. The most general conception is simply that of a place where machines are used for language learning.

Language laboratories differ (1) in what they contain (accommodation and equipment), (2) in the way they work (functioning), (3) in the way they are run (operation), (4) in what they do with the language-teaching material (teaching procedures), and (5) in their relation with what goes on in class and with what is included in the text.

1. ACCOMMODATION AND EQUIPMENT

The first thing that strikes the eye when visiting a language laboratory is its physical aspect—(1) its accommodation, and (2) its equipment.

1.1 ACCOMMODATION

Laboratories vary (1) in the type of quarters used, and (2) in the types of arrangement in them.

1.1.1 **Quarters**

What sort of rooms are used for the language laboratory? How many are there and what is their function? Does the laboratory have one or more practice rooms for the learners, a control room for the instructors, a studio for recording teaching material, a projection cabin for films, storage space for tapes, equipment and spare parts?

Is the laboratory situated in a quiet enough place? Are the rooms acoustically conditioned against background noise? For how many users is the laboratory designed?

Some classrooms may be so equipped that they can be temporarily converted into language laboratories. Although most large and well-equipped laboratories are necessarily fixed installations, there is such a thing as a mobile language laboratory. With the use of portable loudspeakers, gramophones, recorders and projectors, almost any classroom can be converted into a temporary drill-room. The necessary electronic and mechanical equipment can also be built into specially designed tables which can be wheeled into any room when required. Or a small, battery-operated tape recorder on the teacher's desk can transmit lessons individually to students at their seats if their headphones include a small radio which receives in a closed circuit created by laying a wire around the room. This eliminates wiring between the teacher's tape recorder and the headsets of the learners, thus permitting them to move freely about the room.

1.1.2 **Arrangement**

Are the practice rooms furnished with seats for group work, isolation booths for individual practice, or both? If the laboratory is furnished with booths, what sort are they? Are they sound-proof enough to prevent noise from neighbouring booths from disturbing the learner? What sort of design have they and what sort of construction?

(i) *Design*

The design and dimensions of the practice booth may vary according to the amount of sound-proofing required, the type of room, and the height of the ceiling.

We can imagine the practice booth as a large, open-ended box whose interior is lined with sound-absorbing material. Some booths, however, are nothing more than partitions between listening positions.

If the ceiling of the room is low, and there are projecting plaster beams, it may be necessary to include a top to the booth. If, however, the ceiling is high, even and covered with acoustic tile, no top may be necessary.

The dimensions of the booth may vary slightly:

Dimensions	Inches	Centimetres
Height	50 – 72	125 – 180
Width	24 – 36	60 – 90
Depth	24 – 36	60 – 90
Height of counter from floor	26 – 32	65 – 80
Depth of counter	12 – 20	30 – 50

The shorter the counter, the further the learner can get into the booth and the less his voice is likely to disturb others. The counter, however, must be sufficiently large to hold the recording machine, even though it may be placed at an angle ($30°– 90°$). It may also support a screen for work with individual 8 mm. motion-picture projectors, sound-synchronized film-strips and /or closed-circuit television.

(ii) *Construction*

Booths can be made of some combination of material which stops the sound and of material which absorbs it. Most booths are made of some hard material like wood or metal on the outside, and lined with some softer, sound-absorbing material like acoustic tile, insulboard, rock wool, or felt. There may be two or more layers of the sound-absorbing material and an air-space between them and the hard outer wall. It is important that joints and seams should be tightly closed.

The fronts of some booths are made of glass. Although this reflects the sound and may sacrifice some of the sound-proofing, it has certain advantages for groups which must see the instructor, or for audio-visual laboratories where the projection screen must be viewed from the booth. Some laboratories achieve the same results by putting a sliding panel in the front of the booth; by lining the panel with sound-absorbing material, much of the sound-proofing is retained.

How many booths are there? This will depend on the following factors: the length of the laboratory period, the number of learners, the frequency of laboratory periods per learner, and the number of hours a day the laboratory is open (see 3.2).

1.2 EQUIPMENT

What types of machines are there in the language laboratory and how suitable are they?

1.2.1 **Types**

A language laboratory may contain different types of (i) sound recorders, (ii) loudspeakers, (iii) earphones, (iv) microphones, (v) projectors, (vi) radio receivers, (vii) visual teaching machines, (viii) acoustic equipment, and (ix) maintenance equipment.

(i) *Sound Recorders*

(a) Magnetic Tape Recorders:
The vast majority of language laboratories make use of tape recorders in preference to wire or magnetic disc. There are some good reasons for this. Tape can give high fidelity performance at a moderate price. Surface noise can be eliminated. Breakages of tape are easy to repair and may completely disappear with the use of unbreakable tape. Tape recorders are in more common use; they can be purchased and repaired in many shops dealing in gramophones, radio and television sets. Tape recorders are available in single full-track, single half-track, and multi-track types.

Single Full-track:
These were the first type of tape recorders made. They may be quiet adequate for listening and non-simultaneous recording. But there are

certain functions which they cannot perform. Yet they are often preferred for the making and playing of master tapes, because of their greater acoustic possibilities.

Single Half-track:

Although this type of recorder performs the same laboratory functions as the full-track recorder, it doubles the playing time of the tape by recording on only half of the tape-width at a time. It records in both directions using the upper half of the tape in one direction and the lower half in the other But it cannot use both halves simultaneously as two separate tracks.

Double-track:

The big advantage of this type of recorder is that two tracks can be used simultaneously, one for the model (the master track), and the other as a sort of "audio practice pad". This recorder can be adjusted so as not to erase the master track, but only the learner's previous version of it as he tries again and again to approximate to the model. This machine enables him: 1. Simply to listen to the master track. 2. To listen to the master track and, after each pause, to record his sentence-by-sentence imitation of it. 3. To listen at the same time to the master track and to his imitation of it. 4. To erase his own version and to re-record his imitation of the master track as often as desired, without affecting the recording on the master track. 5. To listen only to his own voice. Recorders that can perform these functions are a necessary part of the equipment of some types of practice laboratory with individual recording control. The two tracks may take up only half of the tape-width in one direction and use the other half in the opposite direction, giving double the playing time of a single half-track recorder.

Multiple-track:

Using an extra-wide tape, some recorders can accommodate as many as a few dozen tracks. Each track can be used for a different purpose, level or lesson. One track may be used for student recording, another for timing and indexing, and the remainder may function as master-tracks.

Immediate Playback:

This is achieved by a special recorder or pair of coupled recorders which permits a learner to hear the model sentence and his imitation immediately after having recorded it. It is especially useful in the learning of pronunciation.

(b) Magnetic Wire Recorders:

The main advantage of wire recorders seems to be that wire breaks less easily than tape. But this is counterweighed by the lower fidelity and by the fact that wire cannot be cut, spliced and edited as can magnetic tape.

(c) Magnetic Disc Recorders:

Although the first magnetic disc recorder appeared as a dictaphone, there are some which are especially designed for language students. One model consists of two turntables which can operate simultaneously, one to listen to the model and the other to record the learner's imitation of it. The model can be pre-recorded on a master disc, or it can be recorded on to it while the learner is listening to the taped version sent to his model disc through his earphones from a central control panel. One advantage of the disc is that the learner can immediately turn to the beginning of the record simply by lifting up the pick-up arm. The disc can record much less than tape, does not approach its acoustic quality, and has more problems of surface noise.

(d) Gramophones:

The magnetic recorder has not made the gramophone obsolete in language teaching. It is still an important part of a well-equipped laboratory; indeed, if commercial language discs are to be used, it is indispensable. Gramophones have been highly developed and are easily obtainable. Some laboratories require a solid "professional" turntable and a good pre-amplifier that can be hooked up to a loudspeaker placed anywhere in the room, or in another room.

(ii) *Loudspeakers*

A loudspeaker is an essential piece of equipment for the drill room. It is, however, not necessary in practice laboratories where all sound comes to the learner through his earphones.

In the drill room, the speaker may be mounted high up on the wall facing the audience at an angle aiming at the centre of the group. In examining the loudspeaker, we should check whether its quality is comparable with that of the machine which feeds it. Is it powerful enough to fill the room comfortably at mid-volume? Or does it have to be operated at full-volume, producing a hum or distorting the sound?

(iii) *Earphones*

Earphones are an important part of the equipment of a practice booth. In examining them it is necessary to check whether they match the fidelity of the machine to which they are connected. To connect an expensive tape recorder with a cheap set of earphones is to reduce the performance of the recorder to that of a cheap machine. On the other hand, to use an expensive set of earphones with a cheap gramophone is also wasteful. Some earphones transmit speech from an audio-active microphone back into the speaker's ears (see below).

(iv) *Microphones*

Microphones may vary greatly in quality and type. Even though the microphone selected is of a quality comparable with that of the recorder to which it is connected, there are still several other factors to examine.

Since the function of the microphone in the language laboratory is to record, not music, but the *individual* voice, a wide-angle microphone is not necessary; in fact, it may be quite detrimental since, being sensitive to noises coming from many angles, it may permit voices from neighbouring booths to be recorded. This does not mean that the microphone selected cannot be a sensitive one. It simply means that it ought at best to be a model specially designed to eliminate background noise.

Some types are "audio-active microphones" which channel the learner's voice back into his earphones, if necessary at an increased volume.

(v) *Projectors*

Is the laboratory equipped with projectors—film-strip projectors and/or motion-picture projectors?

Among the points to note in examining film-strip projectors are ease of manipulation and rapidity of adjustment. If the projector is an air-cooled model, is it silent enough, or does the noise of the cooling mechanism reduce the audibility of recorded speech? Can the projector be synchronized with the play-back mechanism of a tape recorder or gramophone? This is especially important if booths are equipped with both tape-recorders and film-strip projectors where frequency signals pre-recorded on one of the tracks are responsible for switching the picture-frame.

Is there an easily operated 16 mm. sound-film projector whose mechanism does not make too much noise? If it is used in a laboratory already equipped with a loudspeaker, it may not be necessary to have the loudspeaker which goes with the projector. At all events, it is important that the loudspeaker used should be one which faithfully transmits the sound track of the film without vibration or distortion.

Provided the sound and picture quality are acceptable, each booth may be equipped with an 8 mm. cartridge-loaded sound projector.

(vi) *Radio Receivers*

Some laboratories make use of short-wave radio receivers in order to get foreign broadcasts, which they record on tape, study, and edit for use as listening comprehension and other drills.

(vii) *Visual Teaching Machines*

These are used for teaching reading and writing. They may vary from simple models which operate on rolls of paper moved by a hand lever, to complex mechanisms storing thousands of frames of microfilm. They may also vary in design. In one type, the information or question appears on a window at the left, and the space to be completed appears simultaneously at the right; by pulling a lever the student brings the correct response into view. This is made possible by printing questions, answer-blanks and responses in an appropriate arrangement on to a continuous roll of paper which is inserted into the machine and unrolled very much like the film in a camera.

(viii) *Acoustic Equipment*

Some laboratories may be equipped with special acoustic apparatus, such as a machine for slowing down speech without distorting it (the speech-stretcher), a machine which may make it possible to adjust to the sounds of foreign speech (the electronic ear), a machine which gives an acoustic picture of each sound according to its length, pitch, force and quality (the acoustic spectrograph), and other equipment normally found in laboratories of experimental phonetics.

(ix) *Maintenance Equipment*

Has the laboratory the right sort of equipment for its own maintenance and proper functioning? One requirement may be an electro-magnetic bulk eraser which permits whole reels of magnetic tape to be demagnetized in a few seconds without unwinding. There may also be a need for frequency response sets and other equipment for testing recording machines. Most laboratories need some sort of work-bench with the necessary tools for repairing the machines.

1.2.2 Suitability

Is the equipment suitable for the purpose for which it is being used? Is it of good enough quality, simple to operate, simple to service? Does it produce a minimum of heat and noise? Has the teaching determined the type of equipment, or has the equipment determined the type of teaching?

(i) *Fidelity*

Any equipment for laboratory use must be good enough in quality to stand up under constant and often rough use. Some types of equipment, although cheap and quite suitable for the home, do not stand up to everyday use in the laboratory.

Cheap equipment has been found to be far too costly in repairs and in time wasted to justify the initial saving. Breakdowns can waste a great amount of the teacher's and learner's time; and if they occur frequently, they may discourage both teacher and learner from using the laboratory.

Sound equipment, in order to be an effective medium for teaching the phonetic features of a language, must meet certain acoustic standards. There is a vast literature on the relation between acoustic fidelity and intelligibility (see bibliographies in Miller[367] and Cherry[363]). The fidelity of recording equipment is generally valued by the range of sound waves it can reproduce, measured in the number of sound vibrations or cycles per second (cps). Most intelligibility is done between 1,000 and 2,500 cps. Ordinary speech gives us so many cues for intelligibility that we normally need to hear only a fraction of them in order to understand what is said. It has been shown that we can block out a random 50 per cent of the syllables of the spoken language, distort others, and still have intelligible speech. That is why speech recorded on equipment of low fidelity can be perfectly understood.

These standards, however, cannot be applied to the evaluation of recording equipment used in foreign language instruction because, in this case, intelligibility does not rest on a previous familiarity with the language and the cues for its intelligibility; it is rather through the equipment that these cues are to be learned and to become familiar. But in order to be learned they must first be heard. The fact that a recording is perfectly comprehensible to a native speaker does not mean that it is clear enough to serve as a model for someone learning the language; for native speakers are so used to their language that they can understand it even under poor acoustic conditions. For example, if we were to hear /s/ or /f/ for the first sound of the word *thin* in the sentence, *It's a thin book*, we would still understand the sentence. But that does not mean that such a sound distortion is a good model for the learner to use in order to find out whether or not he is pronouncing the word *thin* correctly. Some machines cannot distinguish these sounds clearly. A range of 70–10,000 cps, which some have recommended for language laboratory recorders, is not exaggerated.[1704:149]

384

(ii) *Simplicity*

Another important consideration is simplicity of operation of the machines to be used by the learners. Can all the attention of the learner be given to the language, or must he devote part of it to the operation of the machine? In some machines with push-button controls, the push-buttons can be numbered so that the learner goes through the various operations very much as he would open the lock of a safe. What percentage of time is spent in operating the equipment? It has been estimated that re-winding alone takes 5 per cent of the laboratory period. That is why some laboratories record the material on loops that work in both directions. In other laboratories all operations are performed by remote control on banks of tape-recorders placed on racks in another room. Instead of a tape-recorder in each booth there is a telephone dial which permits the learner to signal the number of any exercise, lesson or programme he may require.

(iii) *Servicing*

It is of paramount importance that the laboratory be kept in good working condition at all times. It should be possible to have repairs done rapidly enough to avoid interruption in laboratory work. Some laboratories keep one booth in twenty as a spare to be used in case of a breakdown.

2. FUNCTIONING

How does the language laboratory work? (1) What is its range of uses? (2) How is the recording done? (3) How is its use controlled?

2.1 RANGE OF USES

Does the laboratory make use of a drill-room? Does it use individual practice booths? Some laboratories are simply listening rooms which permit the learner to hear the language, sometimes with the aid of pictures. Others permit the recording of speech, and some give training in reading and writing. The range of uses depends on the difference between drill-room and practice-booth, between the simple auditory medium and the audio-visual medium. Language laboratories differ therefore in types (1) of input, and (2) of output.

2.1.1 **Input**

Some laboratories are exclusively "audio labs" which teach the language exclusively through the sense of hearing; others are audio-visual laboratories which combine the activities of listening and looking. Audio labs may be equipped with such apparatus as loudspeakers, tape recorders, gramophones, language tapes and discs; audio-visual labs in addition to these also have projectors, films and film-strips. An audio-visual drill-room might be used for language-teaching films, film-strips, slides and loops, or for oral work based on sound tracks of films, or speech drill and oral composition based on films and film-strips, or drill in rapid reading. Its equipment might include a wide-range loudspeaker, a large projection screen, a 16 mm. motion-picture sound projector and/or a film-strip and slide projector, a gramophone and/or a tape player.

2.1.2 **Output**

From the point of view of output, language laboratories may be audio-passive or audio-active. Audio-passive laboratories are equipped only to permit the learners to listen. They may be listening rooms or audio-passive laboratories furnished with listening booths. The listening room may be a classroom or club room equipped either with a loudspeaker or individual earphones. It may be a corner of the library, with a table provided with listening outlets and earphones. Learners sign for language discs or tapes of dialogues, plays, songs and literature very much as they would for library books. Or the audio-passive laboratory may be several rows of semi-soundproof listening booths each equipped with a set of earphones connected to one or more centrally controlled playback machines.

The audio-active laboratory, in addition to the above facilities, is also equipped for imitative drill and often for self-evaluation. An audio-active laboratory may be simply a room with a loudspeaker fed by language discs or tapes spaced for repetition; or it may comprise a number of individual semi-soundproof practice booths, each equipped with a microphone, earphones, a tape or disc recorder, and/or an audio-active microphone.

2.2 RECORDING

Does the learner record his responses and correct them? Since the learner cannot correct mistakes until he notices them, a recording of his responses may be considered a necessity. Some laboratories, however, are intentionally designed to avoid recording the learner's responses on the grounds that the accurate learner who makes few errors wastes his time, while the faulty learner simply reinforces his mistakes by hearing them. Instead of recorders such laboratories may be equipped with microphones which feed back the learner's responses into his earphones as fast as he utters them.

The main problem here is to decide whether a person can hear himself critically at the same rate as he speaks. Normal self-hearing reaches the ear at intervals of one-thousandth of a second from the time of utterance. Ordinary earphones can modify this rate, but not to a very great extent; we still appear to hear our utterances almost simultaneously. Is it possible then to think almost simultaneously of what we say, how we say it, how we are saying it, and how we ought to have said it?

In analysing the arguments in this controversy, a distinction must be made between what a person says and how he says it. It may be impossible to hear ourselves and analyse our speech without having recorded it; but that does not mean that we are unable to analyse our errors in grammar and vocabulary without recording them. Moreover, there are individual differences in the self-correction of pronunciation. Some learners hear and imitate everything; others make no progress until they can distinguish each mistake, analyse it and be taught how to correct it.

2.3 CONTROL

The control of laboratory apparatus and its functioning may be (1) centralized, (2) individualized, and (3) optional.

2.3.1 Central Control

Drill-rooms are of course, by their very nature, controlled from a single source—the record player or tape recorder which feeds the loudspeaker. In the practice laboratory, however, central control has to be built in by wiring each booth to a central tape recorder or playback which feeds the sound directly into the earphones of each learner or into his recording machine.

Individual booths are equipped with microphone, earphones and recorder. The central control panel must have one or more tape or disc players, wiring, jacks and switches linking it to each booth. Two-way intercommunication between booths and control panel and dual-track recording are optional. The control panel is located either in a separate booth, in a separate room, or on a counter behind a partition.

This set-up is advantageous if groups of the same level are using the laboratory at the same time, and if enough booths can be provided for each member of the group.

Drill material is played at the central control panel and heard on the earphones located in each booth. This material may at the same time be recorded on the machines located in the booths. If these are double-track or double-turntable recorders, the model transmitted from the control panel can be recorded on one track (or disc), leaving the other free for the learner to use when and as often as necessary. So that once the lesson, spaced for repetition, is recorded on the learner's machine, the rest of the period can be devoted to mastering the lesson.

Individual recorders with only one full or half track have the disadvantage, in this type of laboratory, of erasing the model once the learner re-records his imitation of it. He could, of course, preserve the model by continually and dexterously switching from *play* to *record* within the spaces provided for repetition. But this is rarely expedient since, unless skilfully done, it results in the erasing of parts of the model. Moreover, it forces the learner to divide his attention between operating the machine and learning the language.

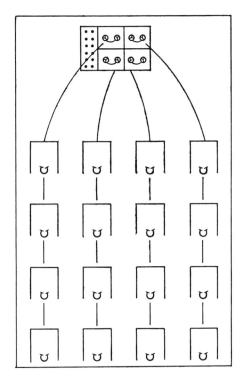

Language Laboratory with Central Control

2.3.2 Individual Control

The central control panel and booth-to-panel wiring is not necessary for individual control; but there must be in each booth at least some sort of playback machine to feed the sound into the learner's earphones. In addition, there may also be individual recording facilities.

Each booth is equipped with the following: a double-track (or double-turntable) recorder, a set of earphones connected to recorder, a narrow-angle microphone. Instead of a recorder there may be simply a dial for remote control work, or special equipment for immediate playback.

Booths are placed in the order which is acoustically the most suitable. This may vary according to the size and shape of the room, the distribution of electrical outlets, etc.

Individually controlled booths may be used for sentence-by-sentence, listen-and-repeat drills after the model on the master track and for substitution drill and pattern practice. Learners may use this sort of laboratory very much like an audio-library. They give their cards or sign for the tape they need and use it in the booth as long as required. In remote control laboratories they simply dial for what they want.

This type of set-up is preferable for situations where there are a number of different levels and relatively few booths.

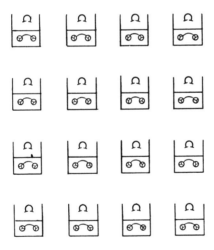

Language Laboratory with Individual Control

2.3.3 Optional Control

The laboratory with optional control combines the advantages of both types; but it may be technically more complex than either. It is essentially a centrally controlled laboratory with play-back and recording equipment in each booth.

The difference is that each machine must have the option either of being used independently or of being tuned in to one of the channels being fed by the central control panel.

It may also be useful to be able to control centrally the recording head of the master track on the machines in the individual booths; otherwise a learner by making a slight mistake in manipulation may unwittingly erase the master track.

Such a laboratory can be used simultaneously for central and individual control. It is the most flexible type of language laboratory, since any number of booths may be grouped into any number of levels under central control, and any number may be left free for individual control. This may be a great advantage where there are different groups of different sizes and levels using the laboratory at the same time. Any of the above types of control may be combined with the audio-visual equipment. Some laboratories are divided into sections, one for central control, another for individual control.

3. OPERATION

How is the laboratory run? What is (1) its staff, (2) its timetable, (3) its routine, and (4) its system of administration?

3.1 STAFF

The size of staff needed to supervise a laboratory will, of course, depend on its size, its functions, and the amount of supervision needed.

There are three types of supervision: technical, clerical and professional. It is possible that any two, and at times all three, of these may be the responsibility of a single person. Or there may be one or more persons responsible for each type of supervision, depending, of course, on the size of the laboratory, and on the size of the budget.

It is possible to operate a laboratory with little or no supervision. But if there is no technical supervision the equipment is likely to be out of order at least part of the time. If there is no clerical supervision, the records of attendance are likely to be inaccurate and teaching materials lost or misplaced. Sometimes it is possible to combine clerical and technical supervision with other work, e.g. library or secretarial work.

The first consideration must of course be technical supervision. For if the laboratory is not in working order its very existence ceases to be justified.

The staffing may be done by a combination of teachers and student assistants. The director may be a senior teacher responsible for general supervision, scheduling, co-ordination and engaging of assistants. A number of teachers may be responsible for preparing and recording scripts on tape. A number of student assistants may take care of the operation of the equipment, the copying of tapes, and some of the paper work. There might also be a number of student teachers to help with all these activities.

3.2 SCHEDULING

The value of frequent and regular practice in the formation of a skill is sufficiently established to be taken seriously. Since language is a complex of skills which can be practised in the language laboratory, frequent and regular use of the laboratory may be advisable. Little and often may be better than a lot from time to time. It may be better to arrange for a learner to have three half-hour periods on three different days than a solid hour-and-a-half session once a week.

The frequency of laboratory periods has generally varied from about three a month to three a week. Daily laboratory periods, however, may be what is needed.

The laboratory timetable may be so organized as to leave a number of booths free for anyone wishing to devote extra time to laboratory work, for learners eager to master the language, and willing to devote as many hours as possible to practising it. The possibility of this type of arrangement may alone be sufficient justification for building a laboratory.

The details of scheduling depend on the type of language laboratory and what is being taught in it. For example, if an individually controlled language laboratory has only five booths at the disposal of groups working at five different levels, one hour a week of individual booth work could be given to 240 learners provided that: the laboratory were open eight hours a day and *either* (a) the timetable was arranged in such a way that no two persons belonging to the same level used the laboratory together, *or* (b) a sufficient number of duplicate tapes be made to allow two or more at the same level to use the laboratory at the same time. On the other hand, if the central control panel has only one playback machine (i.e. one channel), the laboratory timetable must be planned to allow for only one level at a time. Suppose, for example, that a laboratory has ten centrally controlled booths at the disposal of fifty persons belonging to five different levels of ten learners each. Such a laboratory, opening only five hours a week, could give each learner one hour a week of booth work, provided that: *either* (a) all persons belonging to the same level use the laboratory at the same time *or* (b) one channel is installed for each group.

Centrally controlled laboratories may therefore be economical in situations where persons of the same level have to use the laboratory at the same time or where the laboratory can be open for only a few hours a day.

With the optional control type of laboratory, however, it is possible to plan for different groups and individuals at the same time. For example suppose a total of 225 learners were using a 15-booth practice laboratory with optional control, and suppose that these learners belonged to five different levels. If the laboratory has two channels (play-back machines in the control panel), and some or all of the booths have the option of individual control, it would be possible to give the 225 learners one hour a week of booth work by opening the laboratory only three hours a day for five days a week. Groups 1 and 2, the two largest (with say 90 learners each) could be provided for in two groups of six, using the two centrally controlled channels; Groups 3, 4 and 5, the smallest groups (say three groups of 15) could control their booths individually. The distribution would then look something like this:

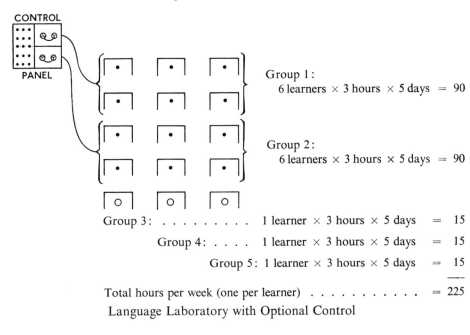

CONTROL

PANEL

Group 1:
6 learners × 3 hours × 5 days = 90

Group 2:
6 learners × 3 hours × 5 days = 90

Group 3: . . . . 1 learner × 3 hours × 5 days = 15

Group 4: . . . . 1 learner × 3 hours × 5 days = 15

Group 5: 1 learner × 3 hours × 5 days = 15

Total hours per week (one per learner) . . . . = 225

Language Laboratory with Optional Control

Of course the scheduling can adjust itself to any change in the size of the groups. Suppose, in the above example, that Group 3 were to increase in size to 30 and Groups 4 and 5 decrease to 8 and 7 learners respectively. The simplest and cheapest solution might be to make an extra copy of the material being used by Group 3 so that two learners from this group could be in the laboratory at the same time at individually controlled booths. Another solution would be to open the laboratory an extra 15 hours a week. A third solution would be to add another channel.

3.3 LABORATORY ROUTINE

This involves (1) orientation, (2) attendance, and (3) monitoring.

3.3.1 **Orientation**

How is the learner initiated into the use of the laboratory? Some language laboratories have a special orientation tape to broadcast to the learner when he first enters a laboratory booth; this tape makes him identify each part of the machine and tells him how to use it. Other laboratories use an orientation motion-picture of the laboratory in action.

3.3.2 **Attendance**

Is laboratory attendance compulsory or optional? How is attendance checked? Can each learner compose his own timetable? Is the laboratory always available for those wishing to put in extra hours?

3.3.3 **Monitoring**

Does someone check the learner's performance in the laboratory? How is it done? Does the teacher listen in from a central control panel? Does he correct or prompt the learner during the drill? Or does someone check the learner's final recording only? Are the drills recorded beforehand, or during the period?

3.4 ADMINISTRATION

What is done to keep track of the tapes, discs, films, scripts of exercises, assignments, and equipment?

What sort of forms does the laboratory keep for administrative purposes? Does the laboratory have such forms as a tape register (in loose-leaf form), a card catalogue, a tape inventory, a laboratory timetable, and attendance records?

Some laboratories have a tape register book which assigns numbers to tapes before they are recorded, keeps track of their length, of when they are needed, of who records them, of what they are about, of the number of duplicates, and of the date when they are erased.

For ease of identification, different levels may be assigned different blocks of numbers (e.g. 1–100 for beginners); and different languages may be colour-coded. For example, if the code colour for French were blue, each tape recorded in French would have a blue card, a blue leader tape, a blue mark on the reel and a blue label.

Care in keeping track of tapes may eventually save a great deal of time, since they can be easily lost if wound on to a different reel or put in the wrong box. That is why some laboratories also record a detailed identification of the tape at the beginning of the reel. The recorded identification might start with a starting signal, followed by a pause, and include the tape number, the type and number of drills included, and directions for using them. This not only identifies the tape but also serves as a starting signal for the learner.

A tape inventory is kept to show how many tapes there are in stock, how many have been bought, recorded, erased and filed.

In addition, there may be a need for a laboratory assignment sheet to permit the learner to prepare the right text and the technician to broadcast it.

Finally, how are the tape scripts catalogued? Are they classified according to the tape number, the text reference, and the subject reference? Can they be easily found when needed?

4. TEACHING PROCEDURES

Arrangement of teaching materials for laboratory use may vary in (1) teaching media, (2) teaching plans, and (3) teaching units.

4.1 TEACHING MEDIA

Through what media is the material presented—written, oral, or pictorial? Does the learner follow a written text while listening and repeating? Do the exercises depend on the reading of a text or on listening only? Do they depend on the use of pictures; if so, are the pictures in a text, on film-strips or on film? Some exercises are built around a series of numbered drawings in the learner's text. The tape asks questions on the drawings, the learner replies and then listens to the tape giving the right answers. Exercises of this pattern may be done with film-strips, synchronized with magnetic tape. Or they may depend on the use of motion picture films the sound-track of which is fed directly into the learner's earphones. The laboratory teaching media may be (1) auditory, or (2) visual.

4.1.1 Auditory Media

A language laboratory may use audio materials available commercially or it may make its own. Among commercial recordings are the "full" courses on disc or tape and the special courses on pronunciation, conversation, pattern drill, etc. Some of these may need adaptation in order to be effective for laboratory work.

(i) *Preparation of Auditory Materials*

Some laboratories may prepare their own courses; others may base the laboratory course on some standard classroom text. Great care is necessary in the preparation of audio materials. Apart from the all-important pedagogical quality of the material (see Part II), the following technical points need to be considered: (a) Are the content and tone those of the spoken language? (b) Is the pronunciation natural and colloquial—*not* that of the lecture room or the pulpit? (c) Is there a pause at the end of each sentence long enough to allow repetition, but not too long to permit a change in rhythm? (d) Is the recording made with a good quality microphone in an acoustically suitable room? (e) Is the voice used one which records well—not one which irritates? Good classroom voices are not always good microphone voices.

(ii) *Use of Auditory Materials*

In the language laboratory the spoken language may take precedence over the written language. Oral proficiency may be the main aim. In some laboratories no books are allowed, and the learner never sees the text he is learning. This is done on the grounds that his pronunciation is influenced not only by reading the text but even by his visual memory of how the words are written. Other laboratories use special books of dialogues or text in phonetic notation, pre-studied at home by the learner.

In some cases, a week's laboratory work may consist of no more than a five-minute dialogue, containing sentences of high frequency and wide usefulness. But the learner may hear it twenty or thirty times during the week until he is able to use the sentences of the dialogue with native-like proficiency. Some pronunciation drills may be based on popular songs, sung with a natural, colloquial pronunciation.

Auditory materials may also be based on appropriate reading selections, preferably passages containing dialogue. There may be questions on the content, recorded on the master track and spaced to permit the learners to respond.

Dictations may also be prepared on tape or disc. The technique used will depend on the aim of the dictation as a test of spelling, a test of auditory comprehension, or as practice in writing.

4.1.2 Visual Media

These may include pictures (drawings, photographs, cartoons, posters), charts, maps, film-strips (designed or adapted for language practice), sound films (language-teaching films or documentary films re-scripted for language practice), and sound film-loops specially designed for drilling the oral skill.

(i) *Preparation of Visual Materials*

Instructors trained in the preparation of audio-visual aids may help in the preparation of visual materials for language teaching. Since the visual material not only furnishes a frame of reference for the oral work, but may, in multilingual classes, be the only source of its meaning, it may be necessary to give a great deal of attention, while preparing the material, to the possible interpretations which the learners may give to it. (See Ch. 8 : 2.3.)

Films and film-strips may range from the beginning look-and-say drill to advanced conversational episodes. There may also be films and film-strips originally intended for other purposes but re-scripted and sound-tracked by the instructors within the language level of the learners.

Film loops are lengths of film with ends spliced together to permit continuous repetition. They come in magazines which fit on to any projector by means of an adapter arm. Each magazine contains a learning unit made up of one or two sequences which run for a few minutes at a time. They are so designed as to allow the learner to repeat a sequence as often as necessary, isolating one skill at a time.

(ii) *Use of Visual Materials*

The main function of visual material is semantic. It permits the learner to understand what he hears, to learn the situation in which language forms are used, and to associate them with what he is learning through imitation and repetition.

If films are used, the learner views each film again and again, listening and looking, until the meaning is clear and the form familiar to the ear. Then he may do concentrated oral drill on the language of the film; transcribed on tape, this becomes his oral homework, to be done in individual booths in the practice laboratory.

At advanced levels, silent films, film-strips, slides and wall-pictures may be used for oral composition. Finally, for groups who have already achieved a certain mastery of the spoken language, films and film-strips may be used to improve reading, writing, and spelling.

4.2 TEACHING PLANS

Does the laboratory have a general, over-all teaching pattern? What sort is it? The following, for example, is one possibility: 1. Dialogue spoken entirely and at normal speed. (Learner listens.) 2. Dialogue broken into five-syllable units, or smaller ones. (*Where* (pause) *can I get* (. . . .) *some matches* (. . . .)?) 3. Learner repeats after each pause. 4. Sequence repeated

three or four times. (*Where* (. . . .) *can I get some matches* (. . . .)? × 3.)
5. Complete sentence at normal speed. (*Where can I get some matches?*)
6. Learner repeats.

Or the pattern may be simply: 1. Bridge phase (revise previous material).
2. Teaching phase (see below). 3. Testing phase (random samples of
items in teaching phase, about a quarter as many). The plan of the teaching phase depends on what is being taught. One plan which has been used
for speech drill is the following: 1. Pre-condition learner (national music,
song, or snatch of dialogue). 2. Elicit responses (echo drill). 3. Mechanize
them (variation drill). 4. Manipulate them (structural meaning). 5. Reinforce them (easy tests). 6. Semanticize them (lexical meaning).[1704:158]

If the presentation is based on a motion-picture film, there may be a plan
of this type: 1. Show sound-films (without previous preparation). 2.
Film-strip based on film. 3. Film sound-track broken up and used in
practice booths. 4. Recorded self-correcting exercises based on sound-
track. 5. Film script distributed for learner to read. 6. Learner studies
script with accompanying recorded text.

When examining the laboratory teaching-plan it is important to find
out whether it takes into account the level of the learner. A learner who
has mastered the pronunciation of a language, for example, may need less
time on recording and playback. Finally, does the plan contain any
measures for preventing learners in the laboratory from practising errors of
which they are not aware?

4.3 TEACHING UNITS

Laboratory teaching units vary in (1) design, (2) repetition, (3) length, and
(4) speed.

4.3.1 **Design**

How are the sentences arranged for presentation and repetition? Here are
some possible types of arrangement:

Type A.   Listen to sentence—imitate sentence.
Type B.   Listen—imitate & record.
Type C.   Listen—imitate, listen & check.
Type D.   Listen—imitate & record—listen & check.
Type E.   Listen—imitate & record—listen & check—repeat & record.

In the place of straight imitation in the above there may be a response
requiring some modification in the sentence. (See Ch. 9 : 2.2.2.)

On a single-track recorder, Types C and A are possible since the learner
does not record. When the learner does not record, there may be a series

of sentences, each recorded in advance, twice in succession. The learner stops the tape after the first utterance, repeats it and checks by starting the tape and listening to the second utterance of the same sentence. Or a key word for each sentence is recorded in advance, followed by a full sentence. The learner listens to the key word, stops the tape, tries to remember and repeat the sentence, checking from the tape after each try. If sentence modification is required the recorded sentences on a single-track are each followed by some change. The learner stops the tape between the model and its changed form, attempts the change, and starts the tape again to hear what he should have said. If he is right, he goes on, if not he starts over again.

On a double-track recorder, Types B, D and E are possible. The learner's attempts are recorded, permitting him later to listen to them and check his performance. For example, a modification drill included in Type E, might go something like this:

1. He's taking a walk. And yesterday
2. *Yesterday he take a walk.
3. Yesterday he took a walk.
4. Yesterday he took a walk.

	1	2	3	4
Master Track:	MODEL or QUESTION	(blank)	CORRECT FORM	(blank)
Practice Track:	(blank)	LEARNER'S ATTEMPT	(blank)	LEARNER'S IMITATION

Another use of the double-track is to record one speaker of a dialogue on one track and the second speaker on the other. The learner after studying the dialogue, listens to one track at a time, and without recording, takes the role of the other speaker; he then switches roles.

The design of language laboratory exercises for reading and writing depends on the sort of machine used. If teaching machines are used, the material may have to be broken up into thousands of small interrelated units, forming easy steps, at each of which the learner is expected to be nearly always right. A writing course for children, for example, might require as many as 25,000 steps.

To teach the spelling of a single word, say *collaborate*, the machine might go through the following steps, each appearing one after the other in the window of the machine.

1. COLLABORATE means to work together. *In making a motion picture many people have to collaborate.*
   Copy the word here: / / / / / / / / / / /
2. Part of the word is the same as the Latin word LABOR meaning *work*.
                    C O L / / / / / A T E
3. The first part of the word, co, comes from a word meaning *with*. Your co-labourer or co-worker is someone who works with you.
                    / / / / L L A B O R A T E
4. Put the same letter in both spaces.
                    C / / L L A B / / R A T E
5. Put the same letter in both spaces.
                    C O L L / / B O R / / T E
6. Put the same letter in both spaces.
                    C O / / / / A B O R A T E
7. IN MAKING A MOTION PICTURE MANY PEOPLE HAVE TO
                    / / / / / / / / / / / /

4.3.2 Repetition

How many times does the learner listen to the unit as a whole? Three hearings have been suggested as the ideal.[1703:34] How many times does the learner listen and repeat or vary each sentence? Some teachers insist on four or five.[888:151] How many times does the learner record and check his responses? More often than he listens to the model, or less? It may be important that he should listen more often to the model than to himself.

How often does the drill repeat the same pattern? It may take at least three listen-and-respond pairs to establish a pattern, and eight to teach it.[1703] For example:

I see her.	8
I see him.	8
I see it.	8
	—
24 repetitions	

4.3.3 Length and Speed

How many units are there per tape? Some laboratories insist on one unit per tape. What is the length of the tape unit? This may vary greatly from an optimum length of three minutes[1704:103] to fifteen minutes for a half-hour laboratory period.[1703:34] The shorter the tape unit, of course, the more often the learner has to repeat.

At what rate is the tape or sound-track spoken? If it is spoken too quickly, the learner will be unable to imitate it accurately; if it is spoken too slowly, it is likely to be unnatural or distorted. What then is the optimum number of syllables per second? This may depend on the level. It has been suggested that five syllables per second is about right for beginners and ten to twelve for advanced learners.[1703]

In addition to the speaking rate, there is the question of rate of repetition. Taking the model-and-response as a pair, an average rate of five pairs per minute has been recommended.

Finally, how long is the time lapse between response and correction or reinforcement? The shorter the gap, the better the learning (see Ch. 4). Immediate playback machines may cut this gap to a minimum for those engaged in self-correction exercises.

5. RELATION TO TEXT AND TEACHER

What is the position of automated language teaching in the general language-teaching programme? What percentage of the teaching does it handle in relation to that done by the text (Part II) and by the teacher in class (Part III)?

Is the material taught in the laboratory different from that taught in class, or is it the same? Does one prepare for the other, revise the other, or test the other? When the learners start the lesson in the laboratory do they first hear material already presented to them in class?

For what purpose is the class time used? Is it used for correction, presentation, drill, testing? Some teachers may use part of the classroom time to make the learner familiar with the type of laboratory drill he will be expected to do. Classroom time may be used to make sure each learner hears the difference between the significant sounds, so that he may be able to check on his own pronunciation in the laboratory. The new words may be presented in class, syllable by syllable, to make their pronunciation clearer. Classroom time may also be used to present the meaning of the texts used in the laboratory drills or to expand the context of the laboratory texts already used.

The same pattern of drills used in the laboratory may be used in class with pictures instead of call-words. For example, if the laboratory uses call-words for echelon drills, the teacher might use pictures with the same drills in class:

> *In the laboratory:*
> Recording: There's a man in the garden.
> Learner: There's a man in the garden.
> Recording: Dog.
> Learner: There's a dog in the garden.

In the classroom:

Teacher: There's a man in the garden.
Learner: There's a man in the garden.
Teacher: (Holds up picture of a dog.)
Learner: There's a dog in the garden.

Some teachers may use machines only to increase the amount of repetition at the end of the lesson. Others may begin the lesson with a presentation on motion-picture film and end it with listen-and-repeat drills in class.

Finally, what is the relation of the laboratory texts with the current reading of the learner? If laboratory materials are chosen from current reading, the contexts of their meaning may be wider, and the content of the laboratory drills consequently more significant.

Whether the teaching is done through the laboratory or in class, its purpose is still to promote language learning. Since the amount of language learning may in turn be used to determine the choice of techniques and materials, it is important for the completion of our analysis to find out how the amount of language learned has been measured.

CHAPTER 16

The Measurement of Language Learning

OUTLINE

0. INTRODUCTION

Although language testing mainly concerns the performance of the learner, the types of tests or examinations that evaluate his knowledge of the language often determine the methods and techniques which teachers use to teach it.

Testing is an activity which may occupy a good portion of the teacher's time, either in administering or choosing the tests or in the actual making of them. It is therefore important for the teacher to know what tests are made of and how they differ.

Language tests may differ in (1) purpose, (2) design, and (3) suitability.

1. PURPOSE

Tests may be designed for four different purposes: (1) to find out how much of the language a person actually knows (proficiency tests); (2) to get an idea of how much of it he will be able to learn (prognostic tests); (3) to find out how much of a course he has actually learned (achievement tests), and (4) to discover what remains to be taught (diagnostic tests).

1.1 PROFICIENCY TESTS

The purpose of a proficiency test is to find out how much of a language a person has mastered. It is not connected with a particular course and is not necessarily based on what the learner may have studied.

Proficiency tests are used to put people into categories according to their knowledge of the foreign language. These categories may be used by governments and employment commissions as a basis for language qualifications, or they may be used for the purpose of finding the level at which a learner should start or continue his study of the language. This may not necessarily be the same for all the language skills. A speech proficiency test may place a learner at one level, and a reading proficiency test at another.

1.2 PROGNOSTIC TESTS

This type of test is intended as a prediction of how well a person is likely to learn a foreign language. It is used to select persons likely to profit from foreign language instruction.

One type of prognostic test for beginners involves the learning of an artificial micro-language containing in miniature all the elements involved in language learning—phonetics, grammar, vocabulary and meaning. The test simulates the conditions of language learning, and includes such activities as imitating sounds and sound patterns, completing pattern changes, and inferring meanings from contexts.

1.3 ACHIEVEMENT TESTS

Achievement tests determine how much of the material of a course has actually been mastered. They include only what has been taught.

The amount of language learned in a course can be measured by giving the same test before and after, or by giving two equal tests, one at the beginning of the course and one at the end. It is important, however, if two different tests are used, that they be tested and proved to be equal.

1.4 DIAGNOSTIC TESTS

The purpose of diagnostic tests is to find out what remains to be taught.

Unless the teacher has a class of absolute beginners, he will be taking over one which has already been taught some of the language, either by himself or by another teacher. What the class has been taught, however, is no indication of what it knows.

Although it may be useful to find out as much as possible about the learners' previous studies of the language, the teacher can determine how much of the language they actually know or do not know only by giving them some sort of test. The purpose of such tests is not to give marks to learners, but to get some information about their knowledge of the language. Diagnostic tests sometimes reveal that the most advanced classes make the most elementary mistakes.

2. DESIGN

The design of a test depends on (1) the skills tested, (2) the types of questioning, (3) the types of response, and (4) the types of correction or scoring.

2.1. SKILLS TESTED

Tests may be classified according to (1) what is tested, and (2) how it is tested.

2.1.1 What is Tested?

What is the test intended to test? Which skill—listening, speaking, reading, writing? Which component of each skill does it test—the discrimination of sounds, the understanding of content, pronunciation, oral expression, reading speed, spelling, composition, translation?

Some tests are frankly labelled according to the skills they include; they may be called reading tests, auditory comprehension tests, pronunciation tests, etc. Other tests, simply called language tests, may include only translations and compositions, assuming that these activities constitute a test of everything that knowing a language involves.

2.1.2 How is it Tested?

A skill may be tested by its use; or it may be broken down into its elements each of which is tested separately. The first approach is based on the assumption that the best way to see whether a person can use a language is to get him to use it. The candidate is forced to show what he can do by doing it. A speaking test requires him to speak; a writing test, to write.

Such tests are easy to give and to compose. As tests, however, this type reveals only what the learner may wish to reveal, since he need not include anything on which he is likely to make a mistake; he may for example avoid sentence structures of which he is unsure. The test may give only a vague idea of the extent of the learner's vocabulary and structure. If the topics of oral or written composition used in such tests are general enough, the candidate can prepare a few compositions in advance, copy and memorize paragraphs from books and articles, and the like.

The correction or scoring of such tests may be highly inaccurate, time-consuming, subjective and at the same time difficult. So many different elements are involved that the causes of errors may be hard to determine. Such an apparently simple test as a dictation, for example, may indicate a number of quite different abilities—the ability to spell, the discrimination of sounds and words, skill in interpreting what is heard and in making sense out of it, a certain knowledge of the structure of the language, skill in writing and punctuation.

In contradistinction to this type is the analytic type of test which aims at breaking a skill down into its elements in order to test one at a time. Such tests can be limited to what the tester wants to know. They can be checked, tested and continually re-designed and improved. The errors can be analysed and their causes determined. Tests of this type can be standardized and used to compare different groups, different individuals or the same individual at different times. Although they are far more difficult to compose, they are quicker and easier to score. Moreover they can be designed in such a way as to be objective, that is, to be entirely independent of the opinions or judgments of the corrector.

Criticisms on the use of analytic objective tests have to do with the mental activities of the learner taking the test. The learner is not required to use the entire complex system of habits simultaneously to the same extent as he does when using the language. For this reason, objective tests often appear to be too easy. Objective tests which give the learner a choice of possible answers may show whether he is right or wrong, but cannot show *how* wrong he may be, for although the right answer may be unique, wrong answers are multiple—all possible guesses and mistakes cannot obviously be shown. Yet for purposes of measuring attainment and proficiency in the language such objections may be irrelevant. Objective tests may be designed not only on the degree of probability of guessing the answers, but also on the probability of specific errors.

The objectivity or analysis in a test may vary in degree. The degree depends on the type of questioning used and the type of response required.

2.2 TYPES OF QUESTIONING

How are the questions of the test posed and arranged?

To begin with, are there clear directions of how the test is to be conducted? Is there an example given before each type of question? Do the questions begin with what is easiest, and increase gradually in difficulty so as to give each learner an opportunity to show what he knows? Do the questions test one thing at a time? Do they test the usual in language, or the unusual?

In what medium is the questioning done—(1) spoken, (2) written, (3) pictorial, or (4) ostensive? If it is spoken or written, which language is used, the native language or the foreign language? What proportion of each?

2.2.1 Spoken Questions

If the spoken language is used, is it recorded or uttered by the person administering the test? Do the learners listen to the recording individually or collectively?

2.2.2 Written Questions

If the questions are written, have the learners individual copies of them, or are they to be put on the blackboard, or projected on a screen?

2.2.3 Pictorial Questions

Are there any questions in the form of pictures? What sort are they? Have learners individual copies or are the pictures posted up or projected? Some tests make use of pictures which have been printed on separate sheets or in separate booklets. These are used by the learners during the tests, but collected for re-use after the test is completed.

2.2.4 **Ostensive Questions**

Tests may also involve the use of objects, actions and situations requiring the learner to say or write what he sees.

2.3 TYPES OF RESPONSE

The type of response required in a test may differ in (1) media used, (2) choices given, and (3) operations required.

2.3.1 **Media**

Responses may involve the use of speech, writing, pictures or actions. The media used in the response, however, may not necessarily be the same as those used in the corresponding question. For example, a test in auditory comprehension might involve written or pictorial responses to spoken sentences. The candidate is required to listen to a recorded text and to select from a printed text the sentence or picture which applies to what he hears. Or the question part may be presented in writing and the response in speech, as in the case of oral reading tests. Or the answers may be actions done in response to spoken commands; the accuracy of the action is used as an indication of how well the spoken command was understood. The spoken or written response may be made in a language different from that of the corresponding question. It may involve a translation into or out of the native language.

2.3.2 **Choice**

Is the learner given a choice of possible responses or does he have to invent his own?

If choices are given, how many are there? Are they of the simple true-or-false type? Or do they present a range of closely related possibilities? On what are these possibilities based, on an analysis of the learner's native language or on a study of the frequency of his past errors?

Multiple-choice responses may involve a number of different operations on the part of the learner, including such things as changing a text or adding to it, answering questions on a text, or explaining some of its elements. (See 2.3.3 below.)

2.3.3 **Operation**

What sort of operation does the response require the candidate to perform? Does he have to (i) give an answer, (ii) give an explanation, (iii) infer something from a text, (iv) add something to the text, (v) change something in the text, or (vi) compose a text himself?

(i) *Answering*

The learner may be required to give an answer to the question on the test. The answer may be entirely of his own invention or it may be chosen from a number of possible alternatives. For example, answering in an auditory comprehension test might involve the following operations:

The description of a context and a series of oral questions on it, recorded on tape or disc, are played to the candidate. For example:

> *Recording:* NUMBER ONE: You're in a station. (*pause*)
> When's the next train for Manchester?

The candidate looks at his answer booklet and selects the most likely answer to the question from such possibilities as: *at the station, five miles away, at five thirty, around the corner.*

The context given may be more or less elaborate. It may include a dialogue, a telephone conversation or a short news broadcast. The candidate may be required to listen to questions on these and select the answers from a list in his answer booklet. Or the telephone conversation may be interrupted at intervals, and during these interruptions the candidate is required to select the next most likely response.

Reading speed may also be tested on the basis of selected answers. A dozen or so short paragraphs may be given, and in the space of five or ten minutes the candidates may be required to read each paragraph and answer a question on it.

(ii) *Explanation*

The response may require an explanation on the part of the candidate. The explanation may be in the native language or in the foreign language. It may be invented by the learner or selected from a list of possible explanations. A vocabulary comprehension test, for example, may be designed with multiple-choice responses. The test may be based on a reading passage containing a number of underlined words, repeated at the end of the passage and followed each by a number of possible synonyms, from which the learner selects. For example:

> . . . These dark, *unfathomed* depths of the ocean have
> never seen the light of day. . . .
> *unfathomed:* A. unexplored; B. unmeasured; C. underwater;
> D. impossible to reach.

(iii) *Inference*

The response may involve the making of inferences from a given text. The choice of a number of possible inferences may be given:

> She turned on the heat in her room.
> A. She was hungry.
> B. She was cold.
> C. She felt too warm.

The test may require the learner to listen to a conversation among a number of speakers, and then to analyse a number of possible inferences based on the conversation. After each inference, the learner checks whether it is true or false.

(iv) *Addition*

The operation required may be that of adding something to the question, either by way of expanding a full sentence by including in it a new element (inclusion) or of finishing an incomplete utterance (completion).

Inclusion may be used in tests of intonation and rhythm. Here a new word or group of words may have to be incorporated into a basic sentence while making the necessary changes in rhythm and intonation. It is similar in form to echelon drill or to that type of pattern practice involving addition (see Ch. 9: 2.2.2). Inclusion may also be used as a test for word-order; here the question gives a basic sentence and a series of words to be included in it. If the questions are oral, the words to be included are uttered after a pause. The inclusion may be cumulative; for example:

> Q: Il faut quitter la piste.
> Ne . . . pas.
> A: (Il ne faut pas quitter la piste.)
> Q: Il ne faut pas quitter la piste. Surtout.
> A: (Il ne faut surtout pas quitter la piste.)

Completion tests of the fill-in-the-blanks type may be used in a variety of ways. The blanks to be filled may be structure words or content vocabulary. They may be presented in isolated sentences or in a running text; the blanks are placed either in the text itself or in sentences based on it.

Completion tests may be used to examine not only grammar and vocabulary but also spelling. They may appear not only as written but also as oral tests. A recording may give an incomplete sentence which the candidate is to complete, either orally or in writing, from a number of possibilities. For example:

> *Recording:* Whenever I have a toothache I immediately go to see....
> *Answer Booklet:* A. the pharmacy; B. the dentist; C. some toothpaste.

A reading comprehension test may involve the completion of statements about a passage read by the candidate. After reading each paragraph he may be required to complete a statement about it, selecting from a list of alternatives. For example:

> Martin has a great deal of admiration for....
>   A. the men who conquered Everest.
>   B. the beauties of the Himalayas.
>   C. the dangers of mountain climbing.
>   D. the Abominable Snowman.

(v) *Alteration*

The question may require some sort of change to be made in the text. The change may involve either conversion or replacement. It may require a conversion of all verbs from the infinitive to the present tense or from the present to the past. Or it may involve replacement of an inappropriate word by a more appropriate one.

The alteration may be from one medium to another, as when the test requires a written passage to be read aloud for the purpose of recording pronunciation, or when an oral passage is put into writing, as in dictation. The alteration may also be in the language, as in the case of translation into or out of the native language. This latter type of test is one which, in the past, has been much used, and much abused.

Another type of alteration is re-statement. The test gives a series of phrases, with instructions to rephrase each in a certain way. These may be recorded and used as an oral expression test. For example:

> *Recording:*   Tell him not to bother.
> *Response:*   (Don't bother.)
> *Recording:*   Ask her to have a seat.
> *Response:*   (Won't you have a seat?)

(vi) *Composition*

The test may require the composition of sentences or paragraphs out of elements of the candidate's own invention or out of a list supplied by the test.

The test may supply a series of words for the learner to unite into a sentence. For example:

> *If   it   not   rain   we   going   country*

Or it may give a number of simple phrases, clauses, and sentences to be linked together into one or more complex sentences, or into a paragraph. For example:

Down the street. I was walking. I met an old friend. My friend asked me to a restaurant. He was an old schoolmate of mine. We had coffee. We talked for a long time. More than two hours. I came home. I was late for dinner.

The question part of the composition test may be a series of pictures. The candidate may be given a booklet of pictures and required to write or record one appropriate sentence for each picture.

Some tests combine a number of different operations into a single theme. For example, each of the recorded responses to the pictures may have to be altered in some way, repeated in the negative, or put into the past.

2.4 SCORING

How is the test designed for scoring? Must it be scored (1) by simple computation, that is, by simply adding up the right answers, (2) by requiring the corrector to discriminate between a right answer and a wrong one, or (3) by the evaluation of different degrees of excellence?

2.4.1 Computation

The simplest type of scoring involves only the counting of right and wrong answers. Tests vary of course in the efficiency of their design for this sort of scoring. A test may, for example, have separate answer sheets, with numbers corresponding to the questions in an answer booklet or question sheet. In such a test, the auditory comprehension test cited above (2.3.3 (i)) might be presented thus:

ANSWER BOOKLET	ANSWER SHEET

1.
  A. At the station.
  B. Around the corner.
  C. At five-thirty.
  D. Five miles away.
	1.
	  A. =
	  B. =
	  C. —
	  D. =

Since the appropriate answer to the oral question "When's the next train for Manchester?" is C, the learner puts a pencil stroke at C in the space provided.

Tests of this design can be corrected rapidly with a perforated key or, if an electrographic pencil has been used, by machine. Applying the perforated key to the answer sheet, the corrector, or the machine, first totals the number of black marks, that is, the rights (R)—let us say 80. He then totals the number of blanks, that is, the mistakes (M)—let us say 20. To compensate for the probability that a learner could guess some of the answers in such a test, the total number of mistakes divided by the number of possible mistakes per question (in this case, $4 - 1 = 3$) is subtracted from the total number of rights. The final score (S) is therefore calculated on the formula:

$$S = R - \frac{M}{n-1} = 80 - \frac{20}{3} = 73\cdot4$$

Such calculations are valid only in the aggregate.

In cases where large numbers of people have to be tested, the ease and rapidity of correction of such tests may be an important argument for adopting them. Moreover, such tests do not require language teachers as correctors.

2.4.2 Discrimination

Tests that require as correctors persons with a knowledge of the language are those where the scoring involves some sort of discrimination between what is correct and incorrect or some sort of evaluation of the candidate's performance.

Those requiring the corrector simply to discriminate between right and wrong may also be designed for rapid scoring. For example, the test may require the candidate to put structure words into the numbered blanks of a written text:

When the child comes ..1.. school age, there is often the question ..2.. deciding where ..3.. send him.

The learner may fill in the blanks on a numbered answer sheet of the same design as the key, so that scoring is simply a matter of applying the key to the answer sheet and marking the mistakes:

KEY	ANSWER SHEET
1. of	1. to X
2. of	2. of ___
3. to	3. to ___
etc.	etc.

If the corrector is not required to take into account a number of possible right answers, the scoring may be left to persons who are not necessarily language teachers.

2.4.3 Evaluation

Tests which require the corrector to judge the answers may involve a considerable amount of time per paper if an accurate evaluation is required. Here again, however, the test may be designed to speed up the scoring. For example, if the test is one in oral expression, it may first be broken down into separate tests of pronunciation, structure and vocabulary. The remaining factors of quickness and appropriateness of response, which may have to be assessed by the corrector, might be scored on a speed scale, where each degree corresponds to a stroke of a metronome. The scoring card for six utterances (centre column) might be designed thus:

SPEED	ACCURACY						SCORE
	1	2	3	4	5	6	21
5				X			5
4			X				4
3	XX						6
2		X			X		4
1						XX	2
0							

The corrector, listening to the recording of the responses, runs his pencil down each column at the rate of one intersection per metronome stroke and stops at the point where he hears a response. If the response is entirely appropriate—regardless of pronunciation and structure, which are tested separately—he makes two check marks at that point; if partly acceptable, one check mark. At the end of the test he simply multiplies each check mark by the point allotted to the speed level at which it was made, and totals the results.

Since each element of each skill may have different scoring techniques used with different types of questioning and response, it is necessary when analysing a test to get a simple, composite picture of all these variable components and their interrelation. This can be done by checking these components on a table. To illustrate, we write into the table the components of our example (in 2.4.1) of an auditory comprehension test.

TYPE OF SKILL	QUESTIONS				TYPES OF RESPONSE															RESULTS		
	media				*media*				*choice*		*operations*						*mechanics*			*scoring*		
Skills Required	Spoken	Written	Pictorial	Ostensive	Speech	Writing	Pictures	Actions	Given	Not Given	Answering	Explanation	Inference	Addition	Alteration	Composition	Checks	Fill-ins	Sentences	Computation	Discrimination	Evaluation
LISTENING: Phonetic Discrimination																						
Auditory Comprehension	√					√			√								√			√		
SPEAKING: Pronunciation																						
Oral Expression:																						
Grammar																						
Vocabulary																						
Context																						
Tempo																						
READING: Visual Discrimination																						
Reading Comprehension		√																				
Reading Speed																						
WRITING: Graphics																						
Spelling																						
Punctuation																						
Grammar																						
Vocabulary																						
Style																						

Framework for Analysing Language Tests

3. SUITABILITY

Is the test suitable for the purpose for which it is going to be used? By referring to the above table we can evaluate the suitability of a test from the points of view of relevance, fairness and usability.

Firstly, is the test relevant? Does it test what it claims to test? Does it test what we are trying to find out? If it is a test of achievement, for example, does it limit itself to the material covered, or does it include material which has no relation to the learner's past training?

Secondly, is it a fair test? Is it of average difficulty; is it too easy, or is it beyond the capacity of those who attempt it? If nothing but errors are produced by a test, it may be the test itself which fails to meet the requirements, and not those taking it who are to blame.

Is the timing of the test right? Does it give the learner enough time to respond? Or does it give him too much? In oral responses, a test may give too much time if it permits the candidate to remember a rule, compose a sentence on it by applying the rule, and then utter the response.

Finally, is the test usable? Can it be applied in the particular circumstances in which it will be given? Can it be administered and corrected by the personnel available? Does it rely too heavily on skilled personnel in situations where these are lacking? Does the test require the use of mechanical equipment which is not available? Some tests may be designed for teaching machines which test what they themselves have taught.

Conclusion

All that has been said in the foregoing pages does not add up to a simple recipe for language teaching. It does try to give some idea of what language teaching involves and of the complex characteristics encountered in its analysis.

These concern three separate but interrelated areas—the language, the text, and the teacher. In analysing the language we encountered the complication of conflicting theories, differences in techniques of describing the language, and numerous factors involved in learning it. In analysing the text, we found that each of its inherent elements—selection, gradation, presentation, and repetition—posed its own problems of analysis and measurement. And in our analysis of the teaching performance of the teacher we had first to take into account the delicate relationship between teacher, text and class, and the necessity for a separate analysis of teaching points, teaching plans, and teaching techniques.

These factors of language, method and teaching have to be taken into account by anyone making an analysis of someone's language teaching or of his own, and by anyone analysing a method or making one. Some of the factors may indeed be more important than others; in the present state of our knowledge the relative importance of some of them remains a matter of opinion. But their existence does not. An inherent factor in a method cannot be brushed aside because one *feels* it to be of no importance. In any fair analysis of language teaching, all factors must be considered, not only those chosen by exponents or opponents of a particular text. In the past, essentially sound language teaching texts have been turned down or discontinued because of certain minor imperfections, well exposed by partisan critics, while fundamentally defective texts have been retained.

One is surprised and shocked to realize how very little real research is devoted to the choice or rejection of language-teaching texts. There may sometimes be a lot of opinions expressed; but these are no substitute for facts. It was to promote factual and textual analysis of language-teaching methods that this book was originally intended. It was designed to provide an analytic framework for those who have to choose language-teaching texts. But since the choice very often depends on the opinions of teachers, it is up to the teacher to analyse his text in relation to his teaching. And this depends largely on an impartial analysis of his own teaching techniques and abilities.

Conclusion

What has been provided is really a framework by means of which a variety of particular cases may be considered. The elements forming the framework still remain to be given their relative values. To do this, a great deal of work is necessary in the correlation of the factors of language teaching with those of language learning. This is the task of special centres for training and research in language teaching. Unfortunately these are very few in number. Some countries have not a single such centre, despite the fact that they may have full-time language teachers in every one of their secondary schools. In this field, there is a great need for centres where specialists in language teaching, in linguistics, in phonetics and in the psychology of language learning may work together and devote all their time to the complex problems of the teaching and learning of foreign languages.

The increase in language-teaching efficiency would alone be worth the trouble and expense involved. For the amount of time lost in language learning is phenomenal. If this book should indirectly contribute to saving a fraction of this time it would very well have served its purpose.

Language Drills

OUTLINE

4. WRITING DRILLS

4.1 Spelling Drills
    4.1.1 Completion Exercises
    4.1.2 Word Building
4.2 Composition Drills
    4.2.1 Look-and-Write Drills
    4.2.2 Do-and-Write Drills
    4.2.3 Question-and-Answer Drills

1. LISTENING DRILLS

Listening involves hearing the sounds and sound patterns of a language and understanding their meaning.

1.1 PERCEPTION DRILLS

The learner must hear the sounds of the language before he can be expected to pronounce them. If the teacher cannot make them himself, he can use recordings with model pronunciations.

Some teachers, especially those who have to teach adults, sometimes start the course by explaining the sounds of the new language to the class. As they utter and explain each sound they put its phonetic symbol on the board with a number underneath. To see whether the learners can identify an individual sound the teacher asks them to give the number of the sound after he has uttered it. For example:

The following is on the board: /iː i e æ aː/
                                1 2 3 4 5

Teacher: /i, i, i, i./
Learner: Number 1.
Teacher: No. /i, i, i, i./
Learner: Number 2.
Teacher: Yes. Number 2. Number 2: /i/, Number 1 /iː/ /i – /iː, /i – iː/, /i – iː/, etc., contrasting Number 2 with Number 1, so that the learner can compare the sound which was pronounced with the sound he thought he heard. The learner can go on to identifying words by the same technique.

This may be useful if the teacher is going to use phonetic symbols. If not, he can sometimes use objects and pictures of things whose names sound alike. For example, take a picture of some sheep and another of a ship. Put the pictures on opposite walls, so that you can see where they point. When you say the word, the learner points to the picture. In this way, the learner learns to hear the difference between /iː/ as in *sheep* and /i/ as in *ship*. Or use two objects like a pin (for /i/) and a pen (for /e/); when you say *pen* the learner holds up his pen, and when you say *pin* he holds up the pin.

Listening exercises are not limited to beginners; they can be continued throughout the course. At a certain stage, learners may be encouraged to listen to long-playing recordings on disc or tape and to recorded radio programmes. For adults, special ear-training exercises involving dictation in phonetic script are sometimes highly effective.

1.2 AUDITORY COMPREHENSION DRILLS

When the learner has begun to get used to hearing the language he can concentrate on developing a certain fluency in understanding its meaning. The teacher can help him achieve this through drills which involve listening and pointing, listening and doing, and through various types of comprehension games (see Appendix B).

1.2.1 Listen-and-Point Drills

Ask the learners to touch, hold up or point to various objects as you name them. For example, after having demonstrated *This is a book* (*pen, pencil, etc.*) ask the learner to touch or hold up each object as you name it. Without indicating the object, say: *This is a book*. (Learner touches book.) *This is a pen.* (Learner touches pen.) Understanding the meaning of structural words like *this* and *that* can also be drilled in this way. If the learner understands "This is a book" he puts his hand on his book; if he understands "That is a book" he points to one on the shelf.

1.2.2 Listen-and-Do Drills

Tell the learner to do something, and if he does what you say, he has probably understood the meaning. For example:

Teacher:	Put your book on your head, Mary. (Mary puts her book on her head.)
Teacher:	Put your pencil on the floor, Tom. (Tom puts his pencil on his head.)
Teacher:	That's your head, Tom. I said: on the floor. Mary? (Mary points to the floor.)
Teacher:	Yes. That's the floor, Tom. Now, put your pencil on the floor. (Tom puts his pencil on the floor.)
Teacher:	That's it. etc.

This drill can be preceded by chorus drill in which you say a sentence and the entire class does the action. Chorus drill may be necessary in large classes.

1.2.3 Recordings with Film-Strips

Listening to recordings along with the pictures which give them meaning is another type of comprehension exercise. The sentences are so spaced as to permit you to change the picture on the screen. Each picture means what is said on the recording.

1.2.4 **Motion-Picture Films**

Special language-teaching films in a limited and graded vocabulary can be useful for beginners, if the films are properly designed. Such films are designed to be shown not once but several times. At a more advanced stage it might be profitable for the class to have regular cinema programmes; let them see two showings or more, in order to get the most language learning value out of the film. Live dialogue, at this stage, may do better teaching than the voice of a commentator.

2. SPEAKING DRILLS

2.1 PRONUNCIATION DRILLS

Before the learner starts drills in oral expression it is important for him to develop an adequate pronunciation of the language. This is better done at the beginning, for every word the learner utters makes his pronunciation of its sounds more and more a habit. If he should develop a faulty pronunciation, correcting it can be very difficult and most time-consuming. If he develops a good pronunciation at the beginning, every sentence he says throughout the course will help in making this pronunciation a habit.

It is not necessary, however, that the learner should be able to pronounce all the sounds correctly before he is allowed to speak. The phonetic drills need not interfere with the rest of the lesson. Nor is it necessary to start drilling individual sounds. It is possible to start with the shorter sentences being taught and, proceeding by approximation, to make their pronunciation more and more precise. The main thing is that the learner's incorrect pronunciation should not become a habit. Along with the stress and intonation of sentences, drill the individual sounds they contain. For this, special phonetic exercises will be needed.

2.1.1 **Phonetic Exercises**

Start with a few short sentences, insisting on the right rhythm and intonation. Have the whole class in chorus imitate either you or the model pronunciation on a recording spaced for repetition. You can beat out the rhythm on the table, on a drum, or by clapping your hands.

As the course advances you can make up special drills for individual sounds like the /θ/, the foreign /r/, or any other sound which does not exist in the native language. You can use all sorts of simple aids to help the learner get the right action out of his speech organs. If the learner has trouble spreading his lips make him hold a pencil between his back teeth. If he has trouble rounding his lips have him whistle or let him try to blow out a flame held about a foot from his mouth. To get the learner to make an /h/ or to add one to initial aspirated /p/, /t/, and /k/, you can tie a small feather to a piece of thread, hang the feather before the learner's mouth and have him blow it away. You can also use this to make him produce a steady stream of air. Suppose, for example, that he gives you a /t/ instead of a /θ/, have him put the tip of his tongue between his teeth, blow on the feather and see how long he can keep it flying. Or you can use the flame of a candle and let him see how long he can keep the flame flat.

When you have enough sounds to make a sequence, drill them in words and sentences. For in speech the sounds of the language appear in groups which are spoken at a certain speed, with a certain stress and a certain intonation. Teach the learners to pronounce correctly and naturally such frequent formulas as *hello, good-bye, good morning, good afternoon, how do you do*, etc. When they can pronounce them well, make them learn them by heart and use them frequently in class when the occasion arises. As the course advances you can make them learn the model sentences in the same way. From the model sentences you can build substitution tables which can also be learned by heart and from which you can get the class to produce hundreds of correctly pronounced sentences. Later these model sentences and formulas can be combined into model dialogues to be studied and memorized.

Formulas, model sentences and dialogues can be based on the pronunciation of the teacher, provided of course that his pronunciation is good enough to serve as a model. If not, it may be advisable for him to use good recordings as models. Those which are spaced for repetition are particularly useful.

2.1.2 Group Singing

Singing is an aid to pronunciation. It gives the learner a great deal of repetition of the sounds and sound patterns which the words of the song contain. It also fixes the words and patterns in the mind of the learner. Since many popular and traditional songs contain words and patterns which are no longer current in everyday speech, great care must be taken in finding the right sort of songs. Many songs put stress on syllables which are normally unstressed in speech; for example, the French song *Il était 'un pe-'tit na-vi-'re*. Such songs give practice in incorrect stress patterns which later have to be corrected. Songs are a great help in language learning, especially when already familiar tunes are used; but words and rhythm have to be carefully chosen so as not to conflict with the other parts of the course.

2.1.3 **Reading Aloud**

We must first distinguish between reading texts in phonetic notation and reading texts in ordinary spelling. If the learners have been taught pronunciation through phonetic notation, the reading of prepared texts in phonetic script may be good practice in putting sounds together. But reading aloud texts in ordinary spelling is another matter. Since the spelling of these texts may be a poor reflection of the sounds of the language, it may contribute to mistakes in pronunciation if it is attempted with learners who do not already know how to pronounce the language. Reading aloud can be used sparingly at a stage where the learners have some knowledge of speech if they are not asked to read aloud sentences which they cannot use in speech. First let them read each sentence silently.

2.2 EXPRESSION DRILLS

From pronouncing ready-made sentences, the learner may go on to saying sentences which he makes up himself. This requires a great deal of careful, graduated teaching. And so much practice is needed in order to make oral expression a habit that the class may sometimes have to do most of the talking; for the more talking the teacher does, the less speech practice they get. Ask the class to look at actions and say what they see, do actions and say what they are doing, ask and answer questions on pictures, and later on written texts. Speech can therefore be drilled through actions, through pictures and through speech.

2.2.1 **Speech through Actions**

First ask the learners to say what they see and say what they do.

(i) *Look-and-Say Drills*

Ask the class to identify and locate persons and things. When teaching a new point, do not miss an opportunity of making the learners identify the objects which you are going to use in your demonstration. For example, if the class already knows the word *knife* and you are going to use a knife to help you demonstrate the structural word *through*, have the class identify it as a build-up for your presentation of the new point. For example:

Teacher:	(Teacher holds up a knife.)
Class:	That's a knife.
Teacher:	(Teacher holds up a piece of paper.)
Class:	That's a piece of paper.
Teacher:	I'll put the knife through the paper.
	Now I'm putting the knife through the paper. etc.

Look-and-say drills may be used again as soon as the learners get the new point. They may be used to review material taught. Take a number of objects and do a number of actions, while the class do the talking. For example:

> (Hold up a key.)
> *Class:* That's a key.
> (Put it in a lock.)
> *Class:* You're putting it in the lock.
> (Hold up a hat.)
> *Class:* That's a hat.
> (Put it on a hook.)
> *Class:* You're putting it on a hook.
> (Hold up a watch.)
> *Class:* That's a watch.
> (Give it to a learner.)
> *Class:* You're giving it to Tom.
> (Gesture to him to put it in his pocket.)
> *Class:* He's putting it in his pocket. etc., etc., etc.

(ii) *Do-and-Say Drills*

Do an action or chain of actions while saying what you are doing. Then let each learner take his turn in doing the same thing. After each sequence the learners can say what they were doing, if they have been taught the structure in which to say it. For example:

> *Teacher* (doing actions): I'm taking a piece of string from my pocket. I'm putting it on the table. I'm taking the pen off the table. I'm putting it in my pocket.
> *Learner* (doing actions): I'm taking a piece of string, etc. (If he cannot remember what to do next, prompt him by miming the action.)
> *Class* (if they have learnt the past tense): He took a piece of string from his pocket. He put it on the table, etc.

Drills of this sort can be put on the board in the form of a table.

Put your	pen pencil book hand	on	your desk. the floor. the table. your head.

Divide the class into two groups. Let one group see how many actions it can get the other group to do by reading off combinations from the table. The person spoken to must say what he is doing. For example:

*A*1 (*to B*1):	Put your book on the floor.
*B*1:	I'm putting it on the floor.
*A*2 (*to B*2):	Put your pencil on your desk.
*B*2:	I'm putting it on my desk, etc.

(iii) *Dramatization*

Another way to give the class practice in speaking, while holding its interest, is to let them perform little skits and short plays. If a learner has to perform before the class, he is more likely to study his part with care, to try to understand it and learn it by heart. If what he learns by heart are colloquial everyday sentences, he will retain some of them and their patterns, and later use them unconsciously in his conversation.

It is important to avoid long plays in which only a few people can speak. Short skits give more practice to more learners. Remember that the purpose of dramatization in class is to make the learners speak.

Classroom dramatization is possible at all levels. At the very beginning when only the pattern THIS IS X has been taught, it is possible to dramatize it as the form of introduction. Have three learners come to the front of the class and introduce one another. A and B are together. C is walking by. A introduces B to C. He can simply say, "C, this is B. B, this is C." If *hello* and *how do you do* have been taught, A can stop C with a "Hello, C." and B and C can add *how do you do* as each is introduced.

A little later on in the course, the class may know enough to dramatize certain actions in their daily lives, like going fishing or going shopping.

Model dialogues may also be dramatized. So can those stories which all the class know or those which they have read in the reader. Well-known events in local or regional history can also be written in dramatic form and presented as little plays. At a certain level the learners can write their own lines, and even their own little plays.

2.2.2 Speech through Pictures

One of the reasons for using pictures to make the learners speak is that the class can thus see and speak about actions and objects which it would be impossible to reproduce in class. Another reason is that it may save valuable classroom time which would otherwise be wasted in changing and setting up situations; for it is sometimes quicker to flash a new picture before the class than to set up a situation. The more different pictures you have, the more different situations you can show. You may draw these pictures yourself, cut them out of picture magazines, buy a ready-made set, or ask the learners to draw them. You can draw some of your pictures on the board before the lesson begins, use ready-made wall-pictures, picture books, pictures in the text, slides, film-strips and even motion-picture films. There are a number of ways of using each of these in order to produce speech.

(i) *Look-and-Say Drills*

Hold up a picture and ask the class, individually or collectively, to say what they see. For example, holding up a picture of a dog, make the class point to it and say, "That's a dog." Suppose you have a picture of a bird sitting on a branch, point to the bird, and let the class say, "That's a bird." Now point out the branch, and they say, "That's a branch." or "That's the branch of a tree." Then point from the bird to the branch as often as it is necessary to get the sentence: "The bird is on the branch," or something equally correct. You can use pictures of persons and things in actions to get such sentences as "Mr. Smith is going to the bank. The train is going up the hill," etc.

The same picture can be used over again at different stages of the course and at different levels of structure. Pictures used in drilling statement forms can later be used to drill question forms. Many pictures like the one of the dog can also be used to drill "What's this?" The learners pick out the pictures and ask the questions. Pictures like the one of the bird on the branch can be used to drill: "Where's the bird?" or "What's on the branch?" Pictures like the one of Mr. Smith can be used to drill: "Where's he going? Is he going to the bank or to the post-office?"

Series of pictures can be arranged in a sequence which tells a story. The learners, prompted by you, tell the story themselves by describing each picture as you show it. When the sequence is finished go over it once or twice again to give practice in continuity. Sequences of pictures in the form of film-strips to be projected on the wall or on a screen are most useful here. The order of the pictures never gets mixed, the picture is large and clear and can be changed with a flick of the wrist as rapidly as your learners can say something about it.

You can also arrange a sequence of pictures in a vertical column and write the story which it tells beside each picture. The learners study both columns—the column of pictures and the column of text. Then the text is covered and the learners try to tell the story while looking only at the pictures.

(ii) *Pictures on the Blackboard*

Some of the pictures and picture sequences can be drawn on the blackboard before the class begins. Or, if you are good at drawing, you can tell the details of a story as you add elements to the picture. Start with a few simple lines and see whether the class can identify anything; as you add more lines—persons, objects or actions—the learners add more sentences to the story. After you have finished ask a learner to come to the board, to point to each picture or part of the picture and re-tell the whole sequence, pausing, if necessary, to ask questions of you or the class. Since nearly every classroom has a blackboard, it is well worth learning how to draw simple pictures on it; you can thus make your lessons clearer, livelier and more interesting. Also encourage the learners themselves to draw pictures on the board and to talk about them.

(iii) *Wall-pictures*

Large pictures with a lot in them can provide a good deal of practice in question-and-answer work. At a certain level of vocabulary and structure, pictures of such things as street scenes, beach scenes, and landscapes with figures are useful for such question-and-answer drills. Learners can ask one another such questions as: "Where's the train going?" "What's on the bridge?" "How many men are there in the field?" Make sure, however, that the learners know enough language to speak about the picture.

(iv) *Flannel-Boards*

This is a device for varying the elements in the picture in order to make the learners vary the elements in the sentence. Since flannel sticks to flannel, one piece can be used for the background of the pictures and other smaller pieces for the main elements. For example, you can have a large piece of grey flannel for your background, a house cut out of red flannel, a tree cut out of green flannel, and a cat out of black flannel. Now put the cat at the door of the house, and let the learners ask and answer questions about it.

Learner A: Where's the cat?
      B: At the door.
         (Put the cat on the roof.)
      B: Where's the cat?
      C: On the roof.
         (Put the cat half way up the tree.)
      C: Where's the cat?
      D: It's going up the tree.

To change the scene, simply remove the house and tree, and stick on a river, a bridge, a train, or other objects, animals or persons about which the learners can speak.

429

(v) *Picture-Books*

Books made exclusively of pictures can be used to encourage the class to speak, provided of course that they have the words for the things pictured. If the pictures are numbered they can be more easily referred to; for example:

Teacher:	Page 24, Number 7.
	What is it?
Class:	It's a lion.
Teacher:	Yes. It's a lion.
	What's the lion doing? Tom?
Tom:	The lion is jumping. etc.

(vi) *Film-Strips*

Film-strips enable the teacher to put a large number of pictures and picture-sequences before the eyes of the learners. He can change these pictures as fast as the learners are able to speak about them. But he must spend a few minutes before the beginning of the class seeing that the projector is properly threaded and ready to operate. One of the many advantages of film-strips is that they save time in changing pictures; if there is a waste of classroom time in threading the projector, this advantage may be lost. Most of the above-mentioned picture drills may also be performed by projecting the picture on a screen. The teacher can make his own black-and-white film-strips simply by having his picture sequences microfilmed on perforated film.

2.2.3 **Speech through Speech**

Once the learners have acquired a certain amount of language, it is possible to use this as a means of making them speak. The important thing is that the learners should have the language to understand the stimulus part of the exercises and enough to respond to it.

In the following drills there is no need for pictures or actions, since they simply use speech to drill speech. Some of them may be of use at the beginning, but most of them are valuable only after the learner has learned to control a certain number of words and patterns.

(i) *Question-and-Answer Drills*

You can begin these by simply questioning the learners. But once the learners have mastered the question patterns, they should practise questioning one another. There are many topics about which questions can be asked, questions about the learners themselves, their surroundings, well-known events (recent and historical), and stories which everyone has read.

It is important however to make the learners use each question form as soon as they have been taught it, so that each form becomes something of a habit before a new form is taught.

If you have just taught the inverted question form and you wish to drill it through speech, you can let the learners ask one another who they are. From time to time put in a question yourself and ask the learner whether he is some well-known person; for example, "Are you the Mayor?" A little humour may thus be attempted if the class is responding well. With the same pattern the learners can ask one another their ages.

After a number of question forms have been mastered, question-and-answer drill can cover a wide variety of topics. For example, the learners are asked to invent all the questions they can about some public figure to see who can answer them.

> Who's the head of the government?
> What's his age?
> Has he a wife?
> Has he any children?
> Has he a car?
> Where is his home? etc.

If the other learners cannot supply the answers, do so yourself, if you can. You can also make the learners ask all the questions they can about a recent sports event, a fire, Mr. X's visit, and other recent events, and likewise well-known past events in the history of the region. Let them ask questions about their own surroundings: "How many people are there in your town?" "What is their language?" "How far is it from here?" and there may be more general questions such as: "What are tables made of?" "Where do oranges come from?" "What do you use for cutting wood?"

If the course includes reading, questions can be asked on the section of the reader which the learners have just read and on any supplementary readers which they may be reading: "Where did the boys go?" "Was anyone in the house?" "How did they get in?" "What did they see in the cellar?" "Who was behind the door?" etc. Learners can be asked to read the text at home or in class with a view to asking the teacher as many questions as they can about it.

(ii) *Verb Series*

At the stage of the course when the number of verbs is being increased, ask the learners to describe a number of natural action sequences such as getting up in the morning, getting dressed, making a parcel, etc. Call on learners individually to describe the series of actions to the class. For example:

> *Teacher:* How do you get dressed in the morning?
> *Learner:* First I get out of bed. Then I put on my shirt. Then I put on my trousers. etc.

Ask the class to prepare such topics as: A day in the life of a schoolboy, a farmer, a fisherman, etc.

(iii) *Topical Talks*

These are useful for expanding vocabulary. First teach the vocabulary of a topic; for example, the weather: *rain, wind, warm, cold, windy, cloudy,* etc. Now let the class ask you as many questions as they can about the weather, and let them copy down your answers. From the answers they have written, the learners prepare a talk on the weather. Next period call one or two to give the talk to the class. After the talk, the learners ask the speakers questions on the topic.

(iv) *Reproduction Exercises*

This type of exercise is a useful device for converting reading vocabulary into speaking vocabulary. Before this type of exercise is attempted, the basic structure of the language must have been mastered.

First ask the class to read silently a passage which they can understand. Then make them close their books and listen to you reading the same passage. Finally call on one or two of them to say in their own words what they have just heard. Then go on to the next passage, which you handle in the same way.

(v) *Descriptive Drill*

Put on the board the name of a person, place or thing; for example, *our town.* Give the class five minutes to make notes on its main characteristics. Then call on one of the learners to give an oral description to the class. When he has finished, others may ask him a number of questions based on their own notes. This drill is for advanced learners.

(vi) *Narrative Drill*

Ask the class to prepare a story, a well-known folk tale or something of their own invention. From his notes, each learner may tell, but not read, the story to the class.

A story may also be composed by the class as a whole. Put the first sentence on the board with a list of related words. Each learner adds to the story using, if possible, some of the words on the board. A secretary is appointed to take down the story, which he later reads to the class. Narrative drills are suitable at the more advanced level.

(vii) *Exposition Drill*

This is similar to verb series, but it applies to a more advanced level. Learners have to explain to the class how certain things are done—riding a bicycle, making a parcel, repairing a fence, trapping animals, baking bread. Try to make the learner be as specific and detailed as possible. If he gives only vague directions, interrupt him with specific questions which will force him to give more detail. For example:

Learner:	To sharpen my pencil, I take a knife and . . .
Teacher:	Where do you get the knife from?
Learner:	I take a knife from my pocket . . .
Teacher:	What sort of knife?
Learner:	I take a small penknife from my pocket and then I sharpen . . .
Teacher:	With the knife closed?
Learner:	No. First I open the knife . . . etc.

To help the learner get the right sequence let him mime the actions.

(viii) *Prepared Speeches*

As the learner's ability to make sentences increases, you can ask him to compose short, two-minute speeches to be given before the class. First he writes out the speech; then you correct it, return it to him, and make him memorize it. But make sure the speech is good enough to be memorized.

3. READING DRILLS

Reading involves the recognition of letters and of words. Since some words are not written the way they are pronounced it is better to make sure the learners have mastered the pronunciation of a word before teaching them to read it. If they read the word first they may develop a wrong idea of how it is pronounced, and you may have to waste a great deal of time in correcting the first false impression.

3.1 RECOGNITION DRILLS

These may be of use only for illiterates, non-alphabetics, and people learning strange scripts. They can be started long before the complete alphabet has been covered and should be continued long after.

433

3.1.1 Making Flash Cards

For each word which your class is able to read, make a card big enough for the entire class to see. About 6 inches or 15 cm. is a good width; the length will depend, of course, on the length of the word. Make the letters thick, high, and black enough to be clearly visible. You can use black ink and a small brush, or a special sign-painter's nib or a felt marker which makes a line about a quarter of an inch thick. These cards are worth making well because they can be used again and again for a great variety of activities. It is a good idea to have two or three sets.

3.1.2 Using Flash Cards

Simply hold up a flash card of a known word until the class, recognizing it, reads the word out loud. Then repeat with another card, and then another, until the class has identified all the words studied. Then test for speed. Hold up the card for a few seconds and see who will be the first to give the word. Show the cards again, calling on individual learners.

3.1.3 Making Sentences with Flash Cards

Give each learner a card with a different word on it. Each says a sentence containing the words distributed. Each learner whose word is part of the sentence comes to the front of the class and stands to the left of the learner whose word comes before his. Then, on a signal from the teacher, they all show their words to the rest of the class, who read the sentence out loud.

As the course progresses, flash cards can be made for groups of words and parts of sentences. These can be treated as individual units and exposed for shorter and shorter periods of time until they can be read fluently.

3.2 COMPREHENSION DRILLS

3.2.1 Find the Object

Put on the table a number of objects the names of which the class knows. Distribute cards with a word on each corresponding to one of these objects. Then ask each learner to find the object the name of which is written on his card. When each learner has found the object which matches his card he takes his turn in showing it to the class, holding the card in one hand and the object in the other and saying "This is —."

3.2.2 Find the Picture

This is similar to the preceding, but instead of objects use pictures of objects and actions. Hang them around the room and ask each learner to find the picture which matches his card.

3.2.3 Find the Missing Half

Each learner is given a card or slip of paper containing one half of a sentence. The other halves are numbered and put on the board. Each learner takes his turn in calling out the number of the half which fits his and reads the complete sentence.

3.2.4 Multiple Choice Drill

Give the learners lists of related words containing one word which does not belong to a series. For example: DOG, CAT, HORSE, APPLE, COW. The learner underlines or crosses out the word that does not belong.

3.2.5 Scrambled Sentences

The sentences of an anecdote are jumbled, put on the board, and numbered. An illustration of the anecdote may be drawn alongside the list of sentences. The learners try to get the number sequence which gives the story.

3.2.6 True-or-False Drills

Put on the board a mixed list of true and false statements. Number them. When you call out a number a learner reads the corresponding sentence silently and says either "Yes" or "No" according as the statement is true or false.

3.2.7 Read-and-Answer Drills

Put a series of questions on the board and number them. Call on individual learners to read the questions silently and give answers to them orally.

You can also place at random around the room a series of questions written on cards. Distribute a set of answers and let the learners match the answers with the questions. You can reverse the process by giving the questions to the learners.

3.3 READING AND ORAL WORK

Reading can be used as revision of the work done orally. A sample of sentences used in the oral lesson can be read silently, either as class-work or as home-work. Picture readers with sentence-by-sentence illustrations of each object and action are most useful in helping the learner to associate the meaning of what he sees with the meaning of what he reads.

4. WRITING DRILLS

Before he can write the learner must be able both to read and to shape the letters of the alphabet. He should ideally be able to say the sentences which he is expected to write. For writing is not primarily a means of teaching the language; it is an aid to remembering it. If he knows the alphabet the learner will still need practice in spelling and composition.

4.1 SPELLING DRILLS

These include completion exercises and word-building exercises. The link between sound and spelling may, if necessary, be drilled through dictation.

4.1.1 Completion Exercises

Put on the board or duplicate an anecdote written in words the learner understands; but in some of the words, leave out certain letters for him to fill in. For example:

One da_, on _is w_y to s_hool, Tom saw a_ old w_man, who, etc.

4.1.2 Word Building

Give the learner a number of initial letters like *t*, *c*, *f*, *b*, and *h*, plus a number of word endings like *-all*, *-ill*, and *-ool*. Let him see how many real words he can make by combining the two.

4.2 COMPOSITION DRILLS

The next stage in learning to write involves a knowledge of how to express meaning in words. The easiest way is to start gradually with sentence-building drills.

4.2.1 Look-and-Write Drills

Hold up a series of objects, and instead of asking the learner to say what he sees let him write it—*That is a pen, That is a book*, etc. Drop your book on the floor, ask the class where your book is, and make them write the answer. Later expand this into getting the learners to write chains of sentences to describe chains of actions.

4.2.2 Do-and-Write Drills

A useful exercise in teaching writing is to expand the association which already exists between action and speech into an association between action and writing. The procedure through which the learner learned to speak can now be repeated for the purpose of teaching him to write.

Convert into writing drills, for example, the above do-and-say speech drills.

4.2.3 Question-and-Answer Drills

Pass around a box full of cards on which questions have been written. Each learner takes one and writes the answer to the question on his card.

Put a list of statements on the board and make the class write all the questions to which these statements are answers.

Language Games

OUTLINE

3. READING GAMES

3.1 Recognition Games
    3.1.1 Matching Cards
    3.1.2 Say the Word
    3.1.3 Find the Word
    3.1.4 Roulette
3.2 Comprehension Games
    3.2.1 The Shop Game
    3.2.2 Find the Sentence
    3.2.3 Read-and-Do Games

4. WRITING GAMES

4.1 Spelling Games
    4.1.1 Crossword Puzzles
    4.1.2 The Magician's Game
4.2 Composition Games
    4.2.1 The Label Game
    4.2.2 Decoding Games

1. LISTENING GAMES

1.1 PERCEPTION GAMES

1.1.1 **The Grape Vine**

Arrange the group in a circle. Whisper a short message (one or two sentences) in the ear of someone in the group. This person whispers it to the person on his left, and so on, until the message has come full circle to its point of origin. It is then compared with the original message.

1.2 AUDITORY COMPREHENSION GAMES

1.2.1 **Find the Object**

Divide the group into two teams. (Let them name the teams themselves.) Put into a large box all the objects the names of which have been taught. As you call out the name of an object, a member of one of the teams comes up and tries to find it in the box. After having found the object named, he holds it up, shows it to the class, and puts it back in the box. If he cannot find the object named, or picks the wrong one, a member of the opposing team has a try, and if he succeeds, wins a point for his team.

2. SPEAKING GAMES

2.1 OBSERVATION GAMES

2.1.1 **Point-and-Say**

This is the simplest of the observation games. Simply divide the group into two teams, and touch or hold up an object the name of which has been taught. Members of each team take their turn in naming the object by pointing and saying: That's an ——, If someone should fail to name the object correctly, his opposite number on the other team can make a point by naming the object.

2.1.2 **Kim's Game**

This is probably the best-known type of observation game. Take half a dozen or more objects the names of which have been taught. Place them on a table, or on the floor, and cover them with a cloth. Remove the cloth for about half a minute and let both teams have a look at the objects. Members of each team alternately take their turn in naming an object. If possible, make them do so within a sentence pattern which has already been taught. Each object may be named only once. As the group becomes used to the game, increase the number of objects and reduce the time exposure. At the intermediate level, require more details about the object named. At this level, for example, it will not be sufficient to identify the object as a *pen*, but as a *red ball-pen*. A point is given for each true statement.

2.1.3 Getting your Own Back

From each member of the group collect one or more of his personal belongings—pens, pencils, books, knives, watches, etc. Put them in a heap on the table or on the floor. Each member of the group tries to get back his possessions by the use of some appropriate formula. Unless what he says is correct in every respect, he does not get back his belongings. The formula used in identifying possessions will depend on the language level reached. At the very beginning level it will be possible to take an object from the collection, say a knife, hold it up and ask the owner to identify it by pointing to it and saying: That's my knife. Do not give it back to the owner until you get the right sentence, and do not let it go until the learner says "Thank you."

At the intermediate level, after the interrogative *whose* has been mastered, let each member of the group take his turn in going up to the collection of belongings, selecting one of the objects, a pencil, for example, showing it to the group and saying: Whose pencil is this? The owner points and replies: That's my pencil.

After the inverted (yes-or-no) question form has been taught, the questioner may be required to guess the name of the owner, with the formula: Martin, is this your watch?

2.1.4 The Here-and-There Game

This is really a variation on the above game. In this case put the objects into *two* piles, one on each side of the room. One team goes to one pile, and the other goes to the second pile. Each person tries to find an object which belongs to him in the pile which his team happens to be searching. If it is in the pile, he must not remove it; if it is not, he is to assume that it is in the other pile, at the other end of the room. Now each person takes his turn in locating his possessions, using such sentences as: My pencil is here. My knife is there. My book is there. He should point to the pile he is referring to, the pile which is near (*here*) or the one which is far away at the opposite end of the room (*there*). Those who have located their belongings in the nearby pile are allowed to take them back after having identified them correctly, in full sentences like "This is my pen (knife, etc.)." Only after all such objects have been removed are the objects which are located at a distance from their owners identified and returned. This is done in the following way: First the owners must locate them again, e.g. (My hat is there); whereupon a person near the object named picks it up and identifies it ("This is your hat"; or "Is this your hat, Mr. X?" if the inverted form has been taught.) The owner replies, and meeting the questioner half way to retrieve his belongings says "Yes, that's my hat . . . Thank you." The type of question form may be elaborated to suit the level of the group.

2.1.5 **Charades**

Among the observation games which can be played at a more advanced level are those of the charade type. This type consists in letting the group observe the miming of an action while trying to guess which action is being mimed. For example, one team may decide—secretly, of course— that one of its members should mime a person getting dressed in an upper berth. While going through the motions, each member of his team takes his turn in asking a member of the opposite team what the action is. ("What's he doing?") The opposing team must reply with complete and correct sentences. Make sure the actions chosen for miming can be described in words the group knows. The more sophisticated, multiple types of charade are generally too difficult for the average language learner, since they often suppose an extensive vocabulary.

2.2 GUESSING GAMES

2.2.1 **What's in it?**

One team is given a bag and the other a box. At the disposal of both teams is a locker full of objects the names of which are known to the group. Each team takes its turn in coming to the locker and selecting an object without showing it to the opposing team, which is then called on to guess what it is. Both teams face each other, and each member of the questioning team (A) takes his turn in asking questions of his opposite number on the guessing team (B). For example:

A1: What's in the box?
B1: A ball?
A1: No. (He passes box with ball in it to A2.)
A2: What's in the box? etc.

Each team keeps the objects which it succeeds in guessing or which the other team fails to guess. The team with the most objects wins the game.

As new question and answer forms are taught they can be included in the pattern of the game. For example, after the inversion forms have been taught, you can have a pattern which goes something like this:

> A1 : What's in the box?
> B1 : Is it a button?
> A1 : No, it isn't.

and later

> A1 : What's in the bag?
> B1 : Is it a part of something?
> A1 : Yes, it is.
> B1 : Is it red?
> A1 : No, it isn't. (Passes bag to A2.)
> A2 : What's in the bag? etc.

In this way, the learners go gradually from habits of uttering colloquial sentences to habits of exchanging dialogue.

Guessing games need not be limited to object questions. They can be used with nearly any question form with which the group is familiar.

2.2.2 **Where is it?**

In this game, one team hides an object somewhere in the room and the other team tries to guess where it is.

> A1 : Where's the key?
> B1 : It's in your pocket. (*or* Is it in your pocket?)
> A1 : No. (*or* No, it isn't.)
> A2 : Where's the key? etc.

If the guessing team is blindfolded or is facing the wall, a greater range of positions is possible—on the table, under the seat, etc. When the game becomes too easy, more precise information might be required.

2.2.3 **Where was I?**

The guessing team is asked where each of the members of the opposing team was at a certain time. For example:

> A: Where was I yesterday at noon?
> B: Were you at the post-office?
> A: No, I wasn't. etc.

2.2.4 **Who has it?**

Arrange for the questioning team to give some small object to one of its members without the guessing team seeing it. Then each member of the guessing team takes his turn in guessing who has the object. For example:

A1: Who has the button?
B1: Tom has it. (*or* Has Tom got it?)
A1: No. (*or* No, he hasn't.)
A2: Who has the button?
B2: You have it. (*or* Have you got it?)
A2: Yes. (*or* Yes, I have.) etc.

2.2.5 Who did it?

Actions can also be elaborated into a guessing game. A member of the questioning team performs some action without the guessing team seeing him. The guessing team must find out who did the action. For example:

> A1: Who took the picture off the wall?
> B1: Did Tom do it?
> Team A: No, he didn't.

2.2.6 What's my line?

This is the well-known television game in which one team tries to guess someone's trade or profession by a series of questions which narrow down the possibilities. In school, learners may assume fictitious trades and professions for the purpose of the game.

2.2.7 Twenty Questions

This is another well-known guessing game made popular through radio and television. The game can be played in a number of ways. For example, one person is asked to write the name of a familiar object on a bit of paper, which is then placed face down on the table. The others take turns in asking questions on the object or in guessing what it is. A maximum of twenty questions is allowed; all of them must be fixed questions of the yes-or-no type. The one who guesses right may pick the new word and answer the questions on it.

This game can also be played as a team game, with one team picking the word and the other team asking the questions. One team writes a word on a card; the other team must find the word in no more than twenty questions.

2.2.8 Riddles

Give a few facts about an object and see whether the group can guess what it is. For example, "It has hands but no feet. It has a face but no head." If the group are unable to guess what it is, add more facts. "I have one in my pocket. It has numbers on it." Encourage learners to bring their own riddles.

Used as a group guessing game, it can be played by two teams. Team A picks a word and Team B tries to guess what it is from the sequence developed by Team A. For example:

A1: I have one in my pocket.	B1: Is it a key?
A1: No, it isn't.	
A2: I got mine on my birthday.	B2: Is it a watch? etc.

2.3 ORAL COMPOSITION GAMES

2.3.1 Let's Tell a Story

This is an attempt at communal composition. Give the first sentence your-self, and let each person take his turn in adding a new one. For example:

> *Teacher*: One day a small boy was going from his house to the school when . . .
> A: He saw a large dog.
> B: The dog went after him, etc.

One of the learners, acting as secretary, makes notes of what is said and when the last sentence has been added reads the entire story to the class.

2.3.2 What's in the Soup?

Ask the group to build up a cumulative recipe from one initial sentence:

> *Teacher*: Mrs. Smith put ten cups of water into the soup.
> A: Mrs. Smith put ten cups of water and three carrots into the soup.
> B: Mrs. Smith put ten cups of water, three carrots and two pounds of meat into the soup.
> C: Mrs. Smith put . . . etc.

The last in line has to repeat the whole recipe. This can also be played as a team game in which any learner who misses an item or gets the order wrong loses a point for his team.

2.3.3 Catch and Say

The group forms a circle with you in the middle. Throw a ball to someone in the circle and as you do so ask for a word or sentence. The person to whom the ball is thrown must catch the ball and produce the word or sentence. For example, a fluency game in opposites might go something like this:

Teacher (throwing ball):	It's hot.
Learner (catching ball):	It's cold.
L. (throwing ball to L.2 or to centre):	It's rough.
L.2 or Teacher (catching ball):	It's smooth, etc.

This type of game is particularly suitable for young learners.

2.3.4 Name the Picture

Divide the group into two teams, hold up a picture and let each team alternate in describing it. Anyone who fails to name what is in the picture loses a point, provided his opposite number in the opposing team succeeds in naming it.

As a question-and-answer game let each member of the questioning team take his turn in picking a picture and showing it, with the appropriate question, to the answering team.

This can be converted into a guessing game by asking the questioning team to pick a picture, and then proceeding as for guessing games with objects.

2.3.5 What's in the Picture

With conversational wall-pictures and other pictures rich in detail, it is possible to organize an observation game very similar to Kim's game. Take a picture which the group has not yet seen, expose it to view for a minute or less; then place the picture face down and ask the group to say what they observed in the picture.

As a team game, let each team alternate in adding new items. Proceed as for Kim's game. Make sure full sentences are used.

2.3.6 Question-and-Answer Game

Use pictures of the conversational wall-picture type. Place the picture in such a way that the group can see the detail. Use names of items in the picture as call-words. When you call out one of these names it is the signal for a member of the questioning team to ask his opposite number a question on it. For example:

> *Teacher:*   Train.
> A1 : Where's the train?
> B1 : It's on the bridge.

Maps can also be used for this sort of game. For example, in response to your call-words, one team can be required to ask their way to a certain point on the map, and a member of the opposing group must tell them how to get there.

2.3.7 The Biography Game

Learners ask questions on the record of a famous person's career. Put the details on the board. For example:

Mr. William X.

Born	1900
Went to X school	1910–1918
Went to X college	1918–1924
Studied law	1924–1927
Worked as lawyer	1928–1932
Elected alderman	1933
Joined the army	1940
Overseas	1943–1945
Wounded	1945
Back home	1946
Opened law office	1947
Elected mayor	1959 etc.

Learners can ask each other such questions as: "When was X born?" "When was he first elected?" "What was he doing in 1925?" "What did he do in 1940?" "Where was he in 1944?" "What is he doing now?" etc. The teacher may first have to give examples of the sort of questions that may be asked.

2.3.8 The Information Desk

Collect all sorts of timetables, programmes, posters, printed invitations, letters, notices, and lists of rules and regulations. Post up some of them in a corner of the room and put the rest of the material on a table next to it. This table will be the information desk. Now pick one of the better learners to act as information clerk. Learners take their turn in going to the information desk and asking for information. For example:

Learner 1:	When's the next bus to X, please?
Information Clerk:	There's a bus at 10.15.
Learner 1:	Thank you.
Learner 2:	What's on at the Capitol, please?
Clerk:	"War and Peace."
Learner 2:	What time does it begin? etc.

Instead of going to the information desk the learners can phone (with a dummy telephone). For example:

Hullo. Is that the information desk?
Is there a letter for me? My name is Tom X.

Before setting up the information desk it is a good idea to begin by posting each document separately, questioning the class on it in order to give them an idea of the variety of questions possible; then ask the class to question you on it. For example, suppose that you have a poster that looks something like this:

```
┌─────────────────────────────────────────────┐
│               PUBLIC LECTURE                  │
│                     by                        │
│                 John Smith                    │
│                     on                        │
│       BIGGER AND BETTER VEGETABLES            │
│                     in                        │
│               The School Hall                 │
│       Thursday, 26 January at 8.30 p.m.       │
│               Admission: Free                 │
│                                               │
└─────────────────────────────────────────────┘
```

Here are some of the questions which could possibly be asked on this poster: Where's the lecture? When's the next public lecture? Who is the speaker? What's he speaking on? What date is the lecture? What day is it? What time is the lecture? What's the price of admission? What's on in the School Hall on Thursday? etc. Rules and regulations can be used in the same way.

If you have a map on your information desk, learners can also ask directions. "Where's X street? Where's the post-office?" etc.

Envelopes from old letters can be distributed to the class and the learners can ask one another various questions, about the letters, such as: "Where's the letter from?" "Who is it for?" "What's his address?" "Who sent the letter?" "When did he send it?" "When did it get here?"

3. READING GAMES
3.1 RECOGNITION GAMES
3.1.1 Matching Cards

Distribute one set of flash cards to the class and hang a duplicate set around the room. Learners compete in matching their cards with those on the wall.

3.1.2 Say the Word

Give each learner a flash card of a word or group of words. Divide the class into two teams. On a signal from you each learner takes his turn in flashing his card to his opposite number for a brief period of time which you control (by raising your hand or by blowing a whistle). During this time his opposite number must read the card.

3.1.3 **Find the Word**

Have three sets of flash cards of words and groups of words. Give one set to each team and keep one for yourself.

From your own set pick a card and hold it up for a short period of time. The first team to find the card in its own set wins a point.

3.1.4 **Roulette**

The learners join hands and form a circle. In front of each learner place a card, face down. In the centre place a stick. Make the circle of learners move around the circle of cards and stop. Then twirl the stick. When the stick comes to a stop the two learners to whom the opposite ends of the stick point must pick up the nearest card and read it. Learners who read their words correctly within a certain time make a point.

3.2 COMPREHENSION GAMES

3.2.1 **The Shop Game**

Give each team a mixed pile of cards containing the names of things to be found in three or four different shops. The team which first succeeds in sorting them all properly into the three shops where they belong wins the game.

3.2.2 **Find the Sentence**

Write on the board such sentences as:

> It is in the sky.
> It is on the water.
> We put it on our letters.
> It is in this room.

Distribute flash cards of such words as *sun, table, boat,* and *stamp* to four learners. Each learner places his flash card beside the appropriate sentence on the board.

3.2.3 **Read-and-Do Games**

Put a series of sentences on the board and number them. The sentences should be about actions which the learners are able to do and describe, for example, "Put your book on the shelf." Call out the number of a sentence and the name of a learner. The learner silently reads the sentence and does the action.

As a variant, write the words on slips of paper or on small cards. Put them into a box and pass them around. Each learner takes a card, reads the sentence and does the action. As he does the action the class says what he is doing or, after the action is completed, what he did. If the learner does the action as written he keeps the card; if not, he puts it back into the box. The learner with the greatest number of cards wins.

With young learners, make the class form a circle, with one learner in the middle holding a pile of cards on which are written sentences with actions to be mimed. The learner in the middle picks a card and flashes it before one of the learners in the circle. If the latter succeeds in reading the sentence correctly and in miming the action, he changes places with the learner in the centre.

4. WRITING GAMES

4.1 SPELLING GAMES

4.1.1 **Crossword Puzzles**

Crossword puzzles seem to be an untiring source of interest, as is attested by their continued appearance in newspapers and magazines. These crossword puzzles, however, often contain rare and archaic words which are really not worth learning; or the words may be too difficult to be of much profit to the learner of a foreign language. What is useful are the specially designed and graded crossword puzzles for different levels of foreign language learning. Booklets of such puzzles are available for English, Russian, and a number of other languages.

4.1.2 **The Magician's Game**

The learner is given the problem of changing one word into another by changing only one letter at a time. Each change must itself constitute a word. For example, change *dog* into *cat*:

DOG			CAT
dog	dot	cot	cat

This type of game is suitable for young learners and non-alphabetics.

4.2 COMPOSITION GAMES

4.2.1 **The Label Game**

The simplest form of this game is one in which the learners write the name of the object they see in the picture. To lead to complete sentences, draw on the board the picture of some sort of action, for example, of a man putting a book on the table. Point to the picture and say: "He is putting a book on the table." Now rub out the book and change it to a hat; ask the class to write the appropriate sentence. The same sort of game can be played on a flannel board.

4.2.2 Decoding Games

Ask the learner to decode a word into a message. For example: Make a message where the first letter of each word adds up to the word MOTHER.

Meeting on Thursday. Have everything ready.

Other games of this type include the rebus and the making and deciphering of anagrams.

Mechanolinguistic Method Analysis

OUTLINE

0. INTRODUCTION

1. PROGRAMMING
    1.1 Data Control Programme
    1.2 Language Analysis Programme
    1.3 Method Analysis Programme
        1.3.1 Routine S (Selection)
        1.3.2 Routine G (Gradation)
        1.3.3 Routine P (Presentation)
        1.3.4 Routine R (Repetition)

2. PRE-EDITING
    2.1 Pre-editing Pictorial Material
    2.2 Pre-editing Textual Material

3. MACHINE ANALYSIS

4. POST-EDITING

0. INTRODUCTION

The great amount of manual compilation and computation necessary in method analysis can be greatly reduced by the use of digital computers. The use of such electronic equipment also makes possible operations which are impracticable by hand.

Since computers are now part of the standard equipment of many universities and boards of education, their use in method analysis becomes a practical proposition. Although any computer can be helpful, the time and amount of work saved depend, of course, on the type used. Since details depend on the type of computer and the sort of linguistic analysis available, only general directions can be given here. The sum of these directions can be known as mechanolinguistic method analysis.

Mechanolinguistic method analysis is the use of mechanolinguistic disciplines in the analysis of language teaching methods. These disciplines include computation of language statistics, linguistic automation (automatic searching, indexing, abstracting and translating), automatic linguistic analysis, and information retrieval.

The two basic requirements of mechanolinguistic method analysis are: (i) the ability to formulate the procedures of the analysis, and (ii) the skill to translate these into machine operations. For the sole function of the digital computer is simply to follow instructions. What it does at any moment depends only on what it has been told to do. A complete sequence of what a computer has been told to do is known as a programme.

After the start button is pressed, the computer takes in the first part of the programme. What it does next depends on what it has taken in. The initial operation may be to bring the programme itself into the storage section of the machine from previously prepared punch-cards or tape. All eventual operations depend on information now located in the storage section, the index register, and the computation section of the computer. The judicious use of these sections and the preparation of texts to go in them is what mechanolinguistic method analysis is about.

Mechanolinguistic method analysis requires four operations: 1. Programming, 2. Pre-Editing, 3. Machine Analysis, and 4. Post-Editing.

1. PROGRAMMING

The programming requires three all-over programmes: 1. The Data Control Programme, 2. The Language Analysis Programme, and 3. The Method Analysis Programme.

1.1 DATA CONTROL PROGRAMME

This programme includes the mechanization of control lists, comprising

454

all the information outside the method itself which may be used as criteria for analysis and measurement. This includes such things as word-lists marking the frequency, range, availability and word-classes of each word. If data from more than one list is required, the computer can be used to combine a number of lists into a more reliable one. It also makes possible the continual revision of the lists by the addition of the results of more recent research. The lists may include grammatical, semantic and even phonological data. It is important, therefore, to be well documented on available language statistics (see Bibliography 6 and 1.3.8).

1.2 LANGUAGE ANALYSIS PROGRAMME

This is a programme which permits the analysis of any text to the extent that the sophistication of the computer-type and advances in mechano-linguistics permit. In some cases even automatic syntactic analysis may be possible; in others, only the identification of phrase structures can be counted on, provided their boundaries are marked off beforehand.

Any effort put into the coding of control lists and the programming of automatic language analysis is well worth while since this material can be used over and over again to process any number of methods in the same language. Techniques for the determination of word-classes and meanings by context searching must be considered along with available procedures of automatic language analysis (see Bibliography 1.3.9).

1.3 METHOD ANALYSIS PROGRAMME

This programme includes four routines: 1. Selection (S), 2. Gradation (G), 3. Presentation (P), 4. Repetition (R).

1.3.1 Routine S (Selection)

S = Q (Quantity), P (Proportion), U (Utility).

(i) *Subroutines of Q (Quantity)*

Q = Count all types (different items) in text: 1. Sentence Structures—SQS. 3. Clause Structures—SQC. 3. Phrase Structure—SQP. 4. Inflection Forms—SQI. 5. Structure Words—SQW. 6. Nouns—SQN. 7. Verbs—SQV. 8. Adjectives—SQA. 9. Adverbs—SQD. 10. Total lexical vocabulary (nouns, verbs, adjectives, adverbs)—SQT.

(ii) *Subroutines of P (Proportion)*

P = Compute the percentages in SQT (total lexical vocabulary) of: 1. Nouns—SPN. 2. Verbs—SPV. 3. Adjectives—SPA. Adverbs—SPD.

Appendix C: Mechanolinguistic Method Analysis

(iii) *Subroutines of U (Utility)*

U = In data control programme find relevant figures (frequency, range, availability) for each item in text. Add and average in each case to give relative: 1. Frequency—SUF. 2. Range—SUR. 3. Availability—SUA.

1.3.2 Routine G (Gradation)

G = T (Textual productivity), C (Combinatorial Productivity), D (Productivity Differential), G (Productivity Gap), I (Intake), R (Rate of Intake).

(i) *Subroutines of T (Textual Productivity)*

T = Total all: 1. Phrases—GTP. 2. Clauses—GTC. 3. Sentences—GTS.

(ii) *Subroutines of C (Combinatorial Productivity)*

C = List relevant structure types. Taking one structure at a time, place in each position—V (Verb), N (Noun), etc.—the corresponding S totals SQV, SQN, etc. Multiply totals in each position of each structure. Select the median. Add the products for all: 1. Phrase Structures—GCP. 2. Clause Structures—GCC. 3. Sentence Structures—GCS.

(iii) *Subroutines of D (Productivity Differential)*

D = What percentage of GC is GT as regards: 1. Phrases—GDP. 2. Clauses—GDC. 3. Sentences—GDS.

(iv) *Subroutines of R (Productivity Rates)*

R = Repeat GC subroutine sequentially for each cumulative 100-token level up to figures for GCP, GCC, GCS. List sequence of R figures for: 1. Phrase Rates—GRP. 2. Clause Rates—GRC. 3. Sentence Rates—GRS.

(v) *Subroutines of G (Productivity Gap)*

G = Repeat GD subroutine sequentially for each cumulative 100-token level; list sequence of G figures for: 1. Phrase Gap—GGP. 2. Clause Gap—GGC. 3. Sentence Gap—GGS.

(vi) *Subroutines of I (Intake)*

I = Total tokens in text; total types in text. Express total types as percentage of total tokens to give figures for: 1. Sentence Intake—GIS. 2. Clause Intake—GIC. 3. Phrase Intake—GIP. 4. Structure-Word Intake

456

—GIW. 5. Noun Intake—GIN. 6. Verb Intake—GIV. 7. Adjective Intake
—GIA. 8. Adverb Intake—GID.

(vii) *Subroutines of K (Intake Rates)*

K = Repeat GI subroutine sequentially for each cumulative 100-token level. List resulting sequence of K figures for: 1. Rate of Sentence Intake—GKS. 2. Rate of Clause Intake—GKC. 3. Rate of Phrase Intake—GKP. 4. Rate of Structure-Word Intake—GKW. 5. Rate of Noun Intake—GKN. 6. Rate of Verb Intake—GKV. 7. Rate of Adjective Intake—GKA. 8. Rate of Adverb Intake—GKD.

1.3.3 **Routine P (Presentation)**

P = S (Staging), C (Spacing), P (Procedure).

(i) *Subroutines of S (Staging)*

S = Group final-position marginal textual sigla (2.2 below) as follows: Listening (*l*, *x*) PSL, Speaking (*e*, *i*, *o*) PSS, Reading (*r*, *s*, *v*) PSR, and Writing (*a*, *c*, *d*, *f*, *q*, *t*, *w*) PSW. Which is represented first, second, third, and fourth?

(ii) *Subroutines of C (Staging)*

C = Indicate number of word-tokens between PSL, PSS, PSR, PSW.
1. Listening (word-tokens between PSL and next skill)—PCL
2. Speaking (word-tokens between PSS and next skill)—PCS
3. Reading (word-tokens between PSR and next skill)—PCR
4. Writing (word-tokens between PSW and next skill)—PCW

(iii) *Subroutines of P (Procedure)*

P = In each case, express second total as percentage of first.
1. Pictorial Procedures (First total: SQS+SQC+SQP+SQI+SQW+ SQT. Second total: Total all instances of initial *p* and *x* in material marked with pictorial sigla—see 2.1)—PPP.
2. Differential Procedures (First total: SQS+SQC+SQP+SQI+SQW +SQT. Second total: Total word-tokens in parts of text marked by textual sigla with *z* in final position)—PPD.

1.3.4 **Routine R (Repetition)**

R = R (Rate of Recurrence), D (Distribution of Recurrence), T (Type of Repetition), S (Skill Ratio), V (Variety of Repetition), C (Verbal Contextualization), P (Pictorial Contextualization).

Appendix C: Mechanolinguistic Method Analysis

(i) *Subroutines of R* (*Rate of Recurrence*)

R = For each type (different word or structure) tally corresponding tokens (number of times it appears) in all parts of text (including those derived from films and recordings). Arrange in order of increasing magnitude and select median for: 1. Sentence Structure Rate—RRS. 2. Clause Structure Rate—RRC. 3. Phrase Structure Rate—RRP. 4. Structure-Word Rate—RRW. 5. Noun Rate—RRN. 6. Verb Rate—RRV. 7. Adjective Rate—RRA. 8. Adverb Rate—RRD.

(ii) *Subroutines of D* (*Distribution of Recurrence*)

D = Total new types in each additional 100-token segment. Number of subsequent 100-token segments in which each type reappears. Number of types reappearing in one subsequent segment, in two, in three, etc. . . . to end. In what percentage of subsequent segments does each type recur? Median percentages represent: 1. Sentence Structure Distribution—RDS. 2. Clause Structure Distribution—RDC. 3. Phrase Structure Distribution —RDP. 4. Structure-Word Distribution—RDW. 5. Noun Distribution— RDN. 6. Verb Distribution—RDV. 7. Adjective Distribution—RDA. 8. Adverb Distribution—RDD.

(iii) *Subroutines of V* (*Variety of Repetition*)

V = Total all word-tokens in parts of text marked with textual sigla, except where last letter is x or z. Total word-tokens for each part of text marked by textual sigla according to difference of letter in final position, and express as percentage of first total.

1. Copying and imitation (c)—RVC. 2. Dictation and transcription (d)—RVD. 3. Reading aloud (e)—RVE. 4. Incremental imitation (i)—RVI. 5. Filling in blanks (f)—RVF. 6. Selecting alternatives (s)—RVS. 7. Altering forms (a)—RVA. 8. Paraphrasing and rephrasing (p)—RVP. 9. Questions and answers (q)—RVQ. 10. Composition (w, o)—RVM. 11. Translating into vernacular (v)—RVV. 12. Translating from the vernacular (t)— RVT. 13. Listening (l)—RVL. 14. Reading (r)—RVR.

(iv) *Subroutines of T* (*Types of Repetition*)

T = Take the average.
1. Rote (RVC + RVD + RVE)—RTR
2. Incremental (RVI)—RTI
3. Variational (RVF + RVS + RVA + RVP)—RTV
4. Operational (RVQ + RVM + RVV + RVT + RVL + RVR)—RTO

(v) *Subroutines of S (Skill Ratios)*

S = Total word-tokens in all texts; total word-tokens for each skill and express as percentage of total word-tokens, obtaining figures by adding word-tokens of skills marked by marginal sigla for:
1. Listening (*r* +*s* in second position)—RSL
2. Speaking (*s* + *p* in second position)—RSS
3. Reading (all tokens in printed texts)—RSR
4. Writing (*o* in second position, except if *x, z, e, l, o, i,* or *r* is final)—RSW

(vi) *Subroutines of C (Verbal contextualization)*

C = Total all word-tokens; add word-tokens in each of the following contexts marked by third position in textual sigla, and express as percentage of first total: 1. Dialogue (*d*)—RCD. 2. Prose (*p*)—RCP. 3. Verse (*v*)—RCV. 4. Song (*m*)—RCM.

(vii) *Subroutines of P (Pictorial contextualization)*

P = Total sentence-tokens in all texts; total pictures (initial *p* or *x* in pictorial sigla) in each of the following, and express as percentage of total sentence-tokens:
1. Textual (*t, e,* or *r* in final position)—RPT
2. Class material (*h, a,* or *g* in final position)—RPC
3. Film-strips and slides (*i,* or *x* in final position)—RPF
4. Motion picture films (*c* in final position)—RPM

Once the three programmes—data control, language analysis and method analysis—have thus been completed have them put on punch-cards or tape. They constitute a permanent instrument of analysis since they have to be elaborated only once and may serve for the measurement of any number of methods. Pre-editing, on the other hand, has to be done for each method.

2. PRE-EDITING

Once the programmes of analysis are completed, the next step is to prepare the methods for analysis by the machine. Since there are certain distinctions which computers are unable to make unless told to do so, a certain amount of editing is necessary before putting the method into the machine. The amount of pre-editing needed depends on how much of the analysis can be programmed for the computer, and this in turn depends largely on the type of machine used.

Appendix C: Mechanolinguistic Method Analysis

The pre-editing can take the form of standardized abbreviations noted in the margin of the text, workbooks, and scripts of accompanying filmed or recorded material.

In pre-editing, one must make a distinction between two types of material—1. Pictorial, and 2. Textual.

2.1 PRE-EDITING PICTORIAL MATERIAL

Pictorial material may be indicated marginally, or on a separate sheet, by the use of a three-letter sign in miniscules. The first letter can be used to indicate whether or not the picture accompanies a text or caption; the second letter can indicate transmission, by distribution or display (including projection); and the third letter can show the type (textbook, exercise book, reader, wall-picture, picture-card, flannel-graph, slide, film-strip or motion picture). This gives us the following:

Pictorial Sigla

	1st position	2nd position	3rd position
1. *Captioning:*			
Titled	p		
Untitled	x		
2. *Transmission*			
Distribution		b	
Display		d	
3. *Type:*			
Textbook			t
Exercise-book			e
Reader			r
Wall-picture			h
Picture-card			a
Flannel-graph			g
Slide			i
Film-strip			x
Motion-picture			c

Examples: *pbt* indicates one captioned picture in the textbook; *xbt* marks an uncaptioned picture in the textbook.

If a series of pictures occurs, simply count the number of pictures and indicate the total after the sigla. For example, *xdx* 16 indicates a film-strip of 16 uncaptioned frames. In the case of composite pictures with a number of captions on different parts of the picture, add one for each caption; for example, *pdh* 6 is a wall-picture (1) with five different items (5) which have their own captions. For motion-picture films, express the total in minutes of running time.

460

2.2 PRE-EDITING TEXTUAL MATERIAL

Whatever the media in which the actual text of the method may appear, it must, in order to be edited, be made available in written form. Secondly, since the digital computer deals with units in sequence, it is important that the beginning and end of any section of the running text of a given type be marked in advance. This can be done by writing in, at appropriate points in the margin, a number of four-letter sigla whose letters represent respectively: 1. media, 2. form, 3. genre and 4. function. This gives us the following:

Textual Sigla

	1st position	2nd position	3rd position	4th position
1. *Media*				
Book, brochure, etc	*b*			
Display material	*w*			
Recorded on tape	*t*			
Recorded on disc	*d*			
Recorded on film	*f*			
2. *Form*				
Recorded but unspaced		*r*		
Recorded and spaced		*s*		
In phonetic notation		*p*		
In ordinary orthography		*o*		
3. *Genre*				
Narrative, descriptive, or expository prose			*p*	
Verse			*v*	
Song with music or notes			*m*	
Dialogue			*d*	
Isolated or listed sentences			*s*	
Isolated or listed phrases or fixed formulas			*f*	
Isolated or listed words			*w*	
4. *Function*				
For practice in reading				*r*
For listening				*l*
Explanation in language being taught				*x*
Explanation in vernacular				*z*

Copying or imitation	*c*
Dictation or transcription	*d*
Reading aloud	*e*
Incremental imitation	*i*
Filling in blanks	*f*
Selecting alternatives	*s*
Altering forms	*a*
Paraphrasing and rephrasing	*p*
Questions and answers	*q*
Oral composition	*o*
Written composition	*w*
To be translated from the vernacular	*t*
To be translated into the vernacular	*v*

Examples: *tsdc* indicates the boundaries of a section of material recorded on tape, spaced, appearing in dialogue form, and used for imitation practice; *bopr* is material in a book, written in ordinary orthography, representing a prose-passage used for reading practice. A method thus edited is ready to be put on tape or on punch-cards, in order to be ready for machine analysis.

3. MACHINE ANALYSIS

We should have on punch-cards or tape three programmes and the entire texts of one or more methods. We can now put these into the machine: 1. Data control programme. 2. Language analysis programme. 3. Method analysis programme—in that order. And we programme the machine so that it also processes the text in that order. Finally we feed the text of the method into the machine from previously prepared punch-cards or tape and press the start button.

What happens then is a successive, automatic comparison of each item in the text of the method with items in each of the programmes. This automatic analysis may be interrupted at any stage for checking or modification. This may be done by having the printer of the computer system type out the results of the analysis up to that point.

4. POST-EDITING

The amount of post-editing required depends on the efficiency of the programming, on the amount of pre-editing and on the capacity of the computer.

Post-editing may begin at any time after the text of the method has been fed into the machine. Even at the first stage, where the text goes through the data control programme, it may be desirable to have the machine print out these first results either in order to check them or to complete them by hand.

The first results will come out on a wide roll of paper on which the running text of the method appears vertically, with analytical indications besides each word or group of words. In this way, ambiguous or false analysis may easily be spotted and rectified before proceeding further with the programme.

It is wise at each stage of the analysis to check the results in this way until one is sure that the programmes are doing the sort of work they were designed to do.

When the final figures come out of the printer, they will have to be gathered and plotted on the appropriate graphs and profiles to produce the sort of image which may be easily read and readily used (see Chapter 10).

Topical Bibliography

Within each section, books and separately published works are listed before articles; the lists are separated by the sign (* * *). Recent works are listed first. Articles appearing in the same publication are grouped together and arranged in reverse chronological order.

Contents

INDEX TO PERIODICALS

1 *AL* Acta Linguistica. Copenhagen (Denmark)

2 *AS* American Speech. A Quarterly of Linguistic Usage. New York (U.S.A.)

3 *Anglia* Anglia. Zeitschrift für englische Philologie. Tübingen (Germany)

4 *AnL* Anthropological Linguistics. Bloomington: Indiana University Department of Anthropology (U.S.A.)

5 *ArchL* Archivum Linguisticum. A review of comparative philology and general linguistics. Glasgow: Jackson (U.K.)

6 *Ba* Babel. Journal of Translation. Official Organ of the International Federation of Translators. Berlin: Langenscheidt (Germany)

7 *Babel* Babel. Journal of the Modern Language Teachers' Association of Victoria. Melbourne (Australia)

8 *BSLP* Bulletin de la Société de linguistique de Paris. Paris (France)

9 *BNML* Bulletin of the New England Modern Language Association. (U.S.A.)

10 *CFS* Cahiers Ferdinand de Saussure. Geneva (Switzerland)

10a *CL* Cahiers de lexicologie. Besançon (France)

11 *CLS* Cahiers de linguistique structurale (*Renamed in* 1961 *as* Cahiers de la psychomécanique du langage). Quebec: Presses de l'Université Laval (Canada)

11a *CMLR* The Canadian Modern Language Review. Published by the Ontario Modern Language Teachers' Association. Toronto (Canada)

12 *Contact* Contact. Publication de la Fédération internationale des professeurs de langues vivantes. Amsterdam: Meulenhoff (Netherlands)

13 *Du* Der Deutschunterricht. Beiträge zu seiner Praxis und wissenschaftlichen Grundlegung. Stuttgart (Germany)

14 *DuA* Deutschunterricht für Ausländer. Zeitschrift für Unterrichtsmethodik und sprachlichen Austausch. Munich (Germany)

15 *EGS* English and Germanic Studies. Cambridge (U.K.)

15a *ELA* Etudes de linguistique appliquée. Publication du Centre de linguistique appliquée de la Faculté des lettres de Besançon. Paris: Didier (France)

16 *ELT* English Language Teaching. London: Oxford U.P. (U.K.)

17 *ENL* English: A New Language. A bulletin for teachers of New Australians in continuation classes. Sydney: Commonwealth Office of Education (Australia)

18 *ES* English Studies. A Journal of English Letters and Philology. Amsterdam (Netherlands)

18a *ETA* English Teaching Abstracts. A quarterly review of studies related to English language teaching appearing in current periodicals. London: British Council (U.K.)

19 *Etc.* ETC. A Review of General Semantics. Chicago (U.S.A.)

20 *FdM* Le français dans le monde. Paris (France)

21	*FM*	Le français moderne. Paris (France)
22	*FR*	The French Review. Baltimore (U.S.A.)
23	*GL*	General Linguistics. Lexington (Ky.) (U.S.A.)
24	*GUMSL*	Georgetown University Monograph Series on Languages and Linguistics. Washington (U.S.A.)
25	*GQ*	The German Quarterly. Cincinnati (U.S.A.)
26	*Hispania*	Hispania. A Teacher's Journal devoted to the Teaching of Spanish and Portuguese. Washington (U.S.A.)
27	*IJaS*	Inostrannye jazyki v škole (Foreign Languages in School). Moscow (U.S.S.R.)
28	*IJAL*	The International Journal of American Linguistics. Baltimore (U.S.A.)
28a	*IRAL*	International Review of Applied Linguistics in Language Teaching. Heidelberg (Germany)
29	*Italica*	Italica. The Quarterly Bulletin of the American Association of Teachers of Italian. Evanston (Ill.) (U.S.A.)
30	*JAcS*	Journal of the Acoustical Society of America. New York (U.S.A.)
31	*JCLA*	Journal of the Canadian Linguistic Association/Revue de l'Association canadienne de linguistique (*Renamed in* 1961 *as the* Canadian Journal of Linguistics/Revue canadienne de linguistique). Toronto & Montreal (Canada)
32	*JEGPh*	The Journal of English and Germanic Philology. Urbana (Ill.) (U.S.A.)
33	*JT*	Journal des traducteurs. Services internationaux de traduction. Montreal (Canada)
33a	*JVL*	Journal of Verbal Learning and Verbal Behavior. New York: Academic Press (U.S.A.)
34	*Lg*	Language. Journal of the Linguistic Society of America. Baltimore (U.S.A.)
35	*LL*	Language Learning. A Journal of Applied Linguistics. Ann Arbor (Mich.) (U.S.A.)
36	*LM*	Les langues modernes. Paris (France)
37	*Lingua*	Lingua. International Review of General Linguistics/Revue internationale de linguistique générale. Amsterdam (Netherlands)
38	*Ling*	Linguistica. Ljubljana (Yugoslavia)
39	*LR*	The Linguistic Reporter. Newsletter of the Center for Applied Linguistics of the Modern Language Association of America. Washington (U.S.A.)
40	*L&S*	Language and Speech. Teddington (Mdx.) (U.K.)
41	*MDU*	Monatsheft für deutschen Unterricht. Madison (Wis.) (U.S.A.)
42	*ML*	Modern Languages. Journal of the Modern Language Association. London (U.K.)
43	*MLF*	Modern Language Forum. Los Angeles (U.S.A.)
44	*MLJ*	Modern Language Journal. Ann Arbor (Mich.) (U.S.A.)
45	*MLN*	Modern Language Notes. Baltimore (U.S.A.)
46	*MLQ*	Modern Language Quarterly. Seattle (Wash.) (U.S.A.)
47	*MLR*	The Modern Language Review. Cambridge (U.K.)

48 *MPhon*   Le Maître Phonétique. Organe de l'Association phonétique internationale. London: University College (U.K.)

49 *MST*   The MST English Quarterly. Organ of the Teachers of English in Manila Public Schools. Manila (Philippines)

50 *MT*   Mechanical Translation. Devoted to the translation of languages with the aid of machines. Cambridge (Mass.): Massachusetts Institute of Technology (U.S.A.)

51 *NS*   Die neueren Sprachen. Vereinigt mit den Fachzeitschriften "Die lebenden Fremdsprachen" und "Neuphilologische Zeitschrift". Frankfurt (Main) (Germany)

52 *Orbis*   Orbis. Bulletin international de documentation linguistique. Louvain (Belgium)

53 *Phonetica*   Phonetica. Internationale Zeitschrift für Phonetik/International Journal of Phonetics. Basel & New York

53a *PJLT*   Philippine Journal for Language Teaching. Quezon City: University of the Philippines (Philippines)

54 *PMLA*   Publications of the Modern Language Society of America. New York (U.S.A.)

55 *RJaS*   Russkij jazyk v nacional'noj škole (The Russian Language in the National Schools). Moscow (U.S.S.R.)

56 *RLaV*   Revue des langues vivantes/Tijdschrift voor Levende Talen. Brussels (Belgium)

57 *RLing*   Revue de linguistique. Bucarest (Rumania)

58 *Sf*   Sprachforum. Zeitschrift für angewandte Sprachwissenschaft. Münster & Cologne (Germany)

59 *SMIL*   Statistical Methods in Linguistics. Stockholm: Språkförlaget Skriptor (Sweden)

60 *SIL*   Studies in Linguistics. Washington & Buffalo (U.S.A.)

61 *SL*   Studia Linguistica. Revue de linguistique générale et comparée. Lund (Sweden)

62 *SNPh*   Studia Neophilologica. A Journal of Germanic and Romanic Philology. Upsala (Sweden)

63 *Sprache*   Die Sprache. Zeitschrift für Sprachwissenschaft. Vienna (Austria)

63a *SRA*   Studia Romanica et Anglica Zagrebiensia. Zagreb: Faculté de philosophie de l'Université. (Yugoslavia)

63b *TA*   La traduction automatique. Bulletin trimestriel de l'association pour l'étude et le développement de la traduction automatique et de la linguistique appliquée (ATALA). The Hague: Mouton (Netherlands)

64 *TCLC*   Travaux du Cercle linguistique de Copenhague. Copenhagen (Denmark)

65 *TCLP*   Travaux du Cercle linguistique de Prague. Prague (Czechoslovakia)

66 *TE*   Teaching English. A Magazine Devoted to the Teaching of the English Language in India. Calcutta: Orient Longmans (India)

67 *TIL*   Travaux de l'Institut de linguistique. Paris: Faculté des lettres de l'Université. (France)

68 *TPS*   Transactions of the Philological Society. Oxford (U.K.)

69	*UCPL*	University of California Publications in Linguistics. Berkeley & Los Angeles (U.S.A.)
70	*VJa*	Voprosy Jazykoznanija. Moscow (U.S.S.R.)
71	*VR*	Vox Romanica. Annales Helvetici explorandis linguis Romanicis destinati. Bern (Switzerland)
72	*Word*	Word. Journal of the Linguistic Circle of New York. New York (U.S.A.)
73	*YWES*	The Year's Work in English Studies. London (U.K.)
74	*YWMLS*	The Year's Work in Modern Language Studies. London (U.K.)
75	*ZPhon*	Zeitschrift für Phonetik, Sprachwissenschaft und Kommunikationsforschung. Berlin: Akademie-Verlag (Germany)

1. SOURCES OF LANGUAGE THEORY

1.1 STUDIES OF LANGUAGE THEORY

1.1.1 Analyses of Language Theory

75a M. Leroy, *Les grands courants de la linguistique moderne*. Brussels: Université libre de Bruxelles 1964

76 P. Hartmann, *Zur Theorie der Sprachwissenschaft*. Assen: Van Gorcum 1961

77 W. F. Mackey, *The Correlation of Linguistic Theories*. Monograph presented to the Canadian Linguistic Association. (mimeographed) June 1959

78 N. L. Wilson, *The Concept of Language*. Toronto: Toronto U.P. 1959

79 H. Güntert, *Grundfragen der Sprachwissenschaft*. (2 ed. rev. by A. Scherer) Heidelberg: Quelle & Meyer 1956

80 G. Pätsch, *Grundfragen der Sprachtheorie*. Halle: Niemeyer 1955

81 W. Luther, *Weltansicht und Geistesleben* (From Homer to Aristotle). Göttingen: Vandenhoeck & Ruprecht 1954

82 B. Malmberg, *Système et méthode*. Lund: Gleerup 1945

* * *

82a W. F. Mackey, A Framework for the Analysis of Language Theories, *Pre-prints of Papers for the Ninth International Congress of Linguists*, Cambridge (Mass.): M.I.T. 1962

83 A. V. Fedorov, Osnovnye voprosy teorii jazykoznanija (Basic problems of linguistic theory), *VJa* 1: 1–22

84 J. Lohmann, "Sprachphilosophie", "Sprachtheorie", und "Allgemeine Sprachwissenschaft", *ZPhon* 5: 59–64

85 A. S. C. Ross, Theory of Language, *EGS* 4: 1–12

86 H. Ammann, Sprachwissenschaft und Sprachtheorie, *Du* 2: 173–79

87 H. Pedersen, Ist eine allgemeine Sprachwissenschaft auf empirischer Grundlage möglich?, *Archiv Orientální* 17: 236–38

88 W. F. Mackey, Fonction d'un schéma de dichotomies croisées dans la comparaison des théories du langage (summary), Montreal: *Les Annales de l'Acfas* 1959

1.1.2 Surveys of Past Language Theories

89 G. L. Bursill-Hall, *The Doctrine of Partes Orationis in the Speculative Grammars of the Modistae.* London: University of London doctorate thesis 1959

90 J. Thorne, *Theories of Language, Logic and Poetry in the Renaissance.* (MS 1959; in the press)

91 H. Arens, *Sprachwissenschaft. Der Gang ihrer Entwicklung von der Antike bis zur Gegenwart.* Freiburg & Munich: Alber 1955

92 P. Chakravarti, *The Linguistic Speculations of the Hindus.* Calcutta: Calcutta U.P. 1953

93 W. S. Allen, *Phonetics in Ancient India.* London: Oxford U.P. 1953

94 R. H. Robins, *Ancient and Mediaeval Grammatical Theory in Europe. With particular reference to modern linguistic doctrines.* London: Bell 1951

95 H. Pedersen, *Linguistic Science in the Nineteenth Century: Methods and Results.* (trans. J. Spargo) Cambridge (Mass.): Harvard 1931 (Reprinted as *The Discovery of Language*, Bloomington: Indiana U.P. 1962)

*   *   *

96 J. Brough, Theories of General Linguistics in the Sanskrit Grammarians, *TPS* 1951: 27–46

96a B. Collinder, Les origines du structuralisme, *Acta Societatis Linguisticae Upsaliensis* 1: 1–15

1.1.3 Surveys of Present-day Theories

97 C. Mohrmann, A. Sommerfelt & J. Whatmough (eds.), *Trends in European and American Linguistics: 1930–1960.* Utrecht: Spectrum 1961

98 P. Guiraud, *La grammaire.* Paris: Presses universitaires 1958

99 R. N. Anshen (ed.), *Language: an enquiry into its meaning and function.* New York: Harper 1957

100 D. C. Menéndez-Pidal, *La escuela lingüística española y su concepción del lenguaje.* Madrid: Románica Hispánica 1955

101 H. Spang-Hanssen, *Recent Theories on the Nature of the Language Sign.* Copenhagen: Nordisk Sprog- og Kulturforlag 1954

*   *   *

102 A. Sommerfelt, Tendances actuelles de la linguistique générale, *Diogène* 1: 77–84

103 G. Herdan, Linguistic Philosophy in the Light of Modern Linguistics, *L&S* 3: 78–85

104 E. Haugen, Directions in Modern Linguistics, *Lg* 27: 211–22

105 M. Leroy, Tendances au doctrinarisme dans la pensée linguistique contemporaine, in *Mélanges G. Smets.* Brussels 1952

106 E. Benveniste, Tendances récentes en linguistique générale, *J. de Psychologie normale et pathologique* 47: 130–45

107 D. Vuysje, The Psycho-linguistic Movement in Holland, *Philosophy of Science* 18: 262–68

108 R. A. Hall, Schools of Linguistics: the old curiosity shop, *SIL* 8: 59–68

(See also **75a** and **77**)

1.2 GENERAL THEORIES

1.2.1 Saussurian

109 F. de Saussure, *Course in General Linguistics*. (trans. of **113** by W. Baskins) New York: Philosophical Library 1959
110 R. Godel, *Les sources manuscrites du Cours de linguistique générale de F. de Saussure*. Geneva: Droz 1957
111 C. Bally, *Linguistique générale et linguistique française*. (2 ed.) Bern: Francke 1944, (4 ed.) 1965
112 A. Sechehaye, *Essai sur la structure logique de la phrase*. Paris: Champion 1926
113 F. de Saussure, *Cours de linguistique générale*. Paris: Payot 1915, 1931, 1949, 1955
114 C. A. Sechehaye, *Programme et méthodes de la linguistique théorique*. Geneva: Eggimann 1908

*   *   *

115 H. Frei, La linguistique saussurienne à Genève depuis 1939, *AL* 5: 54–56
116 F. de Saussure, Cours de linguistique générale (1908–1909): Introduction, *CFS* 15: 1–103
117 H. Frei, Saussure contre Saussure?, *CFS* 9: 7–28
118 A. J. Greimas, L'actualité du saussurisme, *FM* 24: 191–203
119 H. Frei, Langue, parole et différenciation, *J. de Psychologie normale et pathologique* 45: 137–57
120 R. Godel, L'école saussurienne de Genève, in *Trends* (see No. **97** above): 294–98
121 A. Sechehaye, Les trois linguistiques saussuriennes, *VR* 5: 7–48
122 R. S. Wells, De Saussure's System of Linguistics, *Word* 3: 1–31

1.2.2 Bloomfieldian

123 M. Joos (ed.), *Readings in Linguistics. The development of descriptive linguistics in America since 1925*. Washington: American Council of Learned Societies 1957
124 G. L. Trager, *The Field of Linguistics: SIL Occasional Paper I*, Norman (Okla): Battenburg 1950
125 L. Bloomfield, *Outline Guide for the Practical Study of Foreign Languages*. Baltimore: Linguistic Society of America 1942
126 B. Bloch & G. L. Trager, *Outline of Linguistic Analysis*. Baltimore: Linguistic Society of America 1942
127 L. Bloomfield, *Linguistic Aspects of Science*. (*Internat. Encyclopedia of Unified Science*). Chicago: Chicago U.P. 1939
128 L. Bloomfield, *Language*. New York: Holt 1933

*   *   *

129 L. Bloomfield, A Set of Postulates for the Science of Language, *IJAL* 15: 195–201
130 A. A. Hill, Linguistics since Bloomfield, *Quarterly Journal of Speech* 41: 253–60

131 C. C. Fries, The Bloomfield 'School', in *Trends* (see No. **97** above): 196–224
132 M. M. Guchman, Lingvističeskij mexanizm L. Blumfilda i deskrip▸ tivnaja lingvistika, *Trudy Instituta Jazykoznanija* 4: 111–89

1.2.3 Firthian

133 M. A. K. Halliday, *The Language of the Chinese "Secret History of the Mongols"*. (Introduction.) Oxford: Blackwell 1959
134 J. R. Firth, *Papers in Linguistics* (1934–1951). London: Oxford U.P. 1957
135 Philological Society of Great Britain, *Studies in Linguistic Analysis*. Oxford: Blackwell 1957

* * *

136 R. H. Robins, Some Considerations on the Status of Grammar in Linguistics, *ArchL* 11: 91–114
137 J. R. Firth, Ethnographic Analysis and Language with reference to Malinowski's Views, in *Man and Culture: An Evaluation of the Works of Malinowski*. London: Routledge & Kegan Paul 1957
138 R. H. Robins, Aspects of Prosodic Analysis, *Proc. of Univ. of Durham Philos. Soc.* 1957: 1–12
139 T. F. Mitchell, Syntagmatic Relations in Linguistic Analysis, *TPS* 1958: 101–18
140 F. R. Palmer, Comparative Statement and Ethiopian Semitic, *TPS* 1958: 119–143
141 J. R. Firth, Applications of General Linguistics, *TPS* 1957: 1–14
142 M. A. K. Halliday, Grammatical Categories in Modern Chinese, *TPS* 1956: 177–224
143 J. R. Firth, Structural Linguistics, *TPS* 1955: 83–103
144 J. R. Firth, General Linguistics and Descriptive Grammar, *TPS* 1951: 69–87
145 M. A. K. Halliday, Categories of the Theory of Grammar, *Word* 17: 241–92

(See also **450***a*)

1.2.4 Glossematics

146 L. Hjelmslev, *Prolegomena to a Theory of Language* (trans. F. J. Whitfield). Madison: Wisconsin U.P. 1961
147 L. Hjelmslev, *Essais linguistiques*. Copenhagen: Nordisk Sprog- og Kulturforlag 1959
148 H. Spang-Hanssen, *Probability and Structural Classification in Language
1 Description*. Copenhagen: Rosenkilde & Bagger 1959
49 E. Richer, *La glossématique ou le triomphe de la forme linguistique*. Montreal: Section de linguistique de l'Université de Montréal 1958
150 L. Hjelmslev & H. J. Uldall, *Outline of Glossematics. A study in the methodology of the humanities with special reference to linguistics*. Copenhagen: Nordisk Sprog- og Kulturforlag 1957
151 B. Siertsema, *A Study of Glossematics. Critical survey of its fundamental concepts*. The Hague: Nijhoff 1955

152 Cercle Linguistique de Copenhague, *Recherches structurales 1949. Interventions dans le débat glossématique. Publiées à l'occasion du cinquantenaire de M. Louis Hjelmslev.* Copenhagen: Nordisk Sprog- og Kulturforlag 1949

153 Cercle linguistique de Copenhague, *Etudes linguistiques 1944.* Copenhagen: Munksgaard 1945

154 L. Hjelmslev, *Omkring Sprogteoriens Grundlaeggelse.* (English trans., No. **146** above) Copenhagen: Munksgaard 1943

*   *   *

155 W. Haas, Concerning Glossematics, *AL* 8: 93: 110
156 L. Hjelmslev, La comparaison en linguistique structurale, *AL* 4: 144
157 H. Spang-Hanssen, Glossematics, in *Trends* (see No. **97** above): 128–64
158 L. Hjelmslev, La stratification du langage, *Word* 10: 163–88

1.2.5 Psychomechanics

158a G. Guillaume, *Langage et science du langage.* Paris: Nizet 1963
159 G. Guillaume, *L'architectonique du temps dans les langues classiques.* Copenhagen: Munksgaard 1945
160 G. Guillaume, *Temps et verbe.* Paris: Champion 1929

*   *   *

161 R. Valin, La méthode comparative en linguistique historique et en psychomécanique du langage, *CLS* 6
162 R. Valin, Petite introduction à la psychomécanique du langage, *CLS* 3
163 R. Valin, Esquisse d'une théorie des degrés de comparaison, *CLS* 2
164 G. Guillaume, La langue est-elle ou n'est-elle pas un système?, *CLS* 1
165 G. Guillaume, Psycho-systématique et psycho-sémiologie du langage, *FM* 21: 122–36

(See also 270 and 868)

1.2.6 Prague School

166 R. Jakobson & M. Halle, *Fundamentals of Language.* The Hague: Mouton 1956

167 R. Jakobson, C. G. Fant & M. Halle, *Preliminaries to Speech Analysis.* Cambridge (Mass.): M.I.T. Acoustics Laboratory 1955

168 N. S. Trubetzkoy, *Principes de Phonologie.* (trans. of **173** by J. Cantineau) Paris: Klincksieck 1949

*   *   *

169 J. Vachek, Notes on the Development of Language seen as a System of Systems, *J. de la Faculté des Lettres de l'Université de Brno* 1958: 94–107

170 B. Trnka, J. Vachek et al, Prague Structural Linguistics, *Philologica Pragensea* 1: 33–40

171 B. Trnka, On the Combinatory Variants and Neutralization of Phonemes, *Proc. III Internat. Congress of Phonetic Sciences* (Ghent 1939): 23–30

172 J. M. Kořinek, Laut und Wortbedeutung, *TCLP* 8: 58–65
173 N. Trubetzkoy, Grundzüge der Phonologie (French trans., **168** above), *TCLP* 7

174 V. Mathesius, On some Problems of the Systematic Analysis of Grammar, *TCLP* 6: 95–107

175 V. Skalička, La fonction de l'ordre des éléments linguistiques, *TCLP* 6: 129–33

176 S. Karcevski, Du dualisme asymétrique du signe linguistique, *TCLP* 4: 188–227

177 O. K. Leška, K voprosy o strukturalizme (Concerning structuralism— two concepts of grammar in the Prague School), *VJa* 5: 88–103

1.2.7 Soviet Theories

178 L. L. Thomas, *The Linguistic Theories of N. Ja. Marr.* Berkeley: California U.P. 1957

179 A. S. Čikobava & L. A. Bulaxovskij, *Vvedenie v jazykoznanie* (Introduction to Linguistics). 2 vols. Moscow: Učpedgiz 1952

180 E. J. Simmons (ed.), *The Soviet Linguistic Controversy.* (Trans. from the Soviet Press.) New York: Columbia University Slavic Studies 1951

181 I. I. Meščaninov, *Sovetskoe jazykoznanie* (Soviet linguistics). Moscow: Obščee sobranie Akad. Nauk S.S.S.R. 1948

182 R. O. Šor & N. S. Čemodanov, *Vvedenie v jazykovedenie* (Introduction to linguistics). Moscow: Učpedgiz 1945

*   *   *

183 W. K. Matthews, The Soviet Contribution to Linguistic Thought, *AL* 2: 1–23, 97–121

184 N. N. Poppe, The New Stage in Soviet Linguistics, *Bul. Just. Hist. and Culture U.S.S.R.*, Munich 2 (15) 1955: 46, 132, 138, 145

185 A. J. Rožanskij, V. I. Lenin o jazyke (Lenin on Language), *Russkij jazyk* 10: 1–10

186 W. K. Matthews, Developments in Soviet Linguistics since the Crisis of 1950, *Slavonic and East European Review* 34: 123–30

187 G. Jacobsson, La linguistique soviétique de nos jours (On N. J. Marr), *Symbolae Philologicae Gotoburgensis* 401–16, Gothenburg: Wettergren 1950

188 N. A. Kondrašov & V. M. Filippova, V. I. Lenin i voprosy jazykoznanija (Lenin and Linguistics), *VJa* 1: 3–6

189 G. Pätsch, Zur marxistisch- leninistischen Lehre von der Sprache, *Wiss. Z. der Humboldt Universität, sprachwiss. Reihe* 4: 35–46

1.2.8 Individual Theories

189a H. Glinz, *Ansätze zu einer Sprachtheorie.* Düsseldorf: Schwann 1962

189b A. Martinet, *A Functional View of Language.* London: Oxford U.P. 1962

190 P. Hartmann, *Theorie der Grammatik.* 4 vols. The Hague: Mouton 1962

190a E. F. Haden, M. S. & Y. W. Han, *A Resonance Theory for Linguists.* The Hague: Mouton 1962

190b E. Lewy, *Kleine Schriften.* Berlin: D. Akademie der Wissenschaft 1961

191 A. Sommerfelt, *Diachronic and Synchronic Aspects of Language.* The Hague: Mouton 1960

192   K. L. Pike, *Language in Relation to a Unified Theory of the Structure of Human Behavior*. 3 vols. Santa Ana (Cal. U.S.A.): Summer Institute of Linguistics 1960

193   A. B. Johnson, *A Treatise on Language*. (ed. D. Rynin) Berkeley: California U.P. 1959

194   G. Siewerth, *Wort und Bild. Eine ontologische Interpretation.* (French trans., No. **195**) Düsseldorf: Schwann 1958

195   G. Siewerth, *Ontologie du langage.* (trans. M. Zemb). Bruges: Brouwer 1958

196   V. Tauli, *The Structural Tendencies of Languages*. Helsinki: Suomalainen Tiedeakatemia 1958

197   J. H. Greenberg, *Essays in Linguistics*. Chicago: Chicago U.P. 1957

198   P. Hartmann, *Untersuchungen zur allgemeinen Grammatik*. Heidelberg: Winter 1956–57

199   B. Terracini, *Glottologia*. Torino: Gheroni 1956

200   B. L. Whorf, *Language, Thought and Reality* (ed. by J. B. Carroll). New York: Wiley 1956

201   A. Tarski, *Logic, Semantics, Metamathematics*. Oxford: Clarendon 1956

202   I. A. Richards, *Speculative Instruments*. Chicago: Chicago U.P. 1955

203   E. H. Lenneberg, *Language and Cognition.* (mimeographed) Cambridge (Mass.): M.I.T. 1954

204   W. Porzig, *Das Wunder der Sprache*. Bern: Francke 1950

205   A. Marty, *Satz und Wort*. Bern: Francke 1950

206   D. G. Mandelbaum (ed.), *Selected Writings of Edward Sapir in Language, Culture and Personality*. Berkeley & Los Angeles: California U.P. 1949

207   R. Wellek & W. Austin, *Theory of Literature*. New York: Harcourt 1949

208   G. K. Zipf, *Human Behavior and the Principle of Least Effort: An introduction to human ecology*. Cambridge (Mass.): Addison-Wesley 1949

209   R. A. Wilson, *The Miraculous Birth of Language*. New York: Philosophical Library 1948

210   R. Carnap, *Introduction to Semantics*. Cambridge (Mass.): Harvard U.P. 1942

211   C. Morris, *Signs, Language and Behavior*. New York: Prentice-Hall 1946

212   M. G. Bartoli, *Saggi di linguistica spaziale*. Torino: Bona 1945

213   E. Cassirer, *An Essay on Man. An introduction to a philosophy of human culture*. New York: Doubleday 1944

214   V. Brøndal, *Essais de linguistique générale. Publiés avec une bibliographie des oeuvres de l'auteur*. Copenhagen: Munksgaard 1943

215   E. Buyssens, *Les langages et le discours*. Brussels: Office de Publicité 1943

216   G. Révész, *Die Sprache*. Amsterdam: V. K. Neerl. Hb. Wetensch. afd. Lelterk. 1940

217   B. Russell, *An Inquiry into Meaning and Truth*. New York: Norton 1940

218   K. Britton, *Communication*. New York: Harcourt 1939

219   W. M. Urban, *Language and Reality*. London: Allen & Unwin 1939

220   F. Boas, *Language*, in his *General Anthropology*. Boston: Heath 1938

221   C. W. Morris, *Foundations of the Theory of Signs*. (*Internat. Encyclopedia of Unified Science*). Chicago: Chicago U.P. 1938

222   R. Carnap, *The Logical Syntax of Language.* (trans. Countess von Zeppelin) London: Routledge & Kegan Paul 1937

223 B. Malinowski, *Coral Gardens and their Magic. Vol. 2. The Language of Magic and Gardening.* New York: American Library 1935

224 G. K. Zipf, *The Psycho-Biology of Language. An introduction to dynamic philology.* Boston: Houghton Mifflin 1935

225 R. Carnap, *Logische Syntax der Sprache.* Vienna: Springer 1934

226 A. H. Gardiner, *The Theory of Speech and Language.* London: Oxford U.P. 1932

227 C. S. Peirce, *Collected Papers* (ed. C. Hartshorne & P. Weiss) 8 vols. Cambridge (Mass.): Harvard U.P. 1931–35

228 H. Frei, *La grammaire des fautes. Introduction à la linguistique fonctionnelle.* Paris: Geuthner 1929

229 L. Weisgerber, *Muttersprache und Geistesbildung.* Göttingen: Vandenhoeck & Ruprecht 1929

230 A. Meillet, *Linguistique historique et linguistique générale.* Paris: Soc. de Linguistique de Paris 1926

231 M. G. Bartoli, *Introduzione alla Neolinguistica.* Geneva: Olschki 1925

232 J. Vendryes, *Language: a linguistic introduction to history.* (trans. P. Radin). London: Kegan Paul 1925

233 C. K. Ogden & I. A. Richards, *The Meaning of Meaning. A study of the influence of language upon thought and of the science of symbolism.* London: Routledge & Kegan Paul (1 ed.) 1923, (10 ed.) 1949

234 B. Malinowski, Supplement to Ogden & Richards, *Meaning of Meaning* (No. **233** above)

235 E. Cassirer, *Philosophie der symbolischen Formen. I. Teil: Die Sprache.* Berlin: Cassirer 1923

236 L. Spitzer (ed.), *Hugo Schuchardt-Brevier.* 2 vols. Halle: Niemeyer 1922

237 E. Sapir, *Language. An introduction to the study of speech.* New York: Harcourt 1921

1.2.9 Critiques and Comparisons

238 R. Jakobson, Boas' View of Grammatical Meaning, *American Anthropologist* 61: 139–45

239 O. Funke, On the System of Grammar, *ArchL* 6: 1–9

239a B. Pottier, Problèmes de méthode en linguistique structurale, (Guillaume & Hjelmslev) *Bollettino dell'Istituto di Lingue Estere* 6: 24–33

240 H. Frei, Review of S. Ullmann's *Principles of Semantics* in *CFS* 13: 50–61

241 T. C. Pollock, A Theory of Meaning Analyzed, (Review of the *Meaning of Meaning*), *Etc.* 1943

242 M. M. Guchman, Protiv idealizma i reakcii v sovremennom amerikanskom jazykoznanii. (Against Idealism and Reaction in Contemporary American Linguistics), *Izvestija Akademii Nauk S.S.S.R.* 11: 281–94

243 R. B. Lees, Review of Chomsky's *Syntactic Structures*, *Lg* 33: 375–408

244 S. Ceccato, Il linguaggio (1. Empiricism and Idealism 2. Operational Methodology), *Methodos* 1: 229–46

245 G. Bergman, Two Types of Linguistic Philosophy, *Review of Metaphysics* 5: 417–38

246 M. Swadesh, On Linguistic Mechanisms, *Science and Society* 12: 259

247 M. W. Bloomfield, Some Problems of Method in Linguistics, *Studium Generale* 5: 438–43

248 H. J. Pos, Perspectives du structuralisme, *TCLP* 8: 71–8
249 E. H. Cassirer, Structuralism in Modern Linguistics, *Word* 1: 99–120
250 C. F. Hockett, Two Models of Grammatical Description, *Word* 10: 218–34
251 M. K. Jensen, Sur l'objet de la linguistique, *ZPhon* 8: 389–91

1.3 SPECIAL THEORIES

1.3.1 Language and Scientific Method

251a R. Bastide (ed.), *Sens et usages du terme "structure" dans les sciences humaines et sociales.* The Hague: Mouton 1962
251b A. Juilland, *Outline of a General Theory of Structural Relations.* The Hague: Mouton 1961
252 S. Körner, *Conceptual Thinking. A logical inquiry.* New York: Dover 1959
253 P. Winch, *The Idea of a Social Science. And its relation to philosophy.* London: Routledge & Kegan Paul 1958
254 E. R. Leach, The Epistemological Background of Malinowski's Empiricism, in *Man and Culture,* London: Routledge & Kegan Paul 1957
255 A. N. Prior, *Time and Modality.* Oxford: Clarendon 1957
256 S. Körner (ed.), *Observation and Interpretation. A symposium of philosophers and physicists.* London: Butterworth 1957
257 E. Simard, *La nature et la portée de la méthode scientifique.* Quebec & Paris: Presses de l'Université Laval & Vrin 1956
258 M. White (ed.), *The Age of Analysis.* New York: New American Library 1955
259 H. B. Curry, *Outlines of a Formalist Philosophy of Mathematics.* Amsterdam: North-Holland 1951
260 L. Chwistek, *The Limits of Science.* London: Routledge & Kegan Paul 1948
261 B. Russell, *Human Knowledge. Its scope and limits.* New York: Simon & Schuster 1948
262 C. I. Lewis, *An Analysis of Knowledge and Valuation.* La Salle (Ill.): Open Court 1946
263 M. Belin-Milleron, *La réforme de la connaissance.* Paris: Arrault 1942
264 C. Sherrington, *Man on his Nature.* London: Cambridge U.P. 1940
265 A. N. Whitehead, *Process and Reality.* London: Cambridge U.P. 1929
266 C. D. Broad, *Scientific Thought* (8 ed.) London: Kegan Paul 1927
267 A. N. Whitehead & B. Russell, *Principia Mathematica.* 3 vols. (2 ed.) Cambridge: Cambridge U.P. 1925–27
268 A. N. Whitehead, *Science and the Modern World.* London: Cambridge U.P. 1926
269 W. James, *Pragmatism.* London: Longmans 1907

*   *   *

270 C. F. Hockett, Biophysics, Linguistics, and the Unity of Science, *American Scientist* 36: 558–72
270a R. Valin, Le linguiste devant le problème de l'observation, *CLS* 7

271 H. Frei, De la linguistique comme science des lois, *Lingua* 1: 25–34
272 J. W. Yolton, Linguistic and Epistemological Dualism, *Mind* 62: 20–42
273 A. Pap, Semantic Analysis and Psycho-physical Dualism, *Mind* 41: 209–21
274 T. Storer, Linguistic Isomorphisms, *Philosophy of Science* 19: 77–85
275 V. Skalička, The Need for a Linguistics of "Parole", *Recueil* 1: 21–38

1.3.2 Language and Philosophy

275a W. W. Gibson (ed.), *The Limits of Language.* New York: Hill & Wang 1962
275b M. Black, *The Importance of Language.* Englewood Cliffs (N.J.): Prentice-Hall 1962
275c M. Black, *Models and Metaphors.* Ithaca (N.Y.): Cornell U.P. 1962
276 E. Gellner, *Words and Things. A critical account of linguistic philosophy and a study in ideology.* Boston: Beacon 1960
277 L. Rougier, *La métaphysique et le langage.* Paris: Flammarion 1960
278 M. J. Charlesworth, *Philosophy and Linguistic Analysis.* Pittsburgh: Duquesne U.P. 1959
279 L. Wittgenstein, *Tractatus logico-philosophicus.* Oxford: Blackwell 1960
280 P. Henle (ed.), *Language, Thought and Culture.* Ann Arbor: Michigan U.P. 1958
281 A. Pap, *Semantics and Necessary Truth.* New Haven: Yale U.P. 1958
282 L. Wittgenstein, *Philosophical Investigations.* Oxford: Blackwell 1953
283 L. Linsky (ed.), *Semantics and the Philosophy of Language.* Urbana: Illinois U.P. 1952
284 P. Henle, H. Kallen & S. Langer, *Structure, Method and Meaning.* New York: Liberal Arts 1951
285 M. Black, *Language and Philosophy. Studies in method.* Ithaca (N.Y.): Cornell U.P. 1949
286 E. Otto, *Sprachwissenschaft und Philosophie.* Berlin: Gruyter 1949
287 S. K. Langer, *Philosophy in a New Key.* New York: New American Library 1948
288 H. Junker, *Sprachphilosophisches Lesebuch.* Heidelberg: Winter 1947
289 R. Carnap, *Meaning and Necessity.* Chicago: Chicago U.P. 1947
290 C. L. Stevenson, *Ethics and Language.* New Haven: Yale U.P. 1944
291 L. Lachance, *Philosophie du Langage.* Montreal: Levrier 1943
292 H. J. Ayer, *Language, Truth and Logic.* London: Gollancz 1936

*   *   *

293 L. Weisgerber, Sprachwissenschaft und Philosophie zum Bedeutungs-problem, *Blätter f. dt. Philosophie* 4: 17
294 J. Engels, Valeur de la philosophie pour la recherche linguistique, *Neo-philologus* 38: 248–51
295 G. Schmidt, The Philosophy of Language, *Orbis* 6: 164–8
296 I. M. Copi, Philosophy and Language, *Review of Metaphysics* 4: 427–37

1.3.3 Language and Logic

297 W. V. O. Quine, *Word and Object*. New York: Wiley 1960
298 B. F. Huppé & J. Kaminsky, *Logic and Language*. New York: Knopf 1956
299 W. V. O. Quine, *From a Logical Point of View*. Cambridge (Mass.): Harvard U.P. 1953
300 A. G. N. Flew (ed.), *Essays on Logic and Language*. Oxford: Blackwell 1951
301 M. Prot, *Langage et logique. Vers une logique nouvelle*. Paris: Hermann 1949

1.3.4 Language and Psychology

302 J. Church, *Language and the Discovery of Reality*. New York: Random House 1961
303 F. Kainz, *Psychologie der Sprache*. 5 vols. Stuttgart: Enke 1941–61
304 C. G. Hempel, *Fundamentals of Concept Formation in Empirical Science*. Chicago: Chicago U.P. 1952
305 F. Rostand, *Grammaire et affectivité*. Paris: Vrin 1951
306 C. L. Meader & J. H. Muyskens, *Handbook of Biolinguistics*. Toledo (U.S.A.): Weller 1950
307 F. Kainz, *Einführung in die Sprachpsychologie*. Vienna: Sepl 1946
308 A. Marty, *Psyche und Sprachstruktur*. Bern: Francke 1940
309 J. R. Kantor, *An Objective Psychology of Grammar*. Bloomington: Indiana U.P. 1936
310 H. Mulder, *Cognition and Volition in Language*. Groningen: Wolters 1936
311 W. B. Pillsbury & C. L. Meader, *The Psychology of Language*. New York: Appleton 1928
312 J. van Ginneken, *Principes de linguistique psychologique*. Paris: Rivière 1907

* * *

313 G. P. Meredith, Semantics in Relation to Psychology, *AL* 8: 1–11
314 E. L. Thorndike, The Psychology of Semantics, *Am. J. Psych.* 59: 613–31
315 G. A. Miller, Psycholinguistics, in *Handbook of Social Psychology* (II, 693–708). Cambridge (Mass.): Addison-Wesley 1954
316 H. L. Hollingsworth, Meaning and the Psychophysical Continuum, *J. of Philosophy* 20
317 A. Sauvageot, La notion du temps et son expression dans le langage, *J. de psychologie normale et pathologique* 33: 19–27
318 J. Meyer, Language as a Biological Phenomenon, *Proc. 10 Internat. Cong. Philosophy* (II: 951–4) Amsterdam: North-Holland 1948
319 N. H. Pronko, Language and Psycholinguistics: a review, *Psychological Bulletin* 43: 189–239

1.3.5 Language and Thought

320 L. S. Vijgotskij, *Thought and Language*. New York: Wiley 1962
321 W. G. Penfield & L. Roberts, *Speech and Brain-Mechanisms*. Princeton: Princeton U.P. 1959

322 C. A. Lawson, *Language, Thought and the Human Mind.* East Lansing (Mich.): Michigan State U.P. 1958

323 P. von Hartmann, *Sprache und Erkenntnis.* Heidelberg: Winter 1958

324 P. Chauchard, *Le langage et la pensée.* Paris: Presses universitaires 1956

325 J. Holloway, *Language and Intelligence.* London: Macmillan 1951

326 G. Révész (ed.), *Thinking and Speaking. A symposium.* Amsterdam: North-Holland 1954

327 G. Humphrey, *Thinking.* London: Methuen 1951

328 K. Goldstein, *Language and Language Disturbances.* New York: Grune 1948

329 H. Delacroix, *Le langage et la pensée.* Paris: Alcan 1930

*   *   *

330 R. Brain, The Semantic Aspects of Aphasia, *ArchL* 8: 20–7

331 R. W. Brown & E. H. Lenneberg, A Study in Language and Cognition, *J. of Abnormal and Social Psychology* 49: 454–61

(See also under 2.2.6 and 4.4.2)

1.3.6 Language and Meaning

(i) *Semantics*

331a S. Ullmann, *Semantics: An introduction to the science of meaning.* Oxford: Blackwell 1962

332 P. Guiraud, *La sémantique,* Paris: Presses universitaires 1959

333 R. Brown, *Words and Things.* Glencoe (Ill.): Free Press 1958

334 R. M. Martin, *Truth and Denotation: a study in semantical theory.* Chicago: Chicago U.P. 1958

335 K. Baldinger, *Die Semasiologie.* Berlin: Akademie-Verlag 1957

336 V. A. Zvegincev, *Semasiologija.* Moscow: Izdatel'stvo Moskovskogo Universiteta 1957

337 T. Rutt, *Vom Wesen der Sprache.* Ratingen: Henn 1957

338 S. Ullmann, *The Principles of Semantics* (2 ed.). Glasgow: Jackson 1957

339 F. F. Nesbit, *Language, Meaning and Reality.* New York: Exposition 1955

340 P. Kecskemeti, *Meaning, Communication and Value.* Chicago: Chicago U.P. 1952

341 H. Kronasser, *Handbuch der Semasiologie.* Heidelberg: Winter 1952

342 S. Ullmann, *Words and their Use.* London: Muller 1951

343 A. Marty, *Über Wert und Methode: eine allgemein beschreibende Bedeutungslehre.* Bern: Francke 1950

344 J. Bonfante, *Semantics.* Princeton: Ampersand 1950

345 I. J. Lee, *The Language of Wisdom and Folly. Background readings in semantics.* New York: Harper 1949

346 H. M. Woodworth, *The Nature and Technique of Understanding.* Vancouver: Wrigley 1949

347 H. R. Walpole, *Semantics.* New York: Norton 1941

348 S. Chase, *The Tyranny of Words.* London: Methuen 1928

349 K. O. Erdmann, *Die Bedeutung des Wortes.* Leipzig: Haessel 1922

350 W. James, *The Will to Believe.* New York: Longmans 1898

*   *   *

351 C. Bally, L'arbitraire du signe: valeur et signification, *FM* 1940: 193–207
352 H. Gomperz, The Meanings of Meaning, *Philosophy of Science* 8: 160–83
353 A. W. Read, An Account of the Word Semantics, *Word* 4: 18–97

(See also under 2.2.9)

1.3.6 (ii) *General Semantics*

354 T. Longabough, *General Semantics*. New York: Vantage 1957
355 J. S. Bois, *Explorations in Awareness*. New York: Harper 1957
356 S. I. Hayakawa, *Language, Meaning and Maturity, Selections from ETC, A Review of General Semantics, 1943–1953*. New York: Harper 1954
357 M. Gardner, *Fads and Fallacies in the Name of Science*. (Chap. 23: General Semantics, etc.) New York: Dover 1952
358 S. I. Hayakawa, *Language in Thought and Action*. New York: Harcourt 1949
359 A. Korzybski, *Science and Sanity*. Lancaster (Pa.): Science Press 1941
360 I. Lee, *Language Habits in Human Affairs*. New York: Harper 1941
361 S. I. Hayakawa, *Language in Action*. New York: Harcourt 1939

*　　*　　*

362 P. P. Hallie, A Criticism of General Semantics, *College English* 14: 17–23

1.3.7 Language and Communication

362a Union française des organes de la documentation, *Colloque sur les problèmes de la communication*. 2 vols. Paris: Union française des organes de la documentation 1961
362b W. Meyer-Eppler, *Grundlagen und Anwendungen der Informationstheorie*. Berlin: Springer 1959
363 C. Cherry, *On Human Communication. A review, a survey, and a criticism*. New York: Wiley 1957
364 L. Apostel, B. Mandelbrot & A. Morf, *Logique, langage et théorie de l'information*. Paris: Presses universitaires 1957
365 C. Cherry (ed.), *Information Theory*. London: Butterworth 1956
366 B. McMillan et al, *Current Trends in Information Theory*. Pittsburgh: Pittsburgh U.P. 1953
367 G. A. Miller, *Language and Communication*. New York: McGraw-Hill 1951
368 C. Shannon & W. Weaver, *The Mathematical Theory of Communication*. Urbana: Illinois U.P. 1949

*　　*　　*

369 P. Guiraud, Langage, connaissance et information, *J. de Psychologie* 1958
370 G. Peterson, An Oral Communication Model, *Lg* 31: 414–27
371 B. Mandelbrot, Structure formelle des textes en communication: deux études, *Word* 10: 1–27

1.3.8 Language and Mathematics

371a G. Herdan, *The Calculus of Linguistic Observations*. The Hague: Mouton 1962

372 G. Herdan, *Type-Token Mathematics: a textbook of mathematical linguistics.* The Hague: Mouton 1960
373 P. Guiraud, *Problèmes et méthodes de la statistique linguistique.* Paris: Presses universitaires 1960
374 P. Guiraud, *Les caractères statistiques du vocabulaire.* Paris: Presses universitaires, 1960
375 H. H. Somers, *Analyse mathématique du langage: lois générales et mesures statistiques.* Louvain & Paris: Nauwelaerts 1959
376 G. Herdan, *Language as Choice and Chance.* Groningen: Noordhoff 1956
377 P. Guiraud, *Bibliographie critique de la statistique linguistique. Révisée et complétée par T. D. Houchin, J. Puhvel et C. W. Watkins de l'Université Harvard sous la direction de Joshua Whatmough.* Utrecht: Spectrum 1954

*   *   *

378 R. Jakobson (ed.), Structure of Language and its Mathematical Aspects, *Proceedings of the Symposia in Applied Mathematics* 12. Providence (R.I.): American Mathematical Society 1961
379 W. Plath, Mathematical Linguistics, in *Trends* (see No. **97** above): 21–57

(See also Nos. **59** and **1327**)

1.3.9 Language and Technology

379a P. L. Garvin (ed.), *Natural Language and the Computer.* New York: McGraw-Hill 1963
379b A. G. Oettinger, *Automatic Language Translation: lexical and technical aspects.* Cambridge (Mass.): Harvard U.P. 1960
380 E. & K. Delavenay, *Bibliography of Mechanical Translation.* The Hague: Mouton 1960
381 E. Delavenay, *La machine à traduire.* Paris: Presses universitaires 1959
381a A. D. Booth, L. Brandwood & J. P. Cleave, *Mechanical Resolution of Linguistic Problems.* London: Butterworth 1958
382 J. von Neumann, *The Computer and the Brain.* London: Oxford U.P. 1958
383 V. Belevitch, *Langage des machines et langage humain.* Brussels: Lebègue & Nationale 1956
384 W. N. Locke & A. D. Booth (eds.), *Machine Translation of Languages.* New York: Wiley 1955
385 N. Wiener, *Cybernetics.* New York: Wiley 1948

*   *   *

386 G. P. Meredith, The Communication of Scientific Concepts and Models of Semantic Mechanisms, *The Advancement of Science* 18: 110–17
387 F. D. Barrett & H. A. Shepard, A Bibliography of Cybernetics, *Proc. American Acad. of Arts and Sciences* 80: 204–22

1.3.10 Language and Culture

388 H. Hoijer (ed.), *Language in Culture.* Chicago: Chicago U.P. 1954
389 C. Kluckhohn, *Mirror for Man.* Toronto: Whittlesey 1949
390 F. Boas, *Race, Language and Culture.* New York: Macmillan 1940

*   *   *

391   D. D. Lee, Linguistic Aspects of Wintu Acculturation, *American Anthropologist* 45: 435–50
392   A. L. Kroeber, Some Relations of Linguistics and Ethnology, *Lg* 17: 287–91
393   B. W. Wheeler et al, The MLA Interdisciplinary Seminar on Language and Culture, *MLJ* 39: 115–22
394   H. Hoijer, Anthropological Linguistics, in *Trends* (see No. **97** above): 110–27

1.3.11   Language and Society

395   J. Bram, *Language and Society*. New York: Doubleday 1955
396   M. M. Lewis, *Language in Society*. London: Nelson 1947

*   *   *

397   D. Abercrombie, The Social Basis of Language, *ELT* 3: 1–11

1.3.12   Language and History

397a A. S. Diamond, *History and Origin of Language*. London: Methuen 1959
398   H. Goad, *Language in History*. London: Penguin 1958
399   A. Dauzat, *L'Europe linguistique*. Paris: Payot 1953
400   L. Brunschvicq, *Héritage des mots, héritage d'idées*. Paris: Bibl. de philosophie contemporaine 1950
401   A. C. Woolner, *Languages in History and Politics*. London: Oxford U.P. 1938

1.3.13   History of Languages

402   H. M. Hoenigswald, *Language Change and Linguistic Reconstruction*. Chicago: Chicago U.P. 1960
403   M. Schöne, *Vie et mort des mots*. Paris: Presses universitaires 1947
404   A. Meillet, *La méthode comparative en linguistique historique*. Paris: Champion 1925

*   *   *

405   O. Höfler, Stammbaumtheorie, Wellentheorie, Entfaltungstheorie, in *Beiträge zur Geschichte der deutschen Sprache und Literatur*. Tübingen: Niemeyer 1955
406   S. Andrews & J. Whatmough, Comparative and Historical Linguistics in America: 1930–1960, in *Trends* (see No. **97** above): 58–81
407   A. Scherer, Der Stand der indogermanischen Sprachwissenschaft, in *Trends* (see No. **97** above): 225–39

1.3.14   Typology of Languages

408   P. S. Kuznecov, *Die morphologische Klassifikation der Sprachen*. (trans. from Russian by K. A. Paffen) Halle: Niemeyer 1956

*   *   *

409 J. H. Greenberg, A Quantitative Approach to the Morphological Typology of Language, in *Method and Perspective in Anthropology*, ed. by R. F. Spencer. Minneapolis: Minnesota U.P. 1954

410 C. E. Bazell, Syntactic Relations and Linguistic Typology, *CFS* 8: 5–20

411 P. Menzerath, Typology of Languages, *JAcS* 22: 698–701

412 M. Leroy, Les langues du monde et la typologie linguistique, *Mémoires et Publications de la Société des Sciences, des Arts et des Lettres du Hainaut* 74: 169–204

413 E. Lewy, Der Bau der europäischen Sprachen, *Proc. Royal Irish Academy*, 48: C2

414 R. Jakobson, Linguistic Typology, in *Proc. Eighth International Congress of Linguists* (see No. **633** below)

415 S. Ullmann, Descriptive Semantics and Linguistic Typology, *Word* 9: 225–40

2. LINGUISTICS AND THE DESCRIPTION OF LANGUAGES

2.1 GENERAL PROCEDURES

2.1.1 Definitions

416 W. S. Allen, *On the Linguistic Study of Language. An inaugural lecture.* London: Cambridge U.P. 1957

417 B. Terracini, *¿Qué es la lingüística?* Tucumán (Argentina): University of Tucumán 1942

*   *   *

418 A. Martinet, Structural Linguistics, in *Anthropology Today*, 574–86. Chicago: Chicago U.P.

419 C. E. Reed, What is Linguistics?, *GQ* 25: 16–25

420 J. Lohmann, Was ist und was will Sprachwissenschaft?, *Lexis* 1: 128–68

421 A. Reichling, What is General Linguistics?, *Lingua* I: 8–24

422 A. Martinet, The Unity of Linguistics, *Word* 10: 121–5

2.1.1 Techniques of Analysis

422a A. A. Hill (ed.), *Texas Conferences on Problems of Linguistic Analysis in English*. 3 vols. Austin: Texas U.P. 1962

423 D. L. Bolinger, *Generality, Gradients and the All-or-None*. The Hague: Mouton 1961

424 H. Seiler, *Relativsatz, Attribut und Apposition*. Wiesbaden: Harrassowic 1960

425 A. A. Hill, *Introduction to Linguistic Structures: from sound to sentence in English*. New York: Harcourt 1958

426 N. Trubetzkoy, *Anleitung zu phonologischen Beschreibungen*. (2 ed.) Göttingen: Vandenhoeck & Ruprecht 1958

427 A. Martinet, *La description phonologique avec application au parler franco-provençal d'Hauteville (Savoie)*. Geneva: Droz, Paris: Minard 1956

428 V. A. Zvegincev, *Problema znakovosti jazyka* (Problem of the semantic character of language). Moscow: Moskovskogo Universiteta 1956

429 A. N. Chomsky, *Transformation Analysis*. (microfilm) University of Pennsylvania Dissertation 1955

430 H. Frei, *Le livre des deux mille phrases. 1. La méthode des dictionnaires de phrases. 2. Questionnaire de deux mille phrases selon le parler d'un Parisien.* Geneva: Droz 1953

431 Z. S. Harris, *Methods in Structural Linguistics.* Chicago: Chicago U.P. 1951

432 O. Jespersen, *The Philosophy of Grammar.* London: Allen & Unwin 1924

*   *   *

433 R. Quirk, Substitutions and Syntactical Research, *AL* 10: 37–42

434 S. Ullmann, The Concept of Meaning in Linguistics, *AL* 8: 12–19

435 C. H. Borgström, The Technique of Linguistic Description, *AL* 5: 1–14

436 H. Frei, Qu'est-ce qu'un dictionnaire de phrases?, *CFS* 1: 43–56

437 C. F. Voegelin & F. M. Robinett, Obtaining a Linguistic Sample, *IJAL* 20: 89–100

438 M. Joos, Description of Language Design, *JAcS* 22: 701–708

439 A. N. Chomsky, Logical Syntax and Semantics: their linguistic relevance, *Lg* 31: 36–45

440 Y. Bar-Hillel, Logical Syntax and Semantics, *Lg* 30: 230–37

441 C. C. Fries, Meaning and Linguistic Analysis, *Lg* 30: 57–68

442 R. H. Robins, A Problem in the Statement of Meaning, *Lingua* 3: 121–137

443 L. Bloomfield, "Meaning", *MDU* 35: 101–6

443a H. Seiler, Sprachwissenschaftliche Methoden heute: dargestellt am Problem der deutschen Einsilber, *Studium Generale* 15: 22–31

444 W. Haas, Linguistic Structures (criticism of A. A. Hill, *Introduction to Linguistic Structures: from sound to sentence in English*), *Word* 16: 251–75

445 C. E. Bazell, The Choice of Criteria in Structural Linguistics, *Word* 10: 126–35

446 Z. S. Harris, Distributional Structure, *Word* 10: 146–62

447 H. Frei, Critères de délimitation, *Word* 10: 138

448 R. Wells, Meaning and Use, *Word* 10: 235–50

449 G. Gougenheim, Structure et économie en linguistique, *Science* 12: 31–9 1961

450 I. I. Revzin, Struktural'naja lingvistika semantika i problemy izučenija slova, (Structural linguistics, semantics and the problem of the word), *VJa* 6: 59–63

(See also under 2.3)

2.1.3 Levels

450a G. L. Bursill-Hall, Levels of Analysis: J. R. Firth's Theories of Linguistic Analysis, *JCLA* 6: 124–35, 164–91

451 F. R. Palmer, Linguistic Hierarchy, *Lingua* 7: 225–41

452 F. Waismann, The Many-Level Structure of Language, *Synthese* 5: 211–19

2.1.4 Units

453 C. Ebeling, *Linguistic Units*. The Hague: Mouton 1960
454 K. F. Sundén, *Linguistic Theory and the Essence of the Sentence*. Gothenburg: Wettergren & Kerbers 1941
455 J. Ries, *Was ist ein Satz? Beiträge zur Grundlegung der Syntax* 3. Prague: Taussig & Taussig 1931

* * *

456 A. S. C. Ross, The Fundamental Definition of the Theory of Language, *AL* 4: 101–6
457 E. Benveniste, Nature du signe linguistique, *AL* 1: 23–9
458 A. Belić, Constant Features in Language, *ArchL* 4: 17–26
459 R. Godel, La question des signes zéro, *CFS* 11: 31–41
460 E. Sollberger, Note sur l'unité linguistique, *CFS* 11: 45–6
461 R. Godel, Homonymie et identité, *CFS* 11: 5–15
462 R. Valin, Qu'est-ce qu'un fait linguistique?, *FM* 27: 85–93
463 J. Kuryłowicz, Linguistique et théorie du signe, *J. de Psychologie* 42: 170–80
464 C. Bally, Qu'est-ce qu'un signe?, *J. de Psychologie* 1939: 161–74
465 W. Bröcher & J. Lohmann, What is a Sentence?, *Lexis* 1: 24–33
466 P. D. Wienpahl, Are all Signs Signs?, *Phil. Rev.* 58: 243–56
466a H. Frei, L'unité linguistique complexe, *Lingua* 11: 128–40
467 H. Frei, Tranches homophones (à propos de l'article partitif du français), *Word* 16: 317–22
468 F. Hiorth, On Defining "Word", *Studia Linguistica* 12: 1–26
469 C. Stern, The Definition of the Sentence, *SNPh* 20: 37–48
470 S. Halldén, What is a Word?, *Theoria* 8: 55–66
471 W. Haas, On Defining Linguistic Units, *TPS* 1954: 54–84
472 H. Sweet, Words, Logic and Grammar, *TPS* 1876: 4

2.1.5 Notation

473 D. Abercrombie, *English Phonetic Texts* (Introduction and Appendix). London: Faber 1964
474 R. W. Albright, *The International Phonetic Alphabet: its backgrounds and development*. Bloomington: Indiana U.P. 1958
475 B. Collinder, *Ein vereinfachtes Transkriptionssystem*. Upsala: Almqvist & Wiksell 1958
476 International Phonetic Association, *The Principles of the International Phonetic Association. Being a description of the International Phonetic Alphabet and the manner of using it*. London: Department of Phonetics, University College 1949
477 Association phonétique internationale, *L'écriture phonétique internationale. Exposé populaire avec application au français et à plusieurs autres langues*. (2 ed.) London: International Phonetic Association 1921
478 D. Jones, *Intonation Curves*. Leipzig: Teubner 1909

* * *

479 P. A. D. McCarthy, Phonetic Transcription: an attempt at clarification, *ELT* 10: 61–5

480 L. A. Hill, The Length Mark: in Phonetic Transcription, *ELT* 9: 122–31
481 P. A. D. MacCarthy, Phonetic Transcription and the Teaching of Pronunciation, *ELT* 2: 15–20
482 J. Simko, A Contribution to the Problem of a Simplified Phonetic Transcription, *ELT* 1: 182–4
483 L. A. Hill, Stress Marks and Pitch Marks, *MPhon* 108: 32–5
484 L. A. Hill, Transcription of English, *MPhon* 104: 29–30, 107: 5–6

2.2 SPECIAL PROCEDURES

2.2.1 Phonetics

484*a* P. Ladefoged, *Elements of Acoustic Phonetics*, Edinburgh: Oliver & Boyd 1962
485 L. F. Brosnahan, *The Sounds of Language*. Cambridge: Heffer 1961
485*a* W. A. Smalley, *Manual of Articulatory Phonetics: Part One*. Tarrytown (N.Y.): Practical Anthropology 1961
486 J. Carrell & W. I. Tiffany, *Phonetics: theory and application to speech improvement*. New York: McGraw-Hill 1960
487 C. M. Wise, *Introduction to Phonetics*. Englewood Cliffs (N.J.): Prentice-Hall 1958
488 T. Chiba & M. Kajiyama, *The Vowel: Its Nature and Structure*. Tokyo: Phonetic Society of Japan 1958
489 L. Kaiser (ed.), *Manual of Phonetics*. Amsterdam: North-Holland 1957
490 C. M. Wise, *Applied Phonetics*. Englewood Cliffs (N.J.): Prentice-Hall 1957
491 O. von Essen, *Allgemeine und angewandte Phonetik*. (2 ed.) Berlin: Akademie-Verlag 1957
492 B. Malmberg, *La phonétique*. Paris: Presses universitaires 1954
493 R-M. S. Heffner, *General Phonetics*. Madison: Wisconsin U.P. 1952
494 O. von Essen, *Sprechmelodie und Ausdrucksgestaltung*. Hamburg: Phonetisches Laboratorium 1952
495 M. Joos, *Acoustic Phonetics*. (Monograph 23, Supplement to *Language*) Baltimore: Waverly 1948
496 R. K. Potter et al, *Visible Speech*. New York: Van Nostrand 1947
497 K. L. Pike, *Phonetics. A critical analysis of phonetic theory and a technic for the practical description of sounds*. Ann Arbor: Michigan U.P. 1943
498 A. T. Jones, *Sound*. New York: Van Nostrand 1937
499 M. Grammont, *Traité de phonétique*. Paris: Delagrave 1933
500 C. E. Kantner & R. West, *Phonetics*. New York: Harper 1933
501 D. Westermann & I. C. Ward, *Practical Phonetics for Students of African Languages*. London: Oxford U.P. 1933
502 P. Passy, *La phonétique et ses applications*. London: International Phonetic Association 1929
503 IPA, *Miscellanea Phonetica*. London: International Phonetic Association. I (1914), II (1954), III (1958)
504 O. Jespersen, *Lehrbuch der Phonetik*. Leipzig: Teubner 1913
505 H. Sweet, *A Primer of Phonetics*. London: Oxford U.P. 1906

*   *   *

506 S. N. Treviño & J-P. Vinay, Bibliography of Phonetics, *AS* 32: 66–72, 220–7

507 S. N. Treviño, Bibliography of Phonetics, *AS* 15: 99, 198, 322, 439

508 P. Ladefoged, The Classification of Vowels, *Lingua* 5: 113–28

509 K. Hadding-Koch, Recent Work in Intonation, *SL* 10: 77–96

2.2.2 Phonology

510 A. Rosetti, *Sur la théorie de la syllabe*. The Hague: Mouton 1960

511 C. Higounet, *L'écriture*. Paris: Presses universitaires 1959

512 D. Jones, *The History and Meaning of the Term "Phoneme"*. London: International Phonetic Association 1957

513 C. F. Hockett, *A Manual of Phonology*. Baltimore: Waverly 1955

514 D. Jones, *The Phoneme: its nature and use*. Cambridge: Heffer 1950

515 A. Martinet, *Phonology as Functional Phonetics*. London: Oxford U.P. 1949

516 K. L. Pike, *Tone Languages*. Ann Arbor: Michigan U.P. 1948

517 D. Jones, *Differences between Spoken and Written Language*. London: International Phonetic Association 1948

518 K. L. Pike, *Phonemics. A technique for reducing languages to writing*. Ann Arbor: Michigan U.P. 1947

519 R. H. Stetson, *Bases of Phonology*. Oberlin (Ohio): College Oscillograph Laboratory 1945

520 N. van Wijk, *Phonologie*. The Hague: Nijhoff 1939

521 D. Jones, *Concrete and Abstract Sounds*. Off-print from the *Proceedings of the Third International Congress of Phonetic Sciences*. Ghent: University Phonetics Laboratory 1938

522 W. F. Twaddell, *On Defining the Phoneme*. (Monograph 16, Supplement to *Language*) Baltimore: Waverly 1935

*   *   *

523 A. Martinet, Substance phonique et traits distinctifs, *BSLP* 1958: 72–85

524 A. Martinet, Arbitraire linguistique et double articulation, *CFS* 15: 105–116

525 J. Cantineau, Oppositions significatives, *CFS* 10: 11–40

526 C. Bally, Intonation et syntaxe, *CFS* 1: 33–42

527 E. Fischer-Jørgensen, The Phonetic Basis for the Identification of Phonemic Elements, *JAcS* 28: 611–21

528 A. A. Hill, The Audibility of / + /, *JCLA* 5: 81–2

529 R. H. Robinson, D. F. Theall & J. W. Wevers, Interpretation of English Suprasegmentals, *JCLA* 5: 8–16

530 P. D. Drysdale, W. F. Mackey & M. H. Scargill, Pitch and Stress as Phonemes: Analysis or Synthesis, *JCLA* 4: 61–2

531 L. A. Hill, Initial Clusters, *ELT* 14· 118–22

532 W. R. Lee, Some Features of the Intonation of Questions, *ELT* 10: 66–70

533 R. Kingdon, The Semantic Functions of Stress and Tone, *ELT* 3: 178–82

534 K. Malone, Phonemes and Phonemic Correlation in Current English, *ES* 18: 159–64

534a A. A. Hill, Suprasegmentals, Prosodies, Prosodemes, *Lg* 37: 457–68

535 H. Kurath, The Binary Interpretation of English Vowels: a critique, *Lg* 33: 111–12

536 S. Saporta, Frequency of Consonant Clusters, *Lg* 31: 25–30

537 B. Bloch, A Set of Postulates for Phonemic Analysis, *Lg* 24: 3–46

538 E. Haugen & W. F. Twaddell, Facts and Phonemics, *Lg* 18: 228–37

539 H. S. Sørensen, The Phoneme and Phoneme Variant, *Lingua* 9: 68–87

540 H. Contreras & S. Saporta, The Validation of a Phonological Grammar, *Lingua* 9: 1–15

541 H. Mol & E. M. Uhlenbeck, Hearing and the Concept of the Phoneme, *Lingua* 8: 161–85

542 C. Ebeling, Phonemics and Functional Semantics, *Lingua* 3: 295–308

543 W. Haas, The Identification and Description of Phonetic Elements, *TPS* 1957: 118–59

544 B. Trnka, General Laws of Phonemic Combination, *TCLP* 6: 57–62

545 S. Karcevski, Sur la phonologie de la phrase, *TCLP* 4: 188–227

546 A. N. Gvozdev, Obladajut li pozicii različitel'noj funkciej? (Do positions have distinctive features?), *VJa* 6: 59–63

547 P. L. Garvin & M. Mathiot, Fused Units in Prosodic Analysis, *Word* 14: 178–89

548 M. Halle, The Strategy of Phonemics, *Word* 10: 197–209

549 H. Vogt, Phoneme Classes and Phoneme Classification, *Word* 10: 28–34

550 J. D. O'Connor & J. L. M. Trim, Vowel, Consonant, and Syllable—A Phonological Definition, *Word* 9: 103–22

2.2.3 Morphology

551 C. E. Bazell, *Linguistic Form*. Istambul: Istambul U.P. 1953

552 E. A. Nida, *Morphology: the descriptive analysis of words*. Ann Arbor: Michigan U.P. 1946

* * *

553 G. Gougenheim, Morphologie et fonctions grammaticales, *J. de psychologie normale et pathologique*, 56: 417–26

554 Z. S. Harris, From Phoneme to Morpheme, *Lg* 31: 190–222

555 S. Saporta, Morph, Morpheme, Archimorpheme, *Word* 12: 9–14

556 C. E. Bazell, Phonemic and Morphemic Analysis, *Word* 8: 33–8

557 D. L. Bolinger, On Defining the Morpheme, *Word* 4: 18–23

558 D. L. Bolinger, Rime, Assonance and Morpheme Analysis, *Word* 4: 117–36

2.2.4 Syntax

558a A. Henry, *Etudes de syntaxe expressive*. Brussels: Université libre de Bruxelles 1962

558b B. Pottier, *Introduction à l'étude des structures grammaticales fondamentales*. Série A de Linguistique appliquée et traduction automatique. Paris: Publications linguistiques de la Faculté des lettres et des sciences humaines 1962

559 Z. S. Harris, *String Analysis of Sentence Structure.* The Hague: Mouton 1962

560 B. Pottier, *Linguistique des éléments de relation. Etude de morpho-syntaxe structurale.* Paris: Klincksieck 1961

561 N. Chomsky, *Syntactic Structures.* The Hague: Mouton 1957

562 V. Pickett, *An Introduction to the Study of Grammatical Structures.* Glendale (Cal.): Summer Institute of Linguistics 1956

563 M. Sandmann, *Subject and Predicate.* Edinburgh: Edinburgh U.P. 1954

564 E. A. Nida, *Outline of Descriptive Syntax.* Glendale (Cal.): Summer Institute of Linguistics 1951

565 O. Jespersen, *Analytic Syntax.* Copenhagen: Munksgaard 1937

* * *

566 A. V. Isačenko, Morphologie, syntaxe et phraséologie, *CFS* 7: 17–32

567 K. L. Pike, On Tagmemes, née Gramemes, *IJAL* 24: 273–8

568 H. Frei, A Note on Bloomfield's "Limiting Adjectives", *ES* 36: 278–81

568a K. L. Pike, Dimensions of Grammatical Constructions, *Lg* 38: 221–44

568b A. McIntosh, Patterns and Ranges, *Lg* 37: 325–37

569 Z. S. Harris, Discourse Analysis, *Lg* 28: 1–30

570 R. S. Pittman, Nuclear Structures in Linguistics, *Lg* 24: 287–92

571 K. L. Pike, Taxemes and Immediate Constituents, *Lg* 19: 65–82

572 M. Masterman, New Techniques for Analysing Sentence Patterns, *MT* 3: 4–5

573 A. G. Hatcher, Syntax and the Sentence, *Word* 12: 234–50

574 H. Frei, Note sur l'analyse des syntagmes, *Word* 4: 65–70

2.2.5 Parts of Speech

575 L. Tesnière, *Eléments de syntaxe structurale.* Paris: Klincksieck 1959

576 R. Magnusson, *Studies in the Theory of the Parts of Speech.* Lund: Gleerup 1954

577 V. Brøndal, *Les parties du discours.* Copenhagen: Munksgaard, 1948

* * *

578 R. H. Robins, Noun and Verb in Universal Grammar, *Lg* 28: 289–98

579 A. W. de Groot, Structural Linguistics and Word-Classes, *Lingua* 1: 427–500

580 G. Scarpat, Il discorso e le sue parti in Aristotele, *Studi grammaticali e linguistici I* Arona: Paideia 1950

581 A. Penttilä, Concerning the So-called Parts of Speech, *SL* 5: 1–6

582 F. W. Thomas, Parts of Speech, *TPS* 1949: 117–134

2.2.6 Lexicology and Content Analysis

582a H. Gipper & H. Schwarz, Bibliographisches Handbuch zur Sprachinhalts-forschung, Nos. 1 & 2. Cologne: Westdeutscher Verlag 1962 (in progress)

582b F. W. Householder & S. Saporta (eds.), *Problems in Lexicography.* Bloomington: Indiana University Research Center in Anthropology, Folklore and Linguistics 1962

583 E. Leisi, *Der Wortinhalt. Seine Struktur im Deutschen und Englischen.* (2 ed. rev.) Heidelberg: Quelle & Meyer 1961

584 I. de S. Pool (ed.), *Trends in Content Analysis*. Urbana: Illinois U.P. 1959

585 E. H. Lenneberg & J. M. Roberts, *The Language of Experience*. Baltimore: Waverly 1956

586 F. Tschirch, *Weltbild, Denkform und Sprachgestalt*. Berlin: Renner 1954

587 S. Öhman, *Wortinhalt und Weltbild*. Stockholm: Norstedt 1951

588 G. Matoré, *La méthode en lexicologie*. Paris: Didier 1950

589 L. Weisgerber, *Von den Kräften der deutschen Sprache*. 4 vols. Düsseldorf: Schwann 1949–50

590 J. Trier, *Der deutsche Wortschatz im Sinnbezirk des Verstandes: die Geschichte eines sprachlichen Feldes*. Heidelberg: Winter 1931

* * *

591 P. Guiraud, Le substrat informationnel de la sémantisation, *BSLP* 56: 119–33

592 P. Guiraud, Les champs morpho-sémantiques. (Critères externes et critères internes en étymologie), *BSLP* 52: 265–88

593 C. E. Bazell, La sémantique structurale, *Dialogues* 3: 120–32

594 M. R. Snodin, Language in Context, *ELT* 10: 47–50

595 M. H. Roberts, The Science of Idiom. A method of inquiry into the cognitive design of language, *PMLA* 59: 291–306

596 G. Bech, Zum Problem der Inhaltsanalyse, *SNPh* 27: 108–18

597 L. Hermodsson, Zur "glossematischen" Bedeutungsforschung, *SNPh* 26: 35–57

598 S. Öhman, Theories of the "Linguistic Field", *Word* 9: 123–34

599 H. Basilius, Neo-Humboldtian Ethnolinguistics, *Word* 8: 95–105

600 J. Trier, Der neue Sprachbegriff, *Z. für Deutschkunde* 46, 1932

2.2.7 Stylistics

601 T. A. Seboek, *Style in Language*. New York: Wiley 1960

602 P. Guiraud, *La stylistique*. Paris: Presses universitaires 1957

603 C. Bally, *Le langage et la vie*. (3 ed.) Geneva: Droz 1952

604 C. Bally, *Traité de stylistique française*. 2 vols. Heidelberg: Winter 1909

* * *

604a J. Darbelnet, La transposition, *FR* 23: 115–18

(See also **850a** and **851**)

2.2.8 Verbal Behaviour

605 B. F. Skinner, *Verbal Behavior*. New York: Appleton 1957

* * *

606 W. Hively, Implications of B. F. Skinner's Analysis of Behavior for the Classroom, *Harvard Educational Review* 29: 37–42

607 N. Chomsky, Review of Skinner's *Verbal Behavior*, *Lg* 35: 28

608 J. B. Carroll, Analyses of Verbal Behavior, *Psych. Rev.* 51: 102–19

609 P. C. Trotter, Conventional Responses, *ELT* 4: 67–77

2.2.9 Meaning

609a P. Ziff, *Semantic Analysis*. Ithaca (N.Y.): Cornell U.P. 1960
610 C. E. Osgood, G. J. Suci & P. H. Tannenbaum, *The Measurement of Meaning*. Urbana: Illinois U.P. 1957
611 J. J. Jenkins, W. A. Russell & G. J. Suci, *An Atlas of Semantic Profiles for 360 Words*. Minneapolis: University of Minnesota Psychology Dept. 1957
612 L. L. Thurstone, *Multiple-Factor Analysis*. Chicago: Chicago U.P. 1947

* * *

613 R. Wells, A Mathematical Approach to Meaning, *CFS*, 15: 117–36
(See also under 1.3.6)

2.3 DOCUMENTATION ON DESCRIPTIVE LINGUISTICS

2.3.1 General Courses and Popularizations

613a J. P. Hughes, *The Science of Language: an introduction to linguistics*. New York: Random House 1962
613b W. L. Anderson & N. C. Stageberg (eds.), *Introductory Readings on Language*. New York: Holt 1962
613c H. R. Warfel, *Language: a science of human behavior*. Cleveland (Ohio): Allen 1962
614 A. Martinet, *Eléments de linguistique générale*. Paris: Colin 1960
615 S. Potter, *Language in the Modern World*. London: Penguin 1960
616 R. A. Hall, *Linguistics and Your Language*. (2 ed.) New York: Doubleday 1960
617 C. F. Hockett, *A Course in Modern Linguistics*. New York: Macmillan 1958
618 S. Potter, *Modern Linguistics*. London: Penguin 1958
619 J. Perrot, *La linguistique*. Paris: Presses universitaires 1957
620 J. Whatmough, *Language: a modern synthesis*. New York: St. Martin's 1956
621 M. A. Pei, *Language for Everybody*. New York: Devin-Adair 1956
622 H. A. Gleason, *An Introduction to Descriptive Linguistics*. New York: Holt 1955
623 J. B. Carroll, *The Study of Language. A survey of linguistics and related disciplines in America*. Cambridge (Mass.): Harvard U.P. 1953
624 R. M. Estrich & H. Sperber, *Three Keys to Language*. New York: Rinehart 1952
625 M. Cohen, *Le langage: structure et évolution*. Paris: Editions sociales 1950
626 D. Pittman, *Practical Linguistics. A textbook and field manual of missionary linguistics*. Cleveland (Ohio): Baptist Mid-Missions 1948
627 E. H. Sturtevant, *An Introduction to Linguistic Science*. New Haven: Yale U.P. 1947
628 F. Bodmer, *The Loom of Language*. New York: Norton 1944
629 M. Schlauch, *The Gift of Language*. New York: Modern Age 1942
630 L. H. Gray, *Foundations of Language*. New York: Macmillan 1939
631 W. L. Graff, *Language and Languages*. New York: Appleton 1932
632 O. Jespersen, *Language: its nature, development and origin*. London: Allen & Unwin 1922

2.3.2 Collections of Studies

632a *Pre-prints of Papers for the Ninth International Congress of Linguists.* Cambridge (Mass.): M.I.T. 1962

633 *Proceedings of the Eighth International Congress of Linguists.* Oslo: Oslo U.P. 1958

634 *Proceedings of the Seventh International Congress of Linguists.* London: International University Booksellers 1956

635 *Premier congrès international pour le latin vivant.* Avignon: Aubanel 1956

636 *Studies in Communication.* London: Secker & Warburg 1955, 1959 (in progress)

637 *Linguistics Today* (= *Word* 10.2–3). New York: Linguistic Circle of New York 1954

638 *Anthropology Today.* Chicago: Chicago U.P. 1953

639 *Results of the Conference of Anthropologists and Linguists, IJAL* 19 (suppl.) 1953

640 *Actes du sixième congrès international de linguistes.* Paris: Klincksieck 1949

641 *Cinquième congrès international de linguistes: Réponses au questionnaire.* Bruges: St. Catherine 1939

642 *Proceedings of the Third International Congress of Phonetic Sciences.* Ghent: University Phonetics Laboratory 1939

643 *Actes du quatrième congrès international de linguistes.* Copenhagen: Munksgaard 1938

644 *Atti del III congresso internazionale dei linguisti.* Florence: Lemonnier 1935

645 *Actes du deuxième congrès international de linguistes.* Paris: Adrien-Maisonneuve 1933

646 *Actes du premier congrès international de linguistes.* Leiden: Sijthoff 1930

*   *   *

647 The Conference on Archiving, *IJAL* 20: 83–122

648 W. F. Mackey, The Oslo Congress: a critical report, *JCLA* 3: 90–2

649 F. Trojan, Bericht über den X Internationalen Kongress für Logopädie und Phoniatrie, *Phonetica* 1: 124–7

2.3.3 Glossaries of Linguistics

650 J. Knobloch et al, *Sprachwissenschaftliches Wörterbuch.* Heidelberg: Winter 1961

651 J. Vachek & J. Dubsky, *Dictionnaire de linguistique de l'école de Prague.* Utrecht: Spectrum 1960

652 E. P. Hamp, *A Glossary of American Technical Linguistic Usage: 1925–1950.* Utrecht: Spectrum 1957

653 E. de Felice, *La Terminologia linguistica di G. I. Ascoli e della sua scuola.* Utrecht: Spectrum 1957

654 M. A. Pei & F. Gaynor, *A Dictionary of Linguistics.* New York: Philosophical Library 1954

655 J. Marouzeau, *Lexique de la terminologie linguistique: français, allemand, anglais, italien.* (3 ed.) Paris: Geuthner 1951

656 J. B. Hofmann & H. Rubenbauer, *Wörterbuch der grammatischen und metrischen Terminologie.* Heidelberg: Winter 1950

(See also **110**)

2.3.4 Linguistic Bibliographies

657 PICL, *Linguistic Bibliography for the Years 1939–47* (2 vols), *1948–61* (1 vol. per year) Utrecht & Antwerp: Spectrum 1949——(in progress)

658 SIL, *25th Anniversary Bibliography. Summer Institute of Linguistics.* Glendale (Cal.): Summer Institute of Linguistics 1960

* * *

659 W. G. Moulton, A Brief Bibliography of Linguistics for Foreign Language Teachers, *PMLA* 70: 33–5

2.3.5 Periodicals of Linguistics

See Nos. **1, 4, 5, 7, 10, 11, 15**a, **23, 24, 28, 30, 31, 34, 37, 38, 39, 40, 48, 52, 53, 58, 59, 60, 61, 62, 63, 63**a, **63**b, **64, 65, 67, 68, 69, 70, 72, 75**

2.4 SOME DESCRIPTIONS OF ENGLISH

2.4.1 English Dialects

659a H. Orton et al, *A Survey of English Dialects.* Leeds: Arnold 1963

660 H. Kurath & R. I. McDavid, *The Pronunciation of English in the Atlantic States.* Ann Arbor: Michigan U.P. 1962

660a A. Wall, *New Zealand English.* Wellington: Whitcombe & Tombs 1959

661 G. N. Putnam & E. M. O'Hern, *The Status Significance of an Isolated Urban Dialect. Lg.* Dissertation 53. Baltimore: Waverly 1955

662 W. J. Ball, *Conversational English. An analysis of contemporary spoken English for foreign students.* London: Longmans 1953

663 E. Ekwall, *American and British Pronunciation.* Upsala: Lundequistska 1946

664 A. G. Mitchell, *The Pronunciation of English in Australia.* Sydney: Angus & Robertson 1946

665 S. Baker, *The Australian Language.* Sydney: Angus & Robertson 1945

666 H. Mencken, *The American Language* (with 4 supplements). (4 ed.). New York: Knopf 1943–9

667 H. Kurath (ed.) et al, *Linguistic Atlas of New England,* 3 vols. Providence (R.I.): Brown U.P. 1939

668 W. Grant & J. M. Dixon, *A Manual of Modern Scots.* Cambridge: Cambridge U.P. 1921

* * *

669 P. Christophersen, Toward a Standard of International English, *ELT* 14: 127–37

670 M. West, Factual English, *ELT* 12: 121–31

671 M. West, American and British Usage, *ELT* 12: 41–5

672 G. A. Pittman, Trade and Technical English, *ELT* 11: 39–45

673 P. Strevens, English Overseas—Choosing a Model of Pronunciation, *ELT* 10: 123–31
674 D. Abercrombie, English Accents, *ELT* 7: 113–23
675 J. C. Catford, Intelligibility, *ELT* 5: 7–15

(See also **787**)

2.4.2 English Pronunciation

(i) *Articulation and Catenation*
675a A. C. Gimson, *An Introduction to the Pronunciation of English.* London: Arnold 1962
676 D. Jones, *An Outline of English Phonetics.* (9 ed.) Cambridge: Heffer 1960
677 A. J. Bronstein, *Pronunciation of American English.* New York: Appleton 1960
678 B. Nordhjem, *Phonemes of English: an experiment in structural phonemics.* Copenhagen: Gad 1960
679 G. C. Söderberg, *A Typological Study of the Phonetic Structure of English Words. With an Instrumental Phonetic Excursus on English Stress.* Lund: Ohlson 1959
680 R. Lado & C. C. Fries, *English Pronunciation.* (*Intensive course in English.*) Ann Arbor: Michigan U.P. 1958
681 W. Friederich, *English Pronunciation. The relationship between pronunciation and orthography.* (trans. R. A. Martin) London: Longmans 1958
682 E. Kruisinga, *An Introduction to the Study of English Sounds.* (11 ed., rev. by C. Hedeman & J. J. Westerbeek). The Hague: Noordhoff 1957
683 P. Christophersen, *An English Phonetics Course.* London: Longmans 1956
684 A. Stene, *Hiatus in English.* Copenhagen: Rosenkilde & Bagger 1954
685 C. H. Prator, *Manual of American English Pronunciation for Adult Foreign Students.* Los Angeles: California U.P. 1954
686 A. Cohen, *The Phonemes of English.* The Hague: Nijhoff 1952
687 W. F. Mackey, *English Pronunciation Drills.* Quebec: Presses de l'Université Laval 1951
688 D. Jones, *The Pronunciation of English* (3 ed.) Cambridge: Cambridge U.P. 1950
689 G. Faure, *Manuel pratique de l'anglais parlé.* Paris: Hachette 1948
690 C. K. Thomas, *An Introduction to the Phonetics of American English.* New York: Ronald 1947
691 J. S. Kenyon, *American Pronunciation* (9 ed.) Ann Arbor (Mich.): Wahr 1946
692 I. C. Ward, *The Phonetics of English.* Cambridge: Heffer (1 ed.) 1929, (4 ed.) 1945
693 P. A. D. McCarthy, *English Pronunciation. A practical handbook for the foreign learner.* Cambridge: Heffer 1944
694 E. Kruisinga, *The Phonetic Structure of English Words.* Bern: Francke 1942
695 A. Lloyd James, *Our Spoken Language.* New York: Nelson 1938
696 B. Trnka, *A Phonological Analysis of Present-day Standard English.* (Studies in English: 5) Prague: Studies in English 1935
697 W. Ripman, *English Phonetics. A revised version of "The Sounds of Spoken English".* London: Dent 1931

698   E. Kruisinga, *An Introduction to the Study of English Sounds*. Utrecht: Kemink & Zoon (1 ed.) 1914, (5 ed.) 1931

*   *   *

699   E. L. Tibbitts, Pronunciation Difficulties, *ELT* 1: 50, 78, 109–10, 167–8; 2: 47–8, 109–11, 162–6; 3: 53–6

700   J. C. Catford, Word-Linking, *ELT* 4: 115–20

701   H. E. Palmer, Concerning Pronunciation, *BIRET*. Tokyo: IRET 1925

702   J. D. O'Connor, Recent Work in English Phonetics, *Phonetica* 1: 96–117

2.4.2 (ii) *Rhythm*

702a B. L. Milne, *English Speech Rhythm in Theory and Practice*. London: Macmillan 1962

702b A. Vanvik, *On Stress in Present-day English*. Oslo: Norwegian Universities Press 1961

703   R. Kingdon, *The Groundwork of English Stress*. London: Longmans 1958

704   G. F. Arnold, *Stress in English Words*. Amsterdam: North-Holland 1957

705   B. L. Milne, *English Speech Rhythm*. London: Macmillan 1957

706   J. C. Catford & C. K. Ogden, *Word-Stress and Sentence-Stress*. London: Basic English Publishing Co. 1950

707   R. Las Vergnas, *Les Pièges de l'anglais parlé*. Paris: Hachette 1947

708   A. Classe, *The Rhythm of English Prose*. Oxford: Blackwell 1939

*   *   *

709   H. Mol & E. M. Uhlenbeck, The Linguistic Relevance of Intensity in Stress, *Lingua* 5: 205–13

2.4.2 (iii) *Intonation*

710   J. D. O'Connor & G. F. Arnold, *Intonation of Colloquial English: a practical handbook*. London: Longmans 1961

711   W. R. Lee, *An English Intonation Reader*. London: Macmillan 1960

712   R. Kingdon, *The Groundwork of English Intonation*. London: Longmans 1958

713   M. Schubiger, *English Intonation: its form and function*. Tübingen: Niemeyer 1958

714   W. S. Allen, *Living English Speech*. London: Longmans 1954

715   W. Jassem, *Intonation of Conversational English. Educated Southern British*. Warsaw: Wrocławska Drukarnia Naukowa 1952

716   K. L. Pike, *The Intonation of American English*. Ann Arbor: Michigan U.P. 1946

717   L. E. Armstrong & I. C. Ward, *A Handbook of English Intonation*. (2 ed.) Cambridge: Heffer 1931

718   H. E. Palmer, *English Intonation with Systematic Exercises*. Cambridge: Heffer 1924

*   *   *

719   J. Sledd, Review of R. Kingdon's *The Groundwork of English Intonation*, *Lg* 36: 173–9

720   W. R. Lee, English Intonation: a new approach, *Lingua* 5: 345–71

721 M. A. K. Halliday, English Intonation, (mimeographed) Edinburgh: University of Edinburgh 1960

722 D. L. Bolinger, A Theory of Pitch Accent in English, *Word* 14: 109–49

2.4.2 (iv) *English Spelling*

722a W. R. Lee, *Spelling Irregularity and Reading Difficulty in English*. London: National Foundation for Educational Research in England and Wales 1960
723 W. Ripman & W. Archer, *New Spelling*. London: Pitman 1948

*   *   *

723a W. Friederich, Spelling Rules, *ELT* 17: 20–26
724 M. West, English Spelling, *ELT* 9: 133–6

2.4.3 English Grammar

724a B. M. H. Strang, *Modern English Structure*. London: Arnold 1962
724b A. Juilland & J. Macris, *The English Verb System*. The Hague: Mouton 1962
724c R. B. Long, *The Sentence and its Parts: a grammar of contemporary English*. Chicago: Chicago U.P. 1961
725 R. B. Lees, *The Grammar of English Nominalizations*. Bloomington: Indiana U.P. 1960
726 H. Marchand, *The Categories and Types of Present-day English Word-formation. A synchronic-diachronic approach*. Wiesbaden: Harrassowitz 1960
727 J. H. Sledd, *A Short Introduction to English Grammar*. Chicago: Scott 1959
728 G. Scheurweghs, *Present-Day English Syntax*. London: Longmans 1959
729 A. Campbell, *Old English Grammar*. London: Oxford U.P. 1959
730 W. N. Francis & R. I. McDavid, *The Structure of American English*. New York: Ronald 1958
731 H. S. Sørensen, *Word-classes in Modern English*. Copenhagen: Gad 1958
732 D. W. Brown, W. C. Brown & D. Bailey, *Form in Modern English*. New York: Oxford U.P. 1958
733 P. Roberts, *Understanding English*. New York: Harper 1958
734 J. Millington Ward, *Peculiarities in English*. London: Longmans 1957
735 G. H. Vallins, *The Pattern of English*. London: Deutsch 1956
736 P. Roberts, *Patterns of English*. New York: Harcourt 1956
737 D. J. Lloyd & H. R. Warfel, *American English in its Cultural Setting*. New York: Knopf 1956
738 H. Whitehall, *Structural Essentials of English*. New York: Harcourt 1956, London: Longmans 1958
739 P. Roberts, *Understanding Grammar*. New York: Harper 1954
740 J. Millington Ward, *The Use of Tenses in English*. London: Longmans 1954
741 M. H. Scargill, *An English Handbook*. Toronto: Longmans 1954

742 A. S. Hornby, *A Guide to Patterns and Usage in English.* London: Oxford U.P. 1954

743 F. L. Sack, *The Structure of English,* Cambridge: Heffer 1954

744 E. Kruisinga & P. A. Erades, *An English Grammar,* 2 vols. Groningen: Noordhoff, (1 ed.) 1911, (8 ed.) 1953

745 C. C. Fries, *The Structure of English.* New York: Harcourt 1952, London: Longmans 1957

746 L. M. Myers, *American English.* New York: Prentice-Hall 1952

747 G. L. Trager & H. L. Smith, *An Outline of English Structure.* Norman (Okla.): Battenburg 1951

748 O. Jespersen, *A Modern English Grammar on Historical Principles.* 7 vols. Copenhagen: Munksgaard, London: Allen & Unwin 1909–49

749 A. C. E. Vechtman-Veth, *A Syntax of Living English.* (2 ed.) Groningen: Noordhoff 1947

750 R. W. Zandvoort, *A Handbook of English Grammar.* (1st English-Dutch ed.) Groningen: Wolters 1945, (All-English ed.) London: Longmans 1957, (French ed. by G. Bouvet, *Grammaire descriptive de l'anglais contemporain.* Paris: Editions IAC 1949)

751 M. M. Bryant, *A Functional English Grammar.* Boston: Heath 1945

752 C. C. Fries, *American English Grammar. The grammatical structure of present-day American English with especial reference to social differences or class dialects.* New York: Appleton 1940

753 E. Prokosch, *Comparative Germanic Grammar.* Philadelphia: Linguistic Society of America 1939

754 H. E. Palmer & F. G. Blandford, *A Grammar of Spoken English on a Strictly Phonetic Basis.* Cambridge: Heffer 1939

755 A. Blount & C. S. Northup, *Grammar and Usage.* New York: Prentice-Hall 1938

756 H. E. Palmer, *A Grammar of English Words.* London: Longmans 1938

757 H. R. Stoke, *The Understanding of Syntax. Based upon accurate definition and logical application of grammatical terms.* London: Heinemann 1937

758 H. E. Palmer, *Specimens of English Construction Patterns.* Tokyo: Department of Education 1934

759 J. R. Aiken, *A New Plan of English Grammar.* New York: Holt 1933

760 O. Jespersen, *Essentials of English Grammar.* London: Allen & Unwin 1933

761 E. Kruisinga, *A Handbook of Present-Day English. Part II—Accidence and Syntax.* 3 vols. Groningen: Noordhoff (1 ed.) 1911, (5 ed.) 1931

762 H. Poutsma, *A Grammar of Late Modern English.* 5 vols. Groningen: Noordhoff 1914–29

763 W. Wright, *Elementary Historical New English Grammar.* London: Oxford U.P. 1924

764 O. Jespersen, *Negation in English and Other Languages.* Copenhagen: Høst 1917

765 H. Sweet, *A New English Grammar: logical and historical.* 2 vols. Oxford: Oxford U.P. 1891

*   *   *

766 B. Bloch, English Verb Inflection, *Lg* 23: 399–418

2.4.4 English Dictionaries

766a J. L. Roget, *Thesaurus of English Words and Phrases.* (rev. R. A. Dutch) London: Longmans 1962

767 P. B. Gove (ed.), *Webster's Third New International Dictionary of the English Language.* Springfield (Mass.): Merriam-Webster 1961

767a M. P. West & J. G. Endicott, *The New Method English Dictionary.* (4 ed.) London: Longmans 1961

768 *Chambers's Foundation English Dictionary.* Edinburgh: Chambers 1960

769 D. Jones, *Everyman's English Pronouncing Dictionary.* (11 ed.) London: Dent 1958

770 C. L. Barnhart & J. Stein (eds.) *American College Dictionary.* New York: Random House 1956

771 C. E. Funk (ed.), *New College Standard Dictionary.* New York & London: Funk & Wagnalls 1956

772 W. Little et al (rev. C. T. Onions), *The Shorter Oxford English Dictionary.* 2 vols. London: Oxford U.P. 1955

773 J. R. Hulbert, *Dictionaries: British and American.* London: Deutsch 1955

774 A. S. Hornby, E. V. Gatenby & H. Wakefield, *The Advanced Learner's Dictionary of Current English.* London: Oxford U.P. 1953

775 H. G. Emery & K. G. Brewster (eds.), *The New Century Dictionary.* 2 vols. New York: Appleton 1952

776 E. Partridge, *A Dictionary of Slang* (3 ed.). London: Routledge & Kegan Paul 1949

777 B. L. K. Henderson, *A Dictionary of English Idioms.* 2 vols. London: Blackwood 1948

778 J. S. Kenyon & T. A. Knott, *Pronouncing Dictionary of American English.* Springfield (Mass.): Merriam 1944

779 W. A. Craigie & J. R. Hulbert (eds.), *Dictionary of American English on Historical Principles.* Chicago: Chicago U.P. 1938–43

780 C. K. Ogden, *The General Basic English Dictionary.* New York: Norton 1942

781 H. E. Palmer, *A Grammar of English Words.* London: Longmans 1938

782 M. West, *Definition Vocabulary.* Toronto: Toronto U.P. 1935

783 M. M. Mathews, *Survey of English Dictionaries.* London: Oxford U.P. 1933

784 J. A. H. Murray, H. Bradley, W. A. Craigie & C. T. Onions (eds.), *Oxford English Dictionary on Historical Principles.* 12 vols. London: Oxford U.P. 1933

785 R. E. Zachrisson, *An English Pronouncing Dictionary and Spelling List in Anglic.* Cambridge: Heffer 1933

786 H. W. & F. G. Fowler, *Concise Oxford Dictionary.* London: Oxford U.P. 1911

787 J. Wright, *English Dialect Dictionary.* 6 vols. London: Frowde 1898–1905

*   *   *

788 W. F. Mackey, Slang, *Encyclopaedia Britannica* 1959

(See also **845**)

2.4.5 Periodicals on the English Language

See Nos. **2, 3, 15, 16, 17, 18, 32, 45, 62, 73**

2.5 SOME DESCRIPTIONS OF FRENCH

2.5.1 French Dialects

788a P. Nauton, *Atlas linguistique et ethnographique du Massif Central.* 3 vols. Paris: C.N.R.S. 1957

788b P. Gardette et al, *Atlas linguistique et ethnographique du Lyonnais.* 3 vols. Lyon: Institut de linguistique romane des Facultés catholiques de Lyon 1956

788c J. Séguy et al, *Atlas linguistique et ethnographique de la Gascogne.* 3 vols. Paris: C.N.R.S. 1956

789 J. Haust, *Atlas linguistique de la Wallonie.* 2 vols. Liège: Vaillant-Carmanne 1953

790 A. Martinet, *La prononciation du français contemporain.* Paris: Droz 1945

791 Société du Parler français, *Glossaire du parler français au Canada.* Quebec: Action 1932

792 J. Gilliéron & E. Edmont, *Atlas linguistique de la France.* Paris: Champion 1902–12

2.5.2 French Pronunciation

793 P. Fouché, *Traité de prononciation française.* Paris: Klincksieck 1956

793a H. Sten, *Manuel de phonetique française.* Copenhagen: Munksgaard 1956

794 P. Burney, *L'orthographe.* Paris: Presses universitaires 1955

795 M. Peyrollaz & M. L. B. de Tovar, *Manuel de phonétique et de diction à l'usage des étrangers.* Paris: Larousse 1954

796 P. Fouché, *Phonétique historique du français.* (Introduction.) Paris: Klincksieck 1952

797 G. Straka, *La prononciation parisienne, ses divers aspects et ses traits généraux.* Strasbourg: *Bulletin de la Faculté des lettres* 1952

798 B. Malmberg, *Le système consonantique du français moderne. Etudes de phonétique et de phonologie.* Lund: Gleerup 1943

799 M. Grammont, *La prononciation française. Traité pratique.* (10 ed.) Paris: Delagrave 1941

800 G. Gougenheim, *Eléments de phonologie française.* Paris: Belles Lettres 1935

801 H. N. Coustenoble & L. E. Armstrong, *Studies in French Intonation.* Cambridge: Heffer 1934

801a L. E. Armstrong, *The Phonetics of French.* London: Bell 1932

802 O. F. Bond, *The Sounds of French.* Chicago: Chicago U.P. 1925

(See also **790, 821, 822, 862, 864, 1528a** and under 2.5.4)

2.5.3 French Grammar

803 M. Grevisse, *Précis de grammaire française* (25 ed.) Gembloux: Duculot 1959

804 M. Grevisse, *Le bon usage*. (7 ed.) Gembloux: Duculot 1959
805 W. von Wartburg & P. Zumthor, *Précis de syntaxe du français contemporain*. (2 ed. rev.) Bern: Francke 1958
806 C. de Boer, *Syntaxe du français moderne*. Leiden: Leiden U.P. 1948, 1954
807 F. Kahn, *Le système des temps de l'indicatif chez un Parisien et chez une Bâloise*. Geneva: Droz 1954
808 S. Roller, *La conjugaison française. Essai de pédagogie expérimentale*. Neuchâtel: Delachaux & Niestlé 1954
809 J. Damourette & E. Pichon, *Des mots à la pensée. Essai de grammaire de la langue française*. 7 vols. Paris: d'Artrey 1911–52
810 K. Togeby, *Structure immanente de la langue française*. Copenhagen: Nordisk Sprog- og Kulturforlag 1951
811 K. Sandfeld, *Syntaxe du français contemporain*. 3 vols. Paris: Champion 1928, 1936, 1943
812 G. R. Le Bidois, *Syntaxe du français moderne*. 2 vols. Paris: Picard 1935–8
813 F. Brunot, *La pensée et la langue*. Paris: Masson 1926

2.5.4 French Dictionaries

814 *Grand Larousse Encyclopédique*. 3 vols. (+ 7 in progress) Paris: Larousse 1960–
815 P. Robert, *Dictionnaire alphabétique et analogique de la langue française*. Paris: Presses universitaires 1956–1964
816 C. & P. Augé (eds.), *Nouveau Petit Larousse*. Paris: Larousse 1958
817 G. Gougenheim, *Dictionnaire fondamental de la langue française*. Paris: Didier 1958
818 E. Littré, *Dictionnaire de la langue française*. 7 vols. Paris: Pauvert 1956–8
819 R. L. Collison, *Dictionaries of Foreign Languages*. London: Hafner 1955
820 L'Académie française, *Dictionnaire de l'Académie*. 2 vols. (8 ed.) Paris: Hachette 1931–5
821 A. Barbeau & E. Rodhe, *Dictionnaire phonétique de la langue française*. Stockholm: Norstedt 1930
822 H. Michaelis & P. Passy, *Dictionnaire phonétique de la langue française*. (2 ed.) Berlin: Meyer 1914

(See also **845**)

2.5.5 Periodicals on the French Language

See Nos. **20, 21, 42, 43, 44, 45, 46, 47, 54, 62, 63a, 71, 74**

2.6 SOME DESCRIPTIONS OF GERMAN

2.6.1 German Dialects

823 R. E. Keller, *German Dialects. Their Phonology and Morphology*. Manchester: Manchester U.P. 1961
824 F. Wrede, W. Mitzka & B. Martin (eds.), *Deutscher Sprachatlas*. Marburg: Elwert 1953
825 A. Bach, *Deutsche Mundartforschung*. Heidelberg: Winter 1934

2.6.2 German Pronunciation

826 T. Siebs, H. de Boor & P. Diels, *Deutsche Hochsprache, Bühnenaussprache*. (18 ed.) Berlin: Gruyter 1961

827 C. & P. Martens, *Phonetik der deutschen Sprache. Praktische Aussprachelehre*. Munich: Hueber 1961

828 H.-H. Wängler, *Grundriss einer Phonetik des Deutschen*. Marburg: Elwert 1960

829 H.-H. Wängler, *Atlas deutscher Sprachlaute*. Berlin: Akademie-Verlag 1958

830 O. von Essen, *Grundzüge der hochdeutschen Satzintonation*. Düsseldorf: Henn 1956

831 W. L. Wardale, *German Pronunciation*. Edinburgh: Edinburgh U.P. 1955

832 C. Winkler, *Deutsche Sprechkunde und Sprecherziehung*. Düsseldorf: Schwann 1954

833 J. Bithell, *German Pronunciation and Phonology*. London: Methuen 1952

834 A. Egan, *A German Phonetic Reader*. London: University of London Press 1913

835 M. L. Barker, *A Handbook of German Intonation*. Cambridge: Heffer 1925

(See also **849** and **864**)

2.6.3 German Grammar

836 H. Glinz, *Deutsche Syntax*. Stuttgart: Metzler 1961

837 H. Glinz, *Die innere Form des Deutschen*. (2 ed.) Bern: Francke 1961

838 K. Duden & P. Grebe, *Grammatik der deutschen Gegenwartssprache*. Mannheim: Bibliographisches Institut 1959

839 H. Glinz, *Der deutsche Satz*. Düsseldorf: Schwann 1957

840 G. O. Curme, *A Grammar of the German Language*. (3 ed.) New York: Ungar 1952

841 E. Drach, *Grundgedanken der deutschen Satzlehre*. Frankfurt: Diesterweg 1937

842 E. Kruisinga, *Einführung in die deutsche Syntax*. Groningen: Noordhoff 1935

843 O. Behaghel, *Deutsche Syntax*. 4 vols. Heidelberg: Winter 1923–32

2.6.4 German Dictionaries

844 *Der neue Brockhaus*. 6 vols. Wiesbaden: Brockhaus 1958–60

845 W. Zaunmüller, *Bibliographisches Handbuch der Sprachwörterbücher*. Stuttgart: Hiersemann 1958

846 H. Paul, *Deutsches Wörterbuch*. (5 ed. by W. Betz) Tübingen: Niemeyer 1957

847 F. Dornseiff, *Der deutsche Wortschatz nach Sachgruppen*. Berlin: Gruyter 1955

848 A. Götze (ed.), *Trübners deutsches Wörterbuch*. 8 vols. Berlin: Trübner 1939

849 W. Viëtor, *Deutsches Aussprachwörterbuch* (5 ed.) Leipzig: Reisland 1931

(See also **819**)

2.6.5 Periodicals on the German Language

See Nos. **13**, **14**, **15**, **25**, **32**, **41**, **42**, **43**, **44**, **45**, **46**, **47**, **54**, **62**, **74**

3. LANGUAGE DIFFERENCES & APPLIED LINGUISTICS

3.1 DIFFERENTIAL ANALYSIS

849a H. L. Kufner, *The Grammatical Structure of English and German.* Chicago: Chicago U.P. 1962

849b W. G. Moulton, *The Sounds of English and German: a contrastive analysis.* Chicago: Chicago U.P. 1962

849c W. W. Gage, *Contrastive Studies in Linguistics. A bibliographical checklist.* Washington: Center for Applied Linguistics 1961

850 H. Glinz, *Sprachliche Bildung in der höheren Schule. Skizze einer vergleichenden Satzlehre für Latein, Deutsch, Französisch und Englisch.* Düsseldorf: Schwann 1961

850a A. Malblanc, *Stylistique comparée du français et de l'allemand. Essai de représentation linguistique comparée et étude de traduction.* Paris: Didier 1961

851 J-P. Vinay & J. Darbelnet, *Stylistique comparée du français et de l'anglais.* Paris: Didier 1958, London: Harrap 1960

852 W. F. Mackey, *Graded Conversations: with phonetic guides in French, German, Italian, Hungarian and Dutch.* (photo-offset) Ottawa: Citizenship Branch 1958

853 R. Lado, *Linguistics across Cultures. Applied linguistics for language teachers.* Ann Arbor: Michigan U.P. 1957

854 E. Petrovici, *Kann das Phonemsystem einer Sprache durch fremden Einfluss umgestaltet werden? Zum slavischen Einfluss auf das rumänische Lautsystem.* The Hague: Mouton 1957

855 L. Deroy, *L'emprunt linguistique.* Paris: Belles Lettres 1956

856 E. Haugen, *Bilingualism in the Americas. A bibliography and research guide.* University (Ala.): Alabama U.P. 1956

857 K. H. Schönfelder, *Probleme der Völker- und Sprachmischung.* Halle: Niemeyer 1956

858 U. Weinreich, *Languages in Contact. Findings and problems.* New York: Linguistic Circle of New York 1953

859 R. MacQuinghen, *L'anglais moderne—Modern French. 3,000 expressions in constant use with their English equivalents.* Paris: Dunod 1953

860 E. Haugen, *The Norwegian Language in America. A Study in bilingual behavior.* 2 vols. Philadelphia: Pennsylvania U.P. 1953

861 C. H. Bissell, *Prepositions in French and English.* New York: R. Smith 1947

862 P. Genévrier, *Précis de phonétique comparée française et anglaise et Manuel de prononciation française à l'usage des étudiants anglo-saxons.* Paris: Didier 1927

863 H. Rheinfelder, *Vergleichende Sprachbetrachtung im neusprachlichen Unterricht.* Munich: Hueber 1926

864 W. Viëtor, *Elemente der Phonetik des Deutschen, Englischen und Französischen.* Leipzig: Teubner 1923

* * *

865 F. Kahn, Phonétique et grammaire comparatives pour l'enseignement de l'allemand dans les écoles primaires et secondaires de langue française, *CFS* 16: 33–90

866 W. F. Mackey, Bilingualism and Linguistic Structure, *Culture* 14: 143–9

867 A. Katona, Grammatical Difficulties of Hungarian Students in Learning English, *ELT* 14: 70–3

867a L. C. Harmer, Sur l'emploi de la voix passive en anglais et en français, *FdM* 8: 7–8

867b P. R. Léon, De l'allemand au français, *FdM* 4: 45–8

868 G. Guillaume, Examen comparatif des systèmes verbo-temporels français et anglais, *FM* 19: 29–41

869 E. Haugen, Problems of Bilingual Description, *GL* 1: 1–9

869a P. Delattre, Research Techniques for Phonetic Comparison of Languages, *IRAL* 1: 85–97

870 J. Darbelnet, La couleur en français et en anglais, *JT* 2: 4–10

870a W. F. Mackey, Bilingual Interference: its analysis and measurement, (mimeographed). Prepared for the Symposium on Psycholinguistics of the Canadian Psychological Association, Quebec: Laval University Department of Linguistics 1963

871 E. Haugen, The Analysis of Linguistic Borrowing, *Lg* 26: 210–31

872 E. Haugen, The Phoneme in Bilingual Description, *LL* 7: 17–24

873 G. Piroch, The Importance of Bilingual Description to Language Learning, *LL* 6: 51–61

874 A. Malblanc, La représentation du temps dans les verbes allemands et français, *LM* 48: 11–18

875 E. Haugen, Problems of Bilingualism, *Lingua* 2: 271–90

876 A. Steiger, Zur vergleichenden Grammatik im Fremdsprachunterricht, *VR* 13: 1–15

877 N. M. Holmer, Comparative Semantics: a new aspect of linguistics, *Yearbook of the New Society of Letters at Lund* (Sweden) 1949–50: 5–18

(See also **583**, **962** and **966**)

3.2 TRANSLATION THEORY

877a S. B. Wynburne, *Vertical Translation and the Teaching of English*. London: P.R.M. Publishers 1961

878 M. Koessler & J. Derocquigny, *Les faux-amis, ou les trahisons du vocabulaire anglais. Conseils aux traducteurs*. (5 ed.) Paris: Vuibert 1961

879 L. Dupont, *Les faux amis espagnols. Dictionnaire des difficultés espagnoles et françaises*. Geneva: Droz 1961

879a W. W. Bower, *International Manual of Linguists and Translators*. New York: Scarecrow 1959, 1st suppl. 1961

880 R. A. Brower (ed.), *On Translation*. Cambridge (Mass.): Harvard U.P. 1959

881 A. V. Fedorov, *Vvedenie v teoriju perevoda* (Introduction to translation theory). (2 ed.) Moscow: Izd. Literatury na Inostr. Jazykax 1958

882 T. H. Savory, *The Art of Translation*. London: Cape 1957

883 F. Boillot, *Le vrai ami du traducteur anglais-français et français-anglais*. (2 ed.) Paris: Oliven 1956

884 IJAL, *International Journal of American Linguistics 20, Special Issue on Translation*. Bloomington: Indiana U.P. 1954

885 J-P. Vinay (ed.) *Traductions*. Montreal: Inst. de Traduction 1952

886 J. G. Weightman, *On Language and Writing*. London: Sylvan 1947
886a J. Derocquigny, *Autres mots anglais perfides*. Paris: Vuibert 1931
886b H. Veslot, *Les épines du thème anglais*. Paris: Hachette 1928
886c H. Veslot & J. Banchet, *Les traquenards de la version anglaise*. Paris: Hachette 1922

* * *

886d J. Darbelnet, Traduction et stylistique comparée, *FdM* 6: 6–9
886e L. Lecocq, Stylistique et traduction, *LM* 55: 188–93

3.3 APPLIED LINGUISTICS IN LANGUAGE TEACHING

887 S. Belasco (ed.), *Anthology for Use with a Guide for Teachers in NDEA Language Institutes*. Boston: Heath 1961
887a D. N. Cárdenas, *Applied Linguistics: Spanish. A guide for teachers*. Boston: Heath 1961
887b R. L. Politzer & C. N. Stauback, *Teaching Spanish: a linguistic orientation*. Boston: Ginn 1961
887c R. L. Politzer, *Teaching French: an introduction to applied linguistics*. Boston: Ginn 1960
888 N. Brooks, *Language and Language Learning. Theory and Practice*. New York: Harcourt 1960
889 H. B. Allen, *Readings in Applied English Linguistics*. New York: Appleton 1958
890 LL, Selected Articles from *Language Learning*. Series 1: English as a Foreign Language. Ann Arbor (Mich.): English Language Institute 1955
891 E. Pulgram (ed.), *Applied Linguistics in Language Teaching*. Washington: Georgetown U.P. 1954
892 P. Sainte-Marie, *De la nécessité d'une linguistique appliquée*. Paris: Coulouma 1953
893 E. A. Nida, *Learning a Foreign Language. A Handbook for Missionaries*. (2 ed.) New York: National Council of the Churches of Christ 1950
894 K. Wähmer, *Spracherlernung und Sprachwissenschaft*. Leipzig: Teubner 1914

* * *

895 M. R. Haas, The Application of Linguistics to Language Teaching, in A. L. Kroeber (ed.) *Anthropology Today*, Chicago: Chicago U.P. 1953
896 C. C. Fries, Structural Linguistics and Language Teaching, *Classical Journal* 52: 265–68
897 S. Vail, Logical Analysis and Linguistics (The Teaching of Classical Languages), *Classical Journal* 52: 274–8
898 W. R. Lee, Linguistics and the Practical Teacher, *ELT* 13: 159–70
898a M. A. K. Halliday, Linguistique générale et linguistique appliquée, *ELA* 1: 5–42
898b A. Valdman, Vers l'application de la linguistique à l'enseignement du français parlé, *FdM* 7: 10–15
898c B. Quémada, Lexicologie et enseignement des langues étrangères, *FdM* 5: 2–4

899 E. Pulgram, Linguistics for More Language Teachers, *FR* 32: 147–55
900 D. N. Cárdenas, The Application of Linguistics in the Teaching of Spanish, *Hispania* 40: 455–60
900a A. P. van Teslaar, Les domaines de la linguistique appliquée, *IRAL* 1: 50–77
900b J. B. Carroll, Linguistic Relativity, Contrastive Linguistics, and Language Learning, *IRAL* 1: 1–20
901 S. St. Clair-Sobell, Phonology and Language Teaching, *JCLA* 2: 14–18
901a Y. Shen, Linguistic Experience and Language Habit, *LL* 12: 133–50
901b C. Métais, Quelques problèmes immédiats de la linguistique appliquée, *LM* 56: 235–7
902 A. Molès, Acoustique, phonétique et enseignement des langues vivantes, *LM* 46: 33–41
902a B. Siertsema, Language Learning and Language Analysis, *Lingua* 10: 128–47
903 W. Real, Linguistique et pédagogie, in *Mélanges Bally* 63–71, Geneva: Georg 1939
904 A. Perrenoud, Linguistique et pédagogie, in *Mélanges Niedermann* 179–84, Neuchâtel: University of Neuchâtel 1944
905 J. T. Waterman, Linguistics for the Language Teacher, *MLF* 41: 9–16
906 R. B. Long, Linguistics and Language Teaching: Caveats from English, *MLJ* 45: 149–55
907 A. A. Hill, Language Analysis and Language Teaching, *MLJ* 40: 335–45
908 M. L. Perkins, General Language Study and the Teaching of Languages, *MLJ* 40: 113–19
909 E. F. Haden, Descriptive Linguistics in the Teaching of a FL, *MLJ* 38: 170–6
910 E. Haugen, Linguistics and the Wartime Program of Language Teaching, *MLJ* 34: 243–5
911 W. Mues, Kernfragen des modernen englischen Sprachunterrichts, *NS* 4: 14, 66, 117
912 W. Preusler, Sprachwissenschaft und Schulunterricht, *NS* 3: 392–400
913 A. T. MacAllister, The Princeton Language Program, *PMLA* 70: 15–22
914 C. C. Fries, American Linguistics and the Teaching of English, *RLaV* 21: 294–310
915 G. Kandler, Zum Aufbau der angewandten Sprachwissenschaft, *Sf* 1: 3–9
915a W. F. Mackey, Language Didactics and Applied Linguistics, *Suomen Uusien Kielten Opettajien Liitto Vuosikirja* 4: 23–34
916 W. G. Moulton, Linguistics and Language Teaching in the United States: 1940–1960, in *Trends* (see No. 97 above): 82–109
917 N. D. Andreev & L. R. Zinder, Osnovnye problemy prikladnoj lingvistiki (The fundamental problems of applied linguistics), *VJa* 4: 1–9
918 K. H. Glaksch, Zur Frage der theoretischen Grundlagen des Grammatikunterrichts und ihrer methodischen Bedeutung für den Unterricht in den modernen Fremdsprachen, *Wissenschaft. Z. der U. Greifswald* 4 (1954): 139–41

(See also **1254** and **1301**)

4. LANGUAGE LEARNING

4.1 LEARNING THE FIRST LANGUAGE

918a M. Cohen et al, *Etudes sur le langage de l'enfant.* Paris: Scarabée 1962

919 I. & P. Opie, *The Lore and Language of Schoolchildren.* London: Oxford U.P. 1959

920 W. Kaper, *Kindersprachforschung mit Hilfe des Kindes.* Groningen: Wolters 1959

921 A. R. Luria & F. I. Yudovich, *Speech and the Development of Mental Processes in the Child.* (trans. J. Simon) London: Staples 1959

922 H. & R. Kahane & S. Saporta, *Development of Verbal Categories in Child Language.* Baltimore: Waverly 1958

923 C. Landreth, *The Psychology of Early Childhood.* New York: Knopf 1958

924 M. M. Lewis, *How Children Learn to Speak.* London: Harrap 1957

925 M. C. Templin, *Certain Language Skills in Children.* Minneapolis: Minnesota U.P. 1957

926 M. E. Morley, *The Development and Disorders of Speech in Childhood.* Edinburgh: Livingstone 1957

927 F. R. Schreiber, *Your Child's Speech.* New York: Putnam 1956

928 R. Griffiths, *The Abilities of Babies.* London: University of London Press 1954

929 W. F. Leopold, *Bibliography of Child Language.* Evanston & Chicago: Northwestern U.P. 1952

930 M. M. Lewis, *Infant Speech.* London: Routledge & Kegan Paul 1951

931 J. Piaget, *Play, Dreams and Imitation in Childhood.* (trans. C. Gattegno & F. M. Hodgson of *La formation du symbole chez l'enfant.* Neuchâtel: Delachaux & Niestlé 1945) London: Heinemann 1951

932 L. Stein, *The Speech of Infancy and the Infancy of Speech.* London: Methuen 1949

933 R. Jakobson, *Kindersprache, Aphasie und allgemeine Lautgesetze.* Upsala: Almqvist & Wiksell 1941

934 A. Gesell et al, *The First Five Years of Life.* New York & London: Harper 1940

935 A. Grégoire, *L'apprentissage du langage. Les deux premières années.* 2 vols. Paris: Droz 1937

936 H. Delacroix, *Le langage et l'enfant.* Paris: Alcan 1934

937 J. Piaget, *The Language and Thought of the Child.* (2 ed.) (trans. M. Gabain of *Le langage et la pensée chez l'enfant.* Neuchâtel: Delachaux & Niestlé 1923) London: Routledge & Kegan Paul 1932

938 W. Stern, *Psychologie der frühen Kindheit bis zum 6. Lebensjahr.* (6 ed.) Leipzig: Quelle & Meyer 1930

939 C. & W. Stern, *Die Kindersprache.* Leipzig: Barth 1928

*   *   *

940 D. McCarthy, Language Development in Children, in *Manual of Child Psychology* (ed. L. Carmichael), New York: Wiley, 1946

941 J. H. S. Bossard, Family modes of expression, *American Sociological Review* 10: 226–37

942 M. Cohen, Sur l'étude du langage enfantin, *Enfance* 5: 181–249

943 R. A. Hall, Idiolect and Linguistic Super-ego, *SL* 5: 21–7

944 C. P. Darlington, The Genetic Components of Language, *Heredity* 1: 269–86

944a M. D. S. Braine, The Ontogeny of English Phrase Structure: the first phase, *Lg* 39: 1–13

945 W. F. Leopold, Patterns in Children's Language Learning, *LL* 5: 1–14

946 M. Grammont, Observations sur le langage des enfants, *Mélanges Meillet*, Paris: Klincksieck 1902

947 J. S. & R. W. Albright, The Sound System of an Eight-year-old Boy, *MPhon* 107: 3–5

948 J. Berko, The Child's Learning of English Morphology, *Word* 14: 150–77

949 R. W. & J. S. Albright, The Phonology of a Two-year-old Child, *Word* 12: 370–81

4.2 LEARNING SECOND LANGUAGES

949a W. M. Rivers, *The Psychologist and the Foreign-Language Teacher.* Chicago: Chicago U.P. 1964

949b W. E. Lambert et al, *A Study of the Roles of Attitudes and Motivation in Second-Language Learning.* (mimeographed) Montreal: McGill University Department of Psychology 1962

949c J. B. Carroll, *The Prediction of Success in Intensive Foreign Language Training.* (mimeographed) Cambridge (Mass.): Harvard University School of Education 1960

949d Ja. V. Golubev, *Voprosy psixologii načal'nogo izučenija inostrannogo jazyka* (Problems in the psychology of beginning foreign language-learning). Monograph 112. Leningrad: Herzen Pedagogical Institute 1955

950 F. B. Agard & H. B. Dunkel, *An Investigation of Second-Language Learning.* Boston: Ginn 1948

951 H. B. Dunkel, *Second-Language Learning.* Boston: Ginn 1948

952 H. Goldstein, *Reading and Listening Comprehension at Various Controlled Rates.* New York: Columbia Teachers College 1940

* * *

953 J. J. Findlay, The Psychology of Modern Language Learning, *British Journal of Psychology* 2: 319–33

953a R. C. Gardner & W. E. Lambert, Motivational Variables in Second-Language Acquisition, *Canadian Journal of Psychology* 13: 266–72

954 M. West, Learning English as Behaviour, *ELT* 15: 3–10

954a M. West, At What Age should Language Teaching Begin?, *ELT* 14: 21–5

955 M. West, The Adult Learner, *ELT* 11: 50–6

956 D. F. Anderson, A Survey of Abilities Needed in Learning English, *ELT* 5: 171–93

957 E. V. Gatenby, Conditions for Success in Language Learning, *ELT* 4: 143–9, 179–82

958 M. M. Lewis, Fundamental Skills in the Learning of a Second Language, *ELT* 2: 169–72; 3: 29–32

959 E. V. Gatenby, Reasons for Failure to Learn a Foreign Language, *ELT* 2: 102–6, 134–8

959*a* E. V. Gatenby, Second Language in the Kindergarten, *ELT* 1: 178–81
959*b* C. Bouton, Motivation et enseignement des langues, *ELA* 1: 85–94
960 W. Penfield, Human Brain and the Learning of Languages, *Food for Thought* 14: 18–22
961 H. Bonnard, Fonctionnalisme et pédagogie, *FM* 24: 205–12
962 J. Cano, Errores más comunes de sintaxis española que cometen los extranjeros, *Hispania* 4: 227–35
962*a* W. E. Lambert et al, Attitudinal and Congitive Aspects of Intensive Study of a Second Language, *J. of Abnormal and Social Psychology 68*
962*b* W. E. Lambert, Measurement of the Linguistic Dominance of Bilinguals, *J. of Abnormal and Social Psychology* 50: 197–200
963 H. B. Dunkel, The Effect of Personality Type on Language Achievement, *J. of Educational Psychology* 38: 177–82
963*a* L. A. Jakobovits & W. E. Lambert, Semantic Satiation among Bilinguals, *J. of Experimental Psychology*, 62: 576–82
964 W. E. Young, The Relation of Reading Comprehension and Retention to Hearing Comprehension and Retention, *J. of Experimental Psychology* 5: 30–9
964*a* W. E. Lambert, Developmental Aspects of Second-Language Acquisition, *J. of Social Psychology* 43: 83–104
965 F. Thomas, Perspectives psycho-pédagogiques sur l'acquisition des langues étrangères, *LM* 49: 10–21
965*a* H. Lane, Some Differences between First and Second Language Learning, *LL* 12: 1–14
966 J. P. Breckheimer, The Kind and Frequency of Typical Errors in Written French, *MLF* 12: 5–7
966*a* W. E. Lambert, Psychological Approaches to the Study of Language, *MLJ* 47: 51–62, 114–21
967 L. A. Larew, The Optimum Age for beginning a Foreign Language, *MLJ* 45: 203–6
968 P. F. Angiolillo, French for the Feeble Minded: an experiment, *MLJ* 26: 266–71
969 D. T. Spoerl, A Study of Some of the Factors Involved in Language Learning, *MLJ* 23: 428–31
970 A. G. Bovée & G. J. Froelich, Some Observations on the Relationship between Mental Ability and Achievement in French, *School Review* 53: 534–7
971 W. Penfield, The Human Brain and the Learning of Secondary Languages, *TE* 4: 73–5
972 W. von Raffler, Results from Research in American Immigrant Language applied to Foreign Language Teaching, *ZPhon* 10: 66–8

4.3 BILINGUALISM

4.3.1 **General**

972*a* V. Vildomec, *Multilingualism: a study in general linguistics and psychology of speech*. Leyden: Sythoff 1963

973 P. Christophersen, *Bilingualism. An inaugural lecture.* London: Methuen 1948

*   *   *

974 W. F. Mackey, Bilingualism, *Encyclopaedia Britannica* 1959
975 W. F. Mackey, Lingua Franca, *Encyclopaedia Britannica* 1959
976 G. E. Perren, Bilingualism or Replacement? English in East Africa, *ELT* 13: 18–21
977 M. West, Bilingualism, *ELT* 12: 94–6
978 E. Haugen, Some Pleasures and Problems of Bilingual Research, *IJAL* 20: 116–22
979 E. Haugen, Bilingualism and Mixed Languages, *GUMSL* 7: 9–19
980 W. F. Mackey, Towards a Re-definition of Bilingualism, *JCLA* 3: 2–11

(See also bibliographies in **856, 858,** and **1000**)

4.3.2 The Bilingual Child

981 W. F. Leopold, *Speech Development of a Bilingual Child: A Linguist's Record.* 4 vols. Evanston & Chicago: Northwestern U.P. 1939–49
982 D. Tits, *Le mécanisme de l'acquisition d'une langue se substituant à la langue maternelle chez une enfant espagnole âgée de six ans.* Brussels: Veldeman 1948
983 M. Pavlovitch, *Le langage enfantin—acquisition du serbe et du français par un enfant serbe.* Paris: Champion 1920
984 J. Ronjat, *Le développement du langage observé chez un enfant bilingue.* Paris: Champion 1913

*   *   *

985 W. F. Leopold, A Child's Learning of Two Languages, *GUMSL* 7
986 W. Waterhouse, Learning a Second Language First, *IJAL* 15:106–9
987 W. F. Leopold, A Study of Child Language and Infant Bilingualism, *Word* 4: 1–17

4.3.3 The Bilingual School

987a T. Österberg, *Bilingualism and the First School Language.* Umeå (Sweden): Våterbottens 1961
988 W. R. Jones et al, *The Educational Attainment of Bilingual Children in Relation to their Intelligence and Linguistic Background.* Aberystwyth: University College of Wales 1957
989 R. E. Davies, *Bilingualism in Wales, Eire and Belgium—with special reference to language teaching.* (MS). Pretoria: Registrar of Copyright 1952
990 Welsh Dept. Ministry of Education, *Bilingualism in the Secondary School in Wales.* London: H.M. Stationery Office 1949
991 N. Toussaint, *Bilinguisme et éducation.* Brussels: Lamertin 1935
992 E. G. Malherbe, *The Bilingual School.* Johannesburg: Rostra 1934
993 M. West, *Bilingualism.* Calcutta: Bureau of Education 1926

*   *   *

994 W. F. Mackey & J. A. Noonan, An Experiment in Bilingual **Education,** *ELT* 6: 125–32
995 S. M. Ervin & C. E. Osgood, Second Language Learning and **Bilingualism,** *Psycholinguistics IJAL* 20 (suppl.): 139–46
996 H. Singer, Bilingualism and Elementary Education, *MLJ* 50: 444–58
997 W. F. Mackey, Bilingualism and Education, *Pédagogie-Orientation* 6: 135–47
998 J. Wilson, Second Language Teaching and the Problem of Bilingualism, *Studies* (Dublin) 1960
999 E. F. O'Doherty, Bilingual School Policy, *Studies* (Dublin) 1958

4.3.4 The Problems of Bilingualism

1000 J. I. Williams et al, *Bilingualism* (*A Bibliography with Special Reference to Wales*). Aberystwyth: University College of Wales Faculty of Education 1960
1001 University College of Wales, *Bilingualism and Non-verbal Intelligence.* (*Faculty of Education Pamphlet* 4) Aberystwyth: University College of Wales 1957
1002 University College of Wales, *A Review of Problems for Research into Bilingualism.* (*Faculty of Education Pamphlet* 1) Aberystwyth: University College of Wales 1953
1002a A. V. Jarmolenko, *K voprosy o psixologii mnogojazyčija* (On the problem of the psychology of multilingualism.) "*Materialy Universitetskoj psixologičeskoj konferencii*" (University Lectures in Psychology) Leningrad: LGU 1949

*   *   *

1003 W. F. Mackey, The Description of Bilingualism, *JCLA* 7: 53–90
1003a W. E. Lambert, J. Havelka & C. Crosby, The Influence of Language Acquisition Contexts on Bilingualism, *J. of Abnormal and Social Psychology* 56: 239–44
1003b W. F. Mackey, Cadres d'analyses fonctionnelles pour servir de base à la mensuration du bilinguisme (summary), *Les Annales de l'Acfas* 1961
1004 G. B. Johnson, Bilingualism as Measured by a Reaction-time Technique, *J. of Genetic Psychology* 82: 3–10
1005 N. T. Darcy, A Review of the Literature on the Effects of Bilingualism upon the Measurement of Intelligence, *J. of Genetic Psychology* 82: 21–58

(See also: **855, 856, 858, 860, 866, 869, 870a, 871, 872, 875.**)

4.4 THE PSYCHOLOGY OF LEARNING

4.4.1 Theories of Learning

1006 O. H. Mowrer, *Learning Theory and the Symbolic Processes.* New York: Wiley 1960
1007 O. H. Mowrer, *Learning Theory and Behavior.* New York: Wiley 1960
1008 W. Penfield & L. Roberts, *Speech and Brain-Mechanisms.* Princeton: Princeton U.P. 1959

1009 W. R. Russell, *Brain, Memory, Learning.* Oxford: Clarendon 1959

1010 W. Penfield, *The Excitable Cortex in Conscious Man.* Liverpool: Liverpool U.P. 1958

1011 E. R. Hilgard, *Theories of Learning.* (2 ed.) London: Methuen 1958

1012 R. R. Bush & F. Mosteller, *Stochastic Models for Learning.* New York: Wiley 1955

1013 R. S. Woodworth & H. Schlosberg, *Experimental Psychology* (3 rev. ed.). London: Methuen 1955

1014 W. K. Estes & S. Koch et al, *Modern Learning Theory.* New York: Appleton 1954

1015 L. P. Thorpe & A. M. Schmuller, *Contemporary theories of learning, with special applications to education and psychology.* New York: Ronald 1954

1016 W. Penfield, *A Consideration of the Neurophysiological Mechanisms of Speech and Some Educational Consequences.* (Reprint 435) Montreal: Montreal Neurological Institute 1954

1017 B. F. Skinner, *Science and Human Behavior.* New York: Macmillan 1953

1018 L. M. Stolurow (ed.), *Readings in Learning.* New York: Prentice-Hall 1953

1019 J. E. Deese, *The Psychology of Learning.* New York: McGraw-Hill 1952

1020 C. L. Hull, *A Behavior System.* New Haven: Yale U.P. 1952

1021 J. A. McGeogh & A. L. Irion, *The Psychology of Human Learning* (2 ed.). New York: Longmans 1952

1022 H. Helson (ed.), *Theoretical Foundations of Psychology.* New York: Van Nostrand 1951

1023 E. C. Tolman, *Collected Papers in Psychology.* Berkeley: California U.P. 1951

1024 F. S. Keller & W. N. Schoenfeld, *Principles of Psychology.* New York: Appleton 1950

1025 W. Penfield & T. Rasmussen, *The Cerebral Cortex of Man: Localization of Function.* New York: Macmillan 1950

1026 D. O. Hebb, *The Organization of Behavior. A Neuropsychological Theory.* New York: Wiley 1949

1027 E. L. Thorndike, *Selected Writings from a Connectionist's Psychology.* New York: Appleton 1949

1028 J. von Neumann & O. Morgenstern, *Theory of Games and Economic Behavior.* (2 ed.) Princeton: Princeton U.P. 1947

1029 C. L. Hull et al, *Mathematico-deductive Theory of Rote Learning.* New Haven: Yale U.P. 1940

1030 W. D. Ellis, *A Source Book of Gestalt Psychology.* New York: Harcourt 1938

1031 A. A. Brill (ed.), *The Basic Writings of Sigmund Freud.* New York: Modern Library 1938

1032 B. F. Skinner, *The Behavior of Organisms.* New York: Appleton 1938

1033 K. Lewin, *Principles of Topological Psychology.* (trans. F. & G. M. Heider). New York: McGraw-Hill 1936

1034 E. R. Guthrie, *The Psychology of Learning.* New York: Harper 1935

1035 K. Koffka, *Principles of Gestalt Psychology.* New York: Harcourt 1935

1036 E. S. Robinson, *Association Theory Today.* New York: Appleton 1932

1037 E. C. Tolman, *Purposive Behavior in Animals and Men.* New York: Appleton 1932

1038 E. L. Thorndike, *The Fundamentals of Learning.* New York: Columbia Teachers College 1932

1039 J. Dewey, *Experience and Human Nature.* New York: Holt 1929

1040 L. L. Thurstone & E. J. Chave, *The Measurement of Attitude.* Chicago: Chicago U.P. 1929

1041 K. Koffka, *The Growth of the Mind.* (trans. R. M. Ogden) New York: Harcourt 1927

1042 R. S. Woodworth, *Dynamic Psychology.* New York: Columbia U.P. 1918

*   *   *

1043 E. Jacobsen, Electrical Measurements of Neuromuscular States during Mental Activity, *American Journal of Physiology* 41: 567–608; 44: 22–34; 45: 694–712; 46: 115–25; 47: 200–9

1044 E. Jacobsen, Electrophysiology of Mental Activities, *American Journal of Psychology* 44: 677–94

1045 I. Lorge, Psychological Bases for Adult Learning, *Teachers College Record* 41: 4–12

1046 J. F. Dashiell, A Survey and Synthesis of Learning Theories, *Psychological Bulletin* 32: 261–75

4.4.2 Thinking

1047 R. Thomson, *The Psychology of Thinking.* London: Pelican 1959

1048 M. Wertheimer, *Productive Thinking.* (2 ed.) New York: Harper 1959

1049 J. S. Bruner & E. Brunswik et al, *Contemporary Approaches to Cognition.* Cambridge (Mass.): Harvard U.P. 1957

1050 J. S. Bruner, J. J. Goodnow & G. A. Austen, *A Study of Thinking.* New York: Wiley 1956

1051 L. A. Jeffress (ed.), *Cerebral Mechanisms in Behavior.* New York: Wiley 1951

1052 J. Hadamard, *The Psychology of Invention in the Mathematical Field.* Princeton: Princeton U.P. 1949

1053 G. D. Stoddard, *The Meaning of Intelligence.* New York: Macmillan 1943

1054 G. H. Mead, *Mind, Self and Society.* Chicago: Chicago U.P. 1934

1055 B. Erdmann, *Umrisse zur Psychologie des Denkens.* Tübingen: Mohr 1908

*   *   *

1056 G. Révész, Thought and Language, *ArchL* 2: 122–31

1057 L. W. Max, An Experimental Study of the Motor Theory of Consciousness, *J. of Comparative Psychology* 19: 469–86

1058 F. Lotmar, Zur Pathophysiologie der erschwerten Wortfindung bei Aphasischen, *Schweizer Archiv für Neurologie und Psychologie* 30

1059 L. Binswanger, Zum Problem Sprache und Denken, *Schweizer Archiv für Neurologie und Psychologie* 18

1060 E. Buxbaum, The Role of Second Language in the Formation of Ego and Superego, *Psychoanalytic Quarterly* 18: 279–89

(See also under 1.3.3., 1.3.4. and 1.3.5)

4.4.3 Remembering

1060*a* W. Feindel, *Memory, Learning and Language.* Toronto: Toronto U.P. 1961

1061 J-C. Filloux, *La mémoire.* Paris: Presses universitaires 1958

1062 I. M. L. Hunter, *Memory: facts and fallacies.* London: Penguin 1957

1063 G. Katona, *Organizing and Memorizing: studies in the psychology of learning and teaching.* New York: Columbia U.P. 1940

1064 F. C. Bartlett, *Remembering. A study in experimental and social psychology.* London: Cambridge U.P. 1932

1065 M. Halbwachs, *Les cadres sociaux de la mémoire.* Paris: Alcan 1925

*   *   *

1066 J. B. Stroud & R. Maul, Influence of Age on Learning and Retention of Poetry and Nonsense Syllables, *Pedagogical Seminary and Journal of Genetic Psychology* 42: 232–50

1066*a* D. L. Bolinger, Verbal Evocation, *Lingua* 10: 113–27

1067 H. J. Leavitt & H. Schlosberg, Retention of Verbal and of Motor Skills, *J. of Experimental Psychology* 34: 404–17

1068 N. D. Rizzo, Studies in Visual and Auditory Memory Span with Special Reference to Reading Disability, *J. of Experimental Psychology* 22: 208–44

1069 W. C. F. Krueger, Further Studies in Overlearning, *J. of Experimental Psychology* 13: 152–63

1070 W. C. F. Krueger, The Effect of Overlearning on Retention, *J. of Experimental Psychology* 12: 71–8

1071 M. C. Barlow, Role of Articulation in Memorizing, *J. of Experimental Psychology* 11: 306–12

1072 W. E. Young, The Relation of Reading Comprehension and Retention to Hearing Comprehension and Retention, *J. of Experimental Psychology* 5: 30–9

1073 J. G. Jenkins & W. M. Sparks, Retroactive Inhibition in Foreign Language Study, (summary), *Psychological Bulletin* 37: 470

4.5 THE PSYCHOLOGY OF LANGUAGE

4.5.1 General

1073*a* S. Saporta & J. R. Bastian (eds.), *Psycholinguistics.* New York: Holt 1961

1074 H. J. Eysenck, *Sense and Nonsense in Psychology.* London: Pelican 1957

1075 C. E. Osgood & T. A. Sebeok (eds.), *Psycholinguistics: a survey of theory and research problems. (IJAL* 20 suppl.) Baltimore: Waverly 1954

1076 C. Lévi-Strauss & R. Jakobson et al, *Results of the Conference of Anthropologists and Linguists.* Baltimore: Waverly 1953

1077 H. J. Eysenck, *Uses and Abuses of Psychology.* London: Pelican 1953

1078 E. R. Hilgard, *Introduction to Psychology.* New York: Harcourt 1953

1079 C. E. Osgood, *Method and Theory in Experimental Psychology.* New York: Oxford U.P. 1953

1080 J. Eisenson, *The Psychology of Speech.* New York: Crofts 1938

*   *   *

1081 S. Adams & F. F. Powers, The Psychology of Language, *Psychological Bulletin* 25: 241–60

(See also under 1.3.4)

4.5.2 Perception of Language Attributes

1082 W. C. Bagley, The Apperception of the Spoken Sentence, *American Journal of Psychology* 12: 80–130
1083 S. M. Sapon & J. B. Carroll, Discriminative Perception of Speech Sounds as a Function of the Native Language, *GL* 3.2
1084 E. S. Dexter & K. T. Omwake, The Relation between Pitch Discrimination and Accent in Modern Foreign Languages, *J. of Applied Psychology* 18: 267–71
1085 G. A. Miller & P. E. Nicely, Analysis of Perceptual Confusions among some English Consonants, *JAcS* 27: 338–52
1086 H. M. Moser & J. J. Dreher, Phonemic Confusion Vectors, *JAcS* 27: 874–81
1087 L. Carmichael, H. F. Hogan & A. A. Walter, An Experimental Study of the Effect of Language on the Reproduction of Visually Perceived Form, *J. of Experimental Psychology* 15: 73–86
1088 M. D. Vernon, The Functions of Schemata in Perceiving, *Psychological Review* 62.3
1089 J. C. Cotton, Normal "Visual Hearing", *Science* 82: 592–3
1090 E. A. Pritchard, Everyday Language and the Structure of our Total Response System, *Synthese* 5: 226–32
1091 E. Polivanov, La perception des sons d'une langue étrangère, *TCLP* 1931–34: 79–96

5. METHODOLOGY

5.1 GENERAL TEACHING

1092 G. Palmade, *Les méthodes en pédagogie.* Paris: Presses universitaires 1958
1093 W. M. Ryburn & K. B. Forge, *The Principles of Teaching.* (2 ed.) London: Oxford U.P. 1957
1094 J. Comenius, *The Analytical Didactic of Comenius.* (trans. V. Jelinek). Chicago: Chicago U.P. 1953
1095 K. Otto, *Bildung und Leben.* Karlsruhe: Müller 1953
1096 A. G. Melvin, *General Methods of Teaching.* New York: McGraw-Hill 1952
1097 A. D. Woodruff, *The Psychology of Teaching.* (3 ed.) New York & Toronto: Longmans 1951
1098 G. A. Yoakam & R. G. Simpson, *Modern Methods and Techniques of Teaching.* New York: Macmillan 1948
1099 J. H. Panton, *Modern Teaching Practice and Technique.* London: Longmans 1945

1100   W. M. Ryburn, *The Principles of Teaching*. Bombay: Oxford U.P. 1944
1101   M. de Montaigne, *Essais*. (ed. P. Villey) Vol. 1. Paris: Alcan 1922
1102   E. L. Thorndike, *The Principles of Teaching, based on Psychology*. New York: Seiler 1906
1103   R. H. Quick, *Locke on Education*. London: Oxford U.P. 1880

5.2 LANGUAGE TEACHING

1103*a*   R. Lado, *Language Teaching: a scientific approach*. Boston: McGraw-Hill 1964
1103*b*   G. Nason (ed.), *Teaching Modern Languages*. Ottawa: Canadian Teachers' Federation 1963
1103*c*   D. C. Miller, *Beginning to Teach English*. London: Oxford U.P. 1963
1103*d*   G. Pittman, *Teaching Structural English*. Brisbane: Jacaranda 1963
1103*e*   C. J. Dodson, *The Bilingual Method: another approach to the learning of modern languages*. Aberystwyth: University College of Wales 1962
1104   R. A. Close, *English as a Foreign Language*. London: Allen & Unwin 1962
1104*a*   C. C. & A. C. Fries, *Foundations for English Teaching*. Tokyo: Kenkyusha 1961
1104*b*   C. Laird & R. M. Gorrell (eds.), *English as a Foreign Language: backgrounds, development, usage*. New York: Harcourt 1961
1105   B. V. Beljaev, *Psixologija obučenija inostrannym jazykam*. (The Psychology of Teaching Foreign Languages.) Moscow: Učpedgiz 1959
1105*a*   J. Lonjaret & R. Denis, *L'anglais dans le cycle d'observation*. Paris: Borrelier 1959
1105*b*   G. M. N. Ehlers, *The Oral Approach to English as a Second Language*. London: Macmillan 1959
1106   I.A.A.M., *The Teaching of Modern Languages*. (3 ed. rev.) London: University of London Press 1959
1107   T. Huebener, *How to Teach Foreign Languages Effectively*. New York: New York U.P. 1959
1108   P. O'Connor, *Modern Foreign Languages in the Secondary School: pre-reading instruction*. Washington: U.S. Dept. of Health, Education & Welfare 1959
1109   B. C. Brookes & J. C. Catford et al, *The Teaching of English*. London: Secker & Warburg 1959
1110   I. V. Karpov & V. Raxmanov, *Metodika naćal'nogo obučenija inostrannym jazykam*. (Methodology of elementary foreign language teaching.) Moscow: Academy of Pedagogical Sciences 1958
1111   M. C. Johnston (ed.), *Modern Foreign Languages in the High School*. Washington: U.S. Dept. of Health, Education & Welfare 1958
1112   R. M. Regberg, *English as a Second Language*. Tel Aviv: Israel Teachers' Union 1958
1113   R. J. Dixson, *Teaching English as a Foreign Language*. New York: Regent 1958
1114   L. R. H. Chapman, *Teaching English to Beginners*. London: Longmans 1958
1115   M. Finocchiaro, *Teaching English as a Second Language. In elementary and secondary schools*. New York: Harper 1958

1116 UNESCO, *The Teaching of Modern Languages. Report on the Unesco Regional Seminar held in Sydney, January–February,* 1957. Sydney: Australian National Advisory Committee for Unesco 1957

1117 W. R. Parker, *The National Interest and Foreign Languages.* (2 ed.) Washington: U.S. Government Printing Office, 1957

1118 SEVPEN, *Cahiers pédagogiques. Le français, langue étrangère.* Paris: SEVPEN 1957

1119 P. Christophersen, *Some Thoughts on the Study of English as a Foreign Language.* Oslo: Nölis 1957

1120 J. O. Gauntlett, *Teaching English as a Foreign Language.* London: Macmillan 1957

1121 A. W. Frisby, *Teaching English. Notes and comments on teaching English overseas.* London: Longmans 1957

1122 T. K. N. Menon & M. S. Patel, *The Teaching of English as a Foreign Language. Structural Approach.* Baroda (India): Acharya 1957

1123 E. Essen, *Methodik des Deutsch-Unterrichts.* Heidelberg: Quelle & Meyer 1956

1124 *VIe Congrès de la fédération internationale des professeurs de langues vivantes.* Groningen: Wolters 1956

1125 D. Abercrombie, *Problems and Principles. Studies in the Teaching of English as a Second Language.* London: Longmans 1956

1126 T. Andersson (ed.), *The Teaching of Modern Languages.* Paris: Unesco 1955

1127 I. C. Thimann, *Teaching Languages: A note-book of suggestions and recollections.* London: Harrap 1955

1128 A. Roche, *L'étude des langues vivantes.* Paris: Presses universitaires 1955

1129 M. West, *Learning to Read a Foreign Language. And other essays on language-teaching.* (new ed.) London: Longmans 1955

1130 F. M. Hodgson, *Learning Modern Languages.* London: Routledge & Kegan Paul 1955

1131 A. Bohlen, *Methodik des neusprachlichen Unterrichts.* (2 ed.) Heidelberg: Quelle & Meyer 1955

1132 P. Gurrey, *Teaching English as a Foreign Language.* London: Longmans 1955

1133 E. W. Stevick, *Helping People Learn English.* New York: Abingdon 1955

1134 E. A. Méras, *A Language Teacher's Guide.* New York: Harper 1954

1135 A. Cochran, *Modern Methods of Teaching English as a Foreign Language. A guide to modern materials with particular reference to the Far East.* Washington: Educational Services 1954

1136 P. Gurrey, *The Teaching of Written English.* London: Longmans 1954

1137 I. Morris, *The Art of Teaching English as a Living Language.* London: Macmillan 1954

1138 V. Mallinson, *Teaching a Modern Language.* London: Heinemann 1953

1139 E. T. Cornelius, *Language Teaching. A guide for teachers of foreign languages.* New York: Crowell 1953

1140 M. Lachs, *Anfangsunterricht in den lebenden Fremdsprachen.* Vienna: Jugend und Volk 1953

1141 T. Andersson, *The Teaching of Foreign Languages in the Elementary School.* (Preliminary Edition) Boston: Heath 1953

1142 O. F. Bond, *The Reading Method. An experiment in college French.* Chicago: Chicago U.P. 1953

1143 M. West, *The Teaching of English. A guide to the New Method Series.* London: Longmans 1953

1144 F. Closset, *Didactique des langues vivantes.* (2 ed.) Paris & Brussels: Didier 1953

1144a UNESCO, *Modern Languages in Schools.* Paris: Unesco 1953

1145 Association of Assistant Mistresses in Secondary Schools, *Memorandum on Modern Language Teaching.* London: University of London Press 1952

1146 B. Pattison, *English Teaching in the World Today.* London: Evans 1952

1147 R. H. Fife & H. T. Manuel, *The Teaching of English in Puerto Rico.* San Juan, P.R.: Dept. of Education Press 1951

1148 G. Benedict, *L'enseignement vivant des langues vivantes par la méthode directe progressive.* Lausanne: Pro Schola 1950

1149 H.M.S.O., *Modern Languages in Secondary Schools.* Edinburgh: H.M. Stationery Office 1950

1150 C. H. Prator, *Language Teaching in the Philippines.* Manila: U.S. Educational Foundation in the Philippines 1950

1151 R. L. Mehta, *The Teaching of English in India.* Bombay: Longmans 1950

1152 F. G. French, *The Teaching of English Abroad.* 3 vols. London: Oxford U.P. 1948–50

1153 C. C. Fries, *The Teaching of English.* Ann Arbor (Mich.): Wahr 1949

1154 M. Newmark (ed.), *Twentieth Century Modern Language Teaching. Sources and readings.* New York: Philosophical Library 1948

1155 P. F. Angiolillo, *Armed Forces' Foreign Language Teaching: critical evaluation and implications.* New York: Vanni 1947

1156 C. Duff, *How to Learn a Language. A book for beginners and all others who may be interested.* Oxford: Blackwell 1947

1157 R. J. Mathews, *Language and Areas Studies in the Armed Services: their future and significance.* Washington: American Council on Education 1947

1158 V. A. Artemov, I. V. Karpov & I. V. Raxmanov (eds.), *Voprosy psixologii i metodiki obučenija inostrannym jazykam* (Problems in the psychology and methodology of foreign language teaching). Moscow: Učpedgiz 1947

1159 C. C. Fries, *Teaching and Learning English as a Foreign Language.* Ann Arbor: Michigan U.P. 1947

1160 Ministry of Education, *Language Teaching in the Primary Schools.* London: H.M. Stationery Office 1945

1161 H. R. Huse, *Reading and Speaking Foreign Languages.* Chapel Hill (N.C.): North Carolina U.P. 1945

1162 I. Morris, *The Teaching of English as a Second Language.* London: Macmillan 1945

1163 H. G. Doyle et al, *A Handbook on the Teaching of Spanish and Portuguese.* Boston: Heath 1945

1164 E. V. Gatenby, *English as a Foreign Language. Advice to non-English teachers.* London: Longmans 1944

1165 F. B. Agard et al, *A Survey of Language Classes in the Army Specialized Training Program.* New York: M.L.A. 1944

1166 F. G. French, *First Year English. What and how to teach.* London: Oxford U.P. 1943

1167 W. V. Kaulfers, *Modern Languages for Modern Schools*. New York: McGraw-Hill 1942

1168 M. M. Lewis, *Language in School*. London: University of London Press 1942

1169 C. C. Gullette, L. C. Keating & C. P. Viens, *Teaching a Modern Language*. New York: Crofts 1942

1170 M. Graves & J. M. Cowan, *Report on the First Year's Operation of the Intensive Language Program of the American Council of Learned Societies: 1941–42*. Washington: A.C.L.S. 1942

1171 F. L. Sack, *Vom Englischunterricht*. Bern: Francke 1941

1172 A. V. P. Elliott & P. Gurrey, *Language Teaching in African Schools*. London: Longmans 1940

1173 A. Pinloche, *La nouvelle pédagogie des langues vivantes. Observations et réflexions critiques*. (3 ed.) Paris: Didier 1940

1174 L. W. Leavitt, *The Teaching of English to Foreign Students*. London: Longmans 1940

1175 F. Closset, *Les langues vivantes dans l'enseignement secondaire*. Liège: Liège U.P. n.d.

1176 H. E. Palmer, *The Teaching of Oral English*. London: Longmans 1940

1177 D. Benzies, *Learning our Language*. London: Longmans 1940

1178 F. Thomas, *Les langues étrangères et la vie*. Paris: École Nouvelle Française n.d.

1179 P. G. Wilson, *The Student's Guide to Modern Languages. A comparative study of English, French, German, and Spanish*. (2 ed.) London: Pitman 1939

1180 P. Skok, *Metodologija francuskoga jezika*. Zagreb: Hrvatska 1939

1181 M. Löpelmann, *Erziehung und Unterricht an der höheren Schule*. Frankfurt: Diesterweg 1938

1182 E. E. Palmer, *Development of the Eclectic Method of Teaching French in the United States since 1875*. New York: New York University doctorate thesis 1937

1183 R. D. Cole & J. B. Tharp, *Modern Foreign Languages and their Teaching*. New York: Appleton 1937

1184 W. V. Kaulfers & H. D. Roberts, *A Cultural Basis for the Language Arts*. Stanford: Stanford U.P. 1937

1185 W. C. R. Hicks & N. A. Haycocks, *Modern Language Teaching on the Decline?* London: Longmans 1937

1186 M. Bronstein, *Méthodes d'enseignement des langues étrangères aux adultes*. Paris: Lipschutz 1937

1187 S. Denis (ed.), *Troisième congrès international des professeurs de langues vivantes*. Paris: Maison du livre français 1937

1188 *L'enseignement des langues vivantes*. Geneva: Bureau International d'Education 1937

1189 W. F. C. Timmermans, *La réforme de l'enseignement des langues vivantes: le débat des méthodes*. Groningen: Wolters 1937

1190 J. D. Haygood, *The Teaching of Modern Foreign Languages*. Gainesville: University of Florida 1936

1191 R. Münch, *Die dritte Reform des neusprachlichen Unterrichts*. Frankfurt: Diesterweg 1936

1192 J. S. Schmidt, *O ensino scientifico das linguas modernas*. Rio de Janeiro: Briguiet 1935
1193 P. Hagboldt, *Language Learning*. Chicago: Chicago U.P. 1935
1194 L. A. Carneiro, *O ensino das linguas vivas*. San Paulo: Comparlia 1935
1195 T. E. Oliver, *The Modern Language Teacher's Handbook*. Boston: Heath 1935
1196 I. A. Richards, *Basic in Teaching: East and West*. London: Kegan Paul 1935
1197 A. Coleman et al, *Experiments and Studies in Modern Language Teaching*. Chicago: Chicago U.P. 1934
1198 W. Huebner, *Didaktik der neueren Sprachen*. Frankfurt: Diesterweg 1933
1199 H. E. Palmer & H. V. Redman, *This Language-Learning Business*. New York: World Book Co. 1932
1200 H. R. Huse, *The Psychology of Foreign Language Study*. Chapel Hill (N.C.): North Carolina U.P. 1931
1201 R. D. Cole, *Modern Foreign Languages and their Teaching*. New York: Appleton 1931
1202 M. Walter, *Zur Methodik des neusprachlichen Unterrichts*. (4 ed.) Marburg: Elwert 1931
1203 T. Tisken, *Der englische Unterricht*. Leipzig: Quelle & Meyer 1931
1204 M. A. Ravizé (ed.), *Deuxième congrès international des professeurs de langues vivantes*. Paris: Presses universitaires 1931
1205 E. W. Bagster-Collins, *The Teaching of Modern Languages in the United States*. New York: Macmillan 1930
1206 R. Mays, *A Guide for Teachers of Modern Foreign Languages*. Dallas (Texas): Southwest Press 1930
1207 C. Brereton, *Modern Language Teaching in Day and Evening Schools, with Special Reference to London*. London: University of London Press 1930
1208 K. A. Ganshina, *Methodology in Foreign Language Teaching*. Moscow: Akcionernoe Obščestvo Sovetskaja Enciklopedija 1930
1209 C. C. Crawford & E. M. Leitzell, *Learning a New Language*. Los Angeles: University of Southern California 1930
1210 M. West, *Language in Education*. London: Longmans 1930
1211 J. J. Findlay, *Modern Language Learning. A concise sketch of principles and of a programme for the introductory stage*. London: Gregg n.d.
1212 A. Coleman, *The Teaching of Modern Foreign Languages in the United States*. New York: American and Canadian Committees on Modern Languages 1929
1213 M. Müller, *Kursbuch für den neusprachlichen Lesestoff*. Leipzig: Rohmkopf 1929
1214 O. Schmidt, *Methodik des englischen Unterrichts*. Bonn: Dümmler 1929
1215 P. Hartig & H. Strohmeyer, *Moderner neusprachlicher Unterricht*. Braunschweig: Westermann 1929
1216 E. Otto, B. Fehr & P. Hartig et al, *Kulturkunde und neusprachlicher Unterricht*. Marburg: Elwert 1928
1217 H. Strohmeyer, *Methodik des neusprachlichen Unterrichts*. Braunschweig: Westermann 1928
1218 J. Schmidt, *Methodik des französischen Unterrichts*. Leipzig: Gronau 1928

1219 K. Ehrke, *Methodik des neusprachlichen Arbeits-Unterrichts.* Berlin: Herbig 1928

1220 E. Escher, *The Direct Method of Studying Foreign Languages: A contribution to the history of its sources and development.* University of Chicago doctorate thesis 1928

1221 M. A. Buchanan & E. D. MacPhee, *Modern Language Instruction in Canada.* 2 vols. Toronto: Toronto U.P. 1928

1222 W. Münch, *Vom Arbeitsunterricht in den neueren Sprachen.* Leipzig: Teubner 1927

1223 H. Plecher, *Handbuch für die Methodik des deutschen Sprachunterrichts.* Munich: Oldenbourg 1927

1224 G. T. Buswell, *A Laboratory Study of the Reading of Modern Foreign Languages.* New York: Macmillan 1927

1225 L. Marchand, *L'Enseignement des langues vivantes par la méthode scientifique.* Cahors: Coueslant 1927

1226 E. Scherping, *Englischer Unterricht auf der Oberstufe.* Marburg: Elwert 1926

1227 F. L. Fraser, *Lehrverfahren und Lehraufgaben.* Marburg: Elwert 1926

1228 P. Aronstein, *Methodik des neusprachlichen Unterrichts.* 2 vols. Leipzig: Teubner 1926

1229 M. de Valette, *La méthode directe pour l'enseignement des langues vivantes à l'aide des tableaux auxiliaires.* Paris: Perche 1925

1230 A. Streubler, *Neuere Sprachen.* Breslau: Hirt 1925

1231 E. Otto, *Methodik und Didaktik des neusprachlichen Unterrichts.* Leipzig: Teubner 1925

1232 H. E. Moore, *Modernism in Language Teaching.* Cambridge: Heffer 1925

1233 C. H. Handschin, *Methods of Teaching Modern Languages.* New York: World Book Co. 1924

1234 H. E. Palmer, *The Oral Method of Teaching Languages.* Cambridge: Heffer 1923

1235 E. Briod, *L'étude et l'enseignement d'une langue vivante.* Lausanne: Payot 1922

1236 H. Palmer, *Principles of Language Study.* New York: World Book Co. 1921

1237 E. Gourio, *The Direct Method of Teaching French.* Boston: Houghton Mifflin 1921

1238 H. Paul, *Über Sprachunterricht.* Halle: Niemeyer 1921

1239 H. G. Atkins & H. L. Hutton, *The Teaching of Modern Foreign Languages in School and University.* London: Arnold 1920

1240 W. Münch, *Didaktik und Methodik des französischen Unterrichts.* (4 ed.) Munich: Beck 1919

1241 F. Glauning, *Didaktik und Methodik des englischen Unterrichts.* Munich: Beck 1919

1242 *Modern Studies, Being the Report of the Committee on the Position of Modern Languages in the Educational System of Great Britain.* London: H.M. Stationery Office 1918

1243 E. C. Kitson, *Theory and Practice of Language Teaching.* London: Oxford U.P. 1918

1244 J. Adams (ed.), *The New Teaching.* London: Hodder & Stoughton 1918

1245 H. E. Palmer, *The Scientific Study and Teaching of Languages*. London: Harrap 1917

1246 A. Bell, *Psychology of Learning a Foreign Language*. Madison: Wisconsin U.P. 1917

1247 C. A. Krause, *The Direct Method in Modern Languages*. New York: Scribner 1916

1248 T. Cummings, *How to Learn a Language*. New York: Cummings 1916

1249 E. Prokosch, *The Teaching of German in Secondary Schools*. Austin: University of Texas (Bulletin 41) 1915

1250 H. O'Grady, *The Teaching of Modern Foreign Languages by the Organized Method*. London: Constable 1915

1251 *Methods of Teaching Modern Languages. Collection of essays by a group of specialists*. New York: Heath 1915

1252 H. Kappert, *Psychologische Grundlagen des neusprachlichen Unterrichts*. Leipzig: Nemnich 1914

1253 O. Thiergen, *Methodik des neusprachlichen Unterrichts*. Leipzig: Teubner 1914

1254 G. Otten, *Die Verwertung der Ergebnisse der Sprachwissenschaft im französischen und englischen Unterricht*. Leipzig: Quelle & Meyer 1914

1255 G. Müller, *Methodik des neusprachlichen Unterrichts*. Leipzig: Zickfeldt 1914

1256 C. B. Flagstad, *Psychologie der Sprachpädagogik*. Leipzig: Teubner 1913

1257 B. Röttgers, *Methodik des englischen und französischen Unterrichts*. Hanover: Meyer 1913

1258 R. Ackermann, *Das pädagogisch-didaktische Seminar für Neuphilologen*. Leipzig: Freytag 1913

1258a J. Firmery & E. Hovelaque, *Conférences sur l'enseignement des langues vivantes*. Paris: Delagrave 1911

1259 W. Münch, *Didaktik und Methodik des französischen Unterrichts*. Munich: Beck 1910

1260 M. Bréal, *De l'enseignement des langues vivantes*. Paris: Hachette 1910

1261 F. B. Kirkman, *The Teaching of Foreign Languages*. London: London University Tutorial Press 1909

1262 C. T. Lion, *Die praktische Erlernung und Verwertung der neueren Sprachen*. Leipzig: Privately published 1909

1263 E. Pitschel, *Eindrücke und Beobachtungen während eines Studienaufenthaltes in Frankreich*. Frankfurt: Limpert 1909

1263a M. G. Delobel (ed.), *Congrès international des professeurs de langues vivantes*. Paris: Association des professeurs de langues vivantes 1909

1264 A. Matthias, *Geschichte des deutschen Unterrichts*. Munich: Beck 1907

1265 C. Sigwalt, *De l'enseignement des langues vivantes*. Paris: Hachette 1906

1266 L. Bahlsen, *The Teaching of Modern Languages*. Boston: Ginn 1905

1267 O. Jespersen, *How to Teach a Foreign Language*. (trans. S. Y-O. Bertelsen). London: Allen & Unwin 1904

1268 C. Schweitzer & E. Simmonot, *Méthodologie des langues vivantes*. Paris: Colin 1903

1269 S. Le Roy, *Logical Teaching and Studying of Modern Languages*. New York: Harrison 1902

1270 W. Viëtor, *Der Sprachunterricht muss umkehren*. Leipzig: Reisland 1902

1271 C. Thomas (ed.), *Report of the Committee of Twelve of the Modern Language Association of America.* Boston: Heath 1901

1272 H. Oertel, *Lectures on the Study of Language.* New York: Scribner 1901

1273 P. Passy, *De la méthode directe dans l'enseignement des langues vivantes.* Cambridge: Association phonétique internationale 1899

1274 H. Sweet, *The Practical Study of Languages: a guide for teachers and learners.* London: Dent 1899

1275 H. Laudenbach et al, *De la méthode directe dans l'enseignement des langues vivantes.* Paris: Colin 1899

1276 K. Breul, *The Teaching of Modern Foreign Languages and the Training of Teachers.* Cambridge: Cambridge U.P. 1898

1277 F. Gouin, *The Art of Teaching and Studying Languages.* (trans. H. Swan & V. Bétis). London: Philip 1894

1278 W. K. Hill, *William Henry Widgery, Schoolmaster.* London: Nutt 1894

1279 C. Colbeck, *On the Teaching of Modern Languages in Theory and Practice.* London: Cambridge U.P. 1887

1280 G. Heness, *Der Leitfaden für den Unterricht in der deutschen Sprache.* New York: Holt 1885

1281 L. Sauveur, *Introduction to the Teaching of Living Languages.* New York: Holt 1883

* * *

1281a L. Taillon, Basic Issues in Second-Language Teaching, *CMLJ* 18(3): 29–35

1281b E. M. Anthony, Approach, Method, and Technique, *ELT* 17: 63–66

1282 F. Morris, The Persistence of the Classical Tradition in Foreign-Language Teaching, *ELT* 11: 113–19

1283 W. R. Lee, The Linguistic Context of Language Teaching, *ELT* 11: 77–85

1284 W. F. Mackey, English Teaching in Puerto Rico, *ELT* 8: 12–14

1285 E. V. Gatenby, Popular Fallacies in the Teaching of Foreign Languages, *ELT* 7: 21–9

1286 W. F. Mackey, The Meaning of Method, *ELT* 5: 3–6

1286a G. Capelle, L'enseignement du "français, langue étrangère", *FdM* 2: 2–5

1287 L. Landré, L'enseignement des langues vivantes en Europe, *LM* 50: 10–18

1288 R. P. Stockwell, Techniques for Language Learning, *LM* 49: 46–51

1289 P. Pfrimmer, Après un demi-siècle de méthode directe, *LM* 47: 49–57

1290 F. Berges, Des fins de l'étude des langues vivantes, *LM* 46: 21–4

1290a J. Ornstein, Foreign Language Training in the Soviet Union: a qualitative view, *MLJ* 42: 382–92

1291 E. E. & L. V. Ellert, Foreign Language Teaching in Europe, *MLJ* 40: 346–50

1292 P. Smith, On Teaching a Language, *MLJ* 40: 62–68

1293 W. R. Parker, The MLA Foreign Language Program, *MLJ* 39: 146–49

1294 R. A. Hall, Some Desiderata for Elementary Language Texts, *MLJ* 29: 290–5

1295 W. G. Moulton, Study Hints for Language Students, *MLJ* 26: 259–64

1295a W. F. Mackey, Today's Demands on Modern Language Teaching, *Teaching Modern Languages*, Ottawa: Canadian Teachers' Federation 1963

1296 M. Antier, Sur l'enseignement des langues vivantes en France (Bibliographie critique), *RLaV* 23: 165–73

1297 I. A. Richards, How Basic English is Really Taught, *J. of Education* 128: 158–61

1298 D. Braun, Grenzen der direkten Methode beim Anfängerunterricht im Ausland, *DuA* 6: 129

1299 J. C. Catford, The University of Edinburgh School of Applied Linguistics, *ENL* 7: 11–16

1300 M. Kirsten, Zur pädagogisch-psychologischen Grundlegung der neusprachlichen Reform, *NS* 28: 30, 113

1301 W. G. Moulton, Linguistics and Language Teaching in the United States 1940–1960, *IRAL* 1: 21–41

1302 G. A. C. Scherer, The Psychology of Teaching Reading through Listening, *GQ* 23: 151–60

1303 O. Springer, Intensive Language Study as Part of the College Curriculum, *GQ* 17: 226

1304 R. A. Hall, Phonetics and the Technique of Grammar, *BNML* 6: 23–5

1305 H. B. Richardson, Intensive Practical Courses in Language, *BNML* 5: 17–18

1306 W. Steinbeck, Konzentration und Sprachunterricht, *Neuphil. Monatsschrift* 3: 161

1307 E. E. Cochran, Ernst Otto's Contribution to Experimental Didactics, *Festschrift Otto* 107–27, Berlin: Gruyter 1957

1308 H. Klitscher, Welchen Weg weist uns heute der Bildungsauftrag für den Unterricht in den lebenden Fremdsprachen?, *Festschrift Otto* 62–106 Berlin: Gruyter 1957

1309 J. B. Tharp & K. McDonald, Psychology and Methods in High School and College: Foreign Languages, *Review of Educational Research* 8: 34–8

1310 A. Willot, L'études des langues vivantes, *Les études classiques* 25: 207–26

1311 R. A. Hall, Progress and Reaction in Modern Language Teaching, *Bulletin of the American Association of University Professors* 31: 220–30

1312 J. S. Diekhoff, The Mission and the Method of Army Language Teaching, *Bulletin of the American Association of University Professors* 31: 606–20

1313 L. Bloomfield, About Foreign Language Training, *Yale Review* 4: 625–41

5.3 BIBLIOGRAPHIES

1313a M. J. Ollmann (ed.), *MLA Selective List of Materials for Use by Teachers of Modern Foreign Languages in Elementary and Secondary Schools*. New York: Modern Language Association of America 1962

1313b E. M. Eaton & L. L. Norton, *Source Materials for Secondary School Teachers of Foreign Languages*. Washington: U.S. Dept. of Health, Education & Welfare 1962

1313c H. L. Nostrand et al, *Research on Language Teaching: an annotated international bibliography for 1945–61*. Seattle: Washington U.P. 1962

1314 M. Frank, *Annotated Bibliography of Materials for English as a Second Language.* New York: National Association of Foreign Student Advisers 1960

1314a S. Ohannessian, *Interim Bibliography on the Teaching of English to Speakers of Other Languages.* Washington: Center for Applied Linguistics 1960

1314b D. W. Alden (ed.) *Materials List for Use by Teachers of Modern Foreign Languages.* New York: Modern Language Association 1959

1314c H. S. Baker, *A Check List of Books and Articles for Teachers of English as a Foreign Language.* New York: The National Association of Foreign Student Advisers 1949

1315 H. G. Doyle (ed.), *Education and its Environment in the United States and Overseas: A Tentative Selective Checklist of Books and Articles.* Washington: ICA Educational Services 1959

1316 UNESCO, *A Bibliography on the Teaching of Modern Languages. Prepared in collaboration between the International Federation of Modern Language Teachers, the Modern Language Association of America, and UNESCO. Educational Studies and Documents 13.* Paris: Unesco 1955

1317 R. Lado, *Annotated Bibliography for Teachers of English as a Foreign Language.* Washington: U.S. Government Printing Office 1955

1317a J. B. Tharp et al, *Annotated Bibliographies of Modern Language Methodology for the years 1946, 1947, and 1948.* Columbus (Ohio): College of Education, Ohio State University 1952

1318 A. Coleman, *An Analytical Bibliography of Modern Language Teaching. Vol. 1 (1927–32) Vol. 2 (1932–37).* Chicago: Chicago U.P. 1933, 1938

1319 M. A. Buchanan & E. D. McPhee, *An Annotated Bibliography of Modern Language Methodology.* Toronto: Toronto U.P. 1928

1320 H. Breymann & G. Steinmüller, *Die neusprachliche Reform-Literatur von 1876–1909.* 4 vols. Leipzig: Deichert 1895–1909

*   *   *

1321 E. V. Eenenaam, Annotated Bibliography of Modern Language Teaching for 1953, 1954, 1955, *MLJ* 39: 27–52, 40: 83–104, 41: 309–12

1322 W. H. Rice, Annotated Bibliography of Modern Language Methodology (–May 1946), *MLJ* 30: 290–308

1323 W. H. Rice, Annotated Bibliography of Modern Language Methodology: July 1943–December 1944, *MLJ* 29: 431–58

1324 H. W. Machan, Annotated Bibliography of Modern Language Methodology: June 1942–June 1943, *MLJ* 28: 70–103

1325 Bibliography on the Language Arts, *Review of Educational Research*, 28 (1958), 25 (1955), 22 (1952), 16 (1946)

1326 W. F. Mackey, Analytic Survey of Courses for the Teaching of English as a Foreign Language. Vol. 1: Great Britain. (MS) Quebec 1959

5.4 PERIODICALS

See Nos. **7, 9, 11a, 12, 13, 14, 15a, 16, 17, 20, 24, 25, 26, 27, 28a, 29, 35, 36, 41, 42, 43, 44, 46, 47, 48, 49, 51, 53a, 54, 55, 56, 66**

6. SELECTION

6.1 GENERAL STUDIES

6.1.1 Principles of Selection

1327 P. Guiraud, *Caractères statistiques du vocabulaire*. Paris: Presses universitaires 1954

1328 R. Michéa, *Vocabulaire de base et formation intellectuelle*. Antwerp: Sikkel 1949

1329 G. Matoré, *La mesure en lexicologie*. Paris: Thalès 1948

1330 H. Bongers, *The History and Principles of Vocabulary Control. As it affects the teaching of foreign language in general and of English in particular*. Woerden (Netherlands): WOCOPI 1947

1331 H. S. Eaton, *Semantic Frequency List for English, French, German and Spanish*. Chicago: Chicago U.P. 1940

1332 R. Jadot, *Recherche sur l'importance et la fréquence des mots dans l'étude d'une langue étrangère*. Brussels: Archives belges des Sciences de l'Education 1936

1333 H. E. Palmer, *An Essay in Lexicology*. Tokyo: IRET 1934

1334 E. Swenson & M. P. West, *On the Counting of New Words in Textbooks for Teaching Foreign Languages*. Toronto: Toronto U.P. 1934

1335 C. K. Ogden, *Bentham's Theory of Fictions*. New York: Harcourt 1932

1336 L. W. Lockhart, *Word Economy. A study in applied linguistics*. London: Kegan Paul 1931

1337 M. P. West, *The Construction of Reading Materials for Teaching a Foreign Language*. London: Oxford U.P. 1927

1338 M. Walter, *Aneignung und Verarbeitung des Wortschatzes im neusprachlichen Unterricht*. Marburg: Elwert 1914

*   *   *

1339 R. Michéa, Mots fréquents et mots disponibles: Un aspect nouveau de la statistique du langage, *LM* 47: 338–44

1340 R. Michéa, Le vocabulaire de base en France et à l'étranger, *LM* 46: 295–397

1341 R. Michéa, Vocabulaire et physiologie, *LM* 46: 27–32

1342 R. Michéa, Rapports de la fréquence avec la forme, le sens et la fonction des mots, *LM* 45: 191–96

1343 R. Michéa, La culture par la langue, *LM* 44: 328–35

1344 R. Michéa, Vocabulaire et culture, *LM* 44: 187–95

1345 P. Henrion, Un mariage malheureux: statistisque et vocabulaire, *LM* 43: 238–45

1346 R. Michéa, Introduction pratique à une statistique du langage, *LM* 43: 173–86, 314–22

1347 R. Michéa, Le vocabulaire de base aux examens, *LM* 43: 135–40

1348 F. Mossé, Détermination et progression du vocabulaire dans l'enseignement des langues, *LM* 42: 89–104

1349 G. Rogers, Pour un enseignement plus méthodique et plus scientifique des langues modernes, *LM* 29: 172–82

1350 H. Walpole, The Theory of Definition and its Application to Vocabulary Limitation, *MLJ* 21: 398–402

1351 M. P. West, The Present Position in Vocabulary Selection, *MLJ* 21: 433–7

1352 M. P. West, Speaking Vocabulary in a Foreign Language, *MLJ* 14: 509–21

1353 M. V. Keller, The Necessity of Teaching a Basic Vocabulary in Modern Language Work, *MLJ* 8: 35–40

1354 R. Michéa, Limitation et sélection du vocabulaire dans l'enseignement actif des langues vivantes, *RLaV* 22: 467–74

1355 F. Closset, Basis Woordenschat, *RLaV* 6: 3–9

1356 R. Michéa, La normalisation des vocabulaires scolaires, *RLaV* 5: 283–99

1357 G. Vannes, Vocabulaire et grammaire de base, *RLaV* 5: 371–6

1358 H. E. Palmer & M. West, Discussion of Word Frequency, *ML* 18: 136–8

1359 J. J. Findlay, Note on the Acquirement of Vocabulary, *ML* 9: 4–7

1360 R. H. Fife, Frequency Word Lists, *MLF* 15: 125–8

1361 J. Boulouffe, What to Overlook and What to Overload, *ELT* 15: 111–15

1362 M. West, Vocabulary Selection and the Minimum Adequate Vocabulary, *ELT* 8: 121–6

1363 A. S. Hornby, Vocabulary Control—History and Principles, *ELT* 8: 15–20

1364 W. F. Mackey, What to Look for in a Method: (I) Selection, *ELT* 7: 77–85

1365 M. West, Simplified and Abridged, *ELT* 5: 48–52

1366 M. West, Vocabulary Selection for Speech and Writing, *ELT* 4: 17–21, 41–4

1367 I. Morris, Principles of Vocabulary Control, *ELT* 1: 163–6, 189–92; 2: 42–6

1368 R. Michéa, Le vocabulaire comme structure et comme expérience, *Revue Philosophique* 142: 223–32

1369 R. Henkl, Word Similarities and Mnemotechnics, *BIRET* 107: 9–11; 110: 10–11

1370 E. Giesecke, Stem-Meanings and the Vocabulary Problem, *MDU* 29: 73–76

1371 V. A. C. Henmon, The Vocabulary Problem in the Modern Foreign Languages, *MDU* 22: 33–9

1372 T. B. Hewitt, For Briefer Text Vocabularies, *GQ* 9: 25–6

1373 W. R. Price, What Price Vocabulary Frequencies?, *GQ* 2: 1–5

1374 W. N. Rivers, An Experiment in Vocabulary Compilation for Foreign Language Texts, *FR* 6: 50–3

1375 W. A. Scott, Some Causes of Unsatisfactory Results in Teaching Vocabulary, *Bulletin of the Wisconsin Association of Modern Language Teachers* 98: 6–8

1376 B. Q. Morgan & L. M. Oberdeck, Active and Passive Vocabulary, *Publications of the American and Canadian Committees on Modern Languages* 27: 211–21

1377 M. West, A Note on the Inferability of Cognates, *High Points* 16: 23–5

1378 A. de la Court, Rationeel Taalonderwijs, *Pedagogische Studiën* 1940

1379 S. A. Freeman, Some Practical Suggestions for the Teaching of Modern Language Vocabulary, *Education* 55: 20–35

1380 M. Chateauneuf, Study of the Written Vocabulary in a Foreign Language, *Educational Outlook* 1933: 224–34

(See also under 1.3.8)

6.1.2 Size of Vocabularies

1381 J. L. Meriam, *Learning English Incidentally*. Washington: U.S. Dept. of Interior 1937

1382 M. D. Horn, *A Study of the Vocabulary of Children before Entering the First Grade*. Baltimore: Child Study Committee of the International Kindergarten Union 1928

1383 E. Horn, *The Commonest Words in the Spoken Vocabulary of Children up to and including Six Years of Age*. Washington: Yearbook of the National Society for the Study of Education 1925

*   *   *

1384 R. H. Seashore & L. D. Eikerson, The Measurement of Individual Differences in General English Vocabularies, *J. of Educational Psychology* 31: 14–38

1385 F. T. Vasey, Vocabulary of Grammar School Children, *J. of Educational Psychology* 10: 104–7

1386 C. A. Gregory, The Reading Vocabularies of Third-Grade Children, *J. of Educational Research* 7: 127–31

1387 J. A. Magni, Vocabularies, *Pedagogical Seminary* 26: 209–33

1388 A. D. Bush, Vocabulary of a Three-Year-Old Girl, *Pedagogical Seminary* 21: 125–42

1389 M. R. Heilig, A Child's Vocabulary, *Pedagogical Seminary* 20: 1–16

1390 A. Salisbury, A Child's Vocabulary, *Educational Review* 7: 289–90

1391 N. M. Nice, The Size of Vocabularies, *AS* 2: 1–7

1392 E. L. Thorndike, Word Knowledge in the Elementary School, *Teachers College Record*, Sept. 1921

6.2 SPECIAL STUDIES

6.2.1 English

(i) *Vocabulary*

1393 F. J. Schonell, I. G. Meddleton, B. A. Shaw et al, *A Study of the Oral Vocabulary of Adults*. London & Brisbane: University of London Press & Queensland U.P. 1956

1394 M. West (ed.), *A General Service List of English Words: With semantic frequencies and a supplementary word-list for the writing of popular science and technology*. London: Longmans 1953

1395 J. E. Johnsen (ed.), *Basic English. The Reference Shelf* 17: 1. New York: Wilson 1944

1396 E. L. Thorndike & I. Lorge, *A Teacher's Word Book of 30,000 Words*. New York: Columbia Teachers College 1944

1397 I. A. Richards, *Basic English and its Uses*. New York: Norton 1943

1398 H. Mutschmann, *Der grundlegende Wortschatz des Englischen*. Marburg: Elwert 1941

1399 C. C. Fries & A. A. Traver, *English Word Lists. A study of their adaptability for instruction.* Washington: American Council on Education 1940

1400 C. K. Ogden, *A Short Guide to Basic English.* Cambridge: Orthological Institute 1937

1401 L. Faucett, H. Palmer, M. West & E. L. Thorndike, *Interim Report on Vocabulary Selection.* London: P. S. King 1936

1402 M. P. West, *Definition Vocabulary.* Toronto: University of Toronto Department of Educational Research 1935

1403 J. Aiken, *Little English.* New York: Columbia U.P. 1935

1404 C. K. Ogden, *The System of Basic English.* New York: Harcourt 1934

1405 M. P. West & E. Swenson et al, *A Critical Examination of Basic English.* Toronto: Toronto U.P. 1934

1406 C. K. Ogden, *The Basic Words. A detailed account of their uses.* London: Kegan Paul 1932

1407 L. Faucett & I. Maki, *Study of English Word-Values Statistically Determined from the Latest Extensive Word-Counts.* Tokyo: Matsumura Sanshodo 1932

1408 C. K. Ogden, *The ABC of Basic English.* London: Kegan Paul 1932

1409 H. Hefferman, *A Guide for Teachers of Beginning, Non-English-speaking Children.* Los Angeles: California Department of Education 1932

1410 E. L. Thorndike, *A Teacher's Word Book of the 20,000 Words Found Most Frequently and Widely in General Reading for Children and Young People.* New York: Columbia Teachers College 1932

1411 A. E. Rejall, *4000 Commonly Used English Words in Adult Education.* Albany (N.Y.): Interstate Bulletin 1932

1412 H. E. Palmer, *Second Interim Report on Vocabulary Selection.* Tokyo: IRET 1931

1413 N. B. Hunter, *Two Hundred Vital Words.* London 1931

1414 W. H. Coleman, *A Critique of Spelling Vocabulary Investigations.* New York: Columbia U.P. 1931

1415 C. K. Ogden, *The Basic Vocabulary: a statistical analysis.* London: Kegan Paul 1930

1416 C. K. Ogden, *Basic English. A general introduction with rules and grammar.* London: Kegan Paul 1930

1417 E. Horn, *A Basic Writing Vocabulary.* Iowa City: University of Iowa Monographs in Education 1926

1418 A. I. Gates, *Reading Vocabulary for the Primary Grades.* New York: Columbia Teachers College 1926

1419 W. F. Tidyman, *A Survey of the Writing Vocabularies of Public School Children in Connecticut.* Washington: U.S. Bureau of Education 1921

1420 W. N. Anderson, *Determination of a Spelling Vocabulary based on Written Correspondence.* Iowa City: University of Iowa 1921

1421 E. L. Thorndike, *Teacher's Word Book.* New York: Columbia Teachers College 1921

1422 L. P. Ayres, *Spelling Vocabularies of Personal and Business Letters.* New York: Russell Sage Foundation 1913

1423 R. C. Eldridge, *Six Thousand Common English Words, their Comparative Frequency and what can be done with them.* Buffalo: Clement 1911

1424 J. Knowles, *The 'London Point' System of Reading for the Blind*. London: Allen & Unwin 1904

* * *

1425 B. Lott, Graded and Restricted Vocabularies and their Use in the Oral Teaching of English as a Second Language, *ELT* 14: 3–14, 65–9

1426 W. E. Flood & M. P. West, A Limited Vocabulary for Scientific and Technical Ideas, *ELT* 4: 128–36

1427 L. Faucett, Essential Differences between the Vocabulary of the Interim Report on Vocabulary Selection and Vocabularies prepared for the simplification of English, *BIRET* 127: 8–10

1428 A. S. Hornby, The IRET Standard English Vocabulary: The Thousand-Word Radius, *BIRET* 100: 8–9

1429 E. Swenson, A Minimum English Speaking Vocabulary, *BIRET* 92: 4–5

1430 H. E. Palmer, The Testing of the Word-Lists, *BIRET* 85: 1–2

1431 H. E. Palmer, The First 600 English Words for a Classroom Vocabulary. Tokyo: IRET n.d.

1432 H. E. Palmer, The First 500 English Words of Most Frequent Occurrence. Tokyo: IRET n.d.

1433 H. E. Palmer, The Second 500 English Words of Most Frequent Occurrence. Tokyo: IRET n.d.

1434 H. L. Ballenger, A Comparative Study of Vocabulary Content of Certain Standard Reading Tests, *Elementary School Journal* 23: 522–34

1435 W. F. Clarke, Writing Vocabularies, *Elementary School Journal* 21: 349–51

1436 J. D. Houser, An Investigation of the Writing Vocabularies of Representatives of an Economic Class, *Elementary School Journal* 17: 708–18

1437 E. Horn, The Vocabulary of Bankers' Letters, *English Journal* 7: 383–97

6.2.1 (ii) *Meaning*

1438 I. Lorge, *Semantic Count of the 570 Commonest English Words*. New York: Columbia U.P. 1949

* * *

1439 I. Lorge, The English Semantic Count, *Teachers College Record* 39: 65–77

6.2.1 (iii) *Structure*

(a) Sentence and Phrase Structures

1440 A. S. Hornby, *A Guide to Patterns and Usage in English*. London: Oxford U.P. 1954

* * *

1441 E. L. Thorndike et al, Inventory of English Constructions, *Teachers College Record* 28: 587–610

1442 H. E. Palmer, Specimens of English Construction Patterns. Tokyo: IRET 1934

1443 H. E. Palmer, Second Interim Report on English Collocations. Tokyo: IRET 1933

1444 H. E. Palmer, Sentences Worth Memorizing, *BIRET* 91: 1–2

(b) Idioms

1444*a* V. H. Collins, *A Third Book of English Idioms.* London: Longmans 1960
1445 V. H. Collins, *A Second Book of English Idioms.* London: Longmans 1958
1446 V. H. Collins, *A Book of English Idioms. With Explanations.* London: Longmans 1956
1447 W. McMordie, *English Idioms and How to Use Them.* (3 ed. rev. R. C. Goffin) London: Oxford U.P. 1954
1448 J. M. Dixon, *English Idioms.* Edinburgh: Nelson n.d.

(c) Verb forms

1448*a* H. V. George, A Verb-form Frequency Count, *ELT* 18: 31–7

6.2.1 (iv) *Phonetics*

1449 N. R. French, C. W. Carter & W. Koenig, *The Words and Sounds of Telephone Conversations.* New York: Bell Technical Publications 1930
1450 G. Dewey, *The Relative Frequency of English Speech Sounds.* Cambridge (Mass.): Harvard U.P. 1923

6.2.2 **French**

1451 Ministère de l'éducation nationale, *Vocabulaire d'initiation à la critique et à l'explication littéraire.* Paris: Didier 1960
1452 Ministère de l'éducation nationale, *Le français fondamental (2e degré).* Paris: Institut pédagogique national n.d.
1453 G. Gougenheim, R. Michéa, P. Rivenc & A. Sauvageot, *L'élaboration du français élémentaire. Etude sur l'établissement d'un vocabulaire et d'une grammaire de base.* Paris: Didier 1956
1454 M. Cohen. *Français élémentaire? Non.* Paris: Editions sociales 1955
1455 Ministère de l'éducation nationale, *Le français fondamental (1er degré).* Paris: Institut pédagogique national 1954
1456 L. Verlée, *Basis-woordenboek voor de Franse Taal.* Amsterdam: Meulenhoff 1954
1457 B. Schlyter, *Centrala ordförradet i franskan,* Upsala: Almqvist & Wiksell 1951
1457*a* R. E. Clark & L. Poston, *French Syntax List: a statistical study of grammatical usage in contemporary French prose on the basis of range and frequency.* New York: Holt 1943
1458 J. B. Tharp, *The Basic French Vocabulary.* New York: Holt 1939
1459 M. West, O. Bond & L. H. Limper, *A Grouped-frequency French Word List based on the French Word Book of Vander Beke.* Chicago: Chicago U.P. 1939
1460 M. Aristizabal, *Détermination expérimentale du vocabulaire écrit pour servir de base à l'enseignement de l'orthographe à l'école primaire.* Louvain: Laboratoire de didactique expérimentale 1938
1461 J. D. Haygood, *Le vocabulaire fondamental du français. Etude pratique sur l'enseignement des langues vivantes.* Geneva: Droz 1936
1462 R. Dottrens & D. Massarenti, *Vocabulaire fondamental du français.* Neuchâtel: Delachaux & Niestlé n.d.

1463 G. W. F. Goodridge, *Difficult French Words: a Classified Vocabulary.* London: Oxford U.P. 1931

1464 F. D. Cheyd eur, *French Idiom List, Based on a Running Count of 1,830,000 Words.* New York: American and Canadian Committees on Modern Languages 1929

1465 G. E. Vander Beke, *French Word Book.* New York: American and Canadian Committees on Modern Languages 1929

1466 D. A. Prescott, *Le Vocabulaire des enfants et des manuels de lecture.* Geneva: Kundig 1929

1467 V. A. C. Henmon, *A French Word Book Based on a Count of 400,000 Running Words.* Madison: University of Wisconsin Educational Research Bulletin 1924

1468 A. A. Méras, *Le petit vocabulaire.* Boston: Heath 1916

1469 R. Blanchaud, *One Thousand French Words.* New York: Crowell n.d.

1470 B. F. Carter, *French Word Lists.* New York: Holt n.d.

*   *   *

1470a G. Gougenheim & P. Rivenc, Etat actuel du français fondamental, *FdM* 1: 4–7

1471 F. A. Hedgock, Word Frequency in French, *ML* 17: 17–18

1472 J. B. Tharp, A. Bovée et al, A Basic French Vocabulary, *MLJ* 19

1473 J. Fortos, Word and Idiom Frequency Counts in French and their Value, *MLJ* 15: 344–453

1474 G. Gougenheim, Le français élémentaire: Etude sur une langue de base, *International Review of Education* 1: 401–12

1475 G. Waringhien, Le français élémentaire, *Vie et langage* 36: 140–44

1476 G. Gougenheim, A propos de l'enquête sur les verbes d'actions courantes, *Vie et langage* 35: 541–4

1477 G. Gougenheim, Pour le français élémentaire: résultat d'une enquête, *Vie et langage* 35: 87–9

1478 C. D. Frank, French in a Changing World, *High Points* 18: 12–15

6.2.3 German

1479 M. Auber, *Guide de fréquence allemand.* Gap: Ophrys 1953

1480 C. M. Purin, *A Standard German Vocabulary of 2,932 Words and 1,500 Idioms.* Boston: Heath 1937

1481 W. Wadepuhl & B. Q. Morgan, *Minimum Standard German Vocabulary.* London: Harrap 1936

1482 H. Bakonyi, *Die gebräuchlichsten Wörter der deutschen Sprache für Fremdsprachunterricht.* Munich: Goethe-Institut 1934

1483 H. Meier, *The One Thousand Most Frequent German Words.* London: Oxford U.P. 1931

1484 E. F. Hauch, *A German Idiom List, Selected on the Basis of Freqency and Range of Occurrence.* New York: American and Canadian Committees on Modern Languages 1929

1485 B. Q. Morgan, *A German Frequency Word Book, Based on Kaeding's Häufigkeitswörterbuch der deutschen Sprache.* New York: American and Canadian Committees on Modern Languages 1928

1486 P. Hagbolt, *Building the German Vocabulary.* Boston: Heath 1928

1487 H. C. Bierwirth, *Words of Frequent Occurrence in Ordinary German.* New York: Holt 1928

1488 H. C. Thurnau, *Vocabulary-Building German for Beginners.* New York: Crofts 1927

1489 A. A. Méras & M. Miller, *Ein Wortschatz.* Boston: Heath 1914

1490 A. H. Prehn, *Practical Guide to a Scientific Study of the German Vocabulary.* London: Oxford U.P. 1912

1491 J. W. Kaeding, *Häufigkeitswörterbuch der deutschen Sprache.* Steglitz: Der Herausgeber 1897

*   *   *

1492 B. Q. Morgan, A Minimum Standard Vocabulary for German, *MLJ* 18: 145–52

1493 A. A. Ortmann, A Study in First-year German Vocabulary, *GQ* 8: 119–28

1494 A. R. Hohlfeldt, Minimum Standard Vocabulary for German, *GQ* 7: 87–119

1495 C. D. Vail, Basic Vocabulary Studies, *GQ* 5: 123–30

1496 P. Hagbolt, The Relative Importance of Grammar in a German Reading Course, *GQ* 1: 18–21

6.2.4 Spanish

1497 I. R. Bou, J. A. Méndez et al, *Recuento de Vocabulario español.* San Juan: Puerto Rico U.P. 1952

1498 V. G. Hoz, *Vocabulario usual, común y fundamental.* Madrid: Instituto San José de Calasanz 1952

1499 H. Keniston, *Spanish Syntax List.* New York: American and Canadian Committees on Modern Languages 1937

1500 H. Keniston, *A Basic List of Spanish Words and Idioms.* Chicago: Chicago U.P. 1933

1501 H. Keniston, *A Spanish Idiom List, Selected on Basis of Range and Frequency of Occurrence.* New York: American and Canadian Committees on Modern Languages 1929

1502 M. A. Buchanan, *A Graded Spanish Word Book.* Toronto: American and Canadian Committees on Modern Languages 1927

1503 L. A. Wilkins, *Spanish Word and Idiom List.* New York: Doubleday 1927

1504 A. J. Ivy, *Practical Spanish Word Book.* Bloomington (Ind.): Public School Publishing Co.

1505 A. A. Méras & S. Roth, *Pequeño vocabulario.* Boston: Heath 1916

*   *   *

1506 E. J. Jamieson, A Standardized Vocabulary for Elementary Spanish, *MLJ* 8: 325–33

1507 H. Keniston, Common Words in Spanish, *Hispania* 3: 85–96

6.2.5 Italian

1508 D. Zinno, *Il piccolo vocabolario.* New York: Italian Publishers 1933

1509 T. M. Knease, *An Italian Word List from Literary Sources.* Iowa City: State University of Iowa doctorate thesis 1931

6.2.6 Russian

1510 H. H. Josselson, *The Russian Word Count*. Detroit: Wayne U.P. 1953

6.2.7 Dutch

1511 G. Vannes, *Vocabulaire du néerlandais de base*. Antwerp: Sikkel 1952
1512 A. de la Court, *De meest voorkomende woorden en woordcombinaties in het Nederlands*. Batavia: Volkslectuur 1937

* * *

1513 G. Vannes, Basis-Nederlandsch, *RLaV* 4: 164–75

6.2.8 Latin

1514 M. Mathy, *Vocabulaire de base du latin*. Paris: O.C.D.L. 1952

6.3 BIBLIOGRAPHIES

1515 E. Dale & D. Reichert, *Bibliography of Vocabulary Studies*. (rev. ed.) Columbus: Ohio State University 1957
(See also **877** and **1318**)

7. GRADATION

1516 I. A. Richards & C. M. Gibson, *The New Approach to the Teaching of Language Skills*. New York: Seminar Films 1952
1517 I. A. Richards, *Notes for a Discussion of Elementary Language Teaching*. (mimeographed) Paris: Unesco 1947
1518 H. E. Palmer, *The Grading and Simplifying of Literary Material*. Tokyo: IRET 1932
1519 H. E. Palmer, *The First Six Weeks of Reading*. Tokyo: IRET 1931

* * *

1520 J. Boulouffe, La gradation des structures pour l'enseignement de l'anglais au degré inférieur, *RLaV* 23: 70–7
1520a W. R. Lee, Grading, *ELT* 17: 107–111, 174–80
1521 H. V. George, A Note on the Teaching of *a* and *the* to Beginners whose Mother-Tongues do not show Parallel Usage, *ELT* 15: 157–9
1522 P. G. Wingard, "What's This?" or "What is This?", *ELT* 13: 11–17
1523 W. F. Mackey, What to Look for in a Method: (II) Grading, *ELT* 8: 45–58
1523a W. F. Mackey, Rola gradacji w nauczaniu języków obcych, *Wiadomości Nauczycielskie* 5: 4–10

8. PRESENTATION

8.1 GENERAL

1524 W. F. Mackey, What to Look for in a Method: (III) Presentation, *ELT* 9: 41–56

1525 A. S. Hornby, Linguistic Pedagogy, *ELT* 1: 6–10, 36–8, 66–71, 91–5; 2: 21–7

1526 F. O'Brien, A Qualitative Investigation of the Effect of Mode of Presentation upon the Process of Learning, *American J. of Psychology* 32: 249–83

8.2 STAGING

1527 J. A. Bright, Reading or Writing First?, *ELT* 10: 142–3

1528 S. H. Hopper, The Psychology of Skill and its Application to Language Learning, *ELT* 4: 11–16, 37–40

8.3 EXPRESSION

8.3.1 Spoken Language

1528a P. R. Léon, *Introduction à la phonétique corrective à l'usage des professeurs de français à l'étranger.* Paris: Bureau d'étude et de liaison pour l'enseignement du français dans le monde 1962

1529 P. Strevens, *Spoken Language.* London: Longmans 1956

*　　*　　*

1530 P. R. Léon, Les méthodes en phonétique corrective, *FdM* 2: 6–9
(See also under 2.2.1 and 14.4)

8.3.2 Written Language

1531 C. M. Gibson & I. A. Richards, *First Steps in Reading English. A book for beginning readers of all ages.* New York: Pocket Books 1957

1532 W. S. Gray, *The Teaching of Reading and Writing. Monographs on Fundamental Education X.* Paris: Unesco 1956

1533 UNESCO, *Progress of Literacy in Various Countries: A preliminary statistical study of available census data since 1900. Monographs on Fundamental Education VI.* Paris: Unesco 1953

1534 W. F. Tidyman & M. Butterfield, *Teaching the Language Arts.* New York: McGraw-Hill 1951

1535 U.S. Office of Education, *Fundamental Education.* Washington: U.S. Government Printing Office 1948

8.4 CONTENT

8.4.1 Differential Procedures

(i) *Translation*

1535a P. A. Soboleva, Primenenie sopostavitel'nogo metoda pri obučenii leksike inostrannogo jazyka (Application of the comparative method to the teaching of foreign language vocabulary). *Studies of the Lenin Pedagogical Institute 93.* Moscow: Faculty of Foreign Languages 1956

1536 H. A. Cartledge, Teaching without Translating, *ELT* 7: 86–90

1537 W. Stannard Allen, In Defence of the Use of the Vernacular and Translating in Class, *ELT* 3: 33–9

(See also under 3.1)

(ii) *Explanation* (*Grammar*)

1538 R. C. Pooley, *Teaching English Grammar*. New York: Appleton 1957

*　　*　　*

1539 R. Quirk, From Descriptive to Prescriptive: an Example, *ELT* 12: 9–11
1540 L. A. Hill, Compounds and the Practical Teacher, *ELT* 12:13–21
1541 F. T. Noordermeer, Two Types of Grammar Teaching, *ELT* 11: 46–9
1542 M. West, How Much English Grammar?, *ELT* 7: 14–20
1543 I. Morris, Grammar and Language: the prescriptive and descriptive schools, *ELT* 6: 55–9

8.4.2 **Ostensive Procedures**

1544 A. S. Hornby, The Situational Approach in Language Teaching, *ELT* 4: 98–103, 121–7, 150–5
1544a A. S. Hornby, Situations: artificial or natural, *ELT* 6: 118–24

(See also Nos. **1106, 1112, 1114, 1115, 1120, 1121, 1132, 1137, 1144, 1152, 1176**, and under 13 and 14)

8.4.3 **Pictorial Procedures**

1545 A. Bohlen, *Bild und Ton im neusprachlichen Unterricht*. Dortmund: Lensing 1962
1545a B. Landers, *A Foreign Language Audio-Visual Guide*. Los Angeles: Landers Associates 1961
1545b T. Huebener, *Audio-Visual Techniques in Teaching Foreign Languages*. New York: New York U.P. 1960
1545c J. Giraud, *Comment enseigner par les moyens audio-visuels*, (*Bib. Pedagogique 5*). Paris: Nathan 1957
1545d W. L. Sumner, *Visual Methods in Education*. Oxford: Blackwell 1956
1546 H. Alpern & A. I. Katsh, *Audio-Visual Materials in Foreign Language Teaching*. New York: New York U.P. 1950

*　　*　　*

1546a S. P. Corder, A Theory of Visual Aids in Language Teaching, *ELT* 17: 82–86
1546b H. A. Cartledge, Film and Tape, *ELT* 17: 87–89
1547 I. A. Richards & C. M. Gibson, Mechanical Aids in Language Teaching, *ELT* 12: 3–8
1548 E. V. Gatenby, The Use of Wall-Pictures in Language Teaching, *ELT* 5: 115–19
1549 D. B. J. Kensit, An Experiment in Language Teaching with Visual Aids, *ELT* 4: 199–205
1550 G. P. Meredith, Visual Aids: Context—Its Significance and its Visual Generalization, *ELT* 2: 97–100
1551 G. P. Meredith, Visual Aids in the Teaching of English, *ELT* 1: 61–5

1552 J. E. Travis, The Use of the Film in Language Teaching and Learning, *ELT* 1: 145–8

1552a J. Guénot, C. Sturge-Moore & M. Tardy, La lisibilité des vues fixes, *ELA* 1: 104–136

1552b A. J. Greimas, Méthodes audio-visuelles et enseignement des langues, *ELA* 1: 137–155

1552c J. Alhinc, M. Clay & P. Léon, Laboratoire de langues et classes audio-visuelles, *ELA* 1: 156–167

1552d J. Bertrand, Image, langage et tableau de feutre, *FdM* 10: 14

1552e J. Bertrand, Le tableau de feutre, *FdM* 5: 25

1552f L. Riégel, Les croquis et leur utilisation dans la classe de langue, *LM* 55: 247–65

1553 R. Arnaud, Projection fixe et méthode active, *LM* 50: 20–6

1554 A. Bohlen, Audio-visuelle Hilfsmittel für den neusprachlichen Unterricht, *NS* 7: 117–24

(See also **1557, 1560, 1564,** and **1641**)

8.4.4 Contextual Procedures

1554a T. Slama-Cazacu, *Langage et contexte*. The Hague: Mouton 1960.

1555 C. K. Ogden, *Opposition. A linguistic and psychological analysis*. London: Kegan Paul 1932

*   *   *

1555a J. Darbelnet, Quelques exercises de stylistique comparée, *FdM* 6: 42–5

1556 L. C. Seibert, A Study on the Practice of Guessing Word Meanings from Context, *MLJ* 29: 296–322

9. REPETITION

9.1 TYPES OF EXERCISES

1556a F. W. Gravit & A. Valdman (eds.), *Structural Drill and the Language Laboratory*. *IJAL* 29: 2 (III) 1963

1557 G. C. Bateman, *Aids to Modern Language Teaching*. (2 ed.) London: Constable 1960

1558 A. S. Hornby, *Teaching of Structural Words and Sentence Patterns*. London: Oxford U.P. 1959

1559 M. Bernett & J. Alcock, *A Song to Sing*. London: University of London Press 1955

1560 E. V. Gatenby & C. E. Eckersley, *General Service English Wall Pictures*. London: Longmans 1955

*   *   *

1561 D. J. Hicks, Types of Spoken Drills, *ELT* 15: 63–67

1562 J. M. Mitchell, The Reproduction Exercise, *ELT* 8: 59–63

1563 M. West, Catenizing, *ELT* 5: 147–51

1564 E. V. Gatenby, Wall-Picture Practice, *ELT* 5: 163–6

1565 D. Hicks, Some Revision Drills, *ELT* 3: 101–4, 141–5, 188–9

1566 M. West, Types of Exercise in Language Teaching, *ELT* 1: 139–42
1566a G. Mathieu, Oral Pattern Practice, *MLJ* 45: 215–16
(See also under 12 and 15.2)

9.2 LISTENING AND SPEAKING

1567 J. Weston, *The Tape Recorder in the Classroom*. London: National Committee for Visual Aids in Education 1960
1568 P. Strevens, *Aural Aids in Language Teaching*. London: Longmans 1958

* * *

1568a R. Leicher, Die "Klangzeitlupe" im neusprachlichen Anfangsunterricht, *Festschrift Otto* 128–41, Berlin: Gruyter 1957
1569 D. Abercrombie, Practical Uses of Speech Recording, *ELT* 6: 26–9.
1569a A. Gauthier, Pour une utilisation collective du magnétophone, *LM* 56: 219–24
1570 A. Lesage, Comment utiliser un magnétophone unique dans une classe normale, *LM* 52: 16–20
1571 J. Guénot, L'utilisation du magnétophone, *LM* 50: 38–44
(See also under 8.3.1 and 15)

9.3 READING

1571a C. C. Fries, *Linguistics and Reading*. New York: Holt 1963
1572 N. Lewis, *How to Read Better and Faster*. (3 ed.) New York: Crowell 1958
1573 W. F. Mackey, *Reading Materials in Controlled Vocabularies*. Ottawa: Citizenship Branch 1957
1574 F. J. Schonell, *The Psychology and Teaching of Reading*. (3 ed.) Edinburgh: Oliver & Boyd 1951
1575 W. S. Gray, *On Their Own in Reading*. Chicago: Scott 1948
1576 W. B. Pitkin, *The Art of Rapid Reading*. New York: Blue Ribbon 1945
1577 I. A. Richards, *How to Read a Page: A course in effective reading with an introduction to a hundred great words*. New York: Norton 1942
1578 M. West, *Learning to Read a Foreign Language: An experimental study*. London: Longmans 1941
1579 D. D. Durrell, *The Improvement of Basic Reading Abilities*. New York: World Book Co. 1940
1580 M. D. Vernon, *The Experimental Study of Reading*. London: Cambridge U.P. 1931
1581 M. West, *The Construction of Reading Material for Teaching a Foreign Language*. London: Oxford U.P. 1927

* * *

1582 M. West, The Problem of "Weaning" in Reading a Foreign Language, *MLJ* 15: 481–9
1583 M. West, The New Method System of Teaching the Reading of a Foreign Language, *ML* 10: 5–10
1583a A. V. P. Elliott, The Reading Lesson, *ELT* 17: 9–16, 67–72
1583b G. Broughton, Don't Shoot the Editor, *ELT* 16: 199–204
1584 L. A. Hill, The Teaching of Reading, *ELT* 14: 18–20

1585 H. C. Burrow, Reading Cards and Substitution Tables, *ELT* 12: 138–49
1585*a* R. Lichet, Procédés d'initiation à la lecture, *FdM* 2: 30–2

(See also under 8.3.2)

9.4 WRITING

1586 L. A. Hill, *Picture Composition Book*. London: Longmans 1960
1587 P. Gurrey, *The Teaching of Written English*. London: Longmans 1954
1588 UNESCO, *The Teaching of Handwriting*. Geneva: International Bureau of Education 1948
1589 F. J. Schonell, *Essentials in Teaching and Testing Spelling*. London: Macmillan 1945

*　　*　　*

1590 D. L. C. Anderson, Crosswords and Language Teaching, *ELT* 5: 53–5
1591 J. G. Weightman, Translation as a Linguistic Exercise, *ELT* 5: 69–76
1592 A. S. Hornby, Direct Method Composition Exercises, *ELT* 4: 22–6, 45–9, 78–81

(See also under 8.3.2.)

10. MEASUREMENT

1593 W. F. Mackey, Un calcul de la productivité, *Les Annales de l'Acfas* 1958
1594 W. F. Mackey, A Theory of Structural Gradation, *Proceedings of the Eighth International Congress of Linguists* 1958

(See also under 1.3.8)

11. SUITABILITY OF METHODS AND TEACHERS

11.1 AIMS AND METHODS

1594*a* Ministère de l'éducation nationale, *Recherche universitaire et enseignement du français langue étrangère*. Paris: Bureau d'étude et de liasion pour l'enseignement du français dans le monde 1963
1594*b* J. Axelrod & D. N. Bigelow, *Resources for Language and Area Studies*. Washington: American Council on Education 1962
1594*c* Modern Language Association, *Modern Languages in the Universities*. London: Modern Language Association 1961
1594*d* MLA, *Reports of Surveys and Studies in the Teaching of Modern Foreign Languages*. New York: Modern Language Association of America 1961
1595 W. V. Kaulfers & H. D. Roberts, *A Cultural Basis for the Language Arts*. Stanford: Stanford U.P. 1937
1596 R. E. McMurray, M. Mueller & T. Alexander, *Modern Foreign Languages in France and Germany*. New York: Columbia Teachers College 1930
1597 T. Huebener, *The Reading Aim in Foreign Language Teaching*, New York: Board of Education, Foreign Language Monograph 6
1598 T. Huebener, *Can the Slow Pupil learn Foreign Languages?* New York: Board of Education, Foreign Language Monograph 2

*　　*　　*

1598a J. B. Carroll, Research on Teaching Foreign Languages, in *Handbook of Research on Teaching*. New York: Rand McNally 1962

1598b H. Lane, Experimentation in the Language Classroom: guidelines and suggested procedures for the classroom teacher, *LL* 12: 115–22

1598c G. Strauch, Une enquête sur l'enseignement de la grammaire, *LM* 55: 266–81

1598d J. Decreus, The National Defence Education Act and Foreign Language Teaching in the U.S.A., *LM* 55: 37–44

1599 R. H. Fife, Preliminary Report on the Modern Language Study, *MLJ* 9: 339–43

1600 E. F. Hauch, The Reading Objective, *GQ* 4: 96–100

1601 R. H. Fife, The Reading Objective, *GQ* 2: 73–87

(See also under 3.3 and 5.2)

11.2 TEACHERS

1602 H. J. Byrne, *Primary Teacher Training*. London: Oxford U.P. 1960

1603 H. J. Byrne, *The Teacher and His Pupils*. London: Oxford U.P. 1953

1604 J. Hargreaves, *Teacher Training*. London: Oxford U.P. 1948

1605 H. Stuart, *The Training of Modern Foreign Language Teachers for the Secondary Schools in the United States*. New York: Columbia Teachers College 1927

*   *   *

1605a D. A. Smith, The Madras "Snowball"—An Attempt to Retrain 27,000 Teachers of English to Beginners, *ELT* 17: 3–9

1605b L. A. Miquel, The Teaching-Practice Programme at the University of Chile, *ELT* 15: 11–16

1606 M. West, Practice Teaching in the Training of Language Teachers, *ELT* 13: 149–54

1607 M. West, Is a Textbook Really Necessary?, *ELT* 8: 64–7

1607a E. V. Gatenby, The Training of Language Teachers, *ELT* 5: 199–207

1608 E. V. Gatenby, Teacher or Textbook, *ELT* 2: 189–92

1609 I. A. Richards, English Language Teaching Films and their Use in Teacher Training, *ELT* 2: 1–7

1609a F. Closset, Formation et perfectionnement des professeurs de langue vivante, *FdM* 4: 2–5

1609b W. F. Marquardt, The Training of Teachers of English as a Second Language in the Peace Corps, *LL* 12: 103–14

1610 M. L. Roger, Formation des professeurs de langues vivantes, *LM* 51: 19–24

1611 S. A. Freeman, What Constitutes a Well-Trained Language Teacher?, *MLJ* 25: 293–305

1612 M. O. Peters, The Place of the Training School in the Training of a Teacher of French, *Teachers College Journal* 4: 269–70

1613 E. B. de Sauzé, The Training of a Teacher of French, *Education Outlook* 6: 235–44

1614 F. D. Cheydleur, Criteria of Effective Teaching in Basic French Courses at the University of Wisconsin, Part I, 1919–1935, Part II, 1953–1943, *Bulletin of the University of Wisconsin*, Aug. 1945

12. LESSON ANALYSIS: TABULATING

1615 P. Roberts, *English Sentences*. New York: Harcourt 1962
1616 F. G. French, *English in Tables*. London: Oxford U.P. 1960
1617 A. S. Hornby, *Teaching of Structural Words and Sentence Patterns*. London: Oxford U.P. 1959
1618 F. G. French, *Common Errors in English. Their cause, prevention and cure*. London: Oxford U.P. 1949

*   *   *

1619 P. A. D. MacCarthy, Substitution Table Technique, *ELT* 4: 171–8, 214–18
1620 A. S. Hornby, Sentence Patterns and Substitution Tables, *ELT* 1: 16–22, 41–5, 105–8, 135–8

13. LESSON PLANNING

1620a I. V. Karpov, O psixologičeskom analize uroka po inostrannomu jazyku (On the psychological analysis of a foreign language lesson), in *Psixologičeskij analiz uroka* (The psychological analysis of a lesson), ed. by N. F. Dobrynin. Moscow: Učpedgiz 1952
1621 G. H. Green, *Planning the Lesson*. London: University of London Press 1948
1622 W. H. Rice (ed.), *Planning the Modern Language Lesson*. Syracuse (N.Y.): Syracuse U.P. 1946
1623 R. O. Billett, *Fundamentals of Secondary School Teaching: With Emphasis on the Unit Method*. Boston: Houghton Mifflin 1940
1624 R. Schorling, *Student Teaching: an experience program*. New York: McGraw-Hill 1940
1625 H. C. Morrison, *The Practice of Teaching in Secondary Schools*. Chicago: Chicago U.P. 1931
1626 L. C. Mossman, *Changing Conceptions Relative to the Planning of Lessons*. New York: Columbia Teachers College 1924

*   *   *

1627 E. B. Richmond, Critique of Lesson Plans with Suggestions for Improving Them, *Educational Methods* 13: 224–6
1628 H. W. Bechtel, An Attempt to Improve Lesson Planning for Teachers-in-Service, *Educational Methods* 9: 545–53
1628a H. Mauffrais, Leçon de langage (enfants), *FdM* 5: 28–9
1628b J. Pélissié, Leçon de langage (adolescents), *FdM* 5: 29–31
1628c G. Capelle, Acquisition du langage (adolescents), *FdM* 4: 38–40
1628d A. Hammeau, La première leçon de français, *FdM* 3: 40–2
1629 L. L. Stroebe, How to Plan a Grammar Lesson, *MDU* 21: 10–14

14. LANGUAGE TEACHING TECHNIQUES

14.1 GENERAL

1629a M. Finocchiaro, *Teaching Children Foreign Languages*. Boston: McGraw-Hill 1964

1629b F. L. Billows, *The Techniques of Language Teaching*. London: Longmans 1961

1630 D. M. Wolfe, *Creative Ways to Teach English (Grades 7 to 12)*. New York: Odyssey 1958

*   *   *

1630a B. Perren, Classroom English, *ELT* 17: 112–117

1631 A. V. P. Elliott, Disciplined Activities in the English Classroom, *ELT* 13: 155–8

1632 W. F. Mackey, Shipboard Language Teaching, *ELT* 11: 86–94

1633 S. H. Hopper, Overteaching, *ELT* 9: 100–2

1634 I. E. Jago & D. H. Spencer, The Importance of Interest in Language Learning, *ELT* 5: 103–8, 130–6

1635 A. V. P. Elliott, English Manners in the Classroom, *ELT* 4: 164–7

1636 F. Clarke, In Defence of Translation, *ML* 18: 115–16

14.2 TECHNIQUES OF PRESENTATION

1636a E. Minor, *Simplified Techniques for Preparing Visual Materials*. New York: McGraw-Hill 1962

1636b M. M. Lewis, *The Use of Diagrams in the Teaching of English*. London: Ginn 1959

1637 H. G. Ramshaw, *Blackboard Work*. London: Oxford U.P. 1955

1638 J. S. Crichton, *Blackboard Drawing*. Edinburgh: Nelson 1954

1639 M. Critchley, *The Language of Gesture*. London: Arnold 1939

*   *   *

1639a R. Hok, Contrast: an effective teaching device, *ELT* 17: 118–121

1640 D. Abercrombie, Gesture, *ELT* 9: 3–11

1641 M. Kummer, Die Bildkarten und ihre Verwendung im Deutschunterricht für Ausländer, *DuA* 6: 82–4

1642 G. Dykstra, Perspective on the Teacher's Use of Contrast, *LL* 6 (3 & 4): 1–6

1643 W. Kaulfers, Contextual Settings as Auxiliaries to Recall, *MLF* 12: 5–8

14.3 TECHNIQUES OF REPETITION

14.3.1 **Language Drills**

1643a H. V. King, Oral Grammar Drills, *ELT* 14: 13–17

1644 F. M. Hodgson, Language Learning Material, *ELT* 12: 131–37

1645 G. A. Pittman, The "Drill" Situation, *ELT* 7: 124–30

1646 H. A. Cartledge, Classroom Technique, *ELT* 3: 21–4

1647 F. Thierfelder, Georg Lappers "Singendes Lernen", *DuA* 6: 76–8

1648 J. Moreno-Lacalle, The Art of Questioning in Language Teaching, *Middlebury College Bulletin* 15: 17–30

(See also 9.1)

14.3.2 **Language Games**

1649 W. F. Mackey, *Seven Types of Language Games*. Ottawa: Citizenship Branch 1959

1650 M. E. Moyes, *Party Games*. London: Foyle 1953
1651 W. M. Ryburn, *Play Way Suggestions*. Bombay: Oxford U.P. 1952

* * *

1651a B. Woolrich, "Alibi", *ELT* 17: 122–124
1651b E. Zierer, A Social Game for Practising English, *ELT* 16: 83–5
1652 K. M. Willey, Language Games, *ELT* 9: 91–9
1653 M. Kummer, Das Spiel im Unterricht, *DuA* 7: 20–3
1654 H. E. Piepho, Das Spiel im fremdsprachlichen Unterricht, *NS* 7: 273–82
1655 G. C. Chambers, Games for Modern Language Classes, *MLJ* 11: 93–8
1656 S. Hinz, German Games for Club and Classroom, *MDU* 22: 20–8

14.4 PRONUNCIATION

1656a V. H. Harkevič, Psixologičeskie voprosy obučenija proiznošeniju na inostrannom jazyke (Psychological problems in teaching the pronunciation of a foreign language). Vol. 6 in the collection *Eksperimental'naja fonetika i psixologija reči* (Experimental Phonetics and the Psychology of Speech), ed. by V. A. Artemov. Moscow: MGU 1953
1656b L. A. Hill, Some Uses of the Tape-Recorder in and outside the English Classroom, *ELT* 15: 116–19
1657 E. M. Anthony, On the Predictability of Pronunciation Problems, *ELT* 11: 120–2
1658 P. A. D. MacCarthy, Pronunciation Teaching: Theory and Practice, *ELT* 6: 111–17; 7: 91–5
1659 R. & M. Kingdon, The Use of Dictation, *ELT* 6: 11–25
1660 R. Kingdon, The Teaching of English Stress, *ELT* 3: 146–51
1661 D. Abercrombie, Teaching Pronunciation, *ELT* 3: 113–22
1662 R. Kingdon, The Teaching of English Intonation, *ELT* 2: 85–91, 113–21, 141–6; 3: 11–19
1663 C. F. Hockett, Learning Pronunciation, *MLJ* 24: 261–9
1664 W. L. Graff, Phonetics Hints for the Modern Language Teacher, *MLJ* 13: 620–5
1665 F. L. Billows, Dictation as Ear Training, *TE* 4: 81–3

(See also **1701a**)

14.5 SPEECH

1666 K. J. Grebanier, *Audio-lingual Techniques for Foreign Language Teaching*. Valley Stream (N.Y.): Teachers Practical Press 1961
1667 T. Huebener, *The Use of Dialogue in Foreign Language Teaching*. New York: Board of Education, Foreign Language Monograph 3

* * *

1668 M. West, The Problem of Pupil Talking Time, *ELT* 10: 71–3
1669 A. S. Hornby, Using the Group in Oral Work, *ELT* 10: 31–2
1670 H. A. Cartledge, Conversation Groups, *ELT* 8: 98–101
1671 D. Abercrombie, Making Conversation, *ELT* 8: 3–11
1672 D. Hicks, Real Conversation?, *ELT* 3: 57–68
1673 W. Rilz, Die Sprache des Lehrers, *DuA* 6: 106–10

1673*a* P. Burney, Programme d'un cours de conversation, *FdM* 2: 35–5
1674   P. Delattre, A Technique of Aural-Oral Approach, *FR* 20: 238, 311
1675   H. Lenz, Dramatics in the German Club, *GQ* 10:
1676   M. A. Béra, La voix de son maître, *LM* 65: 282–92

14.6 READING

1677   G. T. Burswell, *A Laboratory Study of the Reading of Modern Foreign Languages.* New York: Macmillan 1927
1678   M. V. O'Shea, *The Reading of Modern Foreign Languages.* Washington: U.S. Government Printing Office 1927
1679   E. Watkins, *How to Teach Silent Reading to Beginners.* New York: Lippincott 1922

*   *   *

1680   G. L. Barnard, Reading to the Class "with expression", *ELT* 9: 24–9
1681   M. West, The Technique of Reading Aloud to the Class, *ELT* 8: 21-4
1682   H. A. Cartledge, Reading Aloud, *ELT* 6: 94–6
1683   O. F. Bond, A Reading Technique in Elementary Foreign Language Instruction, *MLJ* 14: 363–74, 532–45
1684   C. F. Sparkman, An Analysis of the Fundamental Problems of Learning to Read a Foreign Language, *MLJ* 13: 1–14
1685   P. Hagbolt, On Inference in Reading, *MLJ* 11: 73–8
1686   R. F. Scott, Flash Cards as a Method of Improving Silent Reading, *J. of Educational Method* 5: 102–12
1687   A. I. Gates, Function of Flash-Card Exercises in Reading, *Teachers College Record* 27: 311–26
1688   E. W. Bagster-Collins, Observations on Extensive Reading, *GQ* 3: 18–27
1689   P. Hagbolt, The Relative Importance of Grammar in a German Reading Course, *GQ* 1: 18-21

15. AUTOMATED LANGUAGE TEACHING

15.1 TEACHING MACHINES AND PROGRAMMED INSTRUCTION

1690   A. A. Lumsdaine & R. Glaser, *Teaching Machines and Programmed Learning: a source book.* Washington: National Education Association 1960
1690*a* E. Galanter (ed.), *Automatic Teaching: the state of the art.* New York: Wiley 1959

*   *   *

1691   F. Carpenter, The Teaching Machine and its Educational Significance. Chicago: AACTE Conference Paper, February 12, 1960
1692   R. Glaser, Four Articles on Teaching Machines, *Contemporary Psychology* 5: 24–8
1692*a* J. B. Carroll, Research on Teaching Foreign Languages, in *Handbook of Research on Teaching* (ed. N. L. Gage), Chicago: Rand McNally 1963
1692*b* J. B. Carroll, A Primer of Programmed Instruction in Foreign Language Teaching, *IRAL* 1: 115–41

1692c I. J. Saltzmann, Programmed Self-instruction and Second Language Learning, *IRAL* 1: 104–14

1693 G. R. Price, The Teaching Machine, New York: Harvard University Educational Testing Service Conference, October 31, 1959

1694 J. G. Holland, Teaching Machines: An Application of Principles from the Laboratory. New York: Harvard University Educational Testing Service Conference, October 31, 1959

1694a R. E. Silverman, Auto-instructional Devices: some theoretical and practical considerations, *J. of Higher Education* 31: 481–6

1695 F. Carpenter, How Will Automated Teaching Affect Education? *The University of Michigan School of Education Bulletin* 31: 8–12

1696 B. F. Skinner, Teaching Machines, *Science* 128: 969–77

1697 D. Porter, A Critical Review of a Portion of the Literature on Teaching Devices, *Harvard Educational Review* 27: 126–47

1698 S. Ramo, A New Technique of Education, *Engineering and Science Monthly* 21: 17–22

1699 S. L. Pressey, A Machine for Automatic Teaching of Drill Material, *School and Society* 25: 549–2

1700 S. L. Pressey, A Simple Apparatus which Gives Tests and Scores—and Teaches, *School and Society* 23: 373–6

1700a E. B. Fry et al, Teaching Machines: an annotated bibliography, *Audio-Visual Communication Review* 8: suppl. 1.

15.2 LANGUAGE LABORATORIES

1701 E. W. Najam (ed.), *Materials and Techniques for the Language Laboratory. IJAL* 28: 1 (II) 1962

1701a P. R. Léon, *Laboratoire de langues et correction phonétique: Essai méthodologique.* Paris: Didier 1962

1702 J. S. Holton et al, *Sound Language Teaching.* New York: University Publishers 1961

1703 E. M. Stack, *The Language Laboratory and Modern Language Teaching.* New York: Oxford U.P. 1960

1703a F. R. Morton, *The Language Laboratory as a Teaching Machine.* Ann Arbor: University of Michigan Language Laboratory 1960

1704 F. J. Oinas (ed.), *Language Teaching Today. Report of the language laboratory conference held at Indiana University, Jan. 22–23, 1960. IJAL* 26: 4 (II) 1960

1705 F. R. Morton, *Linguistic Theory and the Language Laboratory.* Eastern Michigan University, Ypsilanti (Mich.): Michigan Linguistic Society, May 9, 1959

1706 M. C. Johnston & C. C. Seerley, *Foreign Language Laboratories in Schools and Colleges.* Washington: U.S. Government Printing Office 1958

1707 W. F. Mackey, *Language Laboratories: Their Nature, Use and Design.* Quebec: Laval University Language Laboratory 1958

1708 F. L. Marty, *Methods and Equipment for the Language Laboratory.* Middlebury (Vt.): Audio-Visual Publications 1956

* * *

1708a I. Wilcock, Language Laboratories in North America, *Babel* 9: 10–11

1708b G. H. MacNeill, The Language Laboratory: its method and practice, *CMLJ* 18 (3): 54–7

1708c S. P. Corder, The Language Laboratory, *ELT* 16: 184–8

1709 H. Hoge, Testing in the Language Laboratory: a laboratory experiment in Spanish pronunciation, *Hispania* 42: 147–52

1709a P. Delattre, Comment tester la facilité de la parole dans un laboratoire de langue, *FdM* 3: 36–8

1710 E. Hocking, The Purdue Language Program, *PMLA* 70: 36–45

1710a J. Hare, Le laboratoire de langues et l'enseignement de l'anglais, *L'enseignement secondaire* 41: 139–50

1711 W. F. Roertgen, Plans for the Germanic Languages Laboratory at UCLA, *MLF* 42: 25

1712 Z. O. Rust, The Language Laboratory in Southern California, *MLF* 39: 26

1713 G. Mathieu, A Brief Guide to Sound Labmanship, *MLJ* 44: 123–6

1713a J. Guénot, Un laboratorie de langues, *FdM* 19: 24–6

(See also **1556a**)

15.3 TELEVISION AND RADIO

1714 S. P. Corder, *English Language Teaching and Television*. London: Longmans 1961

1714a H. R. Cassirer, *Television Teaching Today*. Paris: Unesco 1960

*   *   *

1714b J. Guénot, Télévision et enseignement d'une langue, *LM* 56: 208–19

1715 MLA, The Teaching of Foreign Languages by Television, New York: *MLA* Foreign Language Bulletin 25

1716 R. J. Quinault, English by Radio, *ELT* 1: 119–124

15.4 EQUIPMENT

1717 A. G. Pickett & M. M. Lemcoe, *Preservation and Storage of Sound Recordings*. Washington: U.S. Government Printing Office 1959

1718 C.S.S.O., *Purchase Guide for Programs in Science, Mathematics and Modern Foreign Languages*. Boston: Council of Chief State School Officers 1959

1719 P. Strevens, *Aural Aids in Language Teaching*. London: Longmans 1958

*   *   *

1719a N. Fattu, Training Devices, *Encyclopaedia of Educational Research* (3 ed.). New York: Macmillan 1960

1720 H. Gauvenet, Le disque, *FdM* 1: 31

1720a D. Abercrombie, Speech Recording, *ELT* 5: 208–13

1721 E. P. Appelt, Das Grammophon im Sprachunterricht, *MDU* 20: 166–9

1722 E. G. Kunze, The Phonograph in Modern Language Teaching, *MLJ* 13: 538–49

1723 E. B. Pattee: The Phonograph as an Aid to Pronunciation of Foreign Languages, *MLF* 12: 12–14

(See also under 9.2)

16. LANGUAGE TESTING

1723a R. Lado, *Language Testing: the construction and use of foreign language tests.* London: Longmans 1961

1723b G. Mialaret & C. Malandain, *Test C.G.M. 62—Français: pour apprécier le niveau des connaissances linguistiques.* Paris: Didier n.d.

1724 J. O. Gauntlett, *Educational Measurement in English.* Tokyo: English Teaching Institute of Ehime University 1959

1725 B. Siertsema, *A Test in Phonetics.* The Hague: Nijhoff 1959

1725a J. B. Carroll & S. M. Sapon, *Modern Language Aptitude Test.* New York: Psychological Corporation 1958

1726 C. McCallien & A. Taylor, *Examination Tests in Oral English.* London: Longmans 1958

1727 F. J. & F. E. Schonell, *Diagnostic and Attainment Testing.* (3 ed.) Edinburgh: Oliver & Boyd 1956

1728 P. E. Vernon, *The Measurement of Abilities.* (2 ed.) London: University of London Press 1956

1729 R. Boyer, *Mental Measurement.* London: University of London Press 1953

1730 A. M. Jordan, *Measurement in Education. An introduction.* New York: McGraw-Hill 1953

1731 E. F. Lindquist (ed.), *Educational Measurement.* Washington: American Council on Education 1951

1732 W. V. Kaulfers, *The Forecasting Efficiency of Current Bases for Prognosis in Junior High School Beginning Spanish.* Stanford: Leland Stanford Junior University doctorate thesis 1933

1733 V. A. C. Henmon et al, *Prognosis Tests in the Modern Foreign Languages.* New York: Publications of the American and Canadian Committees on Modern Languages 1929

1734 V. A. C. Henmon, *Achievement Tests in Modern Foreign Languages.* New York: Macmillan 1929

* * *

1734a H. V. George, Testing—Another Point of View, *ELT* 16: 72–7

1735 P. Strevens, The Development of an Oral English Test for West Africa, *ELT* 15: 17–24

1736 R. Lado, English Language Testing: Problems of Validity and Administration, *ELT* 14: 153–60

1737 D. F. Anderson, Tests of Achievement in English Language, *ELT* 7: 37–68

1738 M. West, Examinations in a Foreign Language, *ELT* 6: 60–3

1739 N. Nardi, A Test to Measure Aptitude in the Hebrew Language, *J. of Educational Psychology* 38: 167–76

1739a J. A. Upshur, Language Proficiency Testing and the Contrastive Analysis Dilemma, *LL* 12: 123–8

1740 C. H. Handschin, A Test for Discovering Types of Learners in Language Study, *MLJ* 3: 1–4

1741 P. Delattre, Testing Students' Progress in the Language Laboratory, *Automated Teaching Bulletin* 1: 3

(See also **1709** and **1709a**)

Index

The italic numbers refer to pages in the bibliography.

Index

Index

Index

Index

Index

Riddles, 445
Riégel, L., *1552b*
Ries, J., *455*, 32
Rilz, W., *1673*
Ripman, W., *697, 723*
Rivenc, P., *1453, 1470a*
Rivers, W. M., *949a*
Rivers, W. N., *1374*
Rizzo, N. D., *1068*
Robert, P., *815*
Roberts, H. D., *1184, 1595*
Roberts, J. M., *585*
Roberts, L., *321, 1008*
Roberts, M. H., *595*
Roberts, P., *733, 736, 739, 1615*
Robinett, F. M., *437*
Robins, R. H., *94, 136, 138, 442, 578*
Robinson, E. S., *1036*
Robinson, R. H., *529*
Roche, A., *1128*
Rodhe, E., *821*
Roertgen, W. F., *1711*
Röttgers, B., *1257*
Roger, M. L., *1610*
Rogers, G., *1349*
Roget, J. L., *766a*, 72
Roller, S., *808*
Ronjat, J., *984*, 113, 120
Rosetti, A., *510*
Ross, A. S. C., *85, 456*
Rostand, F., *305*
Roth, S., *1505*
Rougier, L., *277*
Rožanskij, A. J., *185*
Rubenbauer, H., *656*
Russell, B., *217, 261, 267,* 14, 31
Russell, W. A., *611*
Russell, W. R., *1009*
Russian, *1510*
Rust, Z. O., *1712*
Rutt, T., *337*
Ryburn, W. M., *1093, 1100, 1651*

Sevpen, *1118*
SIL, *658*
Sack, F. L., *743, 1171*
St. Clair-Sobell, S., *901*
Sainte-Marie, P., *892*
Salisbury, A., *1390*
Saltzmann, I. J., *1692c*
Sandfeld, K., *811*
Sandmann, M., *563*
Sapir, E., *237,* 14
Sapon, S. M., *1083, 1725a*
Saporta, S., *536, 540, 555, 582b, 922, 1073a*
Saussure, F. de, *109, 113, 116,* 12, 21, 31, 76, 129
Saussurian theory, *109-122*
Sauvageot, A., *317, 1453*
Sauveur, L., *1281,* 143
Sauzê, E. B. de, *1613*
Savory, T. H., *882*
Scargill, M. H., *530, 741*
Scarpat, G., *580*
Scheduling, 391
Scherer, A., *407*
Scherer, G. A. C., *1302*
Scherping, E., *1226*
Scheurweghs, G., *728*
Schlauch, M., *629*
Schleicher, A., 29
Schlosberg, H., *1013, 1067*
Schlyter, B., *1457,* 181, 182
Schmidt, G., *295*
Schmidt, J., *1218*
Schmidt, J. S., *1192*
Schmidt, O., *1214*
Schmuller, A. M., *1015*
Schöne, M., *403*
Schoenfeld, W. N., *1024*
Schönfelder, K. H., *857*
Schonell, F. E., *1727*
Schonell, F. J., *1393, 1574, 1589, 1727,* 298

Schorling, R., *1624*
Schreiber, F. R., *927*
Schubiger, M., *713,* 61
Schuchardt, H., 27
Schwarz, H., *582a*
Schweitzer, C., *1268*
Scientific method, *251a-275*
Scoring, 412
Scott, R. F., *1686*
Scott, W. A., *1375*
Seashore, R. H., *1384*
Seating, 363
Sebeok, T. A., *601, 1075*
Sechehaye, C. A., *112, 114, 121*
Second language, *949a-972;* age, 120; attitude, 117; cinema, 115; church, 114; community, 113; drive, 124; emotion, 123; ethnic group, 114; home language, 112; interference, 109; intelligence, 112; learning time, 115; learning theory, 127; memory, 123; motives, 112; occupation, 113; personality, 123; play, 115; radio, 115; reading, 115; readiness, 123; school, 114; skills, 117; society, 112; standard, 117; television, 115; uses, 116
Seerley, C. C., *1706*
Séguy, J., *788c*
Seibert, L. C., *1556*
Seidenstücker, J., 143
Seiler, H., *424, 443a*
Selection, *1327-1515;* Dutch, *1511-1512;* English, *1393-1450;* French, *1451-1478;* German, *1479-1496;* Italian, *1508-1509;* Latin, *1514;* Russian, *1510;* Spanish, *1497-1507;* special studies, *1393-1514;* principles, *1327-1380;* bibliography, *1515* —455; grammar, 191; phonetics, 190; meaning, 198; measurement, 295; vocabulary, 195
Semantics—analysis, 341; measurement, 297; pictorial, 246
Sentence—composition, 287; modification, 285; structure, 211; scrambled, 435
Sequence, 212; grammatical, 214; lexical, 217; phonetic, 212; semantic, 219
Seventeenth century, 142
Shakespeare, W., 161
Shannon, C., *368*
Shaw, B. A., *1393*
Shen, Y., *901a*
Shepard, H. A., *387*
Sherrington, C., *264*
Siebs, T., *826*
Siertsema, B., *151, 902a, 1725*
Sievers, E., 144
Siewerth, G., *194,* 195
Sigwalt, C., *1265*
SIL, *658*
Silverman, R. E., *1694a*
Simard, E., *257*
Simko, J., *482*
Simmons, E. J., *180*
Simmonot, E., *1268*
Simpson, R. G., *1098*
Singer, H., *996*
Sinno, D., *1508*
Situations, 367
Size of group, 329
Skalička, V., *175, 275*
Skills, 117, 122, 313, 330, 345; testing, 405; ratios, 459
Skinner, B. F., *605, 1017, 1032, 1696*
Skok, P., *1180*
Slama-Cazacu, T., *1554a*
Sledd, J. H., *719, 727,* 60
Slides, 247
Smalley, W. A., *485a*
Smith, D. A., *1605a*
Smith, H. L., *747,* 41, 44, 60
Smith, P., *1292*
Snodin, M. R., *594*
Soboleva, P. A., *1535a*
Société du Parler français, *791*
Society and language, *395-397*

Index

Twentieth century, 145

UNESCO, *1116, 1144a, 1316, 1533, 1588*
U. S. Office of Education, *1535*
Uhlenbeck, E. M., *541, 709*
Uldall, H. J., *150*
Ullmann, S., *331a, 338, 342, 415, 434,* 37
Union française des organes de la documentation, *362a*
Unit method, 154
Units, *453-472,* 37, 234; articulation, 49; catenation, 49; content, 40; differences, 91; expression, 40; intonation, 51; phonology, 49; rhythm, 51; teaching, 397
University College of Wales, *1001, 1002*
Upshur, J. A., *1739a*
Urban, W. M., *219*
Utility, 298, 456

Vachek, J., *169, 170, 651*
Vail, C. D., *1495*
Vail, S., *897*
Valdman, A., *898b, 1556a*
Valetto, M., de, *1229*
Valin, R., *161, 162, 163, 270a, 462*
Vallins, G. H., *735*
van Ginneken, J., *312*
van Teslaar, A. P., *900a*
van Wijk, N., *521*
Vander Beke, *1465,* 180, 181, 182, 298
Vannes, G., *1357, 1511, 1513*
Vanik, A., *702b*
Vasey, F. T., *1385*
Variation, 218, 225, 258
Varro, 64
Vechtman-Veth, A. C. E., *749*
Vendryes, J., *232*
Verbal Behaviour, *605-609,* 104
Verbs, 197, 218
Verlée, L., *1456*
Vernon, M. D., *1088, 1580*
Vernon, P. E., *1728*
Veslot, H., *886b, 886c*
Viens, C. P., *1169*
Viëtor, W., *849, 864, 1270,* 144, 146
Vijgotskij, L. S., *320*
Vildomec, V., *972a*
Vinay, J-P., *506, 851, 885*
Visual media, 395
Visual recognition, 278
Vocabulary, *1381-1392,* 69, 102; selection, 195
Voegelin, C. F., *437*
Vogt, H., *549*
von Essen, O., *491, 494, 830*
von Hartmann, P., *323*
von Neumann, J., *382, 1028*
von Raffler, W., *972*
von Wartburg, W., *805*
Vowels, 80
Vuysje, D., *107*

Wadepuhl, W., *1481*
Wähmer, K., *894*
Wängler, H-H., *828, 829*
Waismann, F., *452*
Wakefield, H., *774*
Wall, A., *660a*
Wall-pictures, 247, 429
Walpole, H. R., *347, 1350*
Walter, A. A., *1087*
Walter, M., *1202, 1338,* 147
Ward, I. C., *501, 692, 717,* 61
Ward, J. M., *734, 740*
Wardale, W. L., *831*
Warfel, H. R., *613c, 737*
Waringhien, G., *1475*
Wartburg, W., von, *805*
Waterhouse, W., *986*
Waterman, J. T., *905*

Watkins, E., *1679*
Weaver, W., *368*
Weightman, J. G., *886, 1591*
Weinreich, U., *858*
Weisgerber, L., *229, 293, 589*
Wellek, R., *207*
Wells, R. S., *122, 448, 613*
Welsh, 73
Welsh Department Ministry of Education, *990*
Wendt, 147
Wertheimer, M., *1048*
West, M. P., *670, 671, 724, 767a, 782, 783, 954, 954a, 955, 977, 993, 1129, 1143, 1210, 1334, 1337, 1351, 1352, 1358, 1362, 1365, 1366, 1377, 1394, 1401, 1402, 1405, 1426, 1459, 1542, 1563, 1566, 1578, 1581, 1582, 1583, 1606, 1607, 1668, 1681, 1738,* 71, 180
West, R., *500*
Westerman, D. ,*501*
Weston, J., *1567*
Wevers, J. W., *529*
Whatmough, J., 97, *406, 620*
Wheeler, B. W., *393*
White, M., *258*
Whitehall, H., *738*
Whitehead, A. N., *265, 267, 268*
Whitney, W. D., 27
Whorf, B. L., *200*
Wiener, N., *385*
Wienpahl, P. D., *466*
Wijk, N. van, *520*
Wilcock, I., *1708a*
Wilkins, L. A., *1503*
Willey, K. M., *1652*
Williams, J. I., *1000*
Willot, A., *1310*
Wilson, J., *998*
Wilson, N. L., 78
Wilson, P. G., *1179*
Wilson, R. A., *209*
Winch, P., *253*
Wingard, P. G., *1522*
Winkler, C., *832*
Wise, C. M., *487, 490*
Wittgenstein, L., *279, 282*
Wolfe, D. M., *1630*
Woodruff, A. D., *1097*
Woodworth, H. M., *346*
Woodworth, R. S., *1013, 1042*
Woolner, A. C., *401*
Woolrich, B., *1651a*
Word Jumbles, 287
Word-order, 216
Wrede, F., *824*
Wren, Sir C., 72
Wright, J., *787*
Wright, W., *763*
Writing, *1531-1535, 1586-1592,* 236, 282, 287, 288, 328, 355, 370, 436; models, 365; games, 451
Wyld, H. C., 27
Wynburne, S. B., *877a*

Yoakam, G. A., *1098*
Yolton, J. W., *272*
Young, W. E., *964, 1072*
Yudovich, F. I., *921*

Zachrisson, R. E., *785*
Zandvoort, R. W., *750,* 63, 64
Zaunmüller, W., *845*
Zierer, E., *1651b*
Ziff, P., *609a*
Zinder, L. R., *917*
Zinno, D., *1508*
Zipf, G. K., *208, 224,* 20
Zumthor, P., *805*
Zvegincev, V. A., *336, 428*

1.3.3 Language and Logic

297 W. V. O. Quine, *Word and Object*. New York: Wiley 1960
298 B. F. Huppé & J. Kaminsky, *Logic and Language*. New York: Knopf 1956
299 W. V. O. Quine, *From a Logical Point of View*. Cambridge (Mass.): Harvard U.P. 1953
300 A. G. N. Flew (ed.), *Essays on Logic and Language*. Oxford: Blackwell 1951
301 M. Prot, *Langage et logique. Vers une logique nouvelle*. Paris: Hermann 1949

1.3.4 Language and Psychology

302 J. Church, *Language and the Discovery of Reality*. New York: Random House 1961
303 F. Kainz, *Psychologie der Sprache*. 5 vols. Stuttgart: Enke 1941–61
304 C. G. Hempel, *Fundamentals of Concept Formation in Empirical Science*. Chicago: Chicago U.P. 1952
305 F. Rostand, *Grammaire et affectivité*. Paris: Vrin 1951
306 C. L. Meader & J. H. Muyskens, *Handbook of Biolinguistics*. Toledo (U.S.A.): Weller 1950
307 F. Kainz, *Einführung in die Sprachpsychologie*. Vienna: Sepl 1946
308 A. Marty, *Psyche und Sprachstruktur*. Bern: Francke 1940
309 J. R. Kantor, *An Objective Psychology of Grammar*. Bloomington: Indiana U.P. 1936
310 H. Mulder, *Cognition and Volition in Language*. Groningen: Wolters 1936
311 W. B. Pillsbury & C. L. Meader, *The Psychology of Language*. New York: Appleton 1928
312 J. van Ginneken, *Principes de linguistique psychologique*. Paris: Rivière 1907

*   *   *

313 G. P. Meredith, Semantics in Relation to Psychology, *AL* 8: 1–11
314 E. L. Thorndike, The Psychology of Semantics, *Am. J. Psych.* 59: 613–31
315 G. A. Miller, Psycholinguistics, in *Handbook of Social Psychology* (II, 693–708). Cambridge (Mass.): Addison-Wesley 1954
316 H. L. Hollingsworth, Meaning and the Psychophysical Continuum, *J. of Philosophy* 20
317 A. Sauvageot, La notion du temps et son expression dans le langage, *J. de psychologie normale et pathologique* 33: 19–27
318 J. Meyer, Language as a Biological Phenomenon, *Proc. 10 Internat. Cong. Philosophy* (II: 951–4) Amsterdam: North-Holland 1948
319 N. H. Pronko, Language and Psycholinguistics: a review, *Psychological Bulletin* 43: 189–239

1.3.5 Language and Thought

320 L. S. Vijgotskij, *Thought and Language*. New York: Wiley 1962
321 W. G. Penfield & L. Roberts, *Speech and Brain-Mechanisms*. Princeton: Princeton U.P. 1959

271 H. Frei, De la linguistique comme science des lois, *Lingua* 1: 25–34
272 J. W. Yolton, Linguistic and Epistemological Dualism, *Mind* 62: 20–42
273 A. Pap, Semantic Analysis and Psycho-physical Dualism, *Mind* 41: 209–21
274 T. Storer, Linguistic Isomorphisms, *Philosophy of Science* 19: 77–85
275 V. Skalička, The Need for a Linguistics of "Parole", *Recueil* 1: 21–38

1.3.2 Language and Philosophy

275a W. W. Gibson (ed.), *The Limits of Language*. New York: Hill & Wang 1962
275b M. Black, *The Importance of Language*. Englewood Cliffs (N.J.): Prentice-Hall 1962
275c M. Black, *Models and Metaphors*. Ithaca (N.Y.): Cornell U.P. 1962
276 E. Gellner, *Words and Things. A critical account of linguistic philosophy and a study in ideology*. Boston: Beacon 1960
277 L. Rougier, *La métaphysique et le langage*. Paris: Flammarion 1960
278 M. J. Charlesworth, *Philosophy and Linguistic Analysis*. Pittsburgh: Duquesne U.P. 1959
279 L. Wittgenstein, *Tractatus logico-philosophicus*. Oxford: Blackwell 1960
280 P. Henle (ed.), *Language, Thought and Culture*. Ann Arbor: Michigan U.P. 1958
281 A. Pap, *Semantics and Necessary Truth*. New Haven: Yale U.P. 1958
282 L. Wittgenstein, *Philosophical Investigations*. Oxford: Blackwell 1953
283 L. Linsky (ed.), *Semantics and the Philosophy of Language*. Urbana: Illinois U.P. 1952
284 P. Henle, H. Kallen & S. Langer, *Structure, Method and Meaning*. New York: Liberal Arts 1951
285 M. Black, *Language and Philosophy. Studies in method*. Ithaca (N.Y.): Cornell U.P. 1949
286 E. Otto, *Sprachwissenschaft und Philosophie*. Berlin: Gruyter 1949
287 S. K. Langer, *Philosophy in a New Key*. New York: New American Library 1948
288 H. Junker, *Sprachphilosophisches Lesebuch*. Heidelberg: Winter 1947
289 R. Carnap, *Meaning and Necessity*. Chicago: Chicago U.P. 1947
290 C. L. Stevenson, *Ethics and Language*. New Haven: Yale U.P. 1944
291 L. Lachance, *Philosophie du Langage*. Montreal: Levrier 1943
292 H. J. Ayer, *Language, Truth and Logic*. London: Gollancz 1936

*   *   *

293 L. Weisgerber, Sprachwissenschaft und Philosophie zum Bedeutungsproblem, *Blätter f. dt. Philosophie* 4: 17
294 J. Engels, Valeur de la philosophie pour la recherche linguistique, *Neophilologus* 38: 248–51
295 G. Schmidt, The Philosophy of Language, *Orbis* 6: 164–8
296 I. M. Copi, Philosophy and Language, *Review of Metaphysics* 4: 427–37